SSY ... 2

OR ANYTHING. 3

EIR LIBIDO OR THEIR REPRODUCTIVE SYSTEM ... 4

OT AN EXCEPTION. 5

I WOULD HOPE THAT WHEN A WOMAN GOES IN TO A PHYSICIAN WITH A RAPE ISSUE, THAT PHYSICIAN WILL INDEED ASK HER ... WAS THIS PREGNANCY CAUSED BY NORMAL RELATIONS IN A MARRIAGE OR WAS IT TRULY CAUSED BY A RAPE? 20

SFY

ER

CA? 7

WE HAD TERRORIST [SIC] IN THE TEXAS STATE SENATE. 21

I'D LIKE TO MAKE A LAW THAT MANDATES A WOMAN WATCH AN ABORTION BEING PERFORMED PRIOR TO HAVING A SURGICAL PROCEDURE. 22

TION. 8

'T UNDERSTAND WHAT'S GOING ON TO THEIR BODIES. 23

AINE HEADACHE IF I DON'T GET A STRANGE PIECE OF ASS EVERY DAY. 24

D IDEA. 9

THESE PLANNED PARENTHOOD WOMEN, THE CODE PINK WOMEN, AND ALL OF THESE WOMEN THAT HAVE BEEN NEUTERING AMERICAN MEN AND BRINGING US TO THE POINT OF THIS INCREDIBLE WEAKNESS—TO LET THEM KNOW THAT WE ARE NOT GOING TO HAVE OUR MEN BECOME SUBSERVIENT. 25

TO A WOMAN'S

AT MAKE IT BETTER? 13

ABORTION FACTORY, FRANKLY. 26

UT OF

EVER. 27

YOU'VE CREATED AN INCENTIVE FOR PEOPLE ... TO SELL THAT FETAL TISSUE. 28

NALLY MATCHING HITLER'S BODY COUNT. 29

PLANNED PARENTHOOD ISN'T PURELY A "HEALTHCARE PROVIDER" ANY MORE THAN A HEROIN DEALER IS A COMMUNITY PHARMACIST. 31

THE WOMB TO PRESERVE THEIR BODY PARTS. 30

UST RELAX AND ENJOY IT. 32

MOVE OVER. THIS IS YOUR PRESIDENT. 33

IF A WOMAN HAS [THE RIGHT TO AN ABORTION], WHY SHOULDN'T A MAN BE FREE TO USE HIS SUPERIOR STRENGTH TO FORCE HIMSELF ON A WOMAN? THE RAPIST'S PURSUIT OF SEXUAL FREEDOM DOESN'T [IN MOST CASES] RESULT IN ANYONE'S DEATH. 35

36

JT THE COUNTRY, YES, [MY DAUGHTERS ARE] BOTH AVAILABLE. 37

WE HOLD THESE TRUTHS TO BE SELF-EVIDENT.

1 ROGER RIVARD

2 DONALD TRUMP

3 KRIS JORDAN

4 MIKE HUCKABEE

5 JOE WALSH

6 MICHAEL BURGESS

7 DONALD TRUMP

8 RICK SANTORUM

9 MIKE PENCE

10 BEN CARSON

11 HENRY ALDRIDGE

12 STEVE STOCKMAN

13 JOHN KOSTER

14 JAN BREWER

15 STEVE BANNON

16 MILO YIANNOPOULOS

17 TED KENNEDY

18 BOBBY JINDAL

19 BILL CLINTON

20 CHUCK WINDER

21 BILL ZEDLER

22 TERRI PROUD

23 GREG BRANNON

24 JOHN F. KENNEDY

25 ALLEN WEST

26 DONALD TRUMP

27 DONALD TRUMP

28 MARCO RUBIO

29 MILO YIANNOPOULOS

30 CHRIS CHRISTIE

31 MIKE HUCKABEE

32 CLAYTON WILLIAMS

33 LYNDON B. JOHNSON

34 TODD AKIN

35 LAWRENCE LOCKMAN

36 JEB BUSH SR.

37 SCOTT BROWN

by Zoë Buckman and Natalie Frank

50 CONTEMPORARY WOMEN ARTISTS

JOHN GOSSLEE & HEATHER ZISES, EDITORS

FOREWORD BY ELIZABETH SACKLER

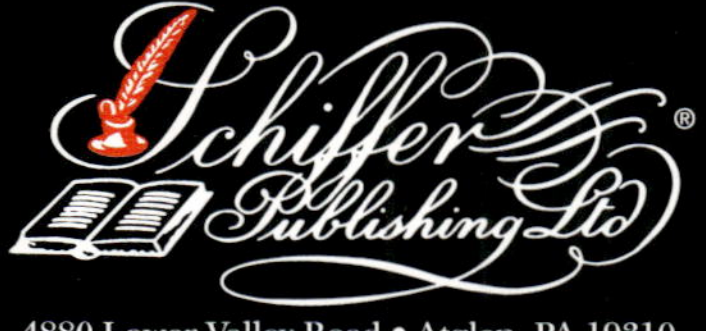

4880 Lower Valley Road • Atglen, PA 19310

Other Schiffer Books on Related Subjects:

Brooklyn On My Mind: Black Visual Artists from the WPA to the Present, by Dr. Myrah Brown Green, Foreword by Chirlane McCray, 978-0-7643-5652-0

Emerging from the Shadows: A Survey of Women Artists Working in California, 1860–1960, by Maurine St. Gaudens
Volume 1: 978-0-7643-4861-7
Volume 2: 978-0-7643-4862-4
Volume 3: 978-0-7643-4886-0
Volume 4: 978-0-7643-4887-7

Library of Congress Control Number: 2018937434

Developmental edit: Jesse J. Marth
Production edit: Kim Hufford
Copyedit: Tod Benedict
Proofreading: Helena Neufeld

Design: Molly Shields
Cover design: Justin Watkinson

Front endsheet: Zoë Buckman & Natalie Frank. *We Hold These Truths to Be Self-Evident*, 2017. Printed vinyl: 31.9 × 10.4 feet. Installation view, New York Live Arts, Ford Foundation Live Gallery, New York City. Designed by Marian Bantjes. Image ©Zoë Buckman and Natalie Frank. Courtesy of the artists

Back endsheet: Zoë Buckman & Natalie Frank. *We Hold These Truths to Be Self-Evident*, 2017. Printed vinyl: 31.9 × 10.4 feet. Installation view, New York Live Arts, Ford Foundation Live Gallery, New York City. Designed by Marian Bantjes. Image ©Zoë Buckman and Natalie Frank. Courtesy of the artists

Type set in Geometr706 Md BT/Futura Bk BT

ISBN: 978-0-7643-5653-7
Printed in China

Published by Schiffer Publishing, Ltd.
4880 Lower Valley Road
Atglen, PA 19310
Phone: (610) 593-1777; Fax: (610) 593-2002
E-mail: Info@schifferbooks.com
Web: www.schifferbooks.com

CONTENTS

FOREWORD

by Elizabeth Sackler, PhD

In a world that now embraces gender neutrality—and with a significant percentage of the current population identifying as gender free, gender fluid, or no gender—discourse on what it means to be feminist, or woman as opposed to female, feels slightly old-fashioned. But, of course, all perspectives do exist at this same moment and so require a shift in consciousness and new nimbleness in thinking. As we learn in John Gosslee's "Preface 1," the editors of *50 Contemporary Women Artists* (*50 CWA*) faced the challenge of winnowing hundreds of artists to a format inclusive of only fifty. And Heather Zises's "Preface 2" addresses the time-honored attributes: woman/women, female/feminist.

In 2017, the Brooklyn Museum celebrated an institution-wide "Year of Yes: Reimagining Feminism at the Brooklyn Museum" in honor of the tenth anniversary of the Elizabeth A. Sackler Center for Feminist Art. The Sackler Center opened in 2007 with a groundbreaking show: *Global Feminisms*. Works by 188 women artists from forty-nine countries, all of whom were born after 1960, heralded *Global Feminisms* as the first major museum exhibition to examine feminist art internationally and at the turn of the twenty-first century. Many of the women included in this volume exhibited in *Global Feminisms* or since at the Sackler Center or in the museum's galleries. During 2018 Brooklyn Museum audiences experienced, for the first time, an encyclopedic museum's exhibitions through a feminist lens. The Sackler Center has shifted the artistic and cultural landscape: since its opening, sales of feminist and women's art has increased worldwide, New York City museums have stepped up solo shows by women artists, and their group shows now include higher percentages of women artists, as do most of the biennials.

Parity is still a distant goal, however. The international art market continues to be a bastion of patriarchy. To those who claim that women's art is not on a par with men's, I remind you that we have been taught to see art, as well as life, through a male gaze—effectively prejudicing our qualitative judgment.

Birthed in the 1970s, the feminist art genre was women artists' contribution to the second-wave women's movement, which addressed women's suppression, misogyny, and the fight for justice—de facto feminist content. The fifty women artists in this volume carry forward our awareness of these inequities. Artists from Seattle to South Africa, from Brooklyn to Bangladesh, and from Montréal to Mexico have faced cultural blockades, familial obstacles, antifemale institutional policies, art-historical omissions, teacher's ridicules, galleries' prejudices, museums' paternalistic systems, and/or collectors' blind spots. In addition, today, the art world turns creativity into a commodity, simultaneously demeaning women's art in the process.

Nevertheless, the artists included herein share brilliance (along with five MacArthur Awards), and embrace morally sound social and political values with fearlessness against patriarchal authority, sexual violence, and the homogenization of the female body. All are taking on high risk with a vengeance! Going back many hundreds of years, women's art has transformed art and architecture—*50 CWA* provides potent pieces from the past sixty years.

At this particular moment, one final point needs to be added: this book may ultimately stand an important test of time as a historic (I prefer "herstoric") marker referencing women's artistic response to the current onslaught of national and global oppression, racism, and abuse. Our turbulent times and the complicity of silence in so many sectors make this book a vitally important statement. These women's voices can be heard through their images—and through the ages.

PREFACE 1

by John Gosslee

My first experience with art was in my childhood home. My parents had a small collection of paintings that hung quietly in our house. Two works that stayed with me were an unsigned painting of ballerinas dancing at night in a forest, surrounded by fireflies as a dim moonlight made their leotards glow, and an old man studying the Bible with bread and cheese and fruit on the desk, next to folded wire-rimmed glasses. I loved how the artist brought out an inner fire on their surfaces; light is something that still excites me in paintings. Later in life, I came to understand the idea of sacred study, embodied in the second piece.

In 2014, I asked editor Heather Zises, who was an ongoing contributor for my first magazine, *Fjords Review*, to curate the art for a special Women's Edition. The issue featured twelve contemporary women artists, including Kate Gilmore, Michelle Hartney, and Allie Pohl, among others, whose artworks were paired with prose by contemporary women writers. The publication served as a platform for my idea of the *50 CWA* book. After some due diligence, I discovered a large gap in the book market: no one had published a book solely dedicated to contemporary living women artists. It was shocking, given how many women are progenitors of styles and movements in contemporary art, and it was in that moment that I realized I had a calling to create this volume.

This book journey has been particularly unique for me, since I'm a male creating a feminist book, a book about women artists that is populated by women. It's a role that I've struggled to grow into, and it's a great responsibility to honor the distinguished work of so many singular great artists.

My first exposure to feminism was through literature. Mary Shelley's mother, Mary Wolstencraft, wrote about social justice and illustrated her fight for equality—one that is still taking place hundreds of years later. Regarding visual artists, there are many women artists whose work I am more drawn to than to male artists', particularly Louise Bourgeois. I saw her work for the first time in a Guggenheim annual catalog that I bought for a dollar from a library sale. I noticed there were dozens of men in the catalog, but only a handful of women. It made me think about how there were almost no women artists in my undergraduate art books, and the ones who were featured, were stigmatized as secondary, ghettoized as making particularly feminine work, or attached to a male artist's history. This widespread absence of acknowledgement both confused and angered me, considering how many women artists create exceptional work. The more I thought about great modernist women artists such as Louise Bourgeois, Agnes Martin, Frida Kahlo, Georgia O'Keeffe, Lee Bontecou, and Joan Mitchell, the more I knew there was much work to be done for the next generation.

Therefore, it is my hope that this book and many more like it will add to the understanding of women's foundational role in art. After the book proposal for *50 CWA* was accepted, I felt an immense responsibility to select artists who have made great strides within their practice—despite being underrepresented—all of whose contributions make the art world one of strength and solidarity through craft, cultural critique, and pure expression.

After three years and countless hours of emails, phone calls and cataloging, I know Heather's curatorial expertise, our dedication to this project, and the artists' commitment to our culture's progress are what made *50 CWA* happen.

PREFACE 2

by Heather Zises

In the summer of 1996, seeking a greater understanding of feminist practices, I interned at Feminist Majority, a women's rights organization founded by Gloria Steinem. Located just outside Washington, DC, the focus of my internship was making Mifepristone (also known as RU-486, an emergency contraception pill) available to American women. In addition to conducting team research on the pill's safety and efficacy, I attended several conferences that featured visible leaders such as Gloria Steinem, Eleanor Smeal, and Kate Michelman from women's liberation groups such as National Organization for Women (NOW), National Abortion Rights Action League (NARAL), and National Women's Political Caucus (NWPC). After my internship, I received a copy of *Feminist Chronicles: 1953–1993* with a personalized note written on the title page from Eleanor Smeal, president of Feminist Majority: "To Heather, Thanks for an excellent internship in making available Mifepristone to American women and encouraging women in sports. But most of all, thanks to your dedication and commitment to Women's Equality. For Feminism, Ellie Smeal." Buoyed by my internship experience and the powerful role models I met, I journeyed through the 1990s and first decade of the twenty-first century as a woman whose consciousness had been seeded by the feminist movement.

Today, my curatorial studies and projects continue to maintain a feminist bent. Historically, the art world—its infrastructure, institutions, marketplace, and so forth—has been an agora in which white, Western male viewpoints are dominant. To level the hierarchy and reform traditional histories of art, *50 CWA* looks away from this androcentric lens by focusing on those artists who have been marginalized, silenced, underrepresented, or omitted altogether in the history of contemporary art. By providing a visual platform where alternative histories can be examined, this book promotes outstanding achievements in contemporary art and architecture by women. And despite the limited number of artist slots, it also advocates intersectional feminism by showcasing a diverse range of differences among women, such as nationality, religion, culture, language, and economic status.

Throughout my research for *50 CWA*, several themes kept surfacing; the predominant one being the book's namesake. I finally gave the matter greater thought after an editor at the *New York Times* wanted to know why the book wasn't called *50 Contemporary Female Artists*. I challenged this inquiry by stating that even though the term "woman artist" may not be grammatically correct, I believe "woman" is a term that rises beyond a scientific gender classification, such as "female," while also being more gender fluid. Looking at today's social landscape, the term "woman" has become increasingly accepted and positively inserted into modern vernacular. We have come a long way from using demeaning terms such as "women's work" in the 1960s, to employing more-empowered terms such as "women's equality," "women's march," "women of color," "women's movement," and, most recently, "nasty woman."

Another theme that repeatedly entered conversation during the making of this book was whether to include the term "woman" in the title. Unfortunately, at this stage in history, when the word "artist" is read or spoken, it typically implies "male artist." Instead of denying statistics, or ignoring the subjects of gender, race, and sexuality, we felt it was best to address some of these imbalances by creating a book specifically focused on contemporary women artists. While some may view this as a categorization, we believe that this choice did not collapse or compromise any of the work featured in *50 CWA*, since gender plays no role in the capacity to create a great work of art. If anything, the decision brought forth notions of how art gets consumed and to what degree all of us maintain a bias. Ultimately, *50 CWA* looks to contemporary art practices that are less polarizing and more focused on identity and gender equality.

The book title also addresses issues on how to name women artists. Given that many historians designate women artists by their surnames or patronyms, we chose to go in the other direction for this book. As such, the title offers a key to how we arranged the order of the artists in the book: alphabetically by first name, a foundational block on which everything else will be built. When we shared this road map with one of the artists in this book, Page Turner, she joyously noted that it was the ultimate nod toward feminism.

By these ideas, the title *50 Contemporary Women Artists* reflects the progress made for and by women in the last few generations. It is my hope that *50 CWA* will be cross-generational in its appeal and contribute to the ongoing dialogue and agency of women in the arts.

In contemplating my formative experiences as a young woman at Feminist Majority, it is exciting to think that we were championing the minority over the majority, and these efforts have not diminished over the last twenty years. Undoubtedly, these persuasions have groomed my post as tireless steward of curatorial activism.

For Feminism.

Art isn't gendered. It's whether you have a vision or not.

—MARILYN MINTER

ALEAH CHAPIN

Aleah Chapin's work with figurative realism unfolds from a childhood spent in the woods of the Pacific Northwest, surrounded by ideas ranging from Buddhism and Celtic mythology to feminism and fairy stories. Using friends and family as her models, Chapin's art is both diaristic and personal. Her work boldly addresses body image in our current culture and the wildness of the natural environment and explores universal human narratives about what it is to inhabit a body.

Chapin received a BFA from Cornish College of the Arts, Seattle, Washington, and an MFA from the New York Academy of Art, New York City. Residencies include the Leipzig International Art Programme in Leipzig, Germany, and the MacDowell Colony in Peterborough, New Hampshire. Exhibitions include the *Invitational Exhibition of Visual Arts*, American Academy of Arts and Letters, New York City; *The Ingram Collection: Bodies*, Woking, United Kingdom; and a solo show, *Body/ Being* at Flowers Gallery, New York City. Chapin is a recipient of the Willard L. Metcalf Award from the American Academy of Arts and Letters, as well as the Elizabeth Greenshields Grant, and she won the BP Portrait Award at the National Portrait Gallery in London.

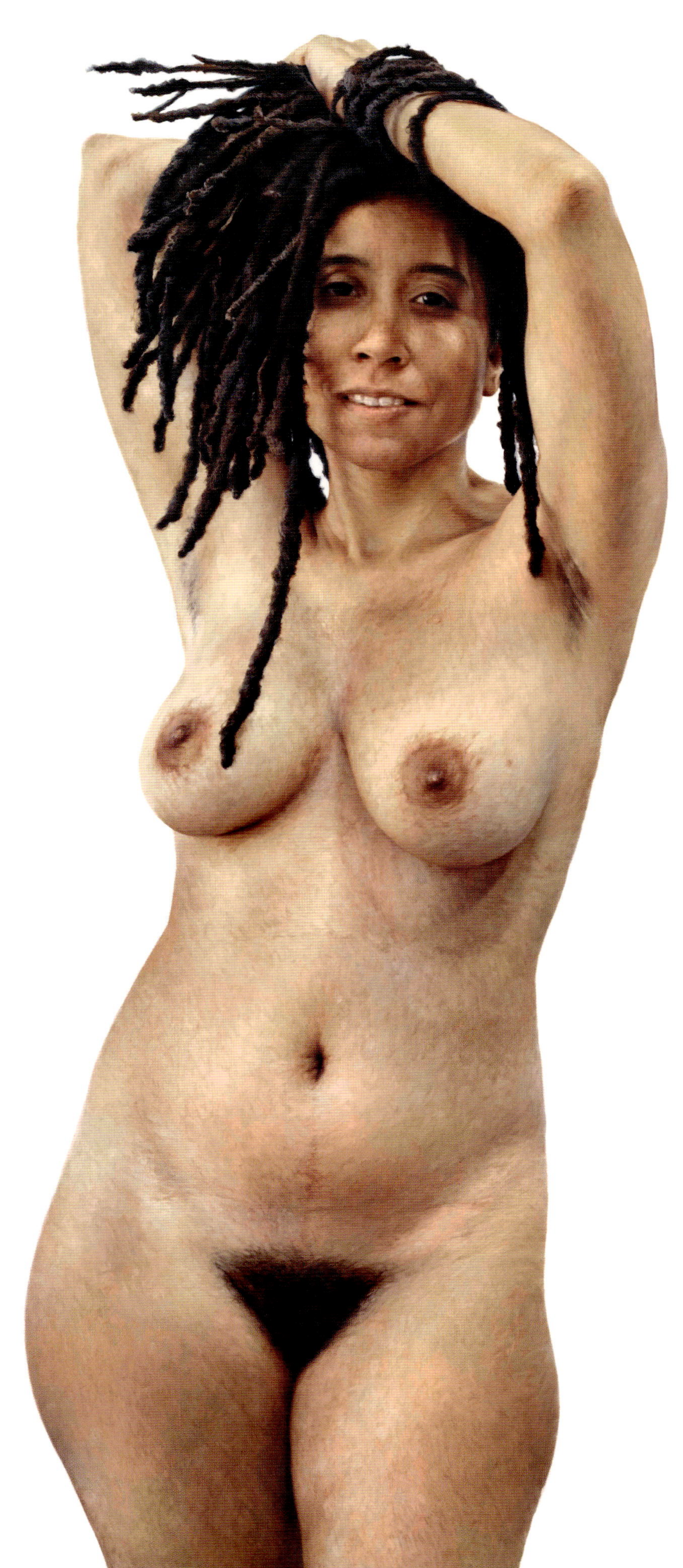

Aleah Chapin. *Kara*, 2015. Oil on canvas: 84 × 50 inches. *Courtesy of the artist and Flowers Gallery London/New York*

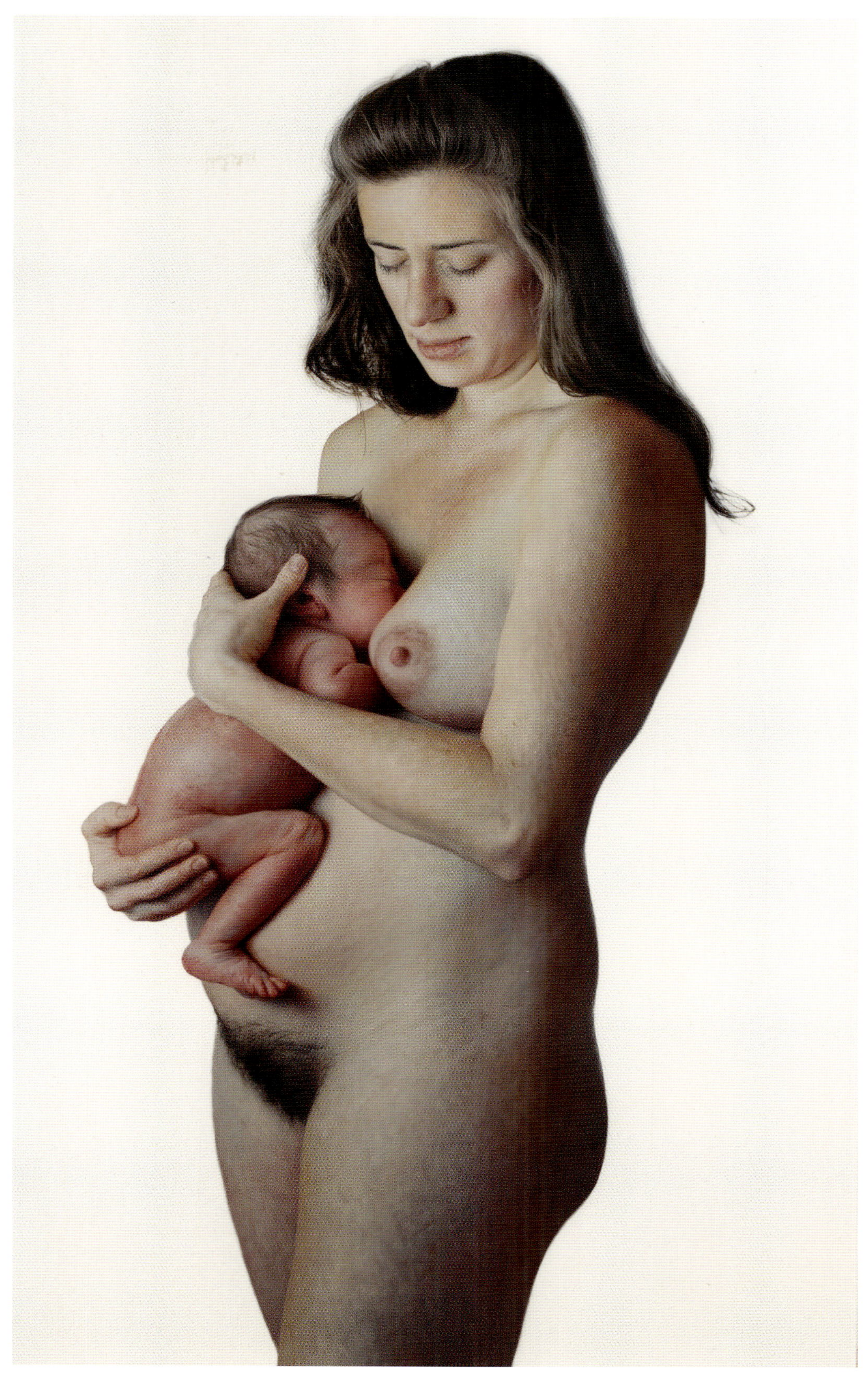

Aleah Chapin. *Rachel and Wes*, 2016. Oil on canvas: 84 × 50 inches. *Courtesy of the artist and Flowers Gallery London/New York*

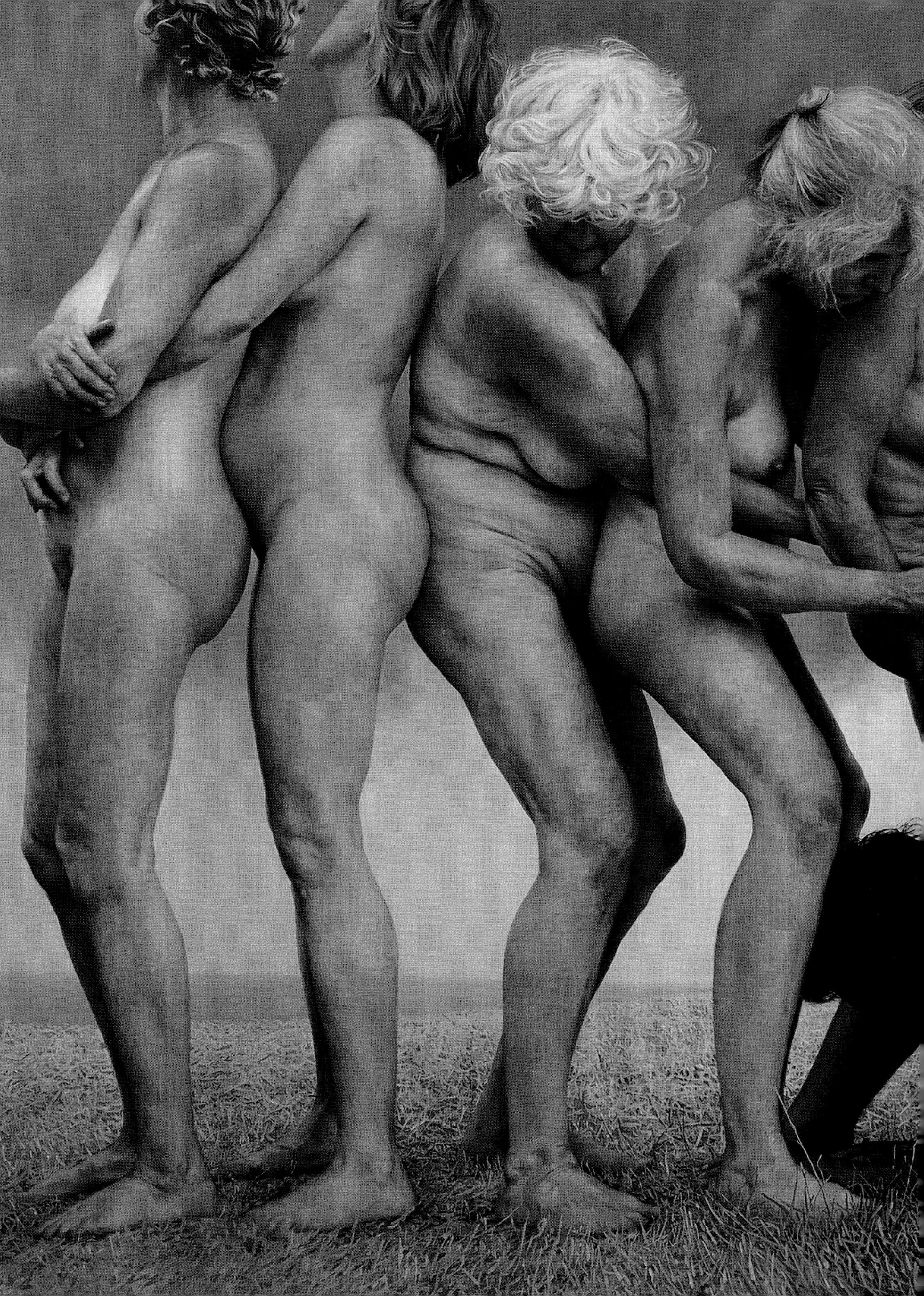

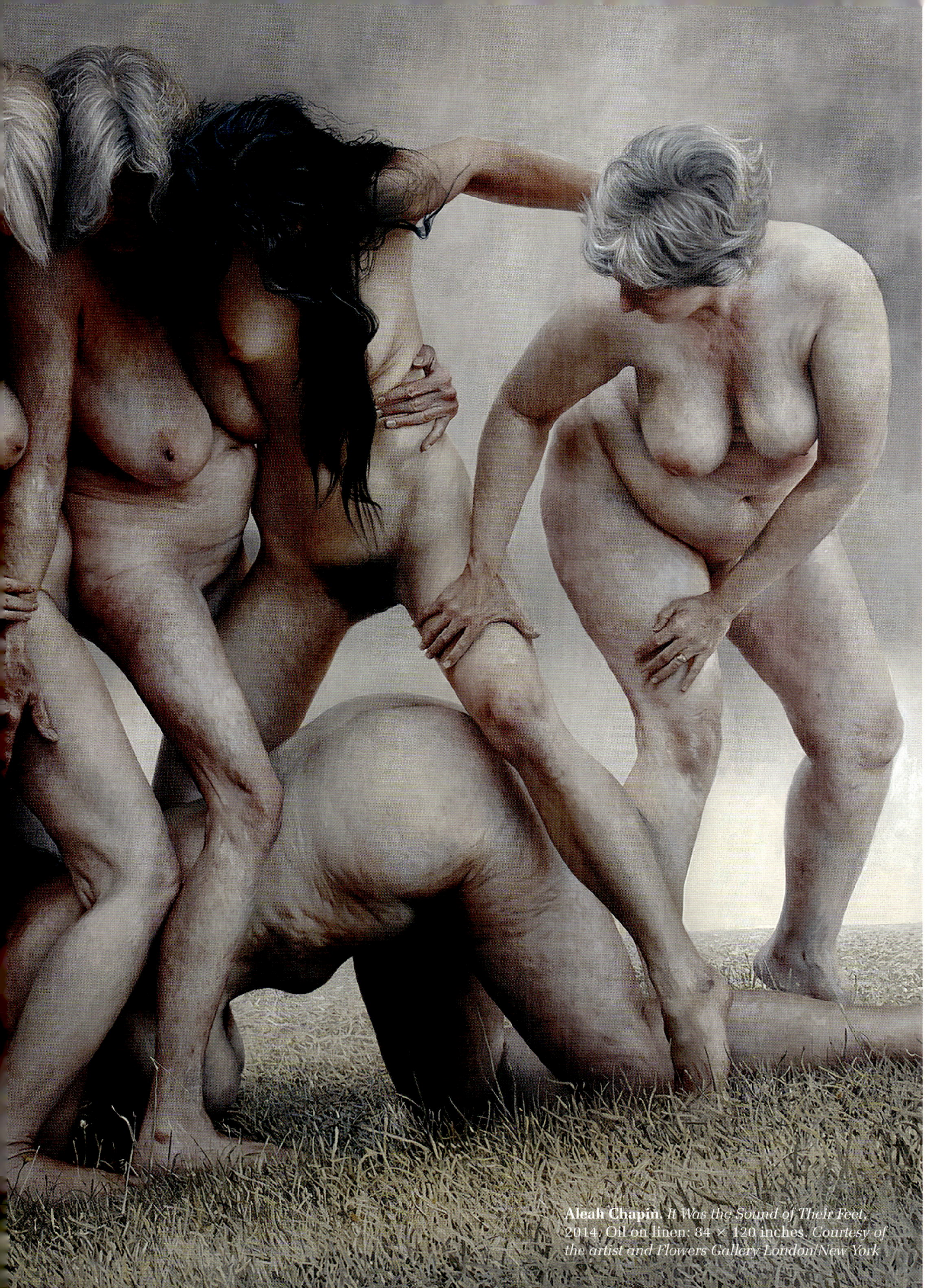

Aleah Chapin. *It Was the Sound of Their Feet,* 2014. Oil on linen: 84 × 120 inches. *Courtesy of the artist and Flowers Gallery London/New York*

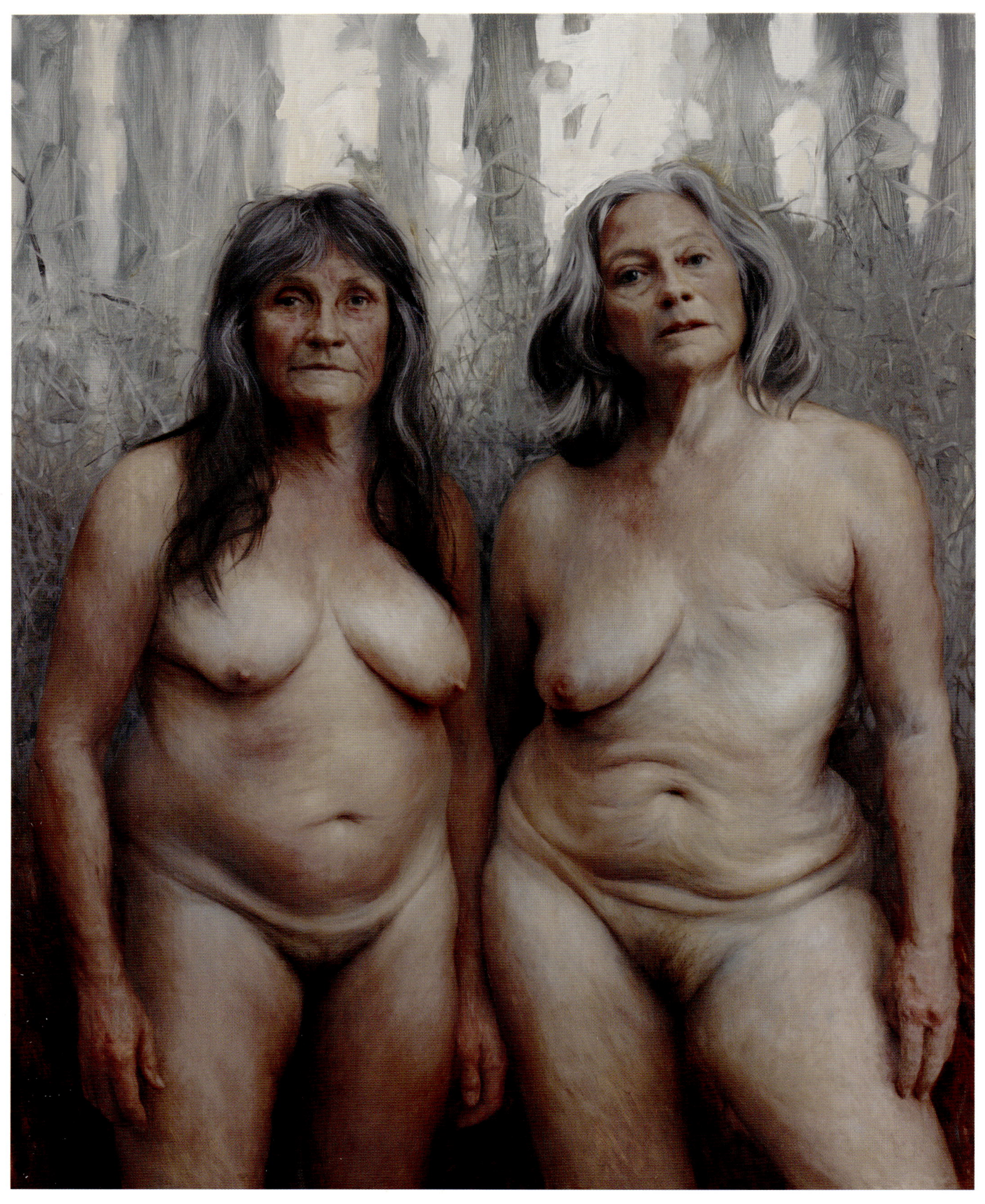

Aleah Chapin. *Shanti and Heather*, 2012. Oil on panel: 60 × 48 inches. *Courtesy of the artist and Flowers Gallery London/New York*

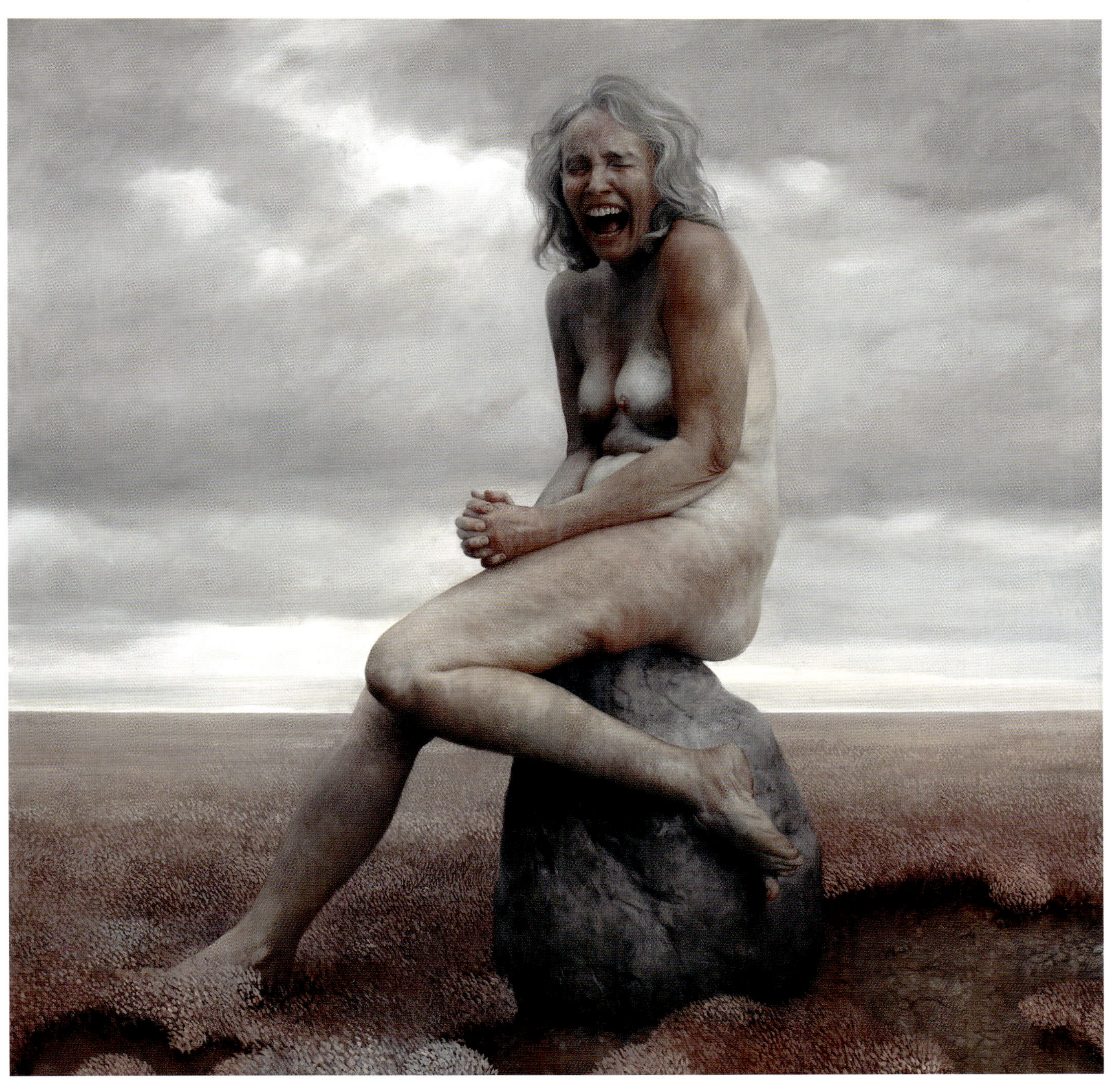

Aleah Chapin. *The Tempest*, 2012. Oil on canvas: 82 × 82 inches. *Courtesy of the artist and Flowers Gallery London/New York*

ANA TERESA FERNÁNDEZ

Through time-based actions and social gestures using her body, Ana Teresa Fernández creates artwork that explores the politics of intersectionality, subverts expectations, and illuminates the psychological and physical barriers that define gender, race, and class in Western society and the Global South. Using performance as a primary research tool in her multimedia practice, Fernández painstakingly renders masterful, larger-than-life oil paintings that stem from her carefully developed, socially conscious video performances.

Fernández's project *Borrando La Frontera (Erasing the Border)* has been the subject of extensive media attention and critical acclaim. Originally staged in 2011, the work has been recommissioned across various US-Mexico border locations and was recorded for a documentary feature by VICE media in 2017. Fernández has had numerous exhibitions of her paintings, including *Mi Tierra: Contemporary Artists Explore Place* at the Denver Art Museum, Denver, Colorado; *Ana Mendieta / Threads of Influence* at Arizona State University Art Museum, Tempe, Arizona; and *Framing Beauty* at the Grunwald Gallery, Indiana University, Bloomington, curated by Deborah Willis. Fernández received her BFA in 2004 and MFA in 2006, both from the San Francisco Art Institute, San Francisco, California. Fernández was born in 1981 in Tampico, Mexico, and lives and works in San Francisco.

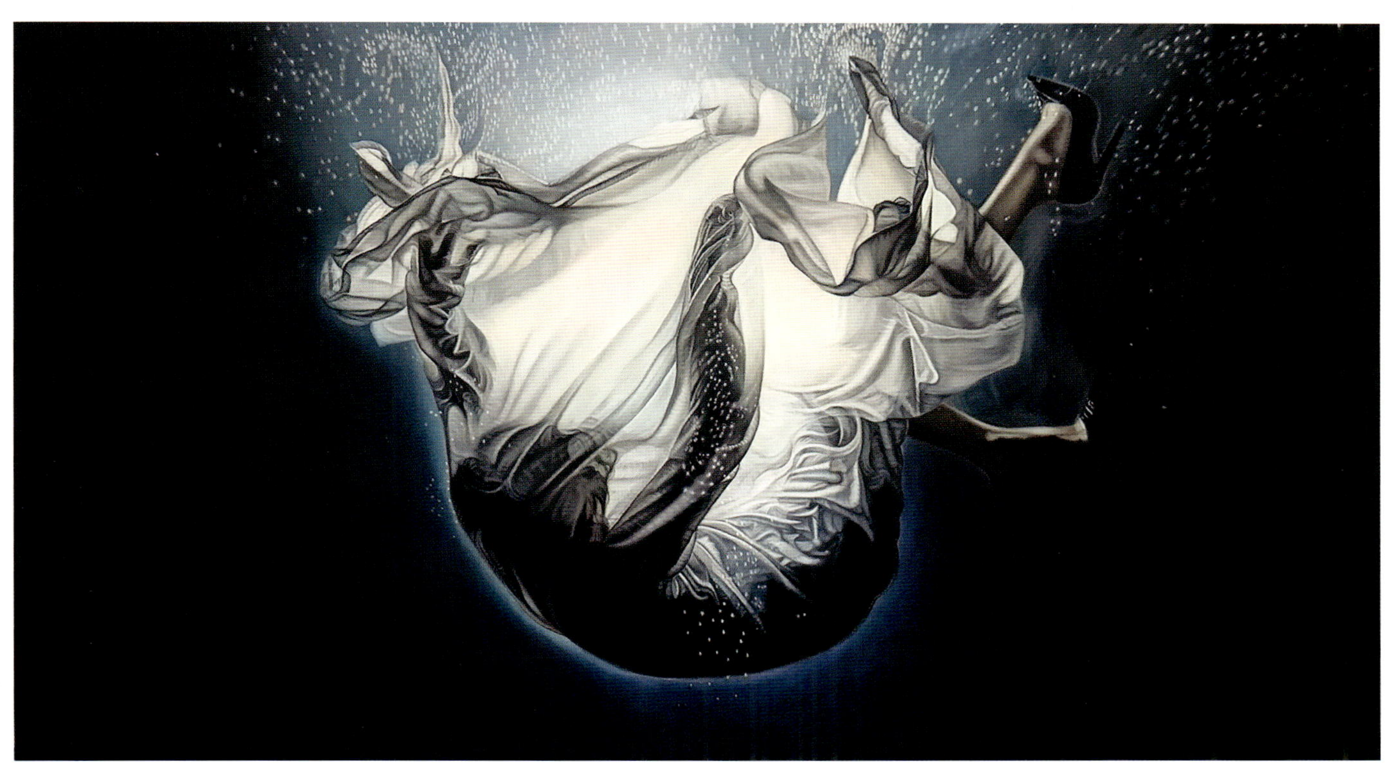

Ana Teresa Fernández. *Gravity*, 2017. Oil on canvas: 53 × 94 inches. *Courtesy of the artist and Gallery Wendi Norris, San Francisco*

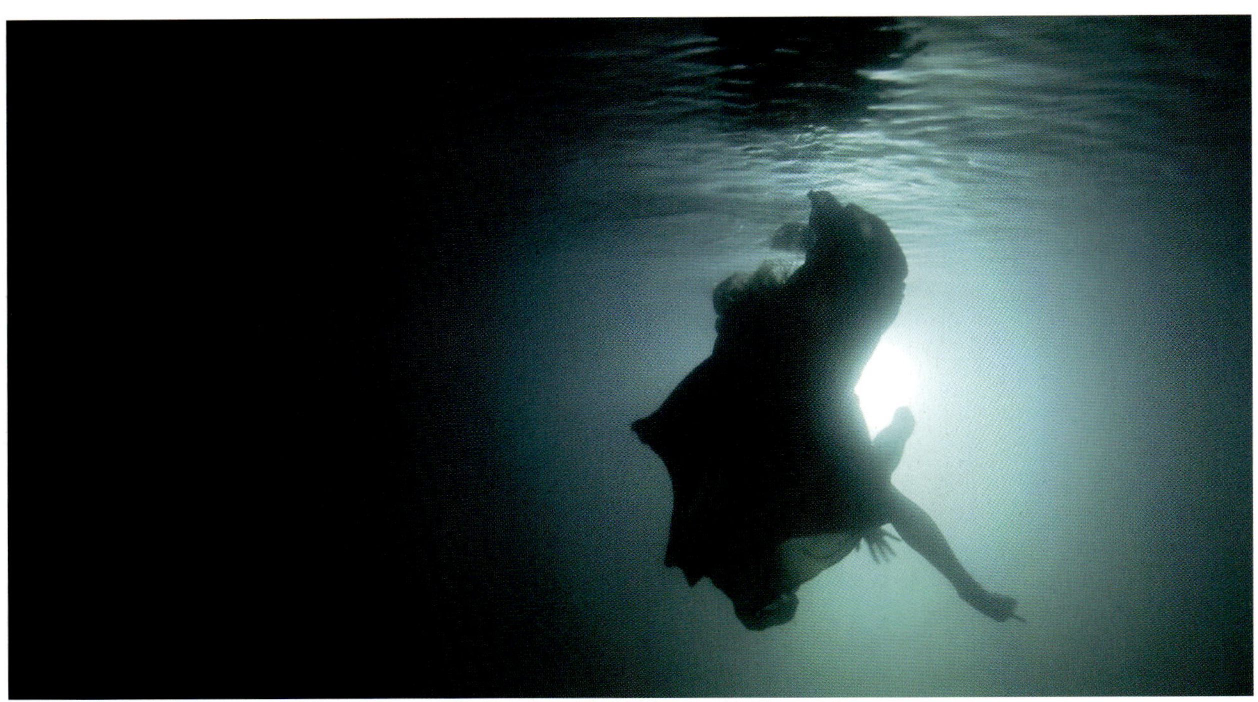

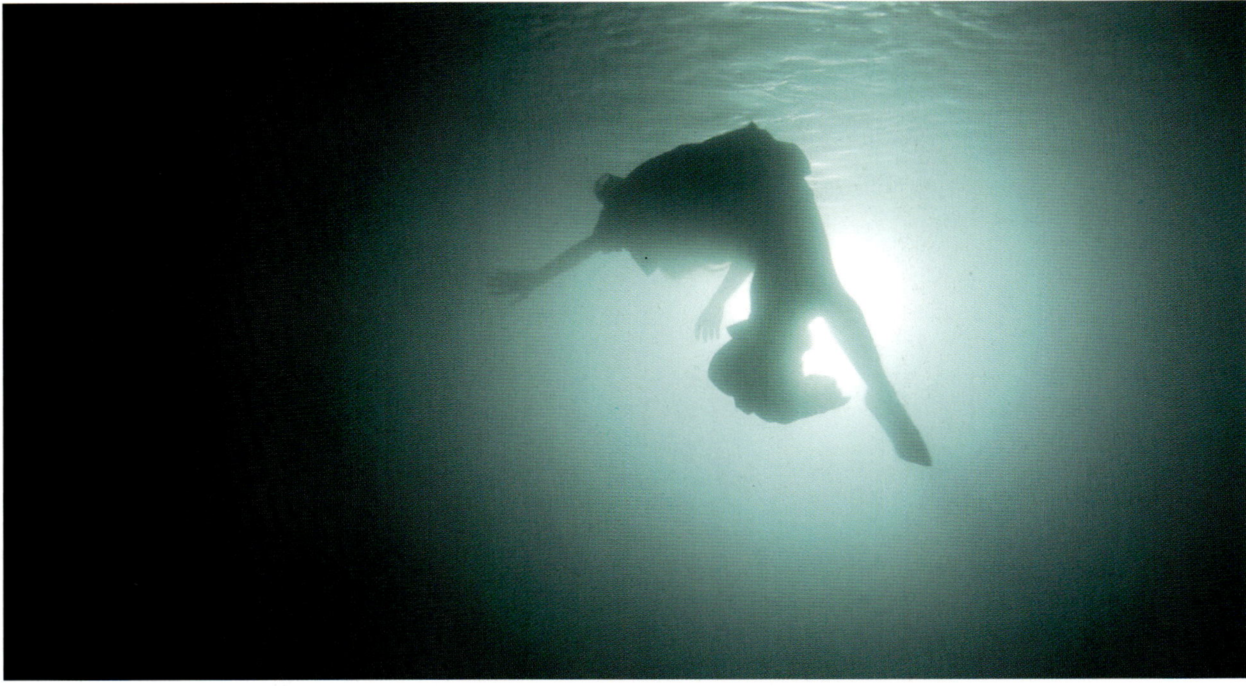

Ana Teresa Fernández. *Untitled* (performance documentation), 2017. Digital Video Stills. *Courtesy of the artist and Gallery Wendi Norris, San Francisco*

Ana Teresa Fernández. *Untitled* (performance documentation), 2017. Digital Video Stills. *Courtesy of the artist and Gallery Wendi Norris, San Francisco*

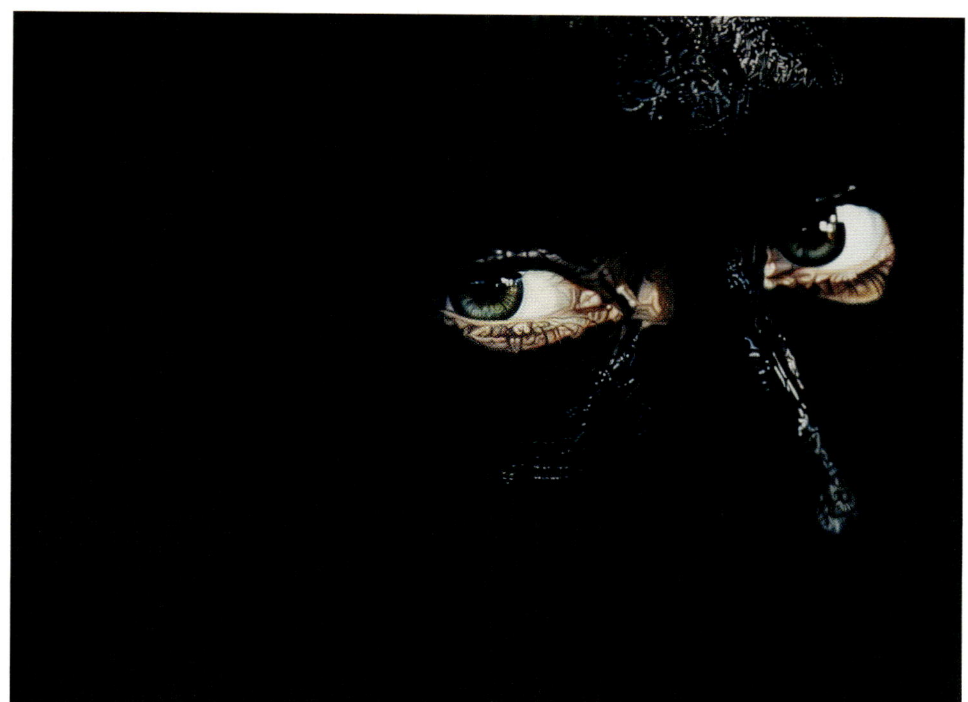

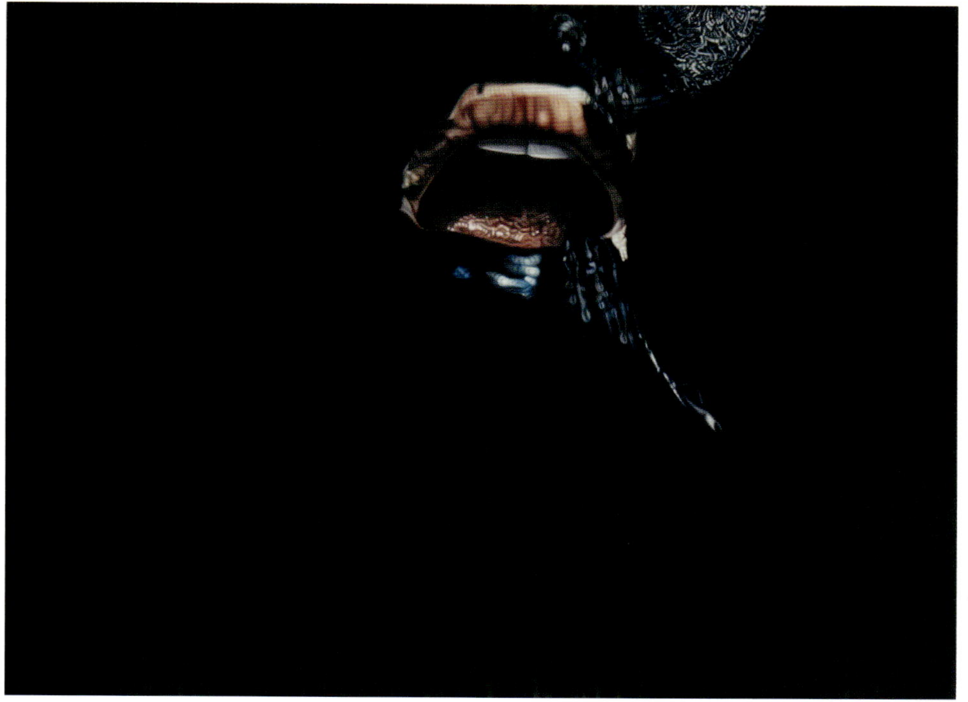

Ana Teresa Fernández. *Erasure 1* (performance documentation), 2016. Oil on canvas: 72 × 98 inches. *Courtesy of the artist and Gallery Wendi Norris, San Francisco*

Ana Teresa Fernández. *Erasure 2* (performance documentation), 2016. Oil on canvas: 72 × 98 inches. *Courtesy of the artist and Gallery Wendi Norris, San Francisco*

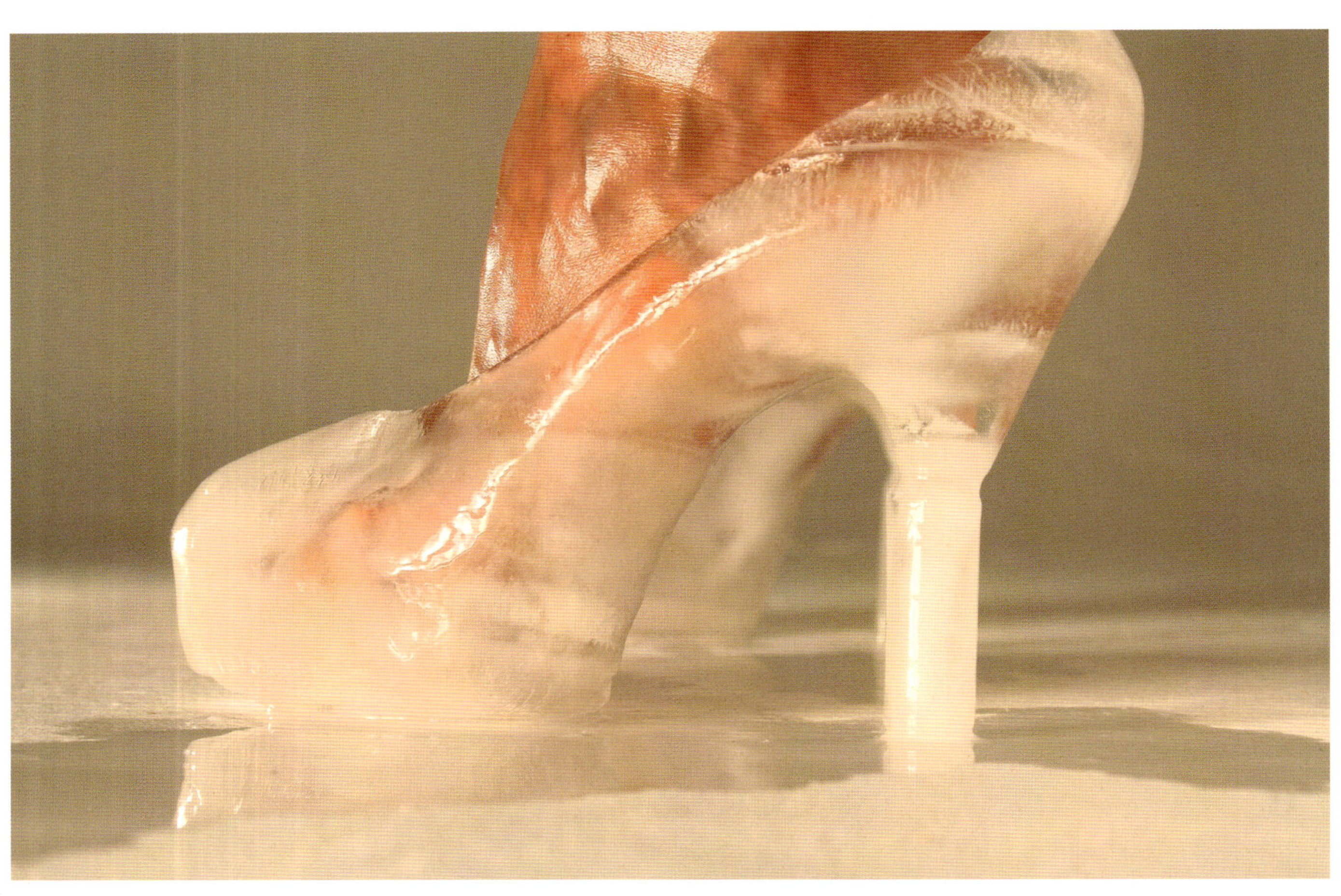

Ana Teresa Fernández. *Ice Queen* (performance documentation), 2013. Digital still from 45 min performance: 18 × 27 inches. Edition 1/5. *Courtesy of the artist and Gallery Wendi Norris, San Francisco*

BARBARA SEGAL

Barbara Segal is a sculptor and master stone carver with an eye schooled in the forms, patterns, and textures of Renaissance and baroque masterpieces. Segal creates pop and fashion icons in rare and exquisite stones. As an ongoing part of her practice, Segal explores ways to merge new technologies with the ancient tradition of stone carving, design, nostalgia, and pop culture. Works such as her *Designer Handbags* series explore society's long-standing obsession with status symbols and their cultural impact, while her *Little Girl's Dresses* turns translucent stones into delicate layers of fabric and lace.

Segal studied at Pratt Institute, New York City, and L'Ècole des Beaux-Arts, Paris. She has worked in some of the finest Italian marble studios and foundries and is represented by multiple US galleries, including Gallery Biba, Palm Beach, Florida; Markowicz Fine Art, Miami, Florida; Krause Gallery, New York City; Vickers Collection, Aspen, Colorado; and Art Angels LA Gallery, Los Angeles. Segal's works are in numerous public and private collections, including MTA Arts for Transit; New York City Department of Parks & Recreation; the White House; Neuberger Museum of Art; Leslie Wexler; Limited; and Malcolm Forbes. Segal's work has been published internationally, including in the *New York Times*, *Sculpture*, the *New York Post*, *Marie Claire*, and *L'Officiel Italia*. She has received an America for the Arts Award, as well as New York State Assembly and Senate citations. Segal teaches stone carving at the School of Visual Arts and the New York Academy of Art in New York City.

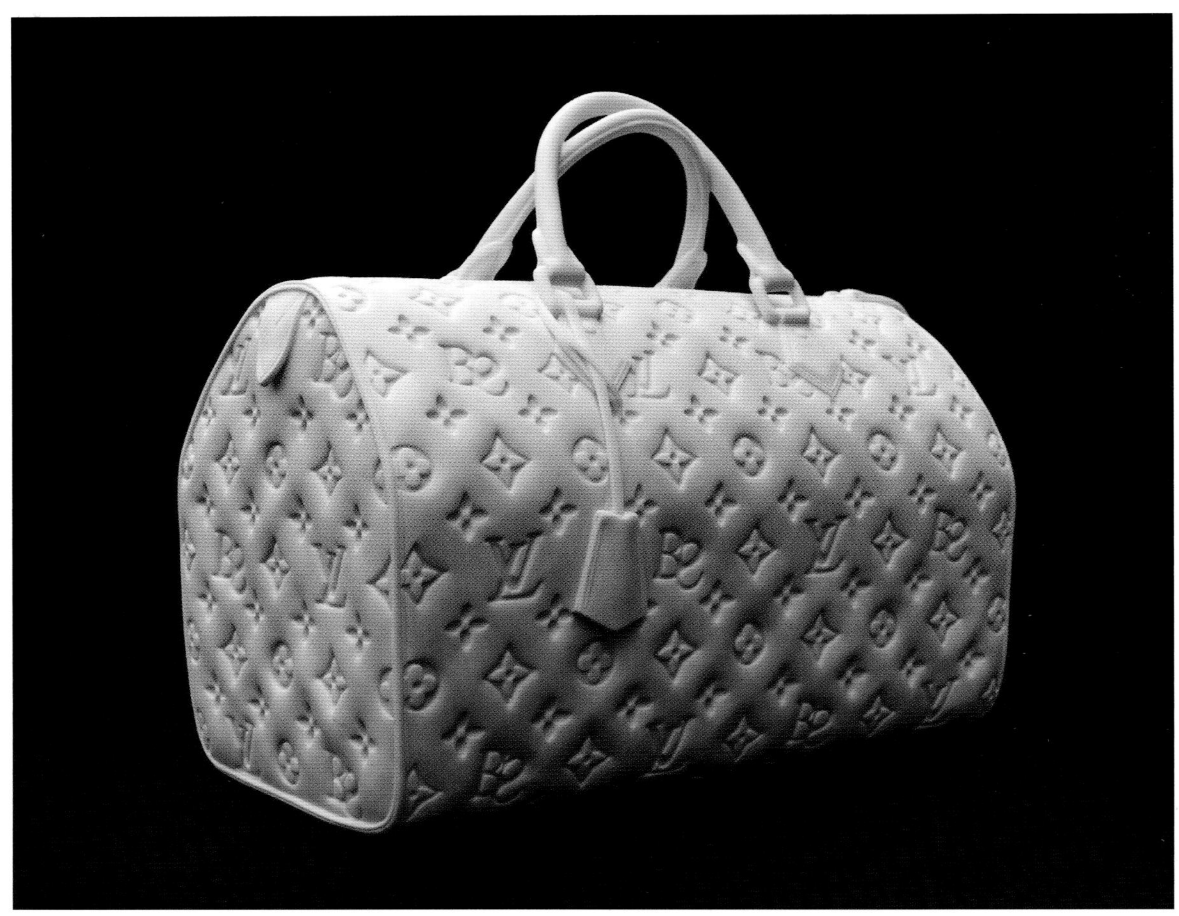

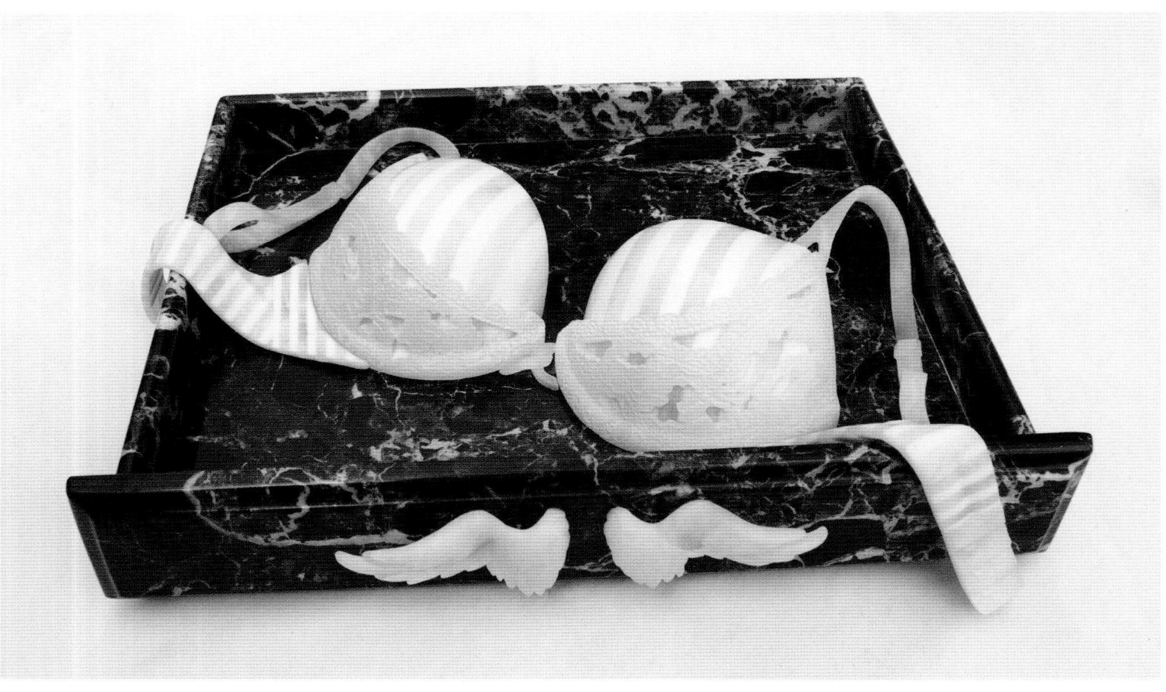

Barbara Segal. *L.V.B.S.*, 2018. White Greek marble: 19 × 22 × 11 inches. *Courtesy of the artist.*

Barbara Segal. *Miraculous Plunge*, 2012. Pink onyx and marble: 4 × 16 × 14 inches. *Courtesy of the artist*

Barbara Segal. *Hot Schott*, 1994. Belgian black marble and steel: 63 × 23 × 8 inches. *Courtesy of the artist*

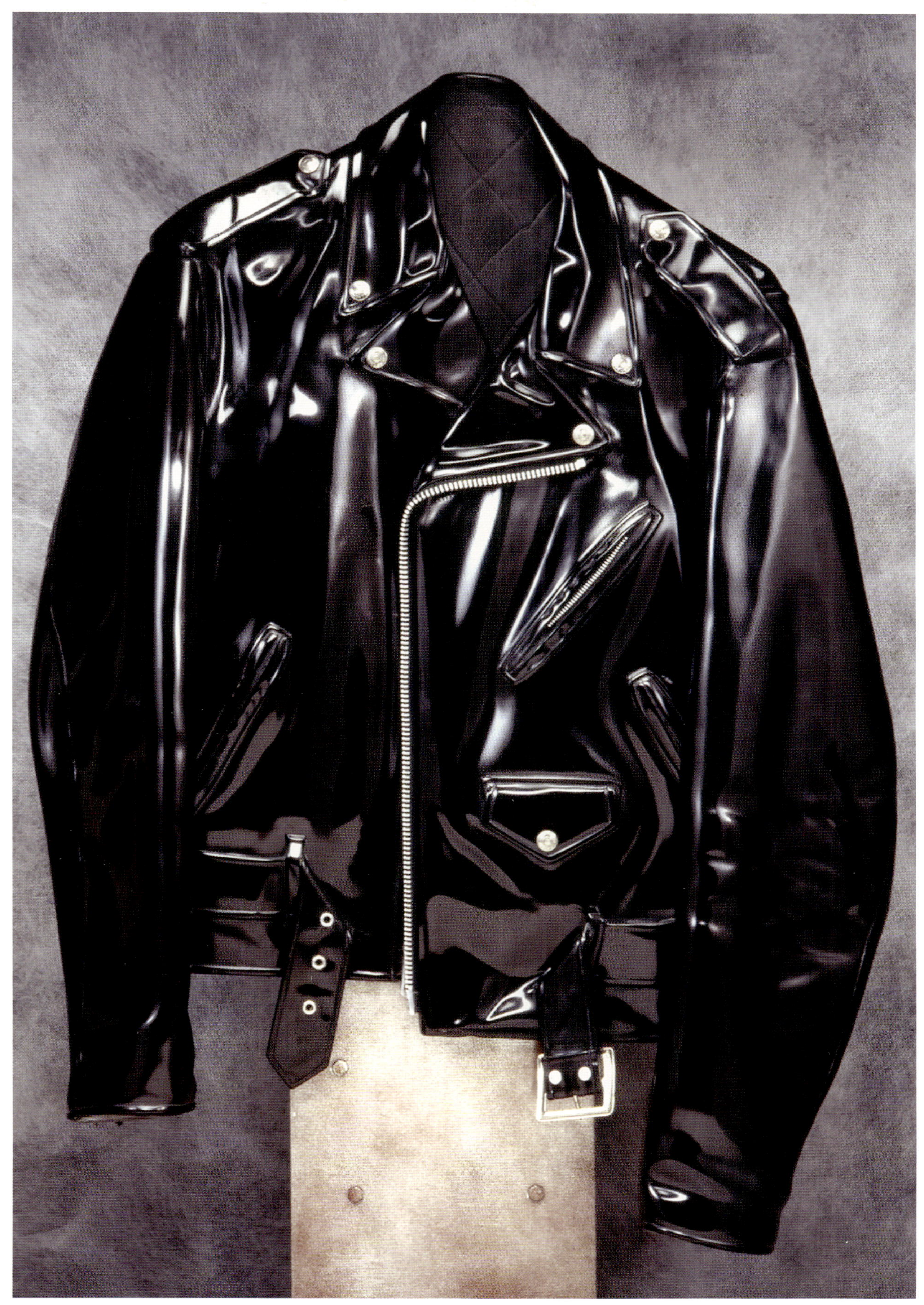

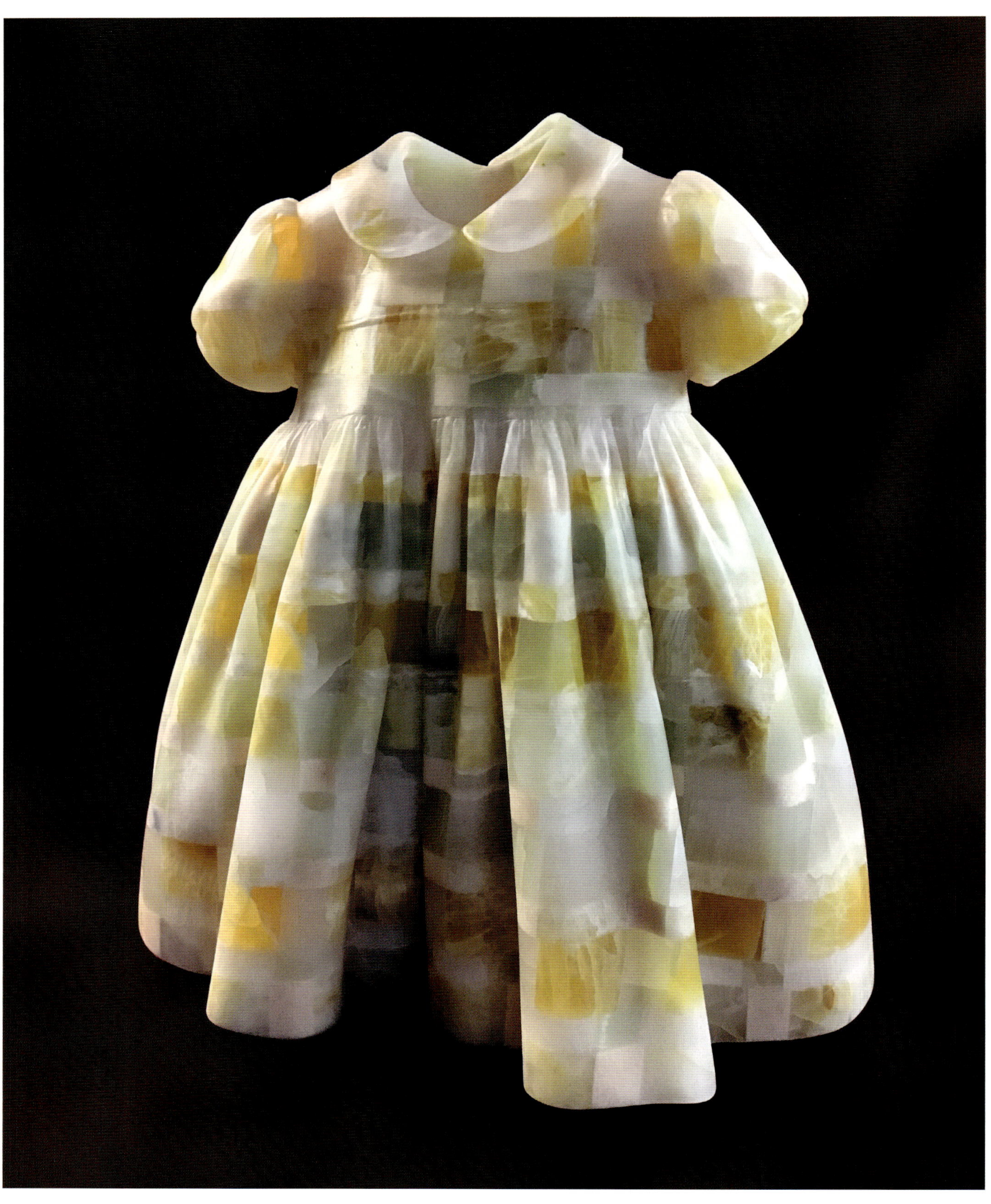

Barbara Segal. *Butterscotch Sunday*, 2016. Constructed marble and onyx: 20 × 18 × 12 inches. *Courtesy of the artist*

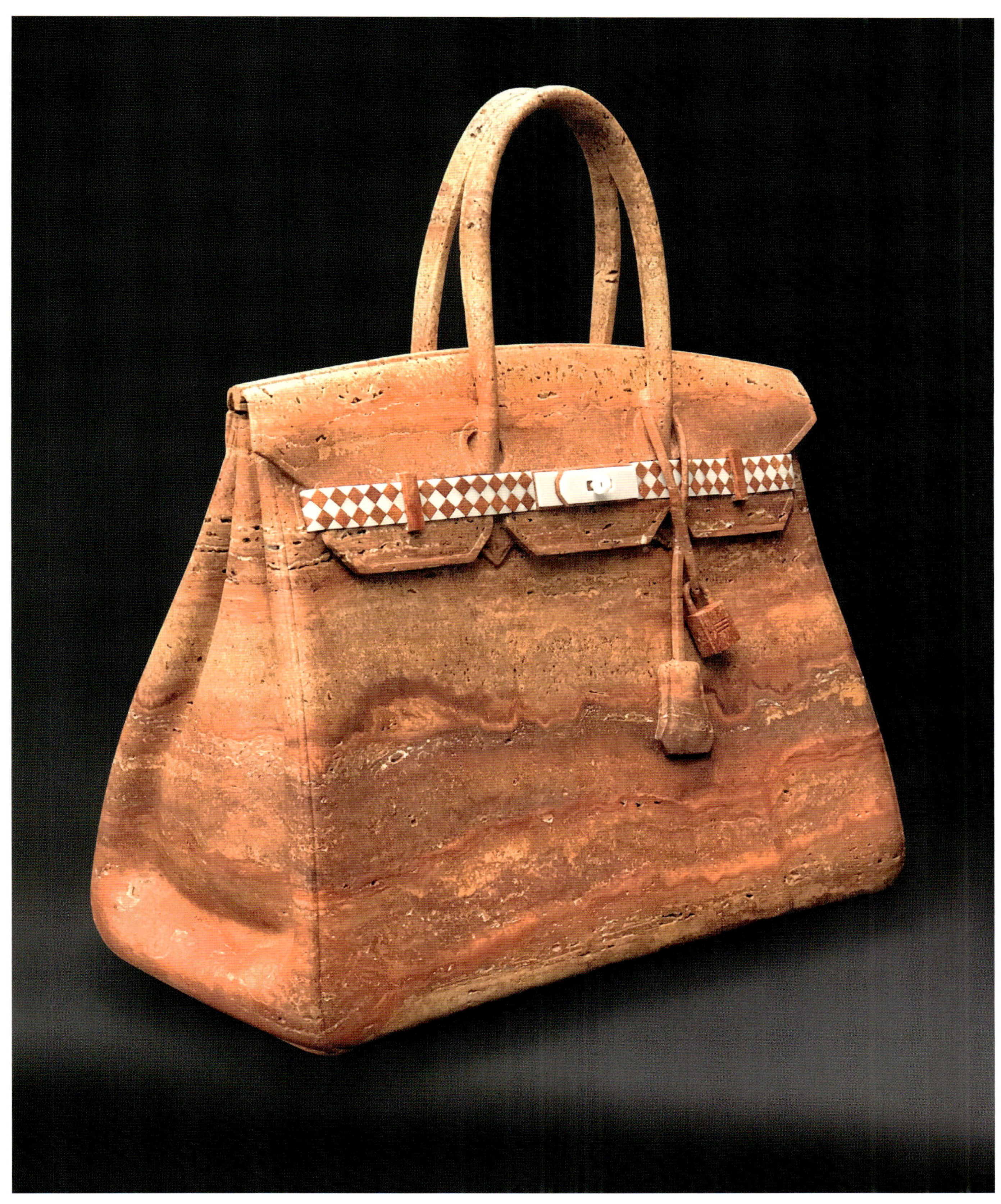

Barbara Segal. *Persian Candy*, 2017. Persian Travertine marble with red and white marble mosaics: 24 × 23 × 10 inches. *Courtesy of the artist*

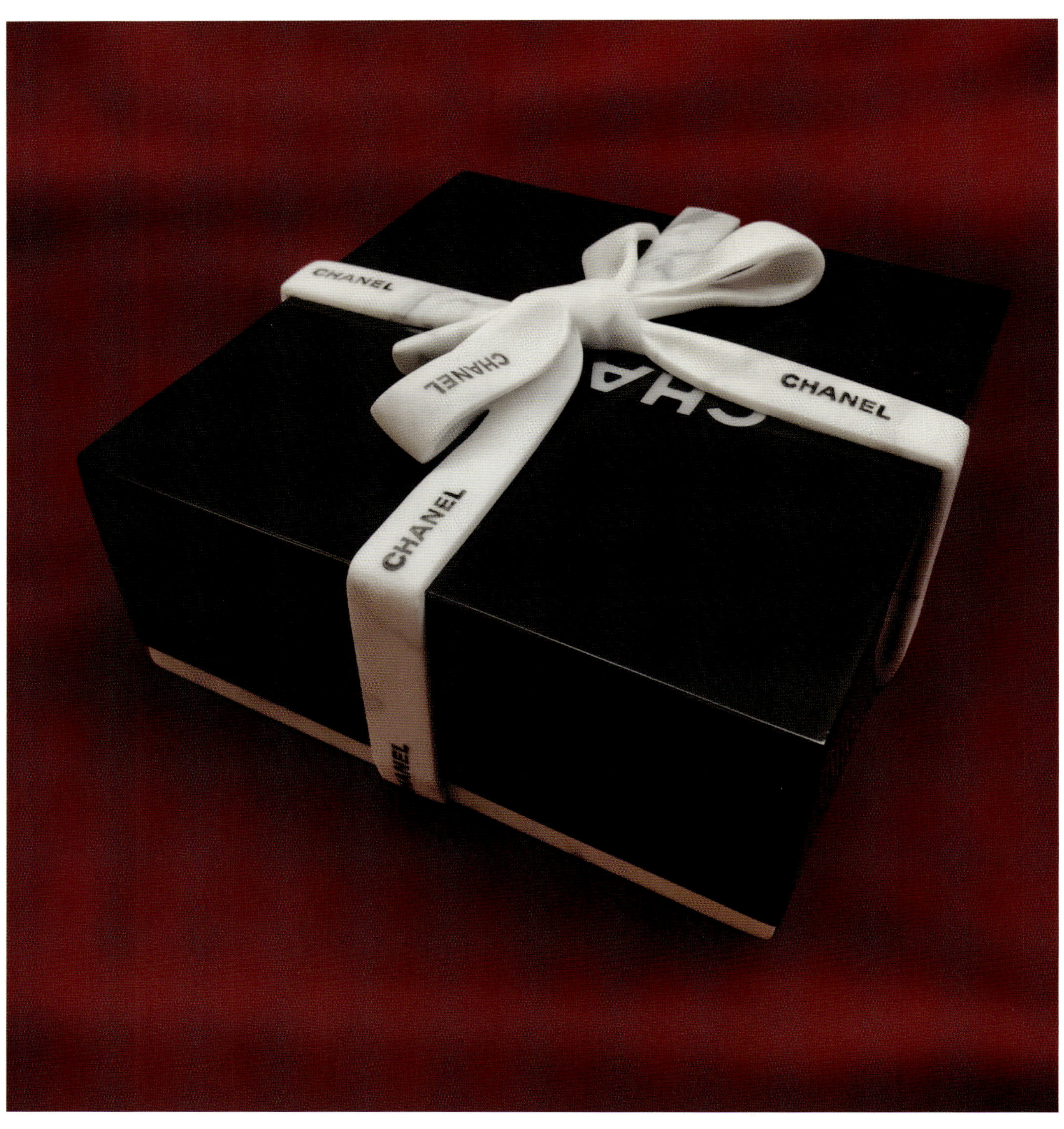

Barbara Segal. *Gift Wrapped*, 2017. Belgian black marble and carrara marble: 13 × 20 × 6 inches. *Courtesy of the artist*

Barbara Segal. *Metamorphose*, 2016. Orange calcite and marble: 13 × 20 × 6 inches. *Courtesy of the artist*

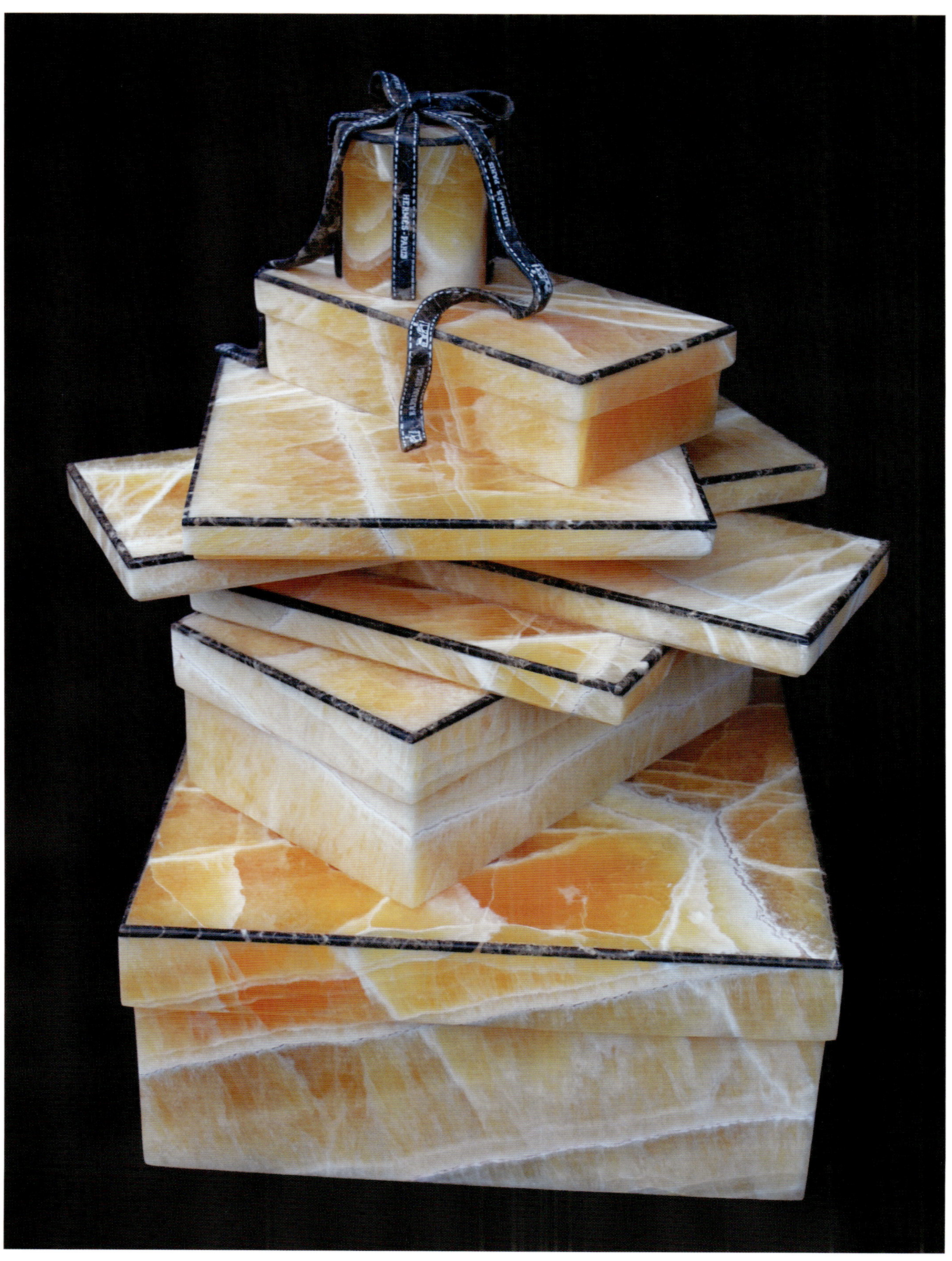
HERMÈS-PARIS
HERMÈS-PARIS

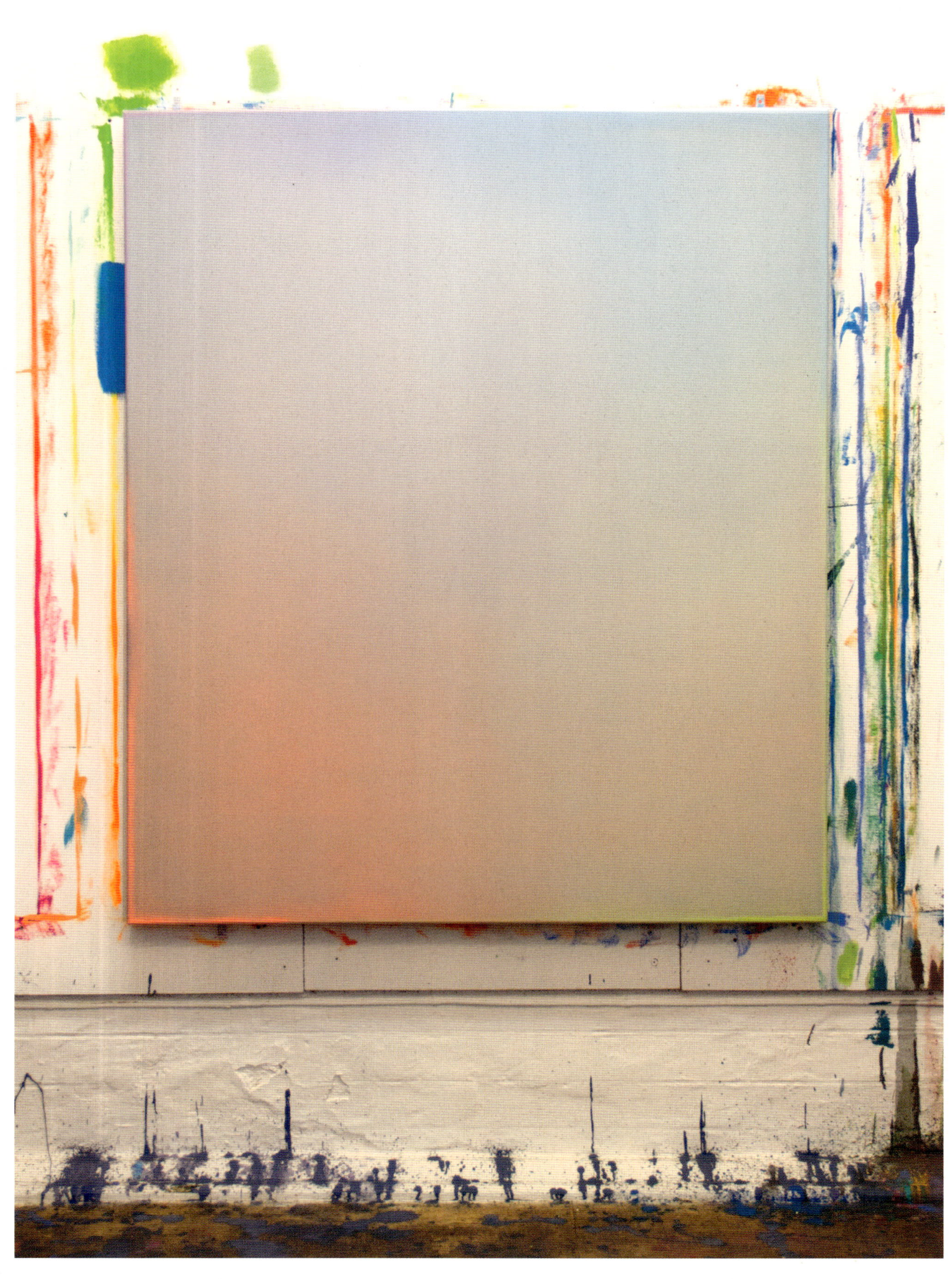

Boo Saville. *Leda*, 2015. Oil on canvas: 43.25 × 51.2 inches. *Courtesy of Davidson Contemporary, New York*

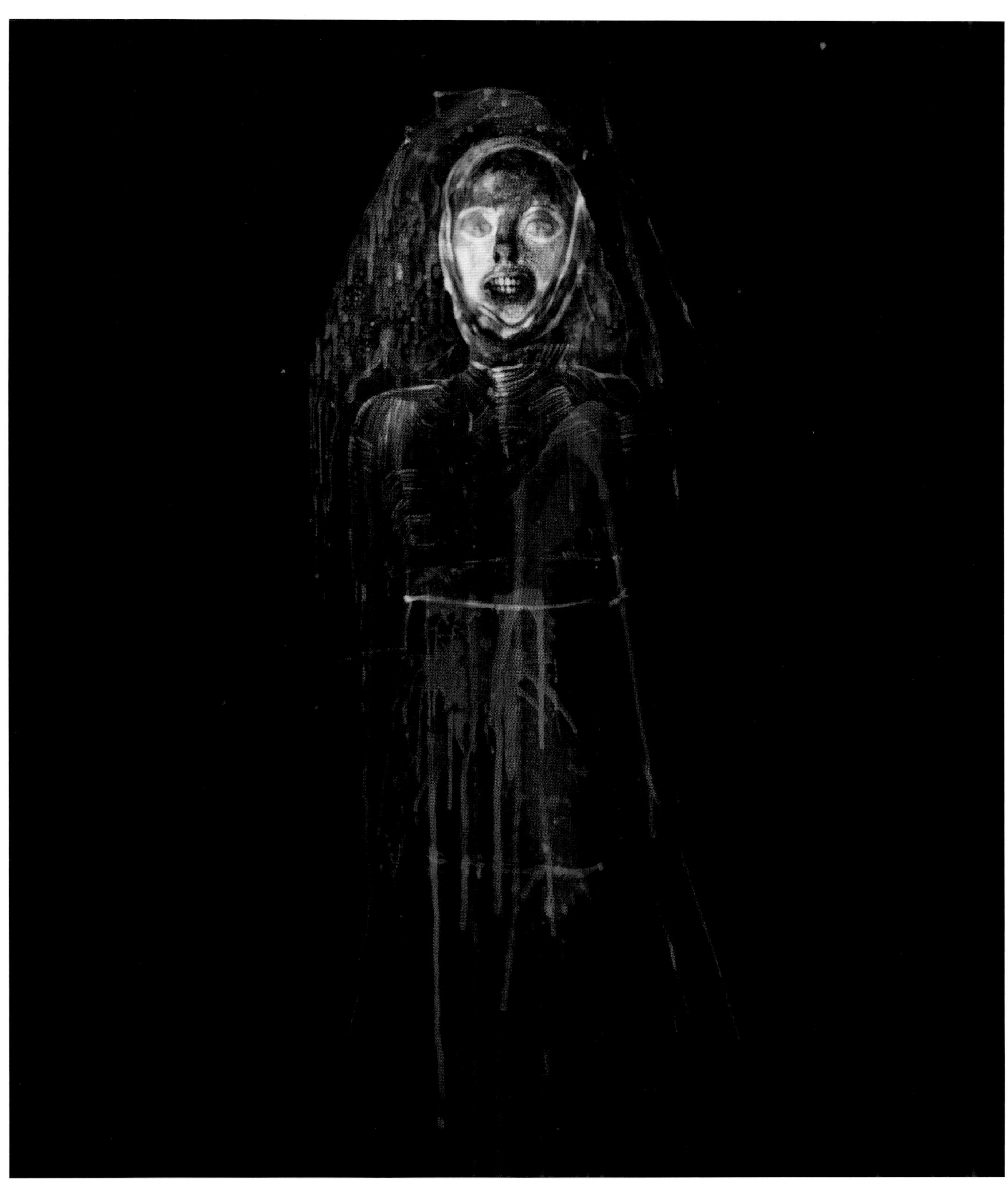

Boo Saville. *The Explorer*, 2009. Household bleach on black cotton: 55 × 65 inches. *Courtesy of Davidson Contemporary, New York*

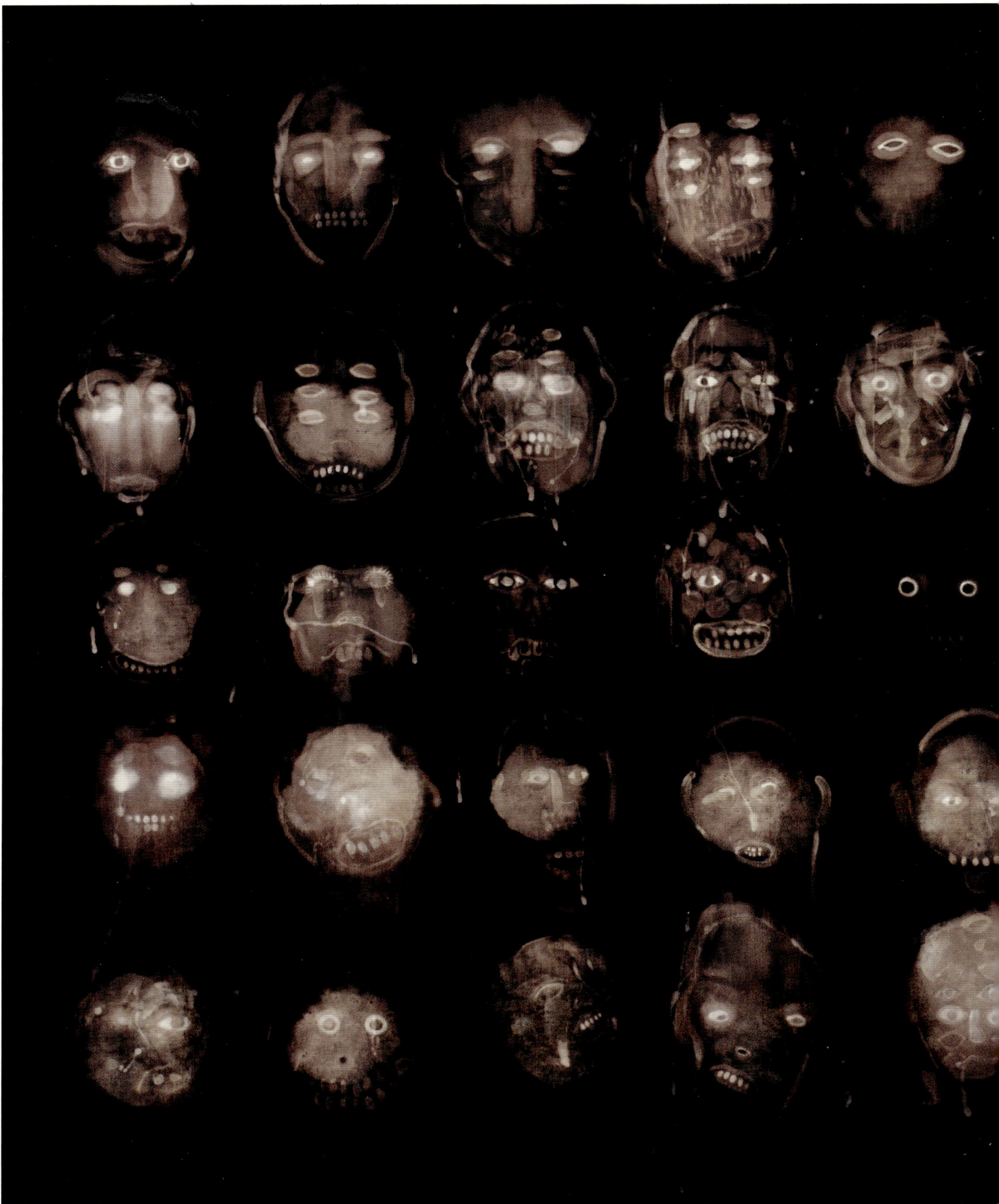

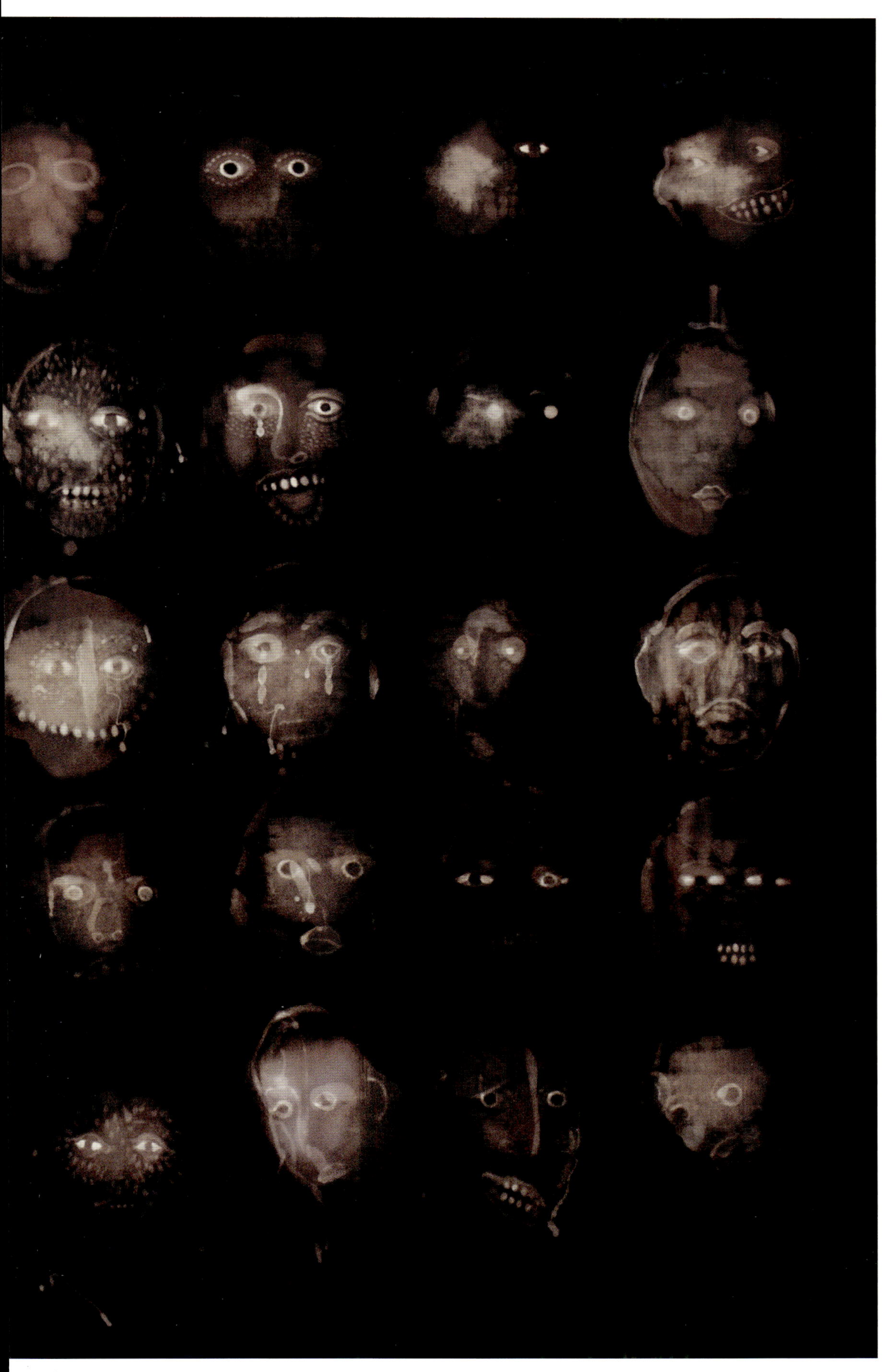

Boo Saville. *How Do We Feel?*, 2010. Household bleach on black cotton: 59 × 78.75 inches. *Courtesy of Davidson Contemporary, New York*

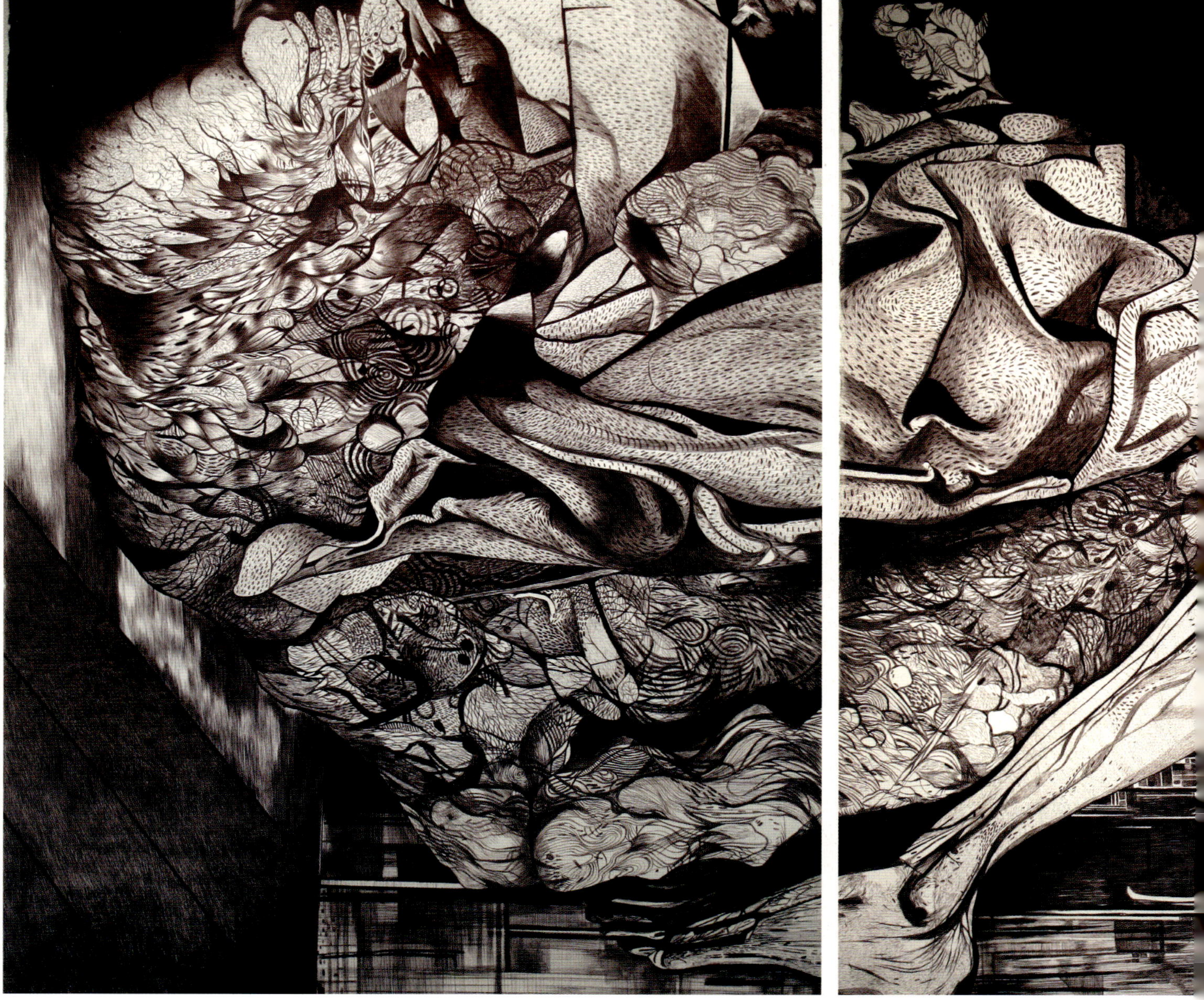

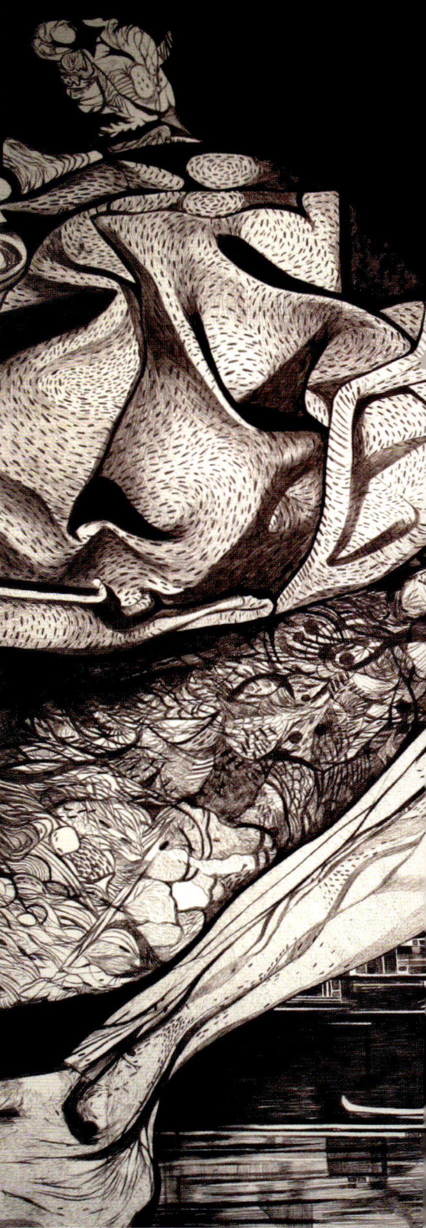

Boo Saville. *Buttersunk*, 2009. Ballpoint pen on paper: 66.1 × 30 inches. *Courtesy of Davidson Contemporary, New York*

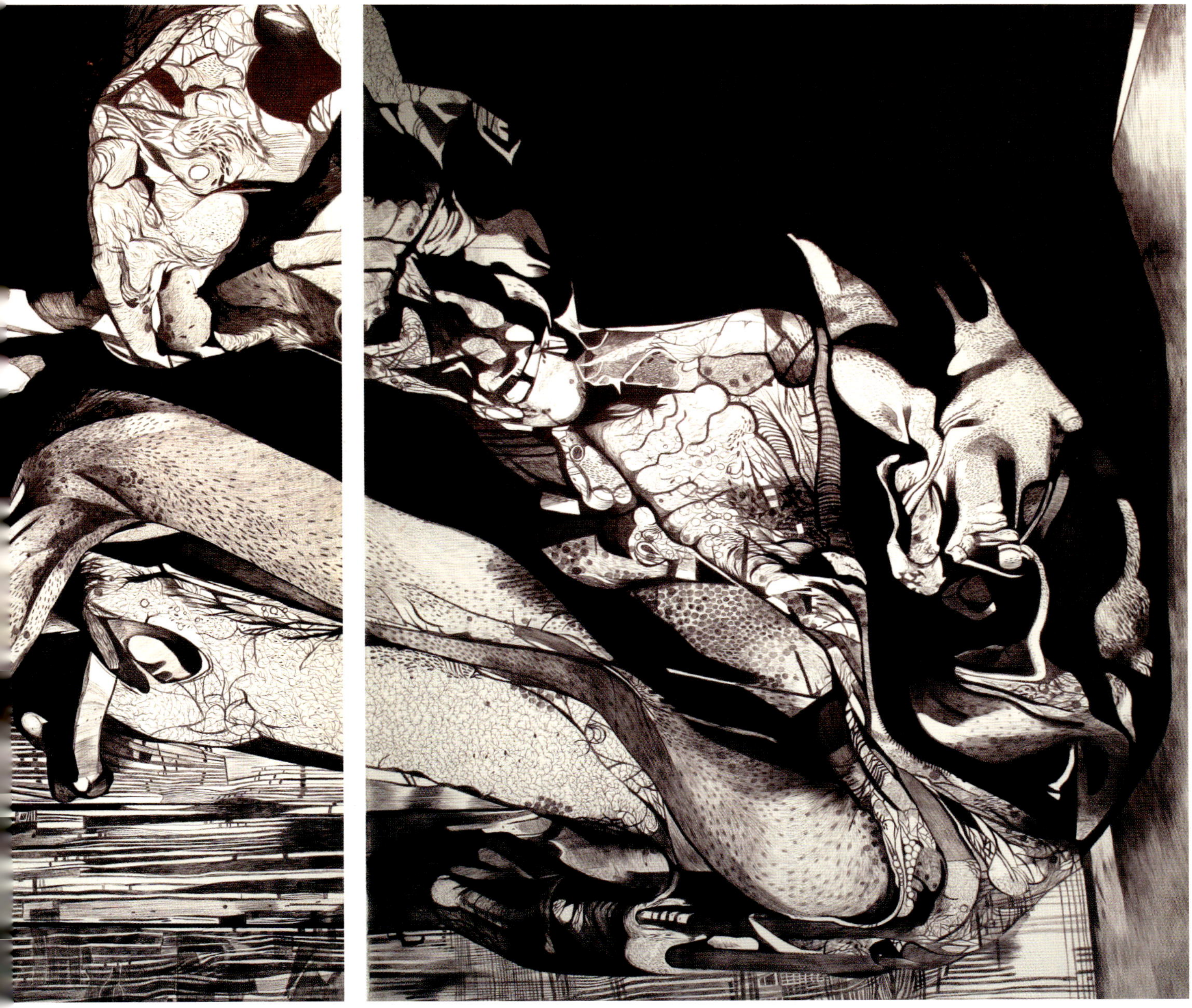

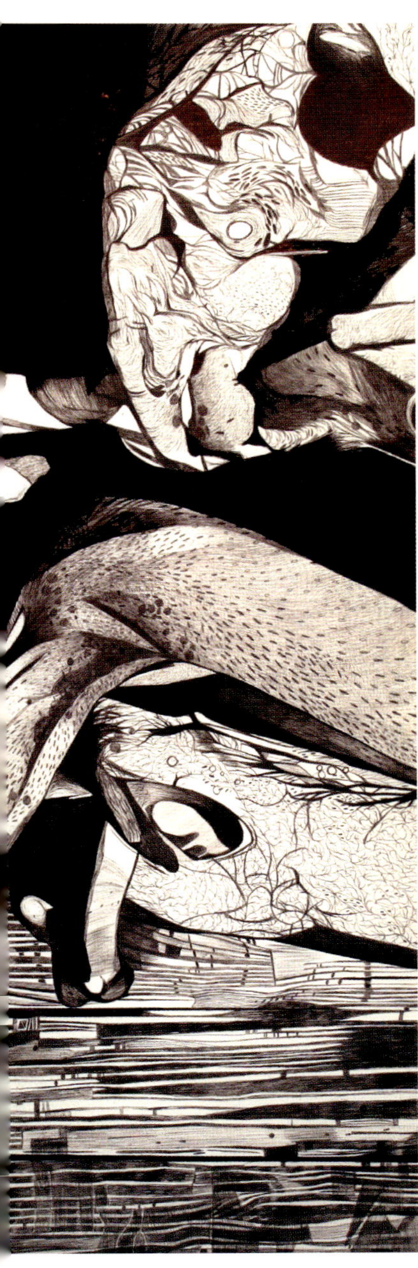

CAROLINE O'DONNELL

Caroline O'Donnell is the winner of MoMA/PS1's Young Architect's Program for *Party Wall* and is the Edgar A. Tafel Assistant Professor and the Director of the Master of Architecture Program at Cornell University. She is principal of the design practice CODA. Other recent projects include *Urchin*, a pavilion for the Cornell Council for the Arts Biennial, and *Bloodline,* a self-consuming grill pavilion for Schloss Solitude, in Stuttgart, Germany. O'Donnell is the editor of the *Cornell Journal of Architecture* and the former founding editor of *Pidgin* magazine. Her first book is *Niche Tactics: Generative Relationships between Architecture and Site*.

O'Donnell was born in Athlone, Ireland, and was raised there and in Derry, Northern Ireland. She received her B.Arch from the Manchester School of Architecture, England, and her M.Arch. from Princeton University, Princeton, New Jersey. Before teaching at Cornell, O'Donnell taught at the Irwin S. Chanin School of Architecture at the Cooper Union and worked at KCAP Architects and Planners in Rotterdam, The Netherlands, and Eisenman Architects in New York, where she was project leader for the Hamburg Library and the Pompei Santuario Railway Station.

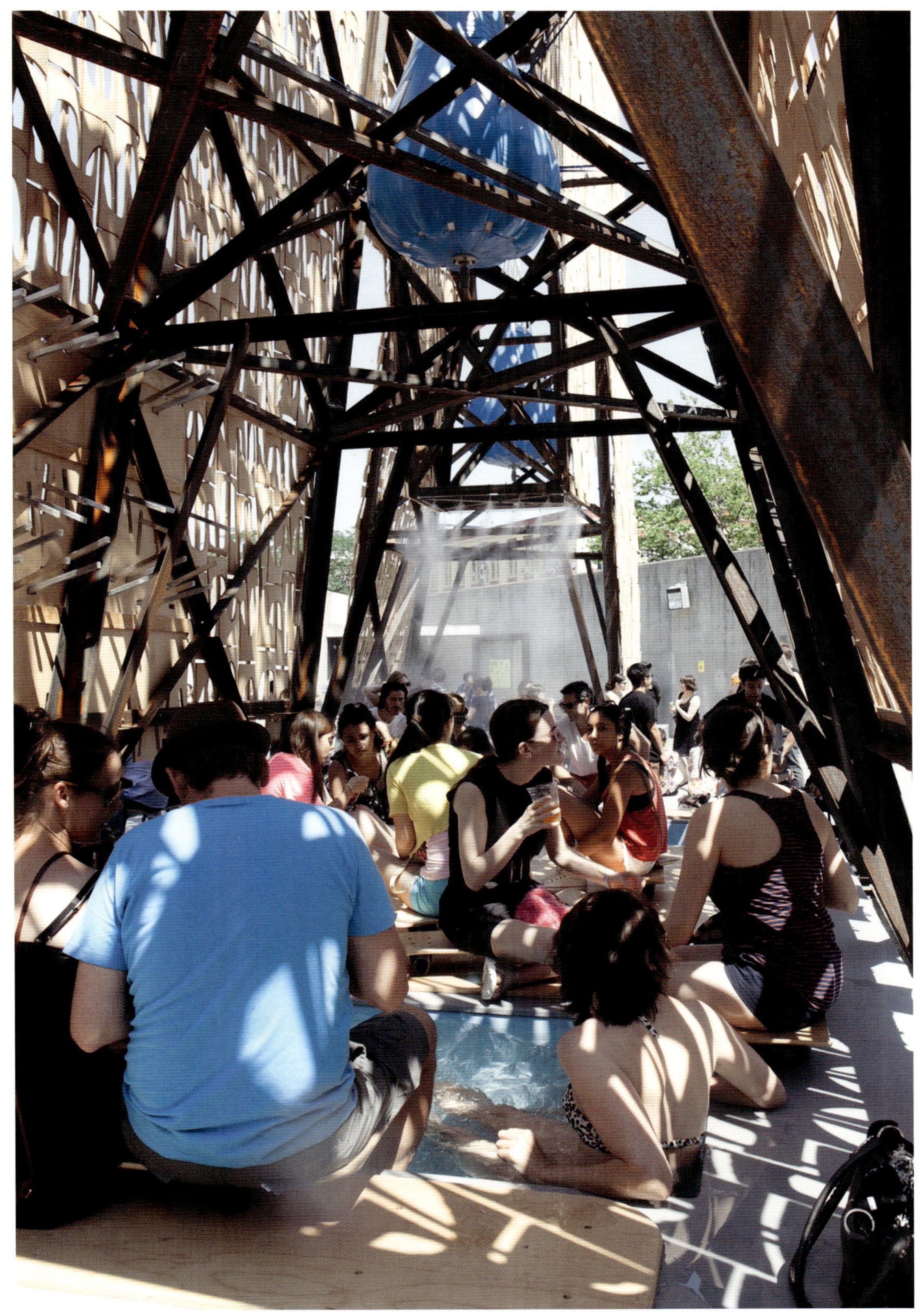

Caroline O'Donnell (CODA). *Party Wall*, 2013. Steel, skateboard bones, and blanks (offcuts): 120 × 40 × 10 feet. Installation view, PS1 MoMA, New York City. Photographer: Zachary Tyler Newton. *Courtesy of the artist*

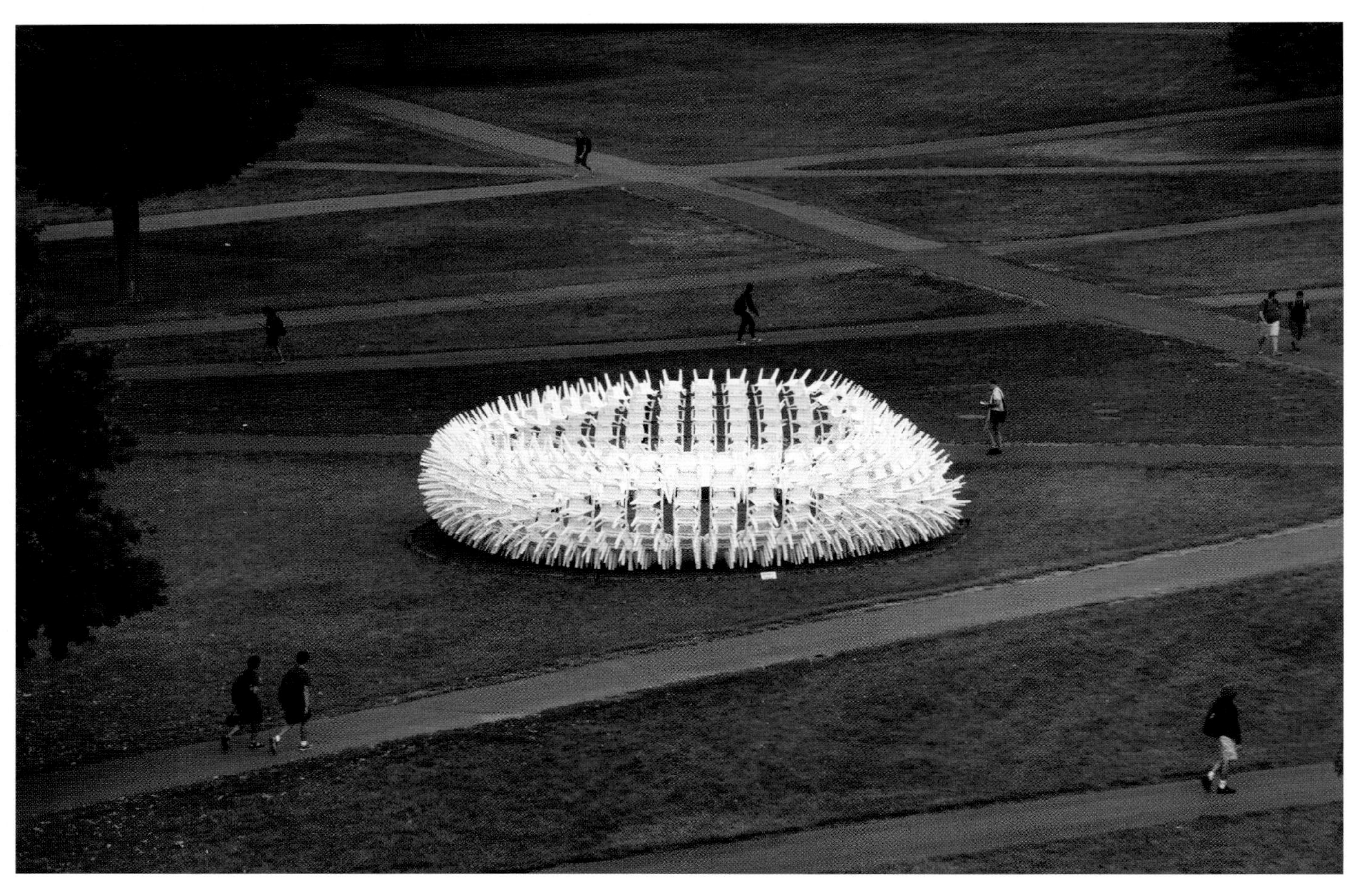

Caroline O'Donnell (CODA). *Urchin: Impossible Circus*, 2016. Plastic chairs, steel rods, and dog spikes: 30 feet in diameter. Installation view, Cornell University, Ithaca, New York. Photographer: John Lai. *Courtesy of the artist*

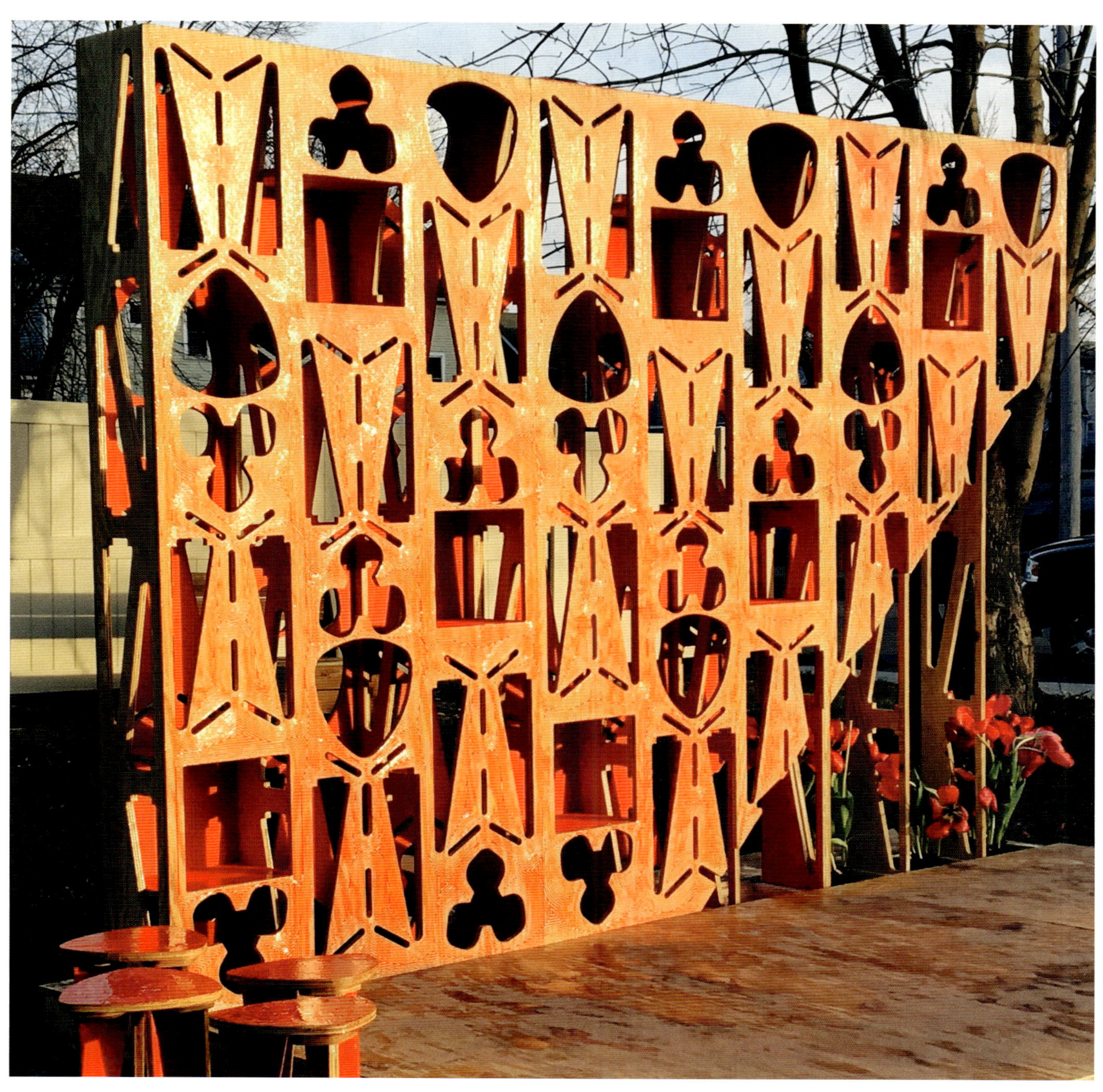

Caroline O'Donnell (CODA). *Tripe*, 2018. Nine plywood sheets and offcuts: 12 × 8 × 9 feet. Installation view, Buffalo, New York. Photographer: Alireza Shojakhani. *Courtesy of the artist*

E. V. DAY

E. V. Day is a New York-based artist whose work explores themes of sexuality and humor while employing gravity-defying suspension techniques. By manipulating iconic imagery from popular culture, Day re-animates the recognizable into new forms that illuminate contradictions in gender roles and stretch the confines of social stereotypes. Day received her MFA in sculpture from Yale University School of Art, New Haven, Connecticut.

Recently awarded the prestigious Rome Prize for Visual Arts by the American Academy in Rome, Day worked for a year in the Eternal City where she continued a twenty-year practice of creating sculptures that interact with, and respond to grand architectural spaces. Her installation *SNAP!* at Philip Johnson's Glass House cast a net, capturing and staking Johnson's playful pavilion "Da Monsta" to the ground, taming the beast through a sound installation inside entitled *Purring Chamber* in 2013. In 2010, she exhibited *Divas Ascending*, a 14-sculpture installation at Lincoln Center created from costumes from the archives of the New York City Opera—an exhibition, that traveled to The Kentucky Center in 2011 and The Houston Grand Opera in 2012.

The first work in her *Exploding Couture* series, *Bombshell*, was included in the 2000 Biennial of the Whitney Museum of American Art, was suspended in the lobby of The Breuer Building, and is now in the Museum's permanent collection. Day has had numerous solo exhibitions, including the installation *G-Force* at the Whitney Museum at Altria in 2001, in which she suspended hundreds of thongs from the ceiling in fighter-jet formations, and a survey exhibition at the Herbert F. Johnson Museum of Art at Cornell University in 2004. *Bride Fight*, a high-tension string-up of two dueling bridal gowns, was exhibited at the Lever House as part of their collection in 2006.

Day's work has been featured in numerous prestigious private and public collections, including the Whitney Museum, New York City; the Museum of Modern Art, New York City; the San Francisco Museum of Modern Art, San Francisco; the Brooklyn Museum, Brooklyn, New York; the National Museum of Women in the Arts, Washington, DC; the New Museum of Contemporary Art, New York City; the New York Public Library, New York City; the Saatchi Collection, London; the Lever House, New York City; and the Smithsonian National Air and Space Museum, Washington, DC.

E. V. Day. *Mimi-Rigor Mortis* from *Divas Ascending*, commissioned by New York City Opera at Lincoln Center, New York City, 2010. Installation view, red velvet opera costume (worn by soprano Renatta Scotto as Mimi in *La Bohème* at New York City Opera), stainless steel rings, monofilament, and hardware: 10 × 6 × 6 feet. *Courtesy of the artist and Deitch Projects, New York*

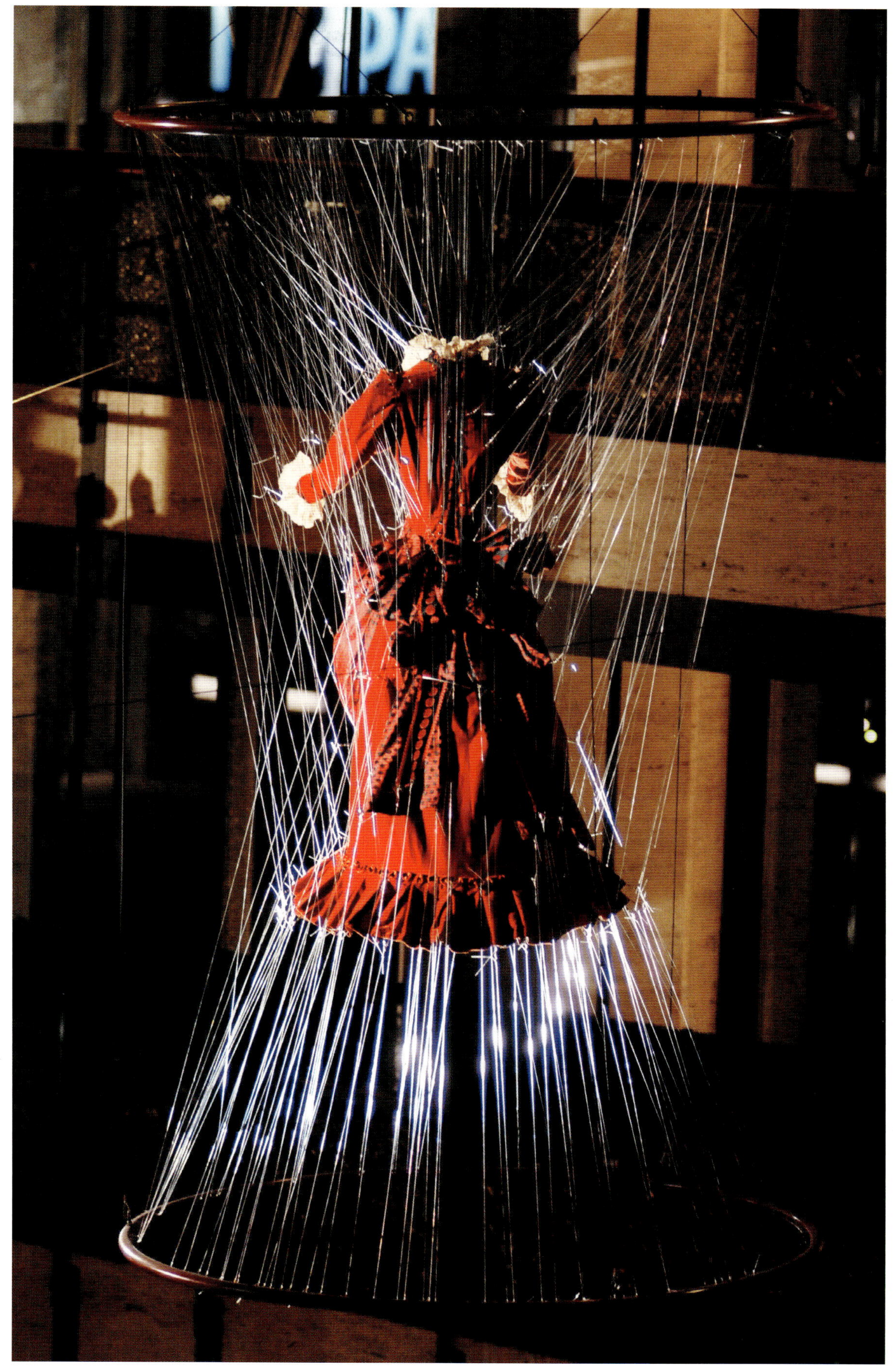

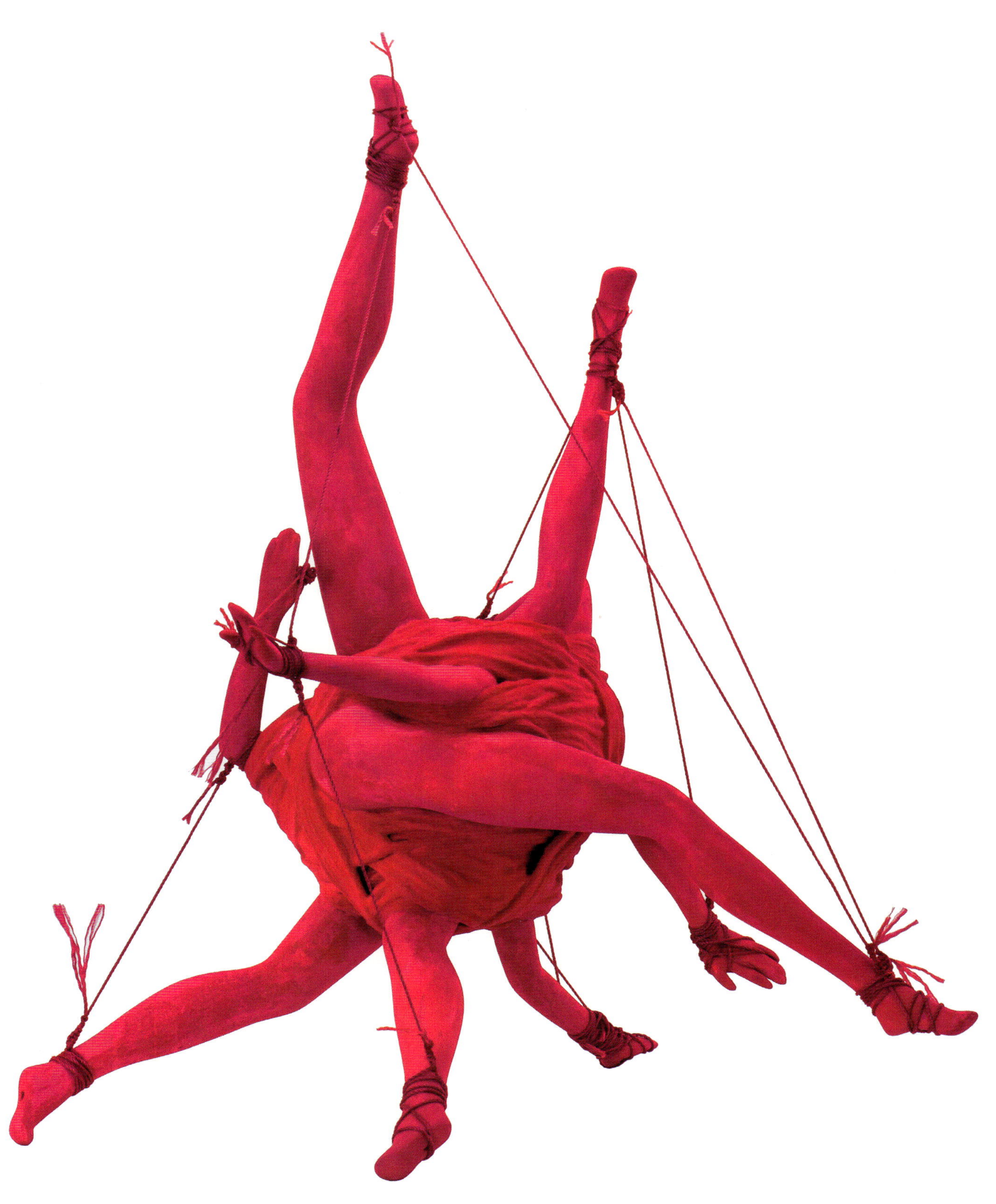

E. V. Day. *Sauvage, Twisted 9*, 2015. Resin, pigment, and satin cord: 24 × 24 × 24 inches. *Courtesy of the artist and Baldwin Gallery, Aspen, Colorado*

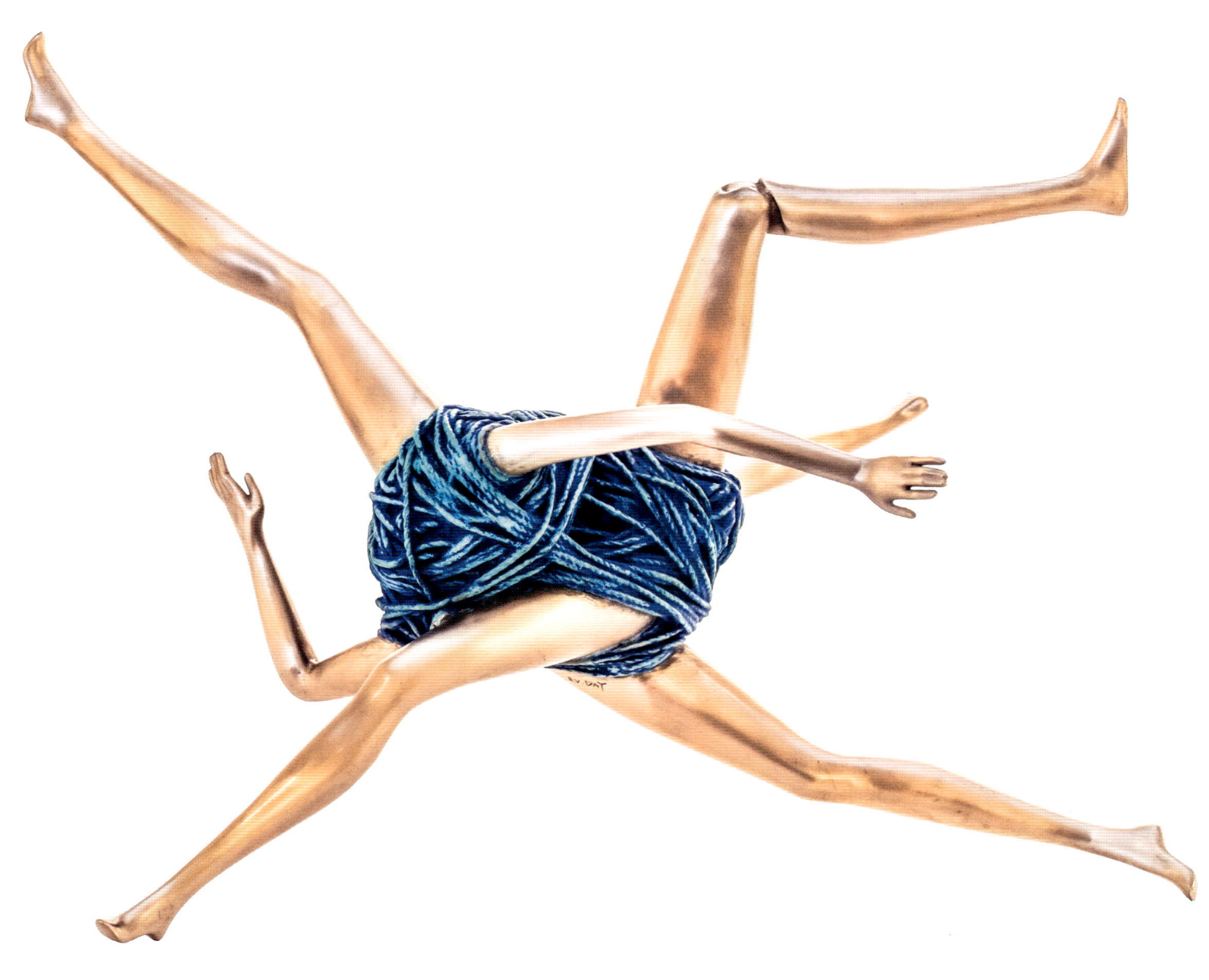

E. V. Day. *Isalovely, Twisted 3*, 2015. Bronze, ultramarine, and cobalt pigment: 24 × 24 × 24 inches. *Courtesy of the artist and Baldwin Gallery, Aspen, Colorado*

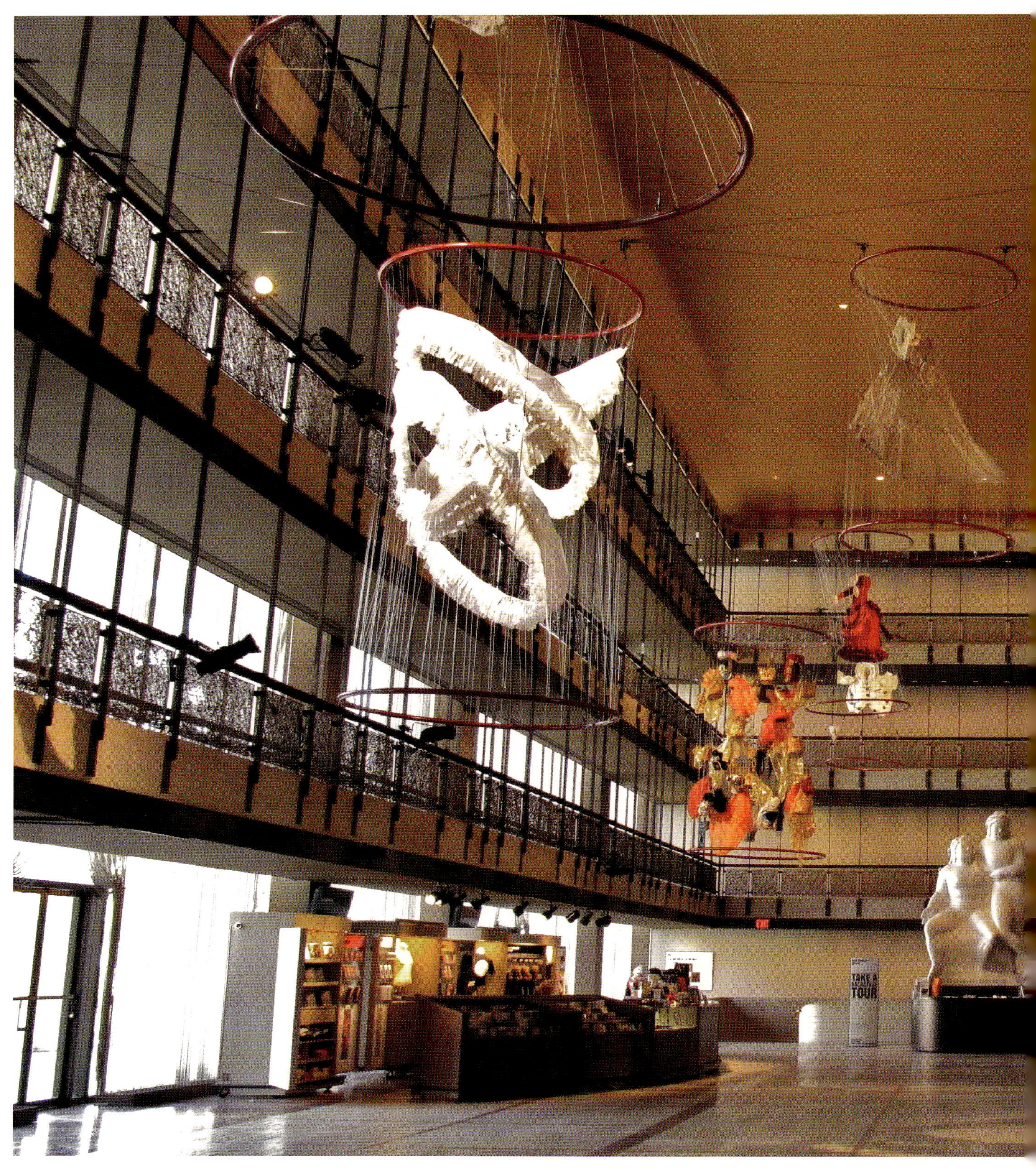

E. V. Day. *Divas Ascending,* commissioned by New York City Opera at Lincoln Center, New York City, 2010. Installation view, fourteen suspended sculptures made from opera costumes worn by principal female roles; stainless steel rings, monofilament, and hardware: 10 × 6 × 6 feet, each. *Courtesy of the artist and Deitch Projects, New York*

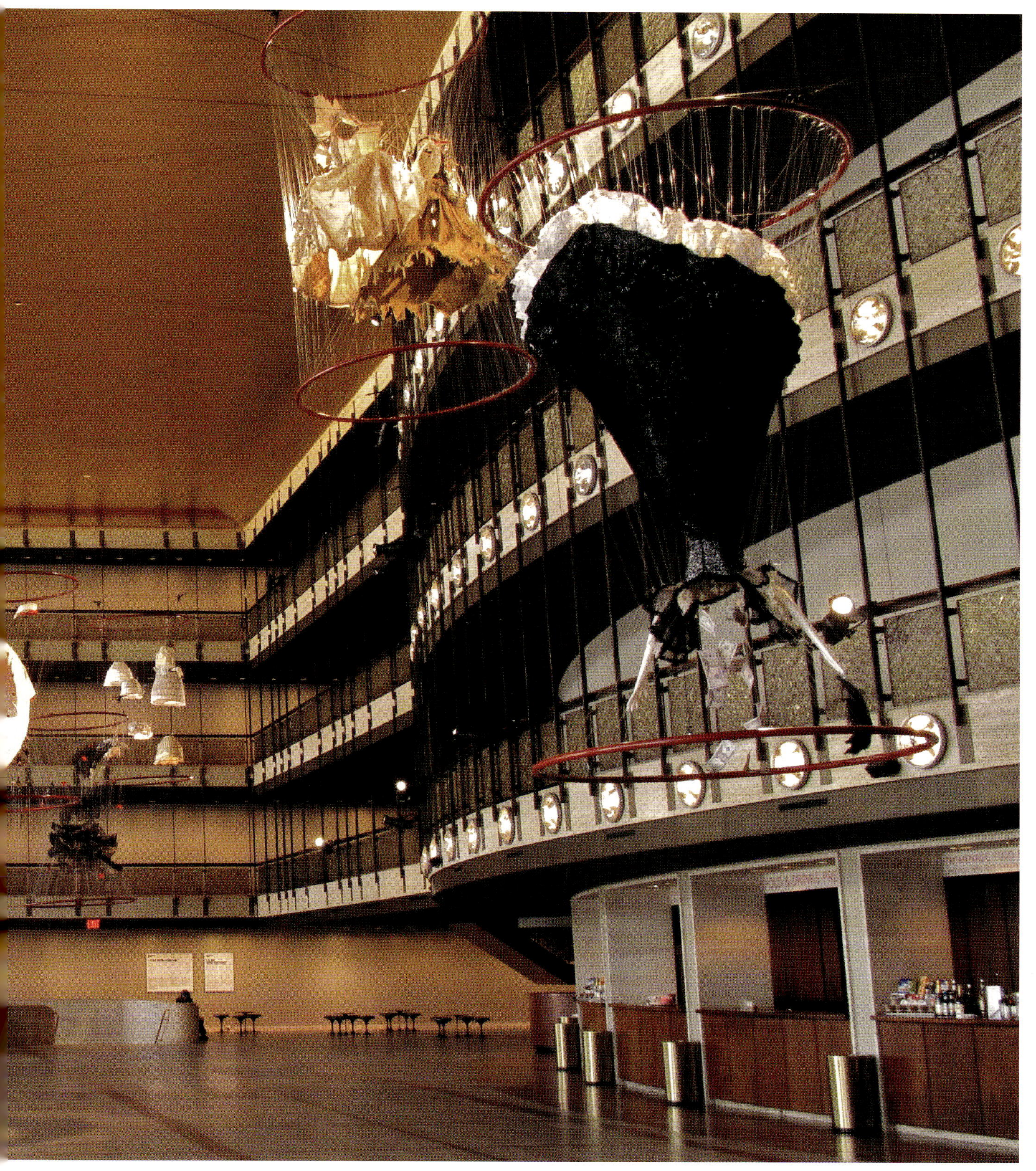

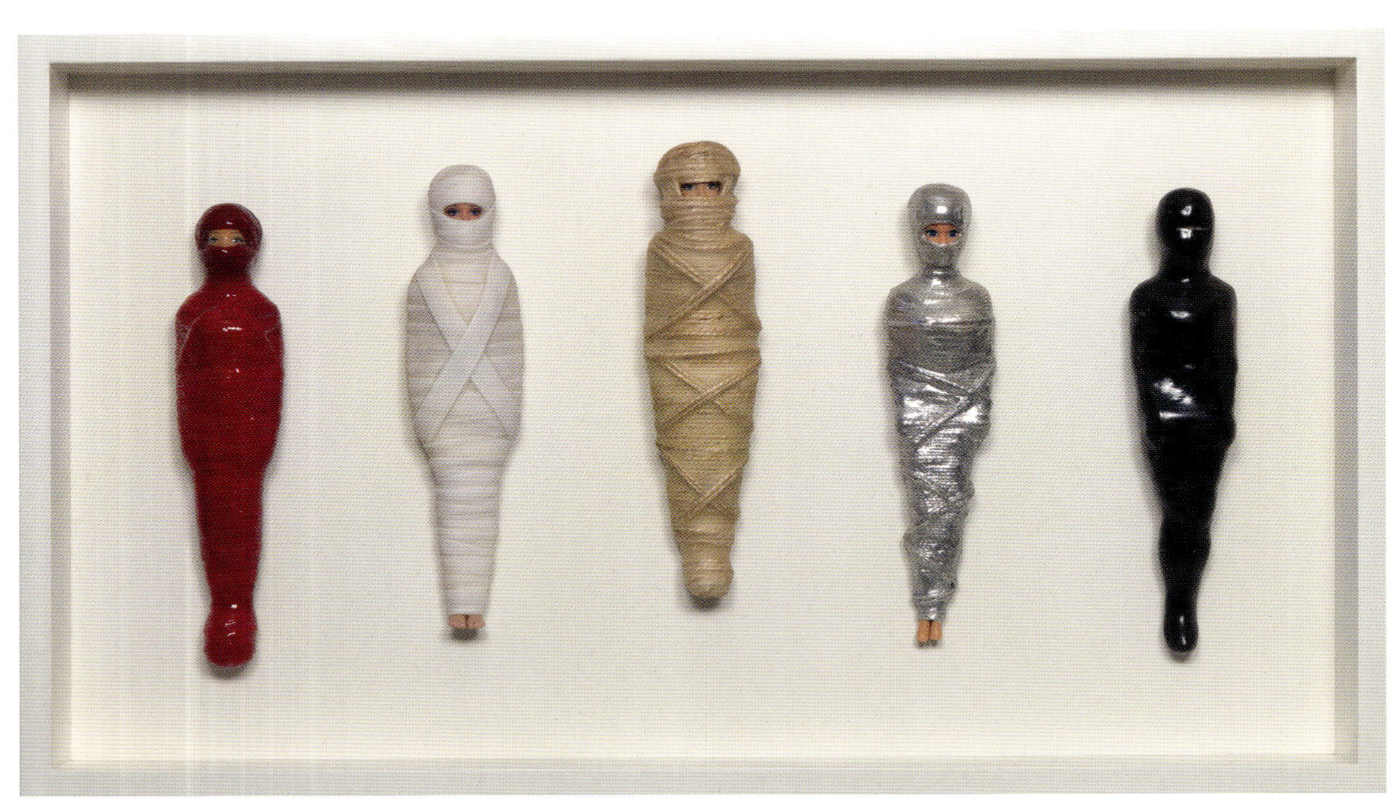

E. V. Day. *Mummified Barbies*, 2015. Barbie dolls, beeswax, and twine: 12 × 2 × 2 inches, each. *Courtesy of the artist and Salomon Contemporary, New York*

ELIZABETH TURK

Elizabeth Turk is internationally recognized for transforming marble into strikingly intricate objects that defy convention and challenge our preconceptions. Her sculpture pushes the medium to its limit, creating a provocative tension between the intrinsic strength of the stone and its inherent fragility. Each work plays with the edge to contradiction; the lightness in weight, the emptiness in mass, the contemporary in the traditional, and extended time in a moment. Her fastidious art-making practice is abandoned when she places completed pieces within larger natural contexts to transform meaning; for example, what was a "lace" marble collar becomes a "skeleton" washed up on the shore.

Turk is a recipient of several awards, including a John D. and Catherine T. MacArthur Foundation Fellowship (2010), a Barnett and Annalee Newman Foundation Fellowship (2010), a Smithsonian Artist Research Fellowship (2011), and a Joan Mitchell Foundation Award (2000). Turk's work resides in numerous prestigious private and public collections, including the Los Angeles County Museum of Art, Los Angeles; the National Gallery of Women in the Arts, Washington, DC; and the Mint Museum, Charlotte, North Carolina. Institutional monographic exhibitions include *Elizabeth Turk: Sentient Forms*, at the Laguna Art Museum, Laguna Beach, California (2015); *Elizabeth Turk: Wings*, at the Dayton Art Institute, Dayton, Ohio (2013); and *Elizabeth Turk, the Collars: Tracings of Thought*, at the Mint Museum of Art, Charlotte, North Carolina (2004). Turk is represented by Hirschl & Adler, Modern in New York.

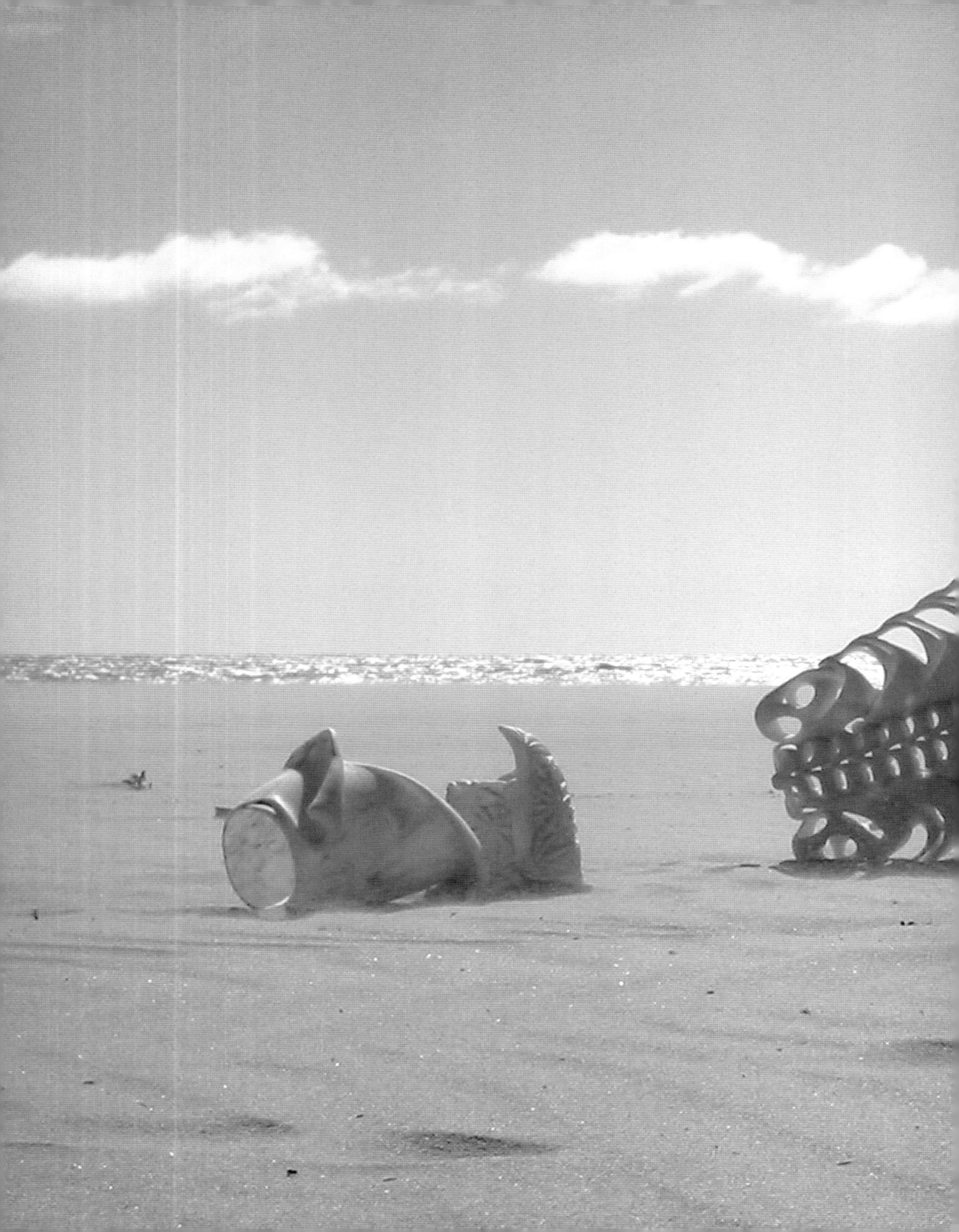

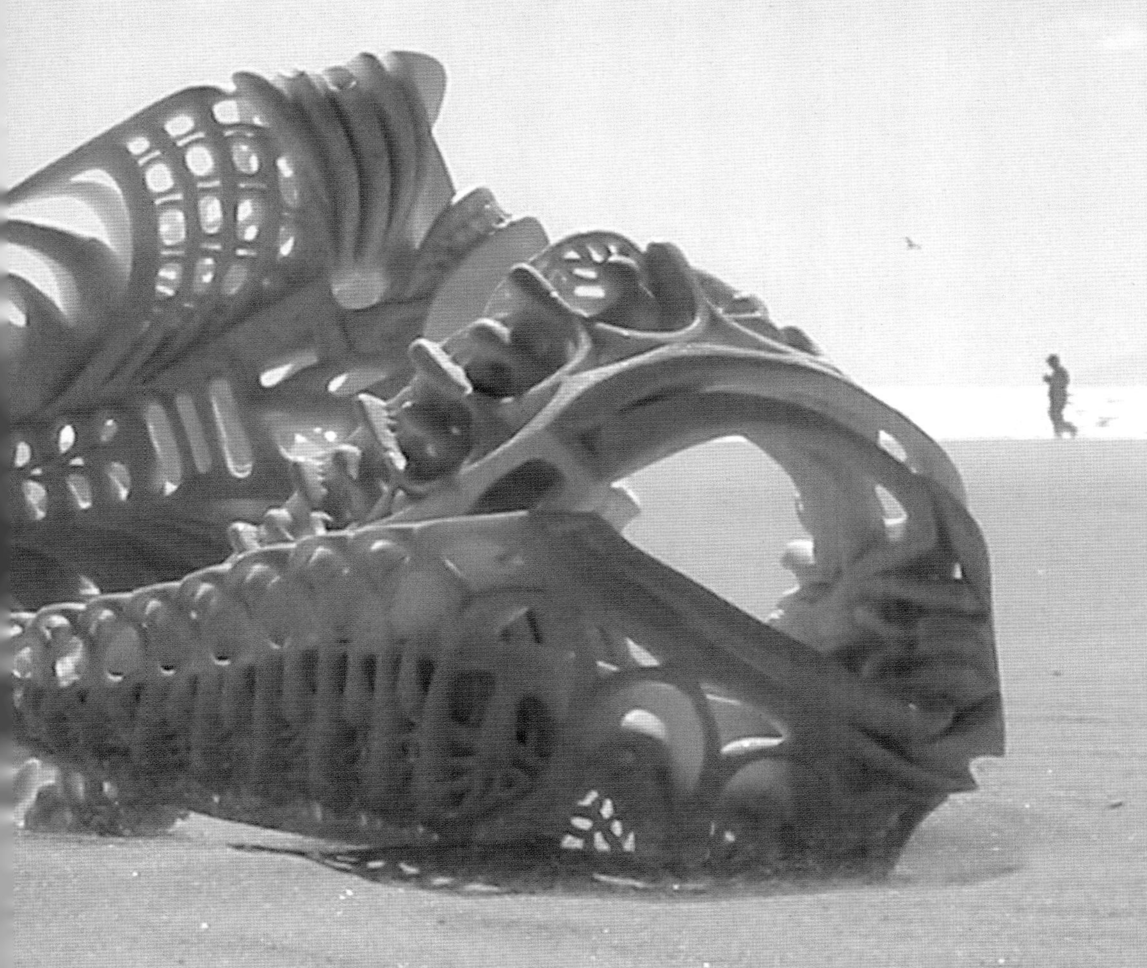

Elizabeth Turk. *Collars 4, 7 & 8, Newport Beach*, 2002–2004. Marble (3 parts): Collar 4: 6 × 4.5 × 5 inches; Collar 7: 16 × 13.5 × 12 inches; Collar 8: 24 × 16.5 × 16 inches. *Courtesy of the artist and Hirschl & Adler, Modern, New York*

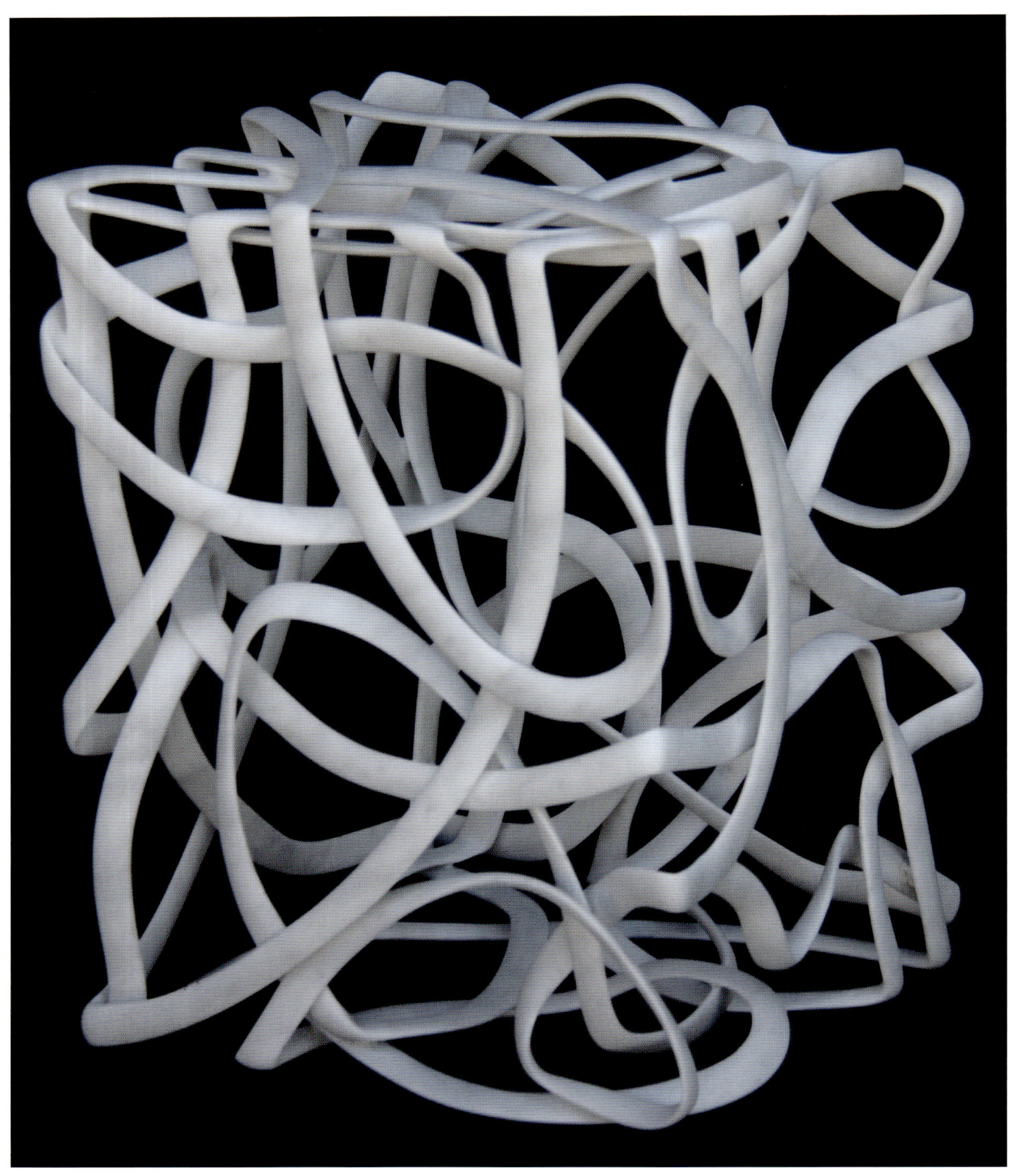

Elizabeth Turk. *Cage: Box 7*, 2012. Marble: 20 × 15 × 15 inches. ©Eric Stoner. *Courtesy of the artist and Hirschl & Adler, Modern, New York*

Elizabeth Turk. *Collar 7, Huntington Pier*, 2003. Marble: 16 × 13.5 × 12 inches. *Courtesy of the artist and Hirschl & Adler, Modern, New York*

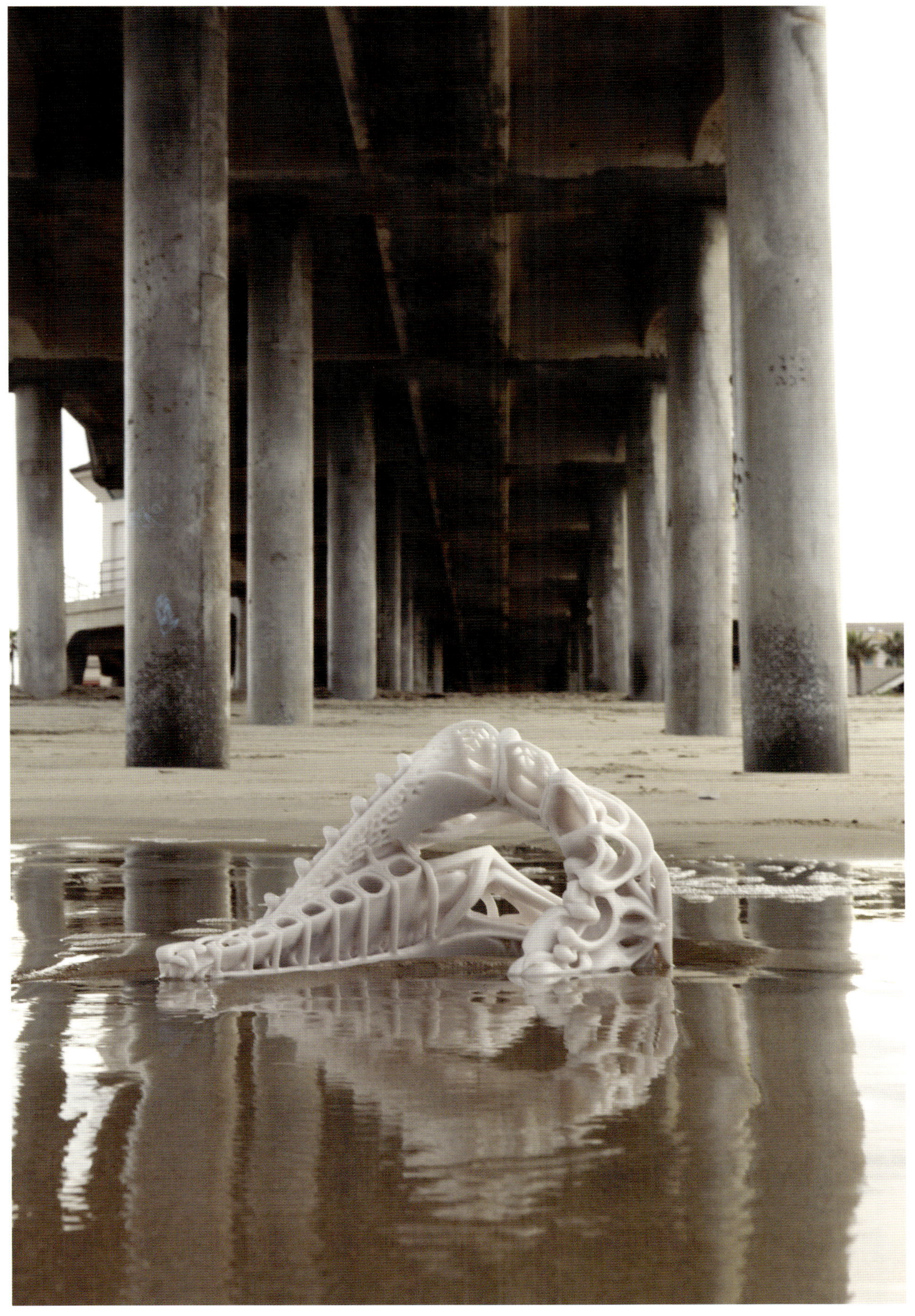

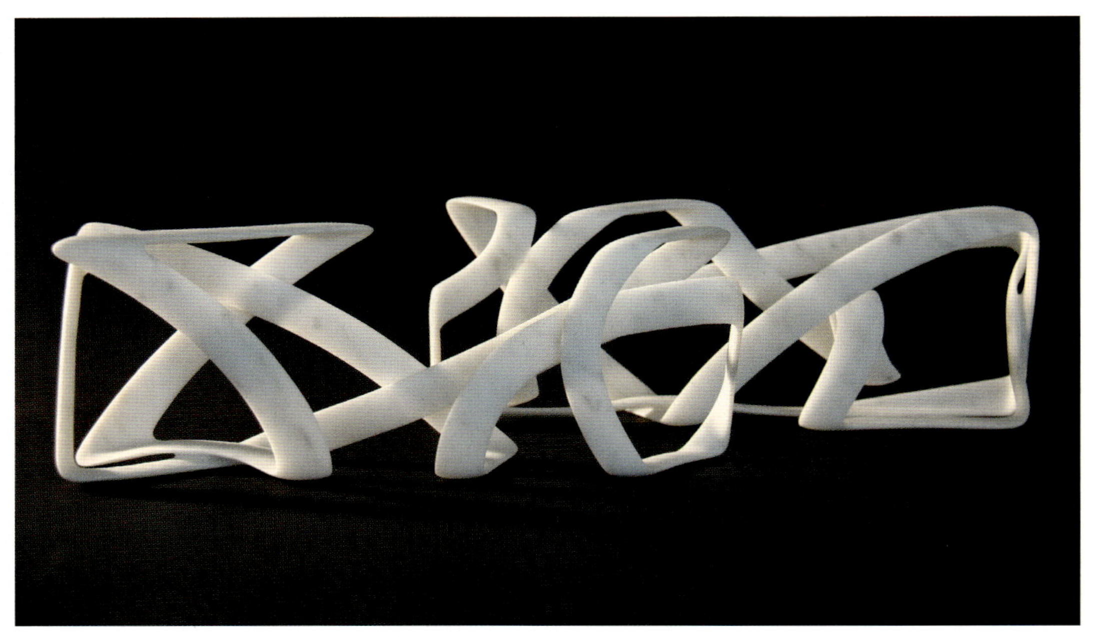

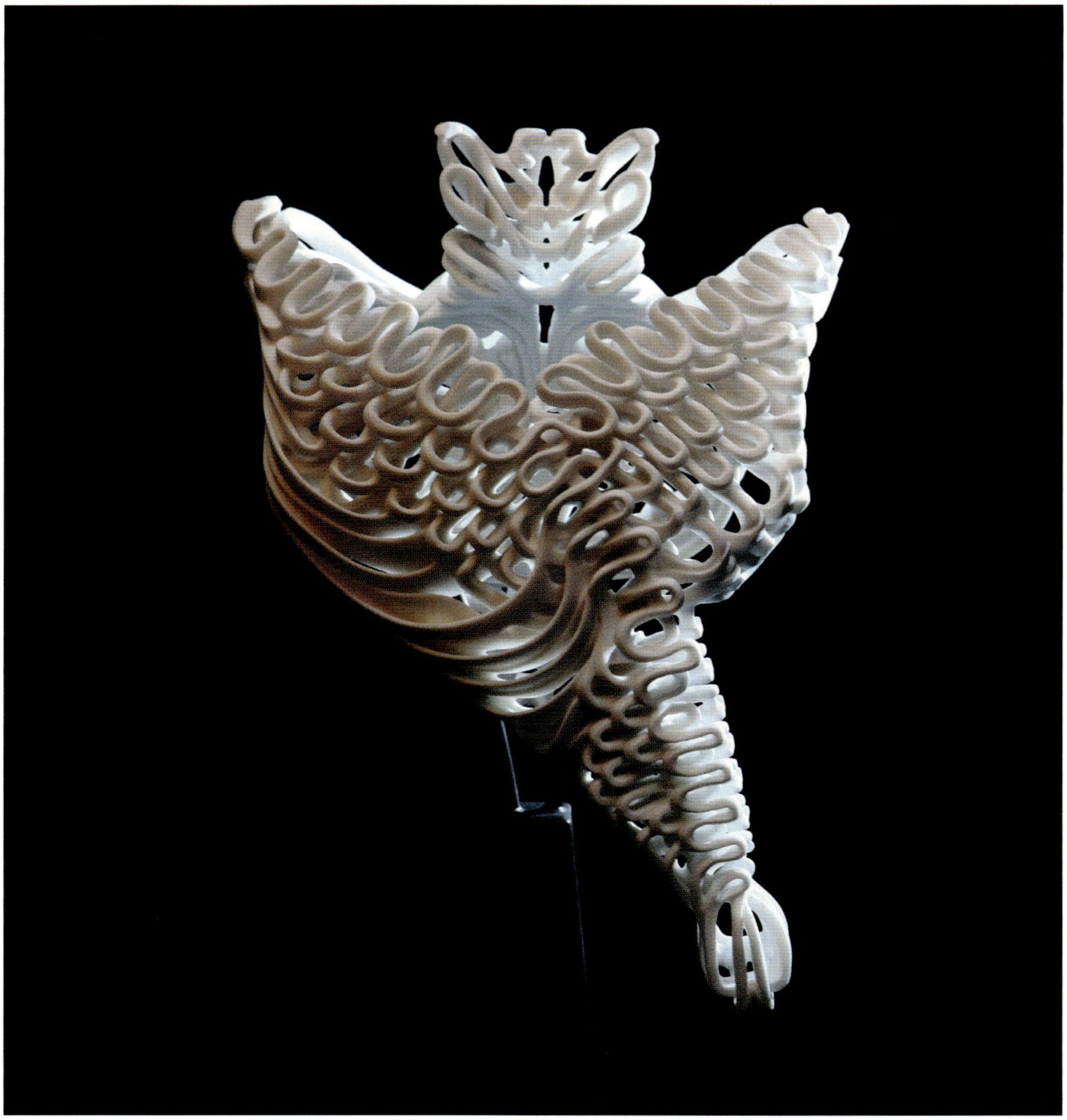

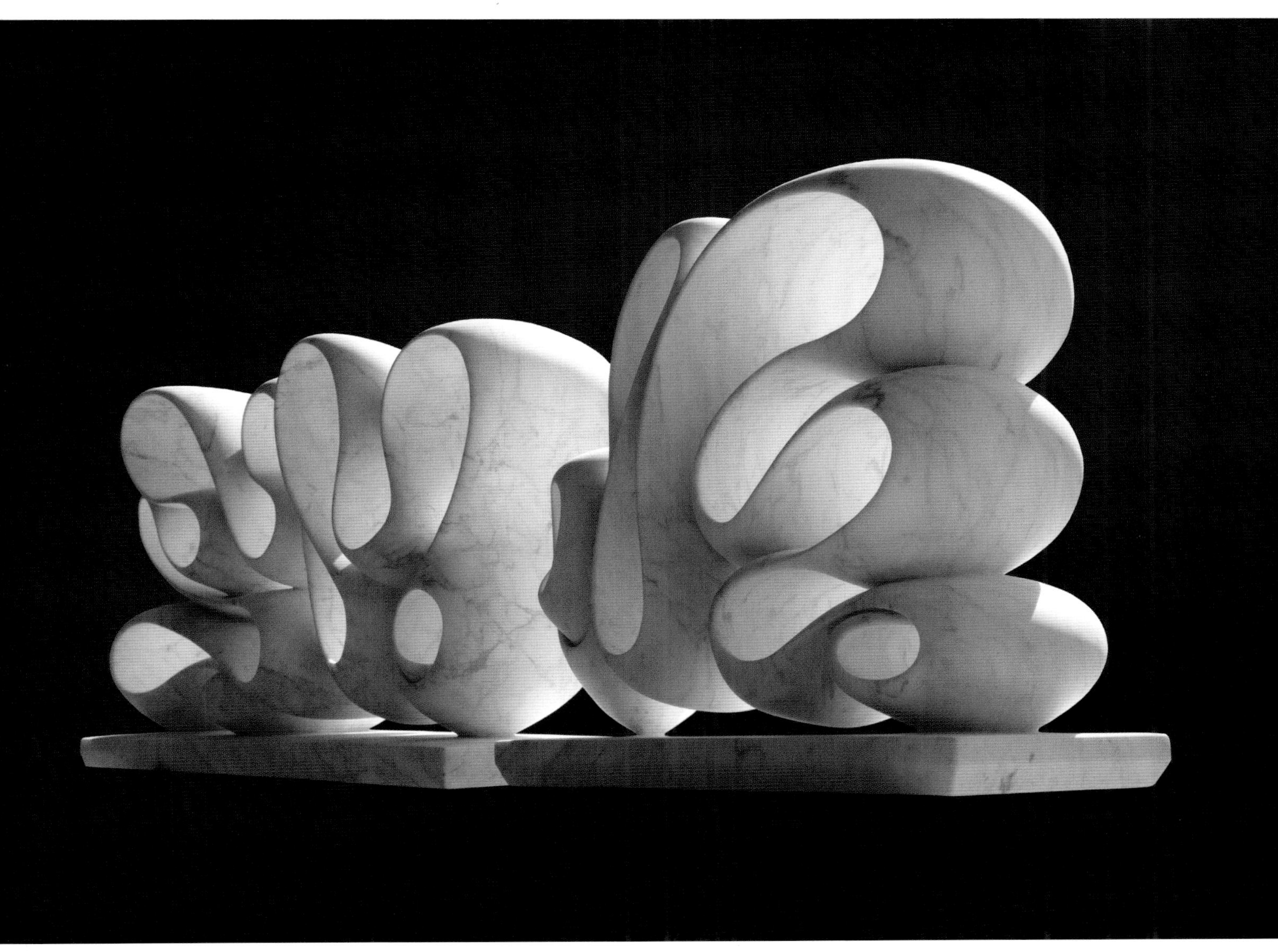

Elizabeth Turk. *Cage: Box 4, Cage: Box 5*, 2012. Marble: 5.5 × 14.5 inches, each. ©Eric Stoner. *Courtesy of the artist and Hirschl & Adler, Modern, New York*

Elizabeth Turk. *Collar #21*, 2010. Marble: 23 × 17 × 14 inches. ©Eric Stoner. *Courtesy of the artist and Hirschl & Adler, Modern, New York*

Elizabeth Turk. *Script Line #255 and #160*, 2014. Marble (2 parts): #255: 24 × 40 × 121 inches; #160: 24 × 24 × 121 inches. ©Eric Stoner. *Courtesy of the artist and Hirschl & Adler, Modern, New York*

EUGENIA LOLI

Eugenia Loli is a collage artist born in Greece. Loli creates vintage collages that depict witty scenes of the strange and the familiar. With a background in filmmaking and technology, Loli builds fictional spaces that tease the viewer with surreal narratives, retro glamour, and compromising perspectives. Working in the vein of Pop and Dada, Loli's imagery produces scenes and environments that evoke a futuristic wonderland. Loli's work has been widely published and exhibited, including in *Vogue.com*, *Town & Country*, *Der Speigel*, *GQ USA*, *Vanity Fair Italia*, *Harper's Bazaar US* and *Harper's Bazaar Australia*, *Wired UK*, *Departures*, *New York Magazine*, *Medium.com*, *Le Monde*, *Glamour Italia* and *Glamour Germany*, *Cosmopolitan US*, and *Entertainment Weekly*. Loli's work has been featured on over thirty book covers, including *Private Novelist* by Nell Zink, which was lauded by the *New York Times* as one of the best book covers of the year in 2016. She is regularly commissioned to create album art for popular indie rock bands, including Highly Suspect and White Denim.

Eugenia Loli. *Knots*, 2016. Digital collage: dimensions variable. *Courtesy of the artist*

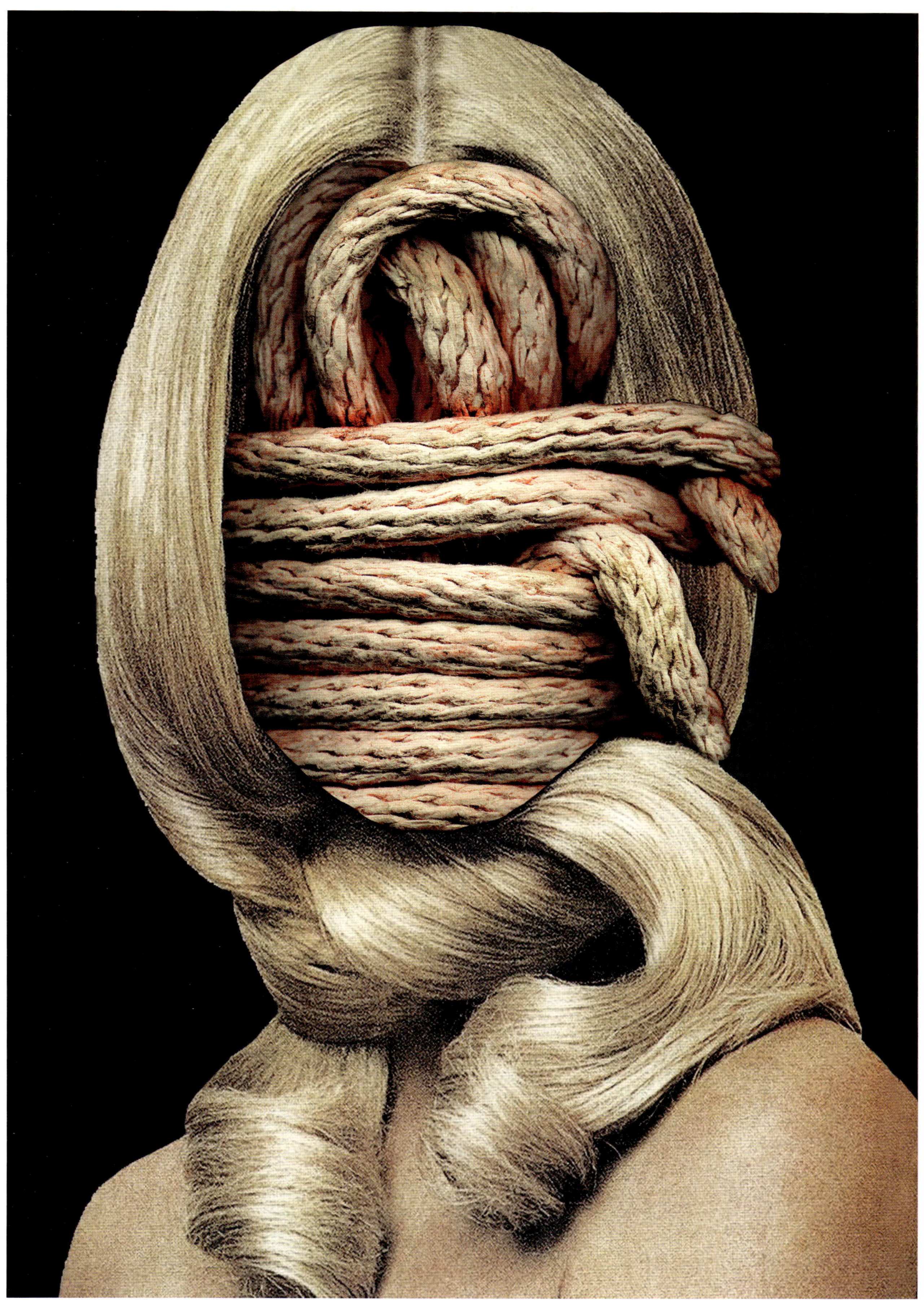

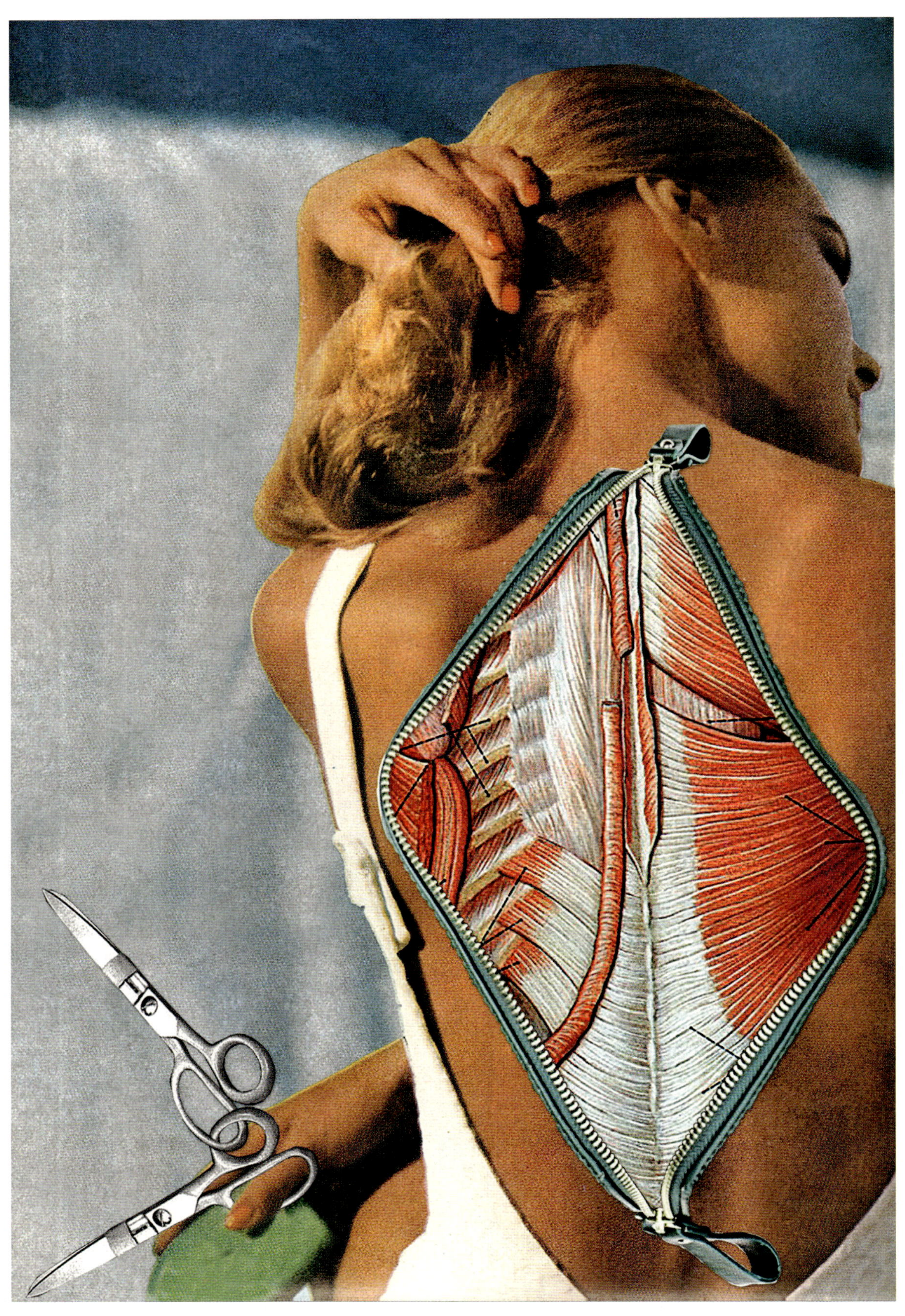

Eugenia Loli. *Underneath It All*, 2014. Digital collage: dimensions variable. *Courtesy of the artist*

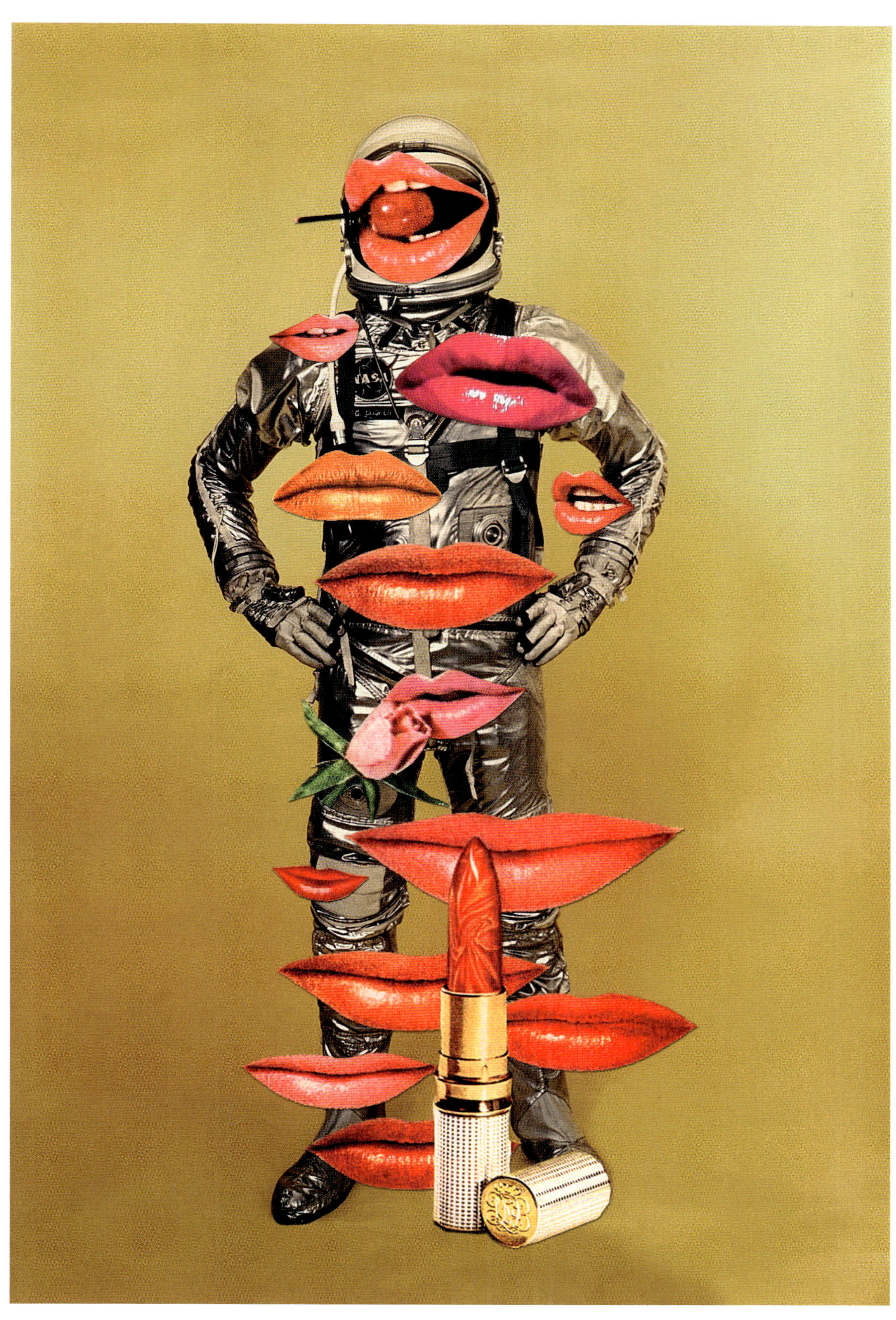

Eugenia Loli. *Rocket Man*, 2014. Digital collage: dimensions variable. *Courtesy of the artist*

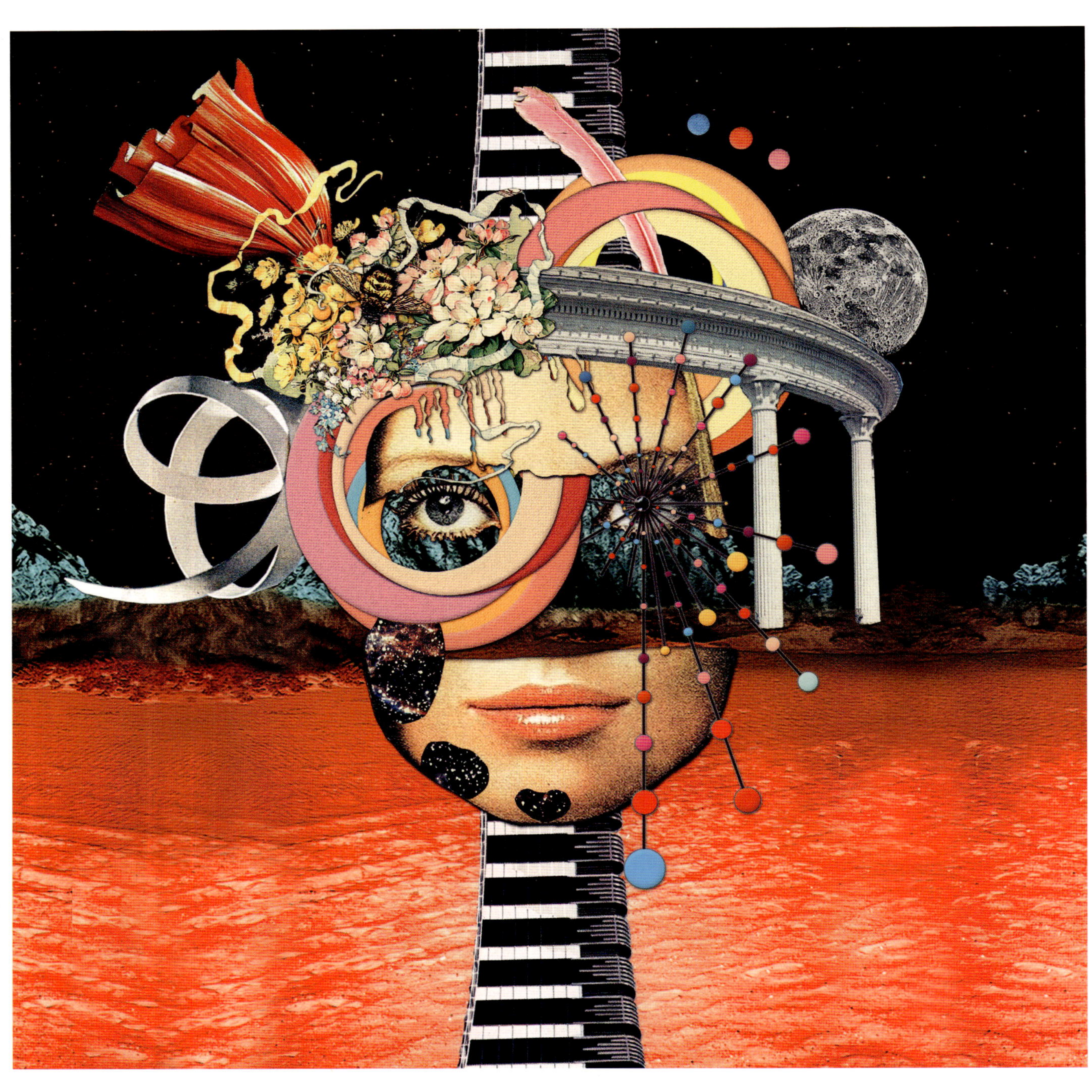

Eugenia Loli. *All about Perspective*, 2016. Digital collage: dimensions variable. *Courtesy of the artist*

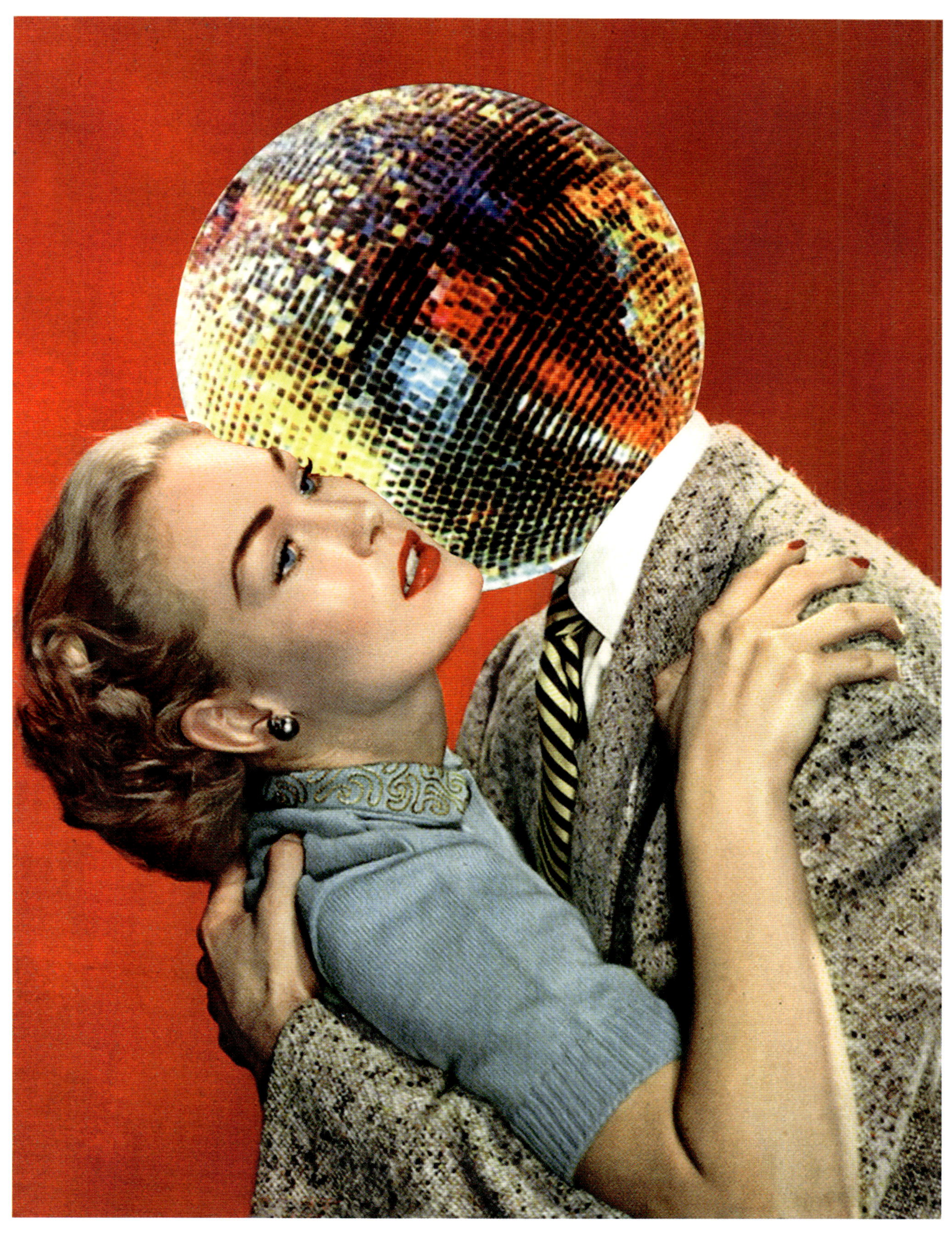

Eugenia Loli. *Discotheque*, 2014. Digital collage: dimensions variable. *Courtesy of the artist*

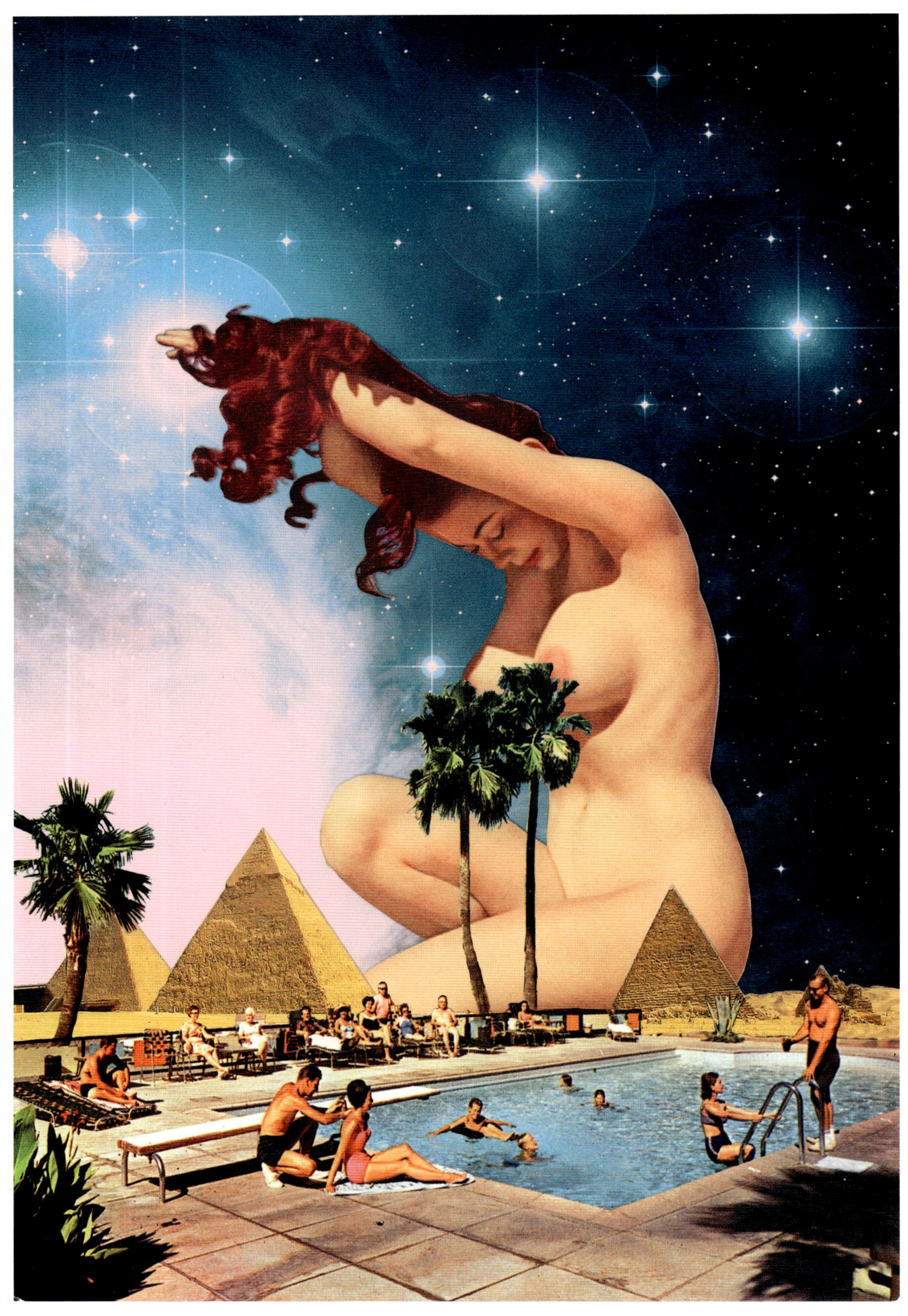

Eugenia Loli. *The Sphinx*, 2012. Digital collage: dimensions variable. *Courtesy of the artist*

FIRELEI BÁEZ

Mining overlooked Caribbean, African American, and female histories, Firelei Báez's work masks confrontational narratives behind luscious, color-rich, and intricate paintings on paper and canvas, as well as large-scale installations. Through a convergence of interest in history, black female subjectivity, and women's work, her art often explores folklore involved in self-making within diasporic societies.

Báez has been included in numerous solo museum exhibitions, including *Bloodlines*,which opened at the Pérez Art Museum Miami, Miami, Florida, in 2015, accompanied by a 120-page publication, and traveled to the Andy Warhol Museum, Pittsburgh, Pennsylvania, in 2016. *Vessels of Genealogies* opened at the Tarble Arts Center, Eastern Illinois University, Charleston, Illinois, in 2016 and traveled to the DePaul Art Museum, Chicago, in 2017. Also in 2017, Báez was included as a finalist in the Pinchuk Foundation's distinguished Future Generation Art Prize exhibition, staged in Kiev, Ukraine, and at the 2017 Venice Biennale as an official collateral exhibition. In early 2018, she was included in *Joy Out of Fire* at the Schomburg Center for the Studio Museum's *inharlem* initiative and *To See Beyond* at the Contemporary Arts Center in Cincinnati. She was also commissioned to produce new work for the 16th International Venice Biennale as well as for the Metropolitan Transportation Authority in New York, later in 2018. This same year, Báez was the recipient of the 2018 CAA Artist Award for Distinguished Body of Work.

Báez received her BFA from the Cooper Union's School of Art, New York City, and studied at the Skowhegan School of Painting and Sculpture, New York City. She also received her MFA from Hunter College, New York City. Firelei Báez was born in Santiago de los Caballeros, Dominican Republic, and lives and works in New York City.

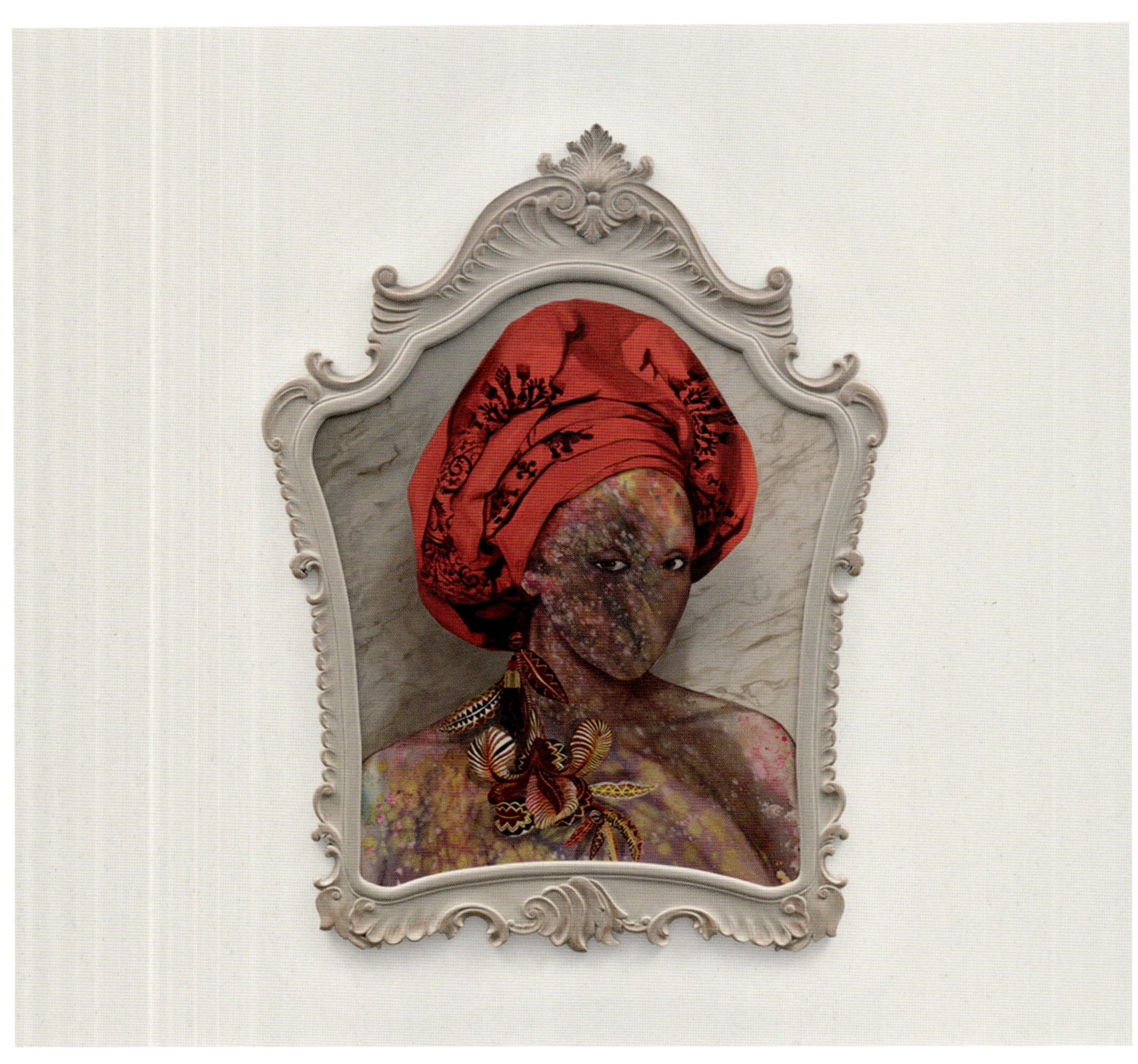

Firelei Báez. *Given the Ground (the fact that it amazes me does not mean I relinquish it)*, 2017. Acrylic and oil on canvas: 49.5 × 42 inches. *Courtesy of the artist and Wendi Norris Gallery*

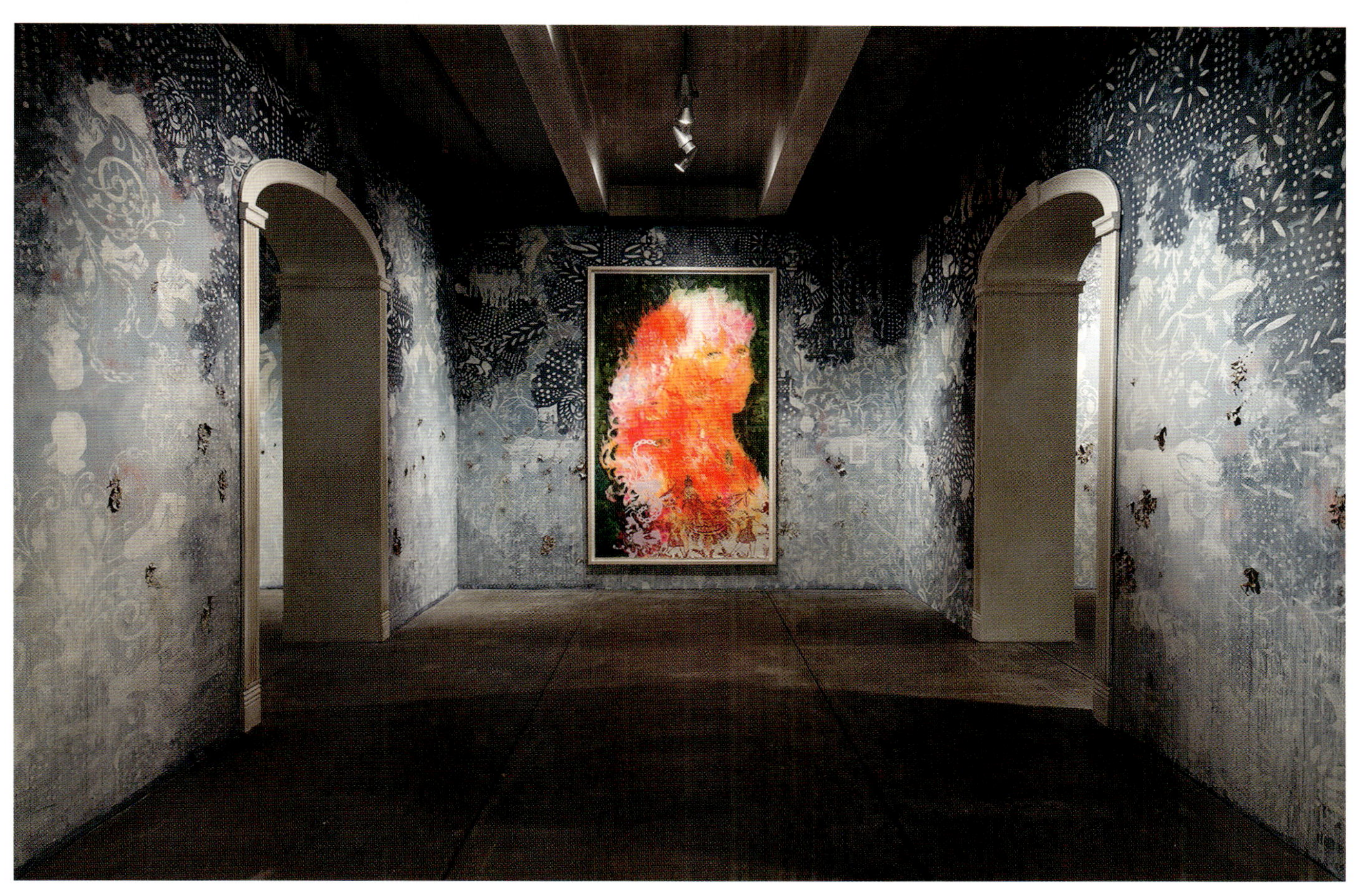

Firelei Báez. *Those Who Would Douse It,* 2017. Acrylic on canvas. *Bloodlines.* Installation view, Andy Warhol Museum, 2017. *Courtesy of the artist and Gallery Wendi Norris, San Francisco*

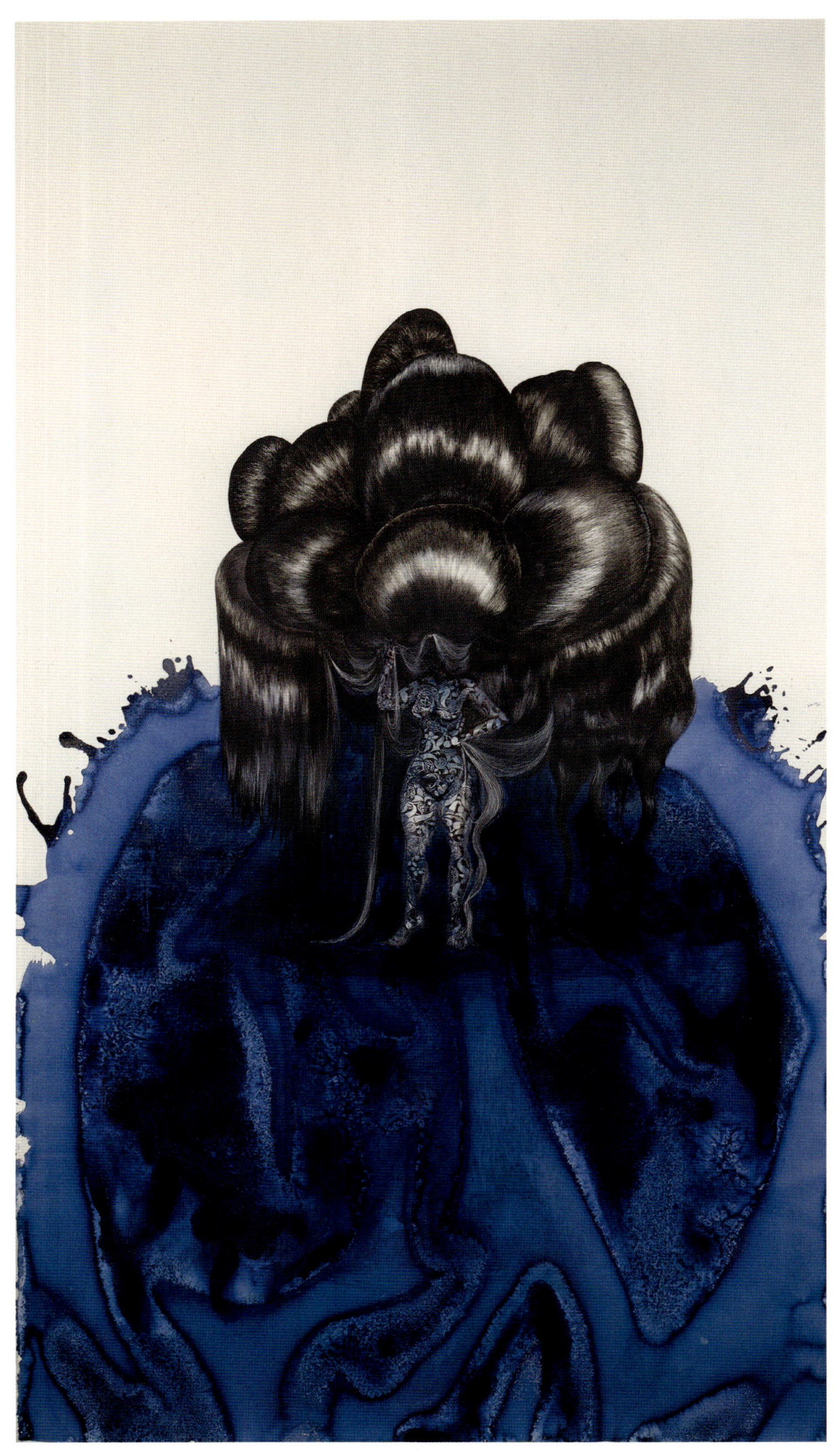

Firelei Báez. *Compulsion to remember and repeat*, 2016. Acrylic, ink, and salt on paper: 93 × 52 inches. *Courtesy of the artist and Gallery Wendi Norris, San Francisco*

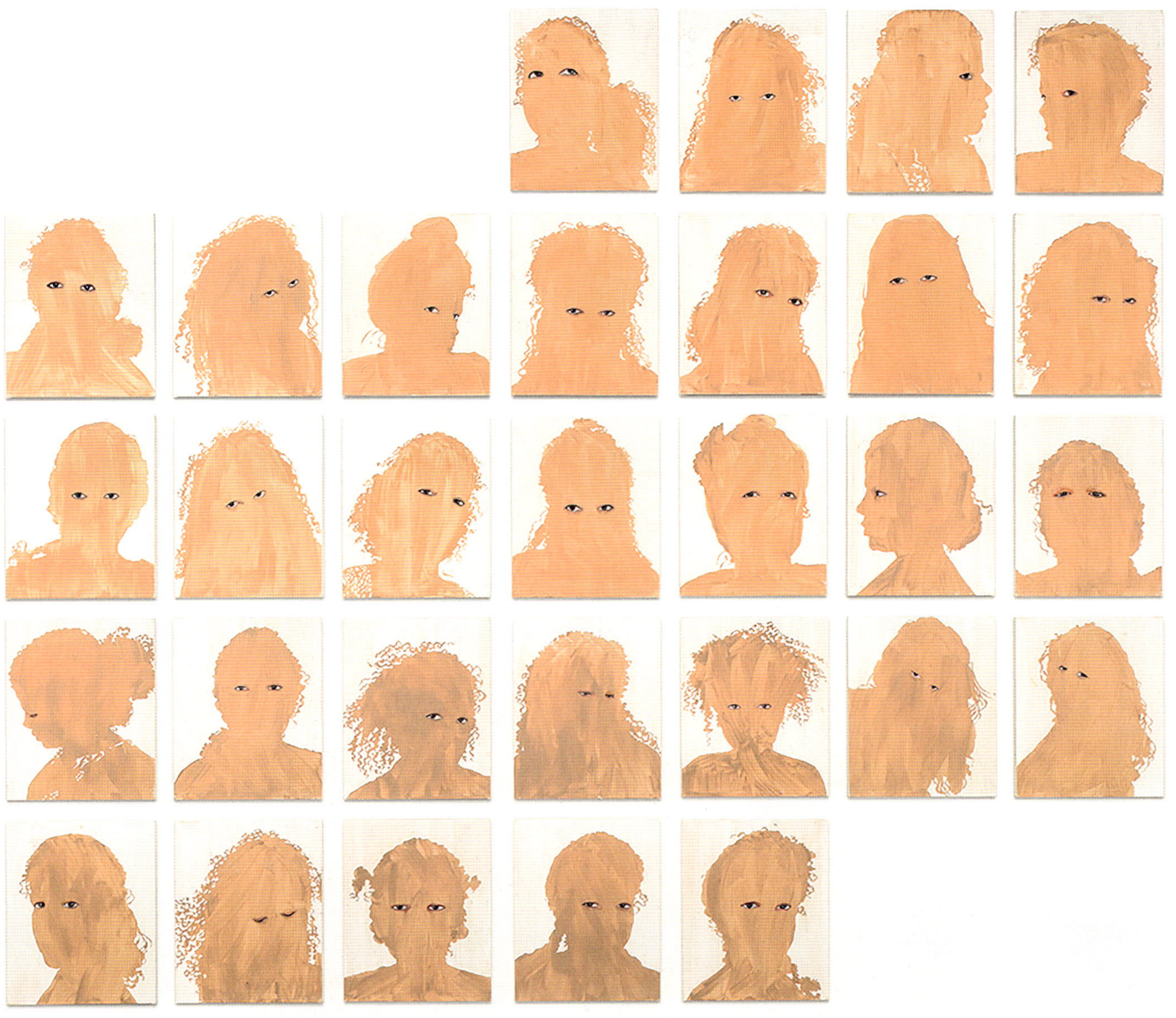

Firelei Báez. *Can I Pass? Introducing the Paper Bag to the Fan Test for the Month of June*, 2011. Gouache, ink, and graphite on panel: 96.1 × 107 inches. *Courtesy of the artist and Gallery Wendi Norris, San Francisco*

FRANCES GOODMAN

Frances Goodman is a multimedia artist born in Johannesburg, South Africa. Working with objects commonly associated with female identity, such as acrylic nails, false eyelashes, and jewelry, Goodman explores how beauty regimes and perfectionism creates obsession and neuroses. Goodman states, "The obsession with appearance, surface, and notions of success and beauty push women to compromising extremes." Her humorously dark sculptures and installations suggest how self-conscious anxieties play a disproportionate role in governing women's lives. In her examination of beauty conventions, marriage traditions, and common material possessions, Goodman reveals both the self-imposed and external pressures to conform to societal expectation. Her works rebel against the influence of the male gaze and a media-obsessed, mainstream culture. Meanwhile, their glossy, sensual surfaces capture the underlying libidinal energy that motivates consumption, from a gleaming car hood to a metallic nail polish sheen. Her work is included in several major international collections, including at the Smithsonian Institution, Washington, DC; the Francis J. Greenburger Collection, 21c Museum Hotel, Louisville, Kentucky; the Sindika Dokolo Collection, Angola; and the University of South Africa, Pretoria, South Africa.

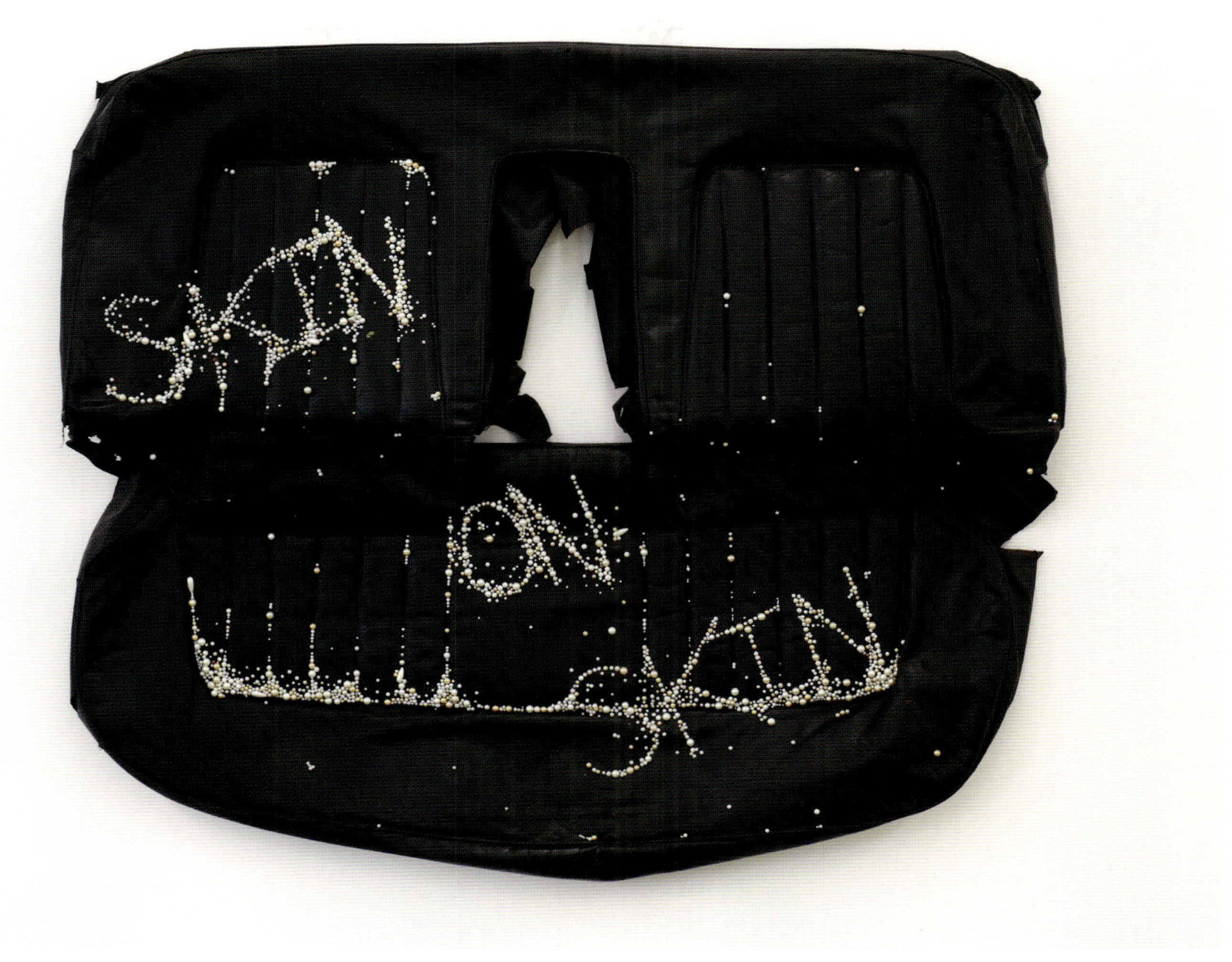

Frances Goodman. *Skin on Skin*, 2012. Car seat and pearls: 53.9 × 48.8 × 3.9 inches. *Courtesy of the artist and Richard Taittinger Gallery, New York*

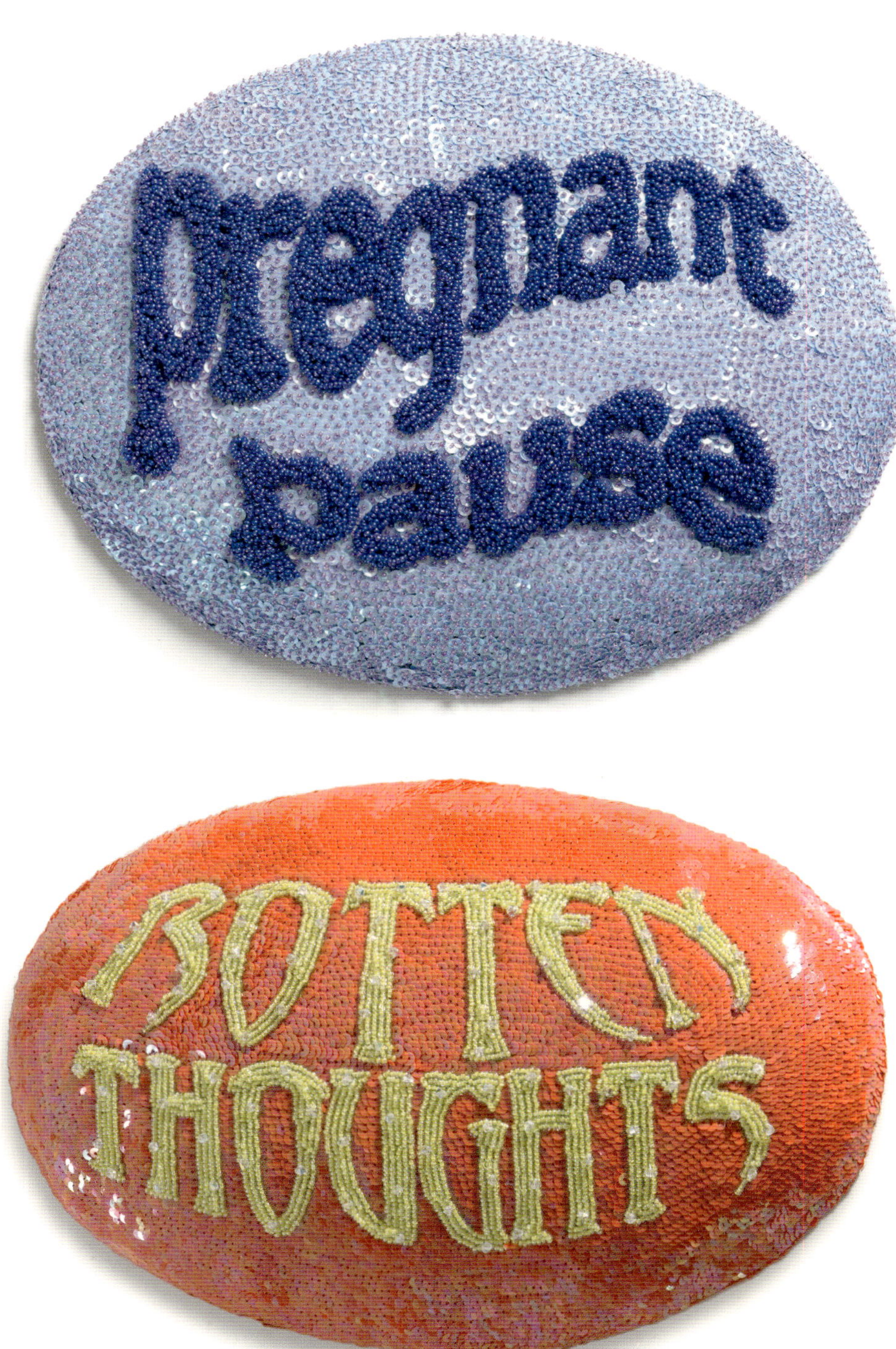

Frances Goodman. *Pregnant Pause*, 2004–05. Glass, beads, cotton, sequins, stuffing, and hardboard: 19.6 × 11.6 × 2 inches. *Courtesy of the artist and Richard Taittinger Gallery, New York*

Frances Goodman. *Rotten Thoughts*, 2004–05. Glass, beads, cotton, sequins, stuffing, and hardboard: 17.6 × 13.6 × 2 inches. *Courtesy of the artist and Richard Taittinger Gallery, New York*

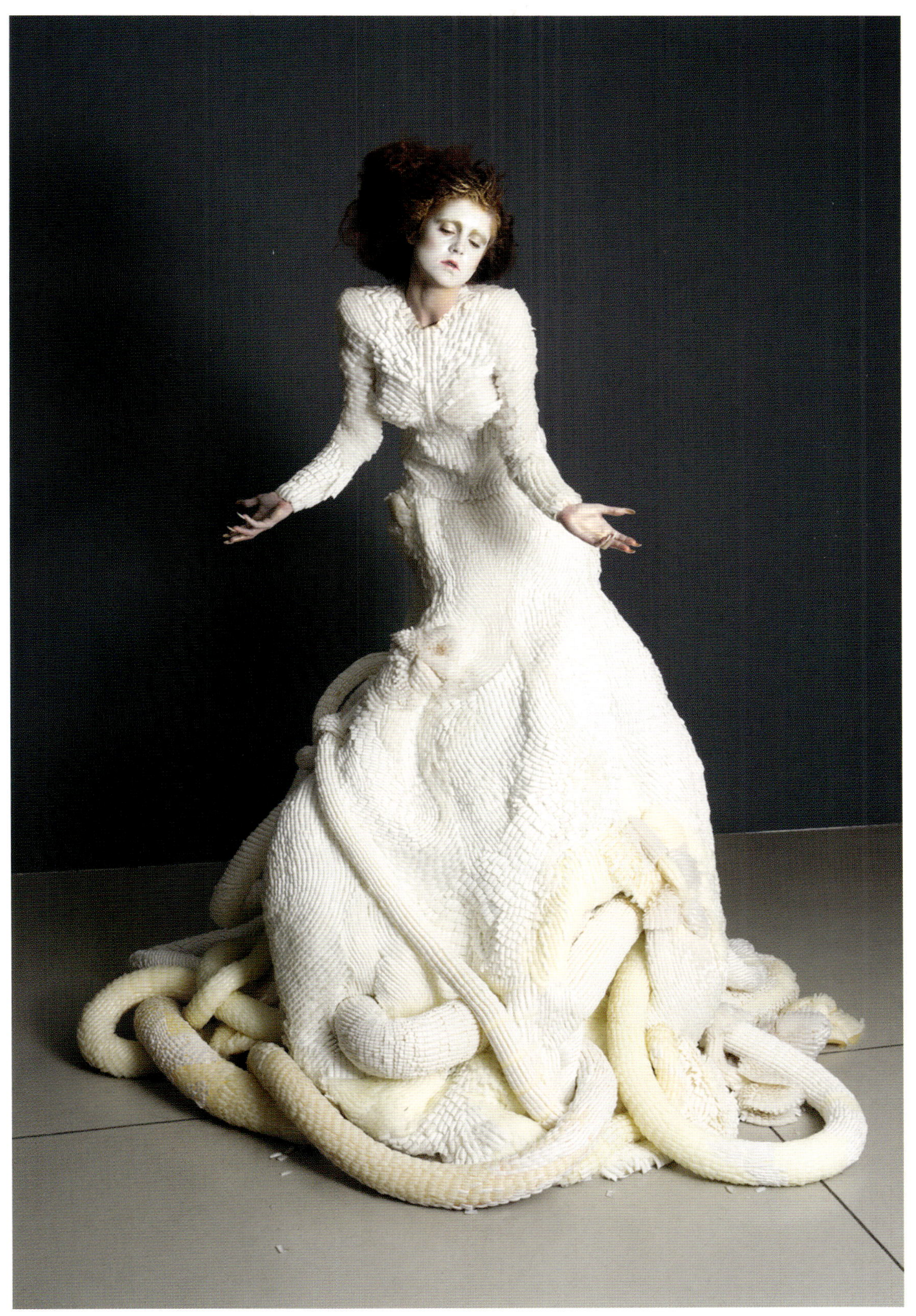

Frances Goodman. *Melusina*, 2014. Acrylic nails, thread, glue, and foam: 78.6 × 59 × 59 inches. *Courtesy of the artist and Richard Taittinger Gallery, New York*

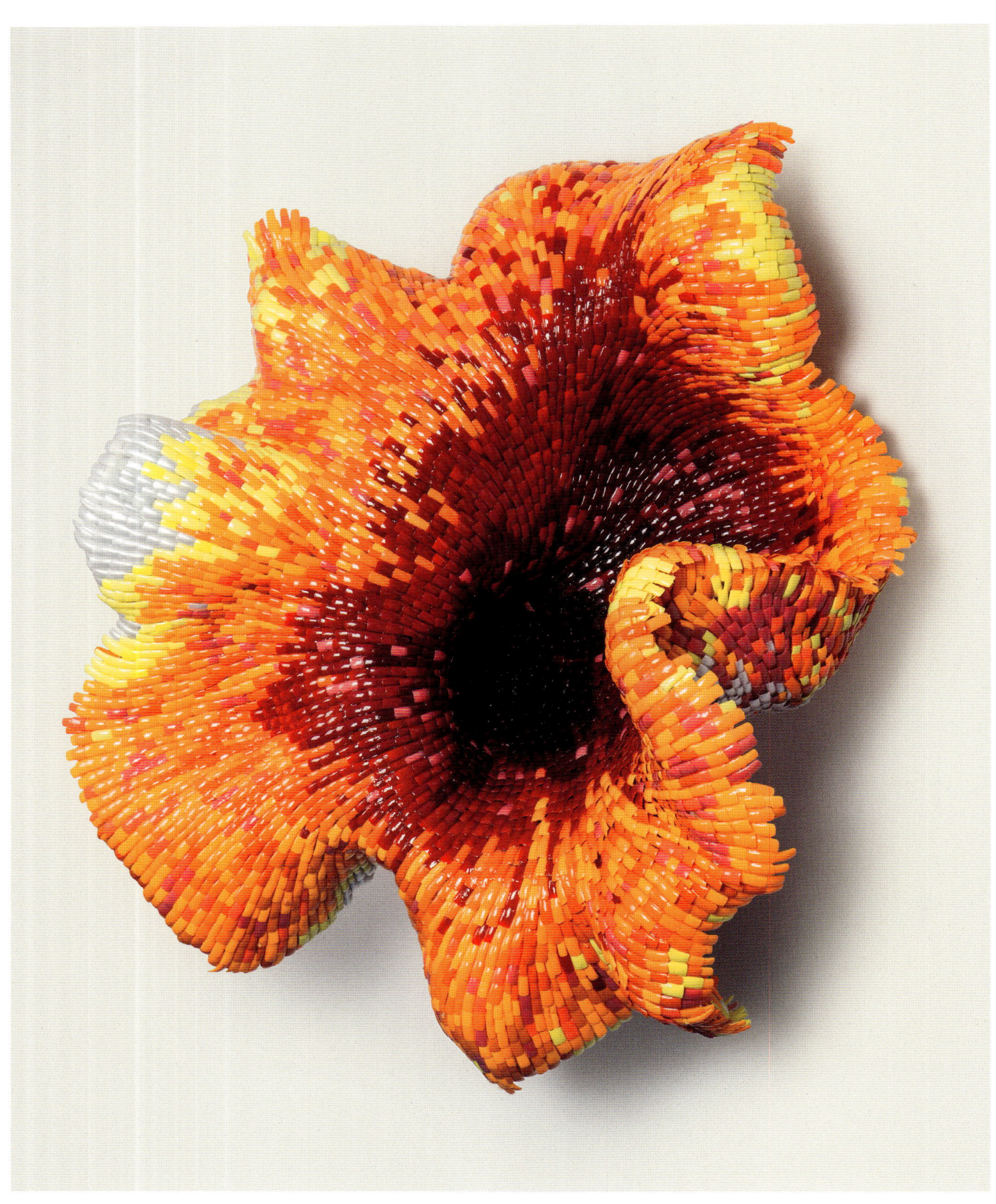

Frances Goodman. *Succubus*, 2016. Acrylic nails, glue, and polyurethane: 40.3 × 40.6 × 20.9 inches. *Courtesy of the artist and Richard Taittinger Gallery, New York*

JADE DOSKOW

Jade Doskow is an architectural and landscape photographer known for her rigorously composed and eerily poetic images that examine the intersection of people, architecture, nature, and time. Based in New York, Doskow holds a BA from New York University and an MFA in photography from the School of Visual Arts. She is best known for *Lost Utopias*, a decade-long photography project on the remaining architecture, art, and landscaping of international world's fairs. Additional projects include a thirteen-year documentation of the waterfront neighborhood of Red Hook, Brooklyn; the architecture of activist buildings such as ABC No Rio in New York; and numerous private commissions of some of New York City's greatest skyscrapers. Throughout all of her work, a sense of timeless monumentality in juxtaposition to modern details highlights the surreality of the modern cityscape.

Doskow's work has been exhibited internationally, including at Cornell University's School of Architecture Gallery in Ithaca, New York; Forma Meravigli Gallery in Milan, Italy; Glass Box Gallery in Seattle, Washington; Tracey Normal Gallery in Asheville, North Carolina; and Front Room Gallery in New York. Additionally, her work has been widely published, including in *U.K. Independent*, *Elle Décor Italia*, *Newsweek Japan*, *Smithsonian*, *Slate*, *Uncube Berlin*, *Business Insider*, *The Atlantic*, *Design Arts Daily*, *NPR Picture Show*, *ArchDaily*, and *Wired*. Doskow is on the photography faculty of the School of Visual Arts, New York City, and the International Center of Photography, New York City, and is represented by Front Room Gallery in New York City, and Tracey Morgan Gallery in Asheville, North Carolina. In December 2016, a monograph of *Lost Utopias* was published by Black Dog London and listed by American Photo as one of the top fifty photo books of the year.

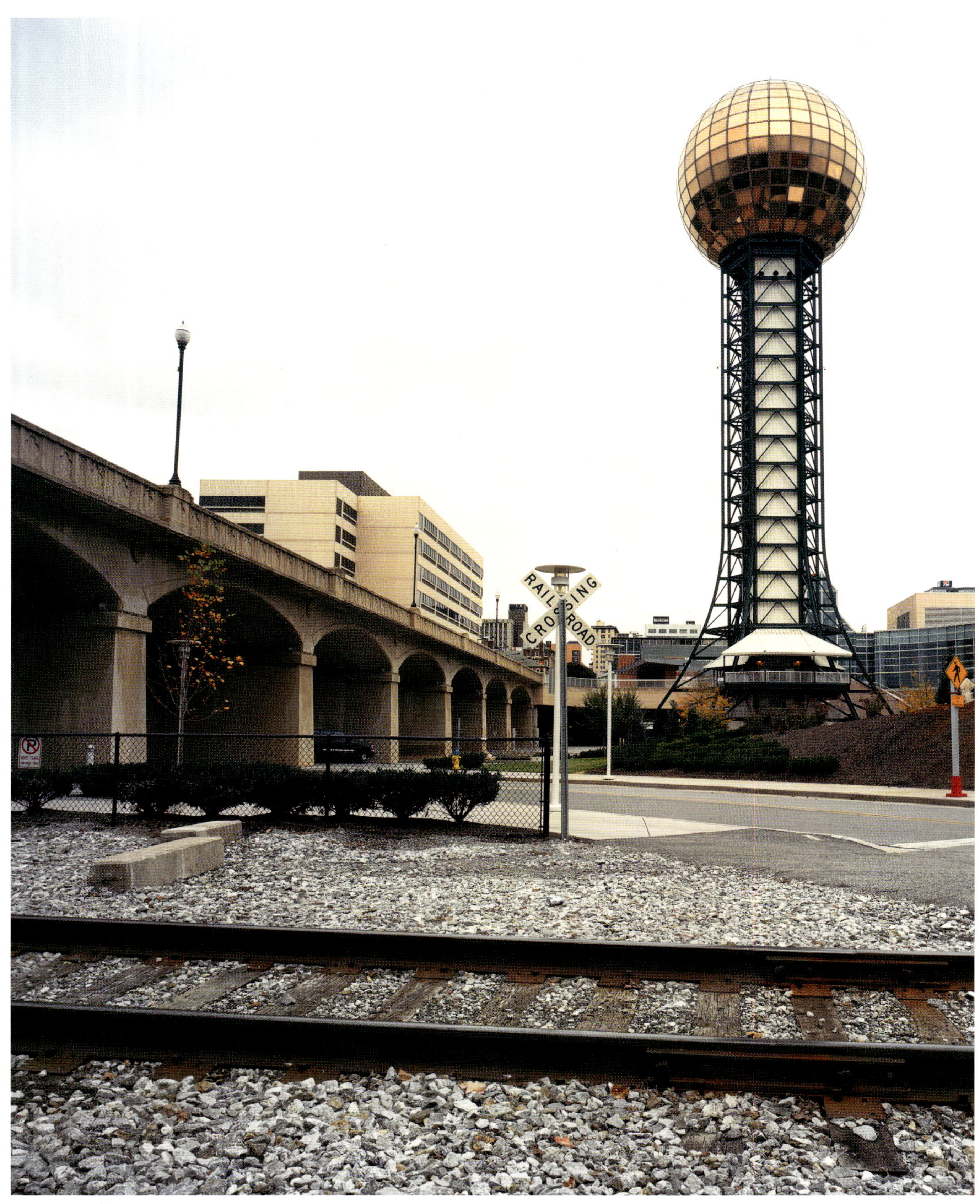

Jade Doskow. *Knoxville 1982 World's Fair, "Energy Turns the World," Sunsphere*, 2009. Digital c-print from 4 × 5-inch negative: 20 × 25 inches. Image ©Jade Doskow. *Courtesy of the artist*

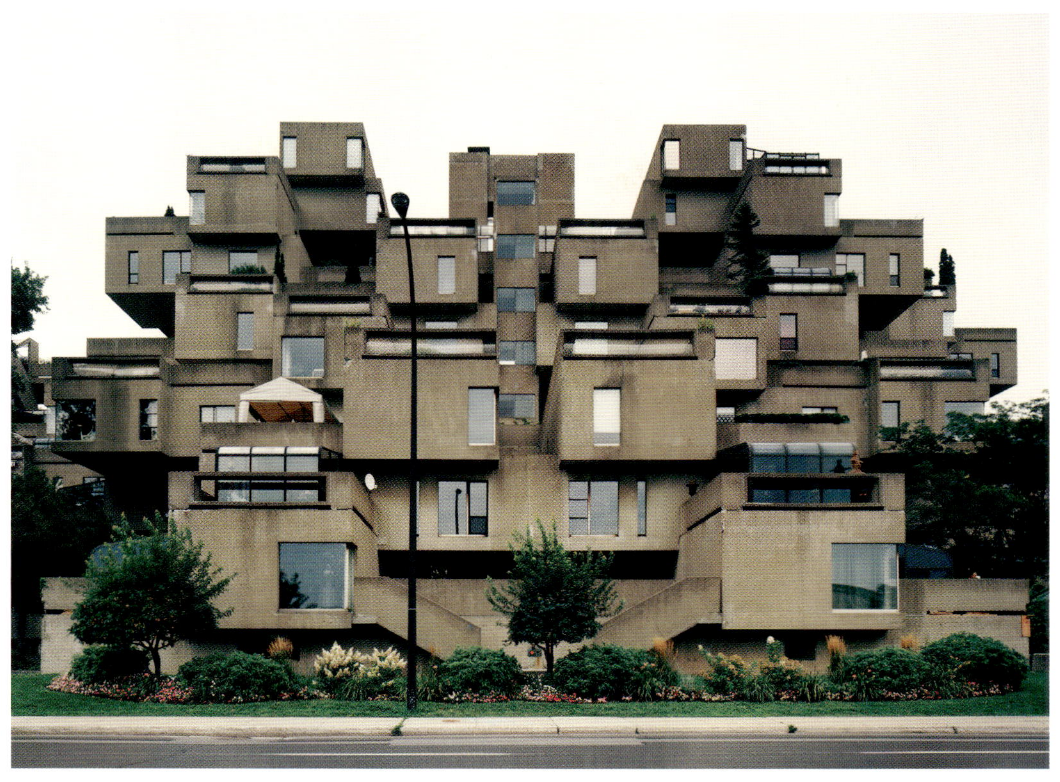

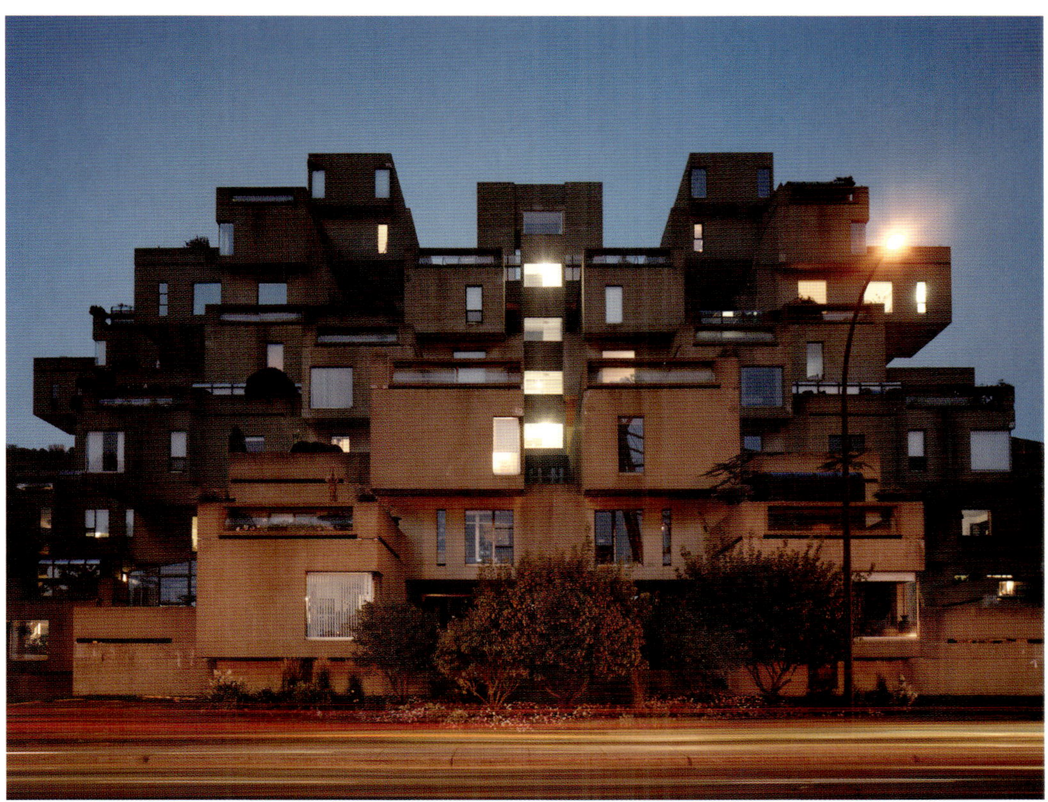

Jade Doskow. *Montreal 1967 World's Fair, "Man and His World," Habitat '67*, 2012. Digital c-print from 4 × 5-inch negative: 22 × 30 inches. Image ©Jade Doskow. *Courtesy of the artist*

Jade Doskow. *Montreal 1967 World's Fair, "Man and His World,"Habitat '67, Night View*, 2012. Digital c-print from 4 × 5-inch negative: 22 × 30 inches. Image ©Jade Doskow. *Courtesy of the artist*

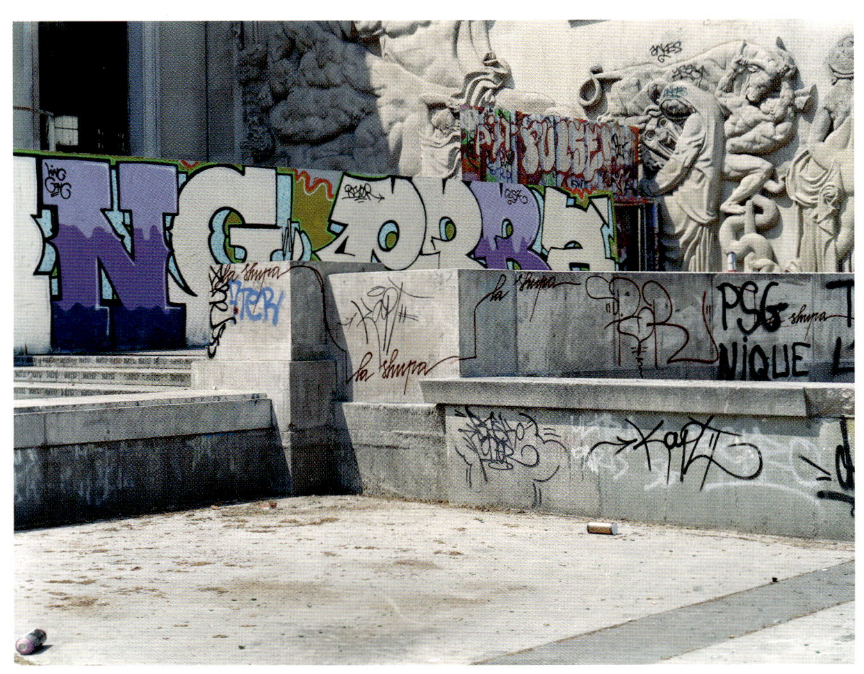

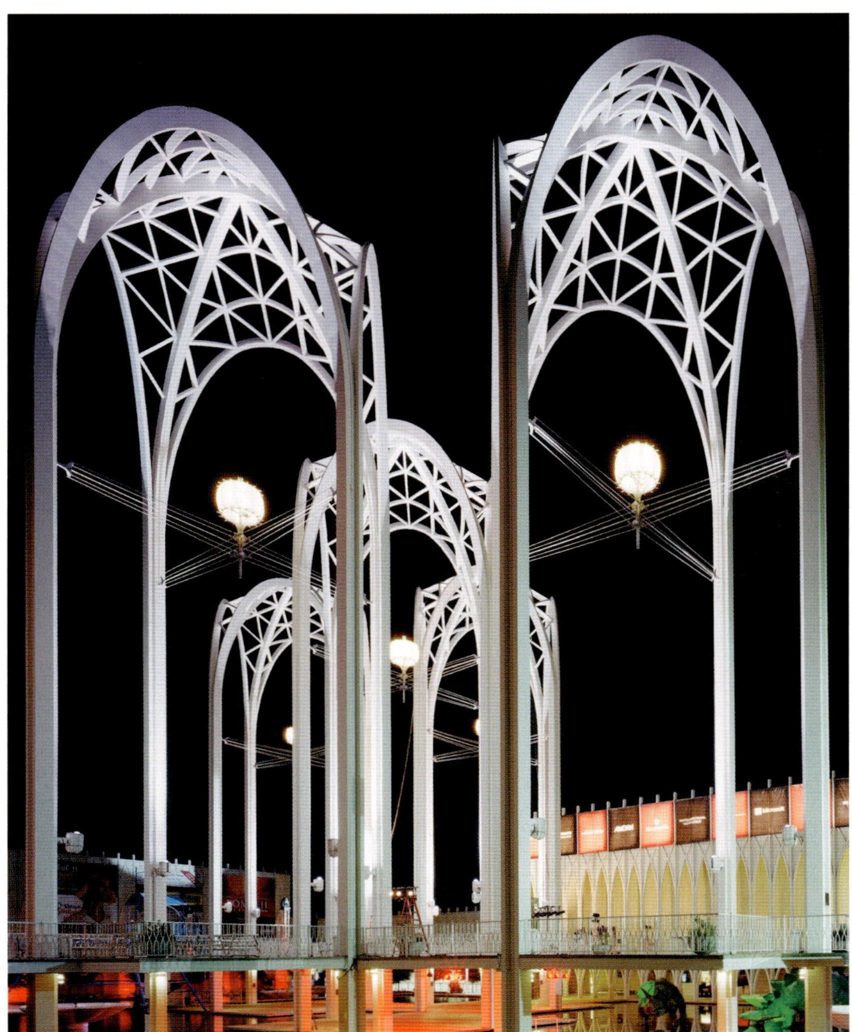

Jade Doskow. *Paris 1937 World's Fair, "Exposition Internationale des Arts et Techniques dans la Vie Moderne", Graffiti, Palais de Tokyo*, 2007. Digital c-print from 4 × 5-inch negative: 30 × 38 inches. Image ©Jade Doskow. *Courtesy of the artist*

Jade Doskow. *Seattle 1962 World's Fair, "Century 21 Exposition," Science Center Arches at Night*, 2014–16. Archival inkjet print from 4 × 5-inch negative: 60 × 50 inches. Image ©Jade Doskow. *Courtesy of the artist*

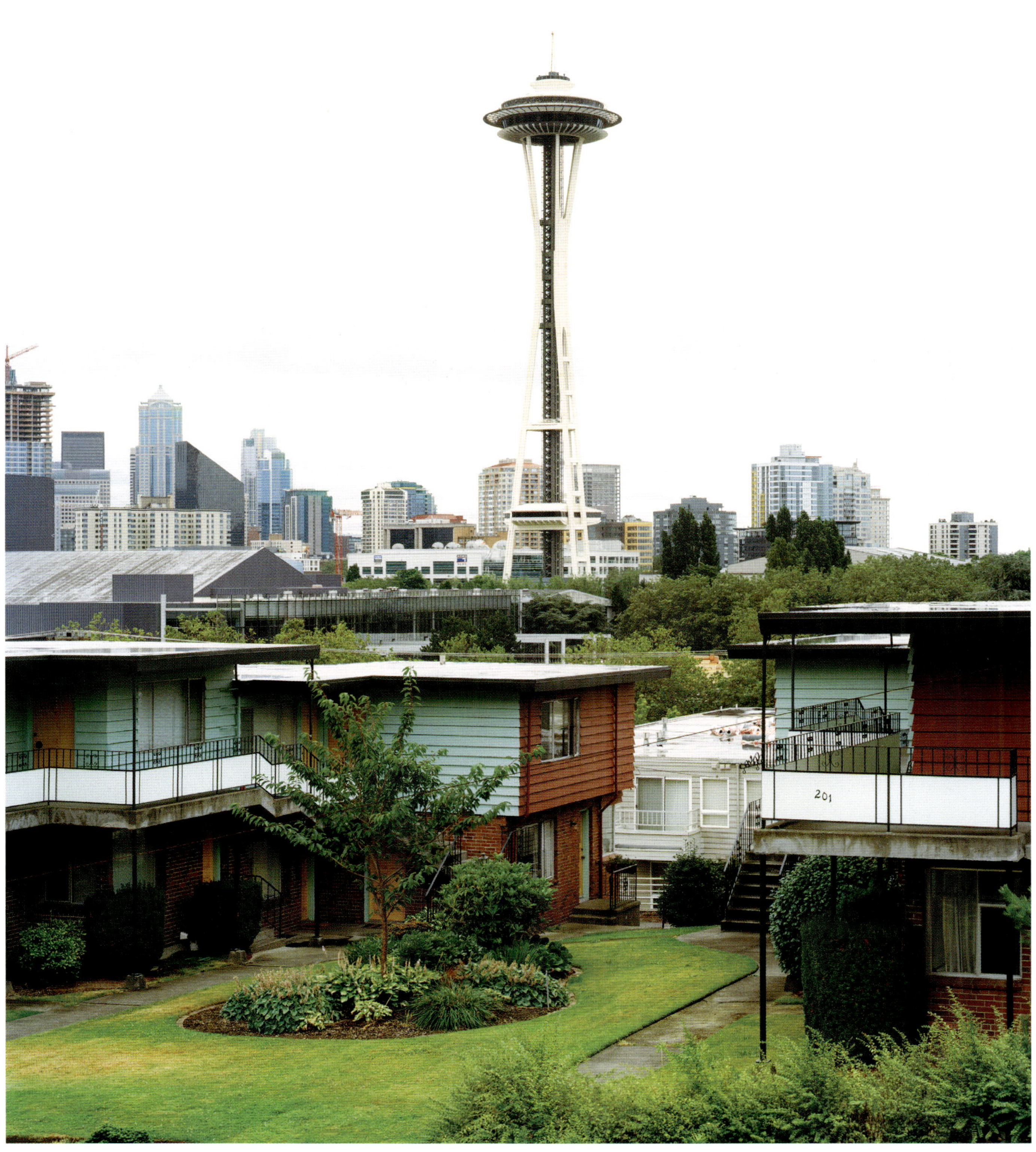

Jade Doskow. Seattle 1962 World's Fair, "The Century 21 Exposition," Space Needle, 2014. Digital c-print from 4 × 5-inch negative: 50 × 40 inches. Image ©Jade Doskow. Courtesy of the artist

JUDY CHICAGO

Judy Chicago is an American artist, writer, and art educator. She coined the term "feminist art" in 1970 and was the founder of the first American feminist art program. Many of her pieces examine stereotypes surrounding skills taught to women and men, such as needlework versus welding. Her most well-known works include, *The Birth Project*, *PowerPlay*, *The Holocaust Project*, and *The Dinner Party*, which is a centerpiece of the Elizabeth A. Sackler Center for Feminist Art at the Brooklyn Museum.

Chicago taught art at Fresno State College, Fresno, California, in 1970 and taught the first women's art class that fall. This class became the Feminist Art Program in 1971, the first of its kind in the United States, and was later reestablished at the California Institute of the Arts, Valencia, California. Her first book, *Through the Flower*, was published in 1975 and told of her struggles with identity and being a female artist. Chicago has permanent collections in many museums around the world, including the British Museum, London; the Brooklyn Museum, Brooklyn, New York; the J. Paul Getty Trust, Los Angeles; the Los Angeles County Museum of Art, Los Angeles; the Museum of Fine Arts, Boston; the National Gallery of Art, Washington, DC; the National Museum of Women in the Arts, Washington, DC; the Pennsylvania Academy of the Fine Arts, Philadelphia; and the San Francisco Museum of Modern Art, San Francisco. Chicago continues to work and still receives awards for her monumental projects. She is regularly recognized for her commitment to art as a vehicle for intellectual transformation and social change, and to women's rights to engage in the highest levels of art production.

Judy Chicago. *Home Sweet Home*, from *Resolutions: A Stitch in Time*, 2000. Counted cross-stitch and embroidery on cotton: 37 × 25.5 inches. Needlework by Pamella Nesbit. ©Judy Chicago/Artists Rights Society (ARS) New York; photo ©Donald Woodman/ARS NY. *Courtesy of the artist and Salon94, New York*

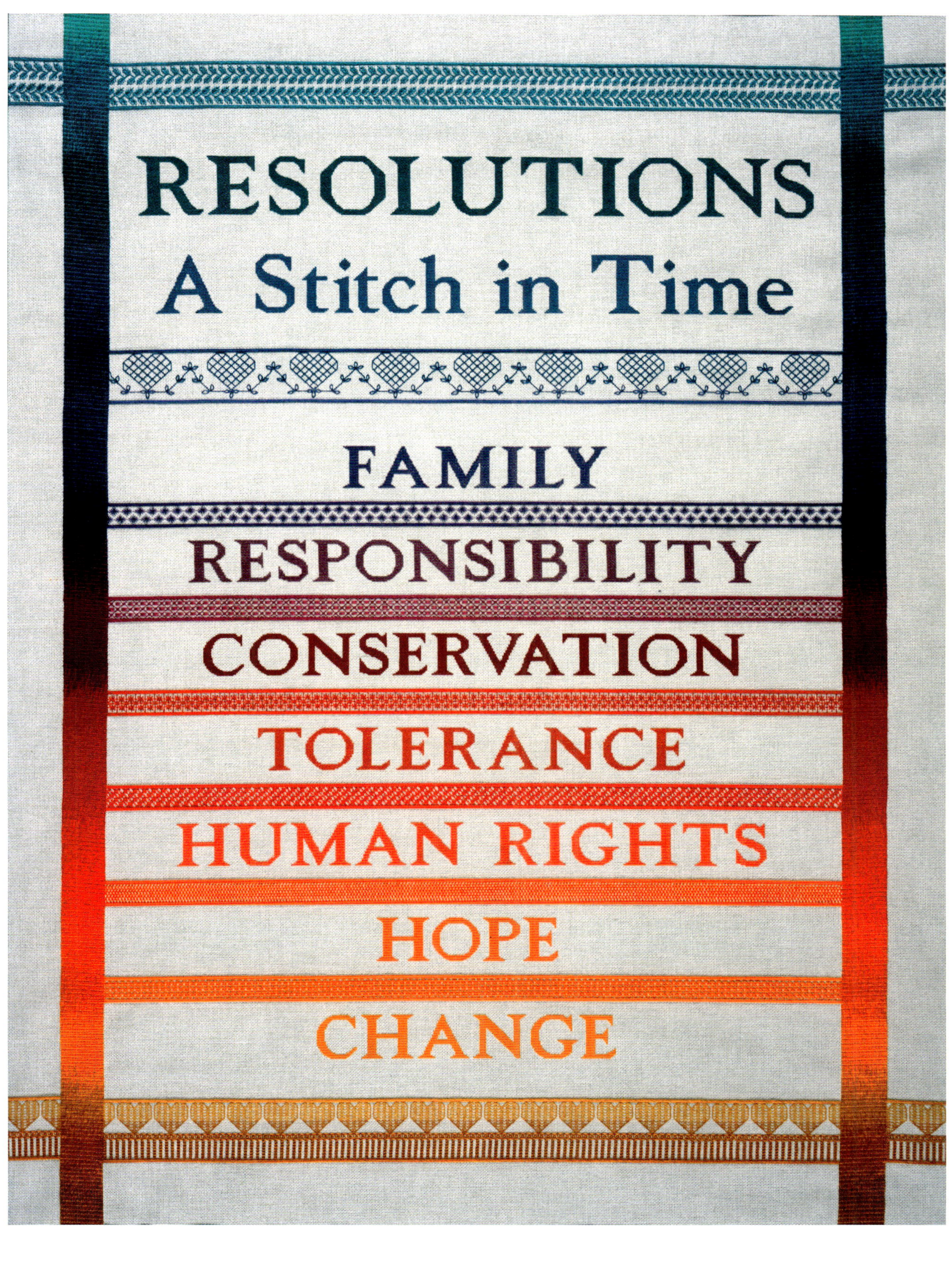
RESOLUTIONS
A Stitch in Time
FAMILY
RESPONSIBILITY
CONSERVATION
TOLERANCE
HUMAN RIGHTS
HOPE
CHANGE

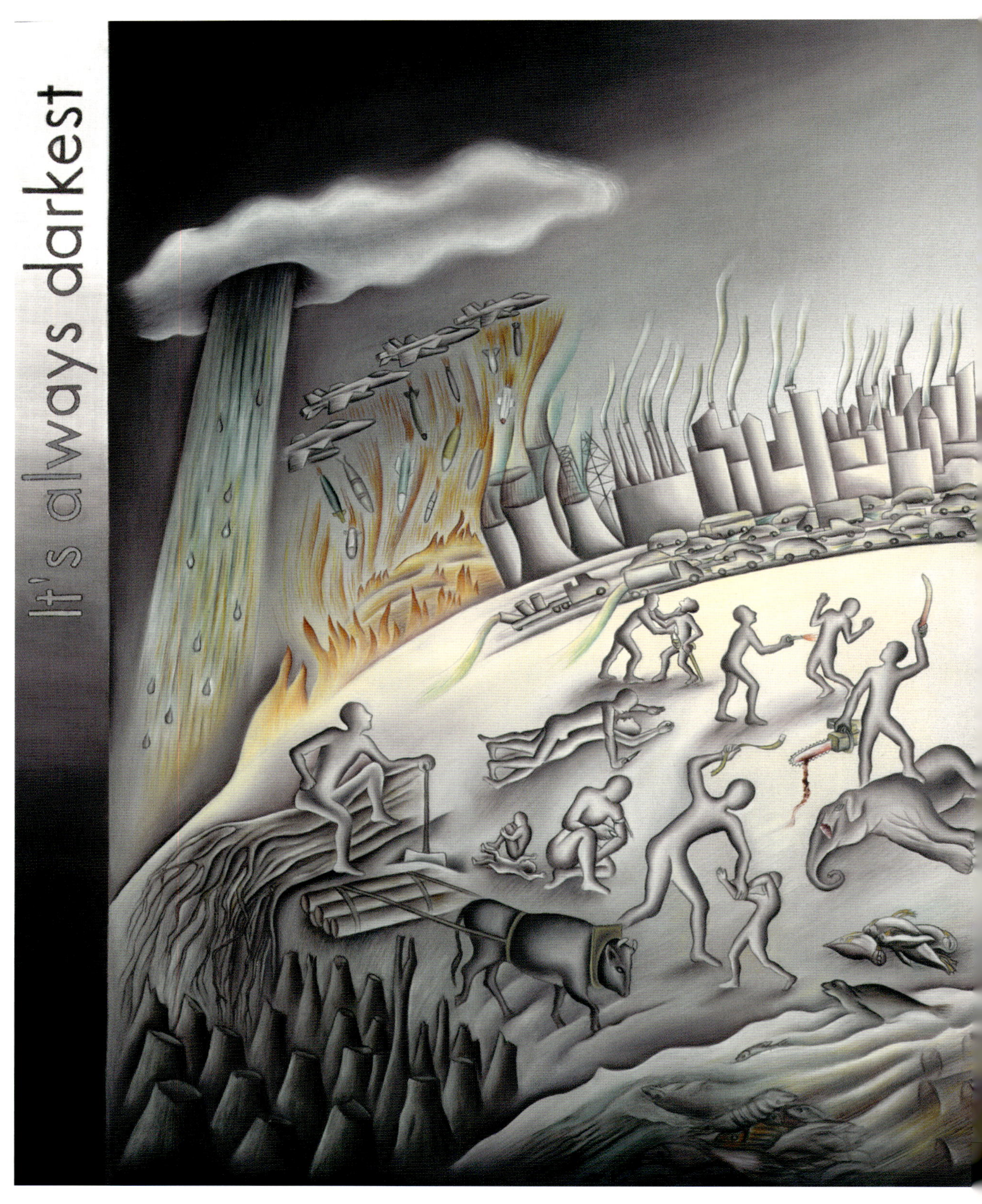

Judy Chicago. *It's Always Darkest before the Dawn*, from *Resolutions: A Stitch in Time*, 2000. Sprayed acrylic, oil paint, and embroidery on portrait linen: 20 × 40 inches. Needlework by Pamella Nesbit. ©Judy Chicago/Artists Rights Society (ARS) New York; photo ©Donald Woodman/ARS NY. *Courtesy of the artist and Salon94, New York*

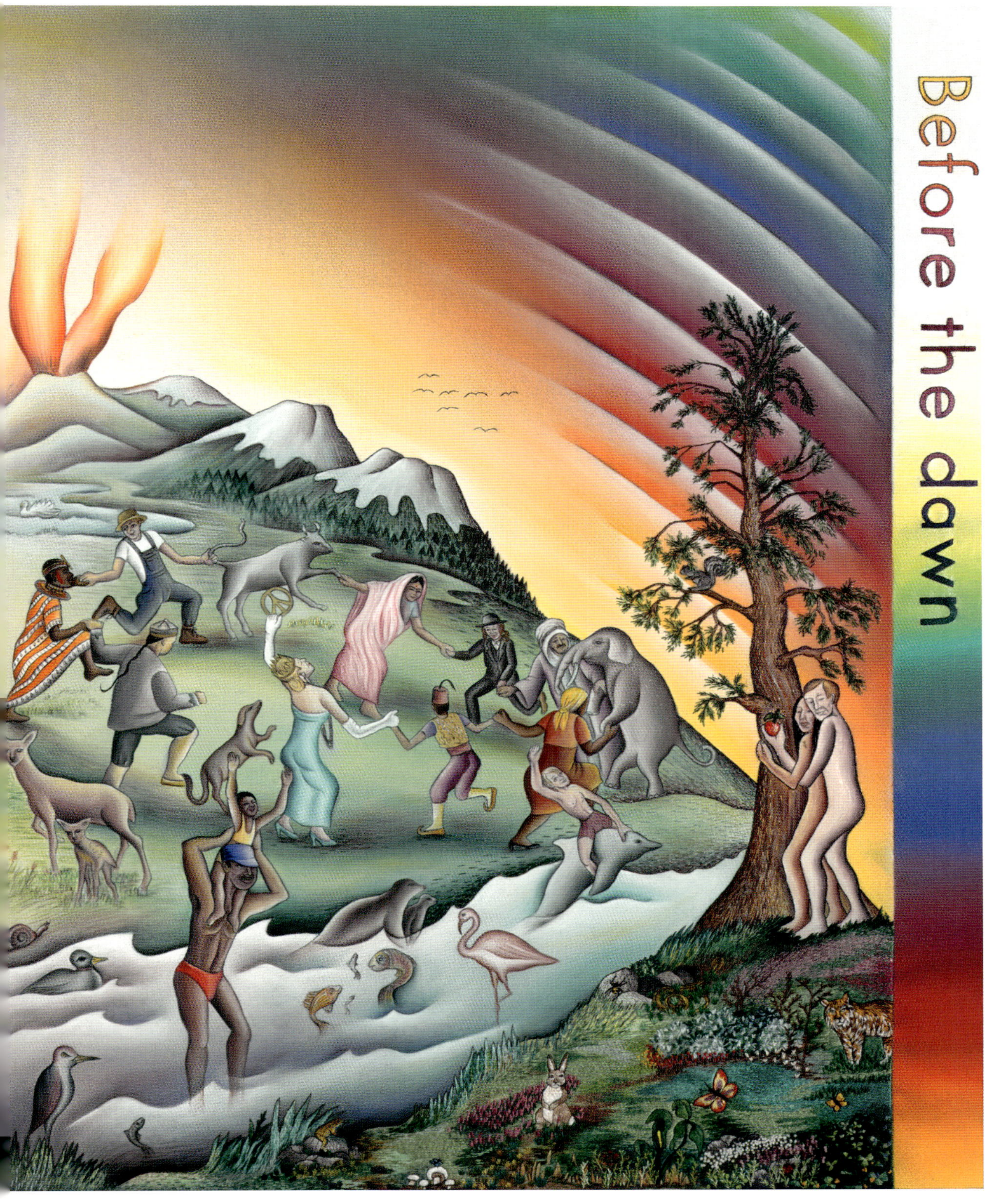

Before the dawn

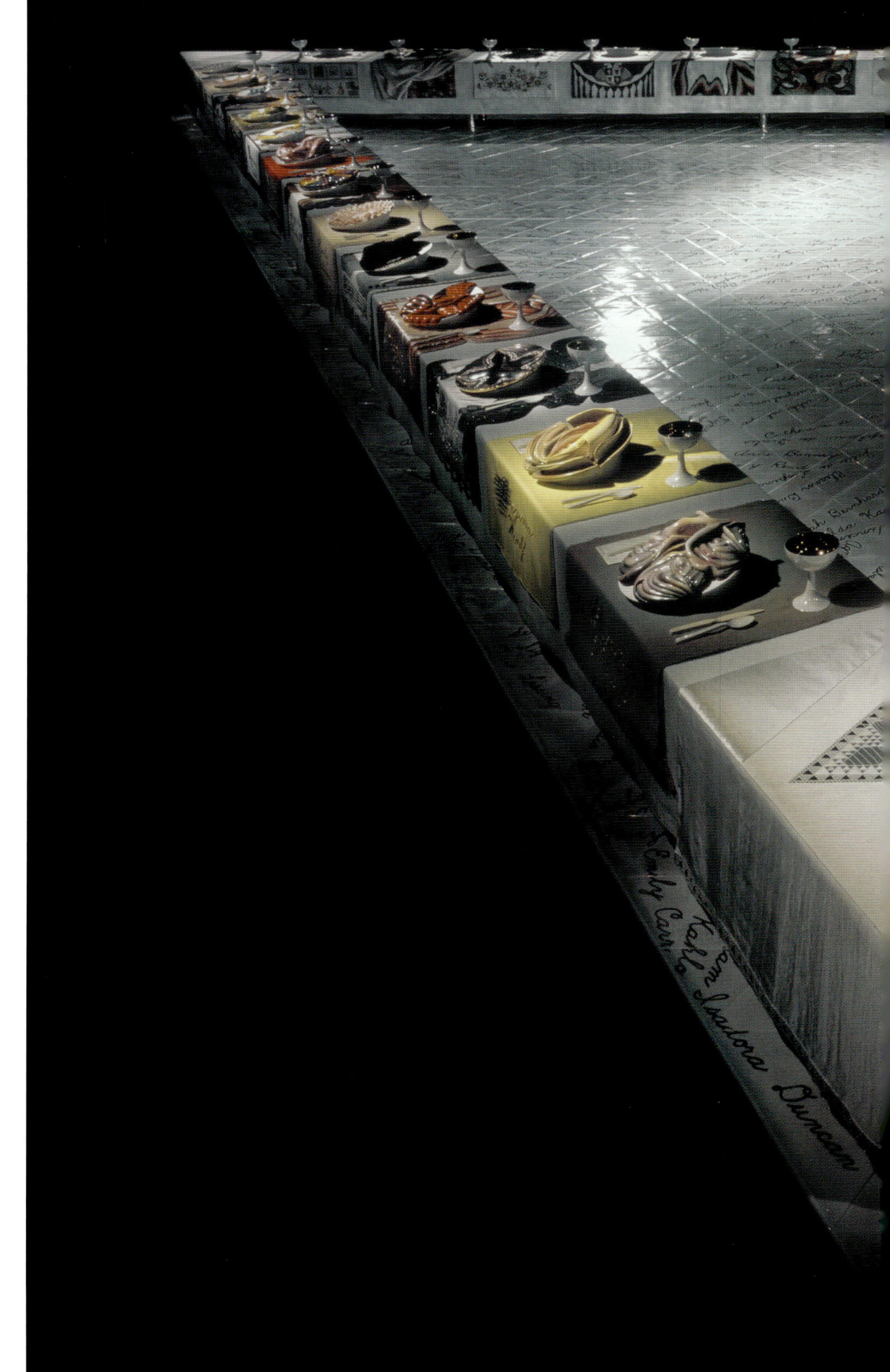
Emily Carr
Isadora Duncan

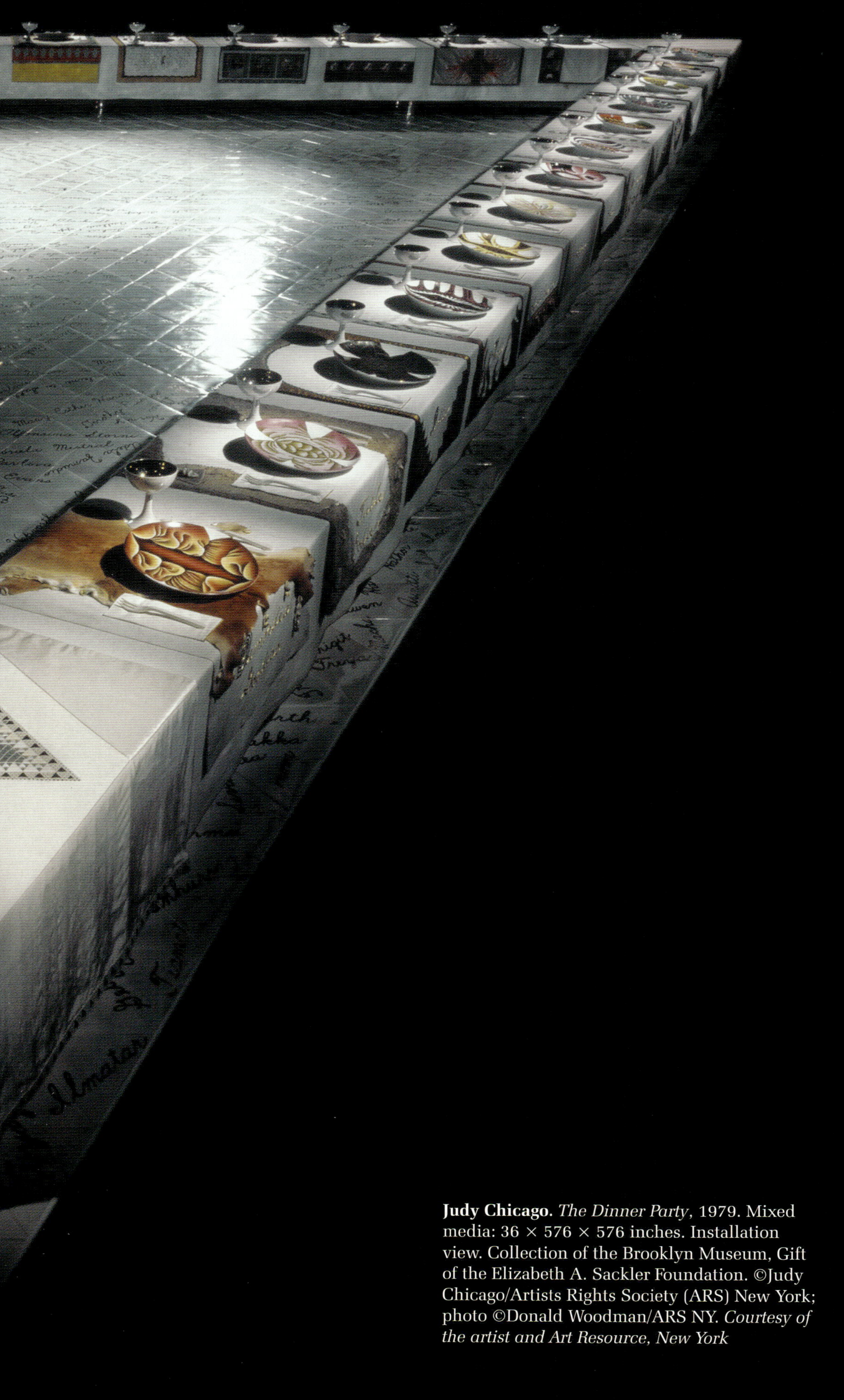

Judy Chicago. *The Dinner Party*, 1979. Mixed media: 36 × 576 × 576 inches. Installation view. Collection of the Brooklyn Museum, Gift of the Elizabeth A. Sackler Foundation. ©Judy Chicago/Artists Rights Society (ARS) New York; photo ©Donald Woodman/ARS NY. *Courtesy of the artist and Art Resource, New York*

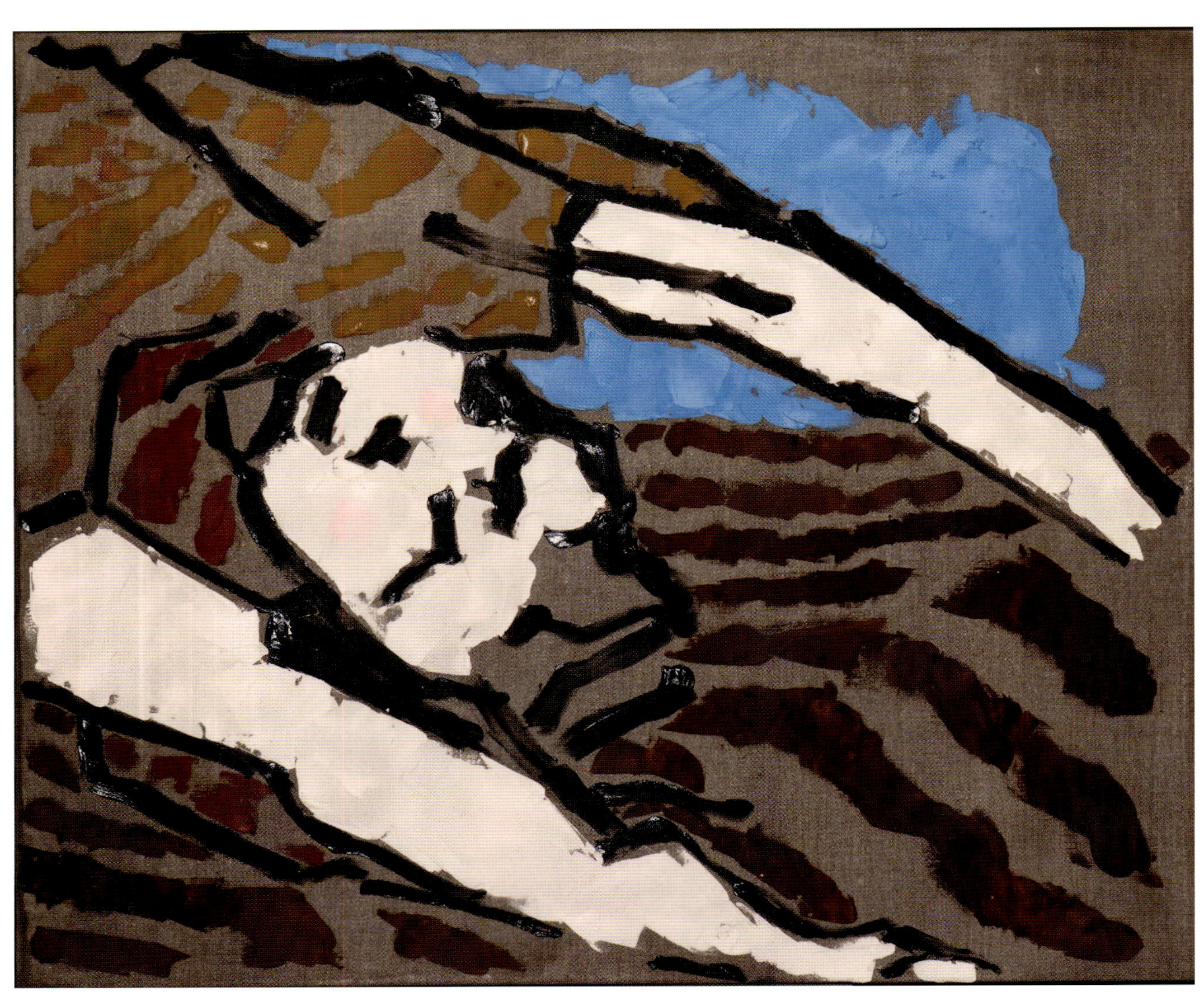

Judy Rifka. *Why Die?*, 1984. Oil paint on linen: 24 × 30 inches. *Courtesy of the artist*

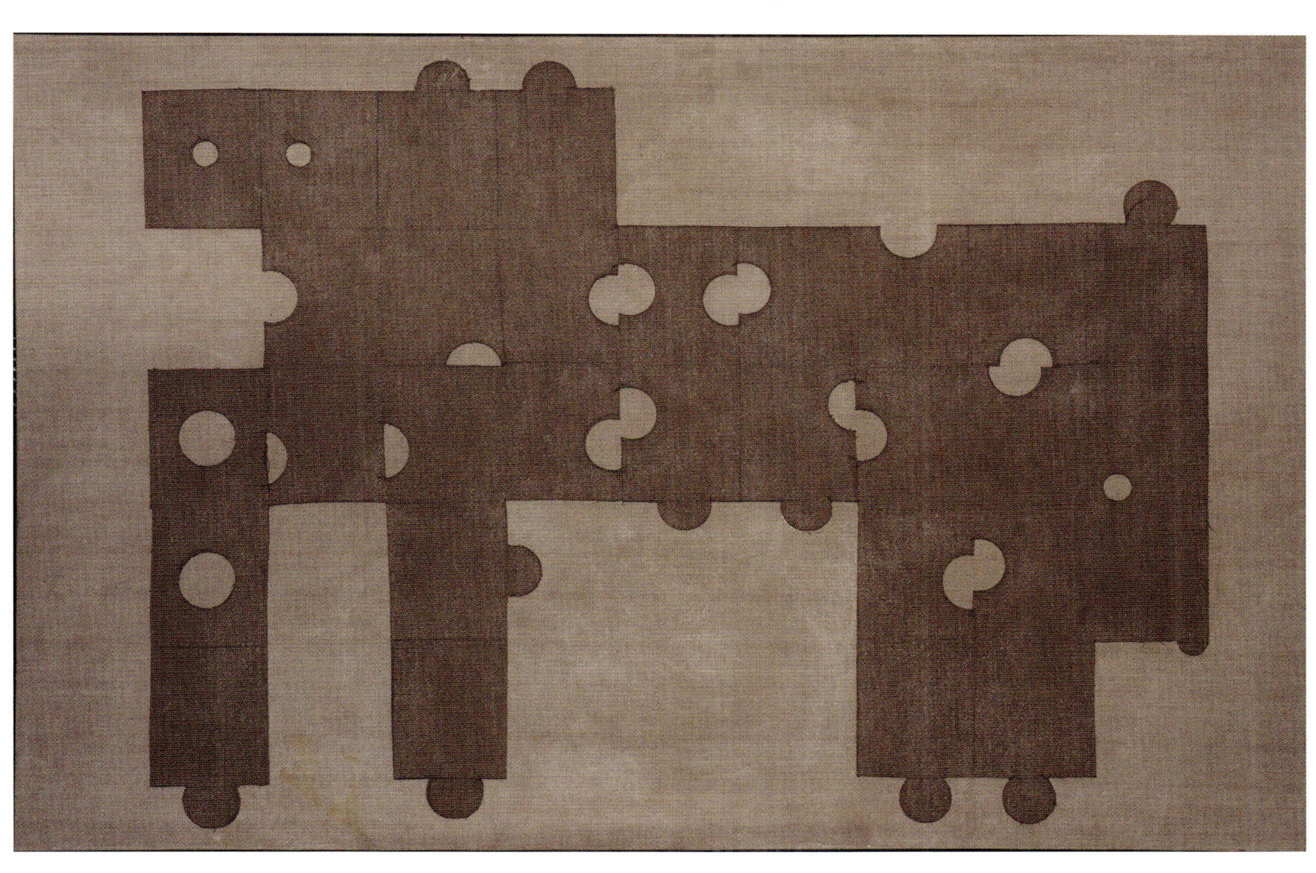

Judy Rifka. *Animal Spirit*, 1995. Linen on linen: 48 × 72 inches. *Courtesy of the artist*

KARA WALKER

Kara Walker is a New York–based artist best known for her candid investigation of race, gender, sexuality, and violence through silhouetted figures that have appeared in numerous exhibitions worldwide. Born in Stockton, California, in 1969, Walker was raised in Atlanta, Georgia, from the age of thirteen. She studied at the Atlanta College of Art, in Atlanta (BFA, 1991), and the Rhode Island School of Design, Providence (MFA, 1994). She is the recipient of many awards, notably the John D. and Catherine T. MacArthur Foundation Achievement Award in 1997 and the United States Artists, Eileen Harris Norton Fellowship, in 2008. In 2012 Walker became a member of the American Academy of Arts and Letters.

A survey exhibition of Walker's work, *Kara Walker: My Complement, My Enemy, My Oppressor, My Love*, was organized by the Walker Art Center in Minneapolis, Minnesota, where it premiered in February 2007 before traveling to ARC / Musée d'Art Moderne de la Ville de Paris, the Whitney Museum of American Art in New York City, the Hammer Museum in Los Angeles, and the Museum of Modern Art in Fort Worth, Texas. During the spring of 2014, Walker's first large-scale public project, a monumental installation titled *A Subtlety: Or . . . the Marvelous Sugar Baby an Homage to the Unpaid and Overworked Artisans Who Have Refined Our Sweet Tastes from the Cane Fields to the Kitchens of the New World on the Occasion of the Demolition of the Domino Sugar Refining Plant*, was on view at the abandoned Domino Sugar Refinery in Williamsburg, Brooklyn, New York. Commissioned and presented by Creative Time, the project—a massive, sugar-covered, sphinx-like sculpture—responded to and reflected on the troubled history of sugar. The installation was seen by over 130,000 visitors over the course of the nine weekends that it was open to the public, and received an overwhelming critical response.

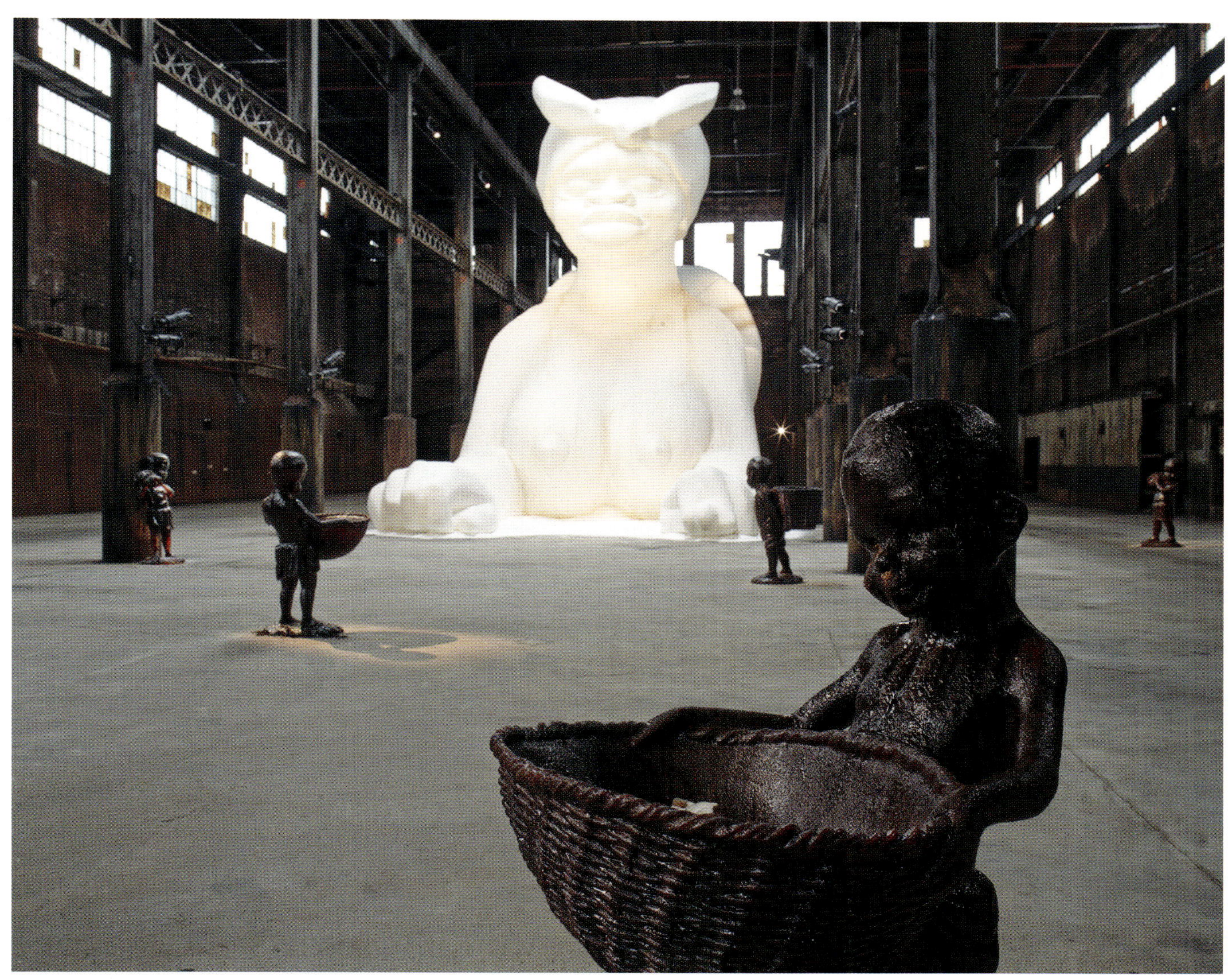

Kara Walker. *A Subtlety: The Marvelous Sugar Baby, an Homage to the Unpaid and Overworked Artisans Who Have Refined Our Sweet Tastes from the Cane Fields to the Kitchens of the New World on the Occasion of the Demolition of the Domino Sugar Refining Plant,* 2014. Powdered sugar, granulated sugar, corn syrup, molasses, foam blocks, steel, resin: dimensions variable. Installation view, a project of Creative Time at Domino Sugar Refinery, Brooklyn, New York. Image ©Jason Wyche. *Courtesy of the artist and Sikkema Jenkins & Co., New York*

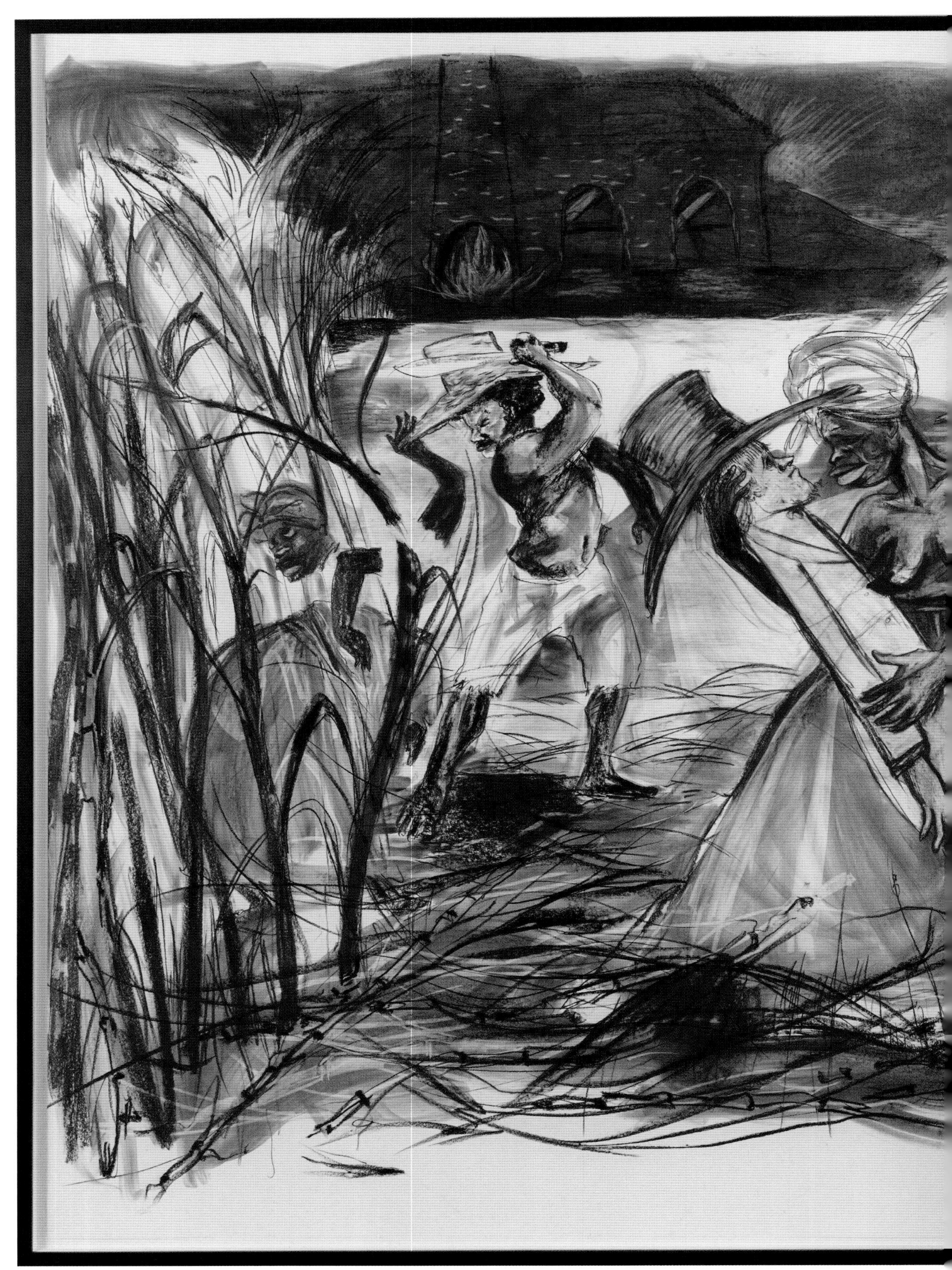

Kara Walker. *Stages of Sugar Production: Cutting, Grinding, Refining*, 2014. Graphite and charcoal on paper (2 parts): 98.25 × 72 inches, each. *Courtesy of the artist and Sikkema Jenkins & Co., New York*

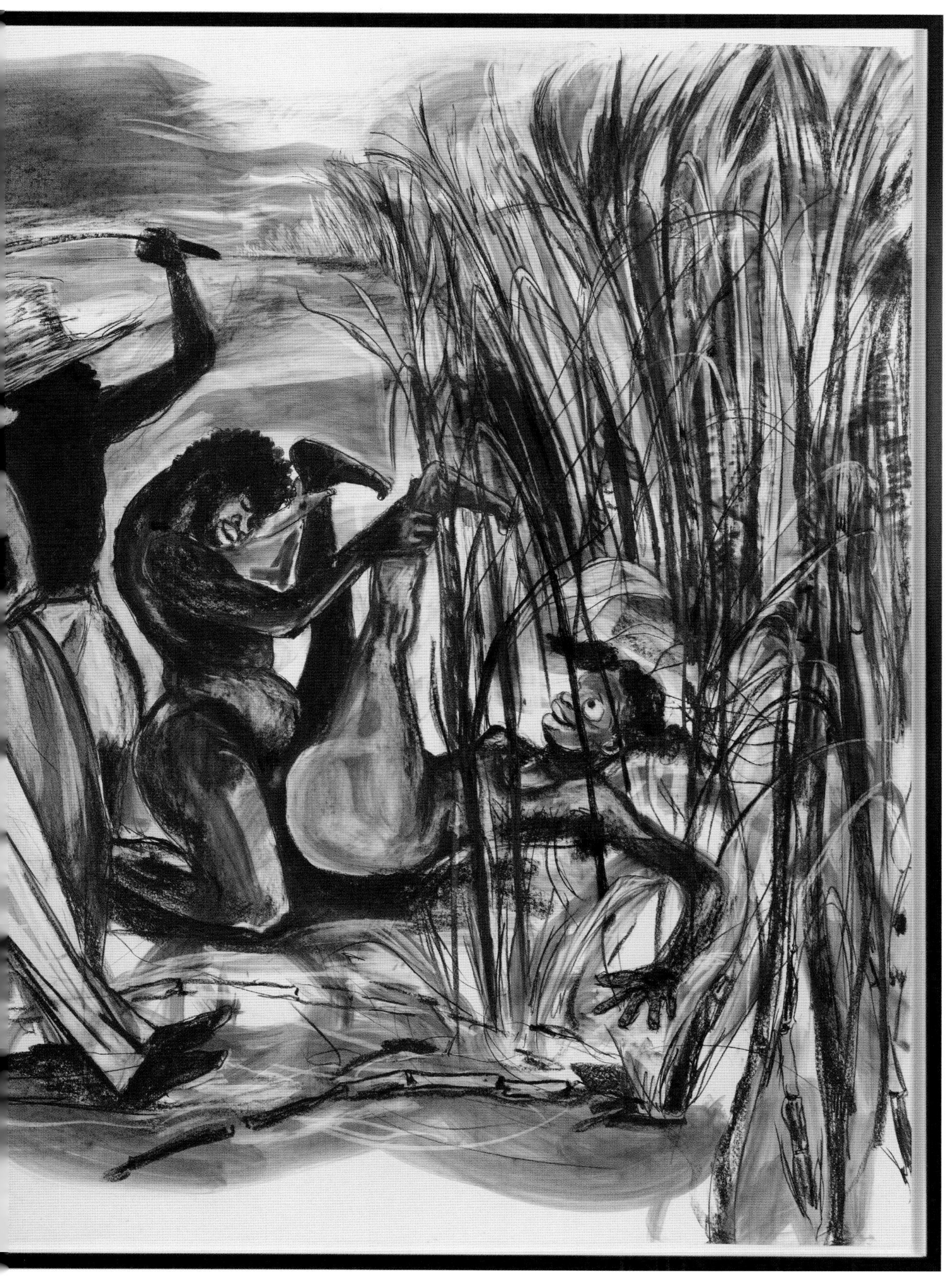

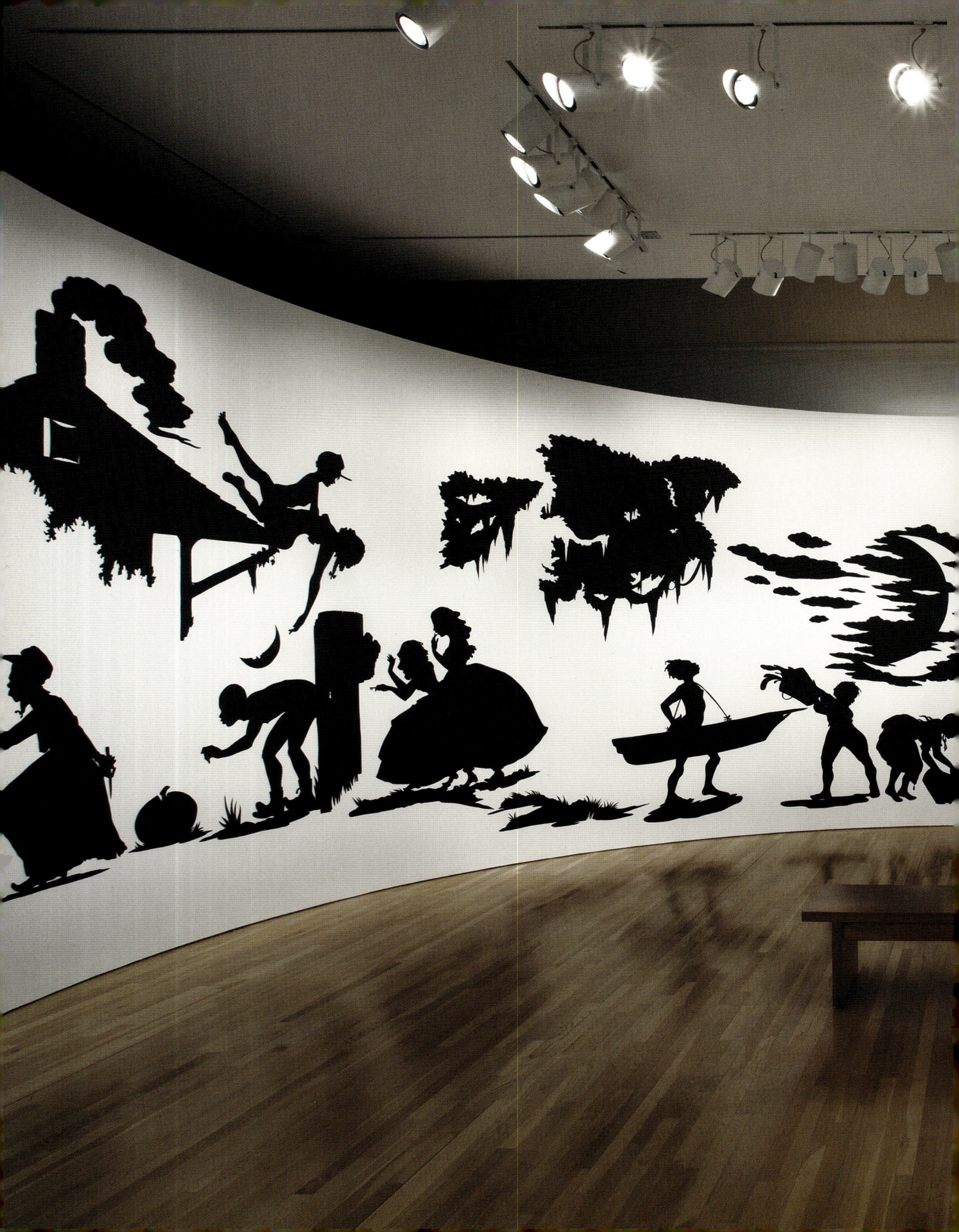

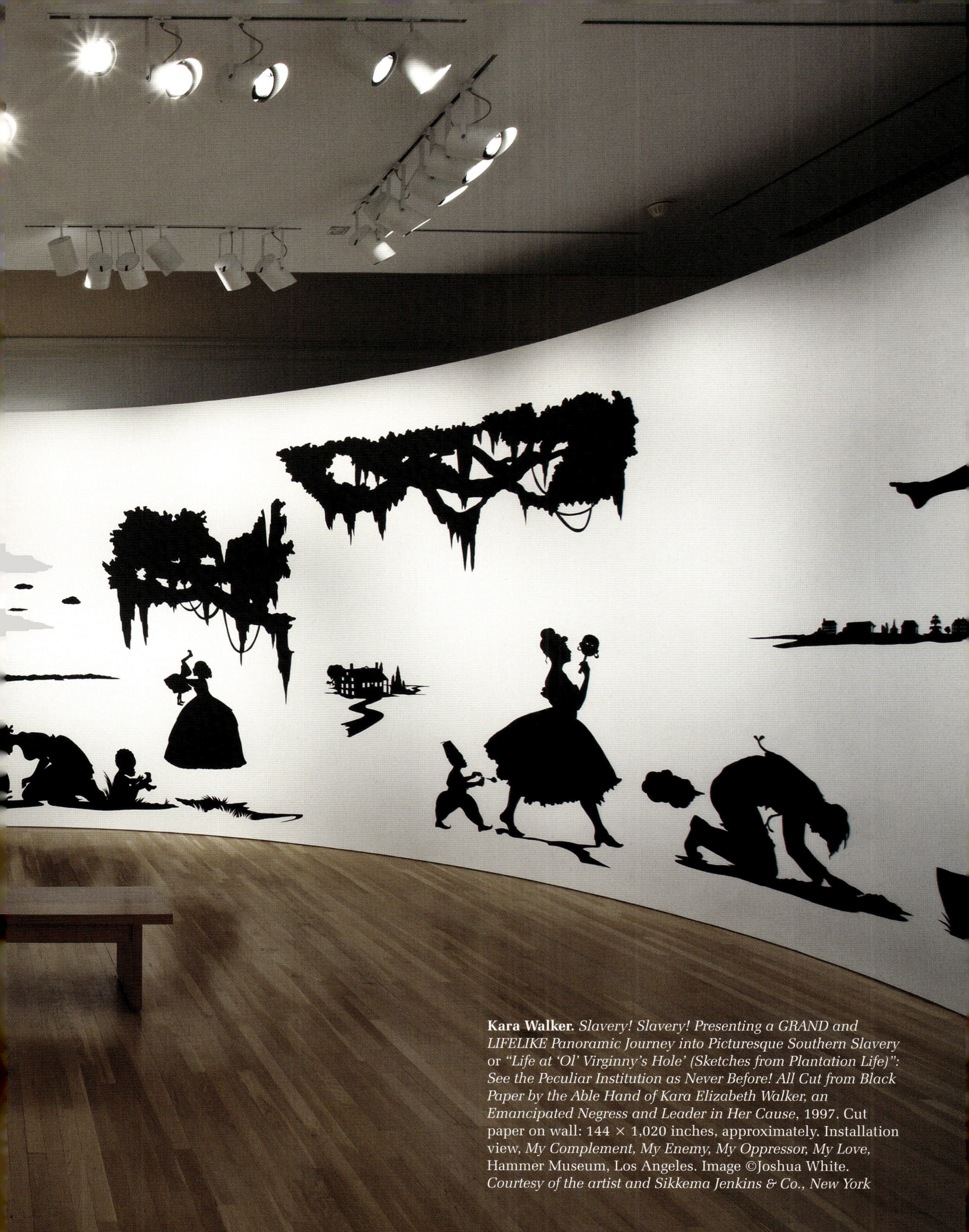

Kara Walker. *Slavery! Slavery! Presenting a GRAND and LIFELIKE Panoramic Journey into Picturesque Southern Slavery or "Life at 'Ol' Virginny's Hole' (Sketches from Plantation Life)": See the Peculiar Institution as Never Before! All Cut from Black Paper by the Able Hand of Kara Elizabeth Walker, an Emancipated Negress and Leader in Her Cause*, 1997. Cut paper on wall: 144 × 1,020 inches, approximately. Installation view, *My Complement, My Enemy, My Oppressor, My Love*, Hammer Museum, Los Angeles. Image ©Joshua White. *Courtesy of the artist and Sikkema Jenkins & Co., New York*

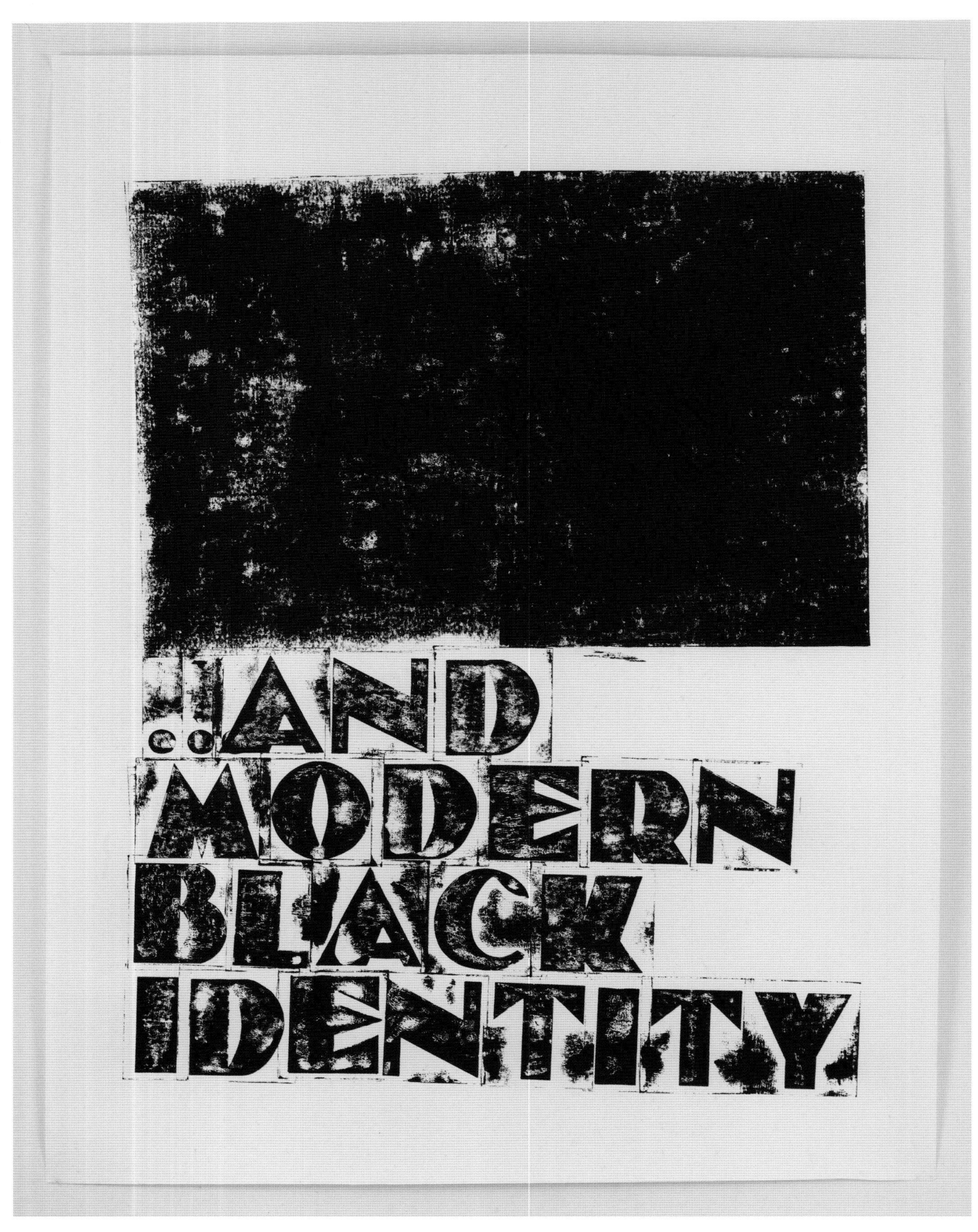

Kara Walker. . . .*(and Modern Black Identity)*, 2010. Unique ink transfer on paper: 94 × 72 inches. *Courtesy of the artist and Sikkema Jenkins & Co., New York*

KAREN JERZYK

Karen Jerzyk is a self-taught photographer who documents subjects in abandoned buildings, fabricated environments, and rustic nature. Using ornate costumes, elaborate scenery, and intense color, Jerzyk presents surreal compositions that read like unforgettable ghost stories. Often the subject of her own narratives, Jerzyk's unsettling self-portraits allow the viewer an abbreviated glimpse into her personal journeys and struggles throughout life. Many of her photos embody the feeling of "future-past"—imagery that is seemingly futuristic yet vintage in nature.

Jerzyk's best-known series are *Last Days of Earth* and *Color*, mainly for their haunting interpretations of a dystopian world. Jerzyk regularly travels throughout the United States for photo projects, and her work has been internationally published in multiple publications, including *Buzzfeed*, *Harper's Bazaar*, *Juxtapoz*, *Shape*, *Artscope Magazine*, *Cosmopolitan Australia*, iTunes, Yahoo.com, MSN.com, and *USA Art News*. Jerzyk graduated with a BA in English from the University of New Hampshire in 2003.

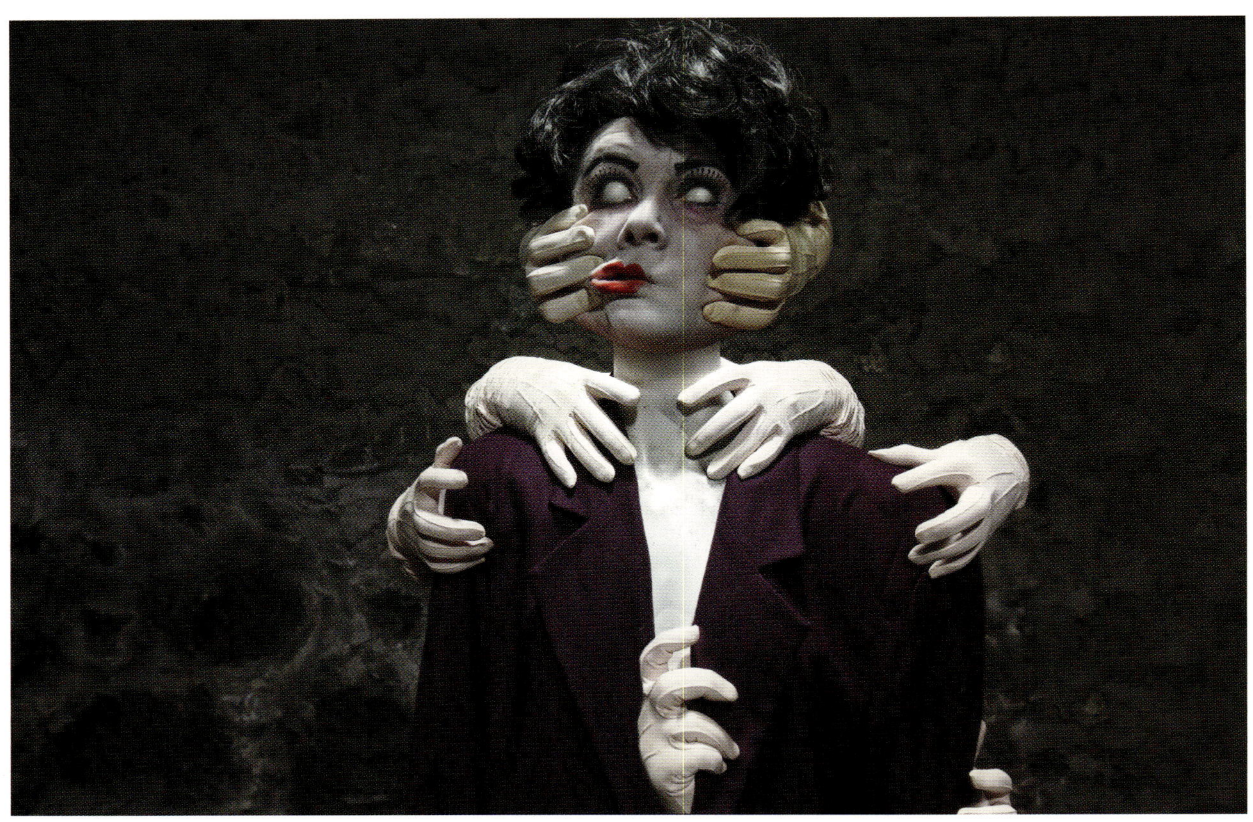

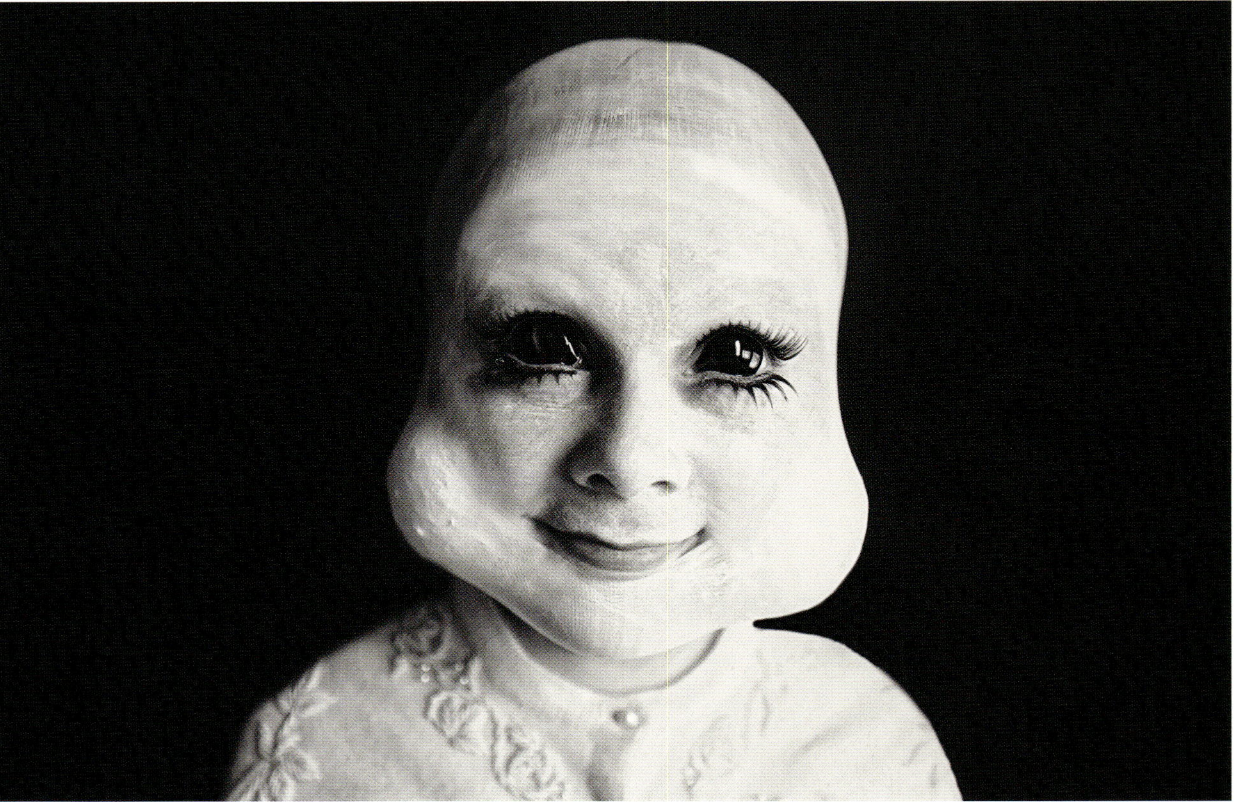

Karen Jerzyk. *I Think I Need to Go to the Emergency Room*, 2014. Digital photograph: dimensions variable. *Courtesy of the artist*

Karen Jerzyk. *Battling the Mumps*, 2014. Digital photograph: dimensions variable. *Courtesy of the artist*

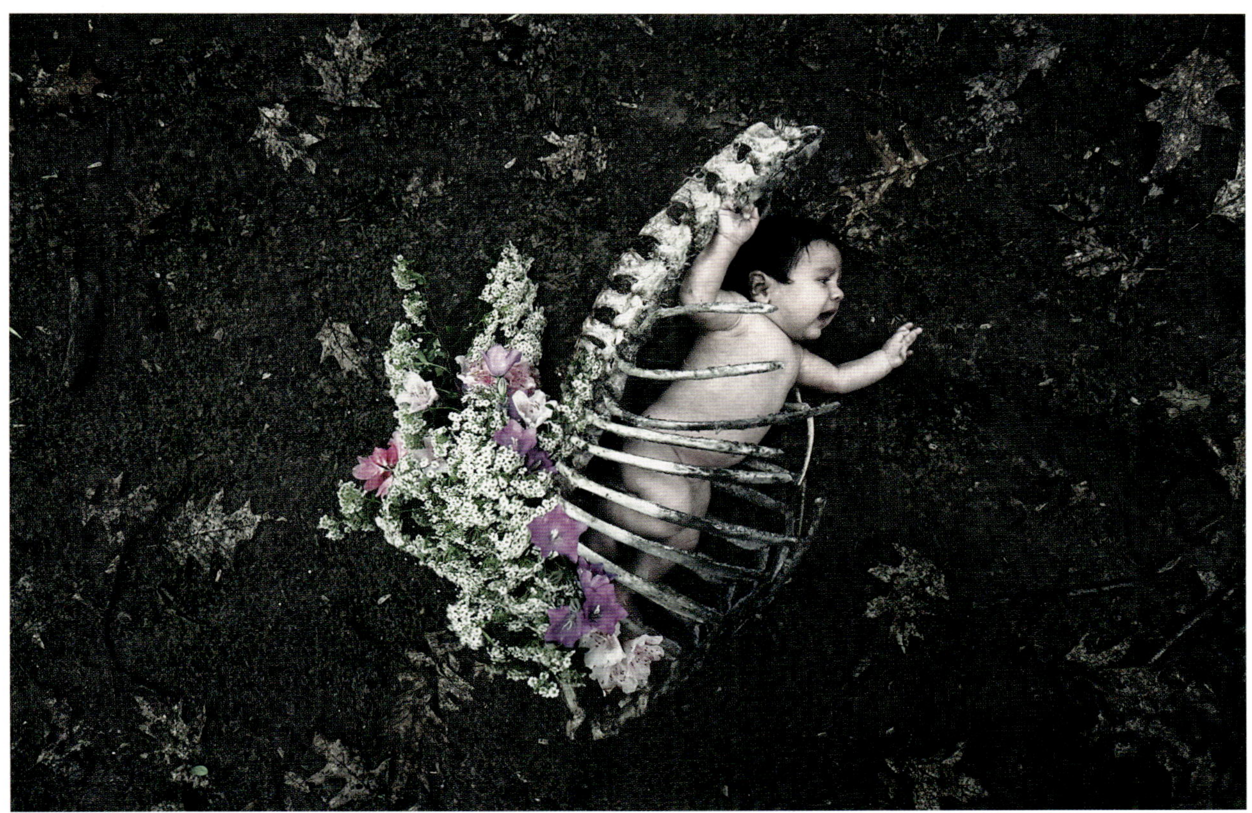

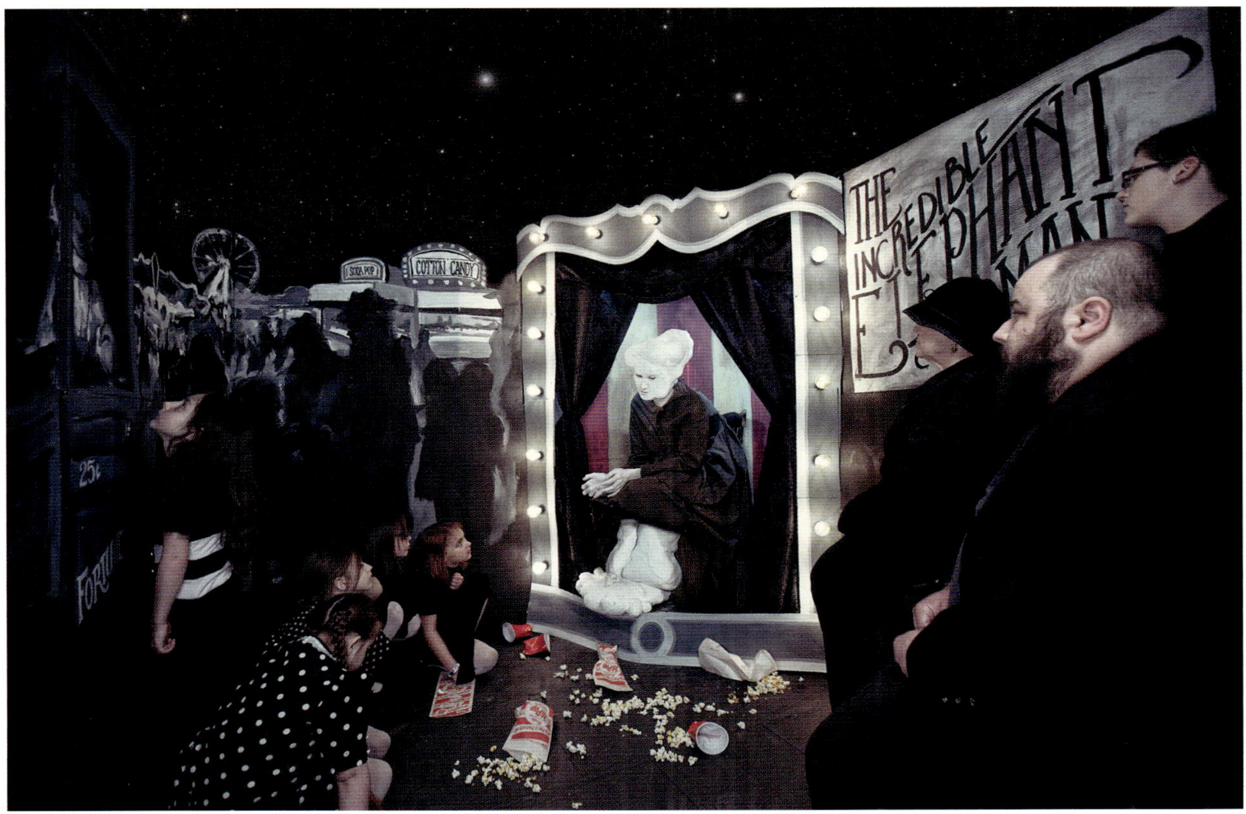

Karen Jerzyk. *Life Support*, 2015. Digital photograph: dimensions variable. *Courtesy of the artist*

Karen Jerzyk. *The Incredible Elephant Woman* (from the *Chromaproscenium Series*), 2017. Digital photograph: dimensions variable. *Courtesy of the artist*

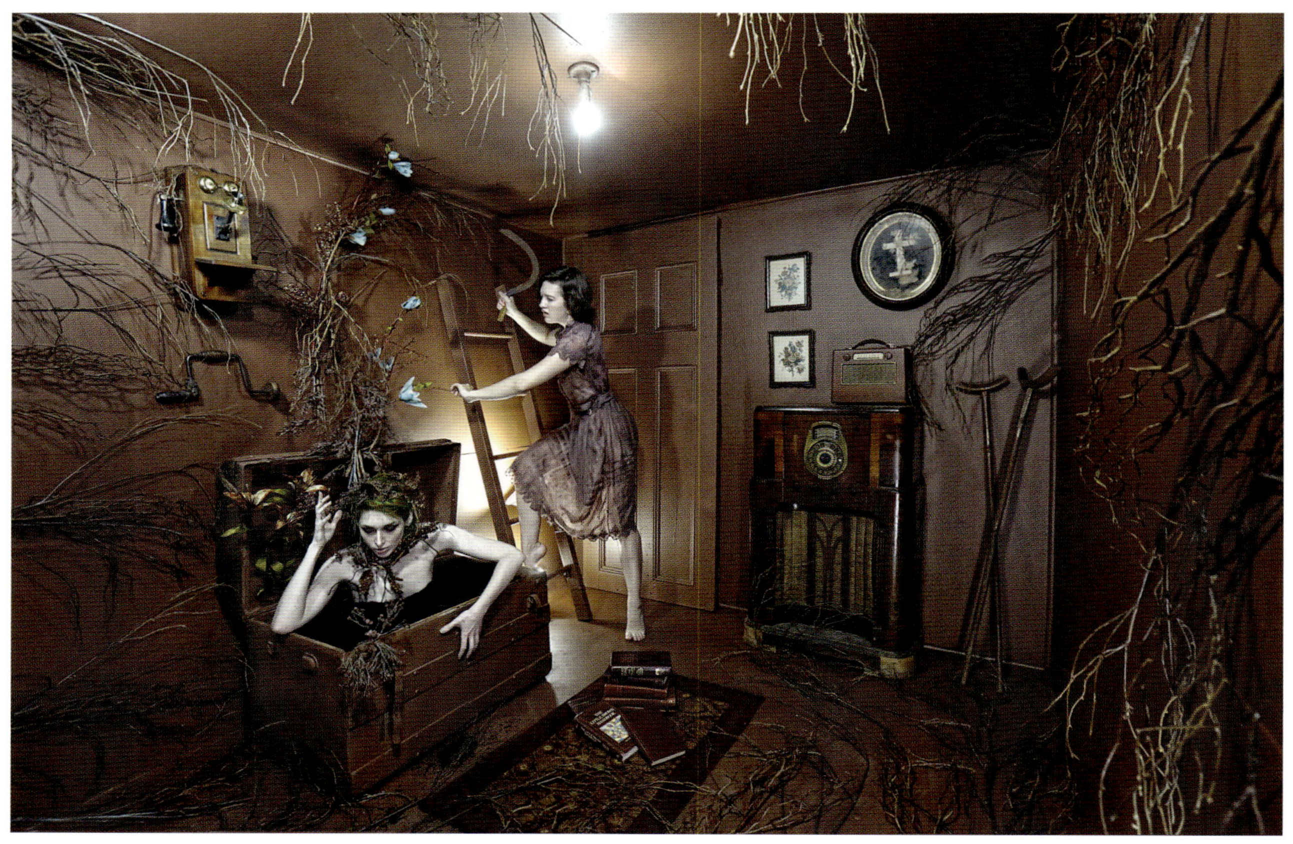

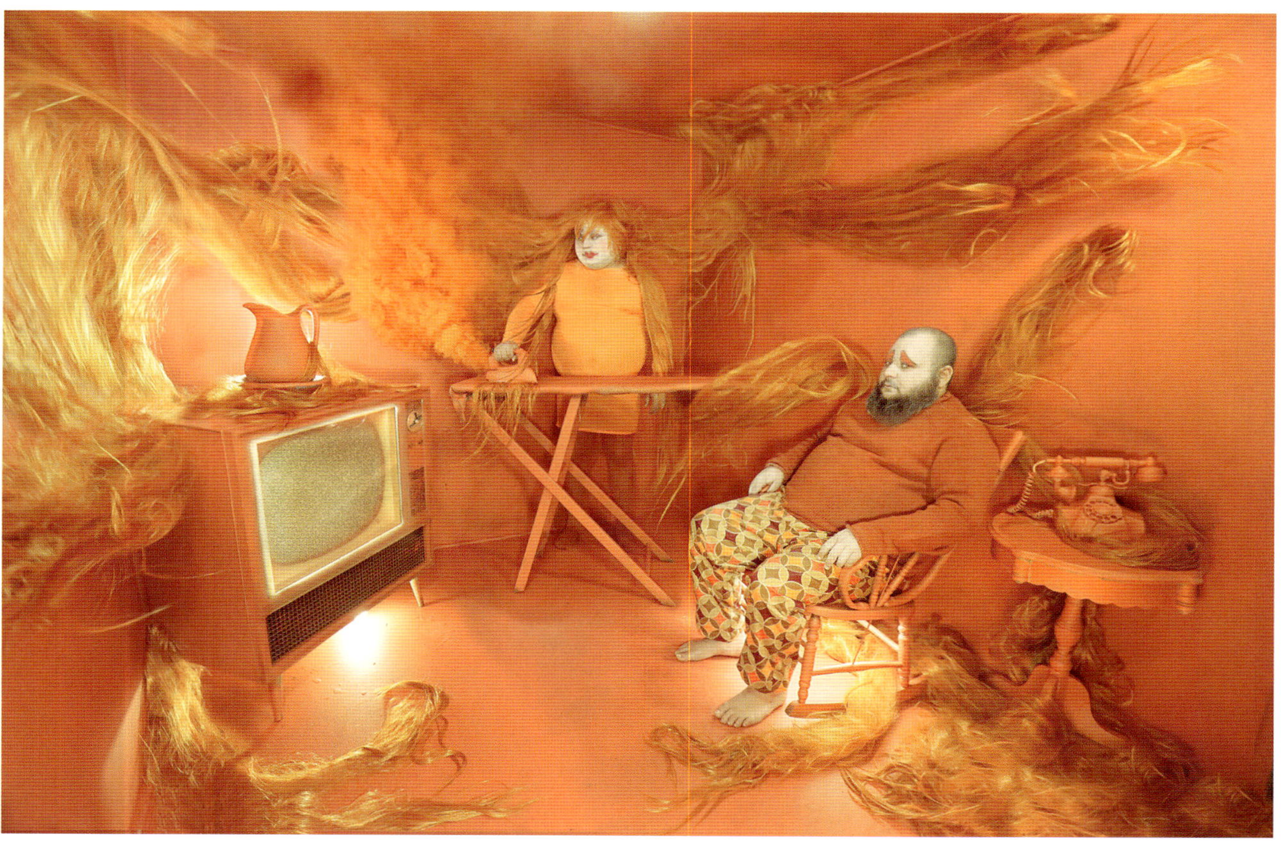

Karen Jerzyk. *Brown*, 2016. Digital photograph: dimensions variable. *Courtesy of the artist*

Karen Jerzyk. *Orange*, 2016. Digital photograph: dimensions variable. *Courtesy of the artist*

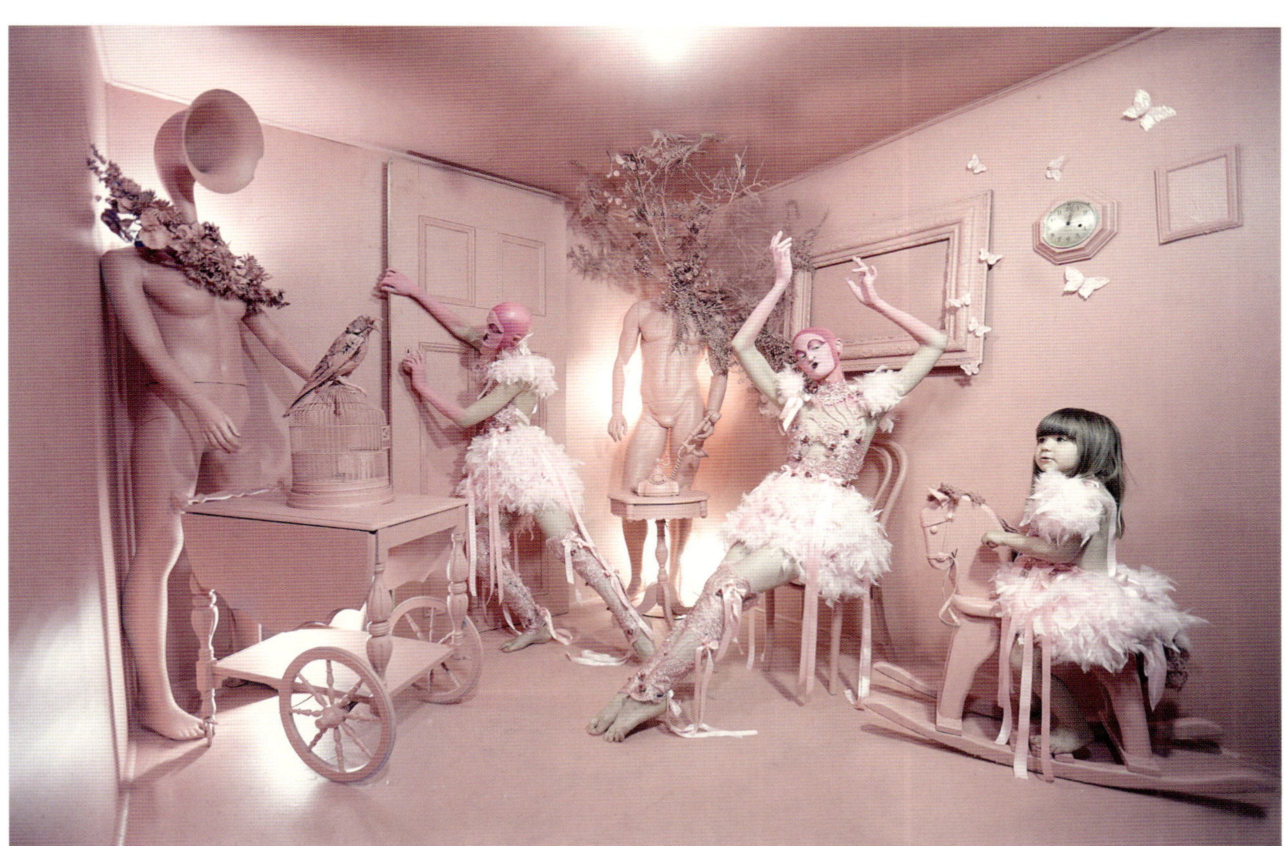

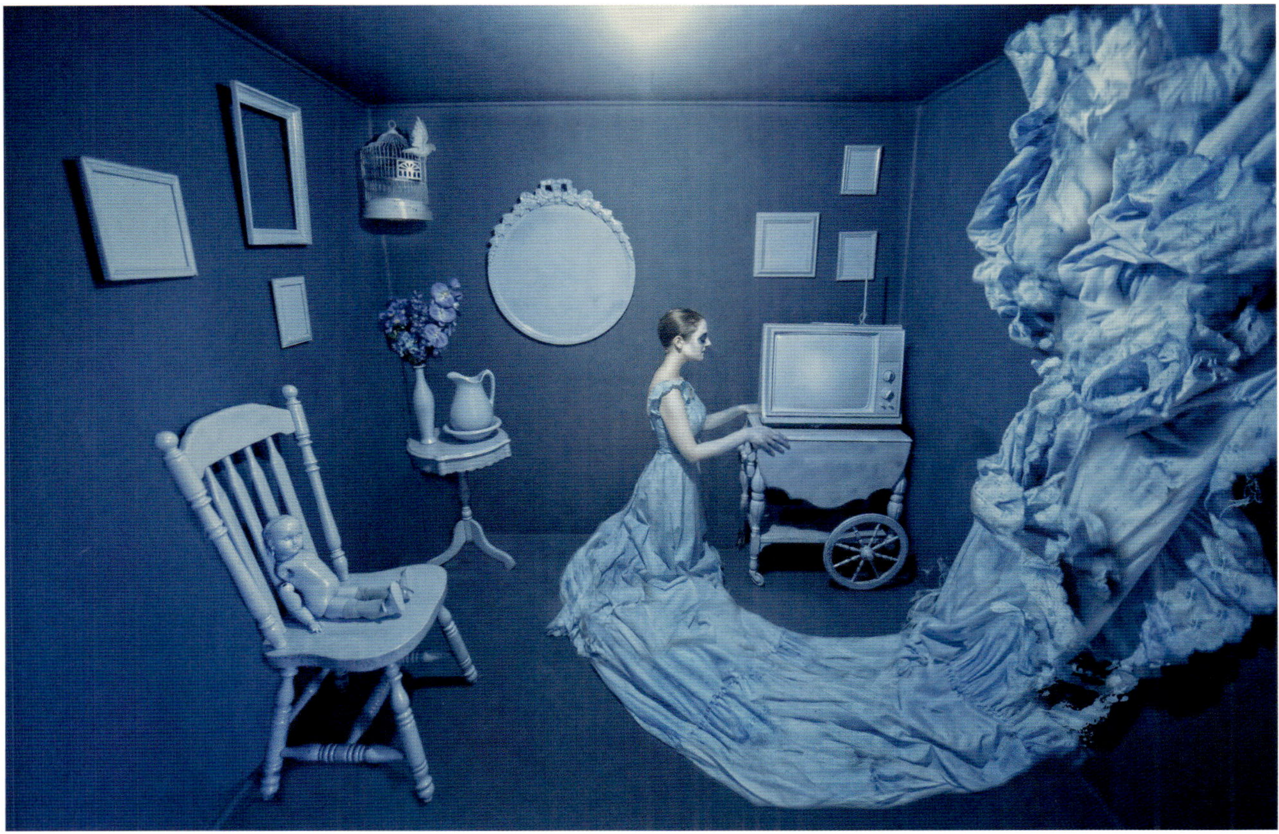

Karen Jerzyk. *Pink*, 2016. Digital photograph: dimensions variable. *Courtesy of the artist*

Karen Jerzyk. *Blue*, 2016. Digital photograph: dimensions variable. *Courtesy of the artist*

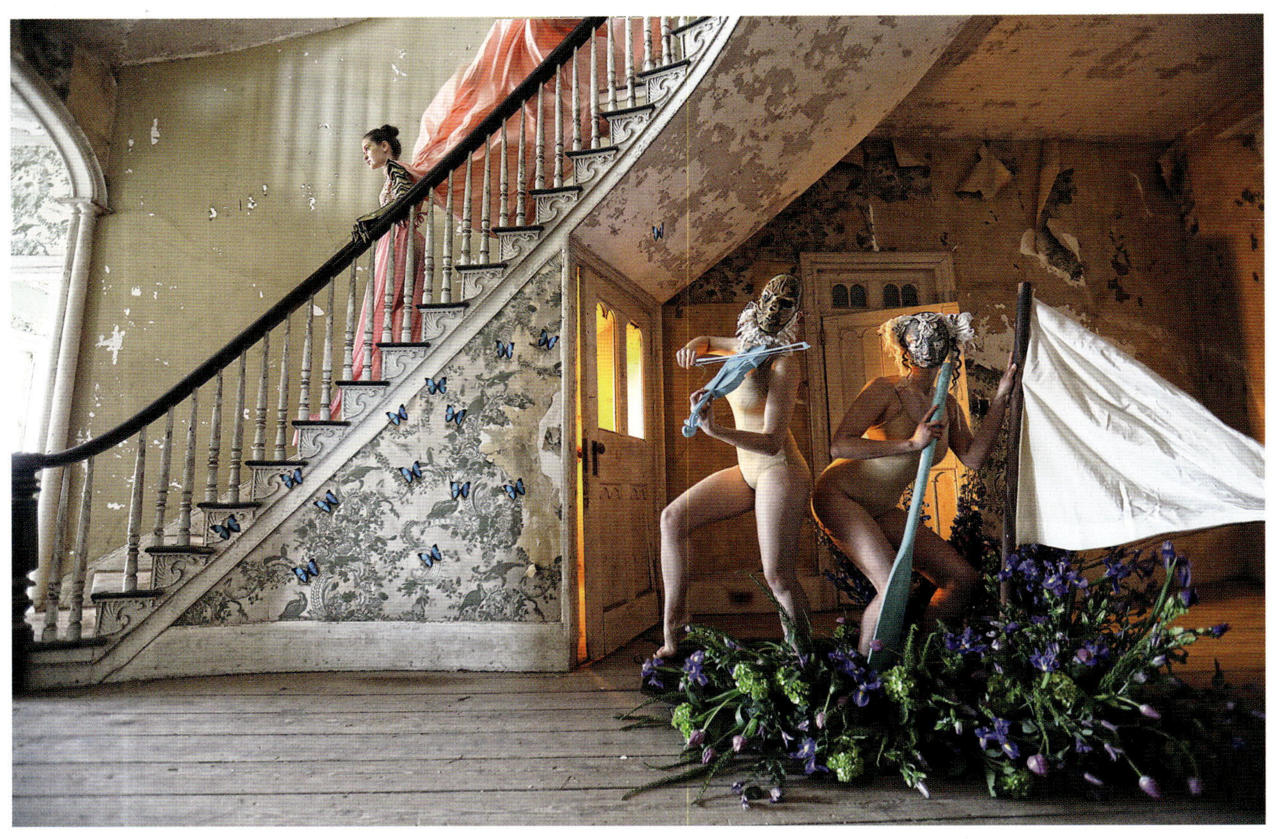

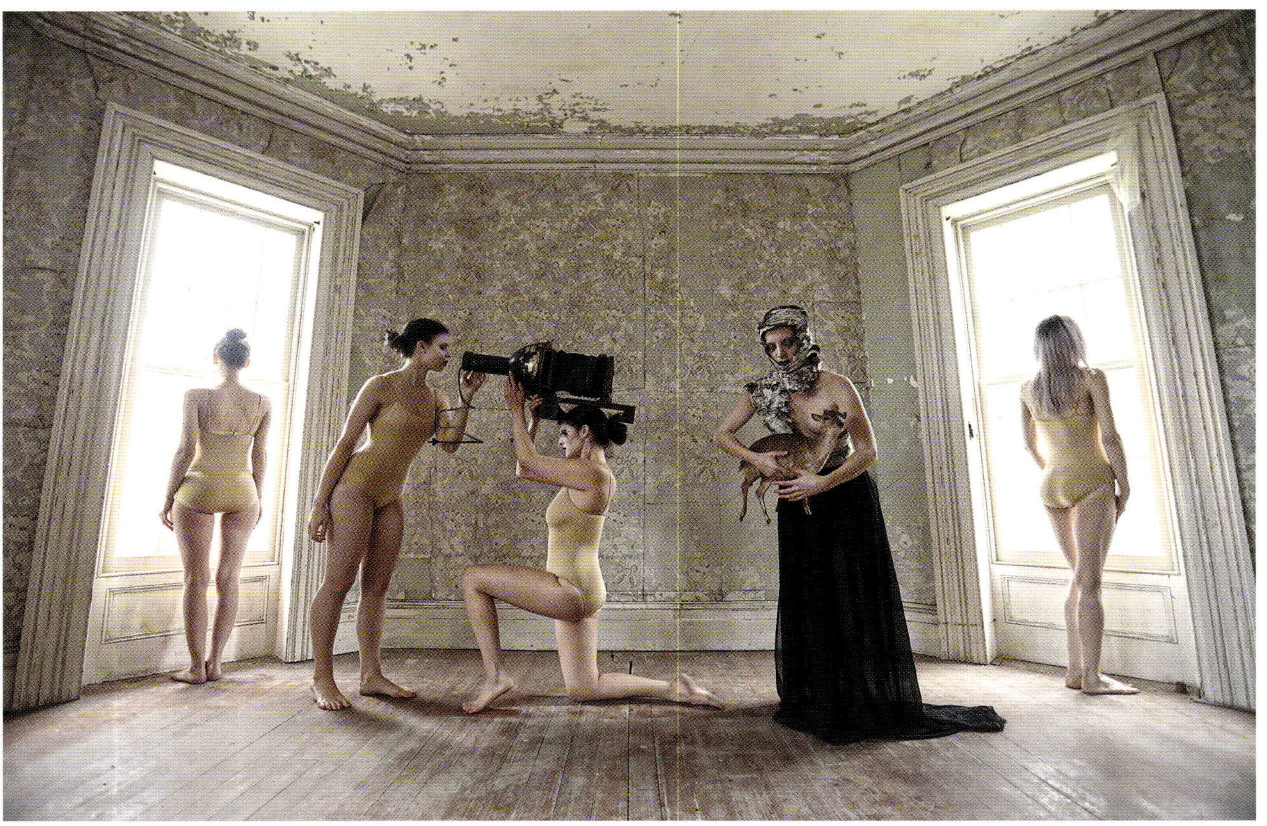

Karen Jerzyk. *Meeting the Weary Travelers*, 2017. Digital photograph: dimensions variable. *Courtesy of the artist*

Karen Jerzyk. *Documenting Mother Nature*, 2017. Digital photograph: dimensions variable. *Courtesy of the artist*

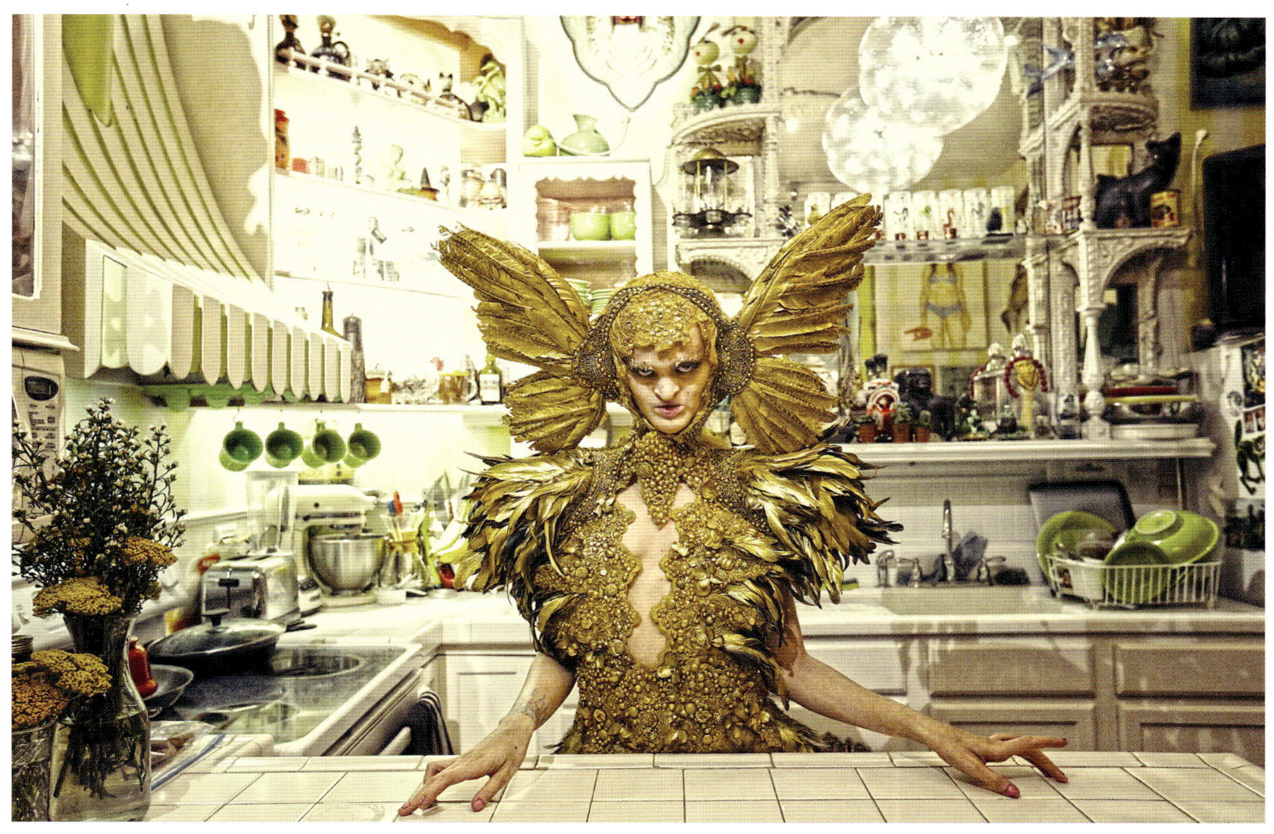

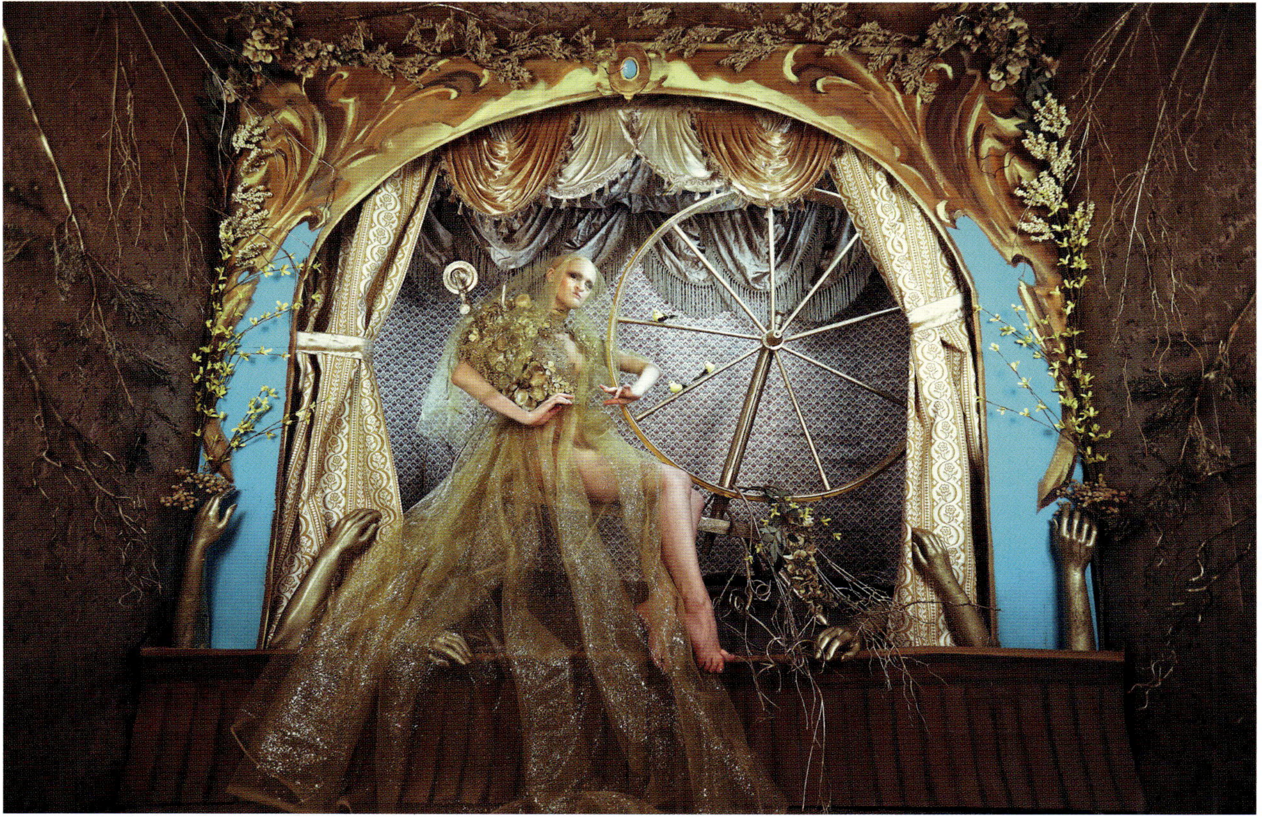

Karen Jerzyk. *Kitchen*, 2016. Digital photograph: dimensions variable. *Courtesy of the artist*

Karen Jerzyk. *Gilded* (from the *Chromaproscenium Series*), 2017. Digital photograph: dimensions variable. *Courtesy of the artist*

KATE GILMORE

Kate Gilmore, a video, and performance-based artist, creates work that addresses one's status and power in society and how one functions in a system of preconceived notions of identity. Gilmore's work often entails the creation of large-scale sculpture in which videos and/or performances occur, either privately for the camera or with large groups of individuals for an audience. Gilmore was born in Washington, DC, in 1975 and lives and works in New York City.

Gilmore received her MFA from the School of Visual Arts, New York, NY (2002) and her BA from Bates College, Lewiston, Maine (1997). She has participated in the 2010 Whitney Biennial, Whitney Museum of American Art, New York, NY; The Moscow Biennial, Moscow, Russia (2011); PS1 Greater New York, MoMA/PS1, New York (2005 and 2010) in addition to solo exhibitions at The Everson Museum, Syracuse; The Aldrich Contemporary Art Museum, Ridgefield, Connecticut (2014); MoCA Cleveland, Cleveland, Ohio (2013); Public Art Fund, Bryant Park, New York (2010); Institute of Contemporary Art, Philadelphia (2008); and Contemporary Art Center, Cincinnati, Ohio (2006). She has been the recipient of several international awards and honors such as the Guggenheim Fellowship (2018); Art Prize/ Art Juried Award, Grand Rapids, Michigan (2015); Rauschenberg Residency Award, Rauschenberg Foundation, Captiva, Florida (2014); Rome Prize from the American Academy in Rome (2007/2008); The Louis Comfort Tiffany Foundation Award, New York (2009/2010); Art Matters Grant, New York (2012); Lower Manhattan Cultural Council Award for Artistic Excellence, New York (2010); the Franklin Furnace Fund for Performance, New York (2006); "In the Public Realm," Public Art Fund, New York (2010); The LMCC Workspace Residency, New York (2005); New York Foundation for The Arts Fellowship, New York (2012 and 2005); and the Marie Walsh Sharpe Space Residency, Brooklyn (2010). Her work is in the collection of the Museum of Modern Art, New York; Brooklyn Museum, Brooklyn; Whitney Museum of American Art, New York; Museum of Fine Arts, Boston; San Francisco Museum of Modern Art, San Francisco; Rose Art Museum, Waltham, Massachusetts; Indianapolis Museum of Art, Indianapolis; and Museum of Contemporary Art, Chicago. Gilmore is an Associate Professor of Art and Design at Purchase College, SUNY, Purchase, NY.

Kate Gilmore. *Higher Ground*, 2015. Performance still. Site-Lab, Grand Rapids, Michigan. *Courtesy of the artist and David Castillo Gallery, Miami*

Kate Gilmore. *Standing Here*, 2010. Video still: 10 minutes 47 seconds. Video/installation at 2010 Whitney Biennial, Whitney Museum of American Art, New York City. *Courtesy of the artist and David Castillo Gallery, Miami*

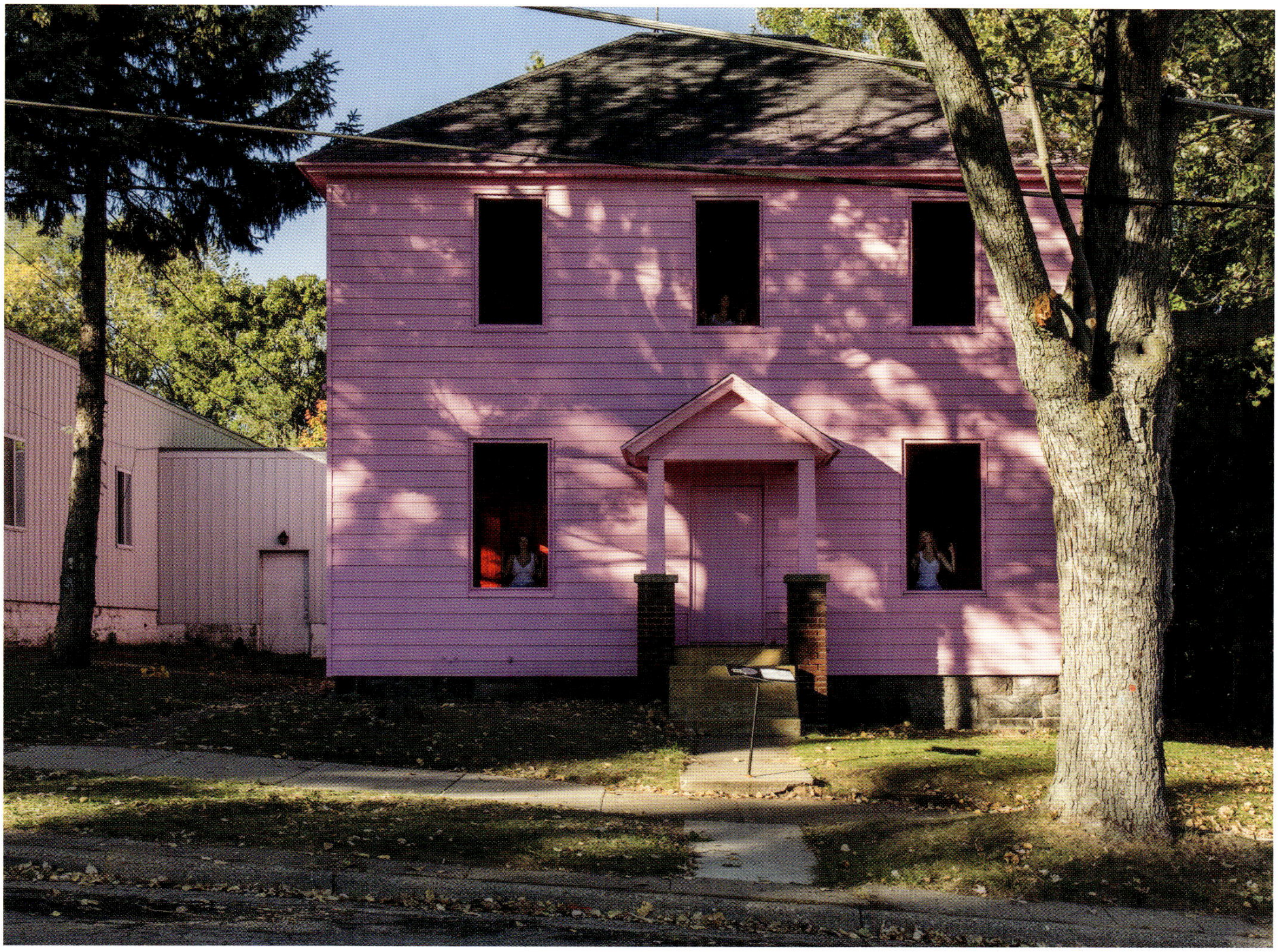

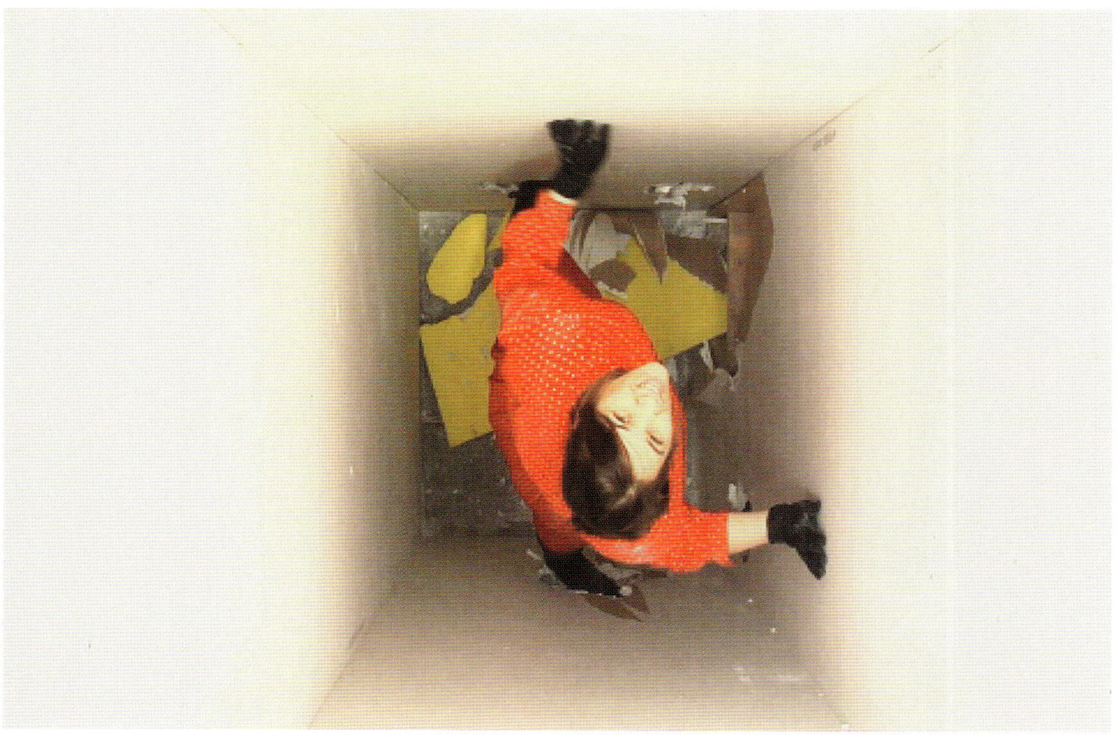

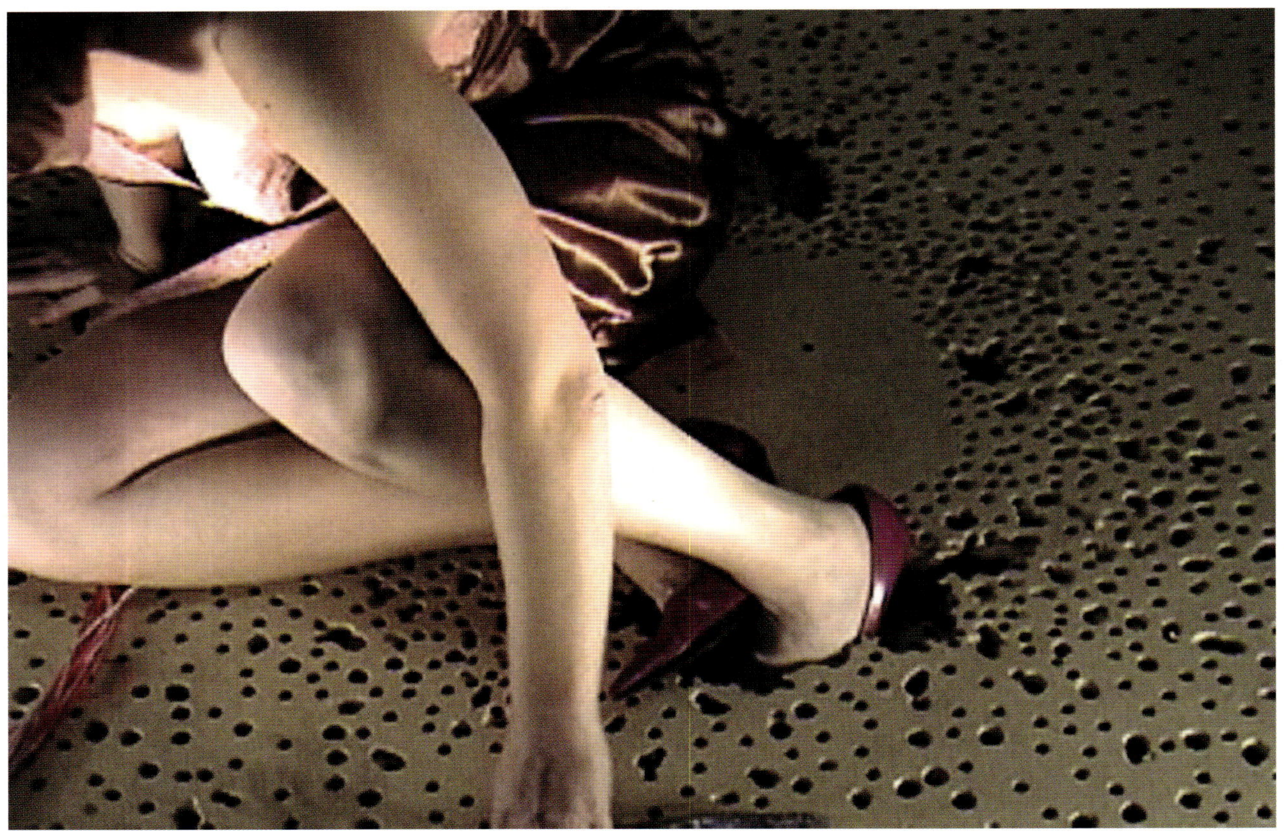

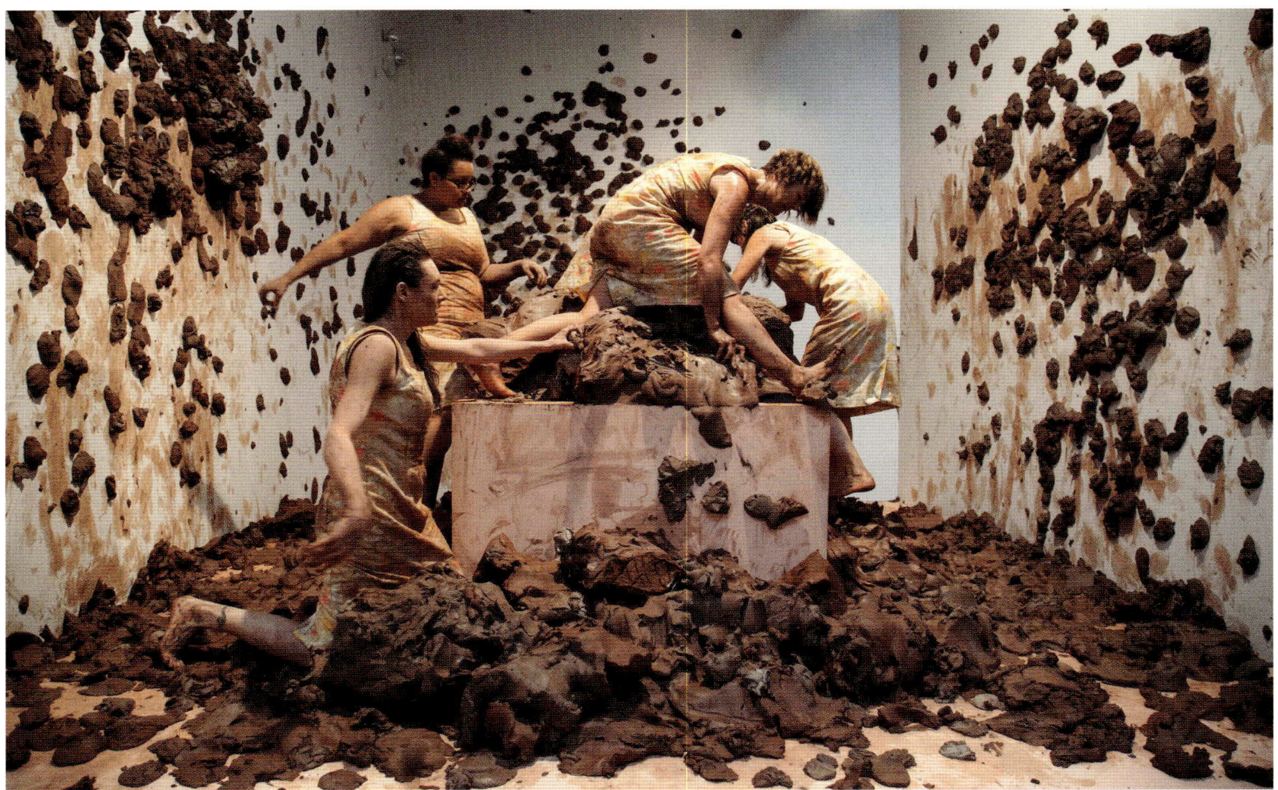

Kate Gilmore. *Double Dutch*, 2004. Video still: 9 minutes 47 seconds. *Courtesy of the artist and David Castillo Gallery, Miami*

Kate Gilmore. *Though the Claw*, 2011. Performance still. Performance/installation at Pace Gallery, New York City. *Courtesy of the artist and David Castillo Gallery, Miami*

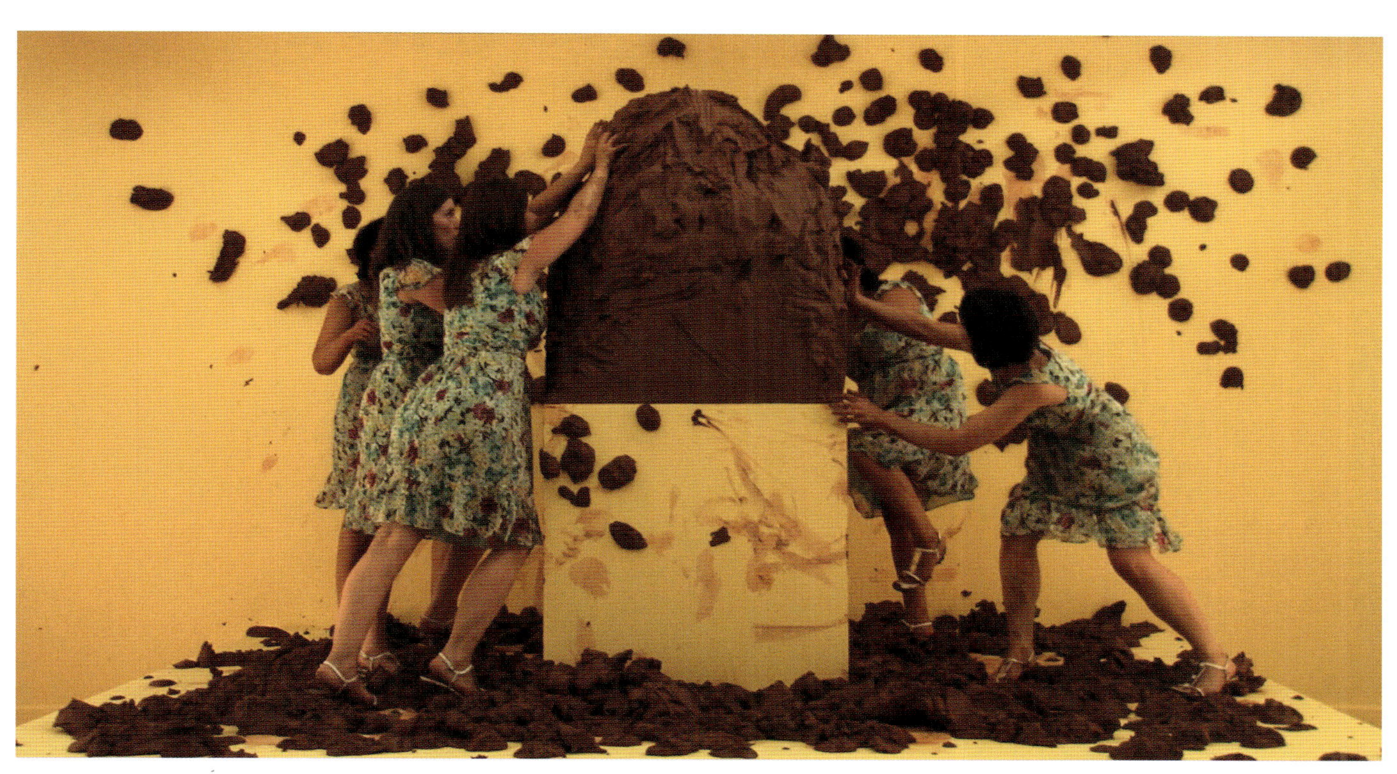

Kate Gilmore. *Sudden as a Massacre,* 2011. Video still: 30 minutes. Video at Time Based Art Festival, Portland Museum of Art, Portland, Oregon. *Courtesy of the artist and David Castillo Gallery, Miami*

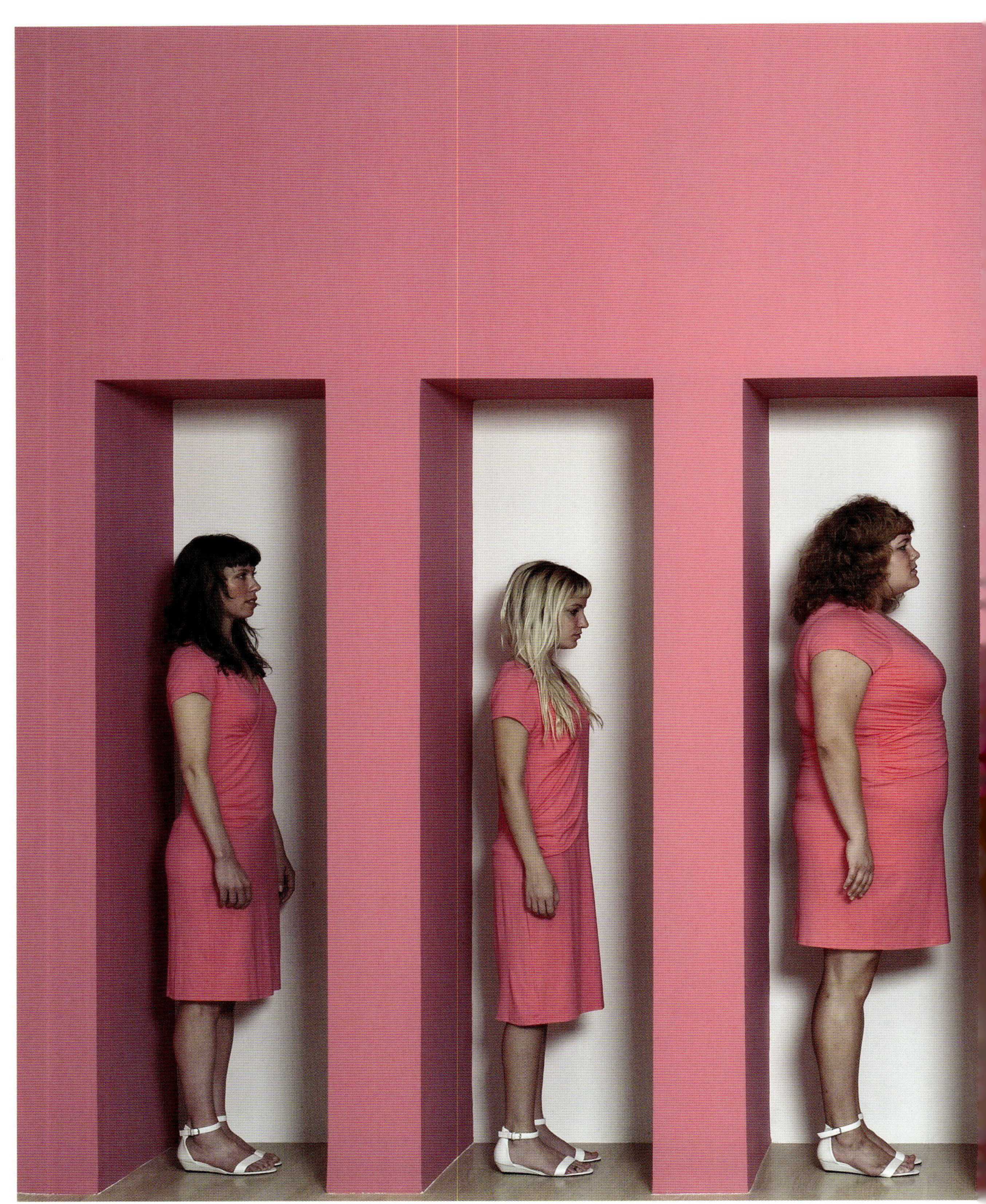

Kate Gilmore. *Wall Bearer*, 2011. Performance still. Performance at Weatherspoon Art Museum, Greensboro, North Carolina. *Courtesy of the artist and David Castillo Gallery, Miami*

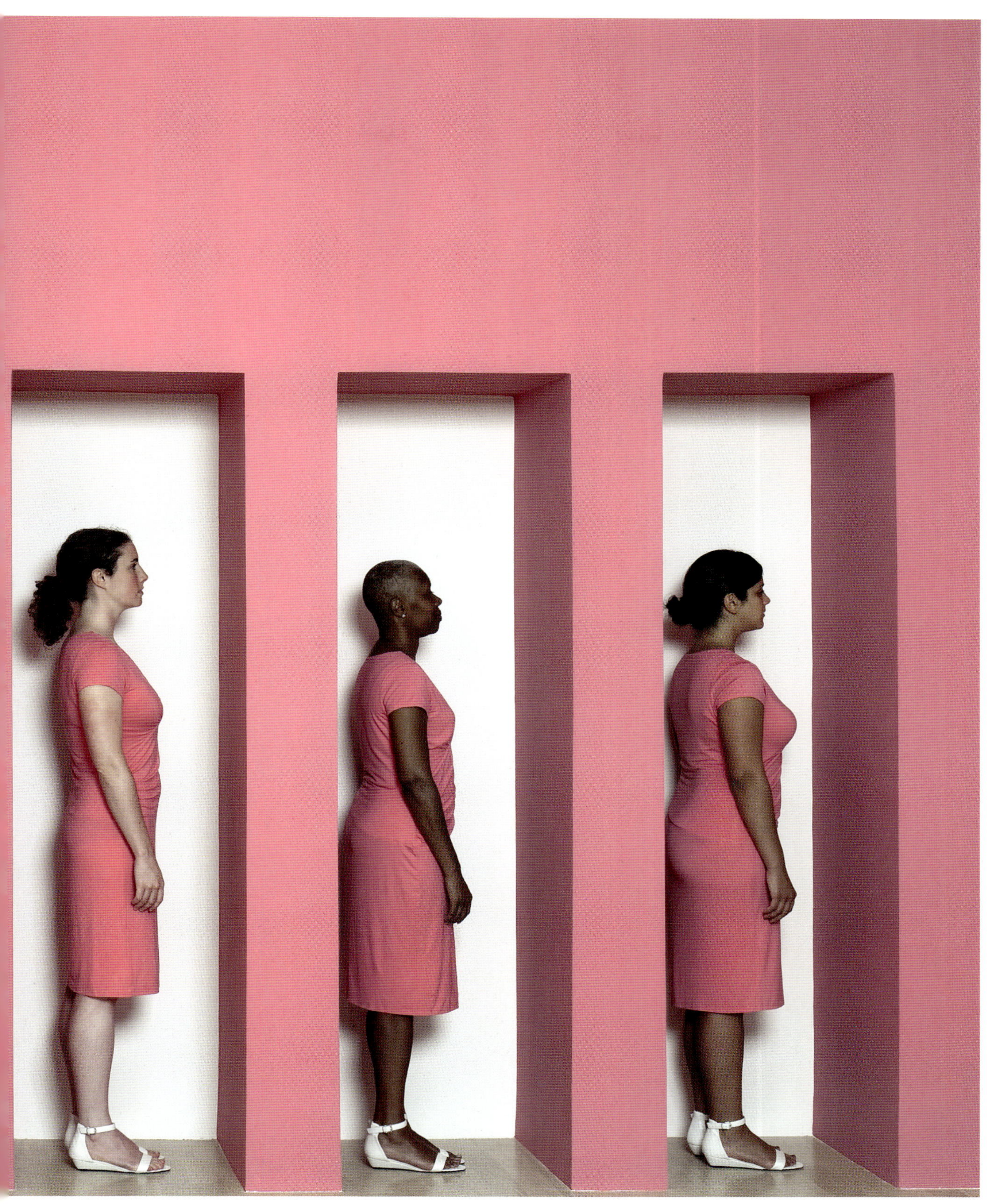

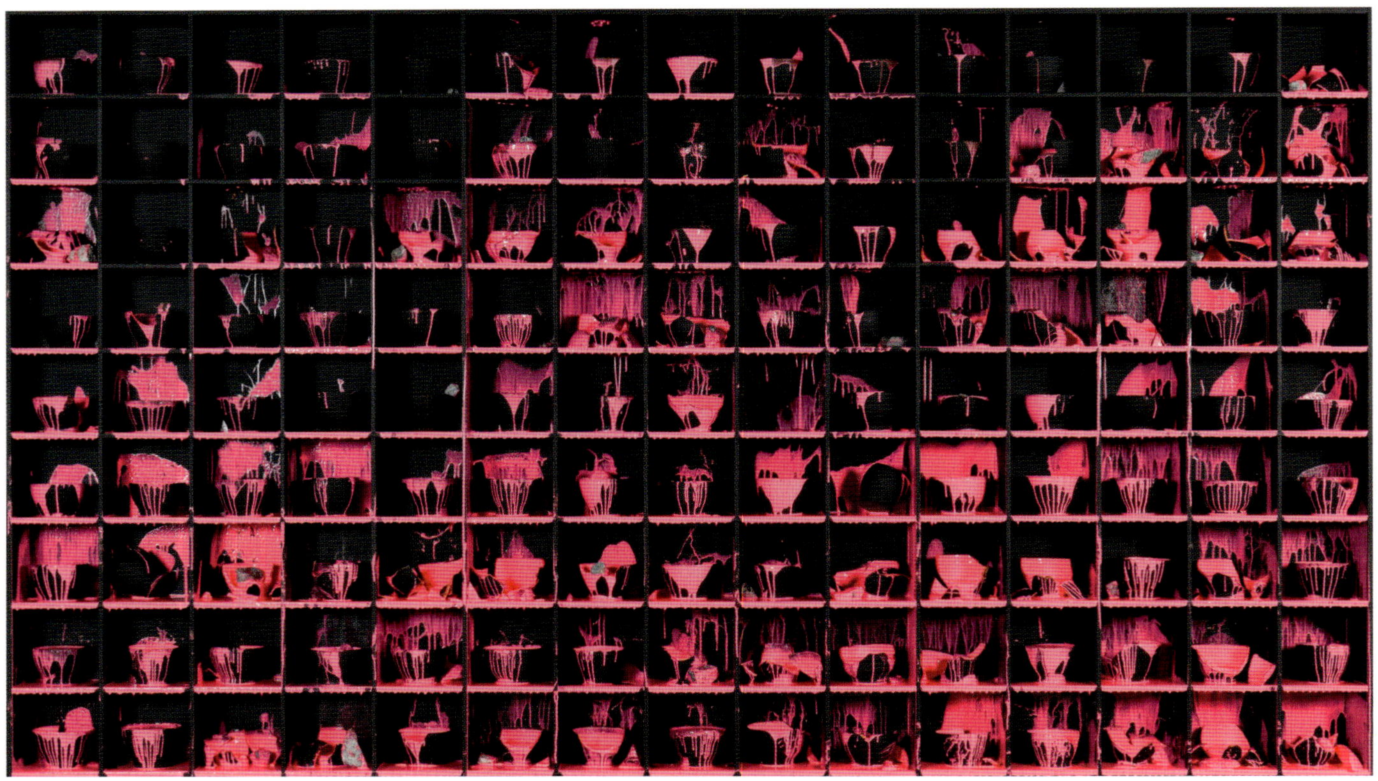

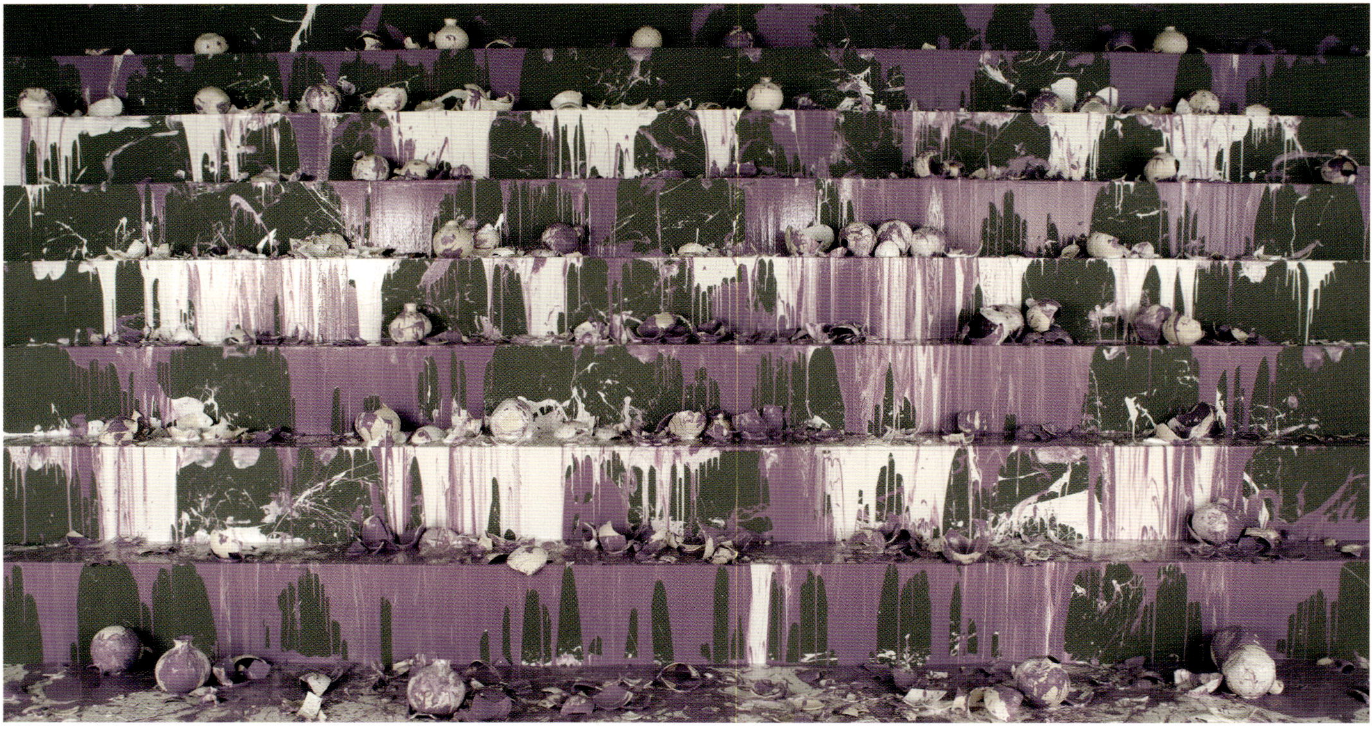

Kate Gilmore. *Rock, Hard, Place*, 2012. Video still: 11 minutes 15 seconds. Video/installation at David Castillo Gallery, Miami, Florida. *Courtesy of the artist and David Castillo Gallery, Miami*

Kate Gilmore. *Buster*, 2011. C-print: 30 × 40 inches. Video/installation at University of Southern Florida Contemporary Art Museum, Tampa. *Courtesy of the artist and David Castillo Gallery, Miami*

KAY ROSEN

Kay Rosen has applied the visual strategies of color, spacing, composition, material, elements of graphic design, and scale to written language to make drawings, collages, paintings, editions, and wall installations that challenge the way that we have read and understood language for over four decades. Born in Corpus Christi, Texas, and based in the Midwest, Rosen turned her attention to art after early academic study of language. Since then, her work has been exhibited in numerous museums and institutions both nationally and internationally. In 1998, the Museum of Contemporary Art, Los Angeles, along with the Otis College of Art and Design, Los Angeles, hosted her midcareer survey *Kay Rosen: Lifeli[k]e*. She is the recipient of numerous awards, including three National Endowment for the Arts fellowships, the 2014 Artist Award for Distinguished Body of Work by the College Art Association, and a 2017 Guggenheim Fellowship. A major publication about her work, *Kay Rosen: AKAK*, was published by Regency Art Press in 2009. Rosen lives in Gary, Indiana, with some time spent in New York City. She was on the faculty at the School of the Art Institute of Chicago for twenty-four years.

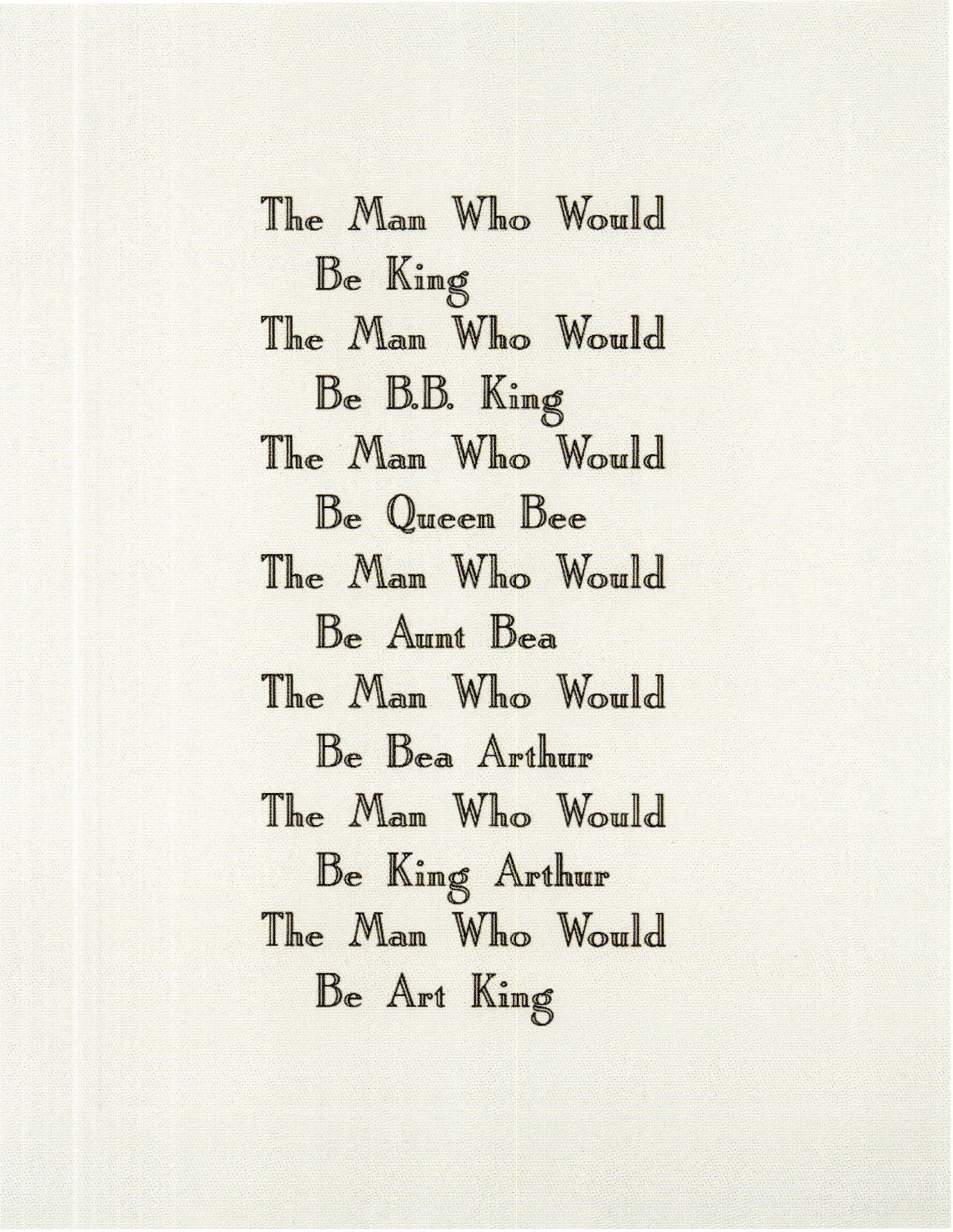

The Man Who Would
Be King
The Man Who Would
Be B.B. King
The Man Who Would
Be Queen Bee
The Man Who Would
Be Aunt Bea
The Man Who Would
Be Bea Arthur
The Man Who Would
Be King Arthur
The Man Who Would
Be Art King

Kay Rosen. *The Man*, 1991. Etching on Rives BFK White paper with deckled edge, Paper size: 25.5 × 19.5 inches, Image size: 15 × 20.75 inches. Edition of 32 with 5 APs and 1 PP. © 2018 Kay Rosen. *Courtesy of the artist and Krakow Witkin Gallery, Boston*

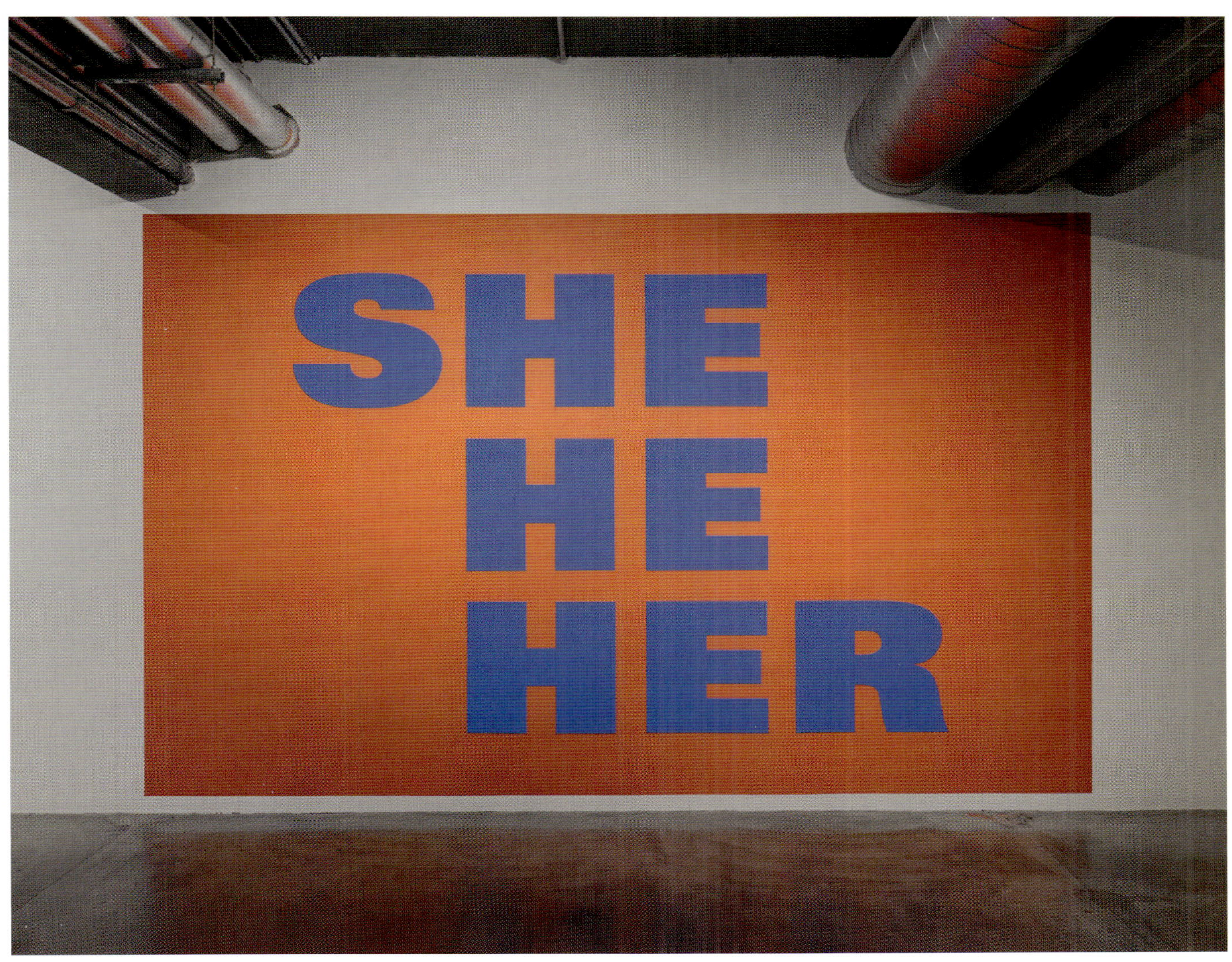

Kay Rosen. *She-Man*, 1996. Paint on the wall: dimensions variable. Installation view, Contemporary Art Museum Houston, Houston, Texas, 2016. Photographer: Tom Dubrock. Additional venues: *Kay Rosen: Lifeli[k]e*, L.A. MoCA, 1998; *Kay Rosen: Big Talk*, Dunedin Public Art Gallery, New Zealand, 2004; Heong Gallery, Cambridge University, UK, 2018. *Courtesy of the artist*

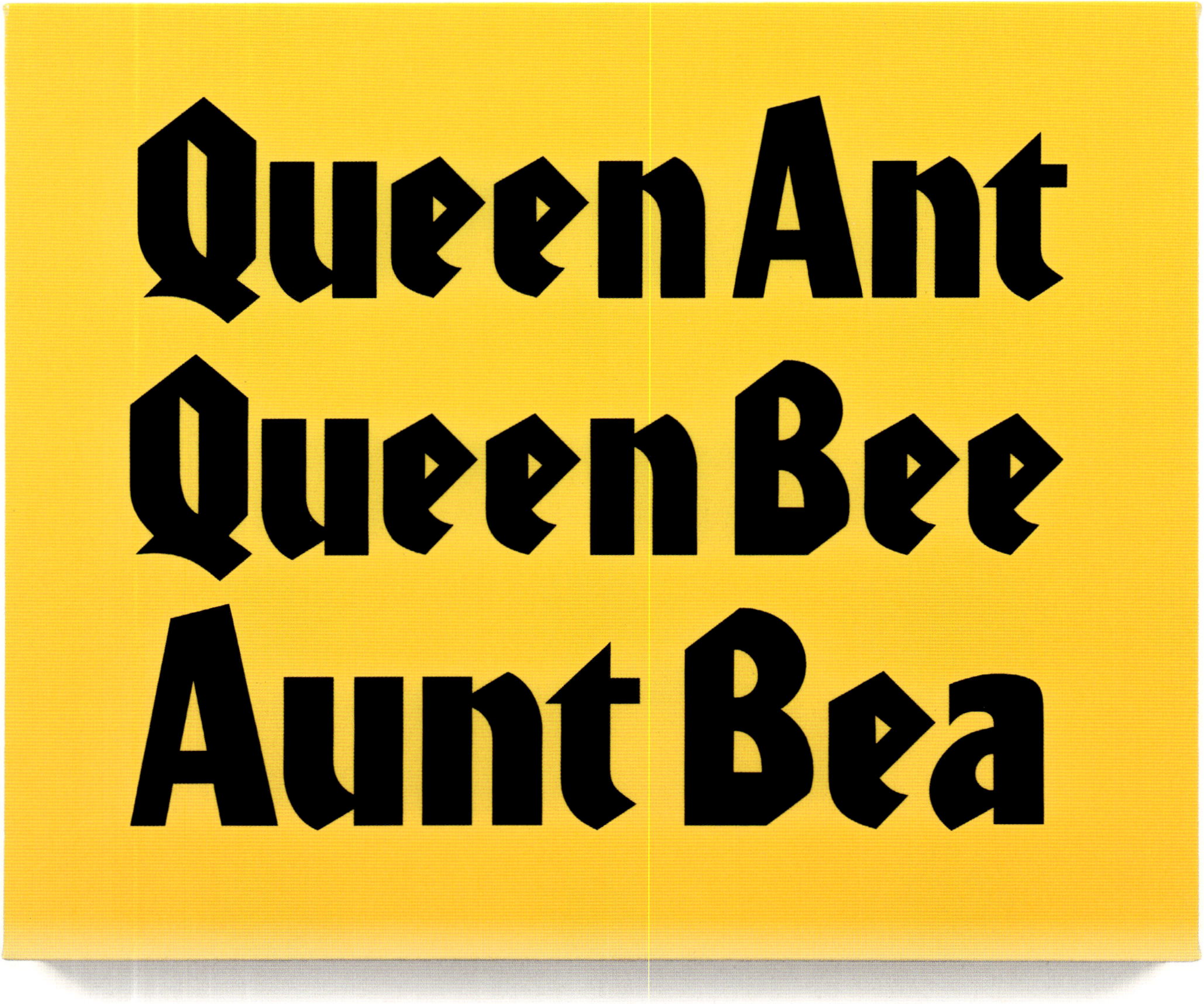

Queen Ant
Queen Bee
Aunt Bea

Kay Rosen. *Aunt Bea*, 1994. Enamel sign paint on canvas: 20 × 24 inches. Photographer: James Prinz. *Courtesy of the artist*

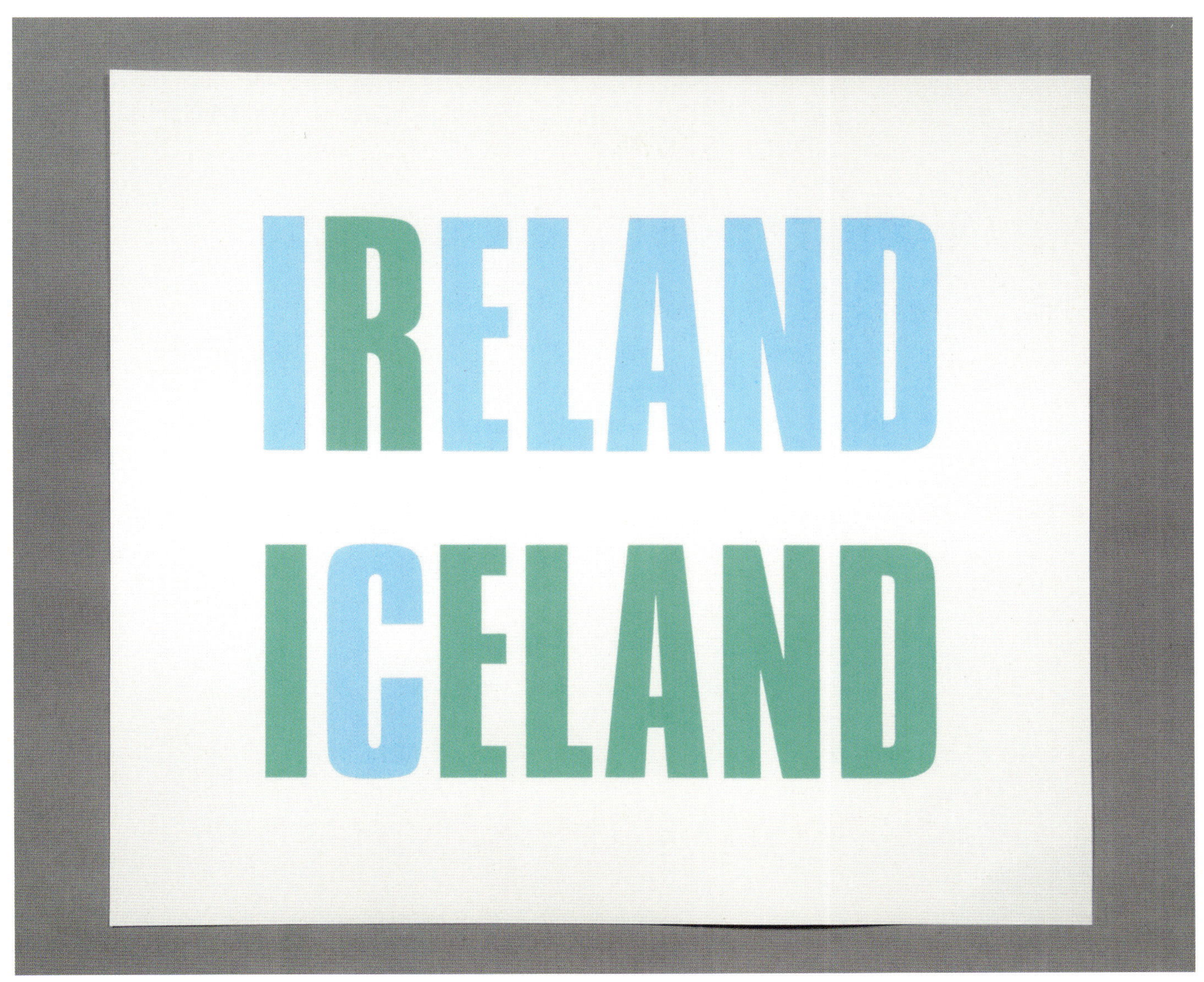

Kay Rosen. *Migration*, 2005. Colored pencil on paper: 18.1 × 20 inches. Photographer: James Prinz. *Courtesy of the artist*

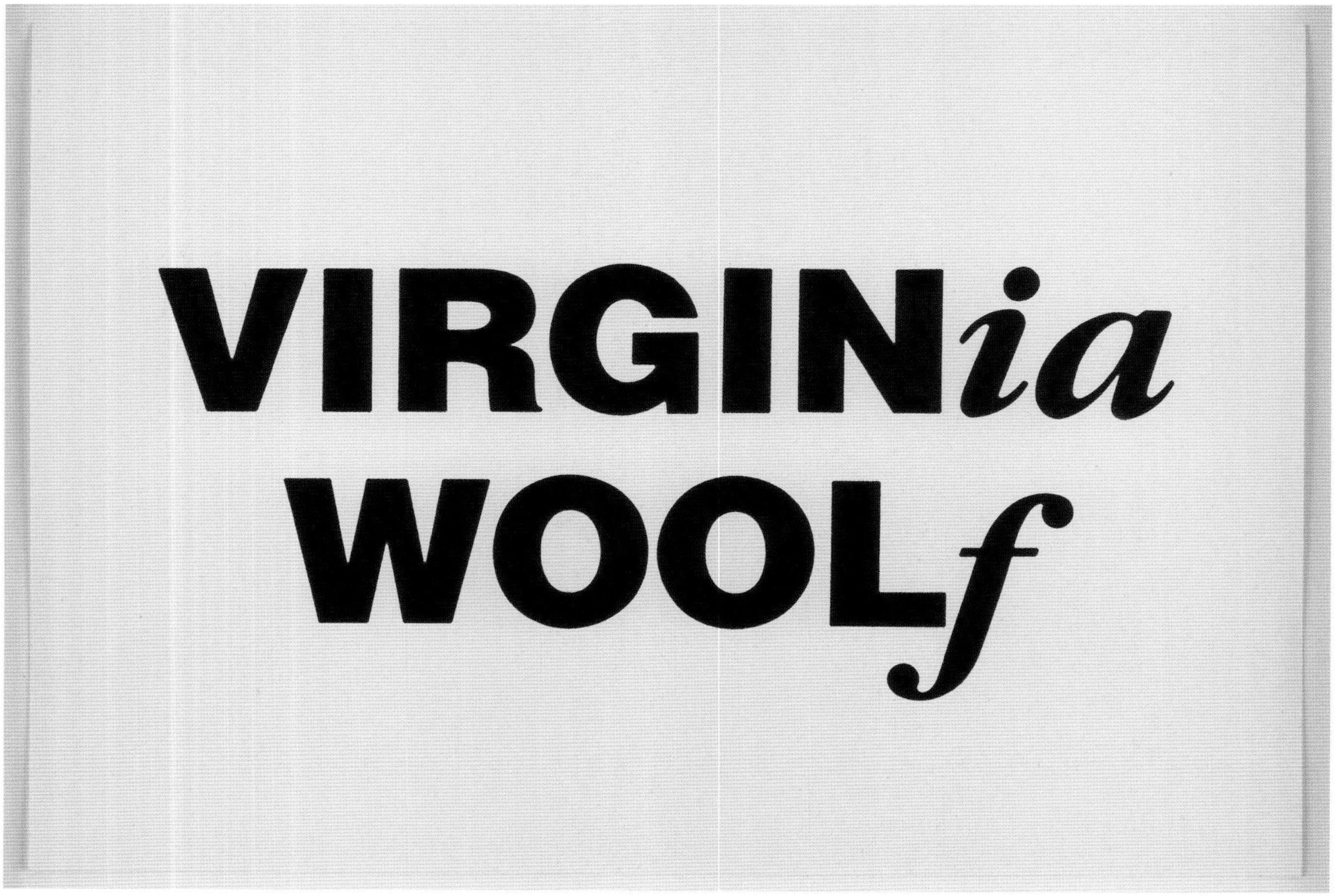

Kay Rosen. *Sheep in Wolf's Clothing*, 1994.
Graphite on paper: 14.6 × 21.1 inches.
Courtesy of the artist

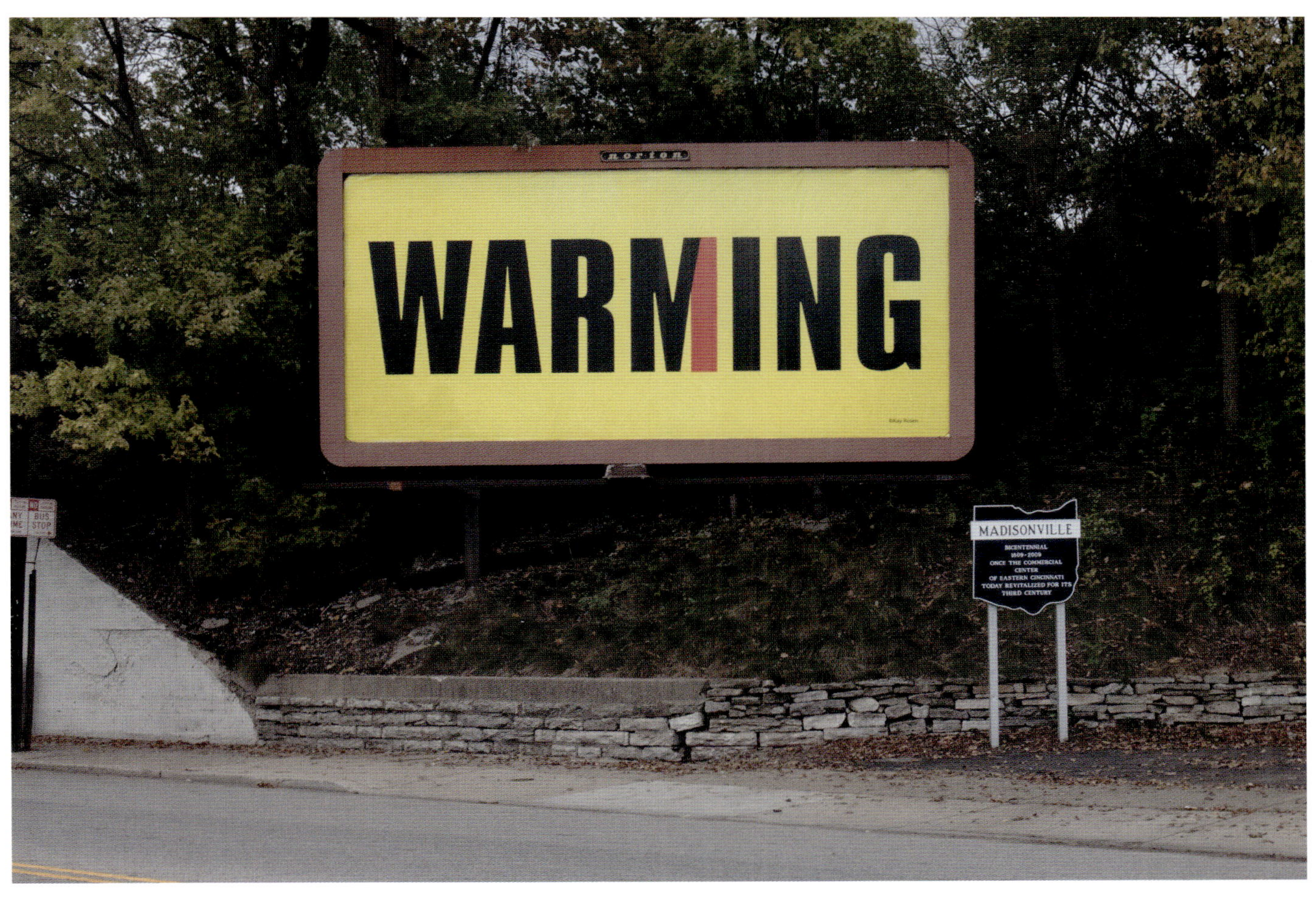

Kay Rosen. *This Means War . . .* , 2015–17. Billboard: dimensions variable. Installation view, the I-71 Project, 2017, copresented by the Contemporary Arts Center, Cincinnati, and the Columbus Museum of Art. Photographer: Anne Thompson. Additional venues: Ludlow 38, New York City, 2015; Ingleby Gallery, Edinburgh, Scotland, 2015; Indiana State Museum, Indianapolis, 2016. *Courtesy of the artist*

LIN TIANMIAO

Lin Tianmiao is part of the "apartment art" generation, and one of the first contemporary Chinese artists to achieve international recognition. She is known for her practice of thread winding, in which she binds the material—silk, hair, cotton, or felt—tightly around found and manufactured objects. Initially tasked by her mother to spool cotton as a young girl, Lin later reclaimed the act. Lin's work studies her own social role and the relationship between identity and social context, questioning the identity of women and conventional ideas of social roles for women. Best known for her large-scale installations, Lin also works in sculpture, photography, video, and other media.

Solo exhibitions of Lin's work have been held around the world. In 2013, the Asia Society Museum in New York City presented *Bound Unbound*, the artist's first major solo museum exhibition in the United States. In fall 2017, Galerie Lelong & Co. presented *Protruding Patterns*, a solo exhibition of Lin's work. Lin was also featured in *Art and China after 1989: Theater of the World* at the Guggenheim Museum, New York City. Lin was born in 1961 in Taiyuan, China, and she now lives and works in Beijing.

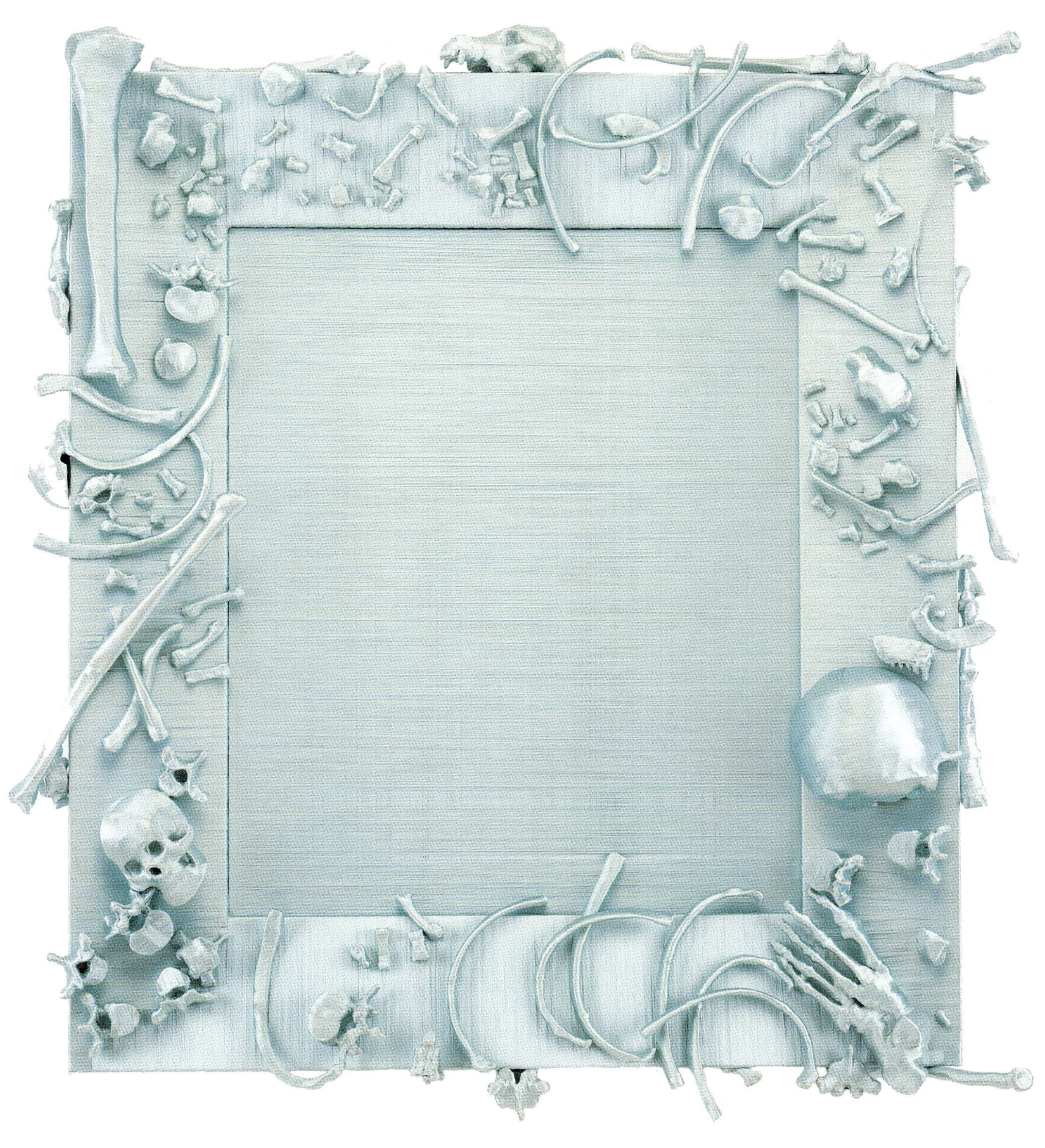

Lin Tianmiao. *Minty Blue*, 2012. Threads, wood frame, synthetic bones: 39 × 35 × 5 inches. Image ©Lin Tianmiao. *Courtesy of Galerie Lelong & Co.*

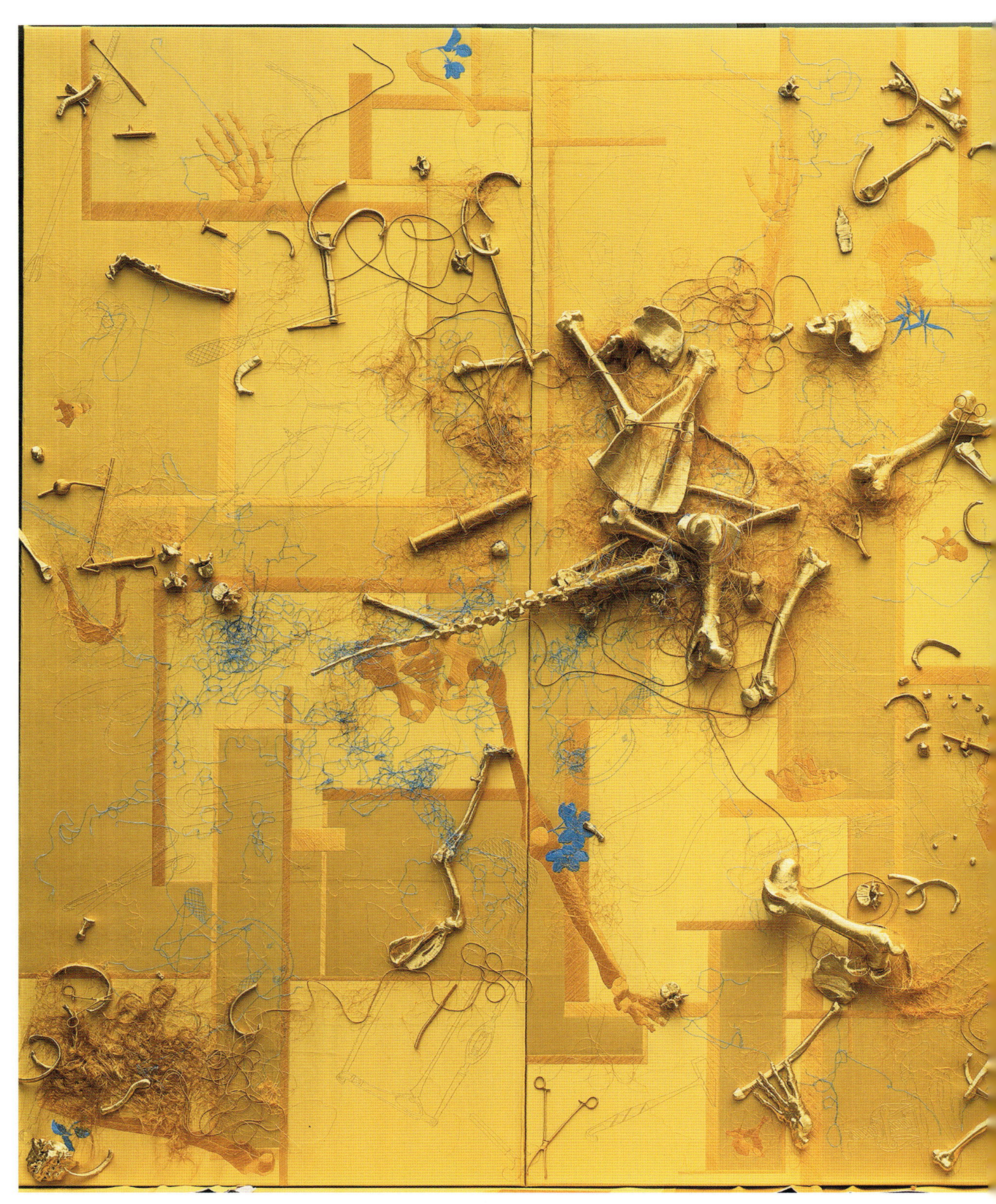

Lin Tianmiao. *The Golden Mean*, 2012. Synthetic resin bones wrapped in gold silk attached to panels: 110.2 × 161.4 inches. Image ©Lin Tianmiao. *Courtesy of Galerie Lelong & Co.*

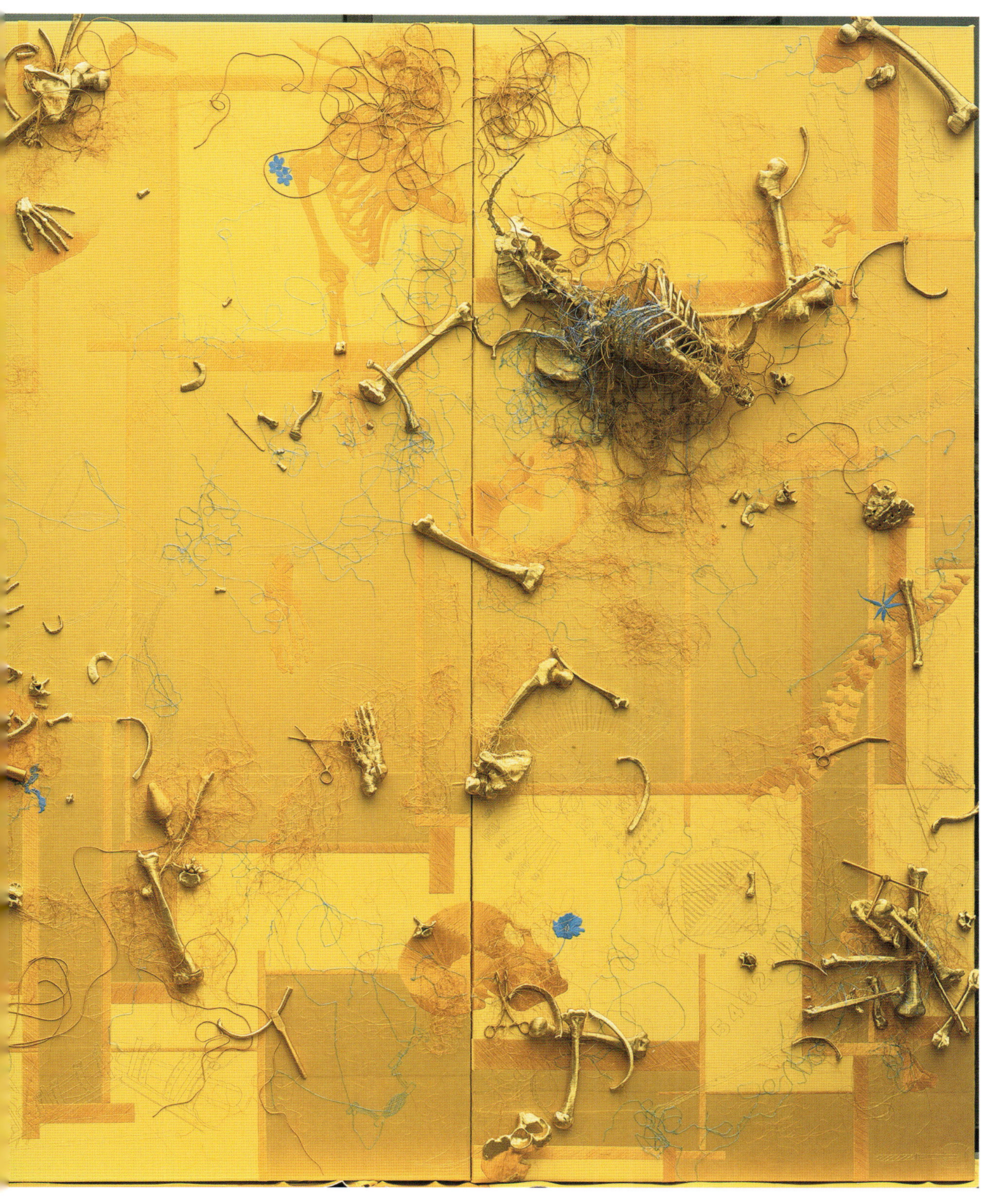

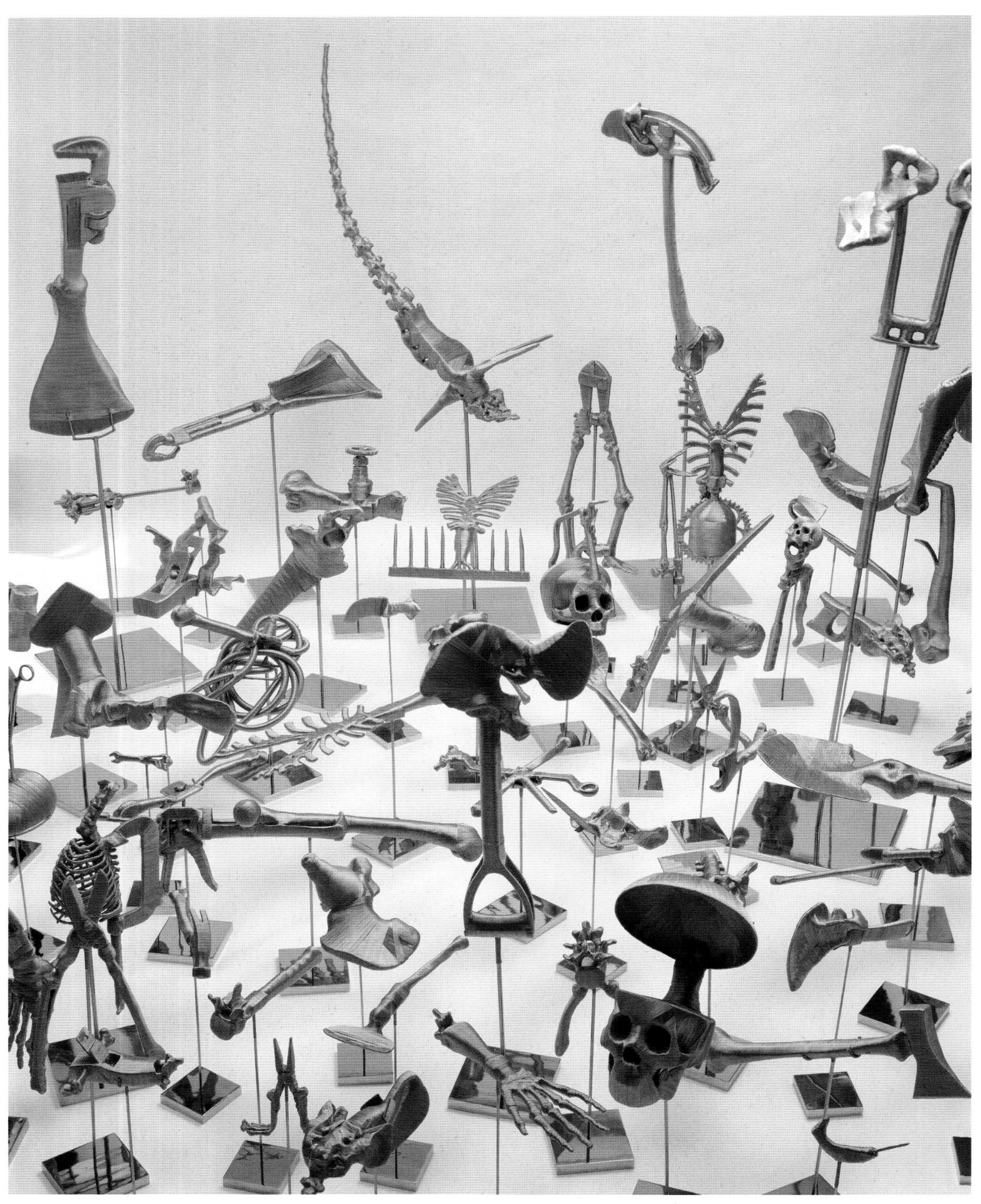

Lin Tianmiao. *More or Less the Same* (detail), 2011. Polyurea, silk threads, and stainless steel: dimensions variable. Image ©Lin Tianmiao. *Courtesy of Galerie Lelong & Co.*

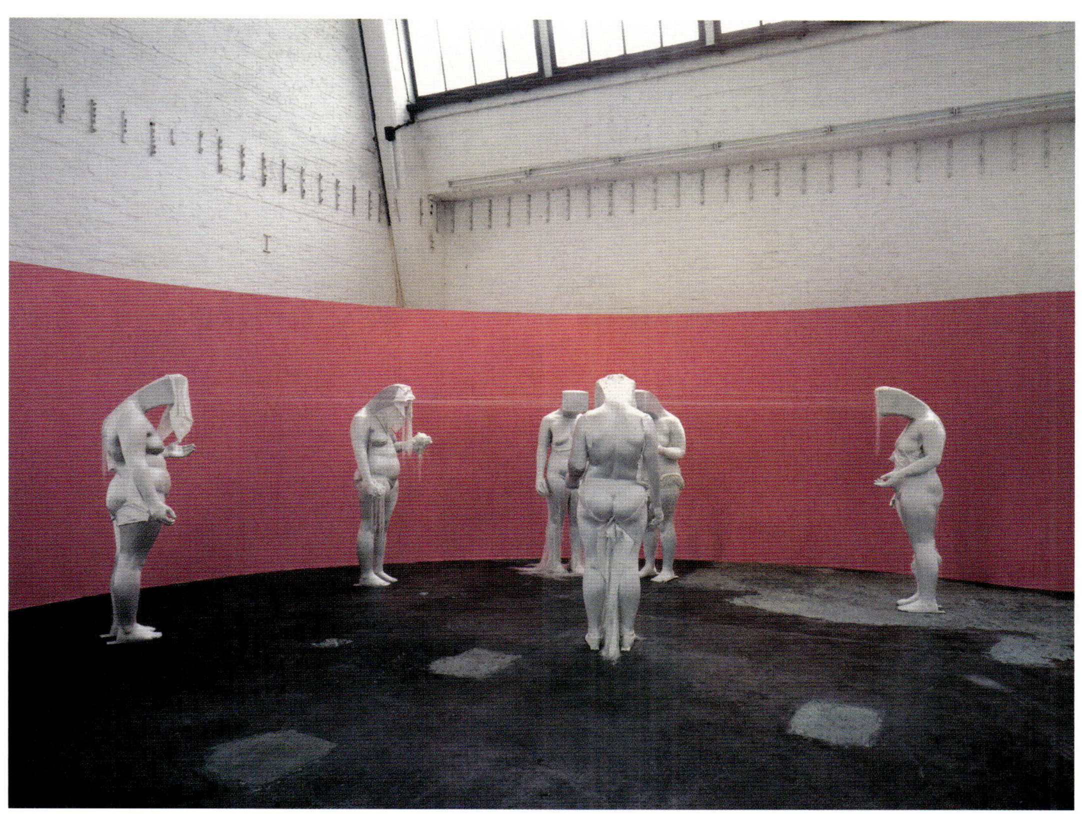

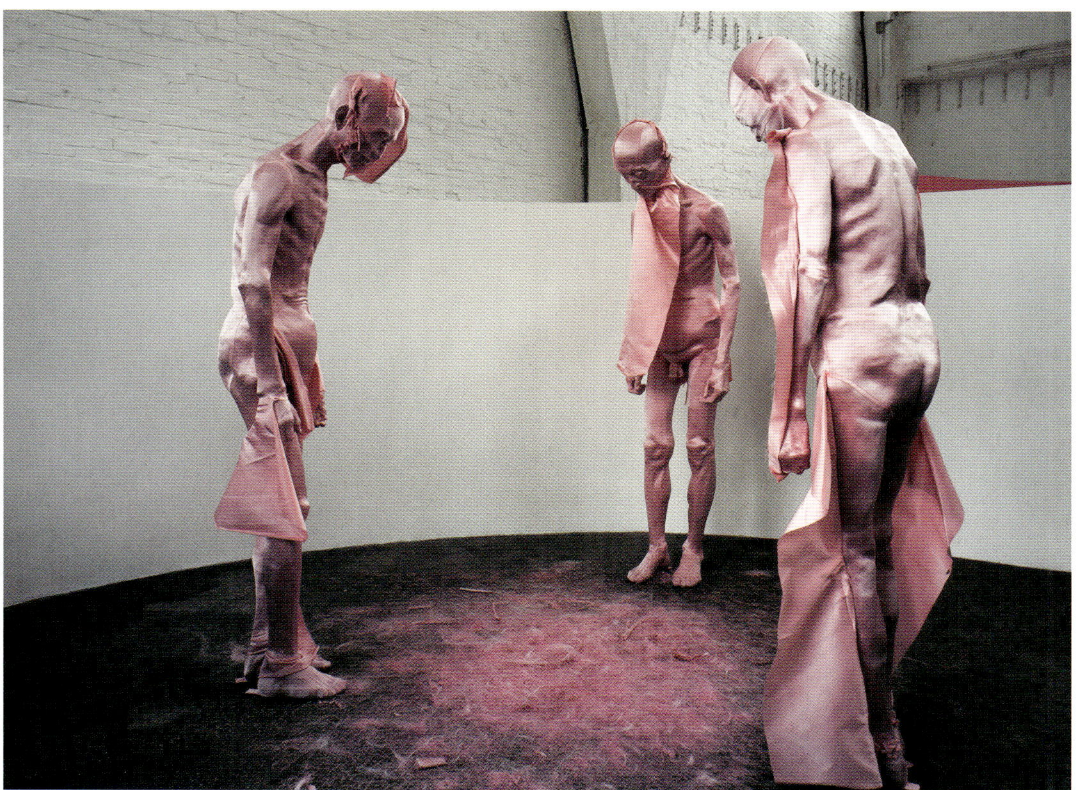

Lin Tianmiao. *Chatting*, 2004. Mixed media, fiberglass, and silk: dimensions variable. Image ©Lin Tianmiao. *Courtesy of Galerie Lelong & Co.*

Lin Tianmiao. *Endless*, 2004. Mixed media, fiberglass, and silk: dimensions variable. Image ©Lin Tianmiao. *Courtesy of Galerie Lelong & Co.*

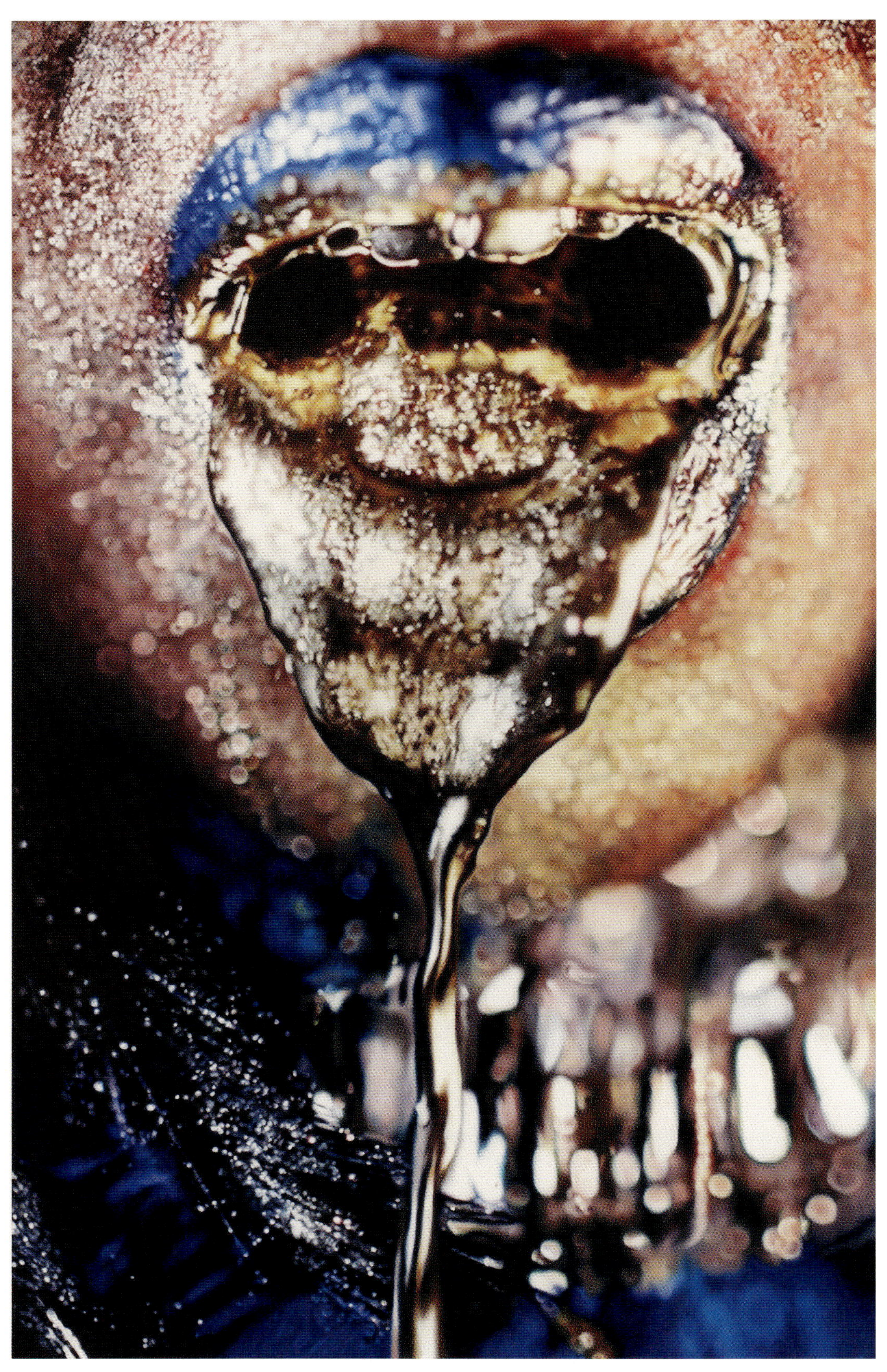

Marilyn Minter. *Drizzle*, 2010. Enamel on metal: 96 × 60 inches. *Courtesy of the artist and Salon94, New York*

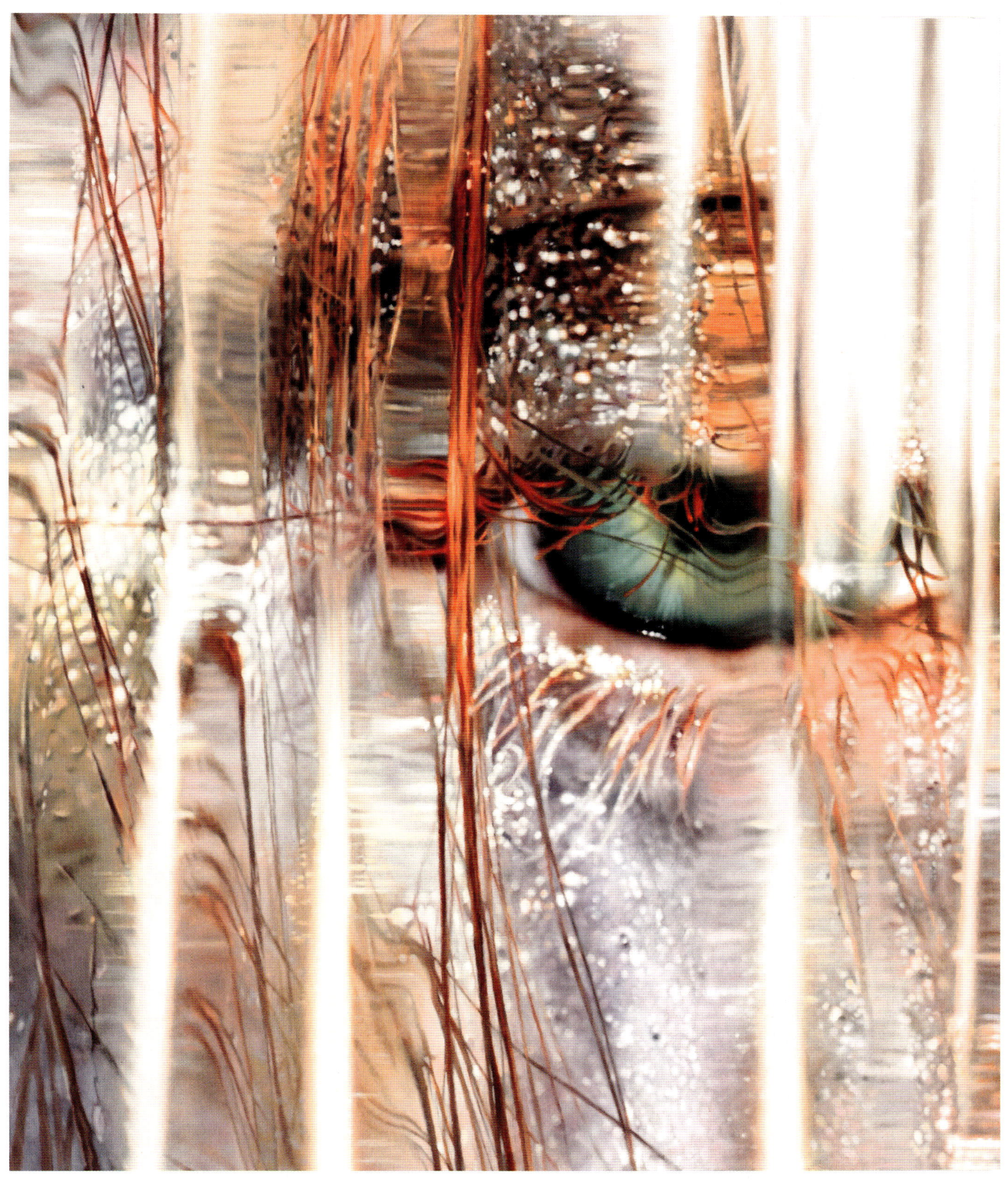

Marilyn Minter. *Redhead*, 2015. Enamel on metal: 72 × 60 inches. *Courtesy of the artist and Salon94, New York*

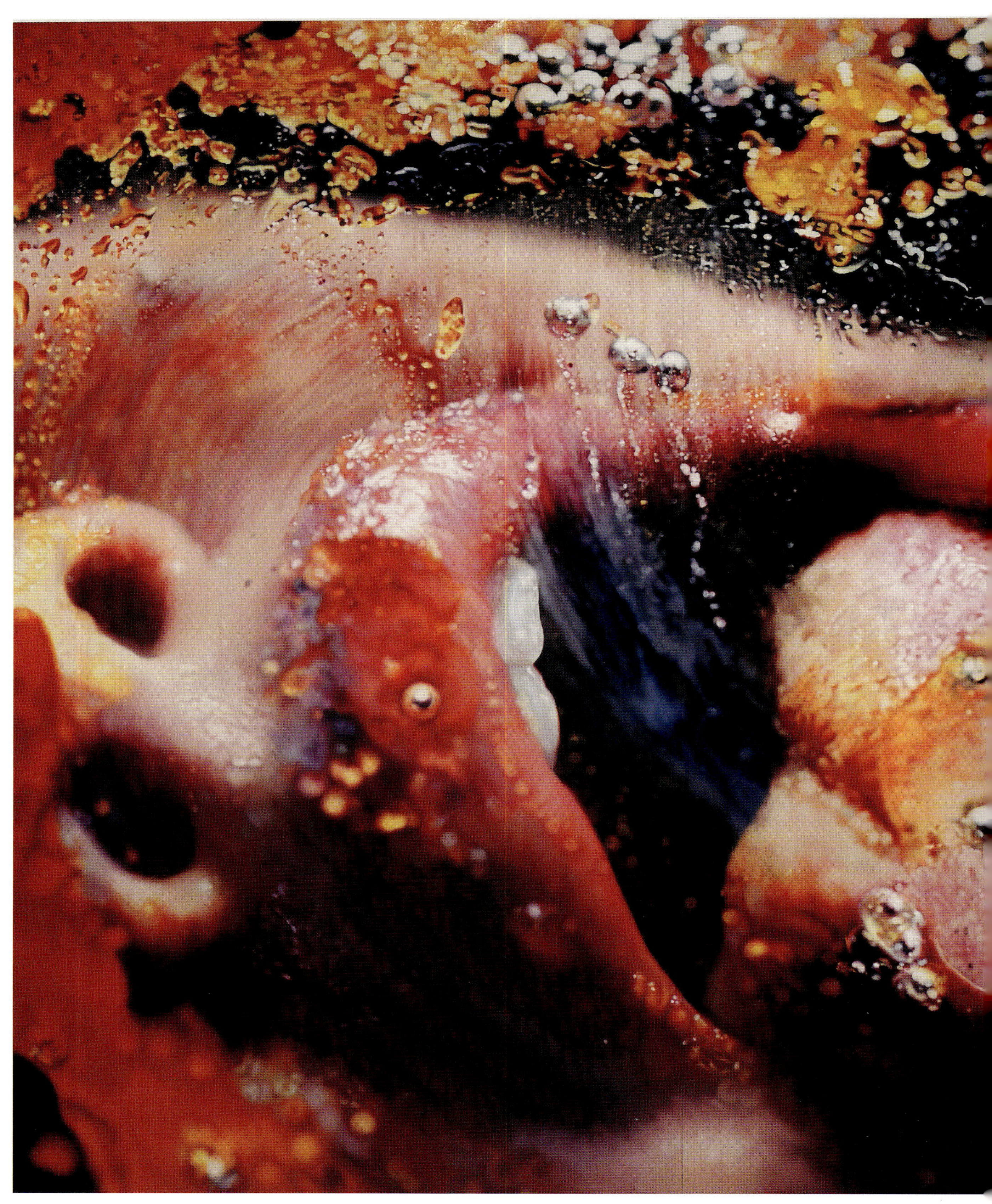

Marilyn Minter. *Orange Crush*, 2009. Enamel on metal: 108 × 180 inches. *Courtesy of the artist and Salon94, New York*

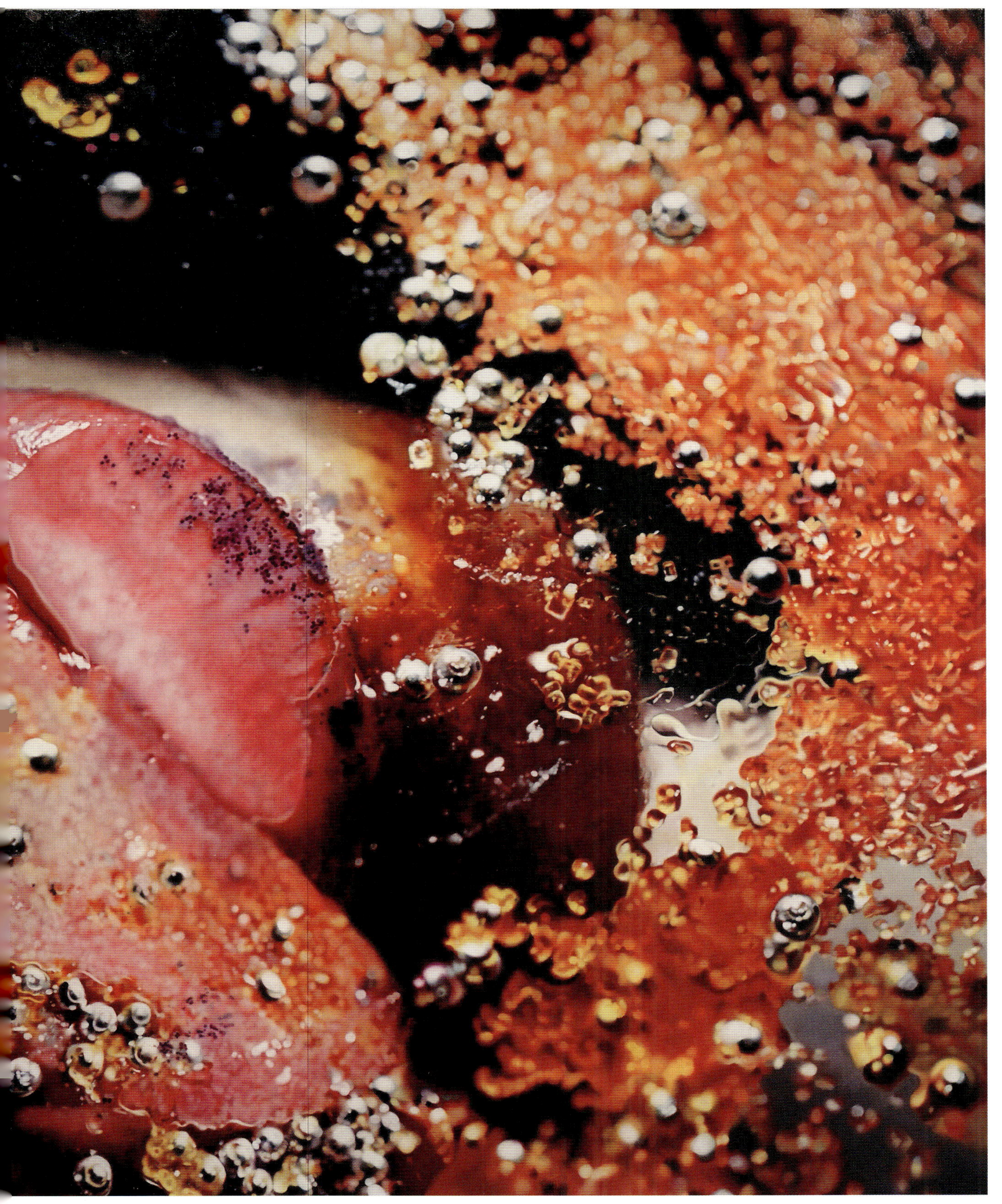

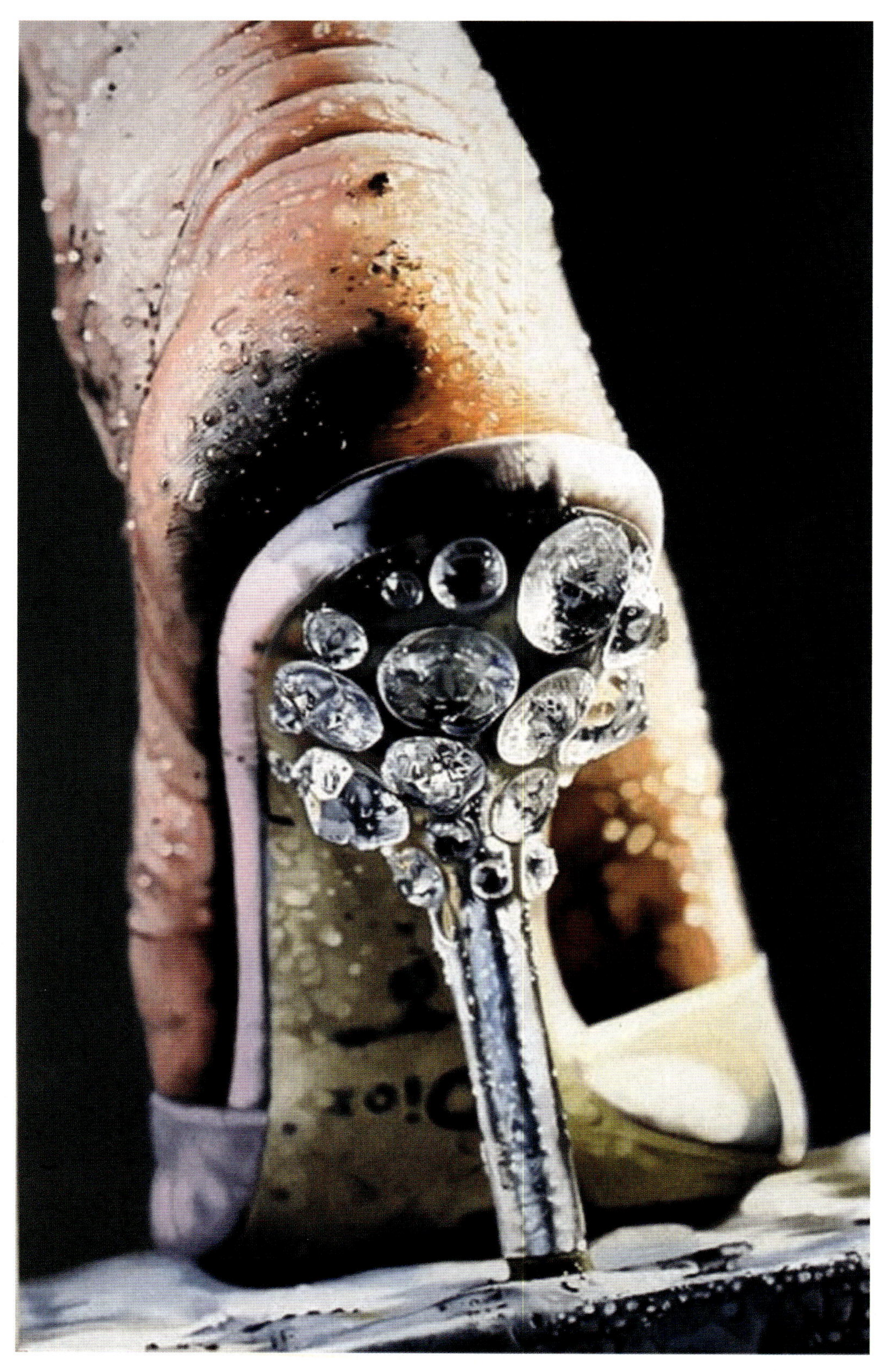

Marilyn Minter. *Strut*, 2005. Enamel on metal: 96 × 60 inches. *Courtesy of the artist and Salon94, New York*

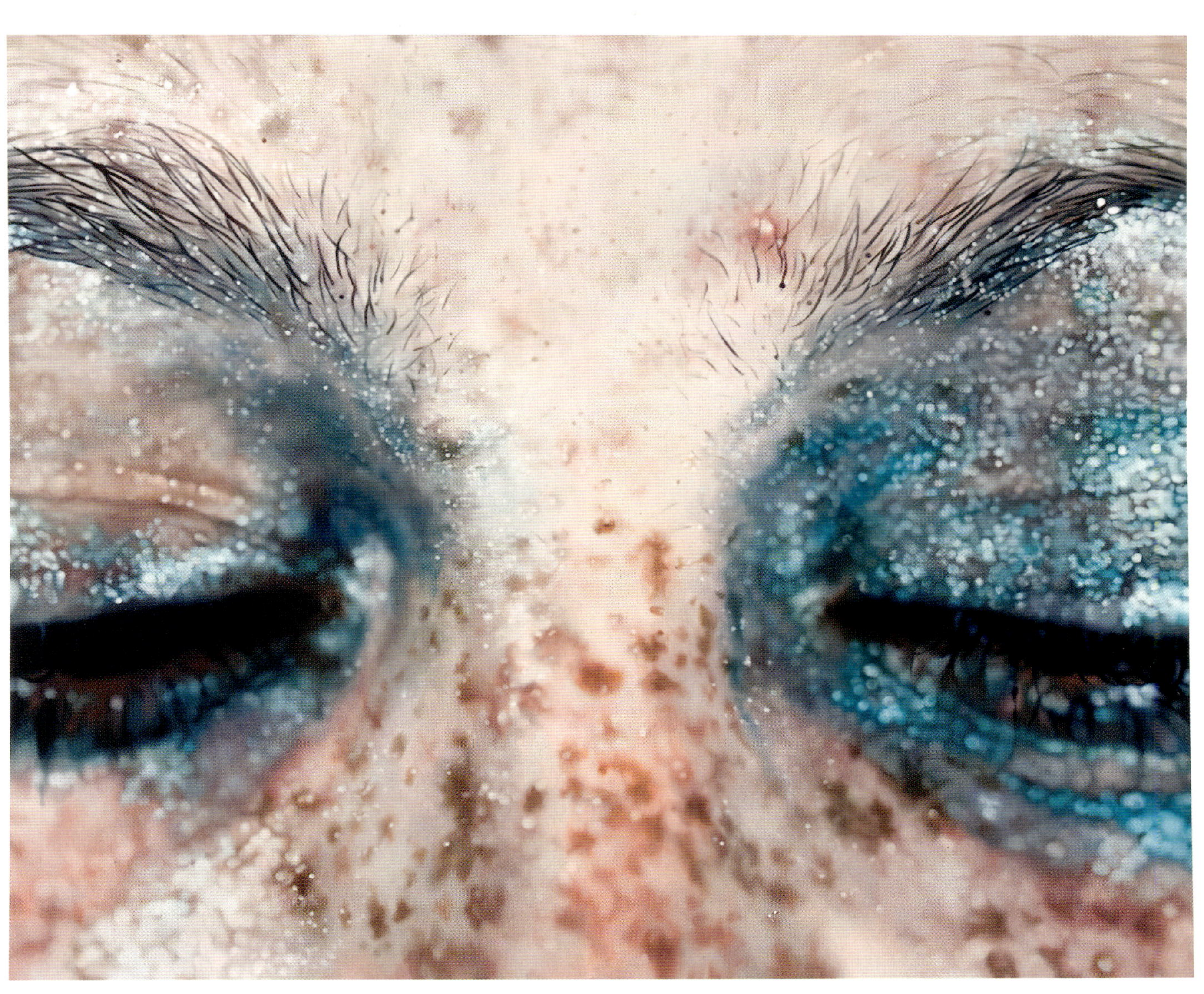

Marilyn Minter. *Blue Poles*, 2007. Enamel on metal: 60 × 72 inches. *Courtesy of the artist and Salon94, New York*

MAYA LIN

Maya Lin's work encompasses large-scale environmental installations, intimate studio artworks, architectural works, and memorials. She redefined the idea of monument with her very first work, the Vietnam Veteran's Memorial, and has since gone on to pursue a remarkable career both in art and architecture, while still being committed to the exploration of time, memory, history, and language. Her artwork interprets the world through a twenty-first-century lens, utilizing technological methods to study and visualize the natural environment. Lin has been the subject of solo exhibitions at museums worldwide and has also created permanent outdoor installations for public and private collections from New York to New Zealand.

Lin's architectural projects are largely undertaken at the request of nonprofit institutions and include the Museum for Chinese in America in New York City and the Riggio-Lynch Interfaith Chapel. Her designs create a close dialogue between the landscape and built environment, and she is committed to advocating sustainable design solutions in all her works. Lin is at work on her final memorial, *What Is Missing?*, a project that raises awareness about the crisis surrounding biodiversity and habitat loss. *Maya Lin: Topologies*, a new monograph covering the past thirty years of her career, has recently been published by Skira Rizzoli. Maya Lin received both her BA and M.Arch. from Yale University, New Haven, Connecticut, in 1981 and 1986, respectively, and has maintained a professional studio in New York City since then. She currently serves on the boards of the What Is Missing? Foundation and the Bloomberg Foundation. Lin is a former member of the Museum of Chinese in America, the Yale Corporation, the Natural Resources Defense Council (NRDC), and the Energy Foundation. She lives in New York City with her husband, Daniel Wolf, and their two children. Lin is represented by the Pace Gallery.

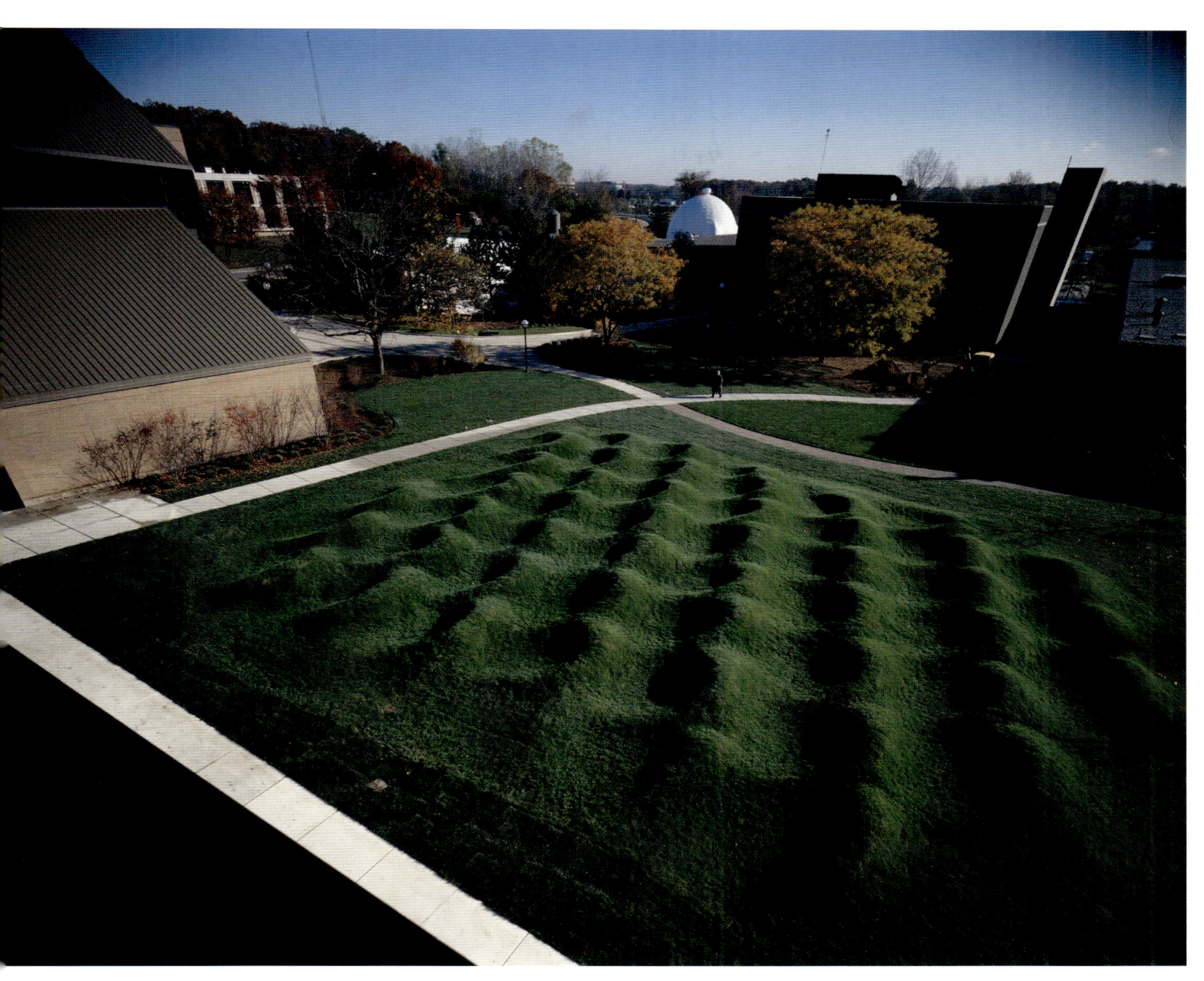

Maya Lin. *The Wave Field*, 1995. Earth: 10,000 sq. feet. Photographer: Balthazar Korab. Image ©Maya Lin. *Courtesy of Maya Lin Studio, New York*

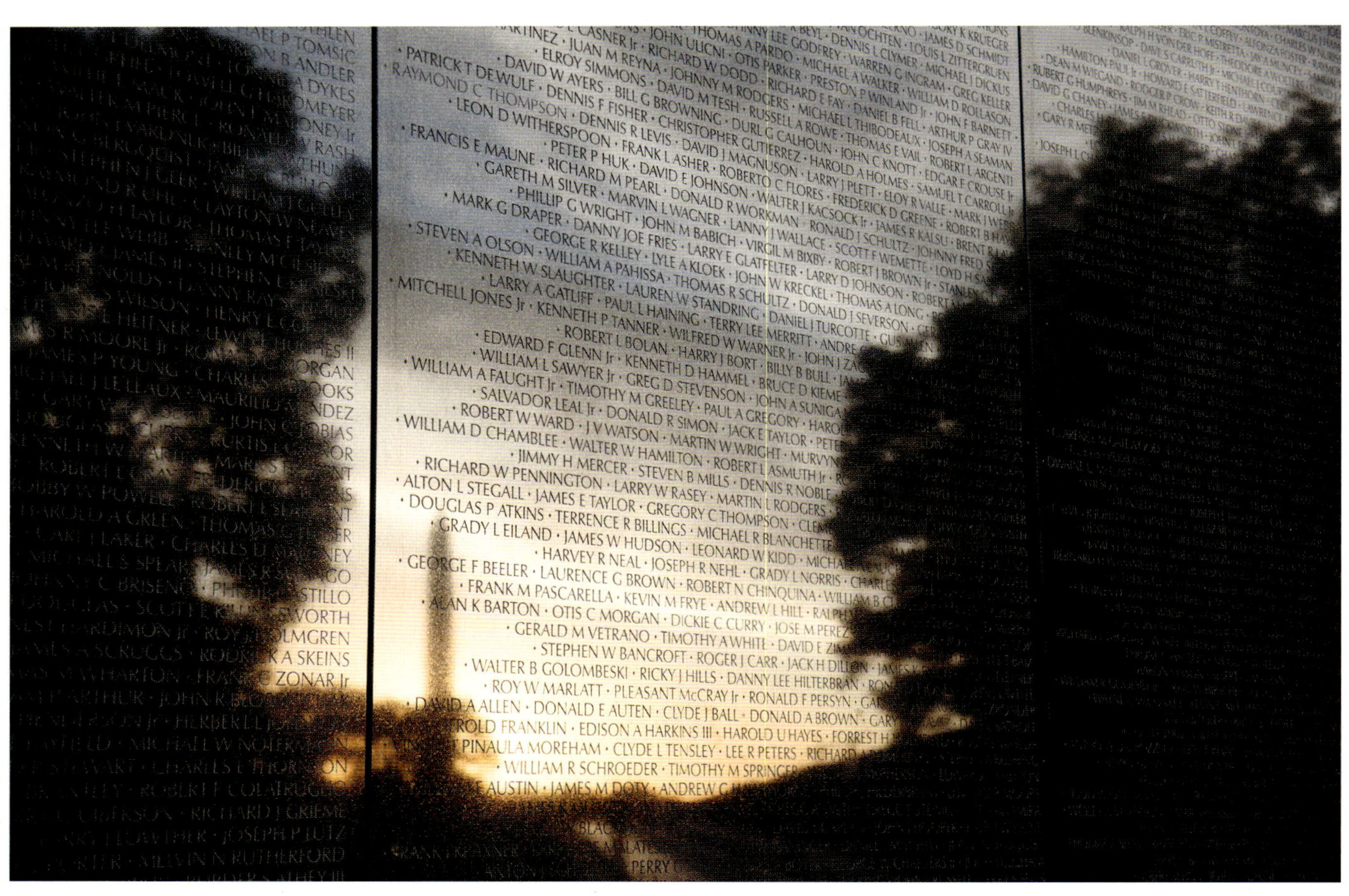

Maya Lin. *Vietnam Veterans Memorial,* 1989. Black granite: 86,000 sq. feet. Photographer: Victoria Sambunaris, Image ©Maya Lin. *Courtesy of Maya Lin Studio, New York*

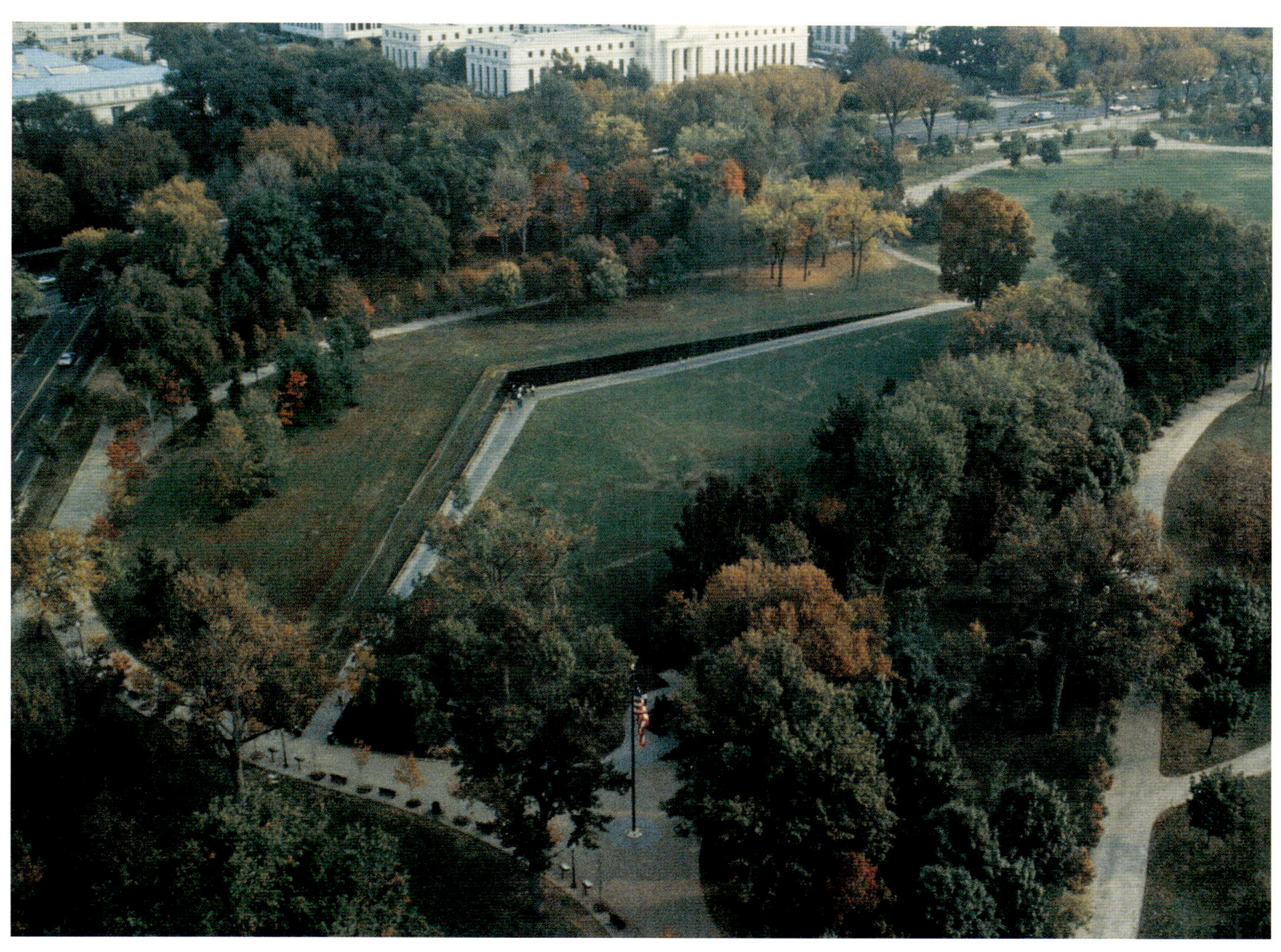

Maya Lin. *Vietnam Veterans Memorial*, 1989. Black granite: 86,000 sq. feet. Photographer: Terry Adams / National Parks Service. Image ©Maya Lin. *Courtesy of Maya Lin Studio, New York*

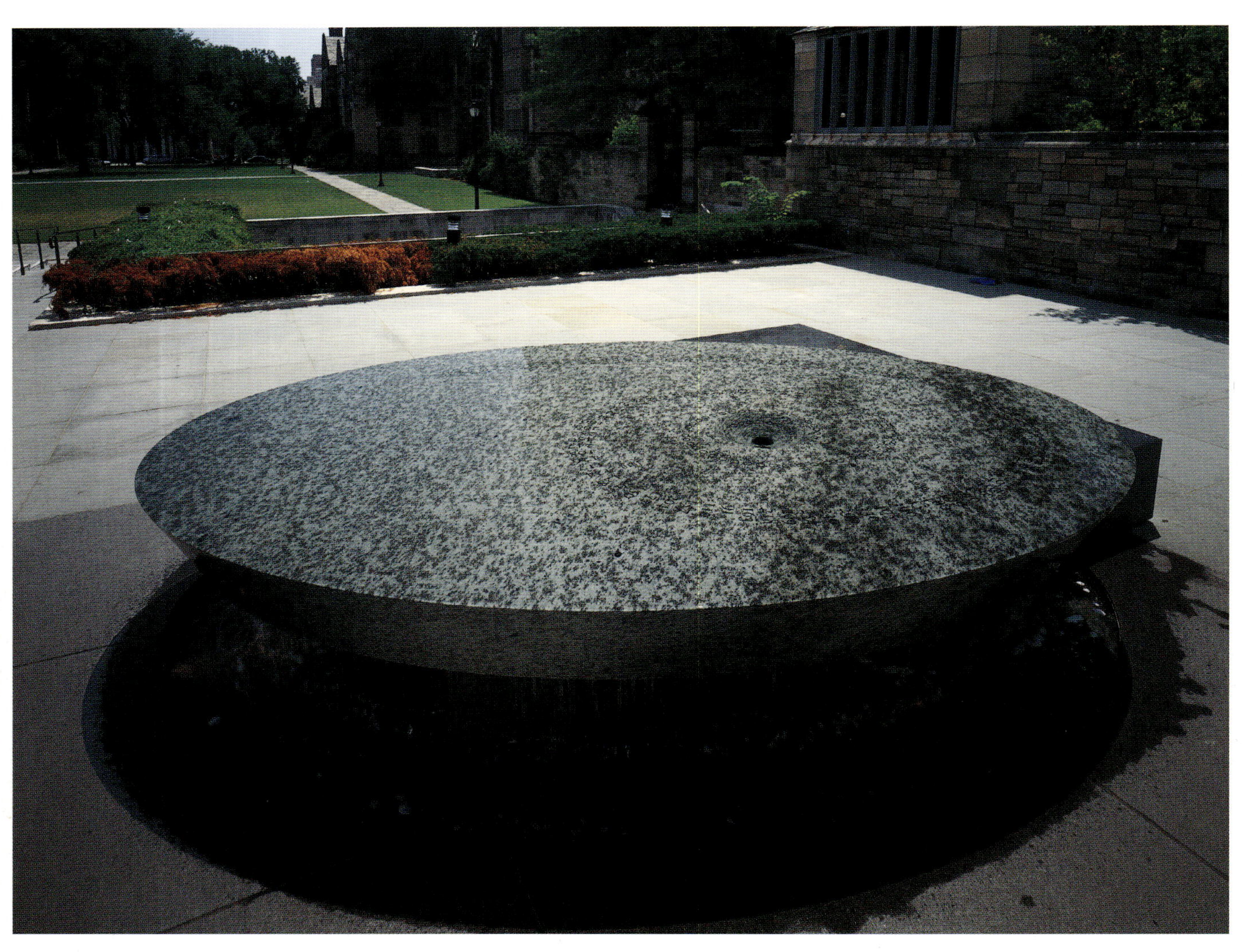

Maya Lin. *The Women's Table,* 1993. Stone and water: 14 × 14 × 2.8 feet. Photographer: Victoria Sambunaris. Image ©Maya Lin. *Courtesy of Maya Lin Studio, New York*

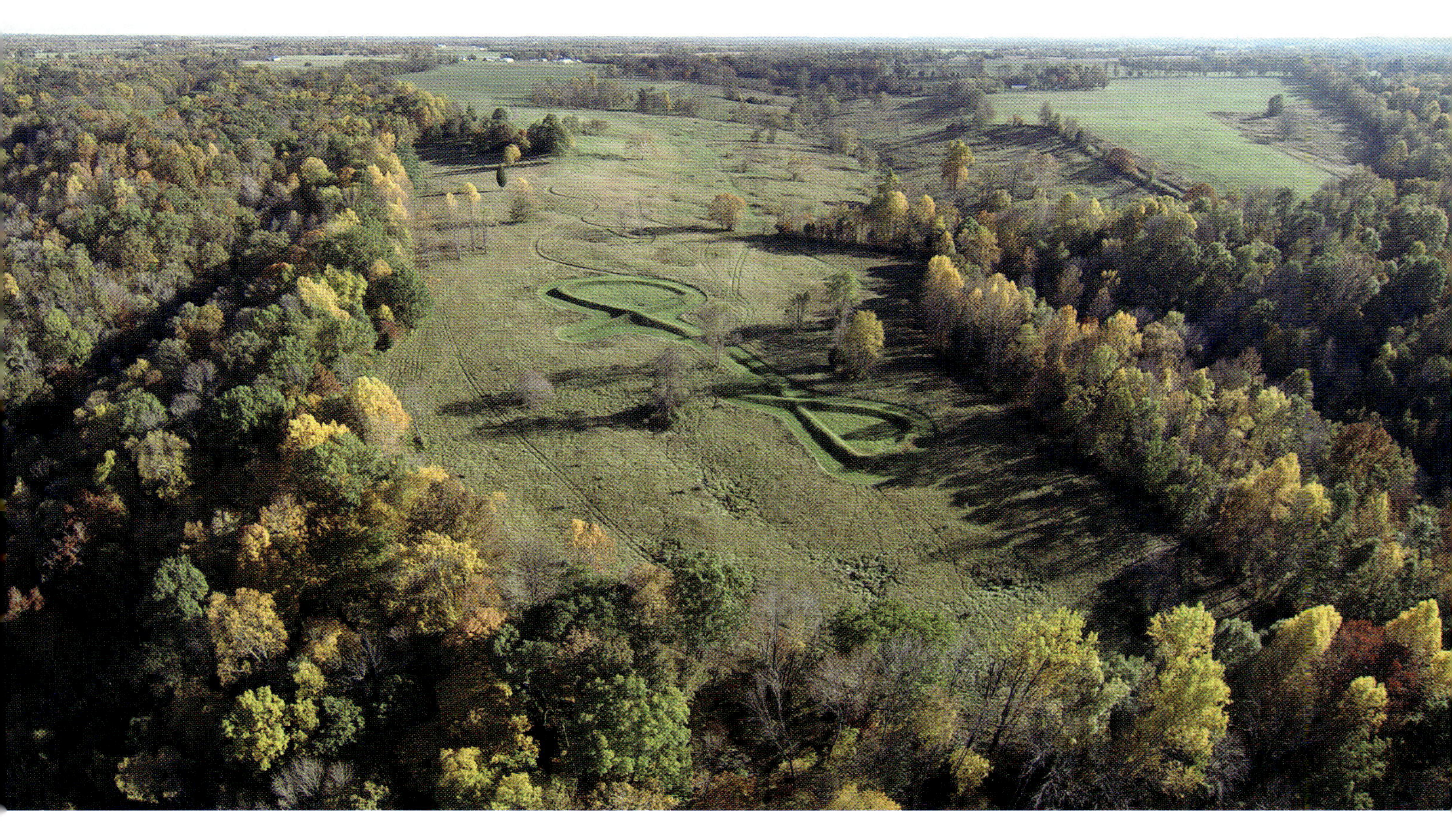

Maya Lin. *Kentucky Line,* 2008. Earth: 29,700 sq. feet. Photographer: William MacLean. Image ©Maya Lin. *Courtesy of Maya Lin Studio, New York*

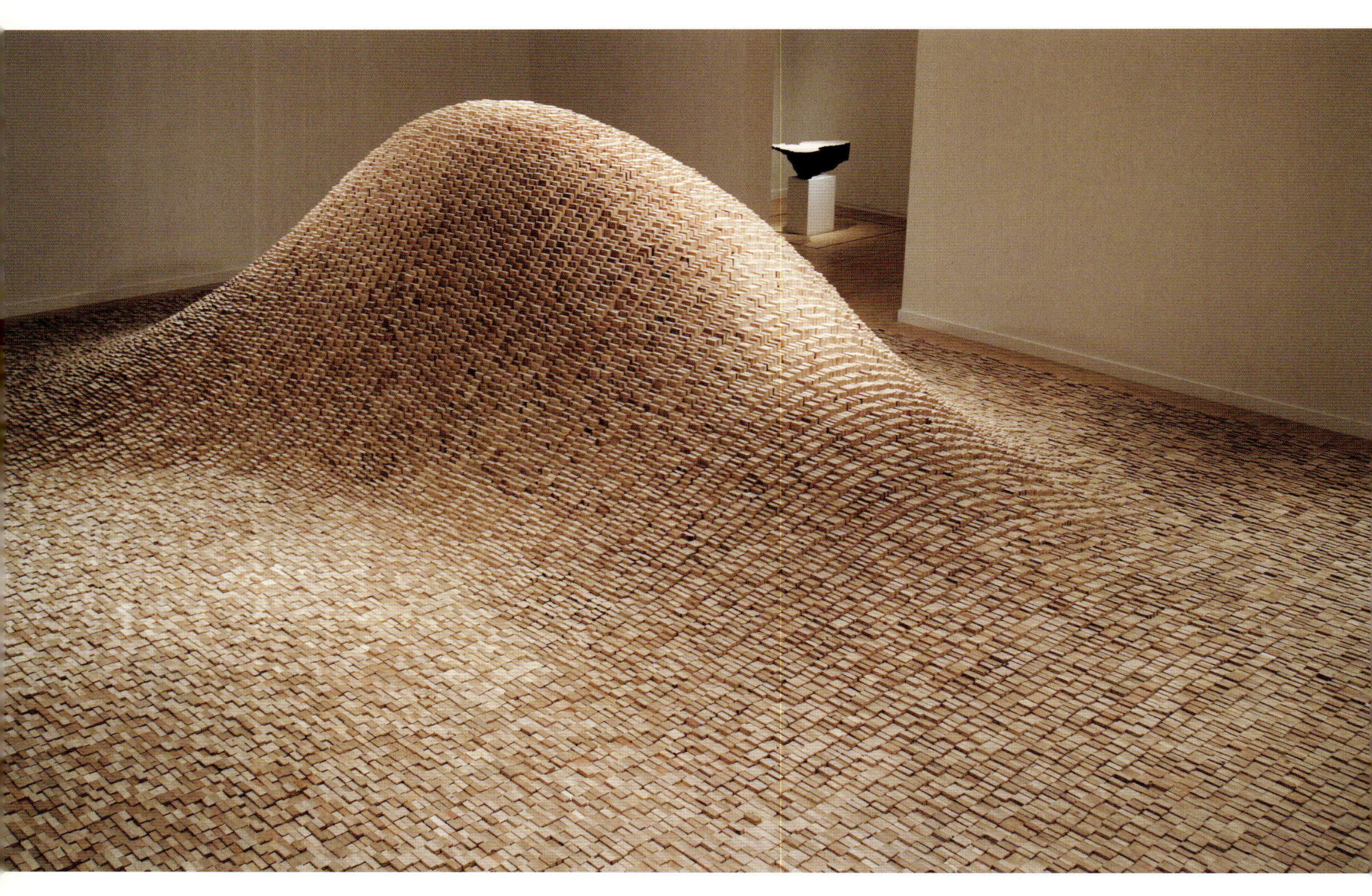

Maya Lin. *2x4 Landscape*, 2006. FSC wood: 10 × 52.7 × 36 feet. Photographer: Colleen Chartier / ART on File. Image ©Maya Lin. *Courtesy of Maya Lin Studio, New York*

MELISSA MURRAY

Melissa Murray creates large-scale, mixed-media compositions on paper. Deeply inspired by psychoanalytics, her drawings are derived from the extensive logging of her dreams and unconscious states.

By combining multiple environments into one still image, Murray creates layered works that freeze an active moment of thought. Each work can be read as a collection of coded memories that are quieted yet clarified through patterns, colors, and space. Murray's current series is derived from a found World War II letter. These paintings are based on consecutive sentences, such that each work combines the transcendental with the mundane and war with domesticity.

Murray has exhibited with Galerie SAS, Montréal; A.I.R. Gallery, New York City; Causey Contemporary, New York City; Lesley Heller Workspace, New York City; Arc Gallery at MOSI Museum in Tampa, Florida; Target Gallery, Alexandria, Virginia; Fuse Gallery, New York City; Chashama, New York City; and 3rd Ward, Brooklyn, New York. She has also shown at SPRING/BREAK Art Show and Pulse Art Fair. Murray's work has been featured and reviewed in *Blouin Artinfo*, *Architectural Digest*, *Time Out*, *Village Voice*, *Juxtapoz Magazine*, and *Wild Magazine*. Murray lives and works in Brooklyn, New York.

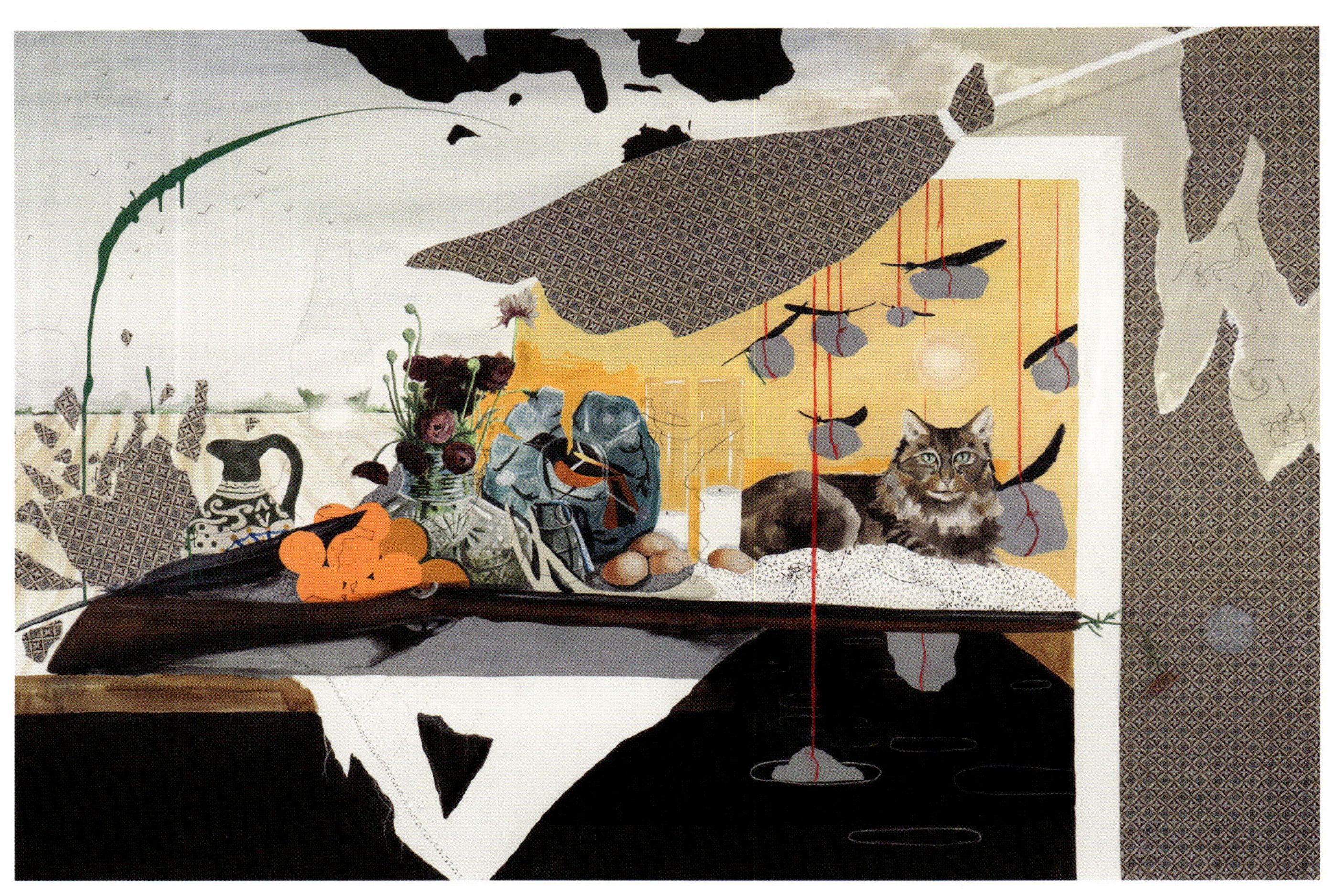

Melissa Murray. *Skylarks wheeled gracefully in the cool gray skies of dawn, unmindful of the strange myriad of sounds that seemed so foreign to this natural serenity,* 2014. Watercolor, acrylic, graphite, colored pencil, and Sumi ink on paper: 40 × 60 inches. *Courtesy of the artist*

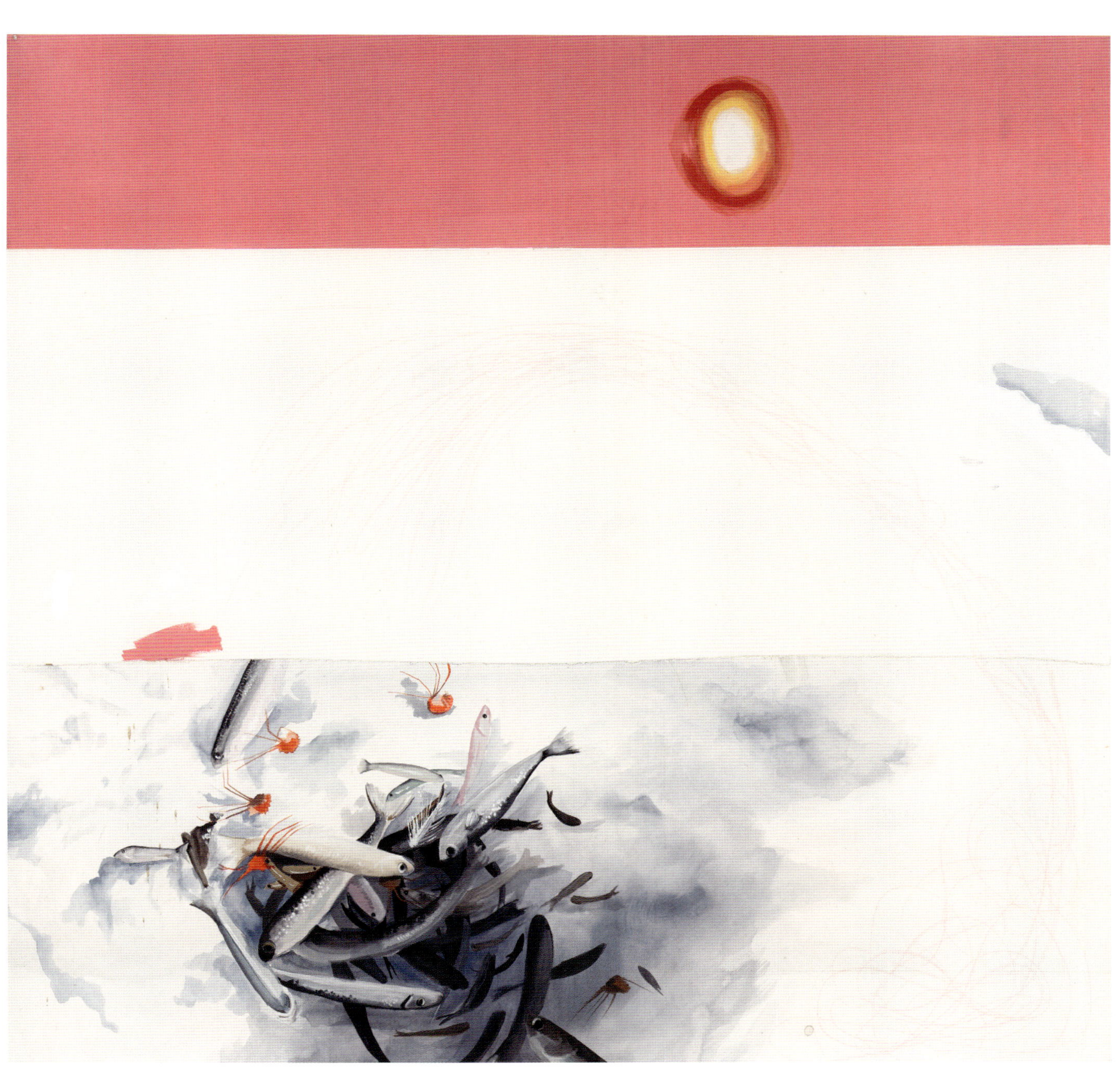

Melissa Murray. *A rose-colored horizon announced the sun, a birth of a new day,* 2014. Watercolor, acrylic, and colored pencil on paper: 42 × 40 inches. *Courtesy of the artist*

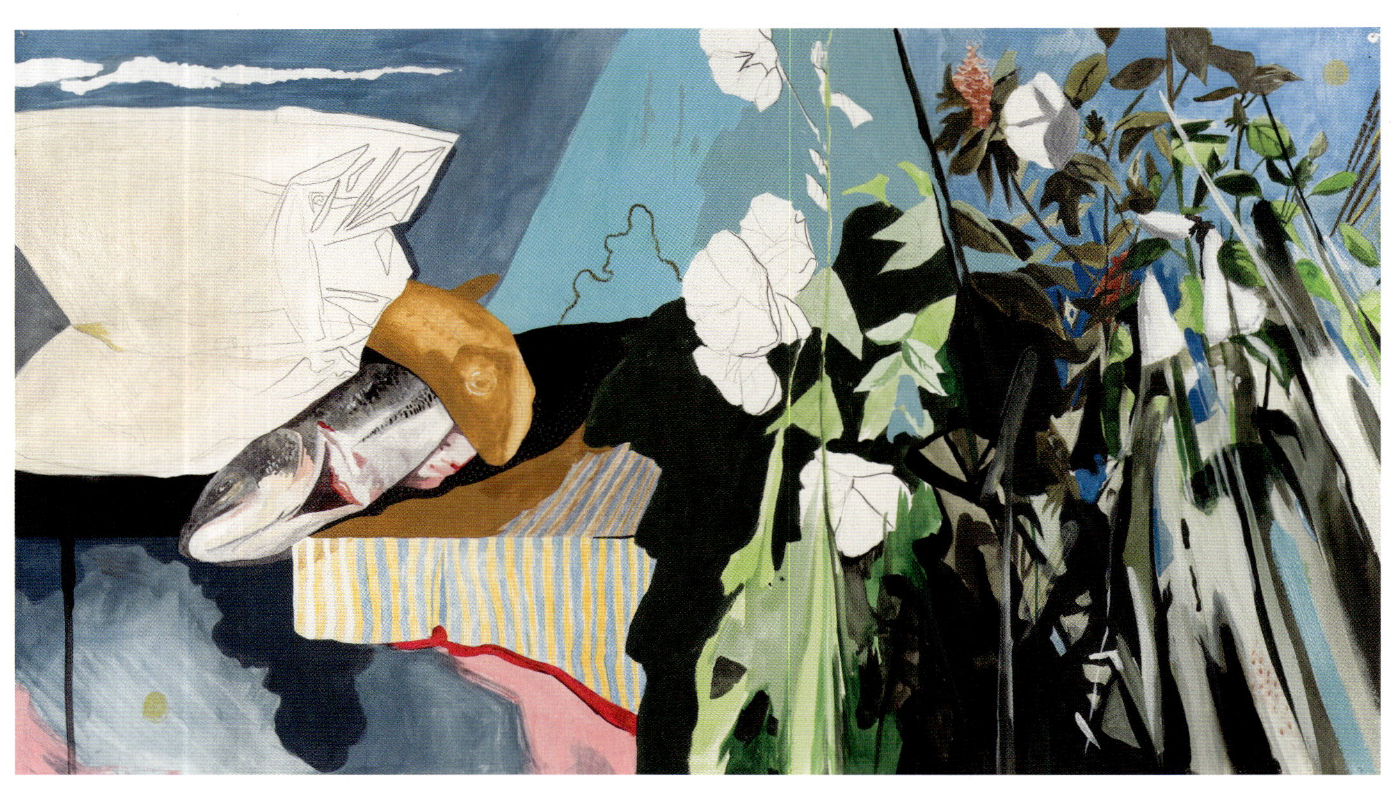

Melissa Murray. *In a few hours I would be five miles above it, in the cold steely blue of enemy skies*, 2016. Watercolor, acrylic, graphite, colored pencil, and Sumi ink on paper: 20 × 40 inches. *Courtesy of the artist*

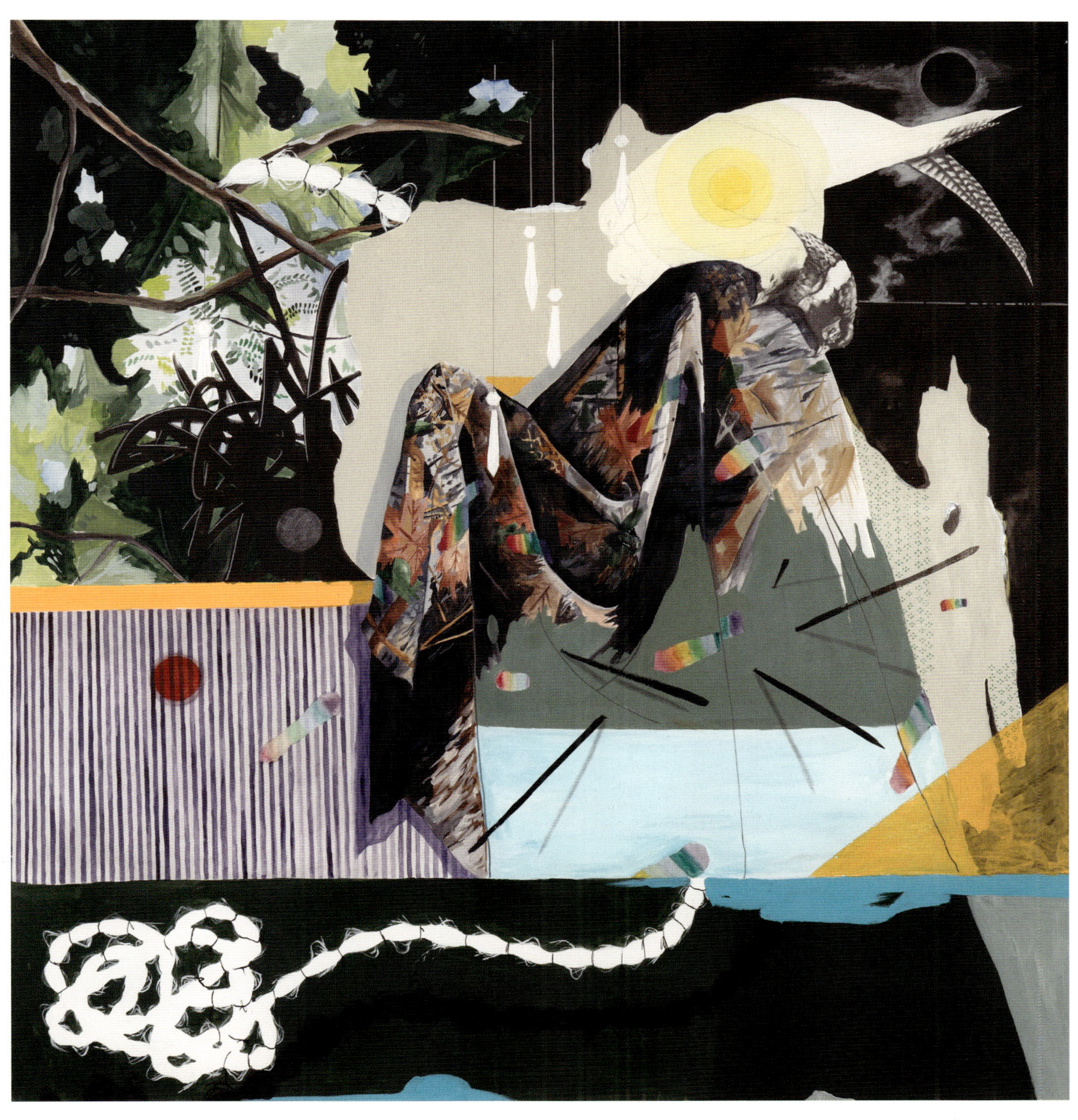

Melissa Murray. *The spectral mists of dawn shrouded the trees and hung low along the landscape*, 2015. Watercolor, acrylic, graphite, colored pencil, and Sumi ink on paper: 42 × 40 inches. *Courtesy of the artist*

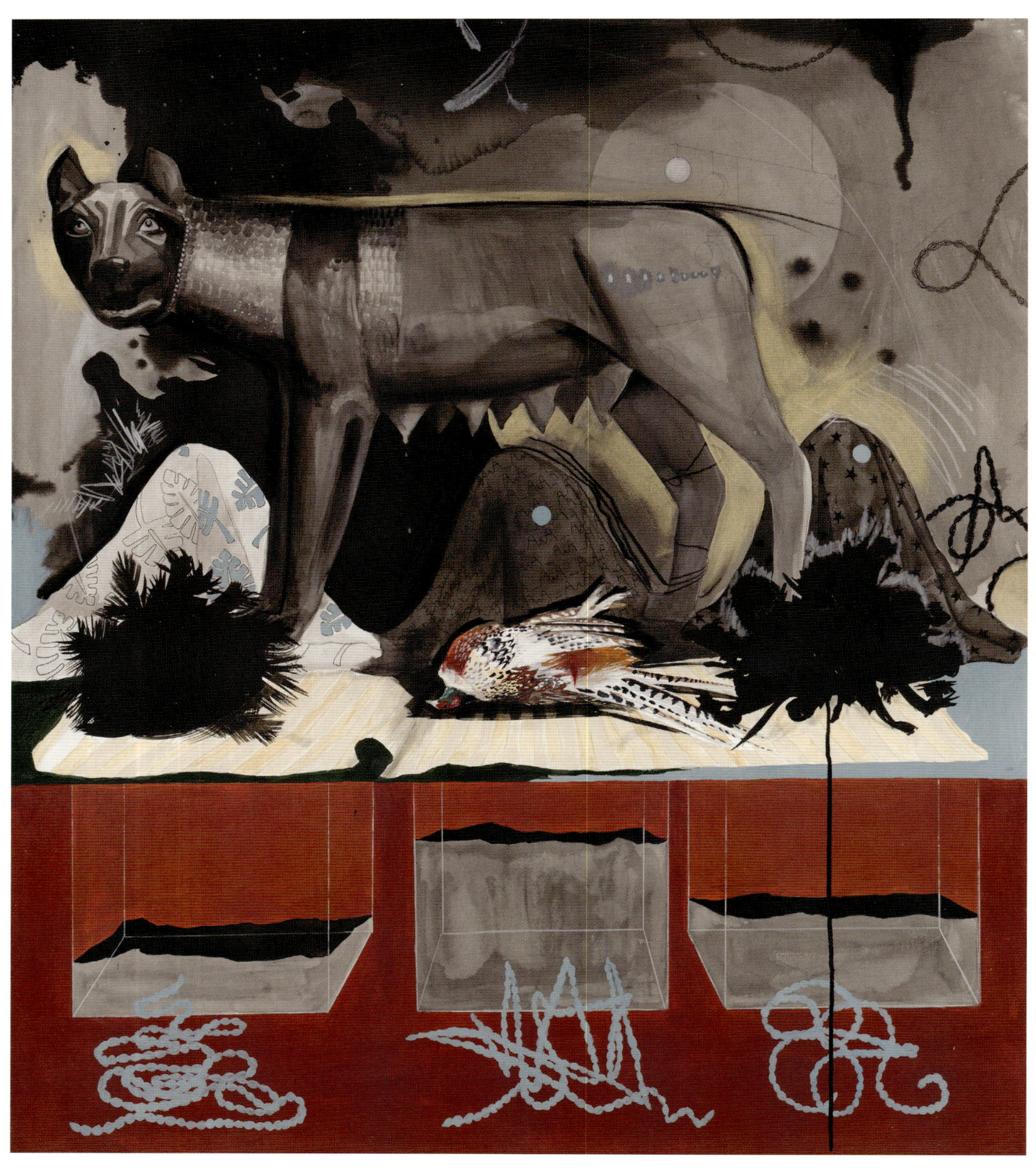

Melissa Murray. *The ground was hard but friendly*, 2016. Watercolor, acrylic, graphite, colored pencil, and Sumi ink on paper: 40 × 40 inches. *Courtesy of the artist*

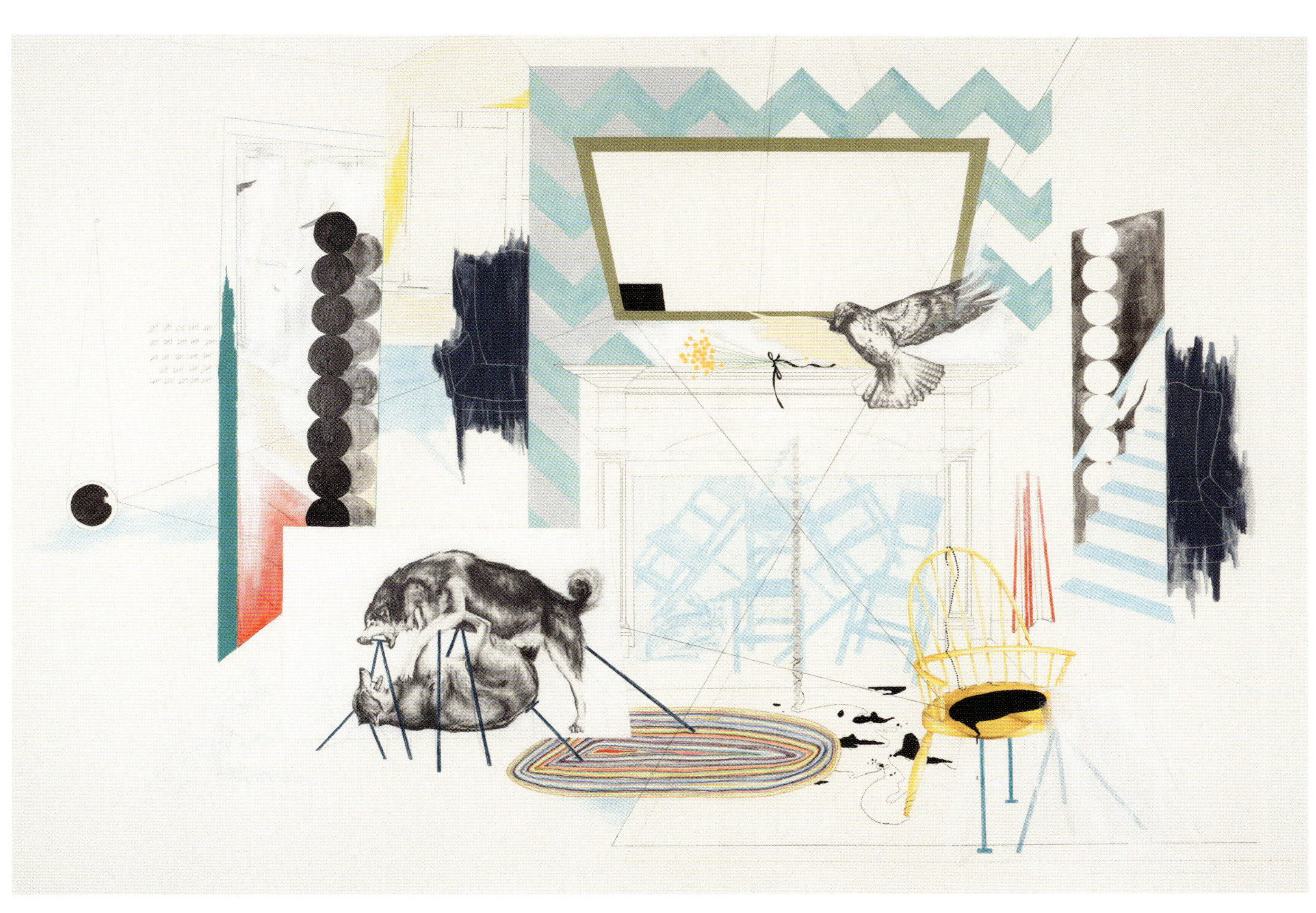

Melissa Murray. *An offering*, 2012.
Watercolor, acrylic, graphite, colored pencil, and Sumi ink on paper: 40 × 60 inches.
Courtesy of the artist

MICHELE OKA DONER

Michelle Oka Doner is an American artist and author. Her work is centered on sculpture, design, and architecture. It draws inspiration from organic beauty and natural creations such as plants, animals, and the human image. One of her most iconic pieces, *A Walk on the Beach*, is on display at the Miami International Airport. It is made up of over 9,000 bronzes embedded in terrazzo with mother-of-pearl, and is one of the largest artworks in the world, reaching a mile and a quarter long. Another iconic piece is *SoulCatchers*, which consists of approximately 400 shamanistic sculptures residing in the kiln room at the Nymphenburg Porcelain Manufactory in Munich, Germany.

Doner was awarded an honorary *Doctor of Fine Arts* degree by the University of Michigan in 2016. She has received several awards and prizes, including the Award of Excellence from the United Nations Society of Writers and Artists; the Pratt Legends Award from Pratt Institute, New York; the American Institute of Architects Citation Award for Art in Architecture for *Wave and Gate* at the Dan M. Russell Jr. US Courthouse; the Certificate of Excellence for Art in Architecture from the American Institute of Architects; the Distinguished Alumnus Award from the Stamps School of Art and Design; an honorary doctorate in fine arts from the New York School of Interior Design; the Best of Show Award and the First Place Award in Concrete Artistry from the American Society of Concrete Contractors; the Honor Award from the National Terrazzo & Mosaic Association for *A Walk on the Beach*; the Concrete Industry Board Award for *Celestial Plaza*; the Standard Ceramic Company Award; and the Lydia Winston Malbin Prize at the Detroit Institute of Arts. Doner has published several books, including *Miami Beach: Blueprint of an Eden*, *What Is White*, and *Into the Mysterium*. Doner was born in Miami, Florida, and now lives and works in New York City.

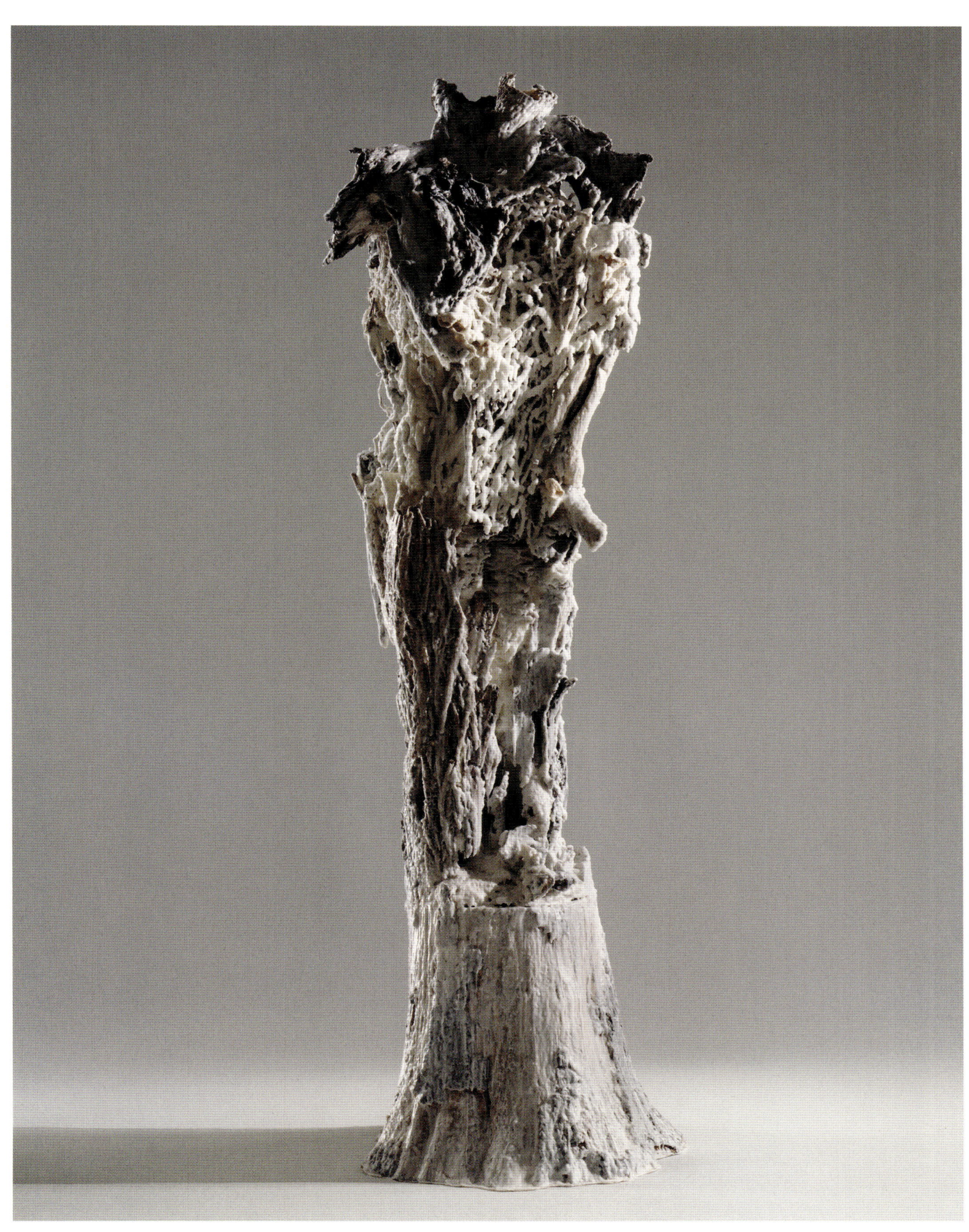

Michele Oka Doner. *Totem*, 2007–15. Wax, organic material, and stainless steel: 100.5 × 33 × 30 inches. *Courtesy of the artist*

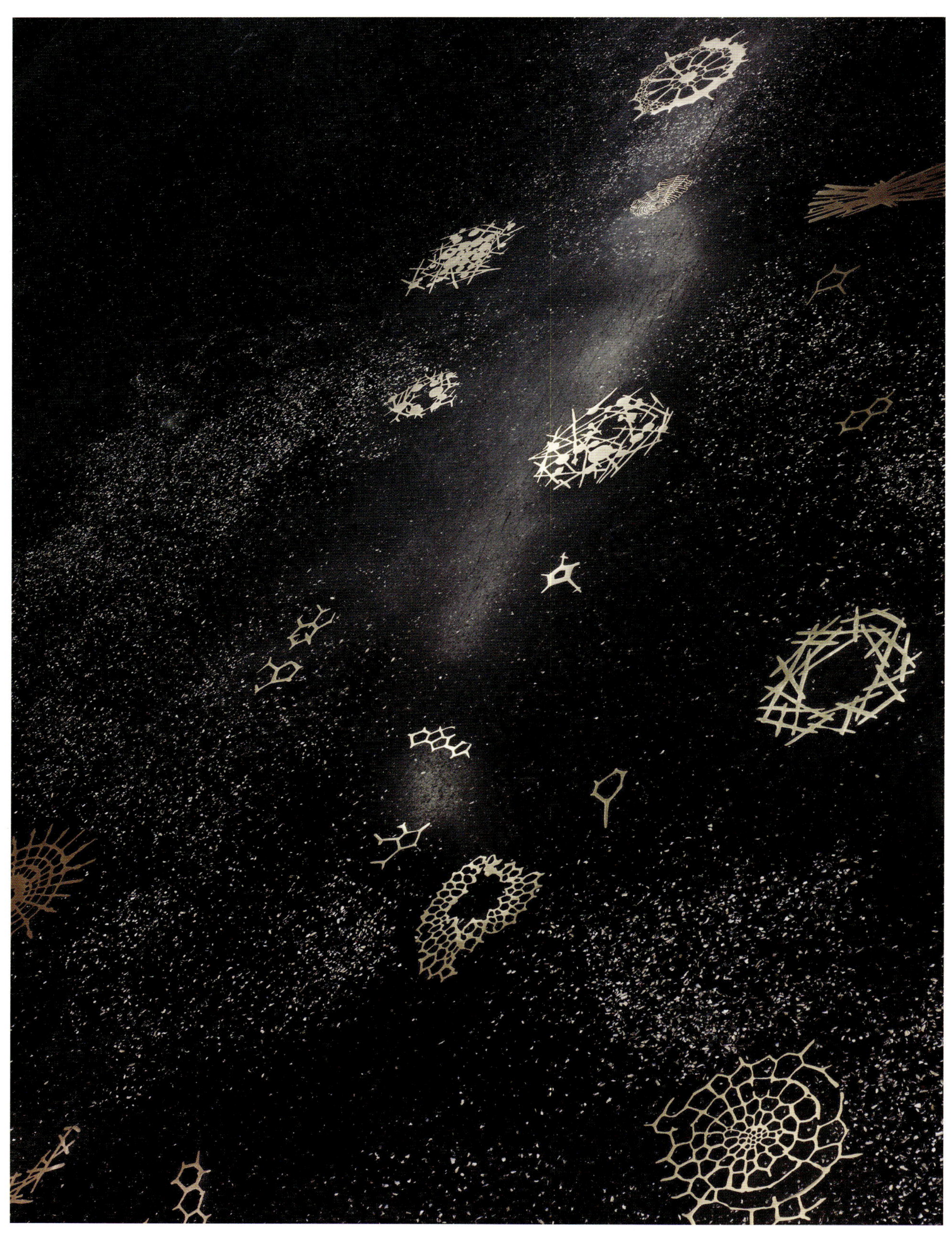

Michele Oka Doner. *Galaxy*, 2008. Black-and-white terrazzo with mother of pearl: 50 × 50 feet. Installation view, Miami International Airport, Miami, Florida. *Courtesy of the artist*

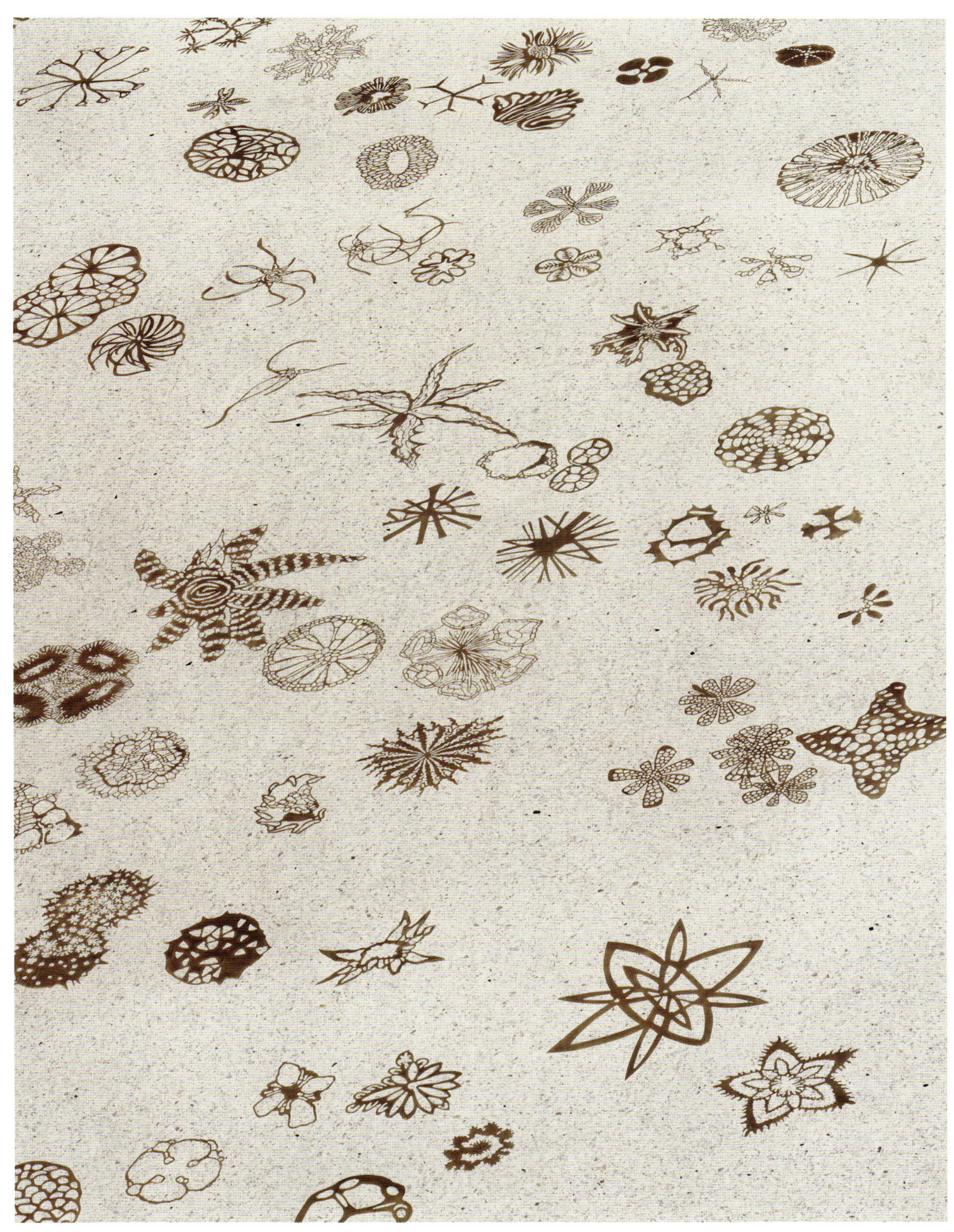

Michele Oka Doner. *Galaxy*, 2008. Black-and-white terrazzo with mother-of-pearl: 50 × 50 feet. Installation view, Miami International Airport, Miami, Florida. *Courtesy of the artist*

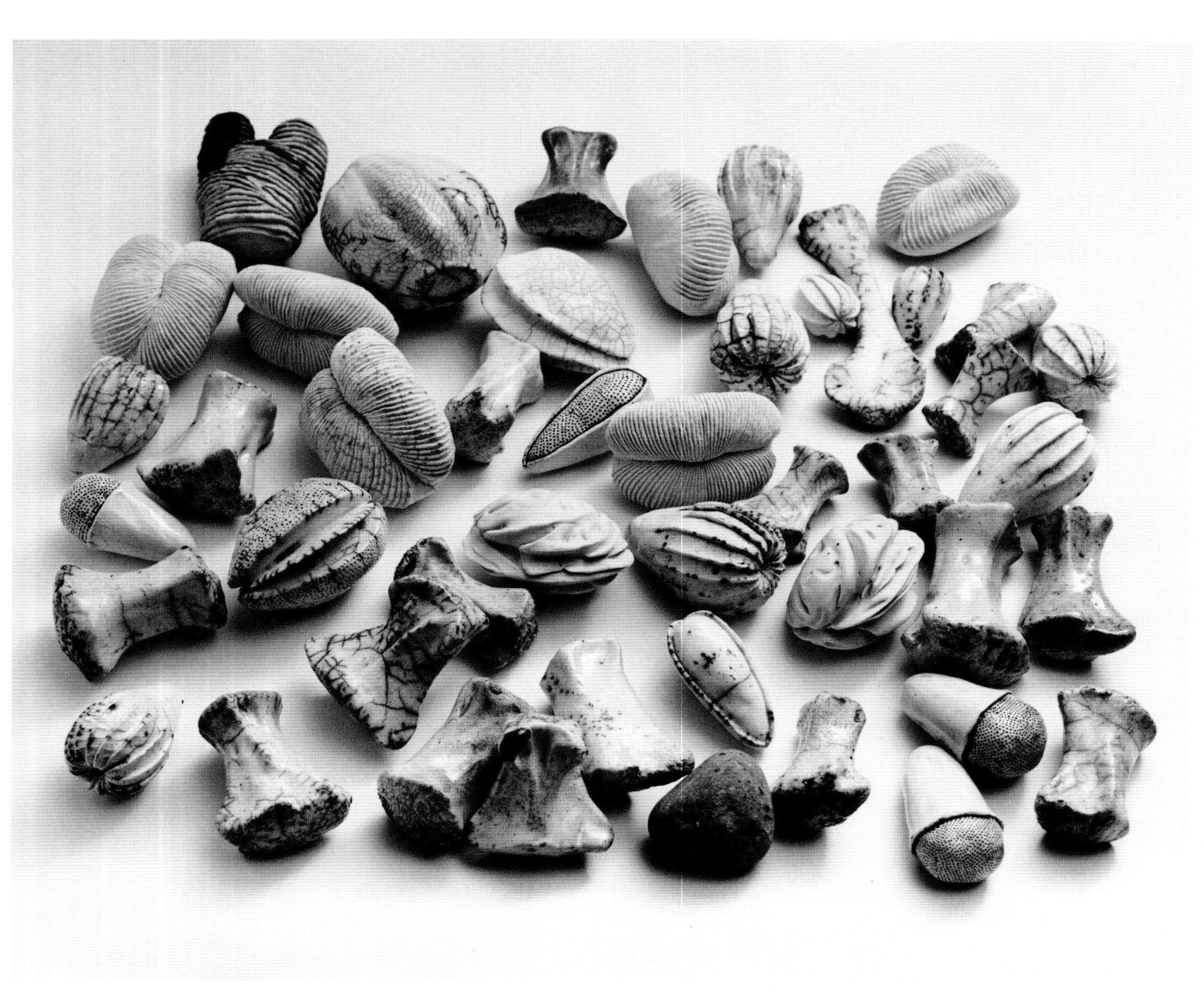

Michele Oka Doner. *Seeds and Pods*, 1977–78. Raku: 2 to 5 inches. *Courtesy of the artist*

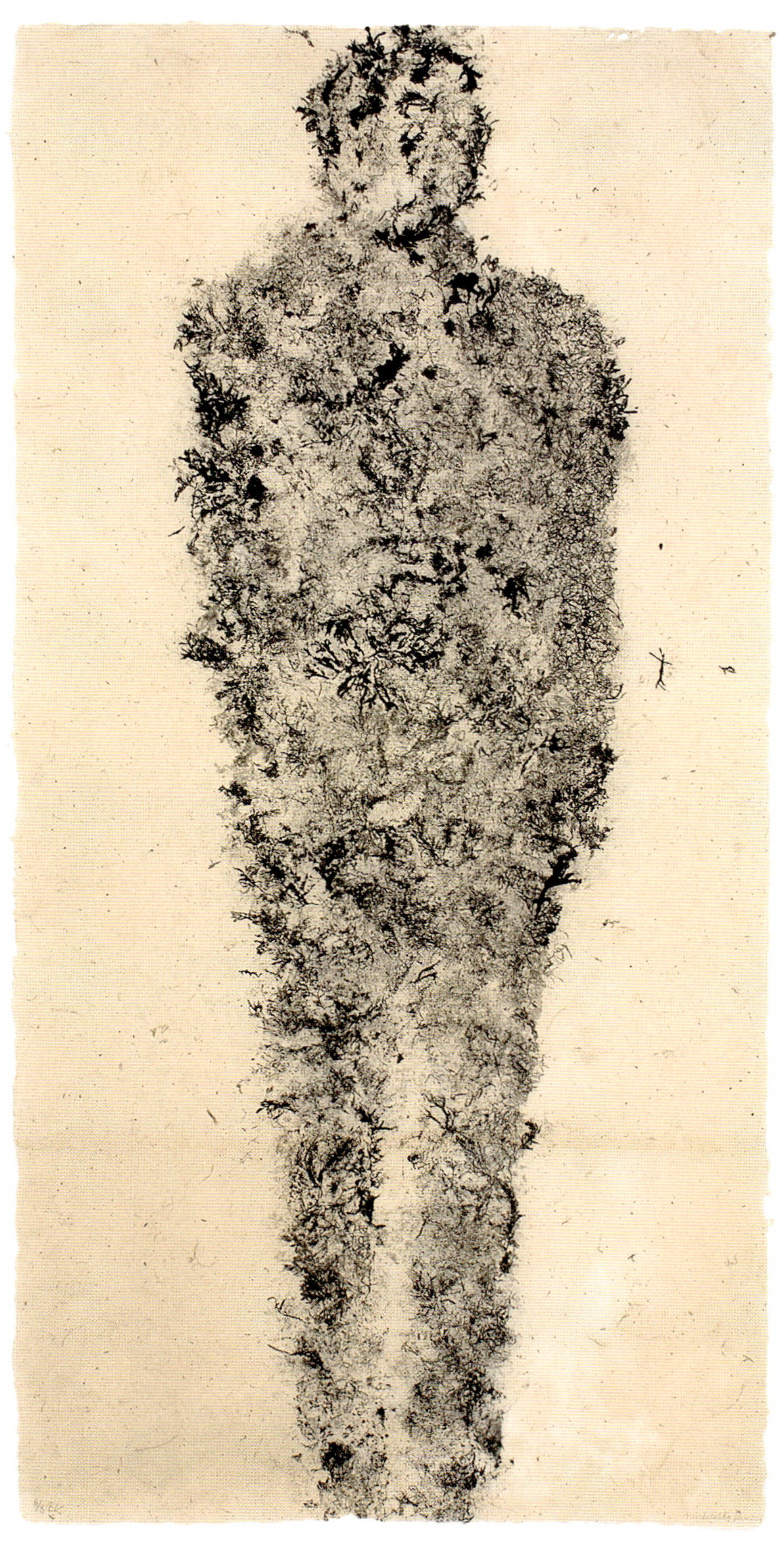

Michele Oka Doner. *Sargassa*, 2008. Relief print from organic material: 101.5 × 53.5 × 1.75 inches. *Courtesy of the artist*

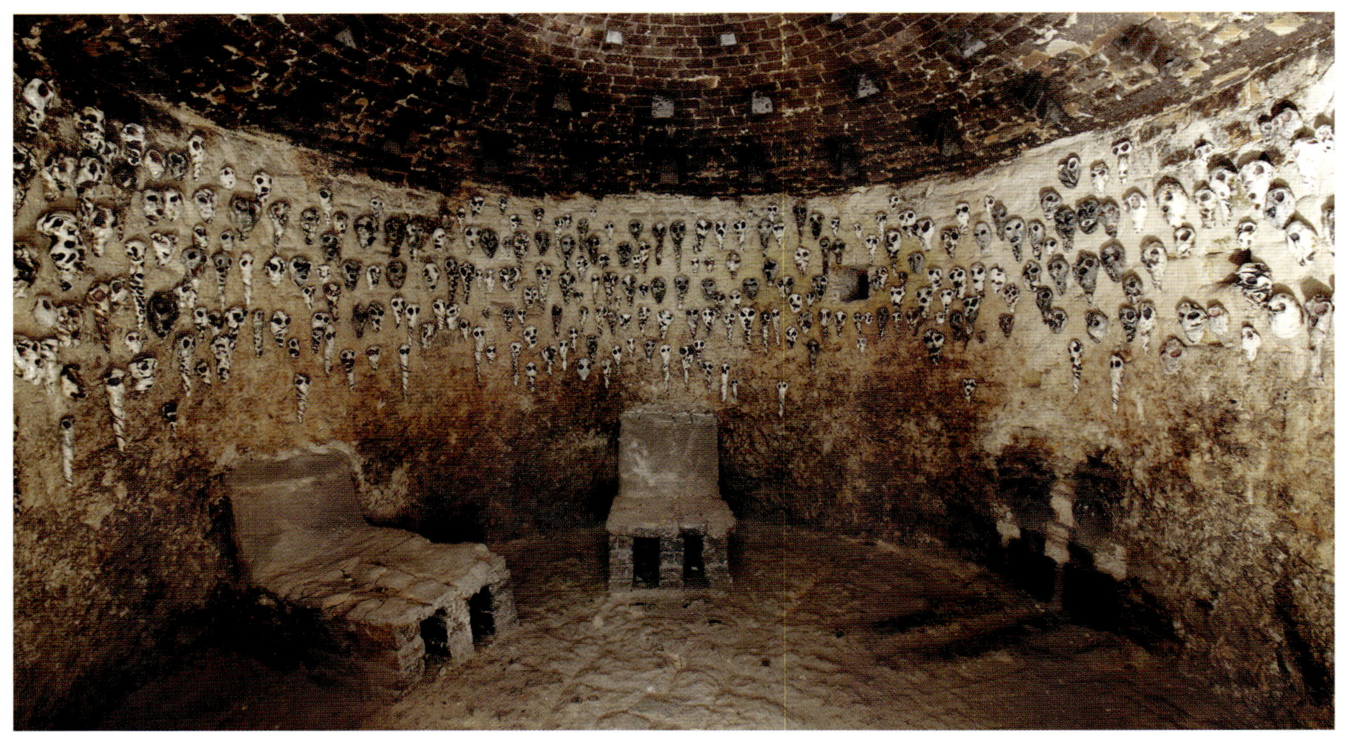

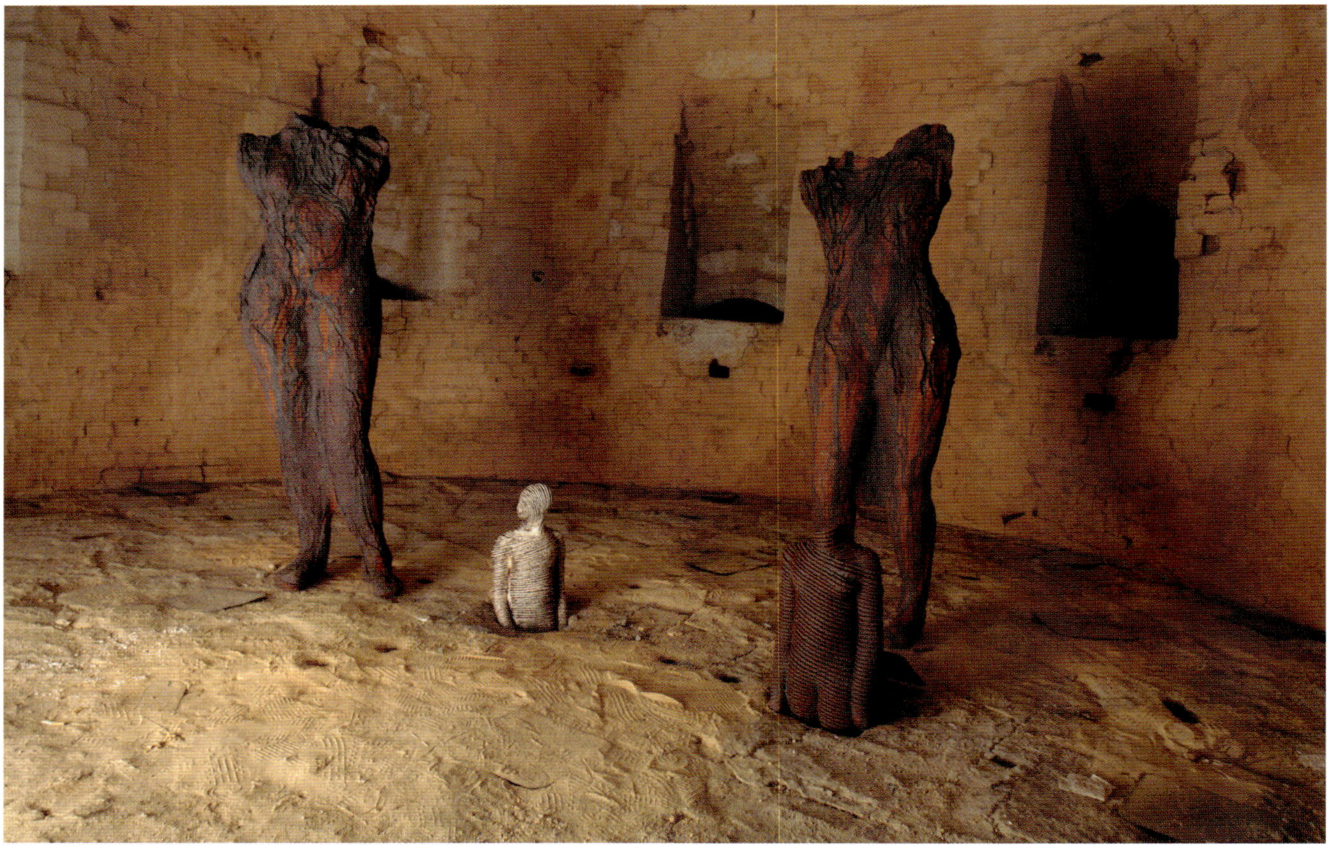

Michele Oka Doner. *SoulCatchers*, 2009. Porcelain: 5 to 12 inches. Installation view, Nymphenburg Manufactory, Munich, Germany. *Courtesy of the artist*

Michele Oka Doner. *Nymphenberg Installation with Four Figures: Distraught Goddess and Her Prophecy, Strabo, Nonus and Hestia*, 2010. Terra-cotta and porcelain: dimensions variable. Installation view, Nymphenburg Manufactory, Munich, Germany. *Courtesy of the artist*

MICHELE PRED

Michele Pred is a Swedish American conceptual artist whose practice includes sculpture, assemblage, and performance. Her work uncovers the cultural and political meaning behind everyday objects, with a concentration on feminist themes such as equal pay, reproductive rights, and personal security. Pred's projects also contain social components that drive the conversation into public spaces. Examples include her exploration of the intersection of personal space and security by using airport-confiscated items after 9/11, the cultural background of the fight for reproductive rights, using thousands of expired birth control pills, and the continuing economic and political struggle for women's rights, represented by her modified vintage handbag editions.

Since Donald Trump took office in 2017, Pred has participated in thirteen group exhibitions throughout the United States in response to the current administration. In December 2017, she organized *Parade Against Patriarchy* in Miami during Art Basel. In November 2018, Pred will lead *Nevertheless We Vote*, an art and social justice parade in New York City, to coincide with the midterm elections. *Nevertheless We Vote* will take place during her solo exhibition *Feminist Vote* at Nancy Hoffman Gallery. Pred has been represented by the Nancy Hoffman Gallery in New York since 2004. Her work is part of the permanent collection at the Berkeley Art Museum, the 21st C Museum, the Fashion Institute of Technology (FIT) in New York, the Contemporary Museum in Honolulu, and the 9/11 Memorial Museum in New York. Pred received a Pro-Choice Leadership Award from Personal PAC, Chicago, and has shown at Jack Shainman Gallery as an original member of the first artist-run super PAC, *For Freedoms*. Pred has exhibited both nationally and internationally at the Neuberger Museum, White Plains, New York; Bild Museet and Kulturhuset in Sweden; University of Westminster, London, Museum of Craft and Folk Art, San Francisco; University of Technology, Sydney, Australia; Omi International Art Center, Ghent, New York; ASU Museum, Tempe, Arizona; the Honolulu Museum of Art; and the Museum of Design Atlanta, among others. Pred received her BFA from California College of the Arts, Oakland, California.

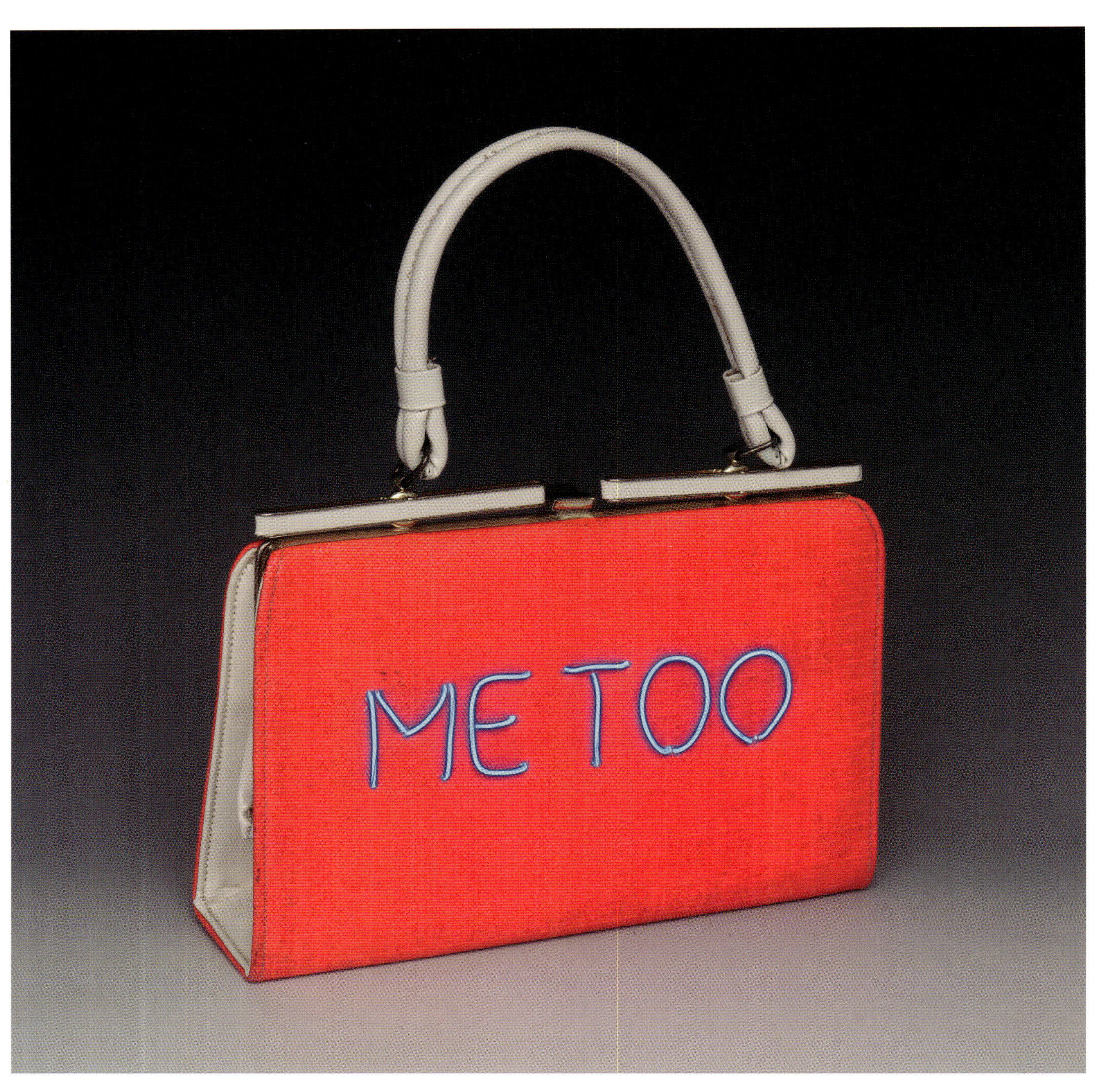

Michele Pred. *Me Too*, 2017.
Electroluminescent wire on vintage purse: 11.5 × 9.5 × 2.5 inches, AP. *Courtesy of the artist and Nancy Hoffman Gallery, New York*

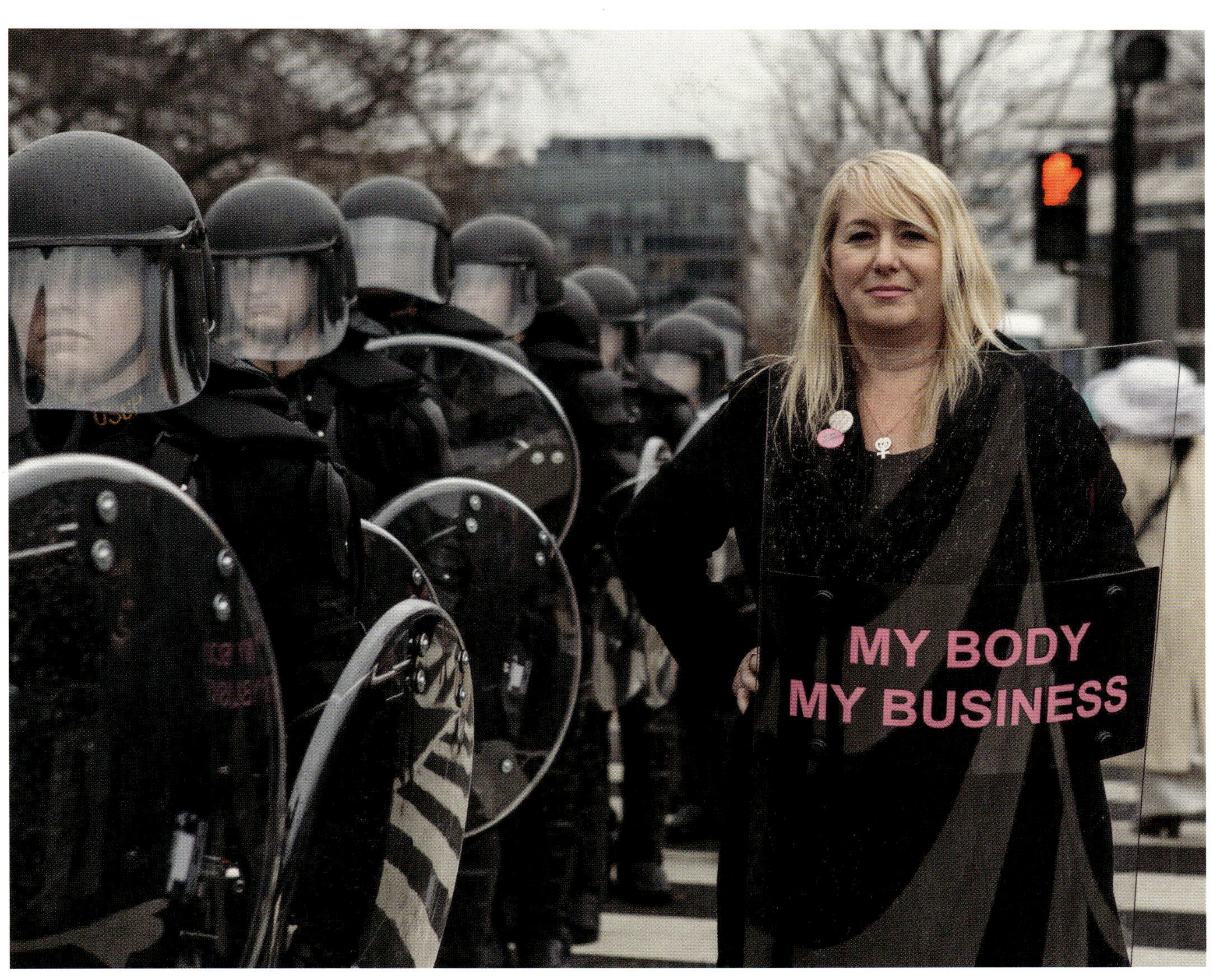

Michele Pred. *ABOUT-FACE, Inauguration Day, Washington, DC, January 20, 2017*, 2017. Digital print: dimensions variable. Photographer: Nick Thomas. Image ©Michele Pred. *Courtesy of the artist*

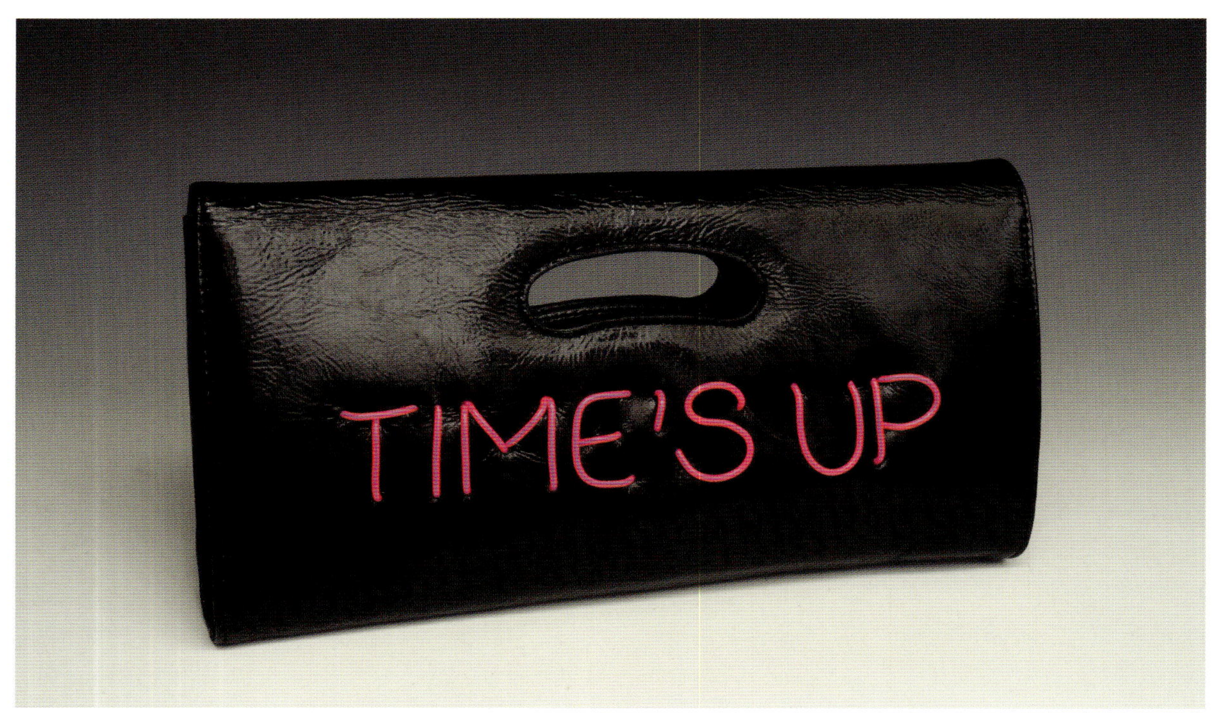

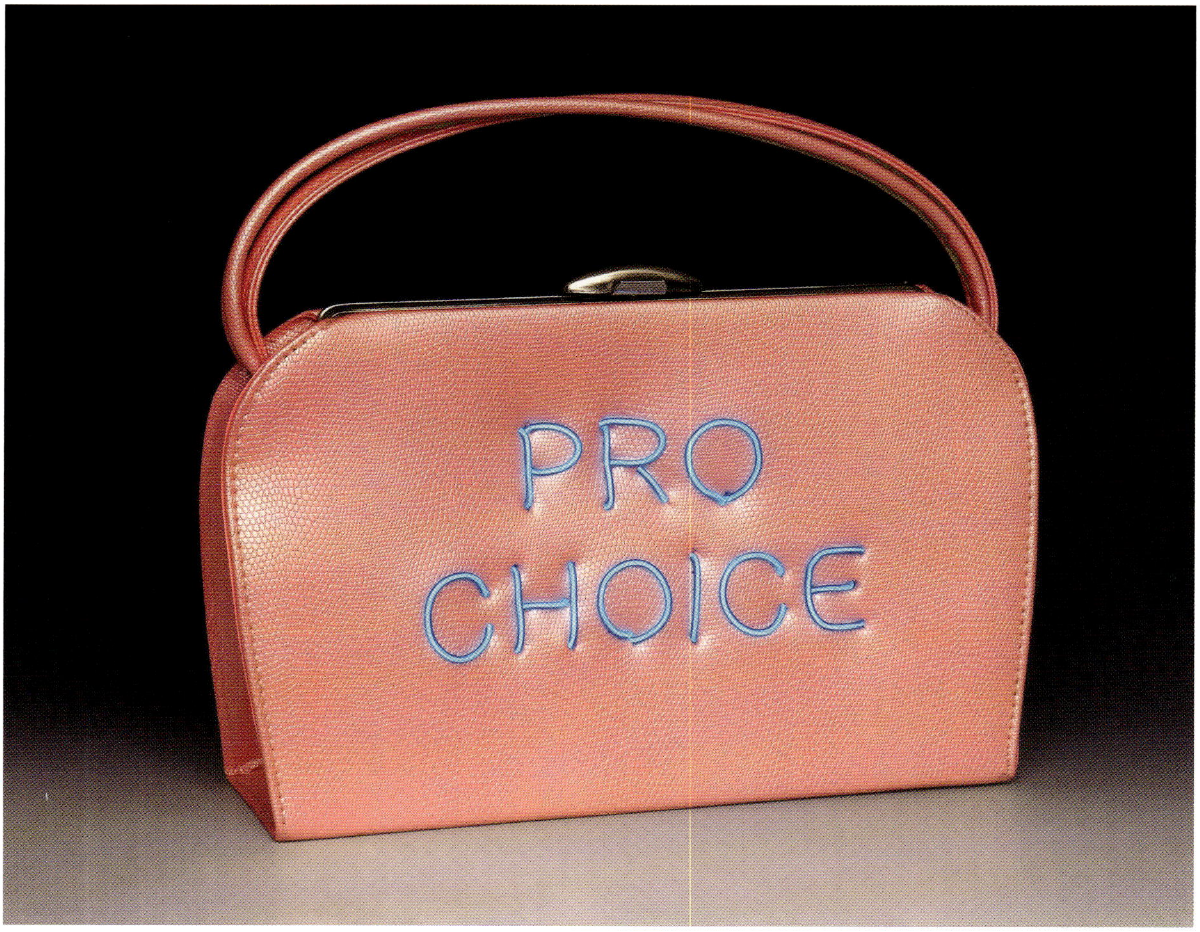

Michele Pred. *Time's Up, 2018.* Electroluminescent wire on vintage purse: 6.5 × 12 × 1.5 inches, AP. *Courtesy of the artist and Nancy Hoffman Gallery, New York*

Michele Pred. *Pro Choice*, 2015. Electroluminescent wire on vintage purse: 11 × 12 × 3 inches. *Courtesy of the artist and Nancy Hoffman Gallery, New York*

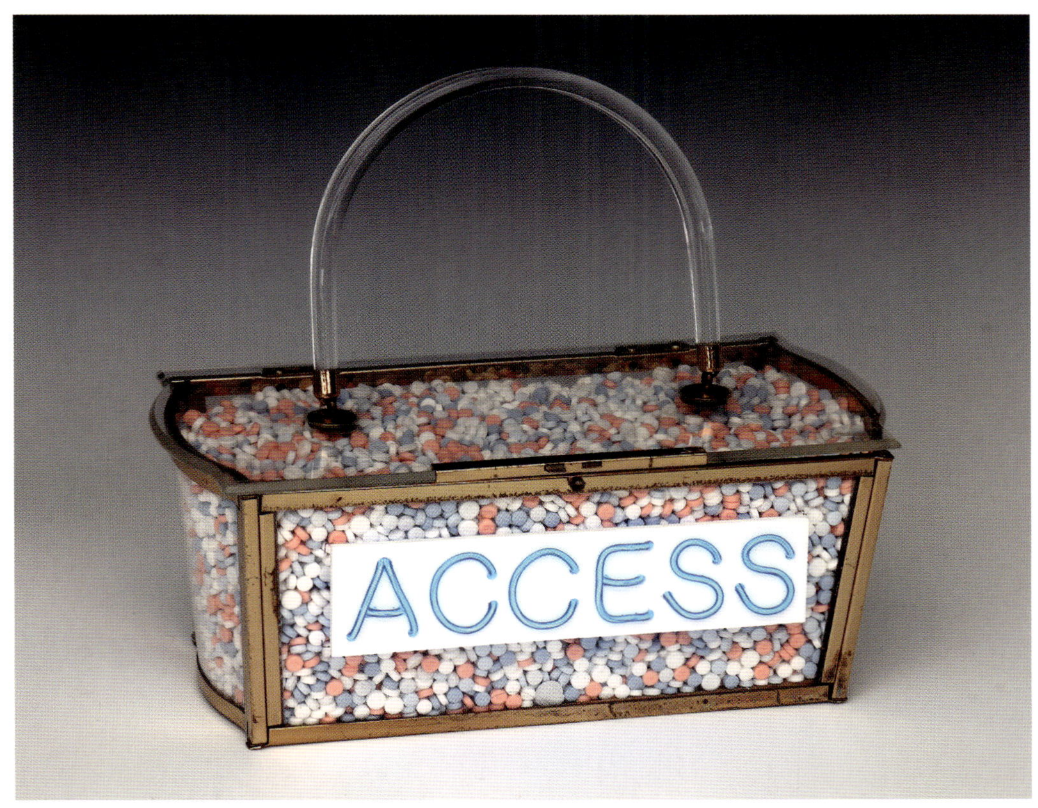

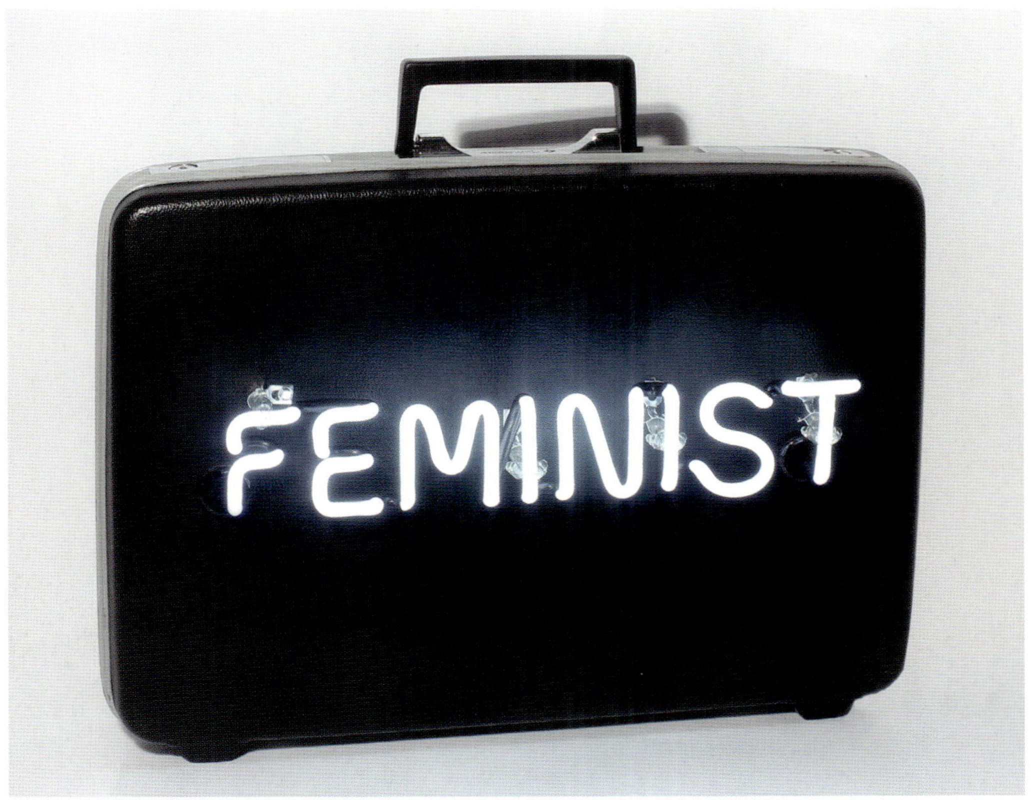

Michele Pred. *Access*, 2015. Expired birth control pills, vintage Lucite purse, electroluminescent wire, enamel, and Plexiglas: 9 × 9 × 5 inches. *Courtesy of the artist and Nancy Hoffman Gallery, New York*

Michele Pred. *Feminist*, 2015. Neon on vintage briefcase: 12 × 18 × 5 inches. *Courtesy of the artist and Nancy Hoffman Gallery, New York*

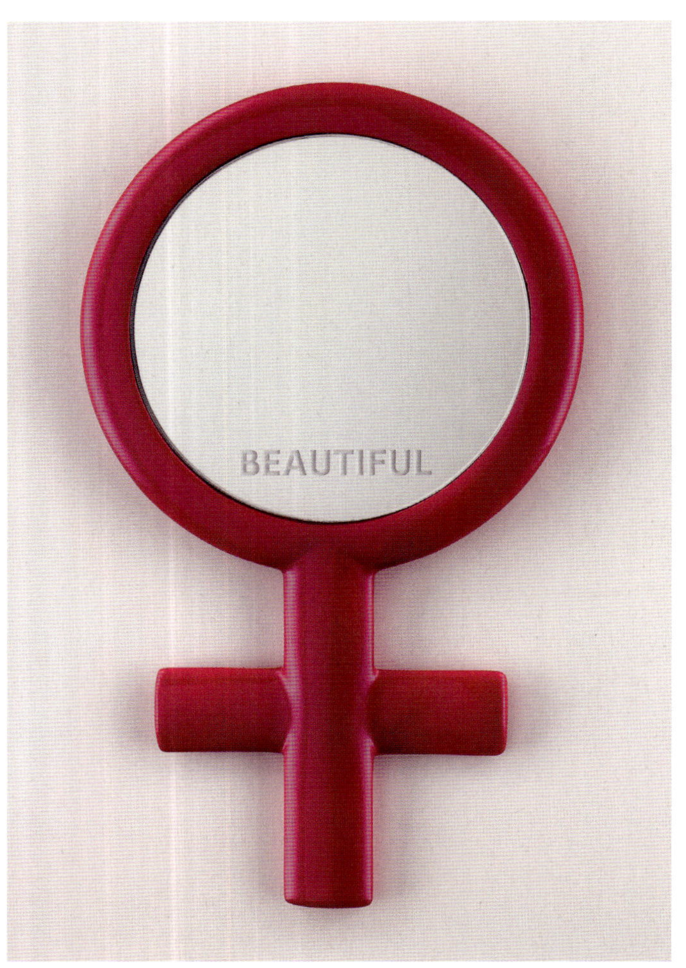

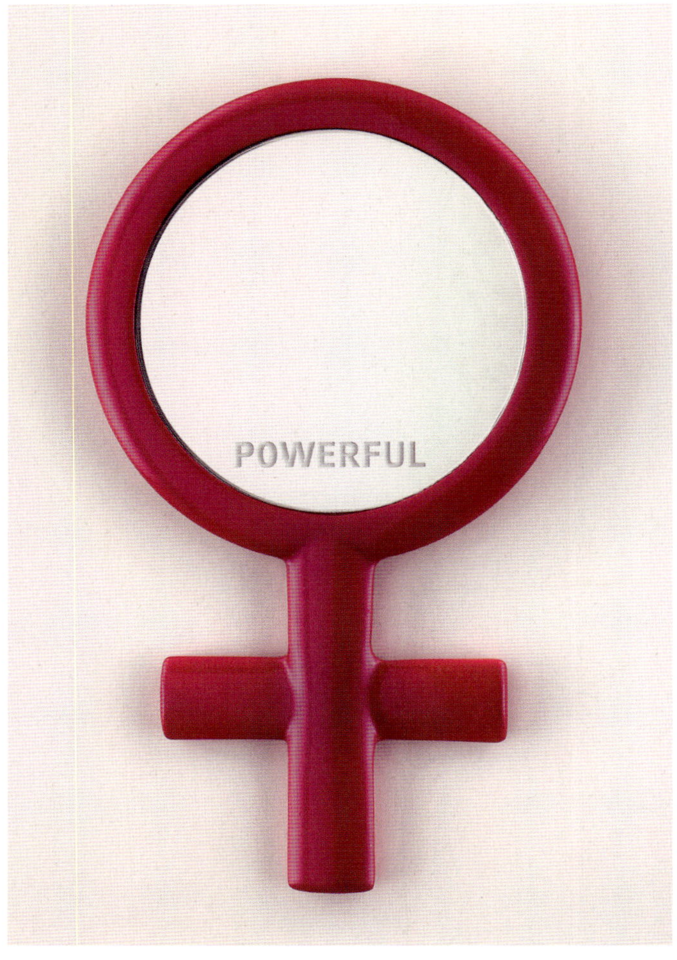

Michele Pred. *Reflections (Beautiful)*, 2015. Resin, mirrored glass, and enamel: 11 × 7 × .5 inches. Edition 1 of 3. *Courtesy of the artist and Nancy Hoffman Gallery, New York*

Michele Pred. *Reflections (Powerful)*, 2015. Resin, mirrored glass, and enamel: 11 × 7 × .5 inches. Edition 1 of 3. *Courtesy of the artist and Nancy Hoffman Gallery, New York*

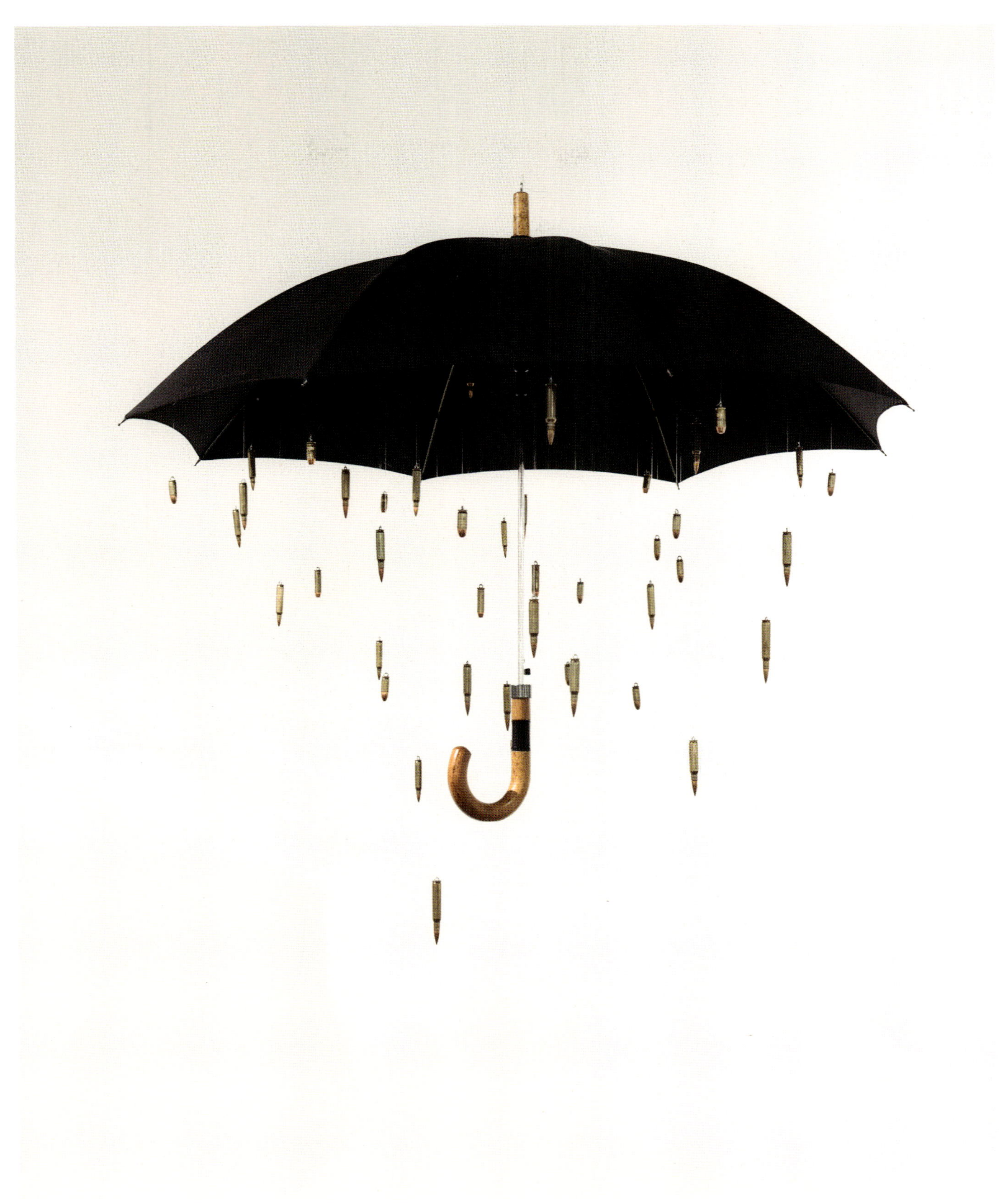

Michele Pred. *Security Storm*, 2016. Umbrella, bullets, and enamel: 40 × 40 × 39 inches. *Courtesy of the artist and Nancy Hoffman Gallery, New York*

MICKALENE THOMAS

Mickalene Thomas is a 2015 United States Artists Francie Bishop Good & David Horvitz Fellow, distinguished visual artist, filmmaker and curator who has exhibited extensively both nationally and internationally. She is known for paintings that combine art-historical, political, and popcultural references. Her work introduces complex notions of femininity and challenges common definitions of beauty and aesthetic representations of women.

Thomas holds an MFA from Yale University and a BFA from Pratt Institute. Her upcoming solo museum exhibitions include *I Can't See You Without Me* at Wexner Center for the Arts, Columbus, Ohio (2018) and *Mentors, Muses, and Celebrities* at Art Gallery of Ontario, Toronto (2018). Recent solo exhibitions include *Mickalene Thomas: Do I Look Like a Lady?* at Museum of Contemporary Art, Los Angeles and *Muse: Mickalene Thomas Photographs* at Aperture Foundation, which features her notably curated exhibition *tête-à-tête* and is scheduled to travel to several venues across the United States in 2019. Previous solo museum exhibitions include *Waiting on a Prime-Time Star* at Moody Center for the Arts (2017); *Waiting on a Prime-Time Star* at Newcomb Art Museum of Tulane (2017); the Aspen Art Museum (2016); L'Ecole des Beaux Arts, Monaco (2014); and the Brooklyn Museum (2012-2013). Recent group shows include *Figuring History* at Seattle Art Museum and *You Are Here* at North Carolina Museum of Art. Thomas's work is in the permanent collections of Museum of Modern Art, New York; the Brooklyn Museum, Brooklyn; the Solomon R. Guggenheim Museum, New York; the Whitney Museum of American Art, New York; the Hammer Museum, Los Angeles; and the Smithsonian American Art Museum, Washington, DC, among others. Thomas is represented by Lehmann Maupin, New York and Hong Kong; Kavi Gupta Gallery, Chicago; and Galerie Nathalie Obadia, Paris and Brussels. She lives and works in New York.

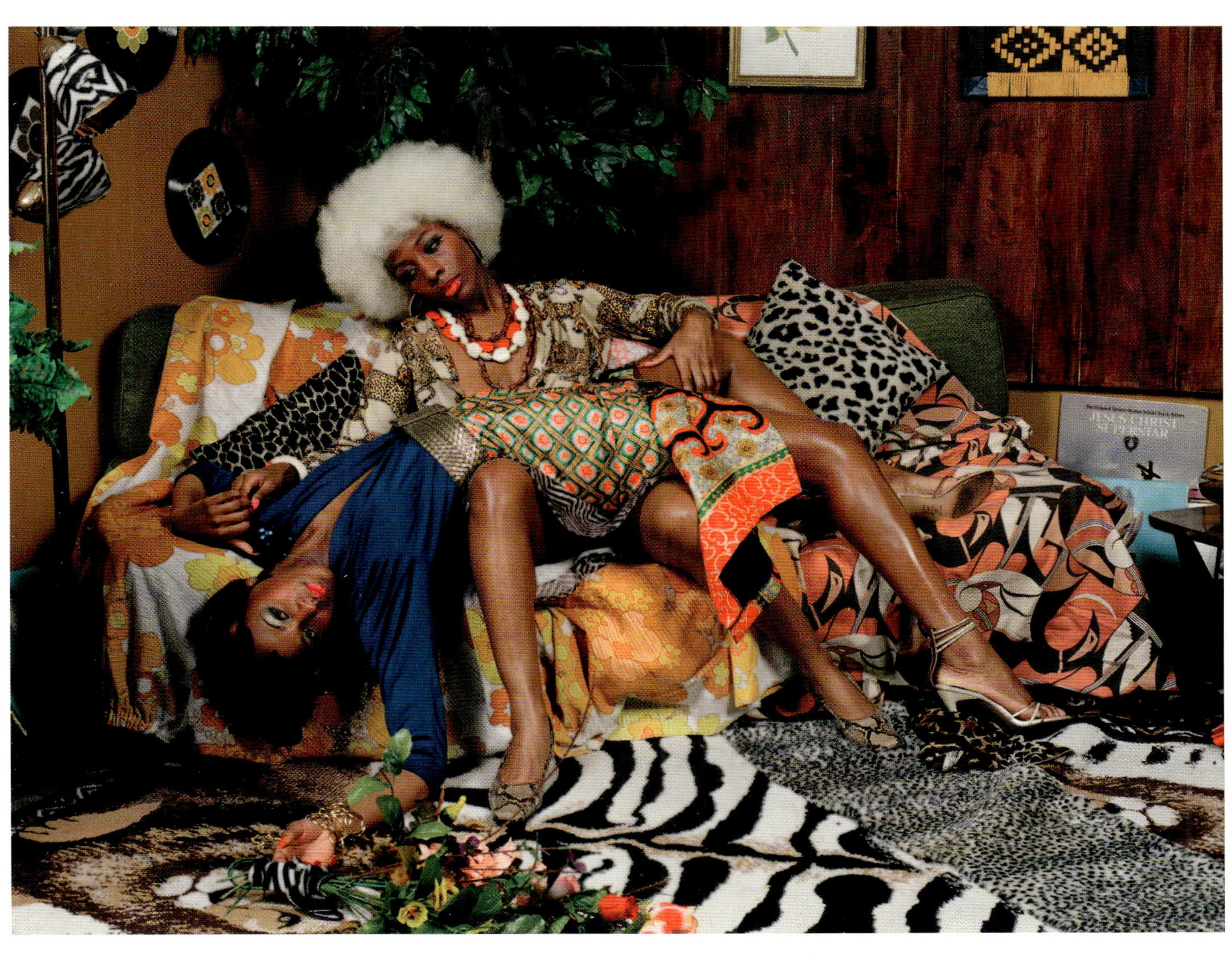

Mickalene Thomas. *La leçon d'amour*, 2008. C-print: 30 × 30 inches. *Courtesy of the artist and Artists Rights Society (ARS), New York*

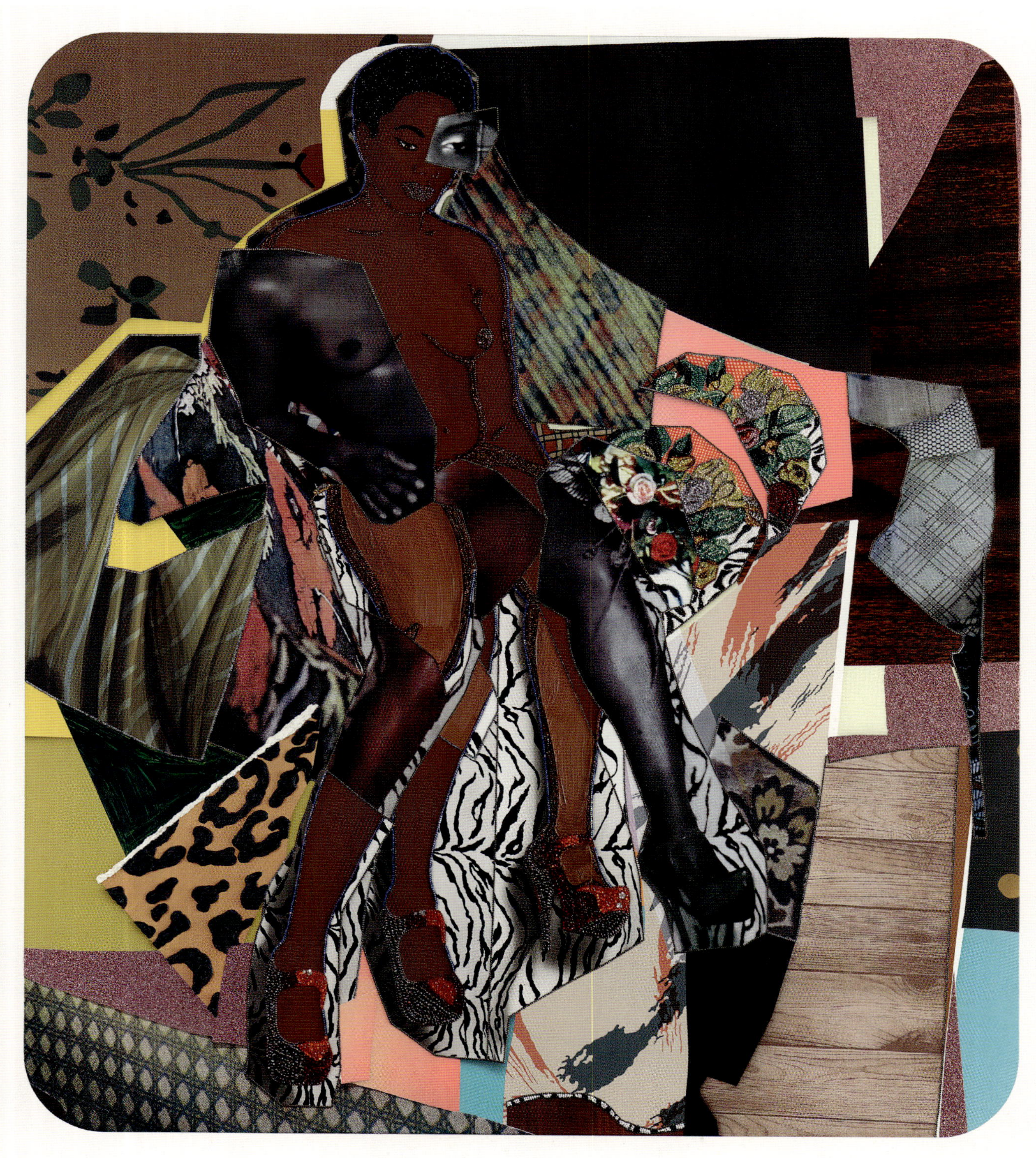

Mickalene Thomas. *Marie with Four Legs*, 2014. Color photograph and paper collage on archival board: 26.5 × 20.5 inches. *Courtesy of the artist and Artists Rights Society (ARS), New York*

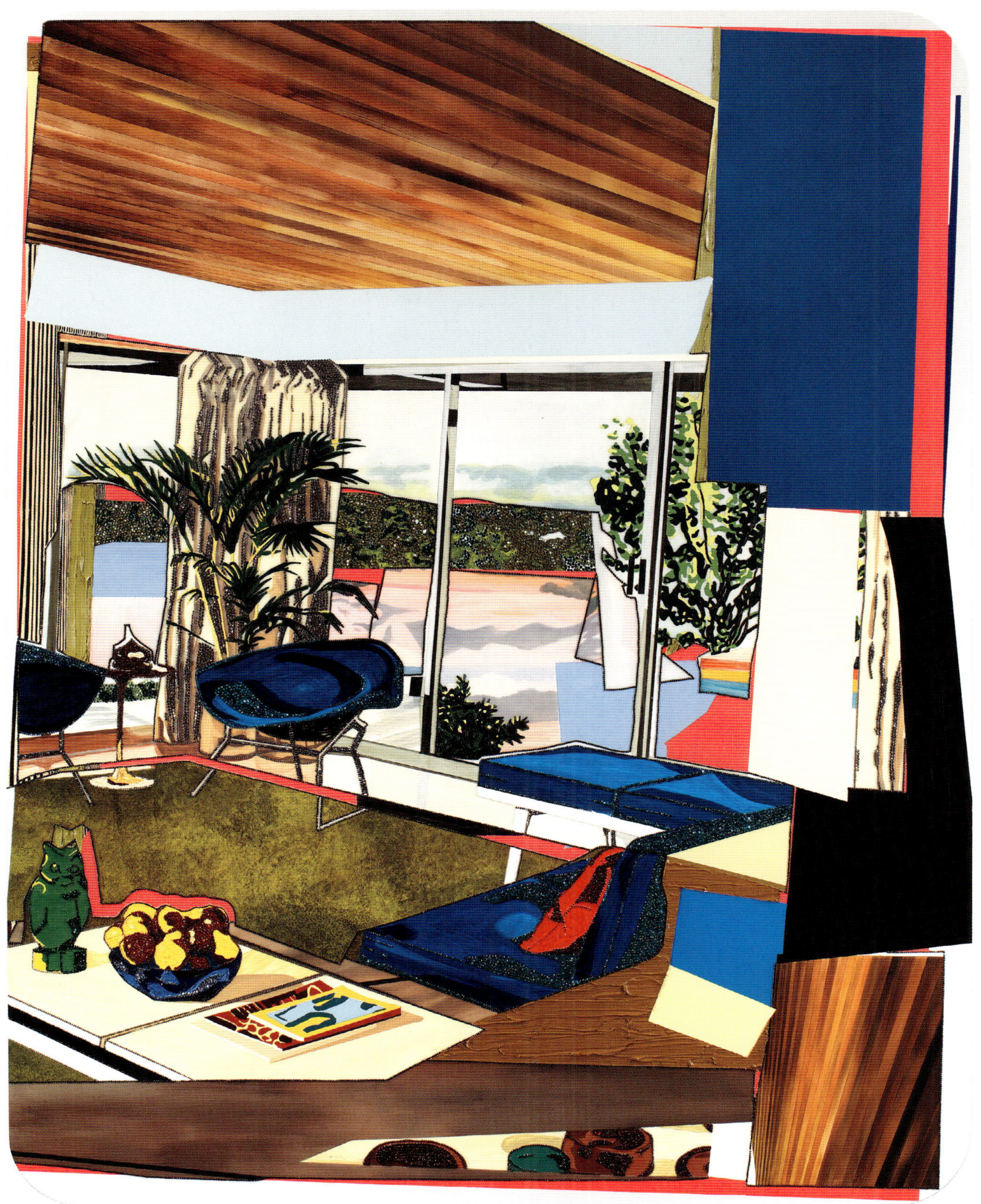

Mickalene Thomas. *Interior: Blue Couch with Green Owl*, 2012. Rhinestones, acrylic, oil, and enamel on wood panel: 108 × 84 inches. *Courtesy of the artist and Artists Rights Society (ARS), New York*

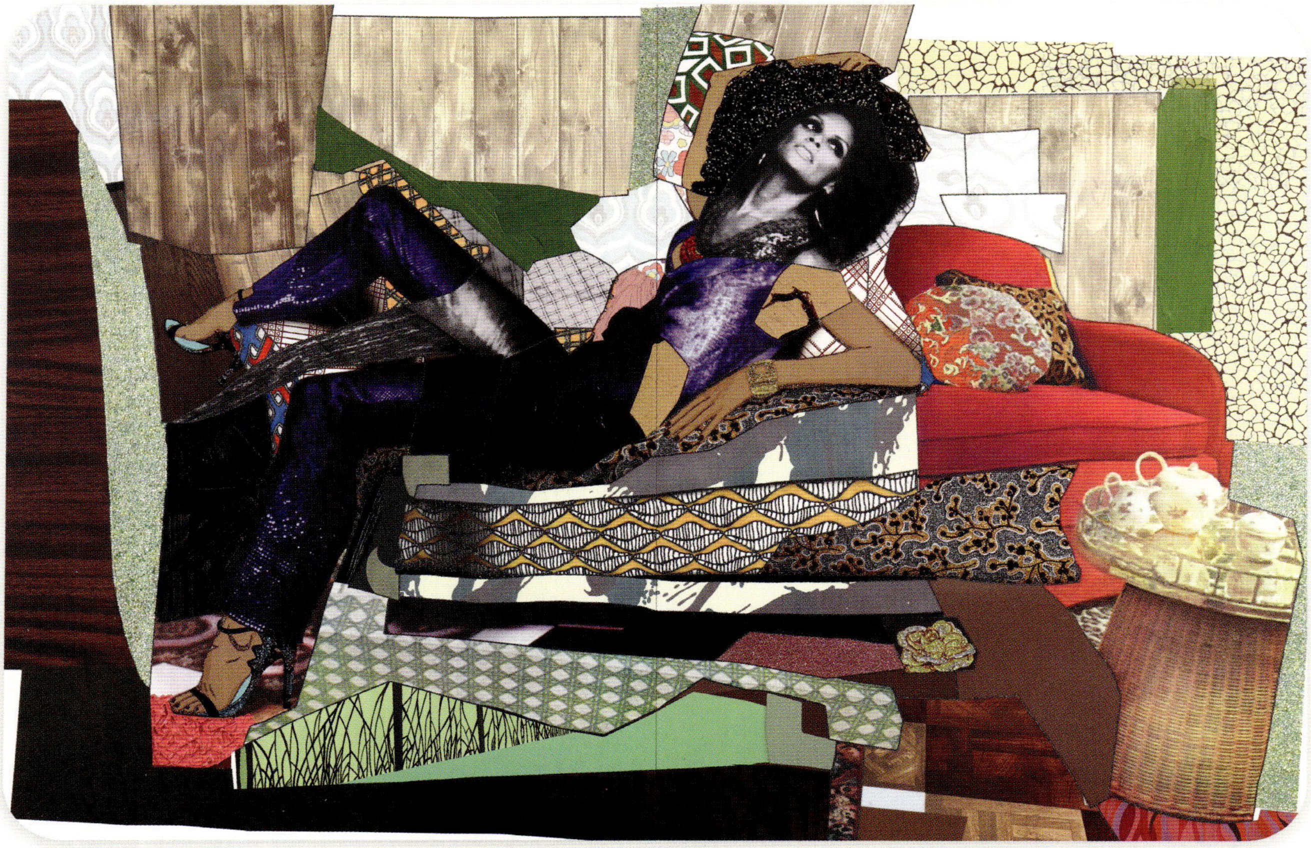

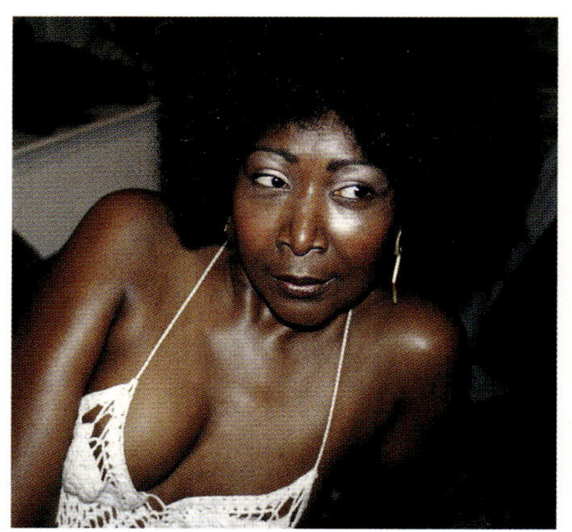

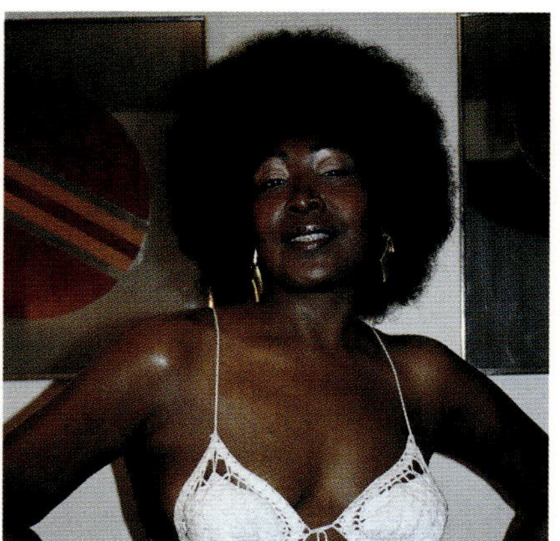

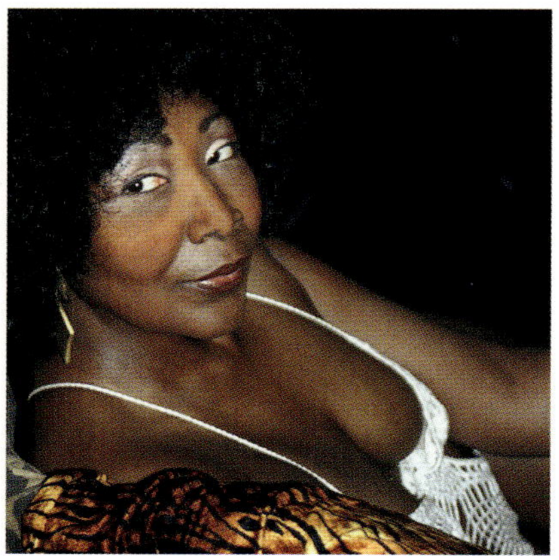

Mickalene Thomas. *Raquel Reclining Wearing Purple Jumpsuit*, 2014. Color photograph and paper collage on archival board: 28 × 41.5 inches. *Courtesy of the artist and Artists Rights Society (ARS), New York*

Mickalene Thomas. *Lounging, Standing, Looking*, 2003. C-print: 30 × 30 inches (each); 30 × 94 inches (overall). *Courtesy of the artist and Artists Rights Society (ARS), New York*

NALINI MALANI

Widely considered the pioneer of video art in India, Nalini Malani explores drawing, painting, and the extension of those mediums into projected animation, video, and film. Her works in new media often take the form of monumental and immersive shadow play pieces that create mesmerizing layers of imagery and sound. Committed to the role of the artist as social activist, Malani focuses on creating dynamic visual stories about those who have been ignored, forgotten, or marginalized by history. Drawn from history, culture, and her direct experience as a refugee of the Partition of India and the legacy of colonialism and decolonization, Malani's work explores violence, the feminine, and the politics of national identity. Malani's work is represented in numerous public collections, including the Asia Society Museum, New York City; Centre Georges Pompidou, Paris; and the Museum of Modern Art, New York City. Malani's solo exhibitions include the Stedelijk Museum, The Netherlands (2017); the Institute of Contemporary Art, Boston (2016); and the Kiran Nader Museum of Art, India (2014). In 2017, the Centre Georges Pompidou presented Part I of Malani's retrospective; Part II was shown in 2018 at Castello di Rivoli Museum of Contemporary Art. Malani was born in 1946 in Karachi, India. She currently lives and works in India and Europe.

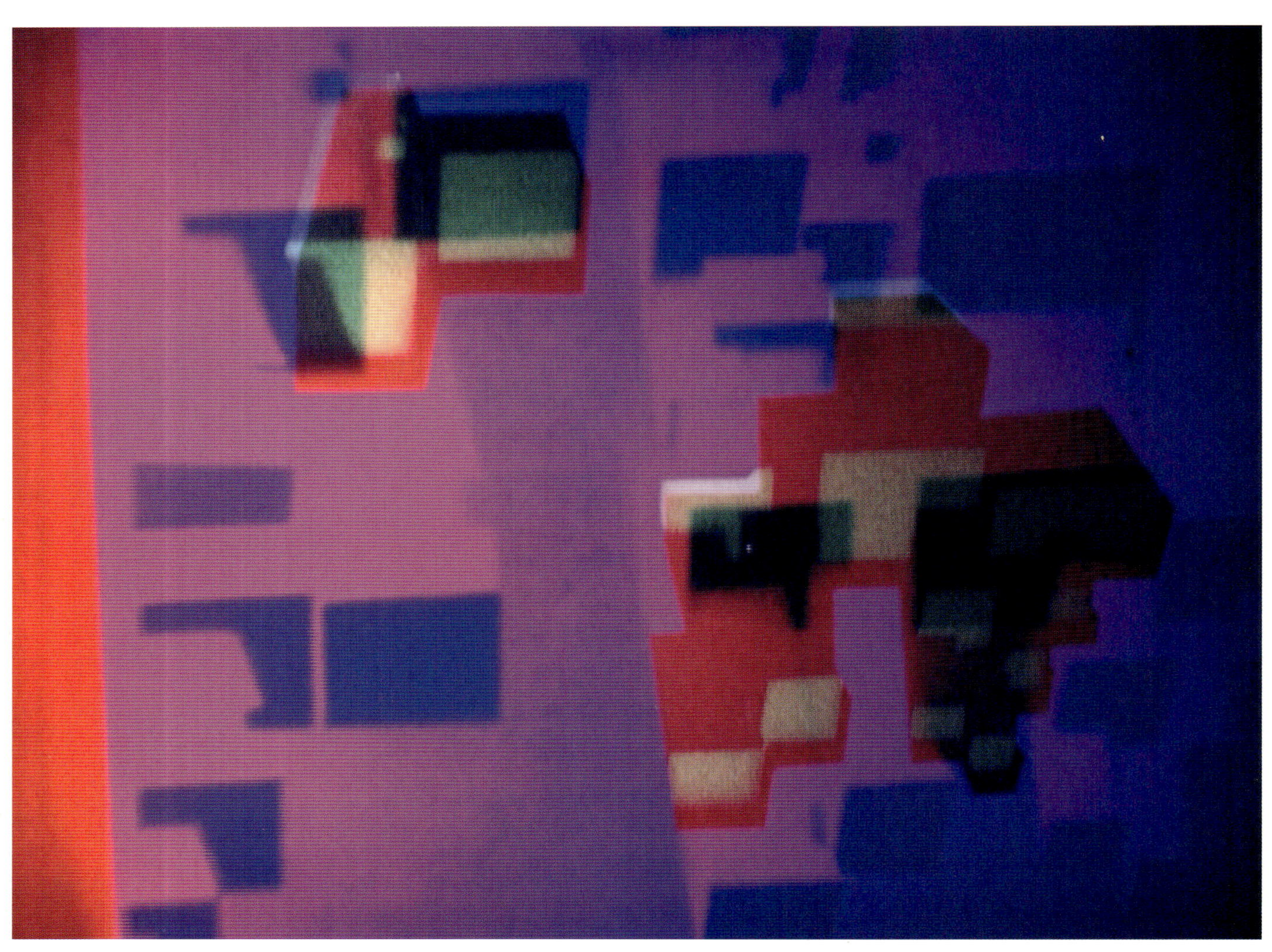

Nalini Malani. *Dream Houses*, 1969. 8 mm color stop motion animation. Collection of the Museum of Modern Art, New York. Image ©Nalini Malani. *Courtesy of the artist and Galerie Lelong & Co.*

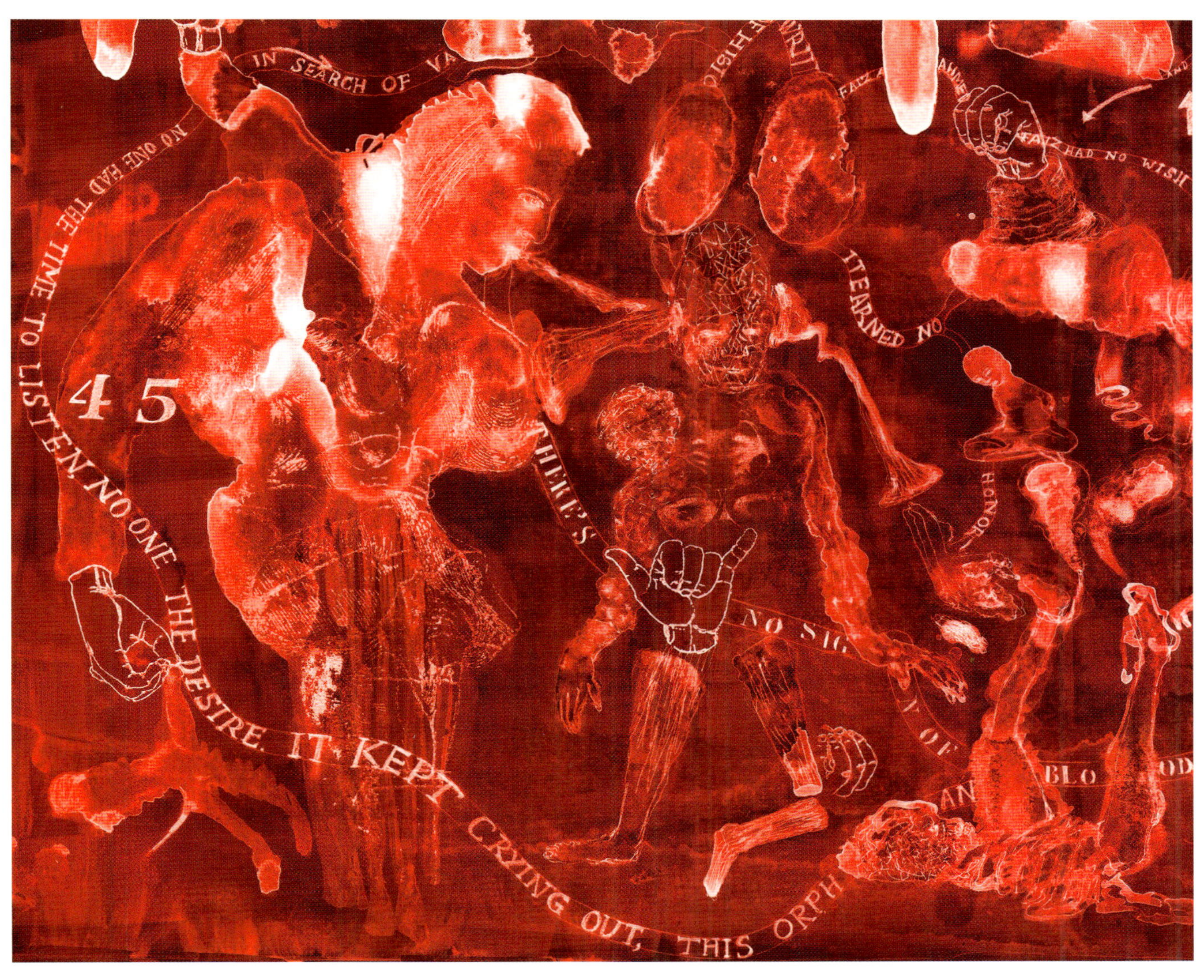

Nalini Malani. *In Search of Vanished Blood,* 2012. Digital pigment print with hand-painted acrylic on Hahnemuhle bamboo paper: 36.5 × 43.5 inches. Image ©Nalini Malani. *Courtesy of the artist and Galerie Lelong & Co.*

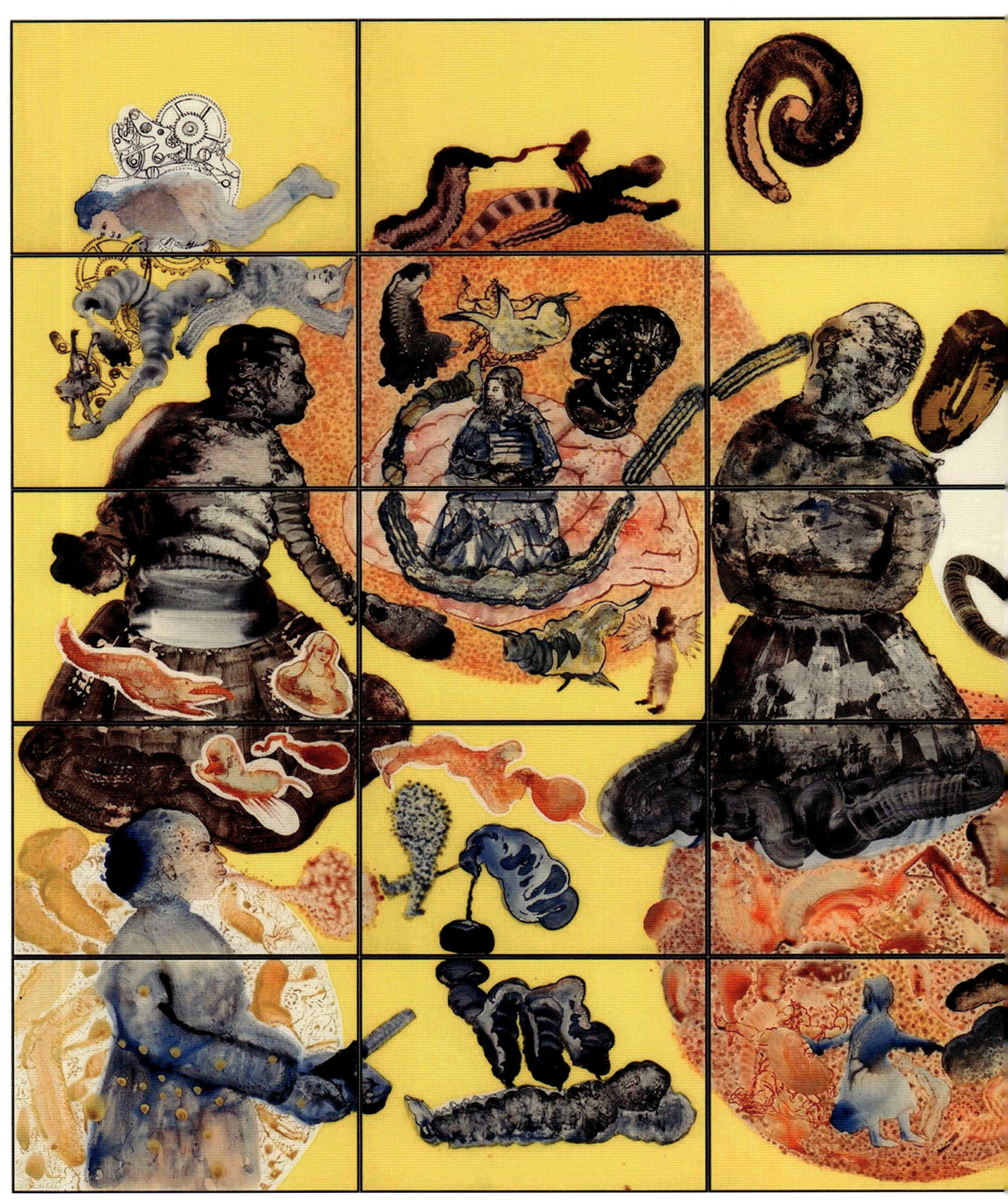

Nalini Malani. *Cassandra*, 2009. Thirty-panel reverse painting on acrylic sheet: 17.7 × 26 inches each. Collection Kiran Nadar Museum of Art, New Delhi. Image ©Nalini Malani. *Courtesy of the artist and Galerie Lelong & Co.*

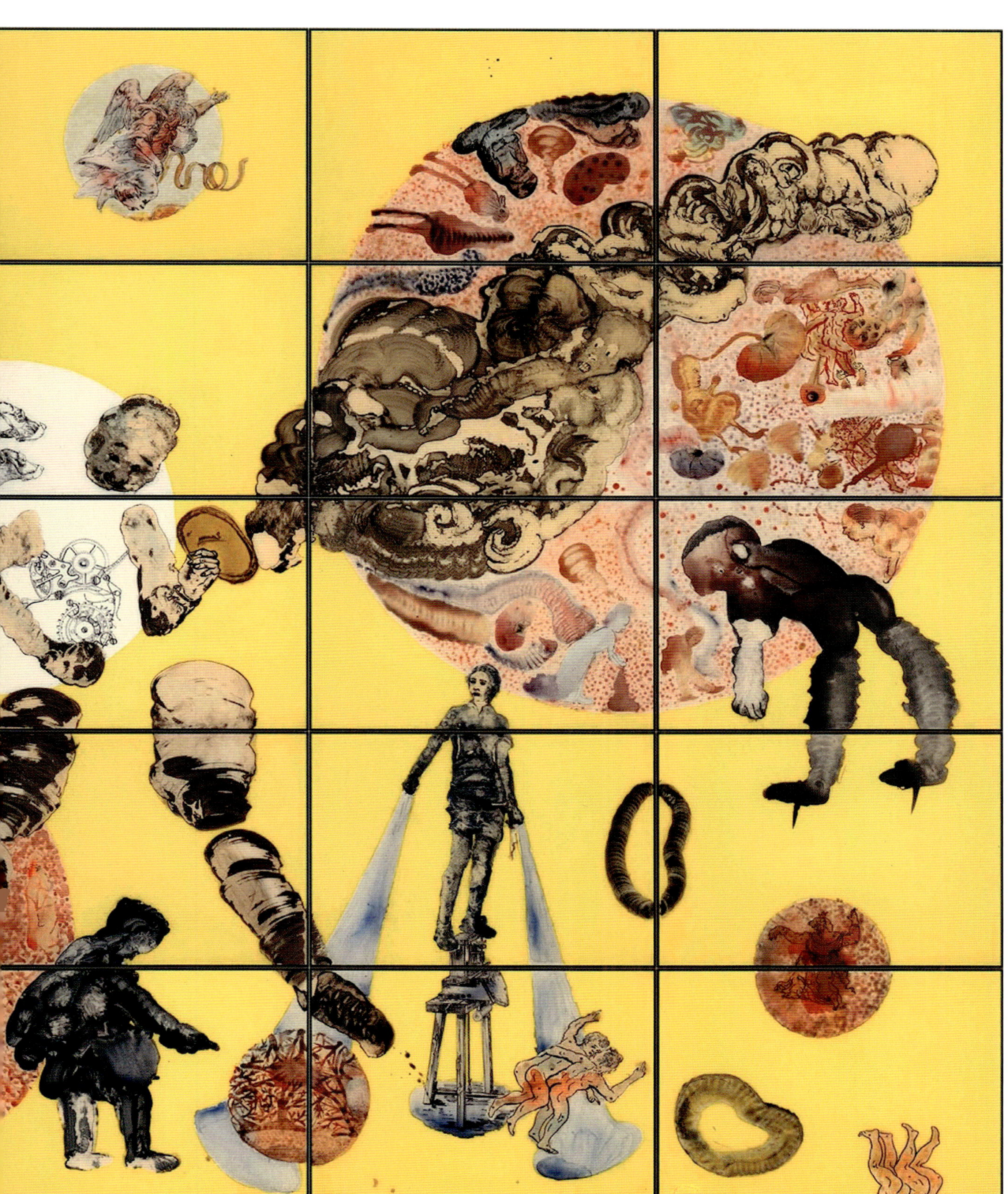

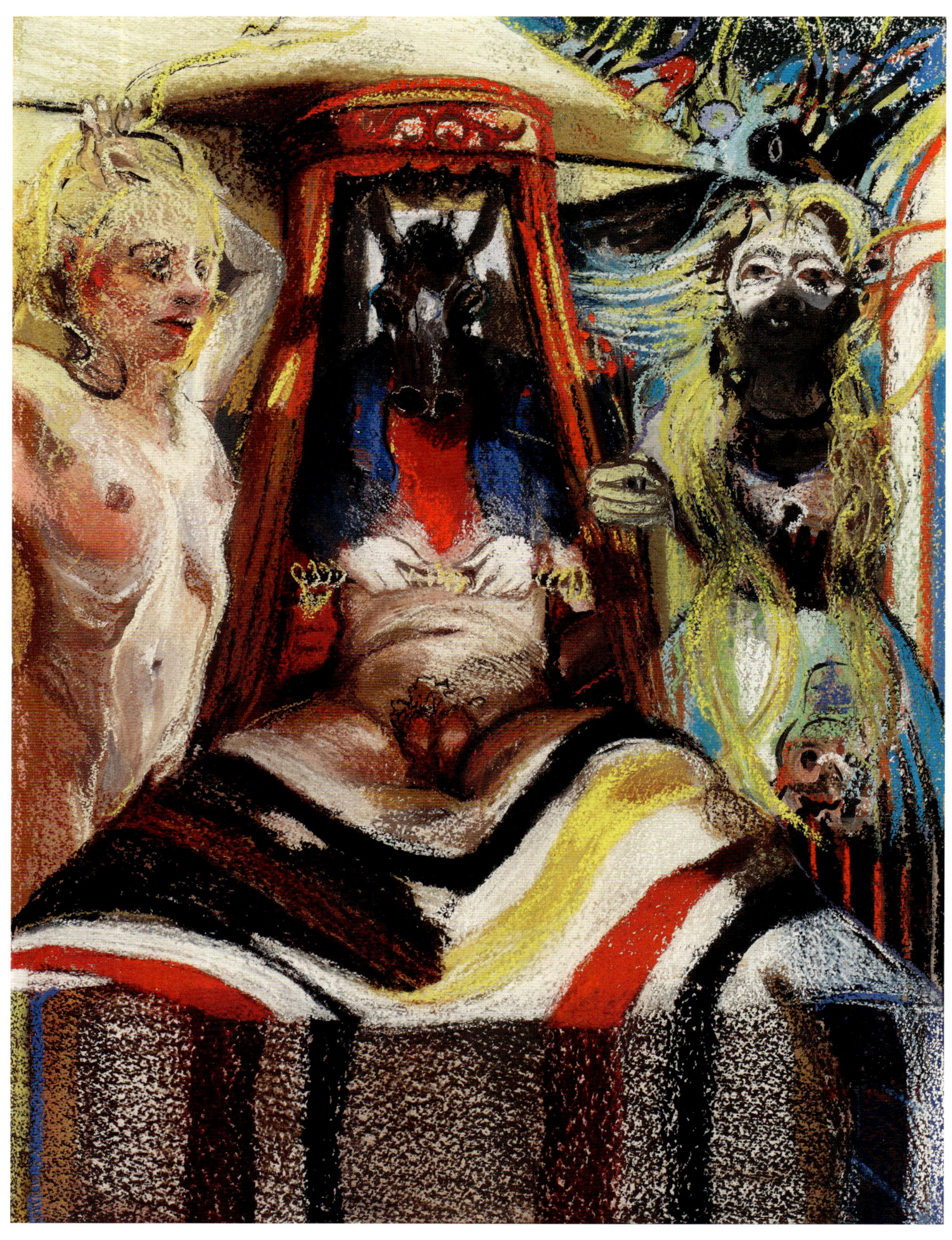

Natalie Frank. *All Fur I*, 2011–14. Gouache and chalk pastel on paper: 22 × 30 inches. *Courtesy of the artist*

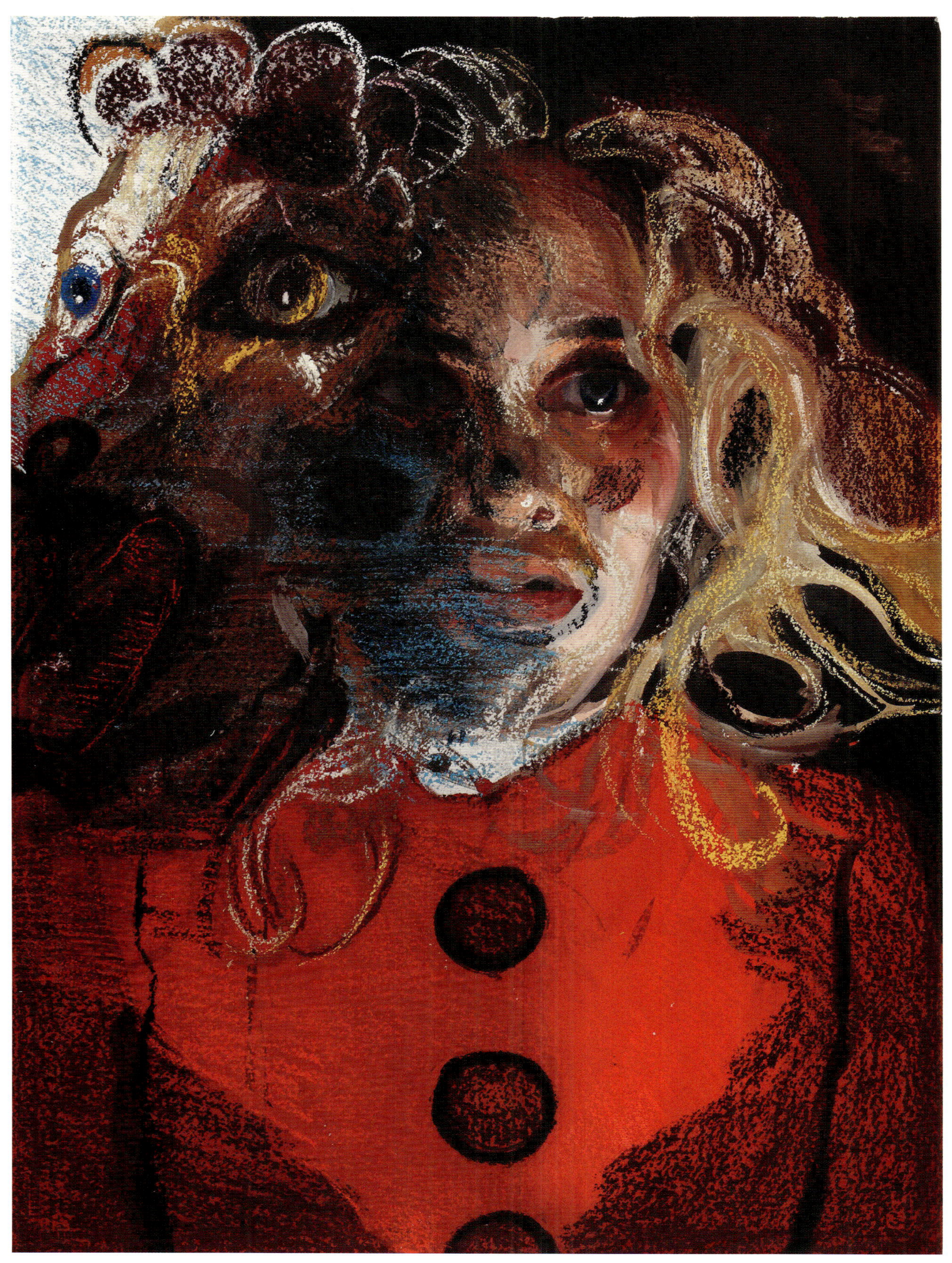

Natalie Frank. *All Fur II*, 2011–14. Gouache and chalk pastel on paper: 22 × 30 inches. *Courtesy of the artist*

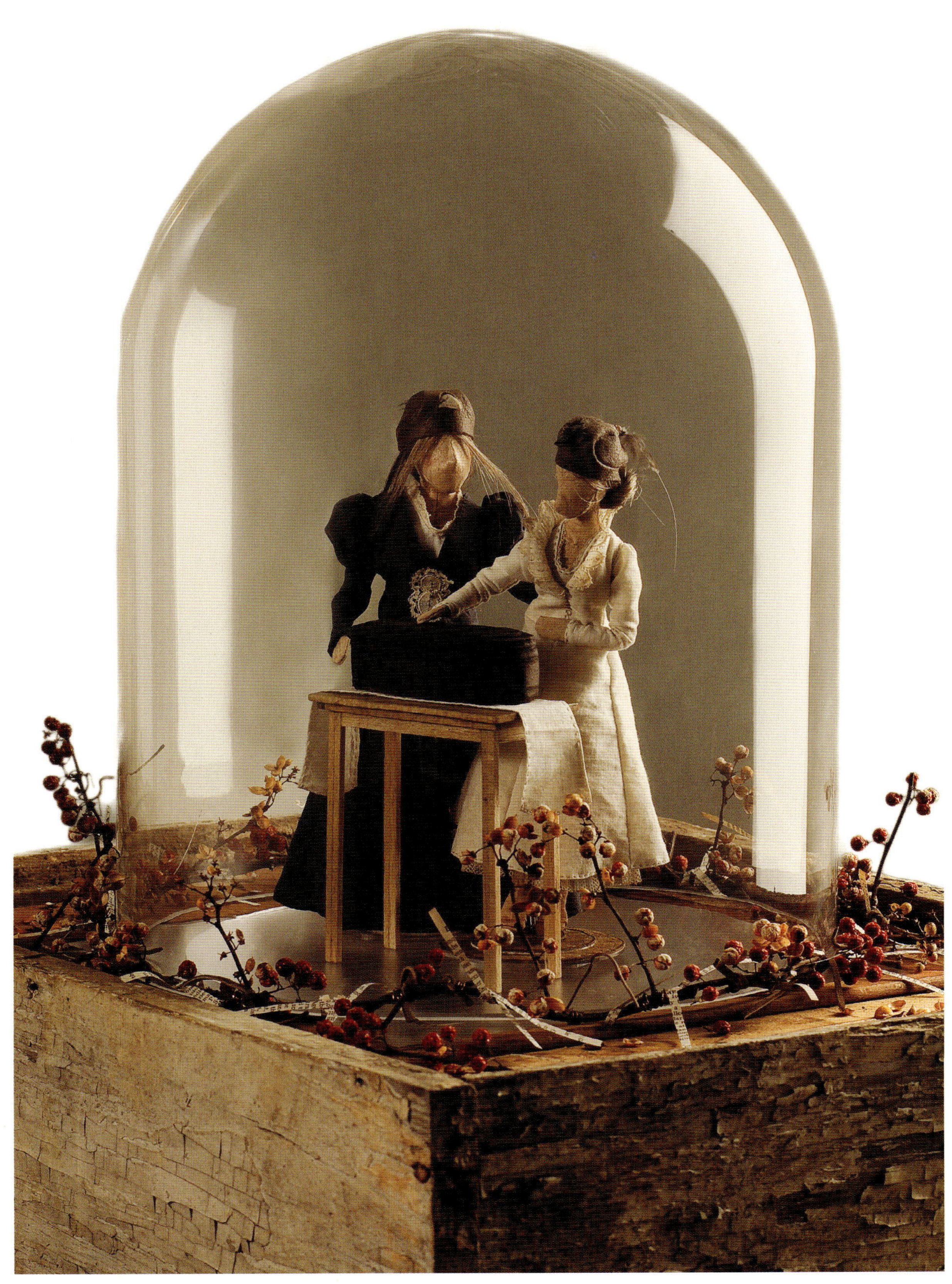

Page Turner. *Beautiful Zion Built Above*, 2015.
Assemblage, hand stitched from personal and found objects: 32 × 22 × 27 inches.
Image ©Sean Cuddy / Cuddy Photography.
Courtesy of the artist

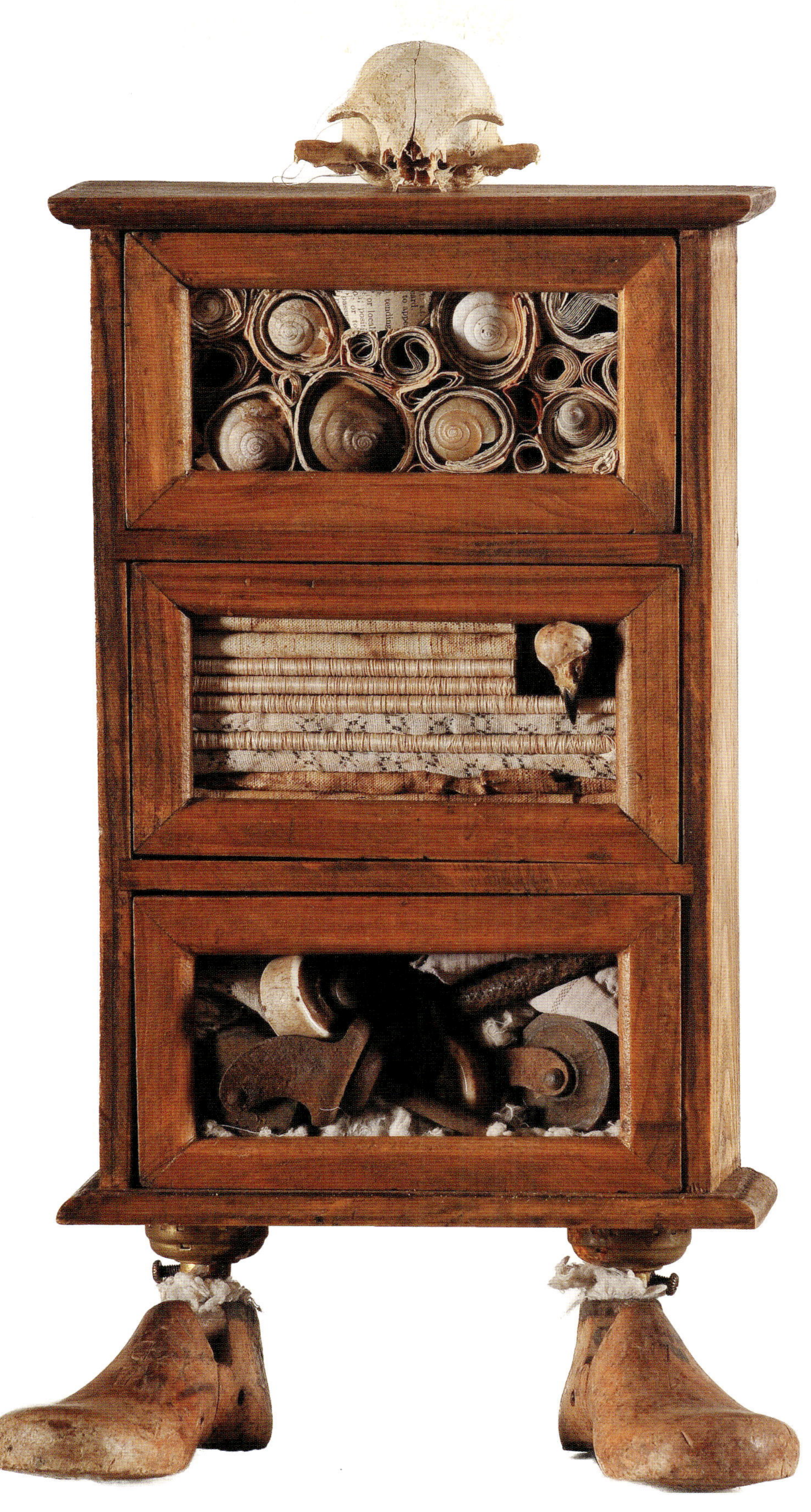

Page Turner. *Tiny Toes*, 2012. Assemblage, found and family objects: 10 × 4 × 3 inches. Image ©Sean Cuddy / Cuddy Photography. *Courtesy of the artist*

PATRICIA PICCININI

Patricia Piccinini is an Australian artist who is known for her work in painting, video, sound, installation, digital prints, and sculpture. Her work depicts the wondrous evolution of nature and organic beauty through warping natural images seen as familiar to society. Although surreal and strange, Piccinini's art often has a message meant to show viewers a new perspective on nature and even their own bodies.

Piccinini's notable work includes *The Stags*, *The Young Family*, *Graham*, and *The Skywhale*, a balloon commissioned for the Centenary of Canberra in 2013. In 2003, her exhibition *We Are Family* represented Australia at the 50th Venice Biennale before touring to the Hara Museum, Tokyo. Her solo survey exhibition *ComCiência* at CCBB toured to São Paulo, Brasília, Rio De Janeiro, and Belo Horizonte in Brazil and was named the most popular contemporary art exhibition in 2016 by the *Art Newspaper*. Other solo museum exhibitions include *Curious Affection* at QAGOMA in Brisbane, Australia, *Relativity* at the Galway International Art Festival, and *Hold Me Close To Your Heart* at Arter, Istanbul. In 2017, Piccinini was appointed as Enterprise Professor in Art at the University of Melbourne.

Patricia Piccinini. *The Strength of One Arm (with Canadian Mountain Goat)*, 2009. Silicone, fiberglass, human hair, clothing, Canadian mountain goat: 70.9 × 60.6 × 22 inches. Photographer: Graham Baring. Image ©Patricia Piccinini. *Courtesy of the artist*

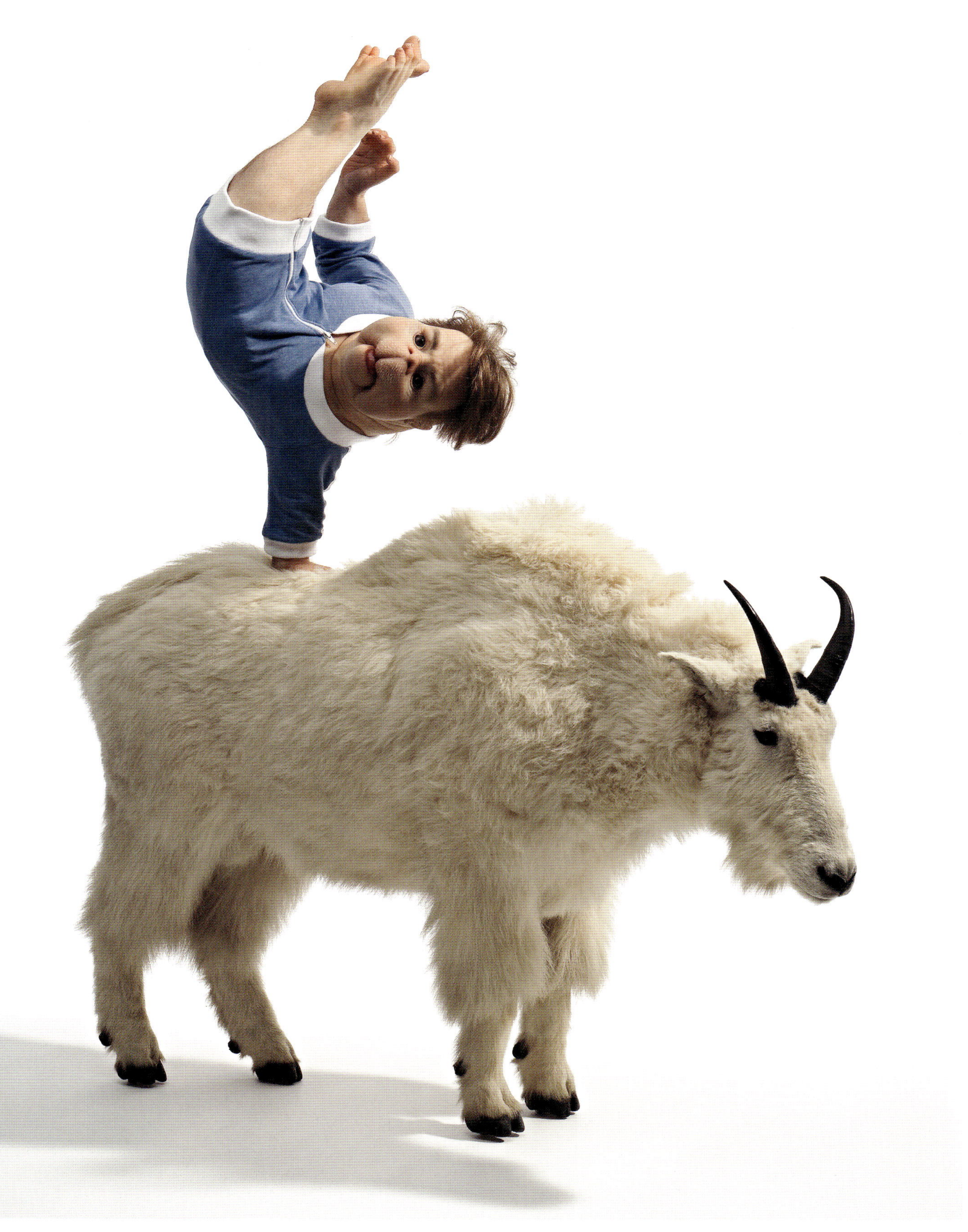

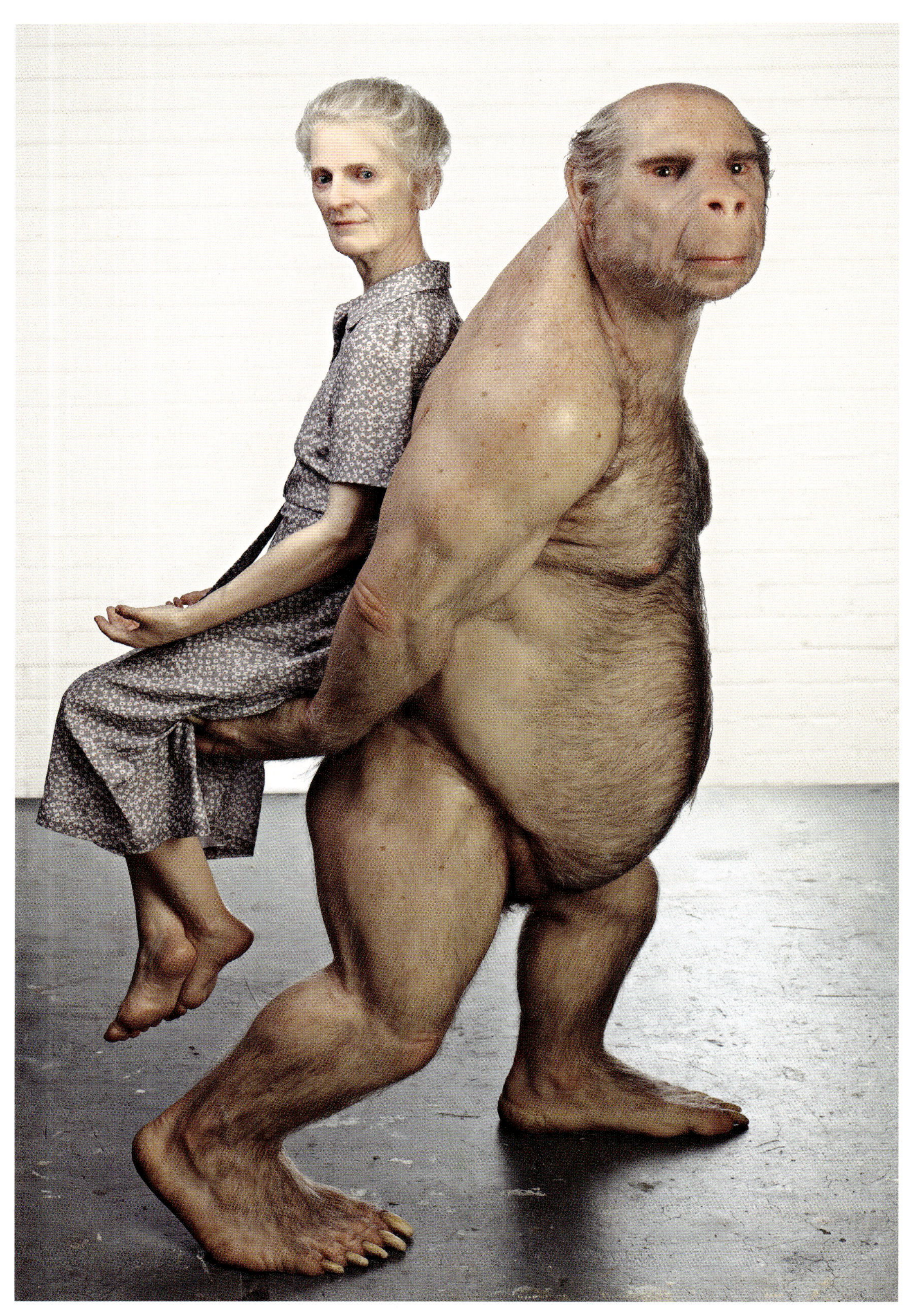

Patricia Piccinini. *The Carrier*, 2012. Silicone, fiberglass, human hair, and clothing: 66.9 × 45.2 × 75 inches. Image ©Patricia Piccinini. *Courtesy of the artist*

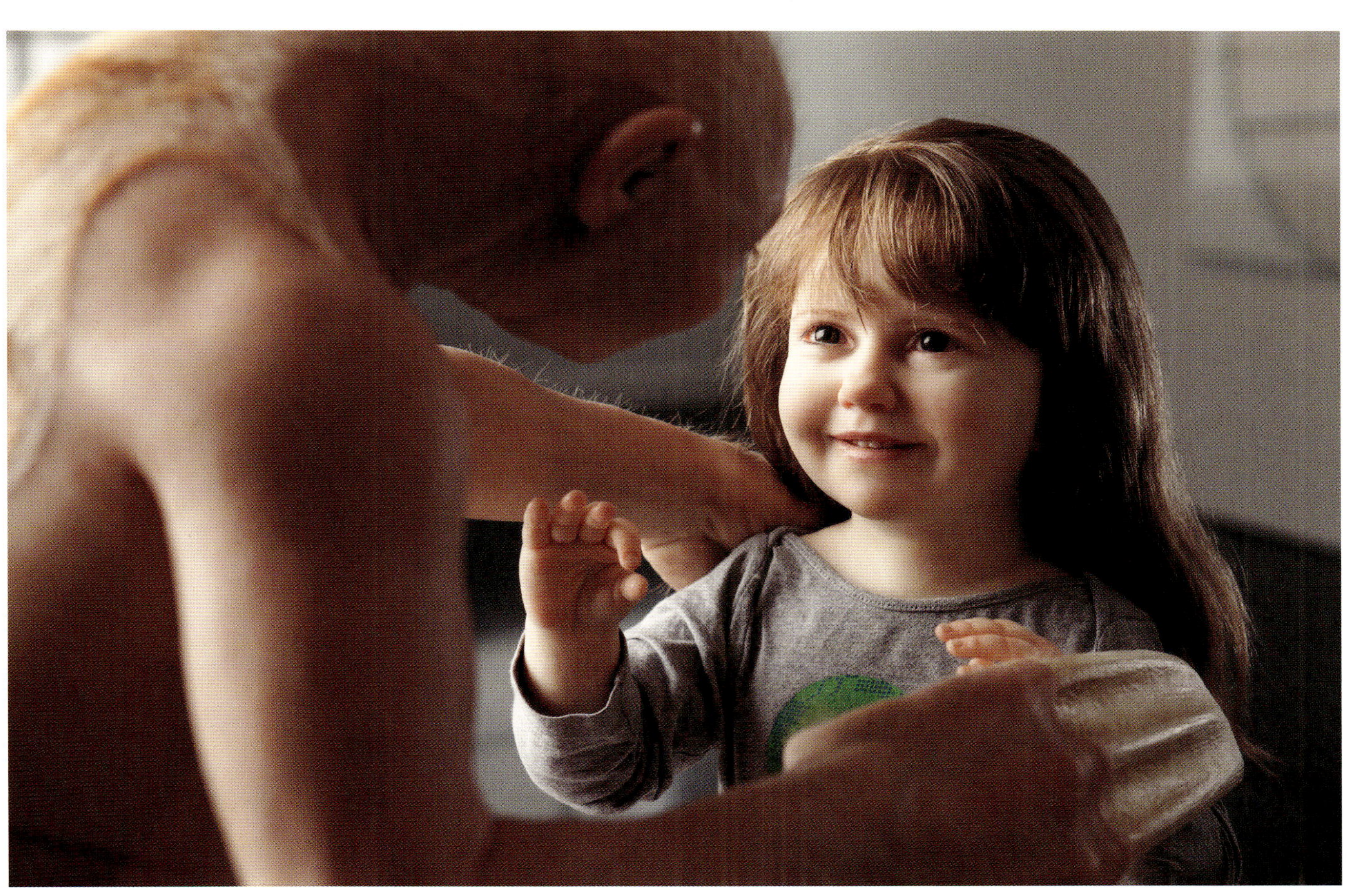

Patricia Piccinini. *The Welcome Guest*, 2011. Silicone, fiberglass, taxidermy peacocks, timber bed, and bed clothes: dimensions variable. *Courtesy of the artist*

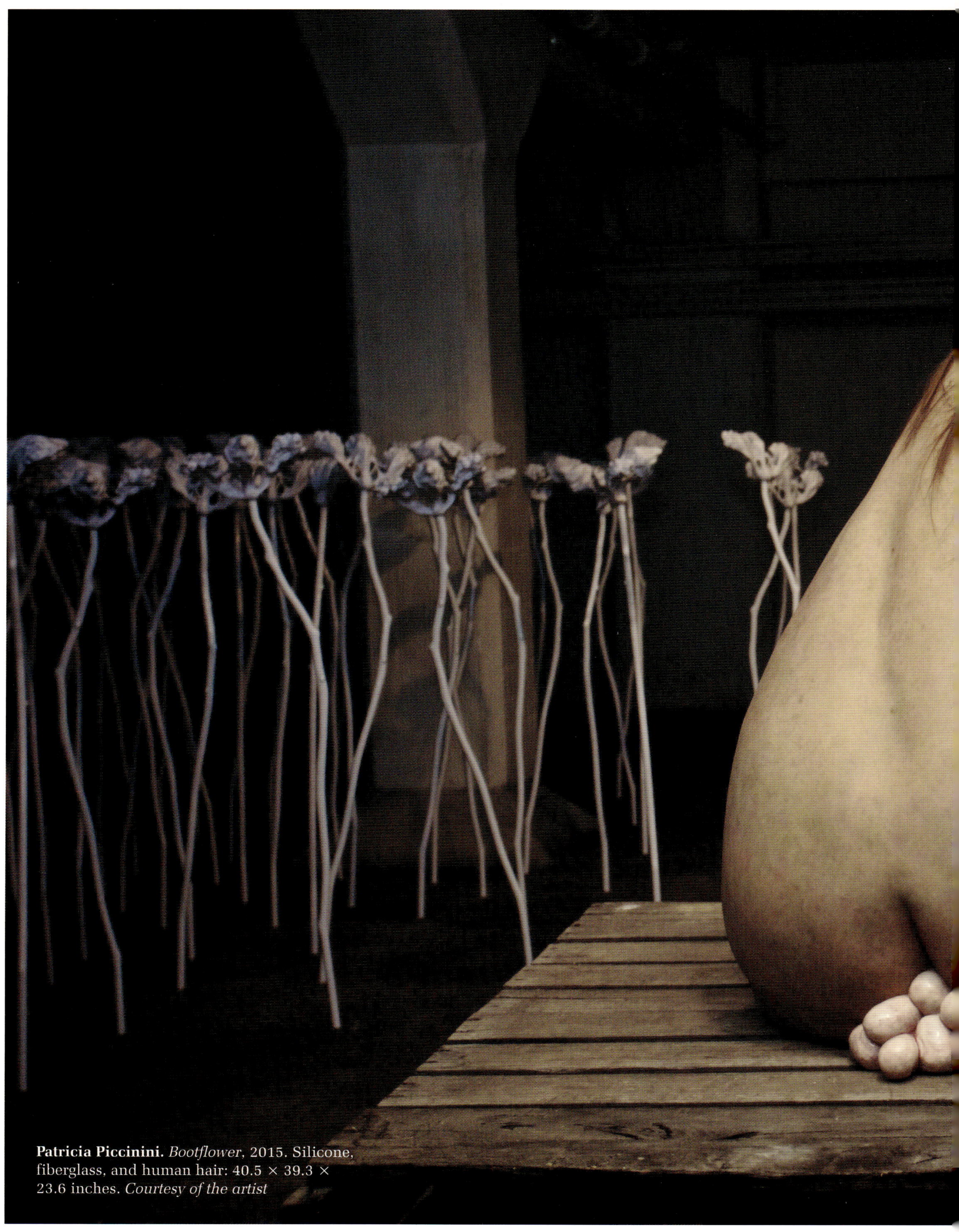

Patricia Piccinini. *Bootflower*, 2015. Silicone, fiberglass, and human hair: 40.5 × 39.3 × 23.6 inches. *Courtesy of the artist*

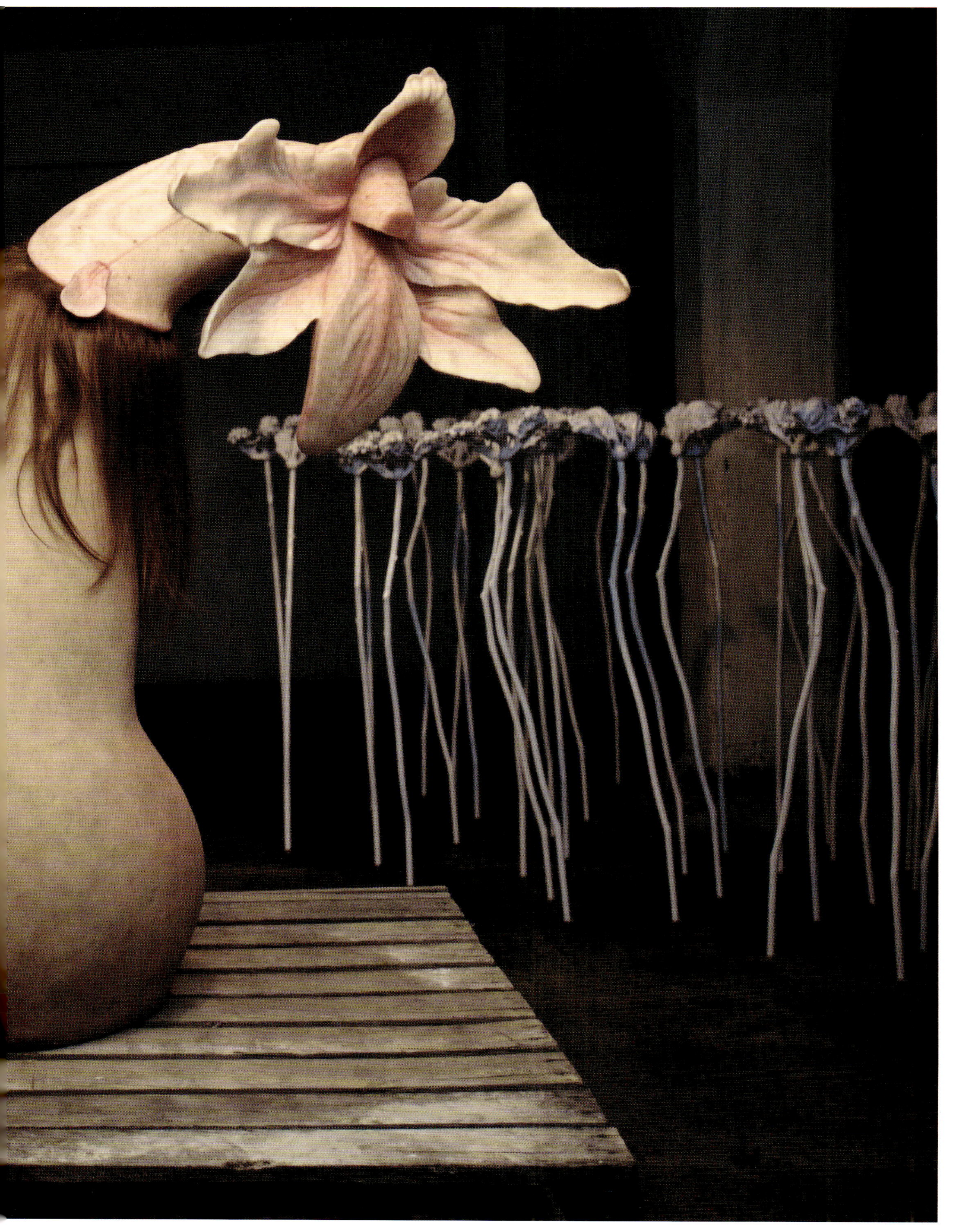

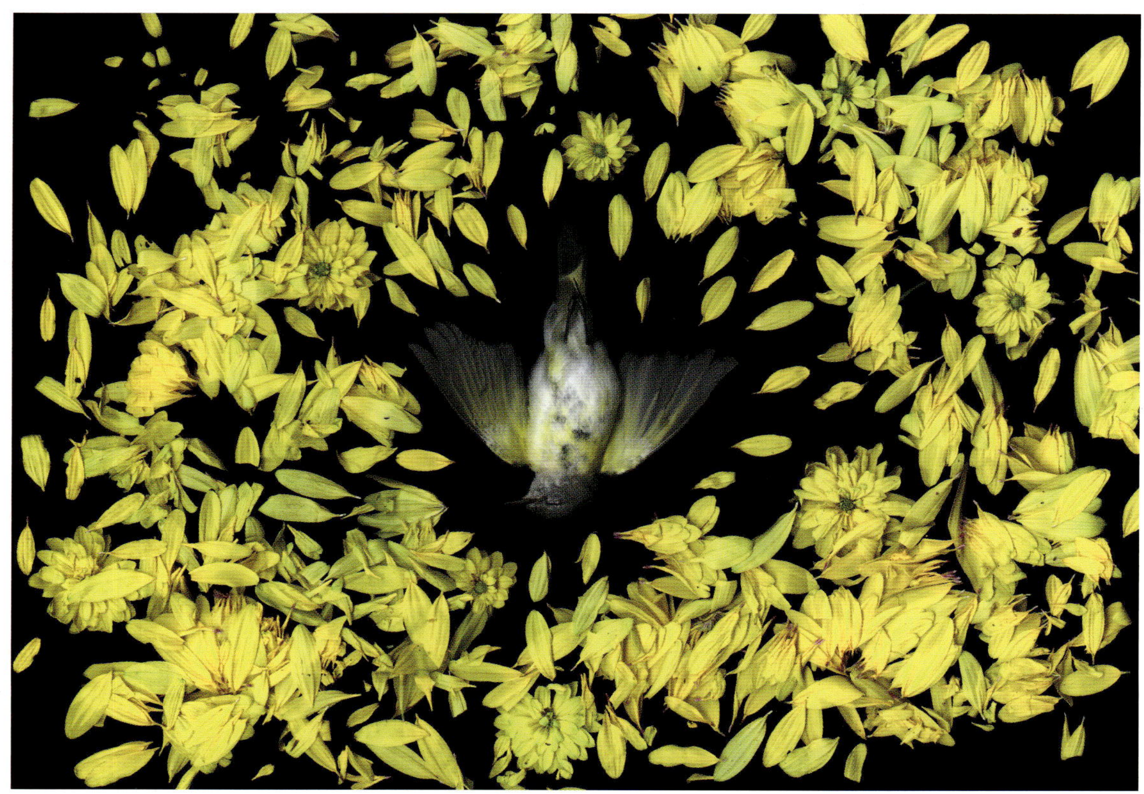

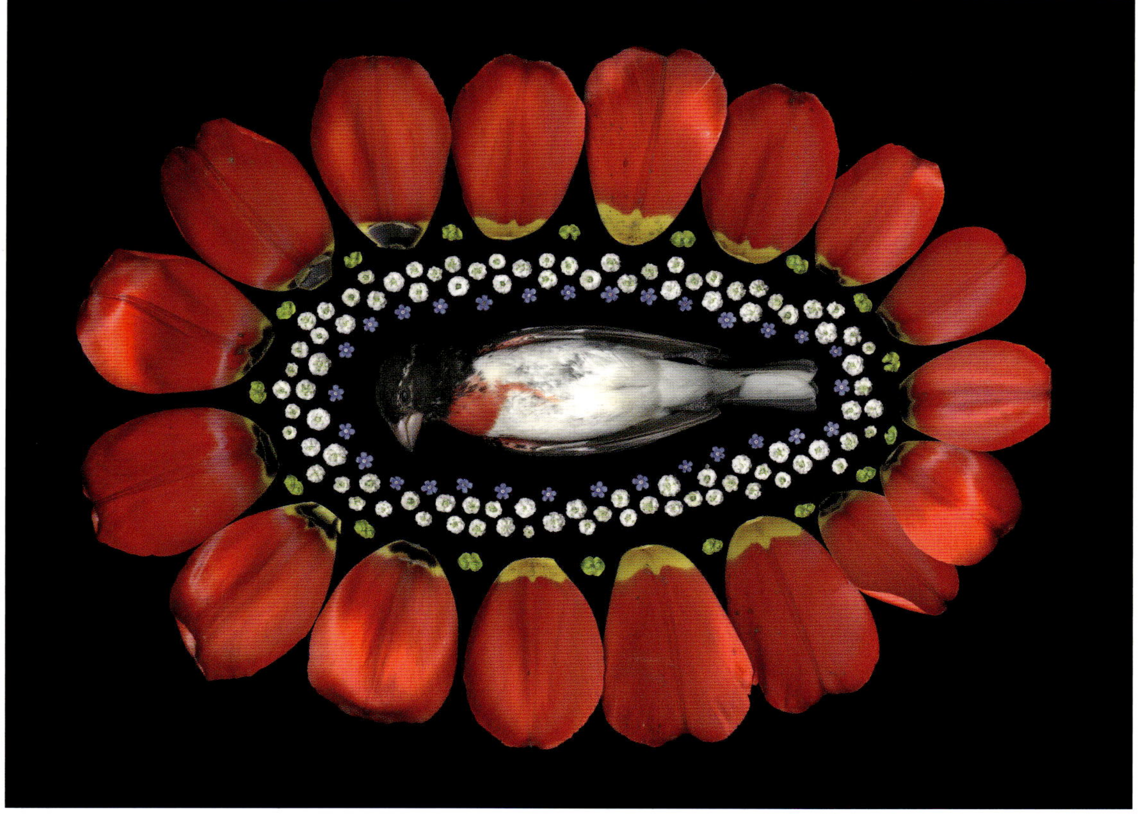

Portia Munson. *Yellow Warbler*, 2015. Pigmented ink on rag paper: 43 × 60.5 inches. *Courtesy of the artist and P.P.O.W. Gallery, New York*

Portia Munson. *Red Breasted Grosbeck*, 2015. Pigmented ink on rag paper: 14.5 × 20 inches. *Courtesy of the artist and P.P.O.W. Gallery, New York*

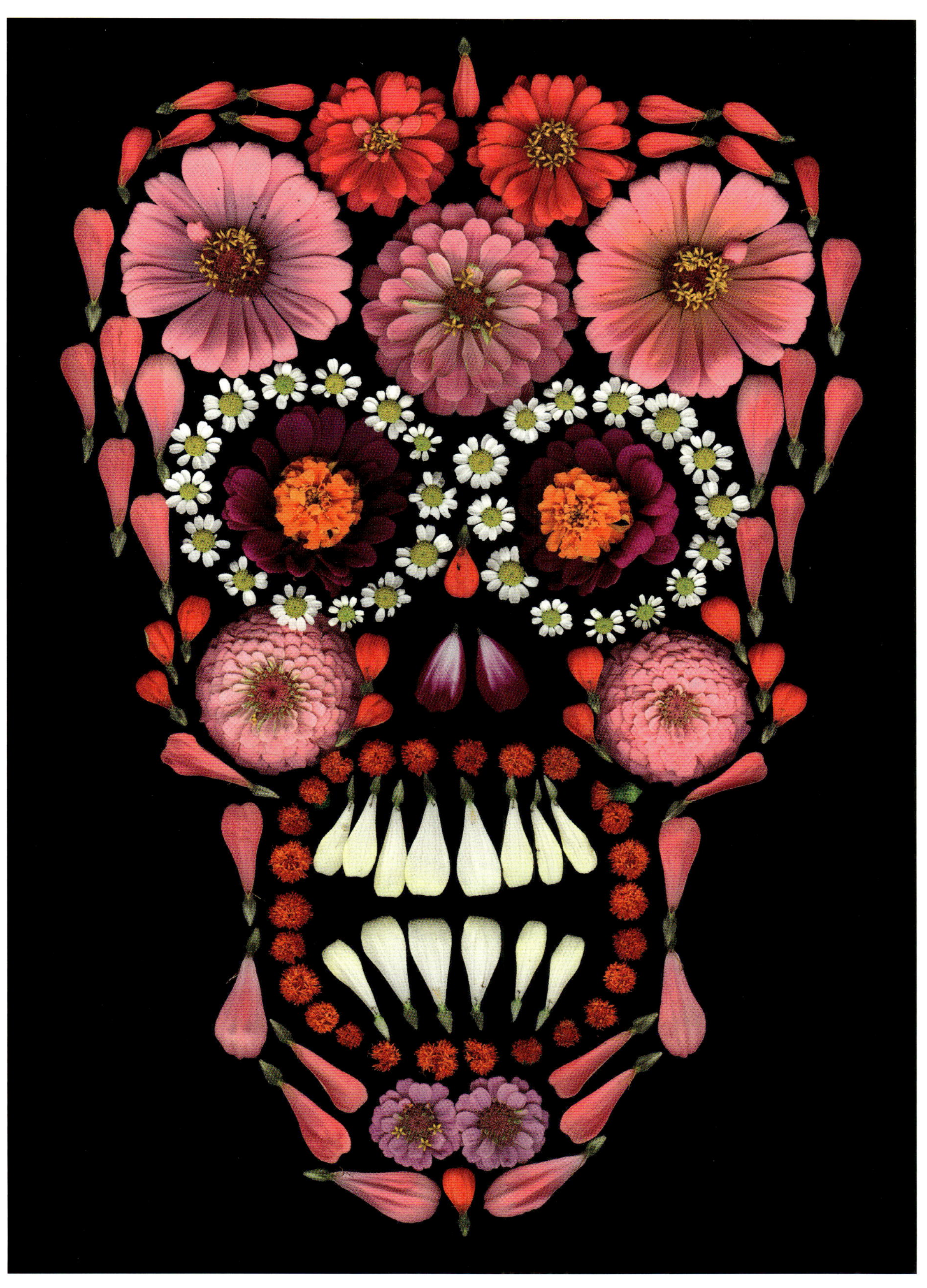

Portia Munson. *Flower Skull*, 2010.
Pigmented ink on rag paper: 42 × 60 inches.
Courtesy of the artist and P.P.O.W. Gallery, New York

RANIA MATAR

Rania Matar was born in Lebanon and moved to the United States in 1984. Her work focuses on women and girls in the United States and the Middle East, with an emphasis on identity and universality. As a Lebanese-born American woman and mother, her cultural background, cross-cultural experience, and personal narrative informs her photography. Matar has dedicated her practice to exploring both sides of this identity by addressing issues of personal and collective identity, through photographs mining female adolescence and womanhood. Originally trained as an architect at the American University of Beirut and Cornell University, she went on to study photography at the New England School of Photography and the Maine Photographic Workshops.

Matar's work has been widely published and exhibited, including most recently in a solo exhibition *In Her Image: Photographs by Rania Matar* at the Amon Carter Museum of American Art, but also at the Museum of Fine Arts, Boston; the Carnegie Museum of Art, Pittsburgh; the National Museum of Women in the Arts, Washington, DC; the Howard Greenberg Gallery, New York City; and the National Portrait Gallery, London. In 2018, Matar was the recipient of a Guggenheim Fellowship. Additionally, she has received several grants and awards, including 2017 Mellon artist-in-residency grant at Kenyon College, Gambier, Ohio; 2011 Legacy Award at Griffin Museum of Photography, Winchester, Massachusetts; 2007 and 2011 Massachusetts Cultural Council artist fellowships; first place from New England Photographer's Biennial and from Women in Photography International. In 2008, she was a Foster Prize finalist at the Institute of Contemporary Art, Boston, with a solo exhibition. Matar's images are in permanent collections of several museums, institutions, and private collections worldwide, and she has published three books: *L'Enfant-Femme* (2016), *A Girl and Her Room* (2012), and *Ordinary Lives* (2009). In 2017, Matar was selected by *Artnet* as one of "10 Remarkable Photographers to Discover at AIPAD." Matar is an associate professor of photography at the Massachusetts College of Art and Design, Boston.

Rania Matar. *Clara 8, Beirut, Lebanon*, 2012. Archival pigment print on Baryta paper from medium-format scanned negatives: 28.8 × 36 inches. Image ©Rania Matar. *Courtesy of the artist and Robert Klein Gallery, Boston*

Rania Matar. *Lindsey 10, Needham Massachusetts*, 2013. Archival pigment print on Baryta paper from medium-format scanned negatives: 28.8 × 36 inches. Image ©Rania Matar. *Courtesy of the artist and Robert Klein Gallery, Boston*

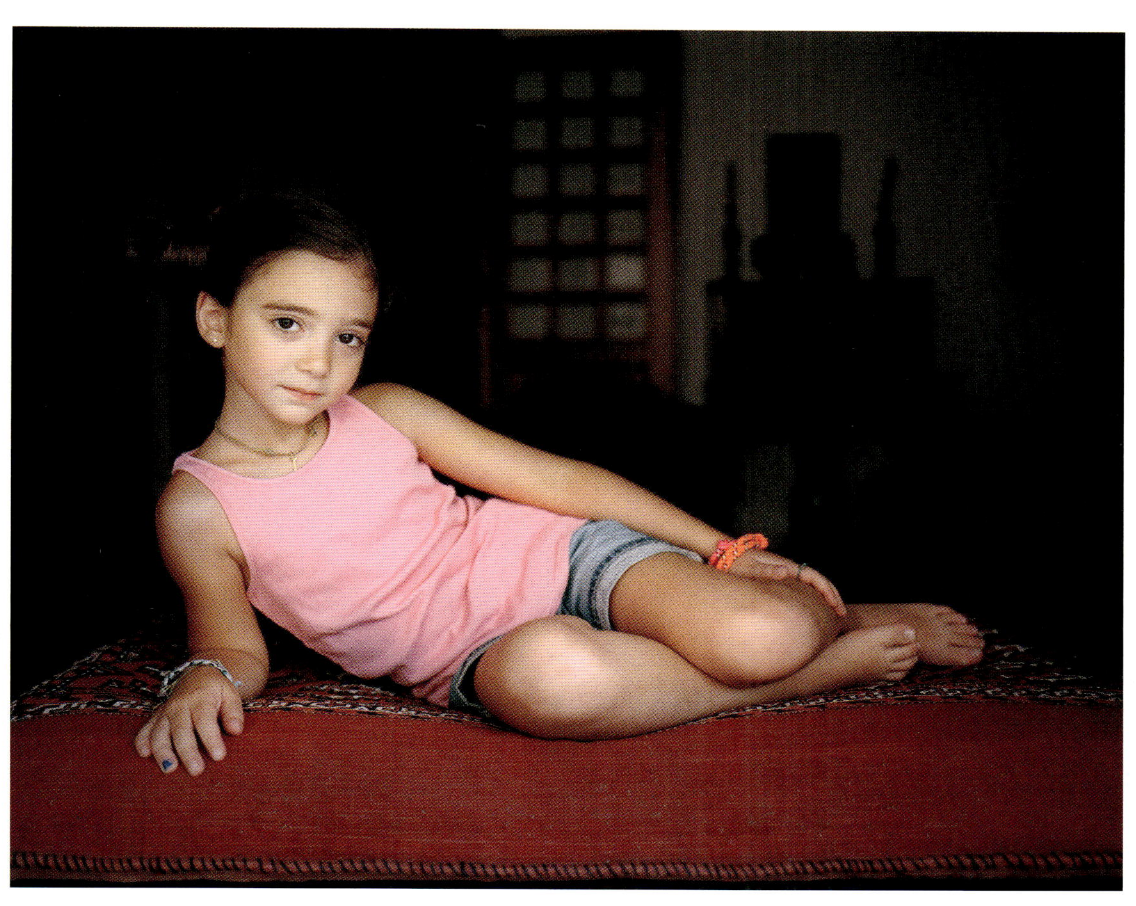

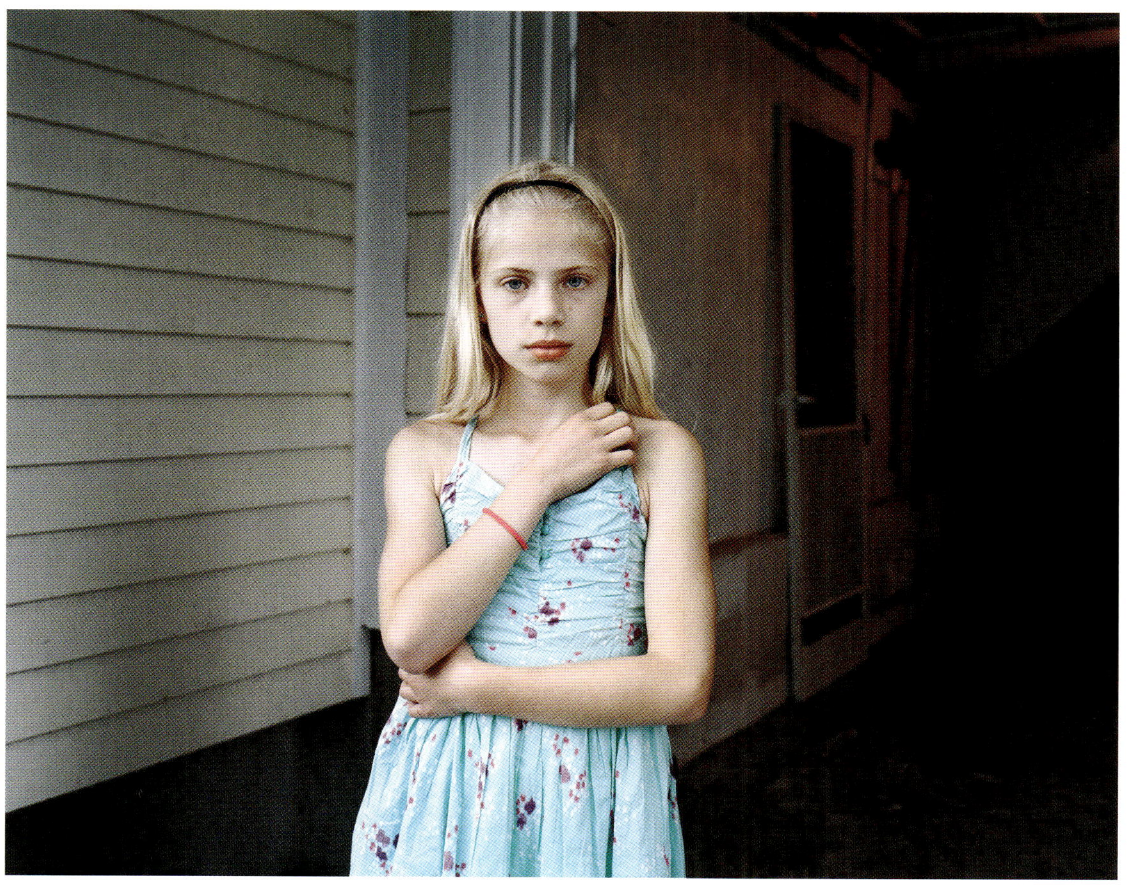

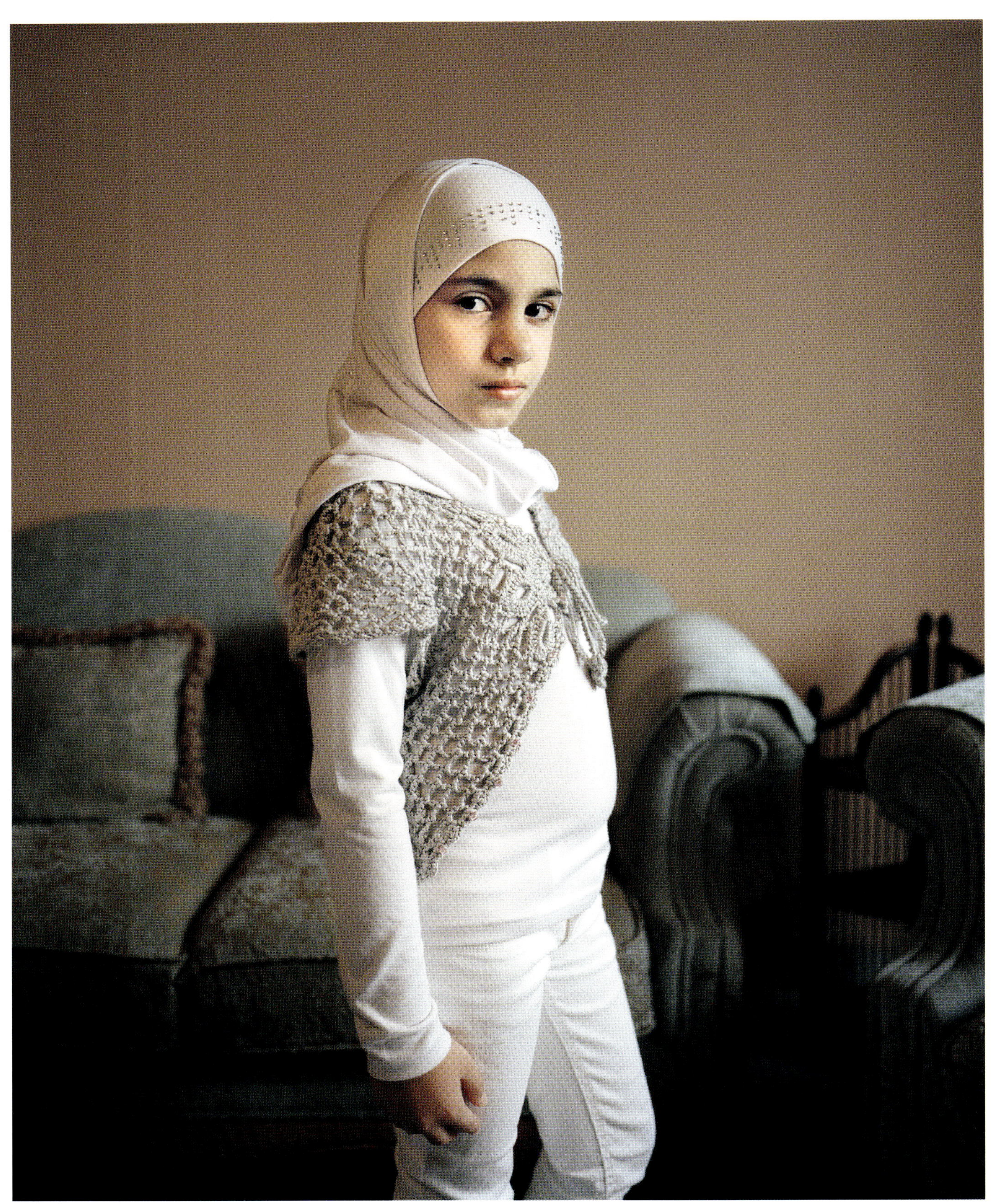

Rania Matar. *Maryam 9, Beirut Lebanon*, 2011. Archival pigment print on Baryta paper from medium-format scanned negatives: 28.8 × 36 inches. Image ©Rania Matar. *Courtesy of the artist and Robert Klein Gallery, Boston*

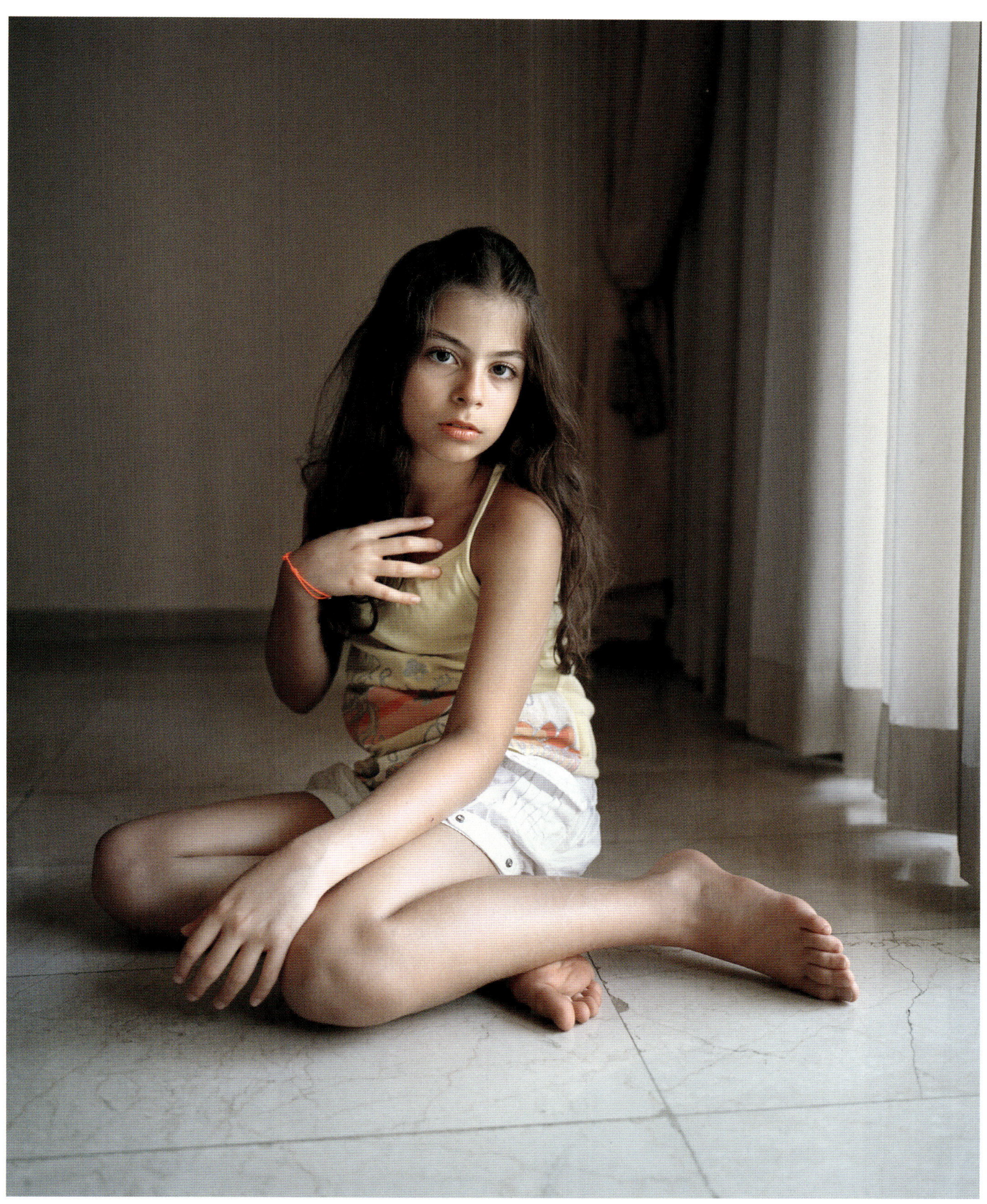

Rania Matar. *Yasmina at 10, Beirut Lebanon,* 2011. Archival pigment print on Baryta paper from medium-format scanned negatives: 28.8 × 36 inches. Image ©Rania Matar. *Courtesy of the artist and Robert Klein Gallery, Boston*

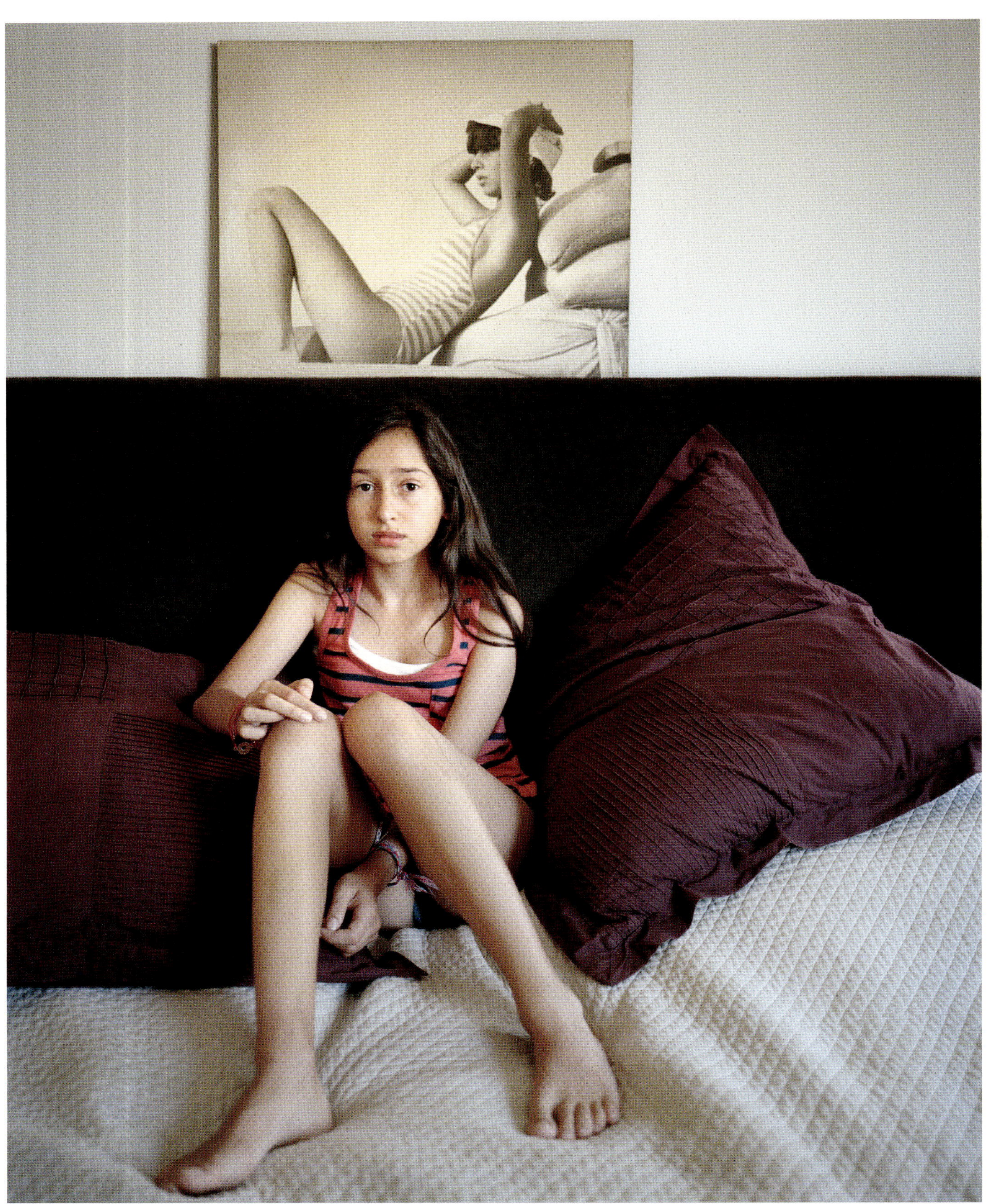

Rania Matar. *Charlotte at 11, Beirut Lebanon*, 2012. Archival pigment print on Baryta paper from medium-format scanned negatives: 28.8 × 36 inches. Image ©Rania Matar. *Courtesy of the artist and Robert Klein Gallery, Boston*

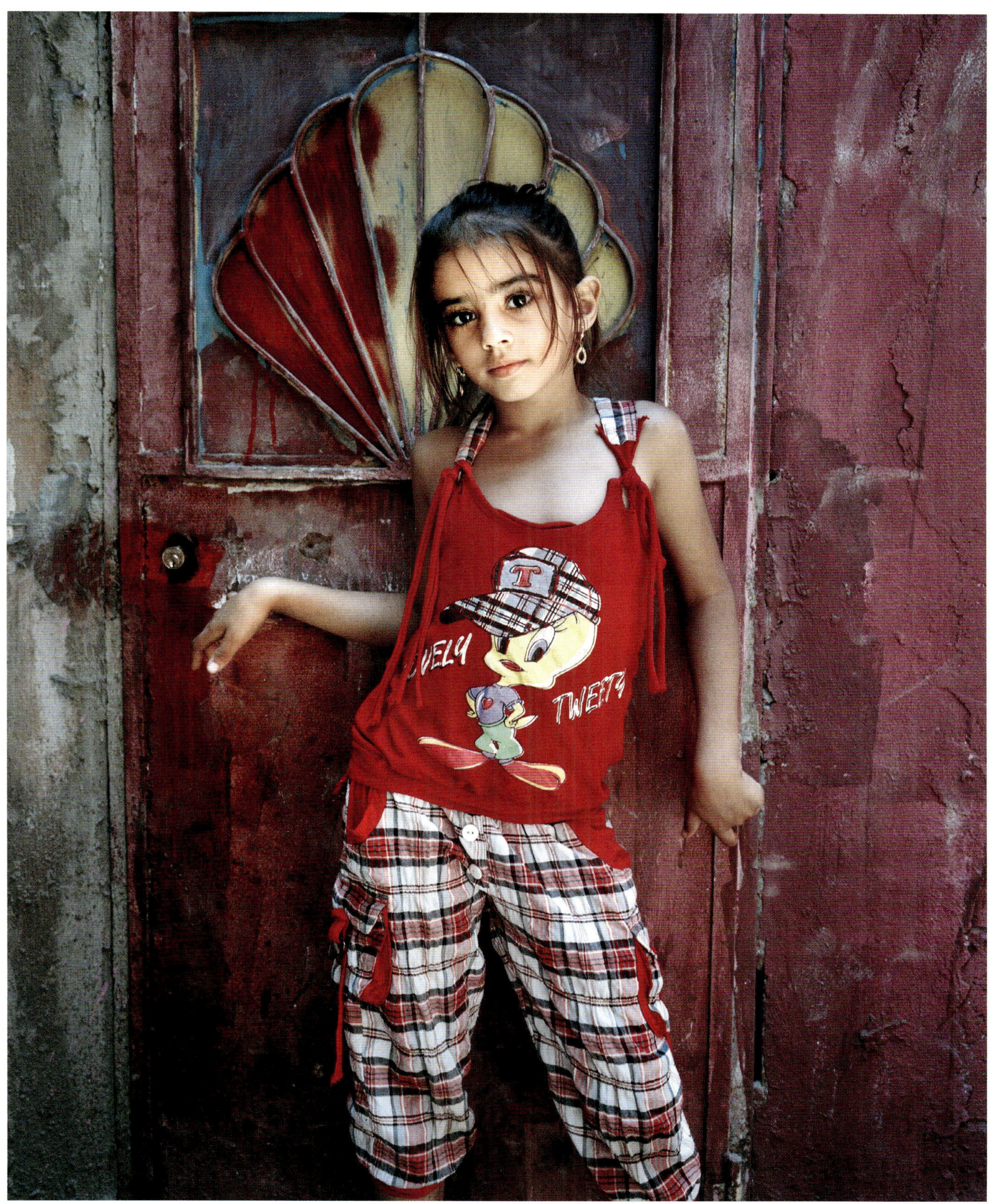

Rania Matar. *Alia 9, Bourj El Barajneh Refugee Camp, Beirut Lebanon*, 2011. Archival pigment print on Baryta paper from medium-format scanned negatives: 28.8 × 36 inches. Image ©Rania Matar. *Courtesy of the artist and Robert Klein Gallery, Boston*

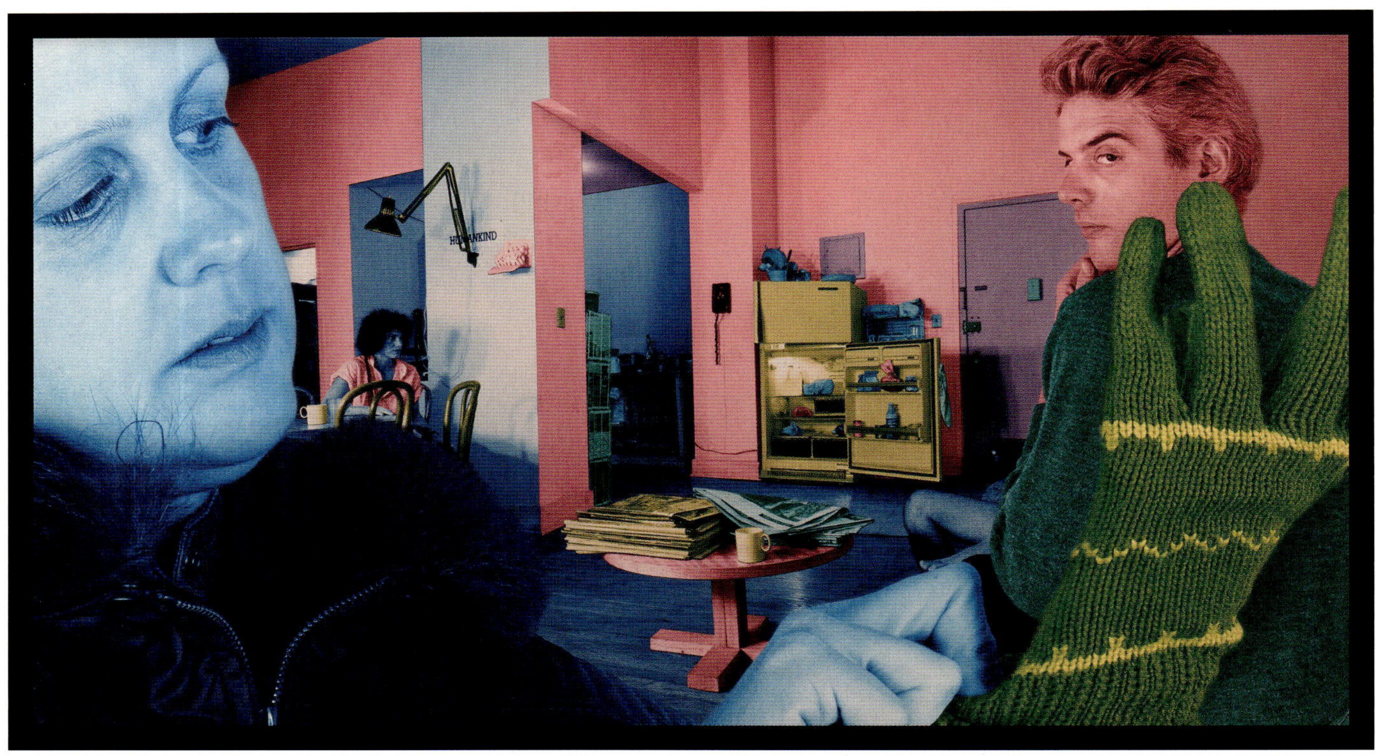

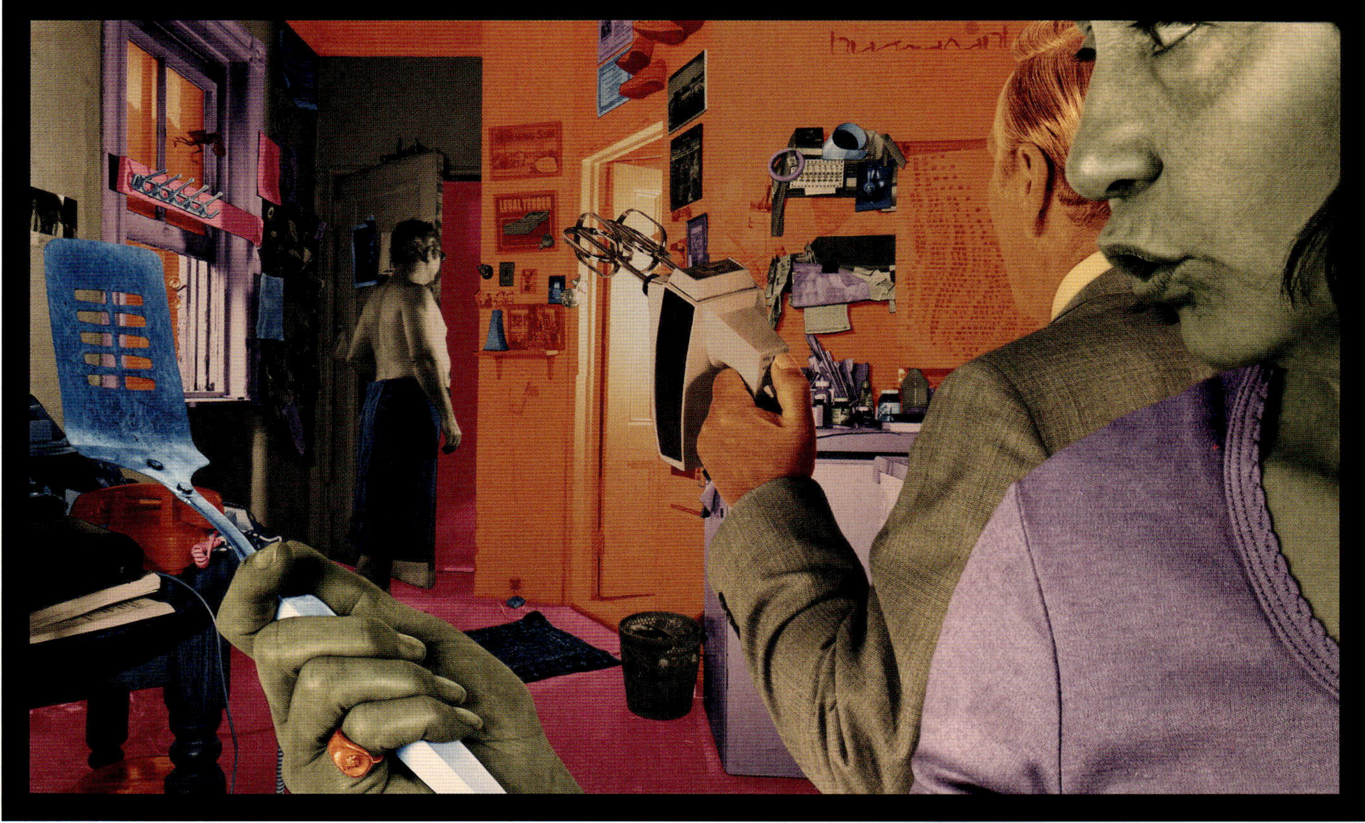

Sandy Skoglund. *Green Glove* (from *True Fiction Two* series), 2004. Color photograph: 14 × 24 inches. Image ©Sandy Skoglund. *Courtesy of the artist*

Sandy Skoglund. *Parallel Thinking* (from *True Fiction Two* series), 2004. Color photograph: 14 × 24 inches. Image ©Sandy Skoglund. *Courtesy of the artist*

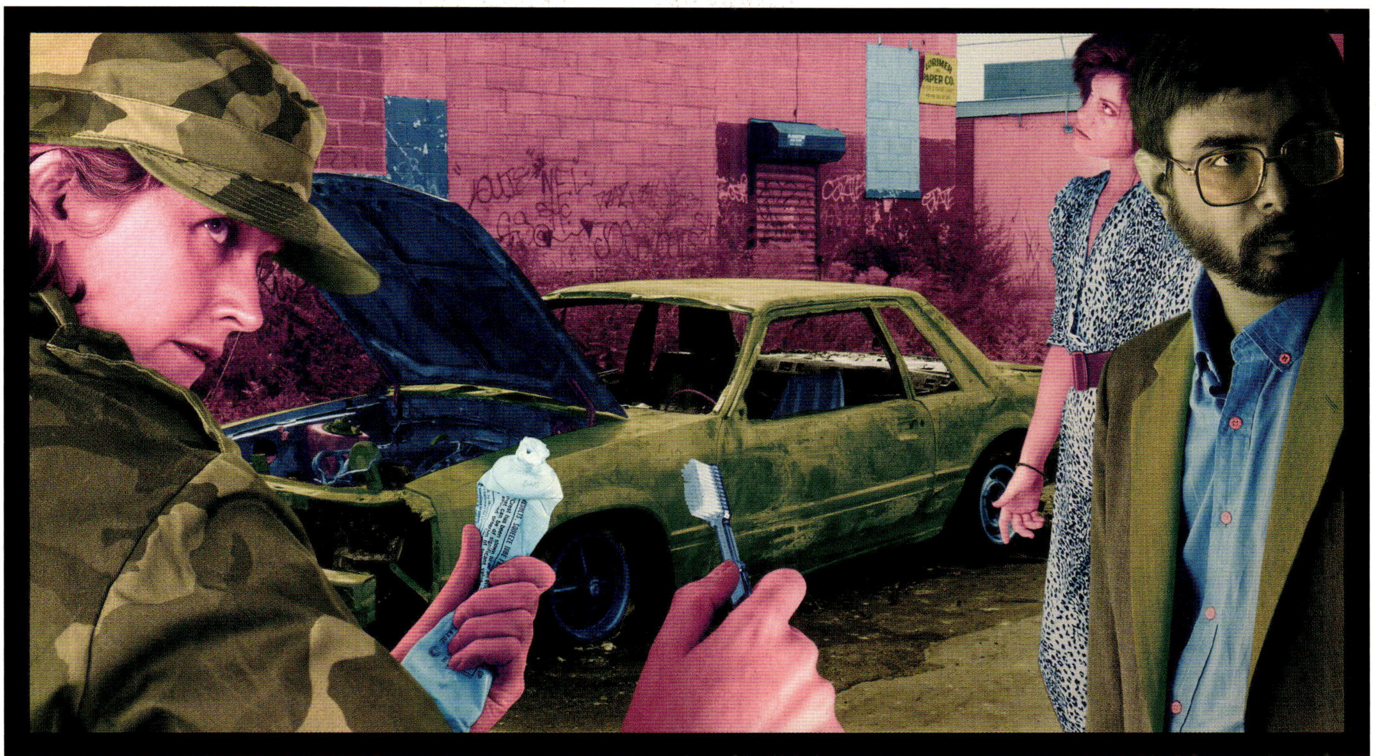

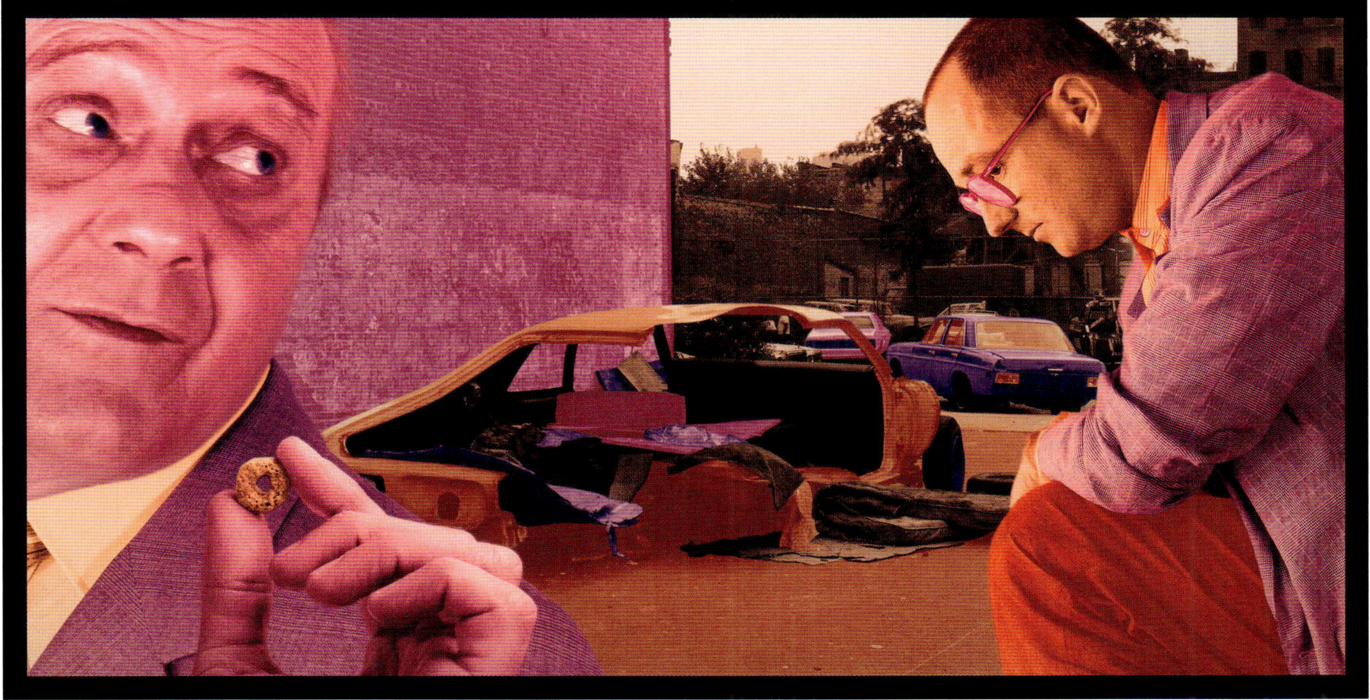

Sandy Skoglund. *Laws of Interior Design* (from *True Fiction Two* series), 2004. Color photograph: 14 × 24 inches. Image ©Sandy Skoglund. *Courtesy of the artist*

Sandy Skoglund. *Invention of the Wheel* (from *True Fiction Two* series), 2004. Color photograph: 14 × 24 inches. Image ©Sandy Skoglund. *Courtesy of the artist*

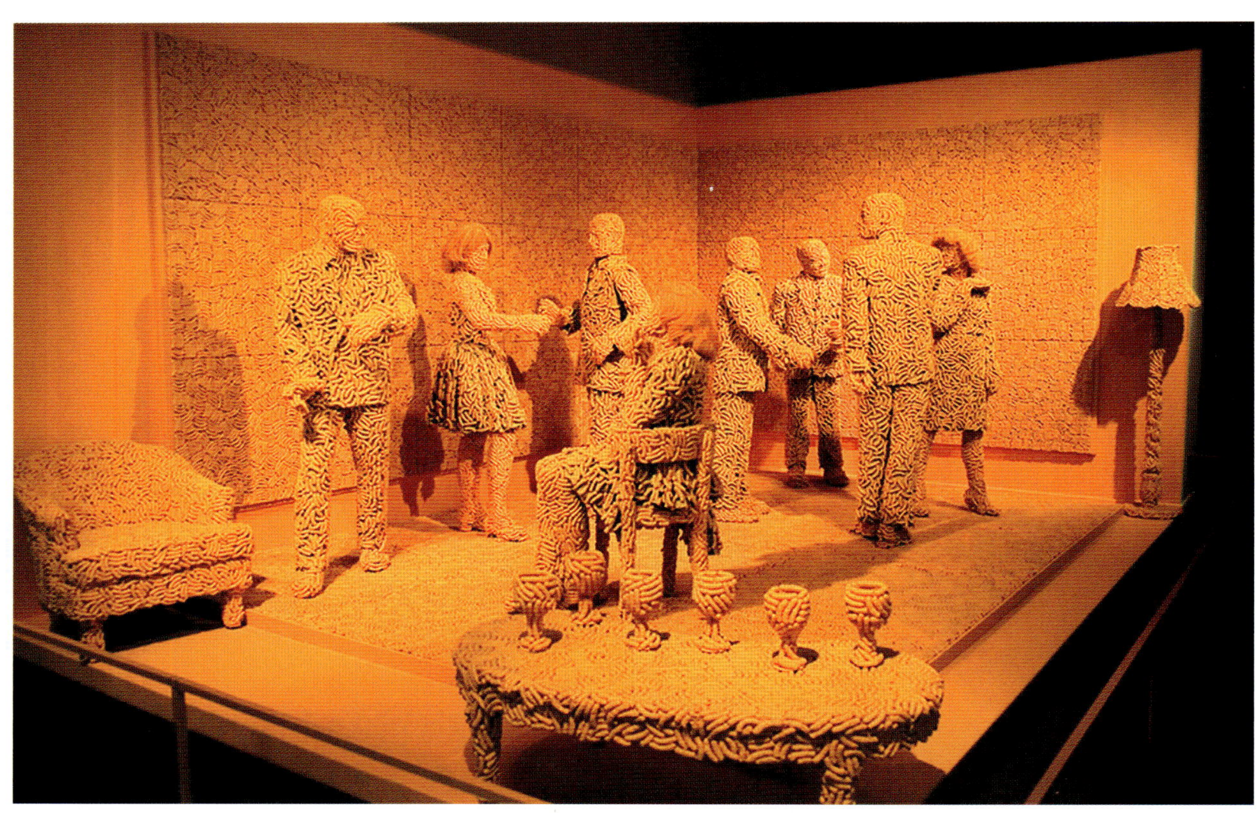

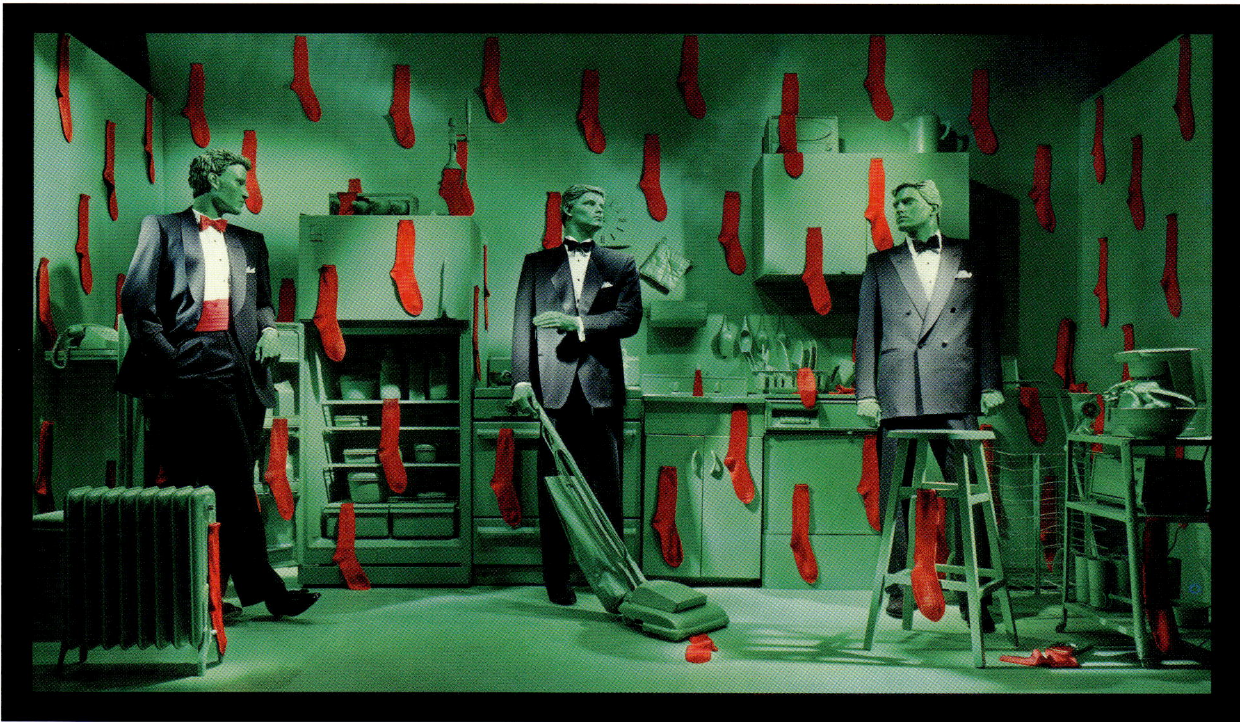

Sandy Skoglund. *The Cocktail Party*, 2004. Mannequins and furniture covered in snack food Cheez Doodles and painted: dimensions variable. Installation view, Copia Artspace, California. Image ©Sandy Skoglund. *Courtesy of the artist*

Sandy Skoglund. *Sock Situation*, 1986. Color photograph: approximate image area 21.25 × 37.5 inches. Installation view, Barney's street window, New York; Christmas display of socks, painted props, and mannequins. Image ©Sandy Skoglund. *Courtesy of the artist*

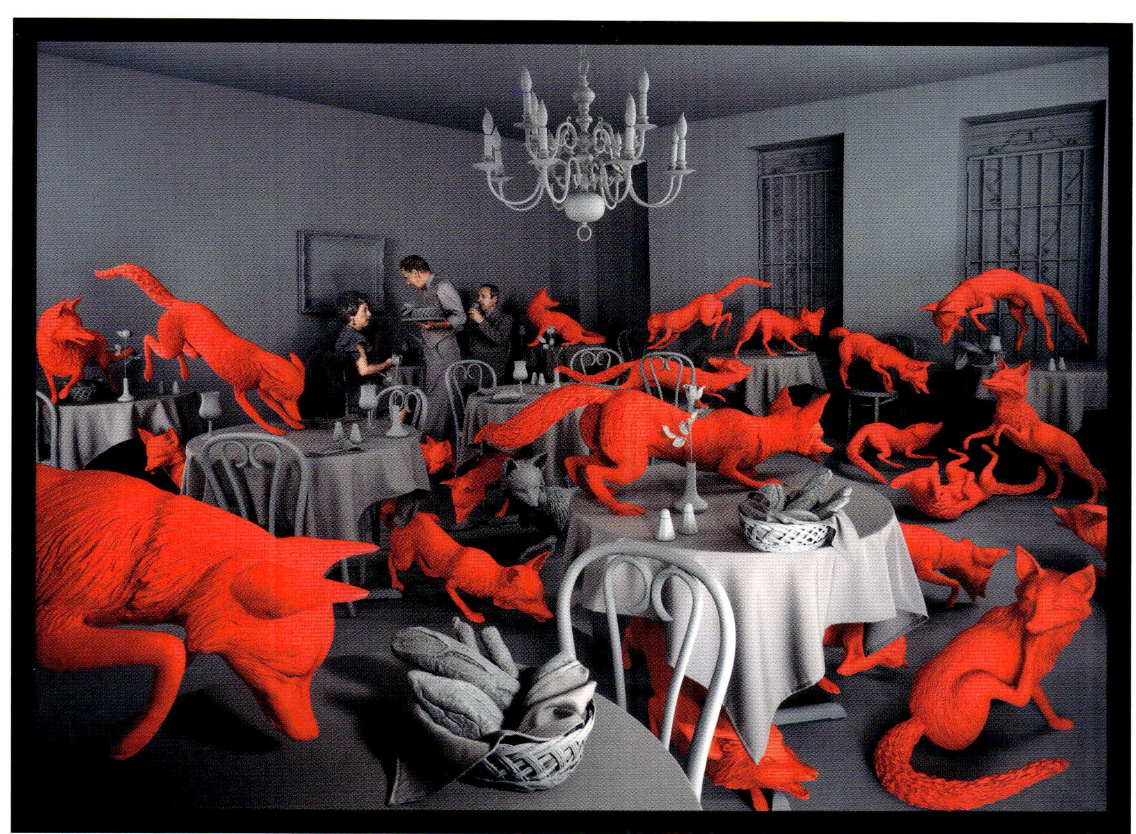

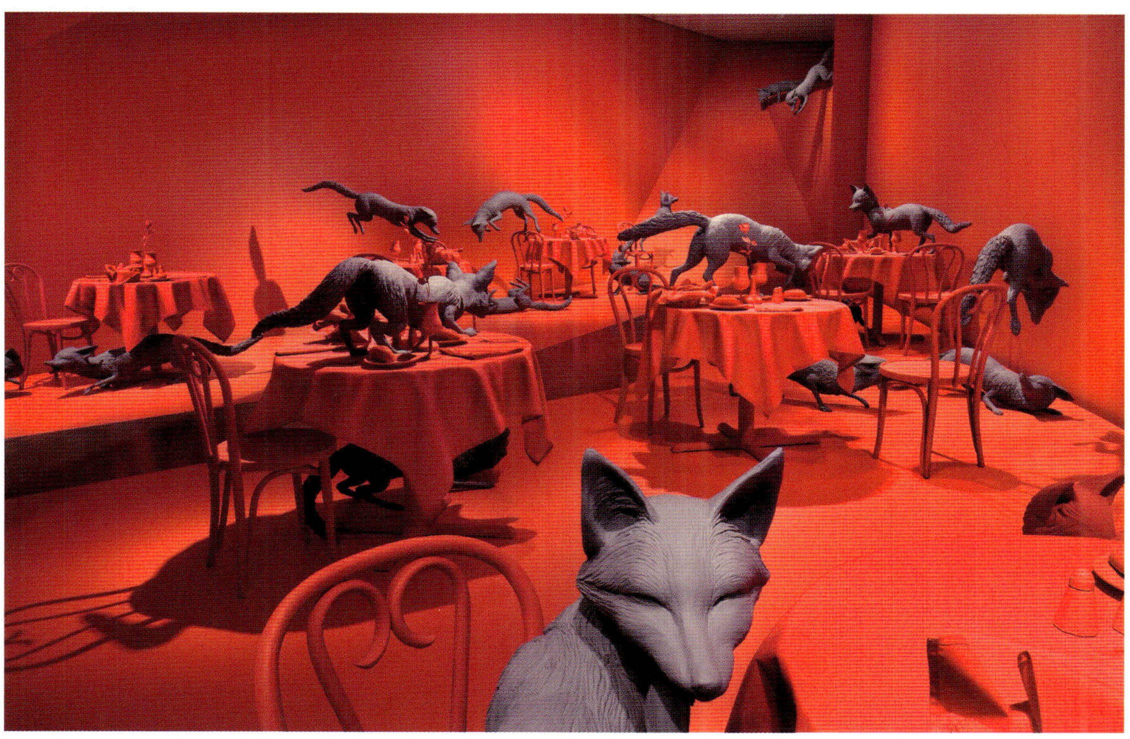

Sandy Skoglund. *Fox Games*, 1989. Color photograph: approximate image area 46.25 × 63 inches, hand-sculpted epoxy resin foxes by the artist and live models. Image ©Sandy Skoglund. *Courtesy of the artist*

Sandy Skoglund. *Fox Games*, 2008. Plastic cast sculpted foxes, tables, chairs, cutlery, and dinnerware painted: dimensions variable. Installation view, Denver Art Museum, Colorado. Image ©Sandy Skoglund. *Courtesy of the artist*

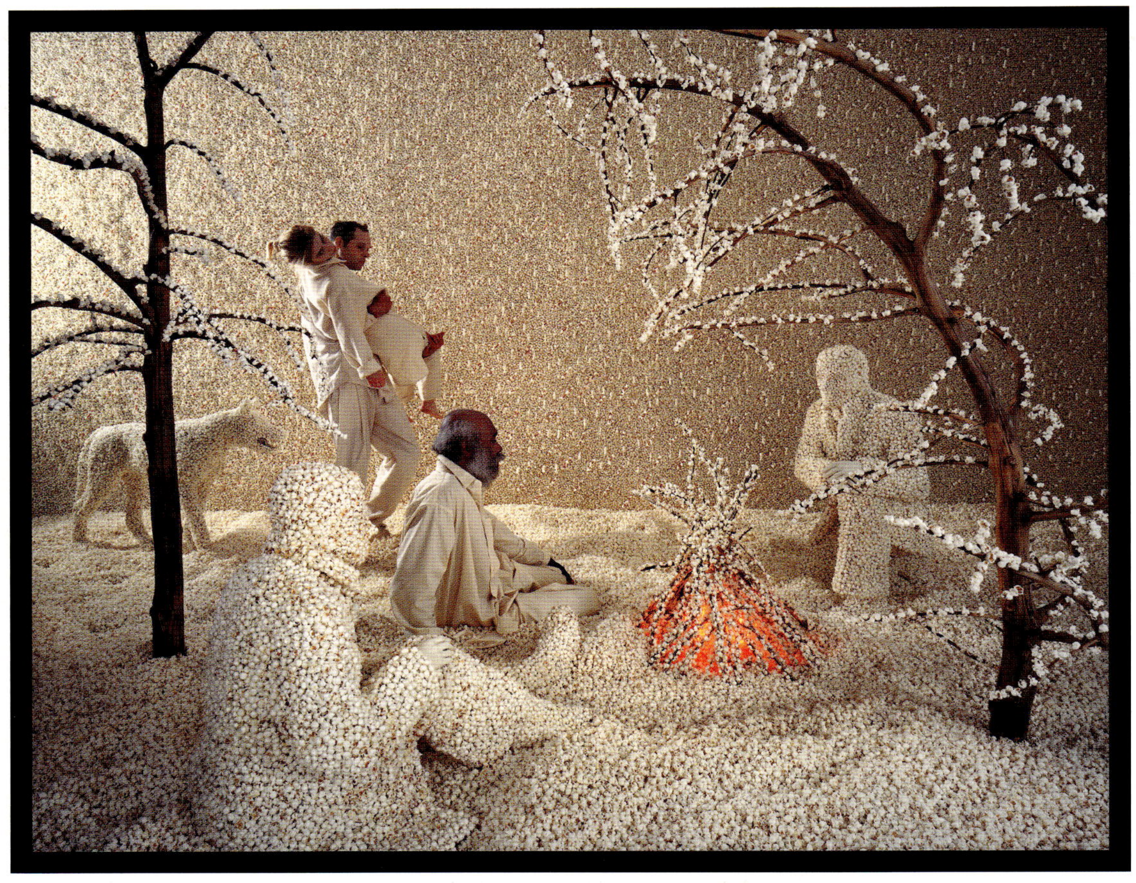

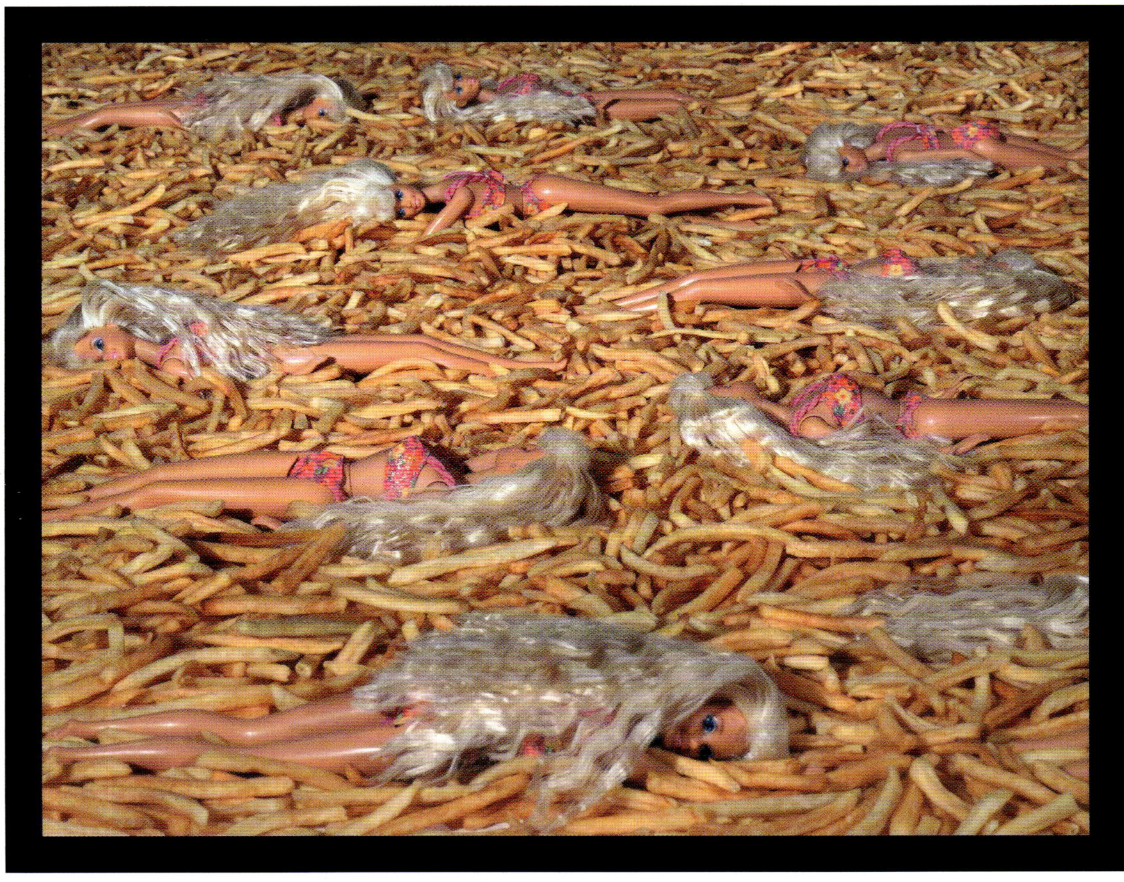

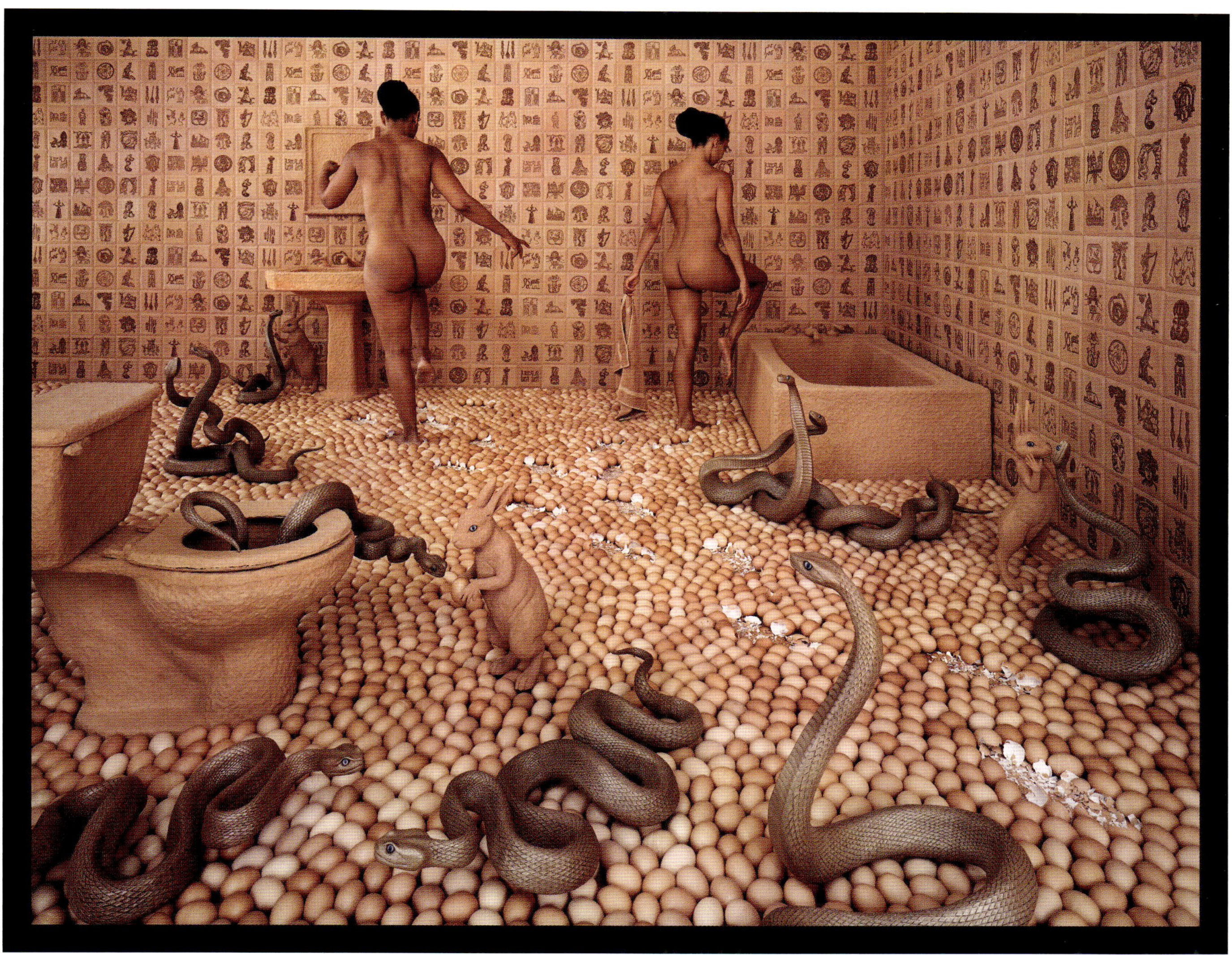

Sandy Skoglund. *Raining Popcorn*, 2001. Color photograph; approximate image area: 39 × 49.5 inches, sculpted figures coated with popcorn, mechanical wall panels of popcorn, and tree branches; live models. Image ©Sandy Skoglund. *Courtesy of the artist*

Sandy Skoglund. *At the Shore*, 1994. Color photograph: approximate image area 11 × 14 inches, French fries and Barbie dolls. Image ©Sandy Skoglund. *Courtesy of the artist*

Sandy Skoglund. *Walking on Eggshells*, 1997. Color photograph: approximate image area: 47 × 61 inches—eggshells on floor; wall tiles of hand-cast paper; sink, tub, and toilet of cast paper with sculpted epoxy resin snakes; sculpted epoxy resin rabbits, with live models. Image ©Sandy Skoglund. *Courtesy of the artist*

SARA CWYNAR

Sara Cwynar is a Canadian multimedia artist who works in film, photography, collage, installation, and bookmaking. In her practice, she explores the limitations of photography and image making through mixed-media motifs such as graphic design and the written word. Cwynar uses her work to challenge images seen in everyday life, such as kitsch, in which ordinary objects become icons because of their sentimental value.

Cwynar has a B.Des from York University, Toronto, and an MFA in photography from Yale University, New Haven, Connecticut. Her work is featured in many permanent collections, including the Solomon R. Guggenheim Museum, New York; MMK Museum für Moderne Kunst, Frankfurt; Art Gallery of Ontario, Toronto; Minneapolis Institute of Art; Milwaukee Art Museum; Fondazione Prada, Milan; Kadist Art Foundation, San Francisco; Zabludowicz Collection, London; the Dallas Museum of Art, Dallas, Texas; and the FOAM Photography Museum, Amsterdam. Cwynar has published two books: *Kitsch Encyclopedia: A Survey of Universal Knowledge* and *Pictures of Pictures*. She has received numerous awards, including the the 2018 MAST Foundation for Photography Grant on Industry and Work; the 2018 International Film Festival Rotterdam; the Ammodo Tiger Short Prize; the 2016 Bâloise Prize; the 2013 Printed Matter Emerging Artist Publication Series Grant; the 2011 Print Magazine 20 under 30 New Visual Artist Award; the 2011 Art Director's Club Young Guns Award; and the 2009 Kondor Fine Arts Award. Cwynar lives and works in New York City.

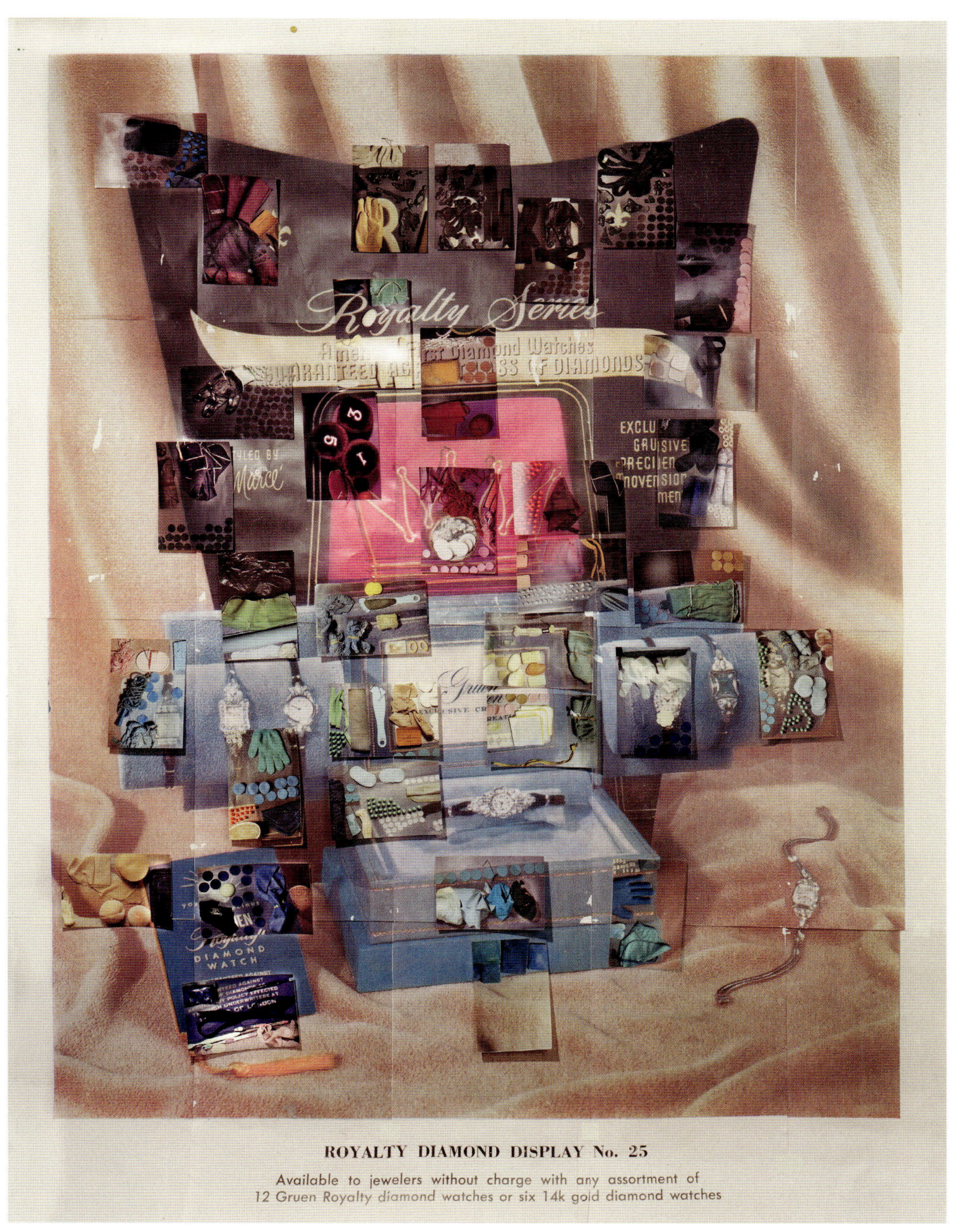

Sara Cwynar. *Royalty Diamond Display No. 25*, 2016. Archival inkjet print: 48 × 36 inches. Edition of 3, 2 AP. ©Sara Cwynar. *Courtesy of the artist and Cooper Cole, Toronto*

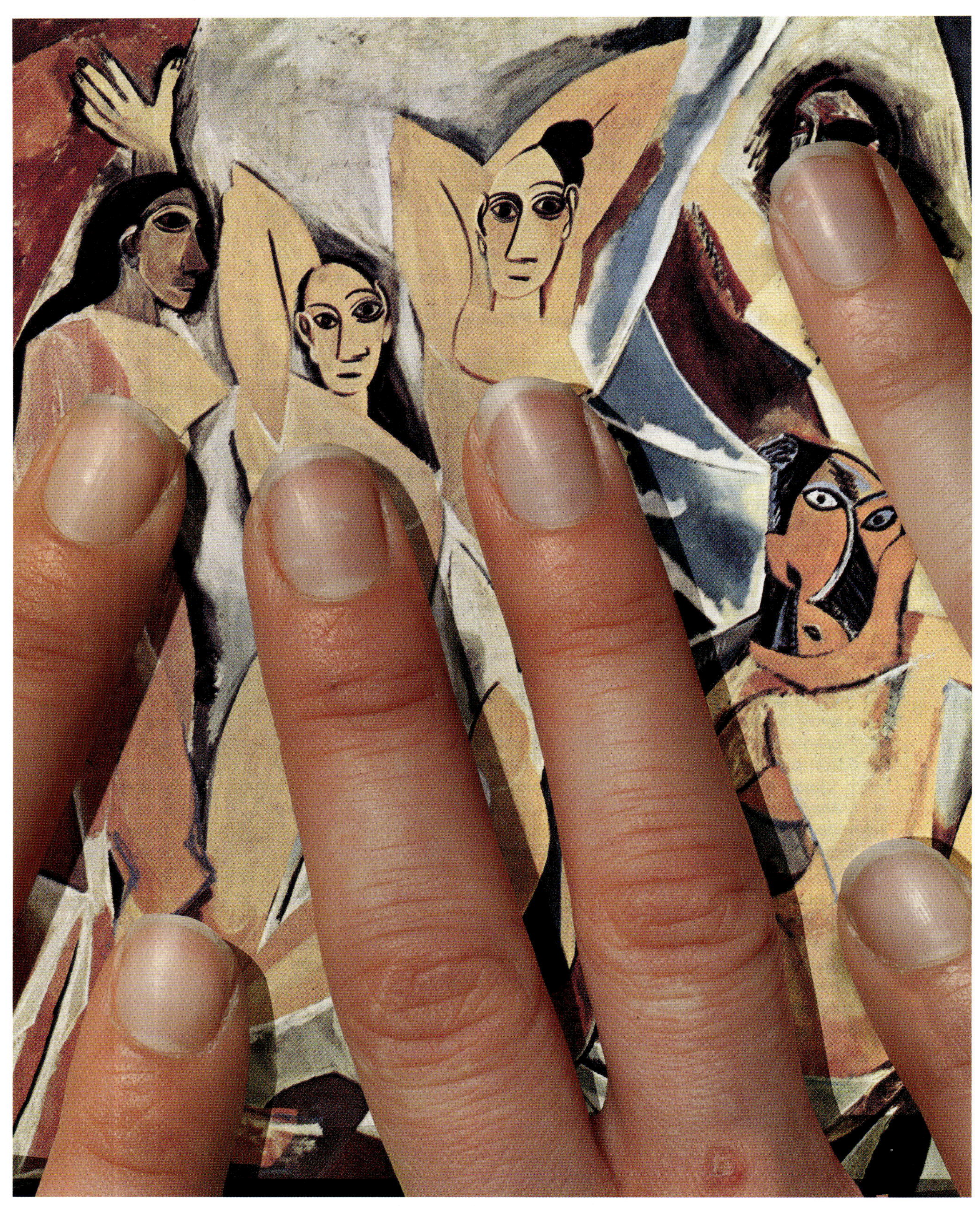

Sara Cwynar. *Women*, 2015. Archival pigment print mounted to Plexiglas: 32 × 25 inches. Edition of 3, 2 AP. ©Sara Cwynar. *Courtesy of the artist and Foxy Production, New York*

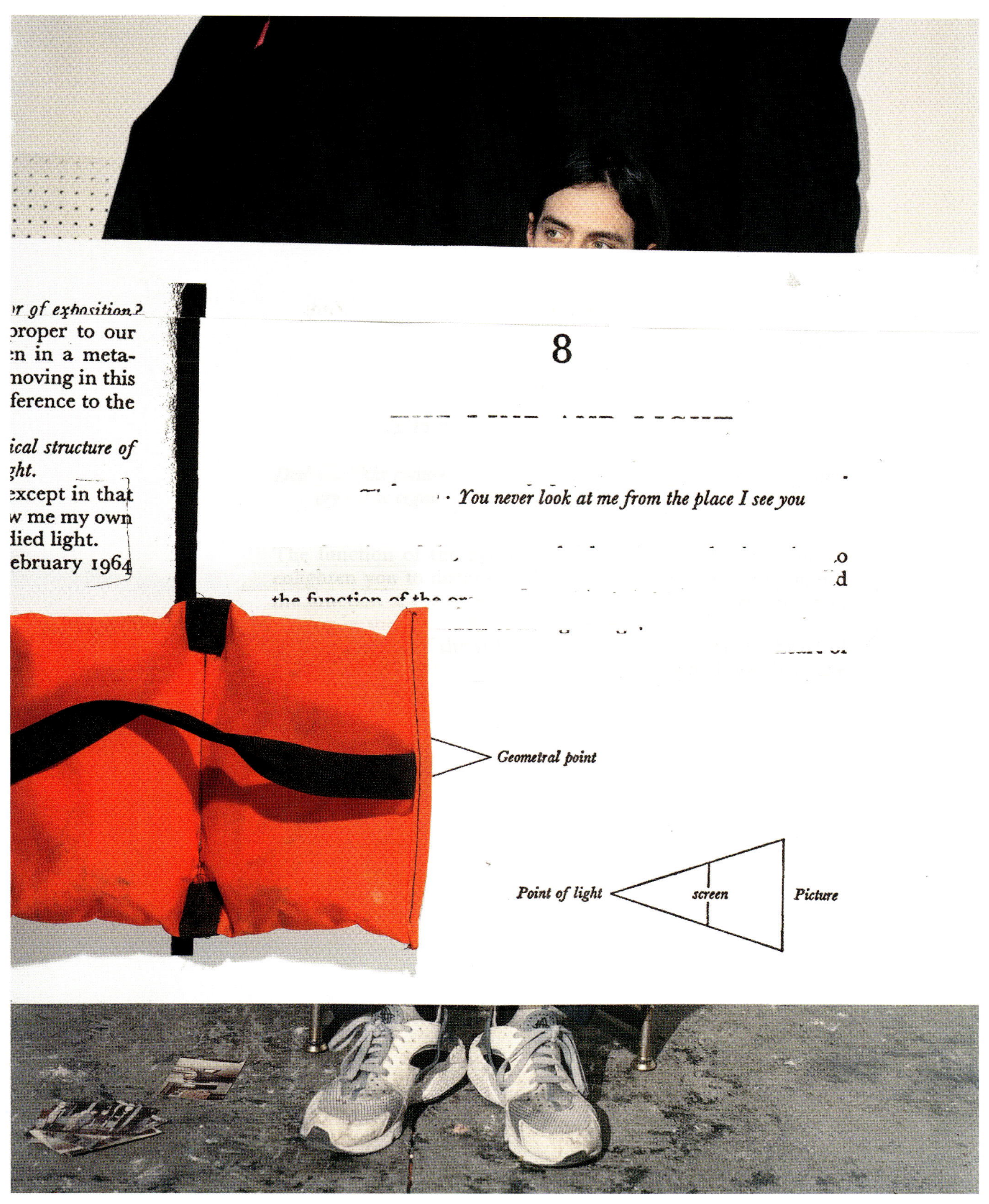

Sara Cwynar. *You Never Look at Me from the Place I See You 2*, 2016. Archival inkjet print: 30 × 24 inches. Edition of 3, 2 AP. ©Sara Cwynar. *Courtesy of the artist and Cooper Cole, Toronto*

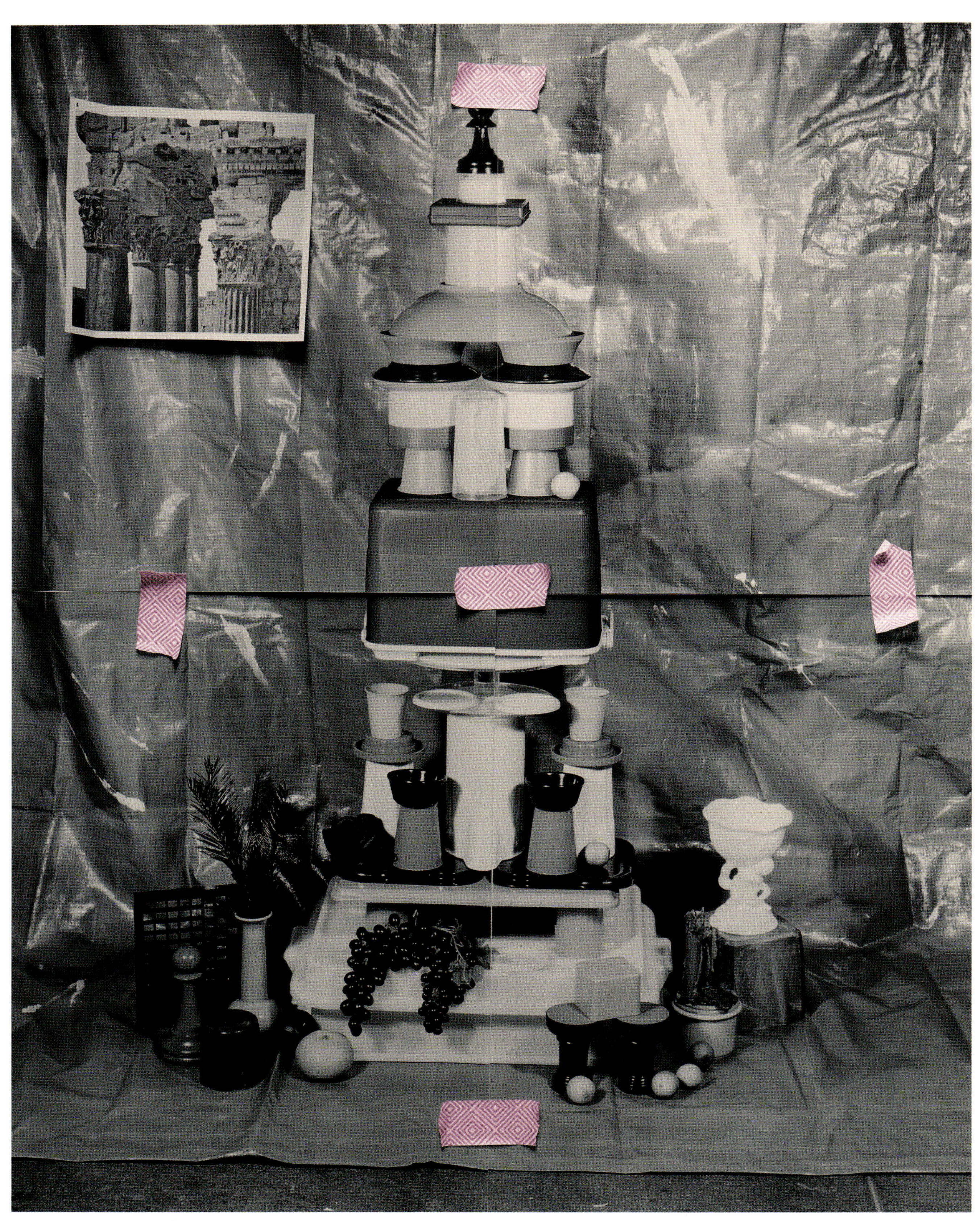

Sara Cwynar. *Corinthian Column (Plastic Cups)*, 2014. C-print mounted on Plexiglas: 30 × 24 inches. Edition of 3, 2 AP. ©Sara Cwynar. *Courtesy of the artist and Foxy Production, New York*

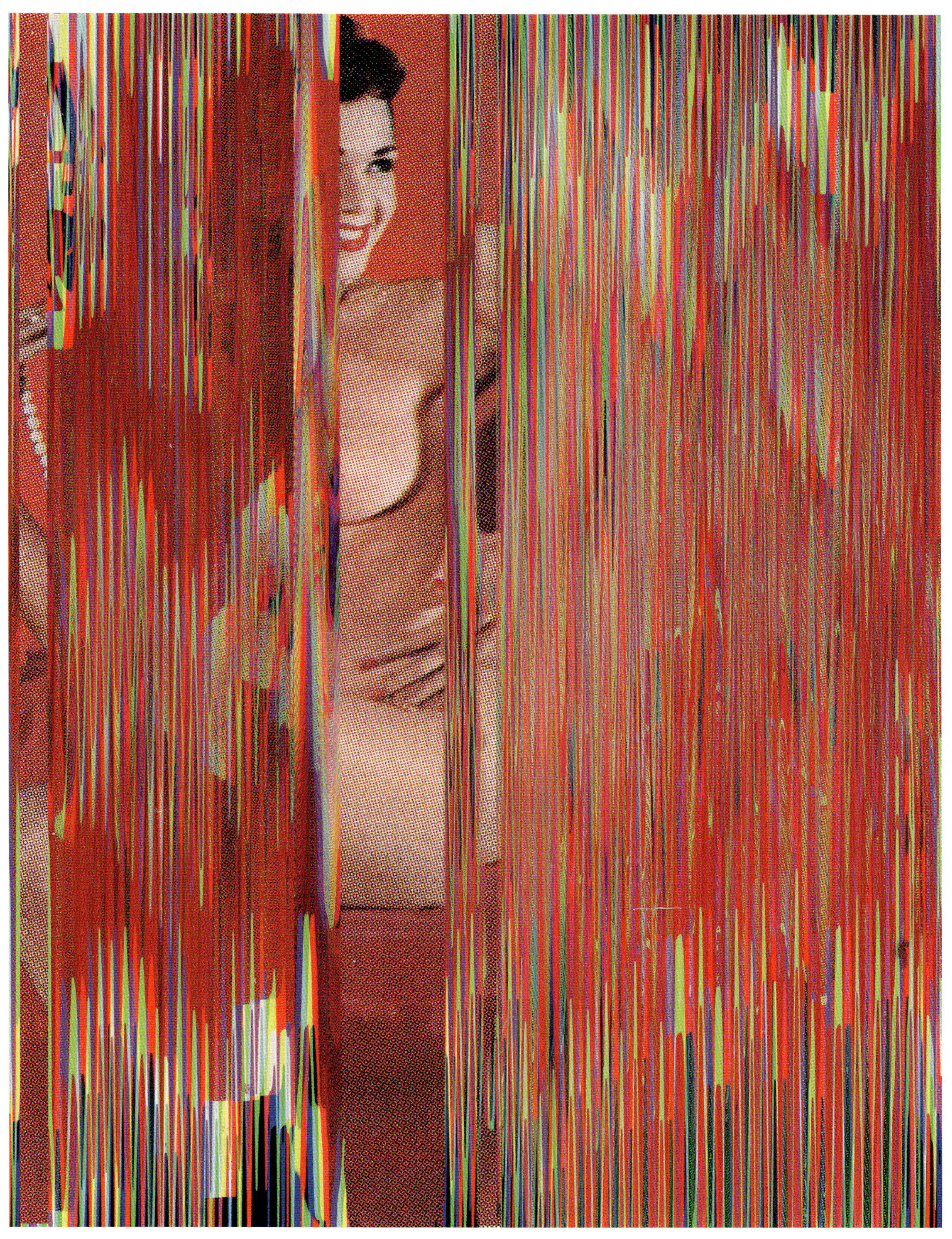

Sara Cwynar. *Woman 6 (Cards)*, 2015.
C-print: 40 × 30 inches. Edition of 3, 2 AP.
©Sara Cwynar. *Courtesy of the artist and Cooper Cole, Toronto*

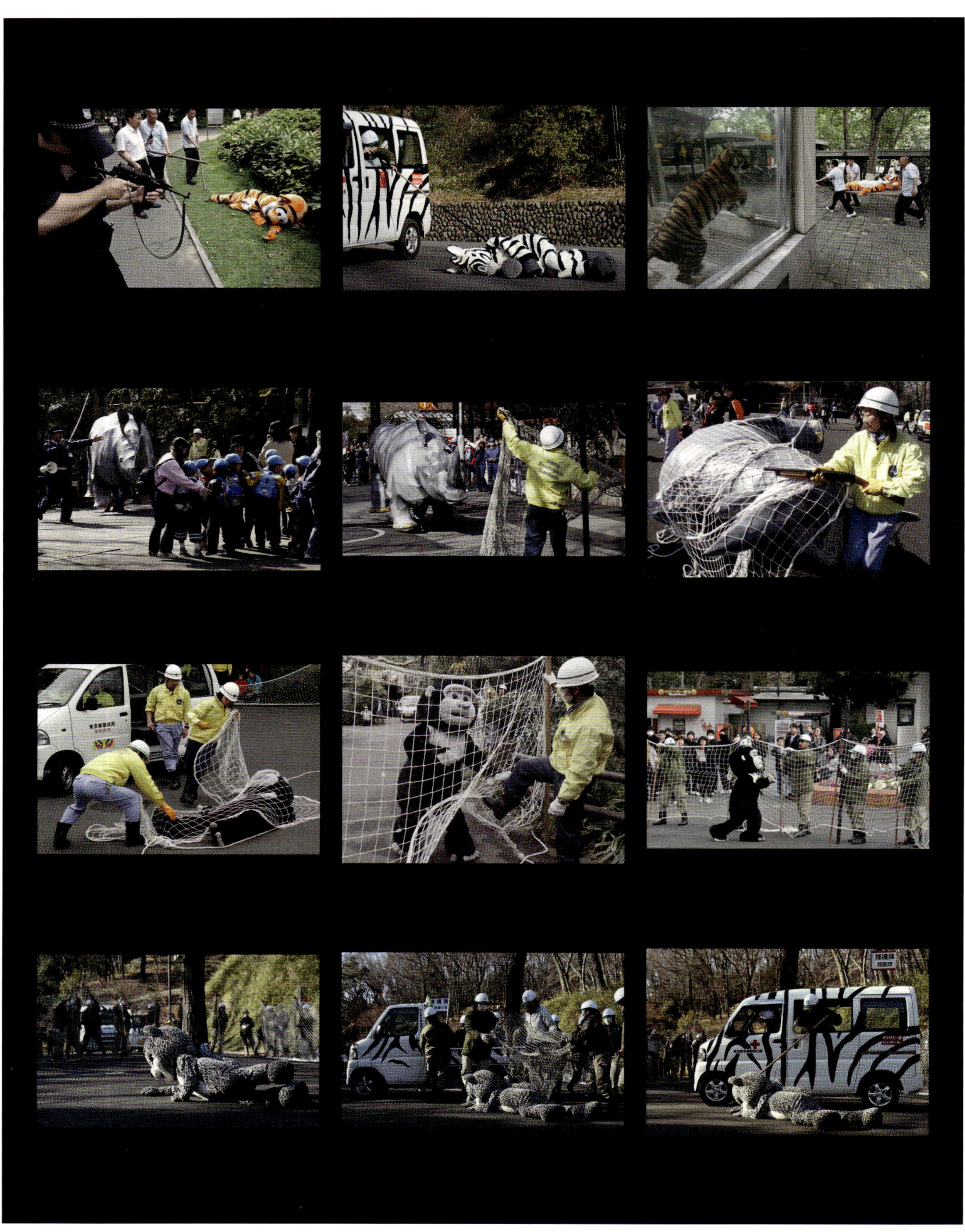

Sara Ludy. *Zoo Drill* (from *Low Prim Room*), 2012–16. HD video: an animal escape drill at Tama Zoo in Hino, Japan. *Courtesy of the artist and bitforms gallery, New York*

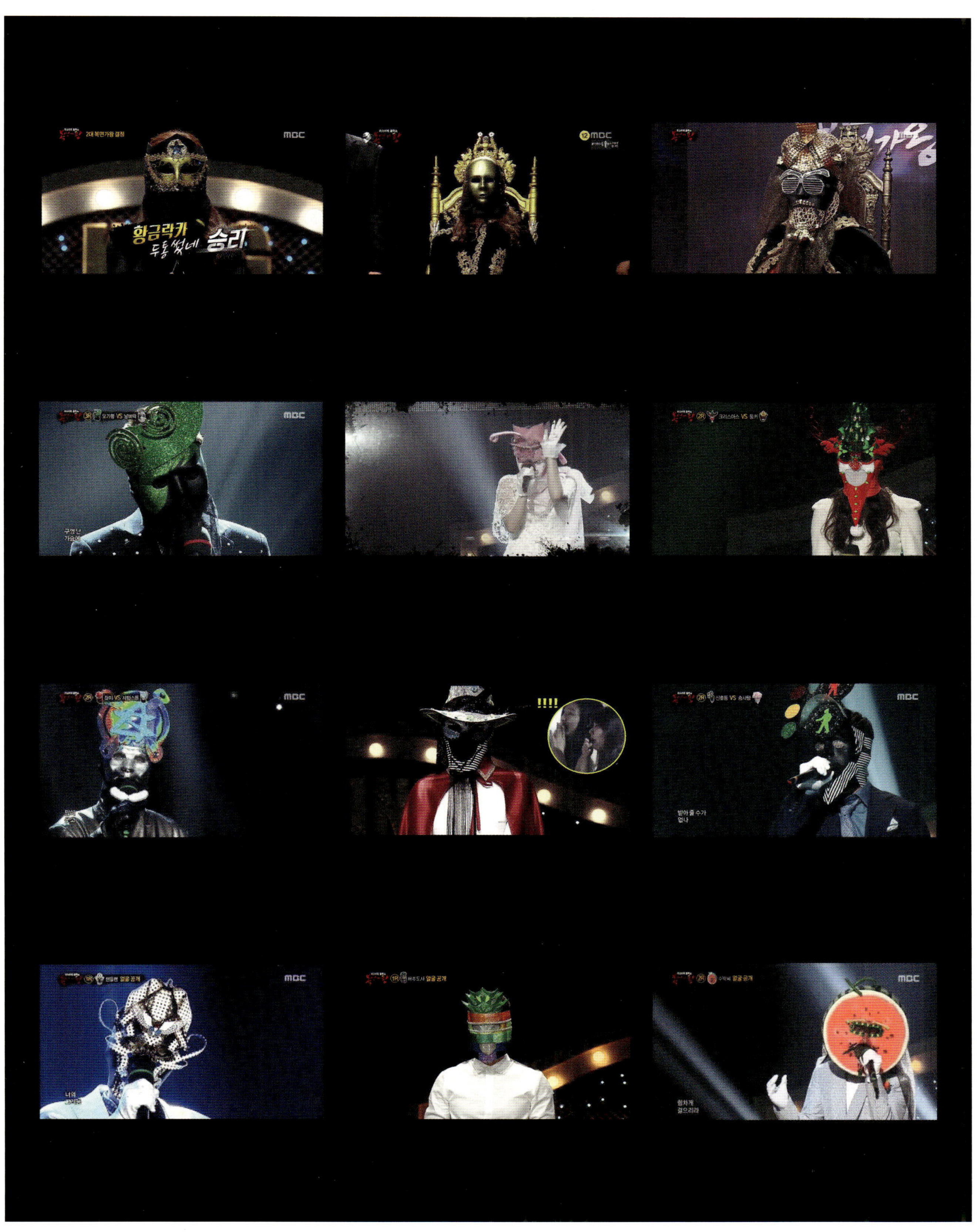

Sara Ludy. *King of Mask Singer* (from *Low Prim 1-87*), 2012–16. HD video: images from King of Mask Singer, a South Korean singing competition. *Courtesy of the artist and bitforms gallery, New York*

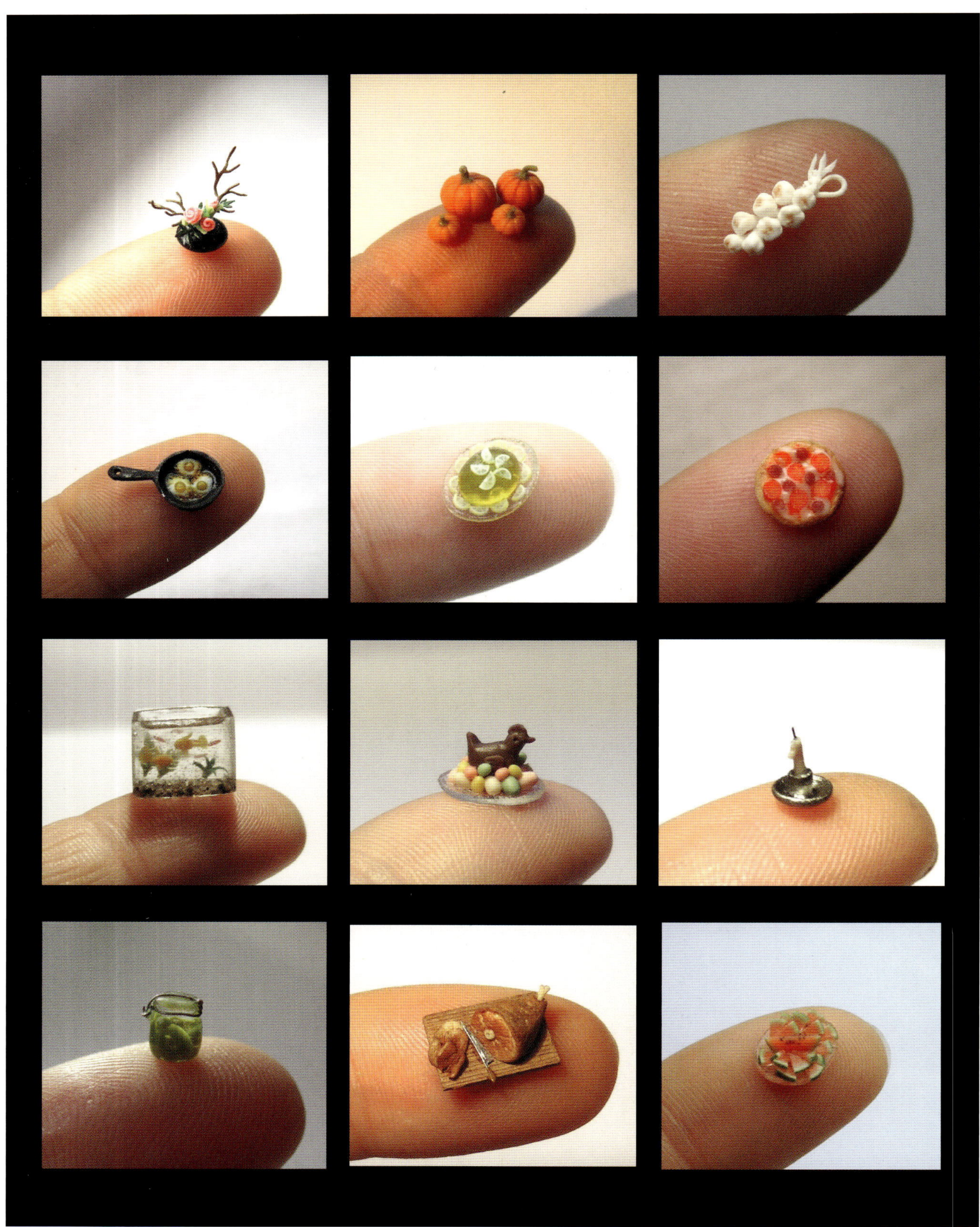

Sara Ludy. *Miniatures* (from *Low Prim 1-87*), 2012–16. HD video: miniatures made by Signe Alvarstein. Images found on Etsy via Google image search. *Courtesy of the artist and bitforms gallery, New York*

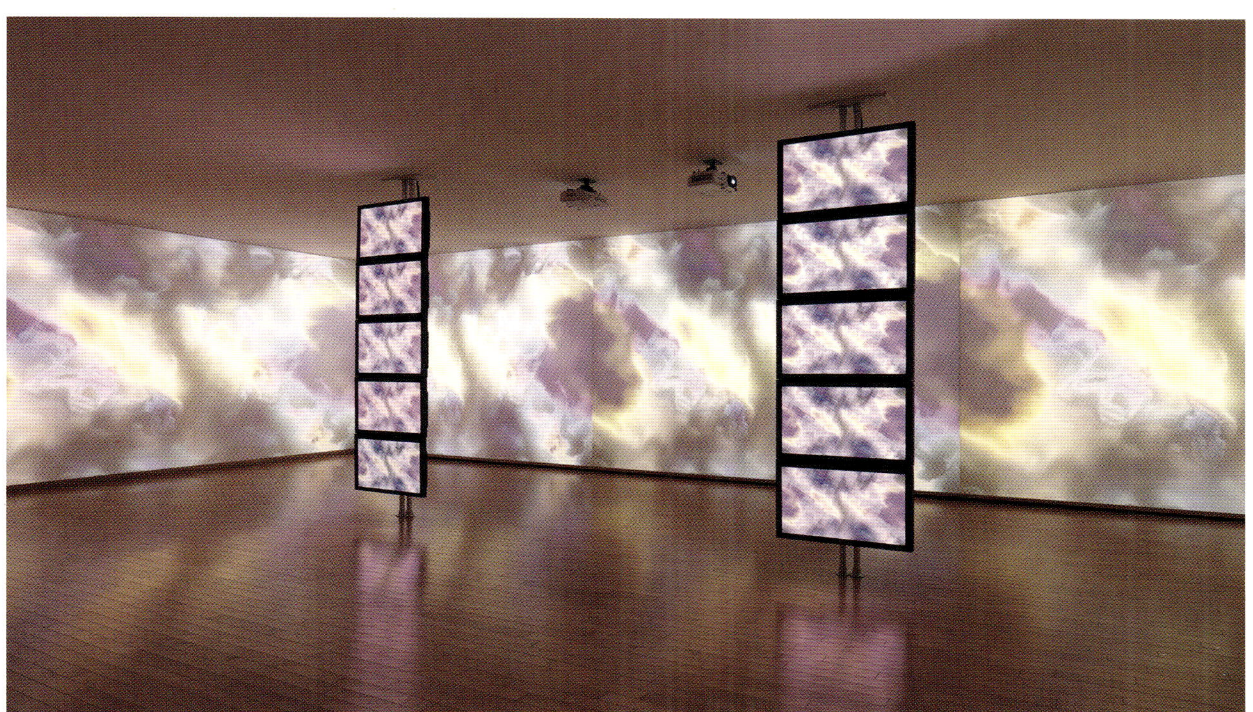

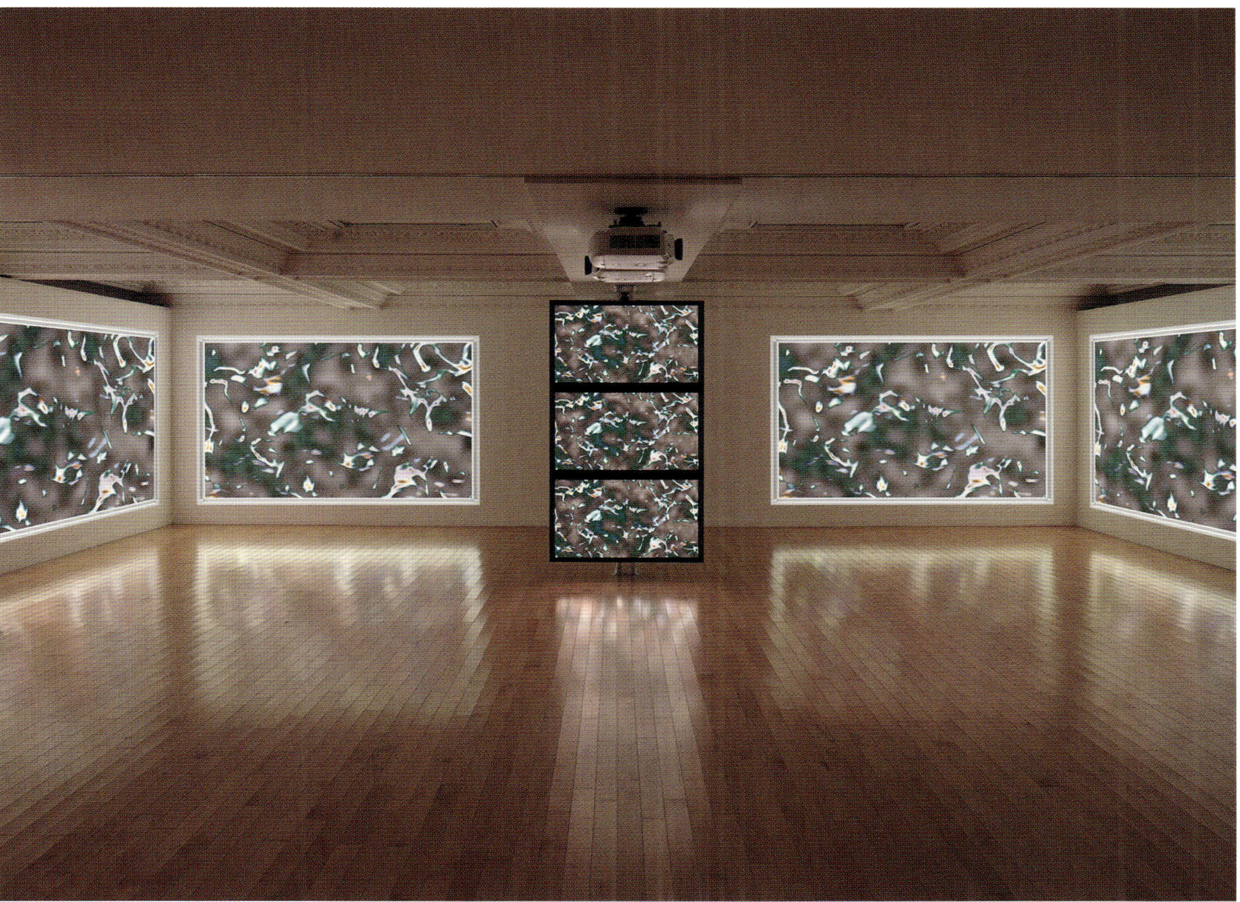

Sara Ludy. *Acid Cloud*, 2015. Computer-generated HD animation: 2 minutes, loop. *Courtesy of the artist and bitforms gallery, New York*

Sara Ludy. *Spectral Pond*, 2015. Computer-generated HD animation: 2 minutes, loop. *Courtesy of the artist and bitforms gallery, New York*

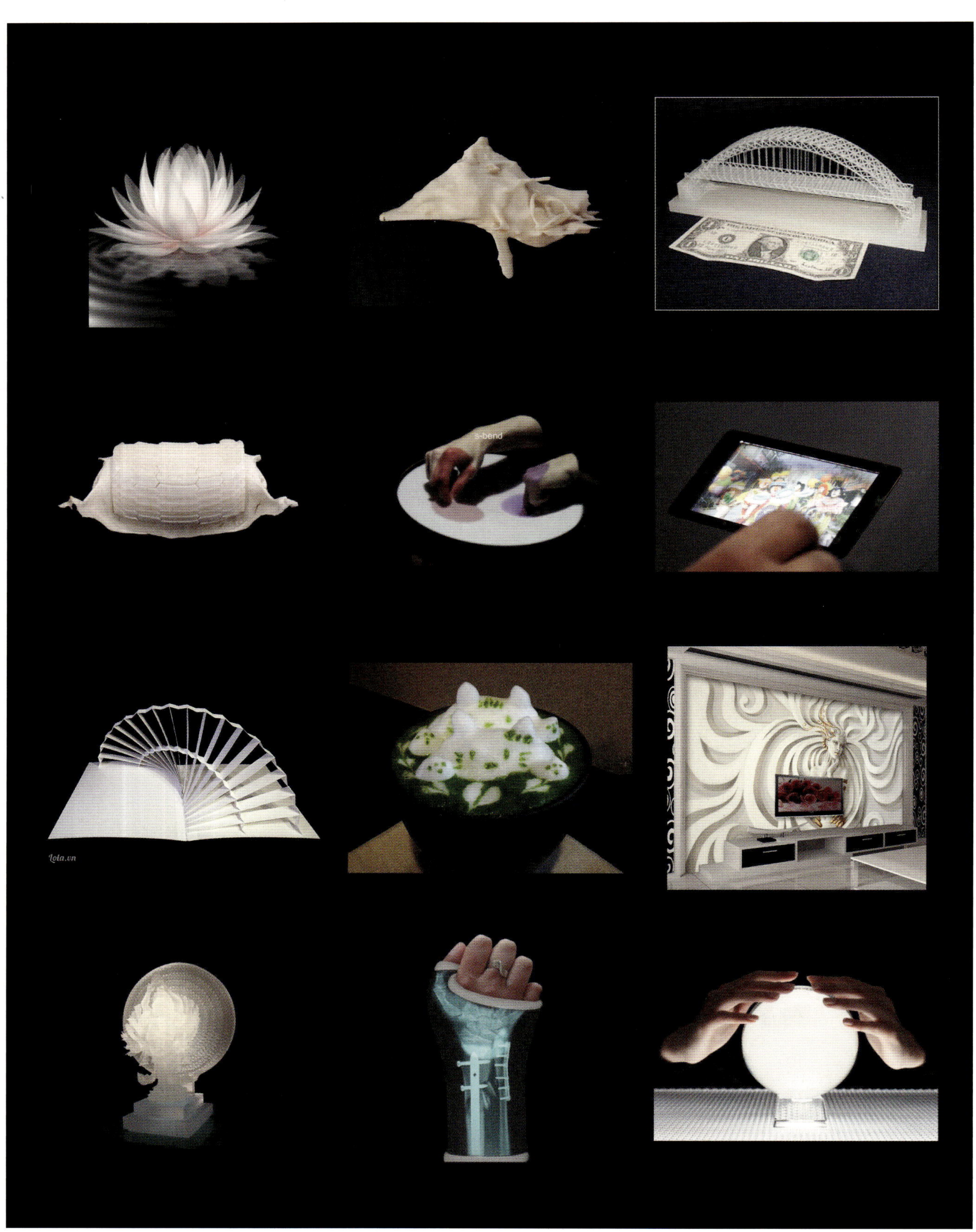

Sara Ludy. *Similar Images 33* (from *Low Prim Room*), 2012–16. HD video: a selection of images from Google similar images. *Courtesy of the artist and bitforms gallery, New York*

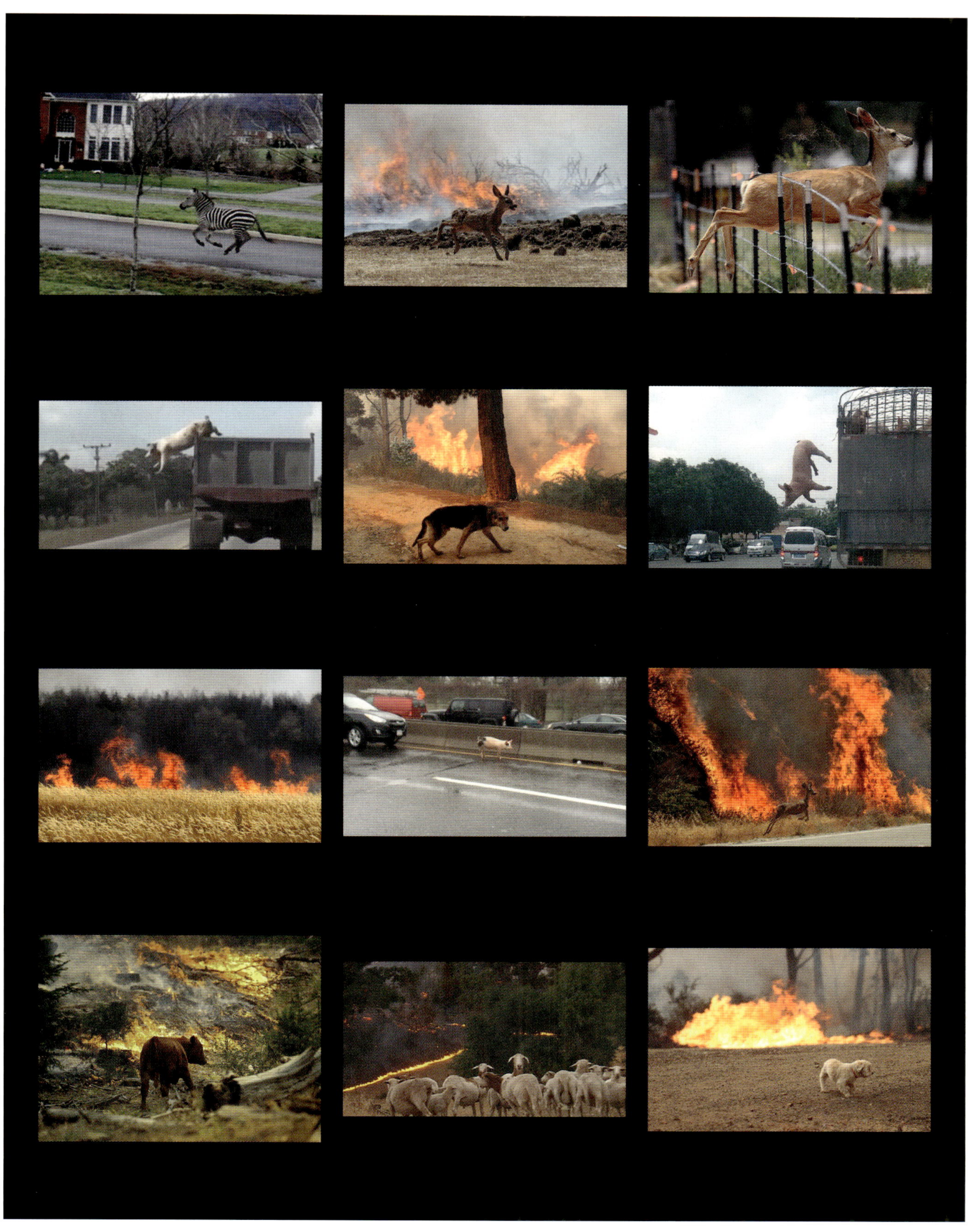

Sara Ludy. *Similar Images 34* (from *Low Prim Room*), 2012–16. HD video: a selection of images from Google similar images. *Courtesy of the artist and bitforms gallery, New York*

SHAHZIA SIKANDER

Shahzia Sikander is a Pakistani-American multidisciplinary artist who works in drawing, painting, animation, large-scale installation, performance, and video. Her practice began by creating traditional-style Indo-Persian miniature paintings based on Persian, Rajput, and Mughal techniques and culture. *The Scroll*, a semiautobiographical manuscript completed in 1989–90, was a turning point in contemporary miniature painting. For her digital animations, she uses techniques of layering and ink drawings to bring her videos to life. *Parallax*, created in 2013, is an animation inspired by Sikander's journey through the unique landscape of the United Arab Emirates. The work examines contested histories of colonialism and cultural authority and tensions over the control of the Strait of Hormuz in the Persian Gulf.

Sikander's work has been widely exhibited, and she has held numerous solo shows throughout the United States, the United Kingdom, Germany, Ireland, Australia, and Hong Kong. She earned her BFA from the National College of Arts Lahore in Pakistan and earned her MFA in painting and printmaking at the Rhode Island School of Design, Providence. Recent awards include the Tamgha-e-imtiaz National Medal of Honor from the government of Pakistan in 2005; the John D. and Catherine T. MacArthur Foundation Fellowship in 2006; Young Global leader, World Economic Forum in 2006; the Medal of Art from the US State Department in 2012; Asia Society Award for Significant Contribution to Contemporary Art in 2015; the American Academy of Religion, Religion and the Arts Award (2016); and the Shahneela and Farhan Faruqui Popular Choice Art Prize at the Karachi Biennale in 2017.

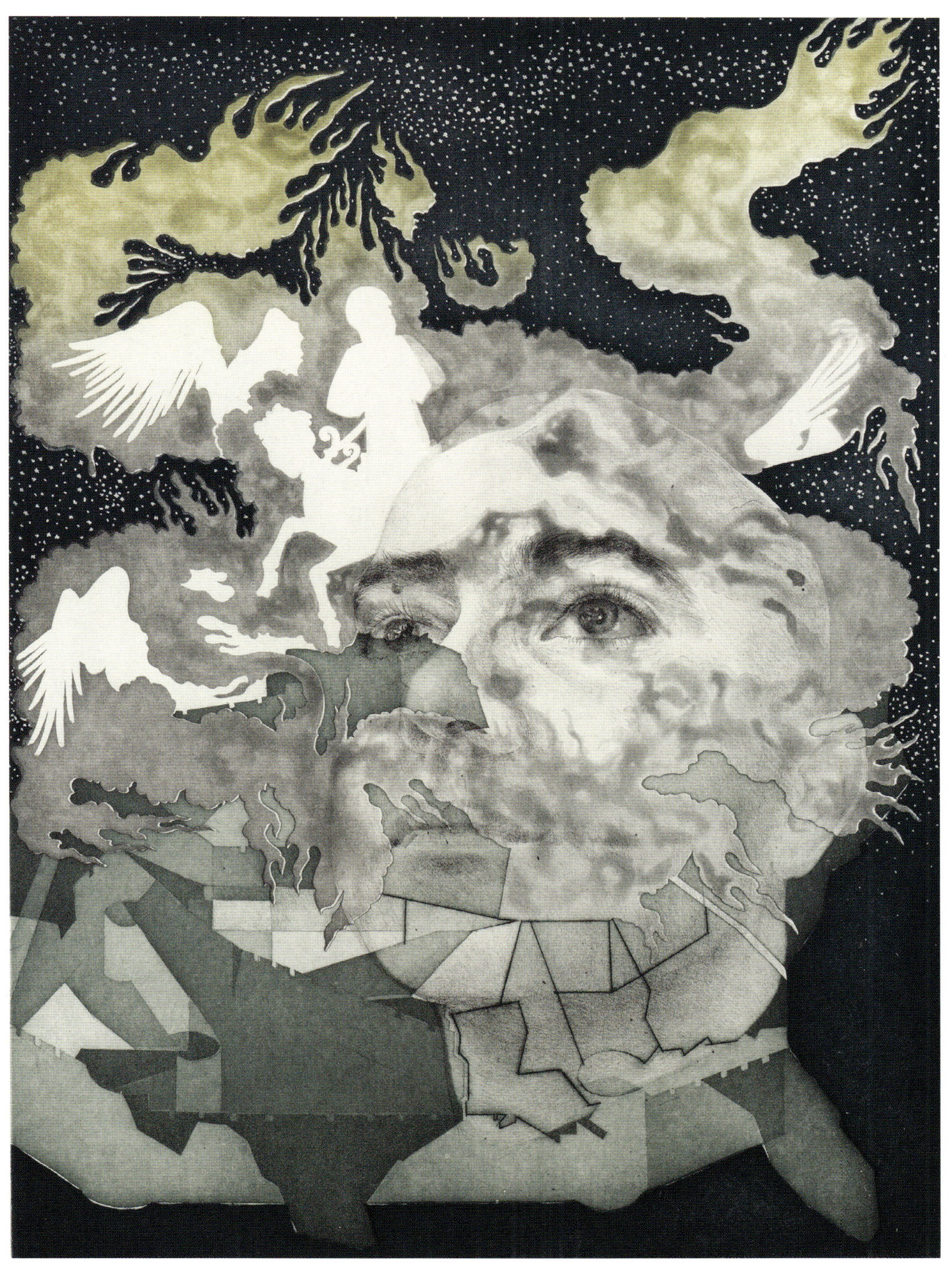

Shahzia Sikander. *Portrait of the Artist*, 2016. Etching, from a suite of four, with colophon text by Ayad Akhtar: Paper size: 27 × 21 inches, Image size: 22 × 17 inches. Edition of 40, Published by Pace Editions, Inc. Image ©Shahzia Sikander. *Courtesy of the artist and Sean Kelly, New York*

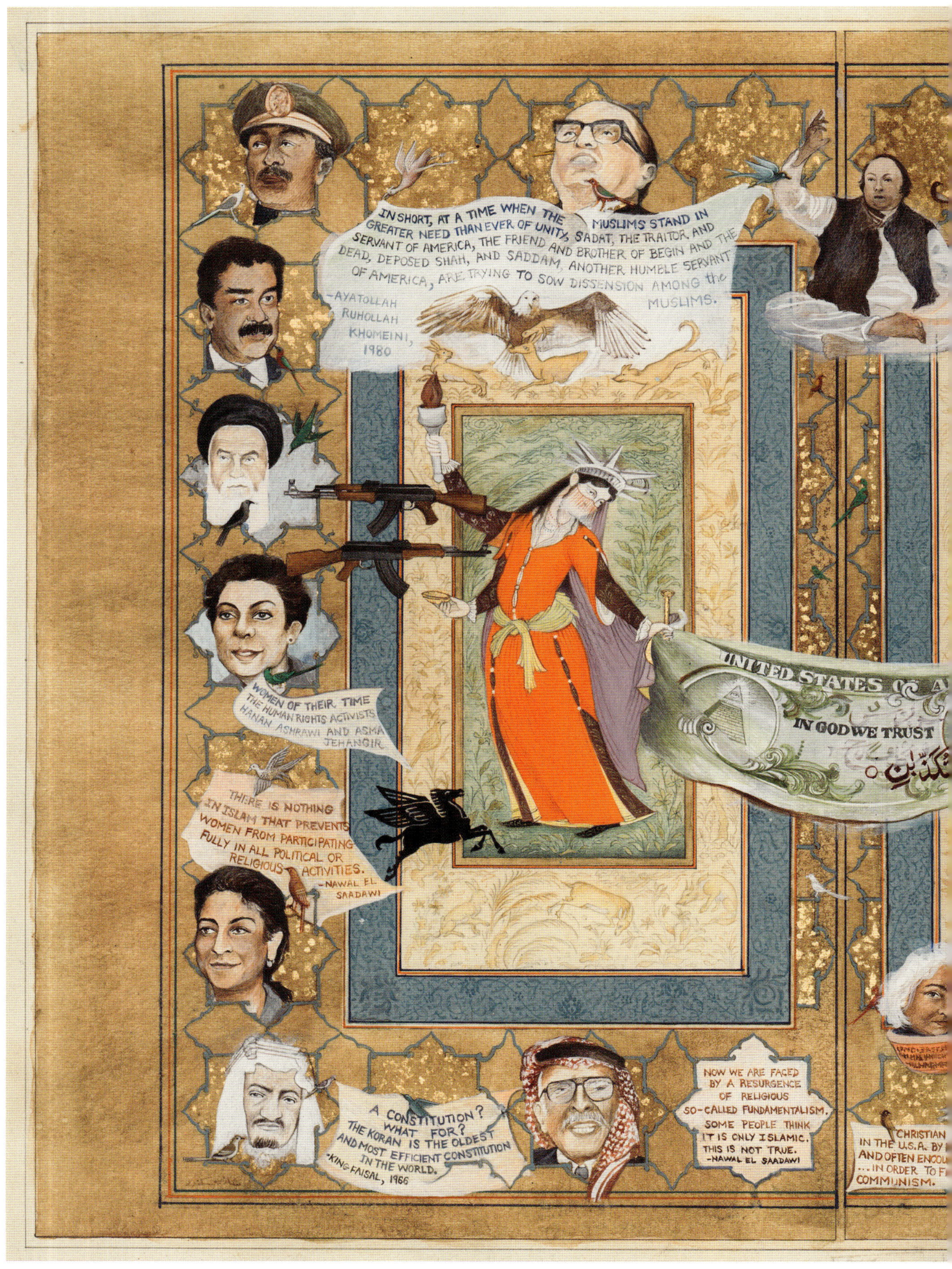

IN SHORT, AT A TIME WHEN THE MUSLIMS STAND IN GREATER NEED THAN EVER OF UNITY, SADAT, THE TRAITOR AND SERVANT OF AMERICA, THE FRIEND AND BROTHER OF BEGIN AND THE DEAD, DEPOSED SHAH, AND SADDAM, ANOTHER HUMBLE SERVANT OF AMERICA, ARE TRYING TO SOW DISSENSION AMONG the MUSLIMS.
-AYATOLLAH RUHOLLAH KHOMEINI, 1980
WOMEN OF THEIR TIME THE HUMAN RIGHTS ACTIVISTS HANAN ASHRAWI AND ASMA JEHANGIR
THERE IS NOTHING IN ISLAM THAT PREVENTS WOMEN FROM PARTICIPATING FULLY IN ALL POLITICAL OR RELIGIOUS ACTIVITIES.
-NAWAL EL SAADAWI
UNITED STATES
IN GOD WE TRUST
A CONSTITUTION? WHAT FOR? THE KORAN IS THE OLDEST AND MOST EFFICIENT CONSTITUTION IN THE WORLD.
-KING FAISAL, 1966
NOW WE ARE FACED BY A RESURGENCE OF RELIGIOUS SO-CALLED FUNDAMENTALISM. SOME PEOPLE THINK IT IS ONLY ISLAMIC. THIS IS NOT TRUE.
-NAWAL EL SAADAWI

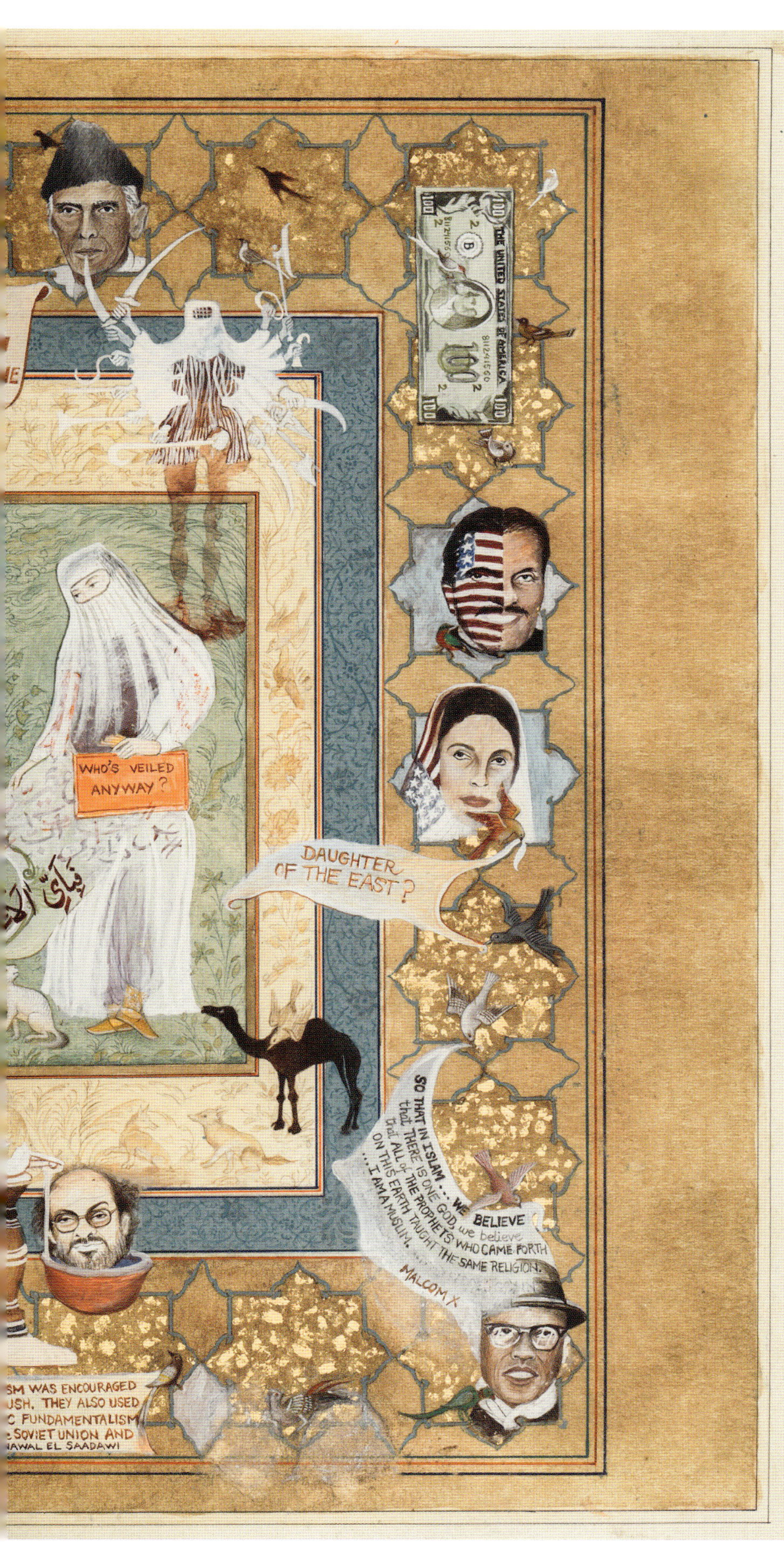

Shahzia Sikander. *Many Faces of Islam*, 1993–99. Gouache, vegetable color, watercolor, tea, and goldleaf on Wasli paper: 24 × 28 inches. Commissioned by the *New York Times Magazine* (September 19, 1999) for special issue *Imagining the Millennium* by living artists. Image ©Shahzia Sikander. *Courtesy of the artist and Sean Kelly, New York*

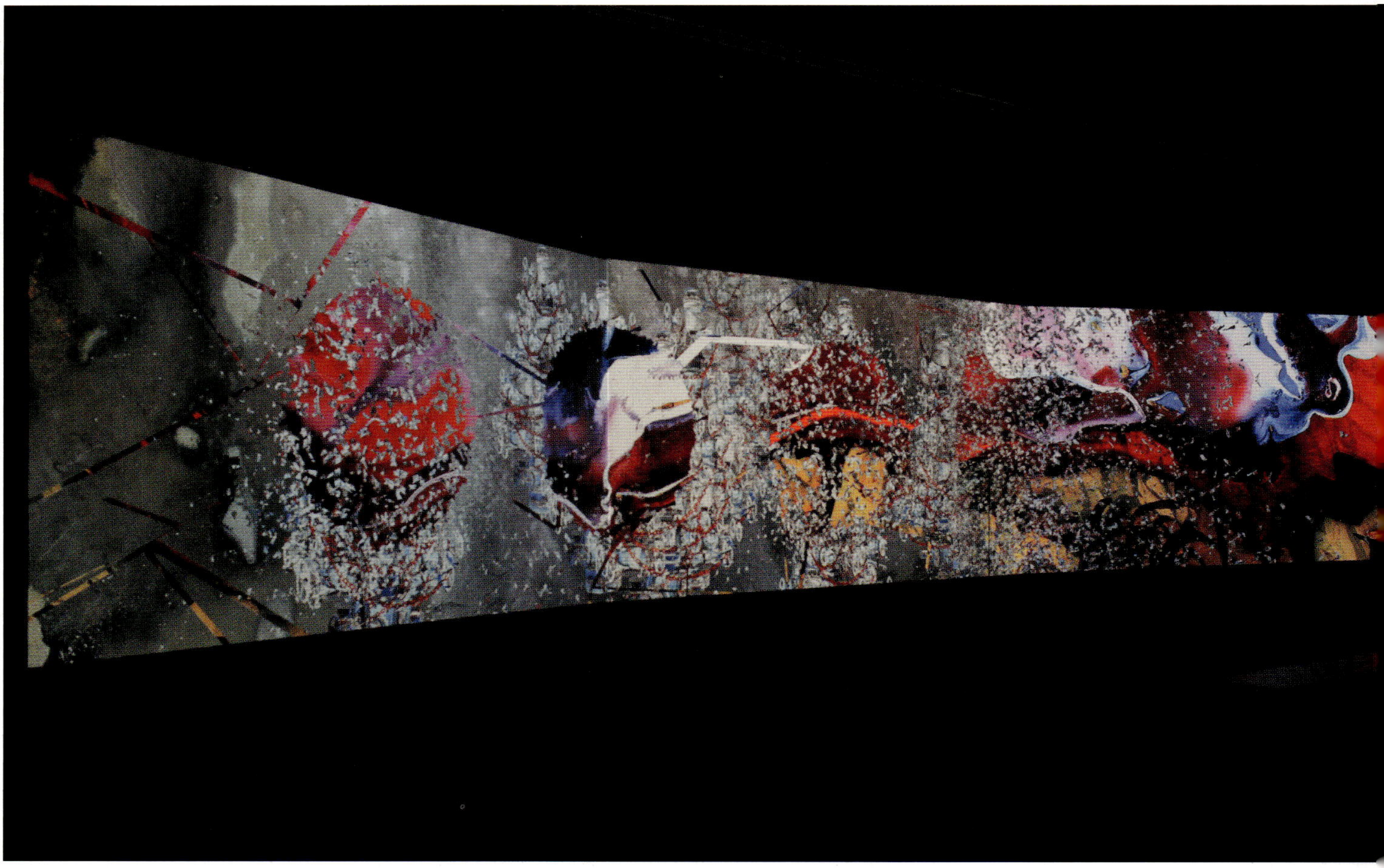

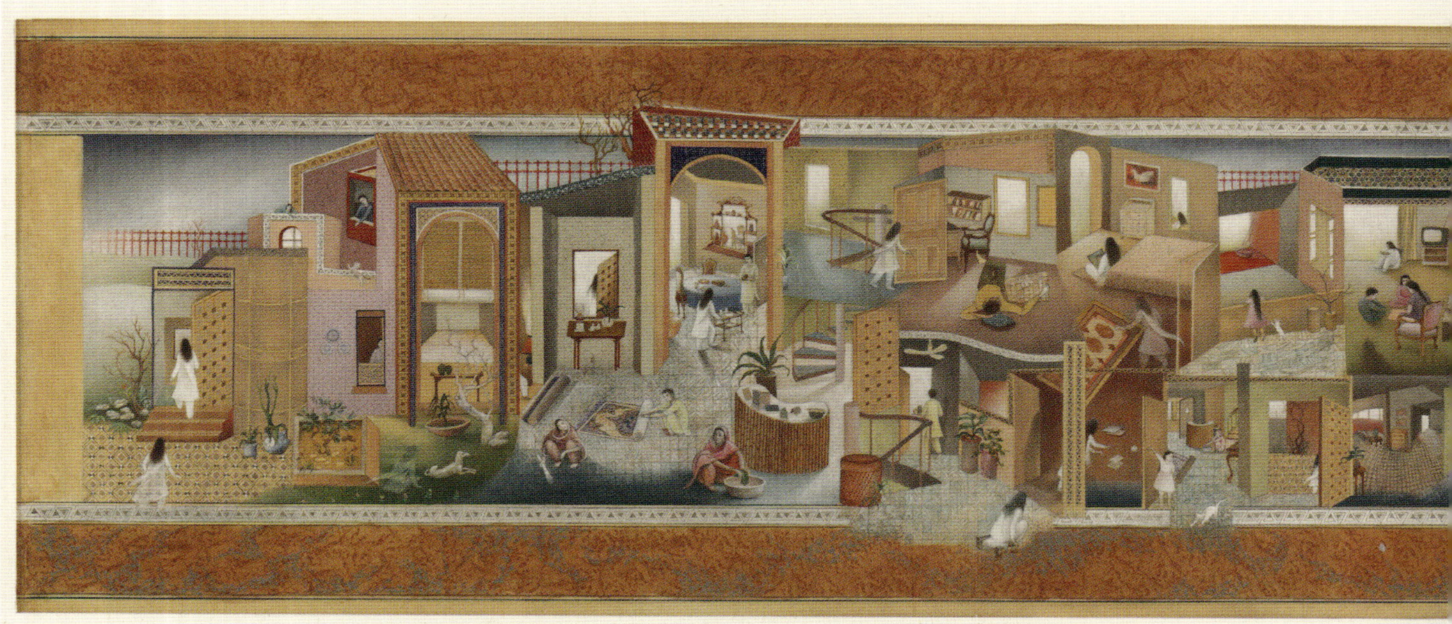

Shahzia Sikander. Mirrored view of *Parallax*, 2013. Three-channel, single-image HD video animation with 5.1 surround sound, 15:26 minutes; original score by Du Yun. Image ©Shahzia Sikander. *Courtesy of the artist and Sean Kelly, New York*

Shahzia Sikander. *The Scroll*, 1989–90. Vegetable color, dry pigment, watercolor, and tea on Wasli paper: 13 × 65 inches. Image ©Shahzia Sikander. *Courtesy of the artist and Sean Kelly, New York*

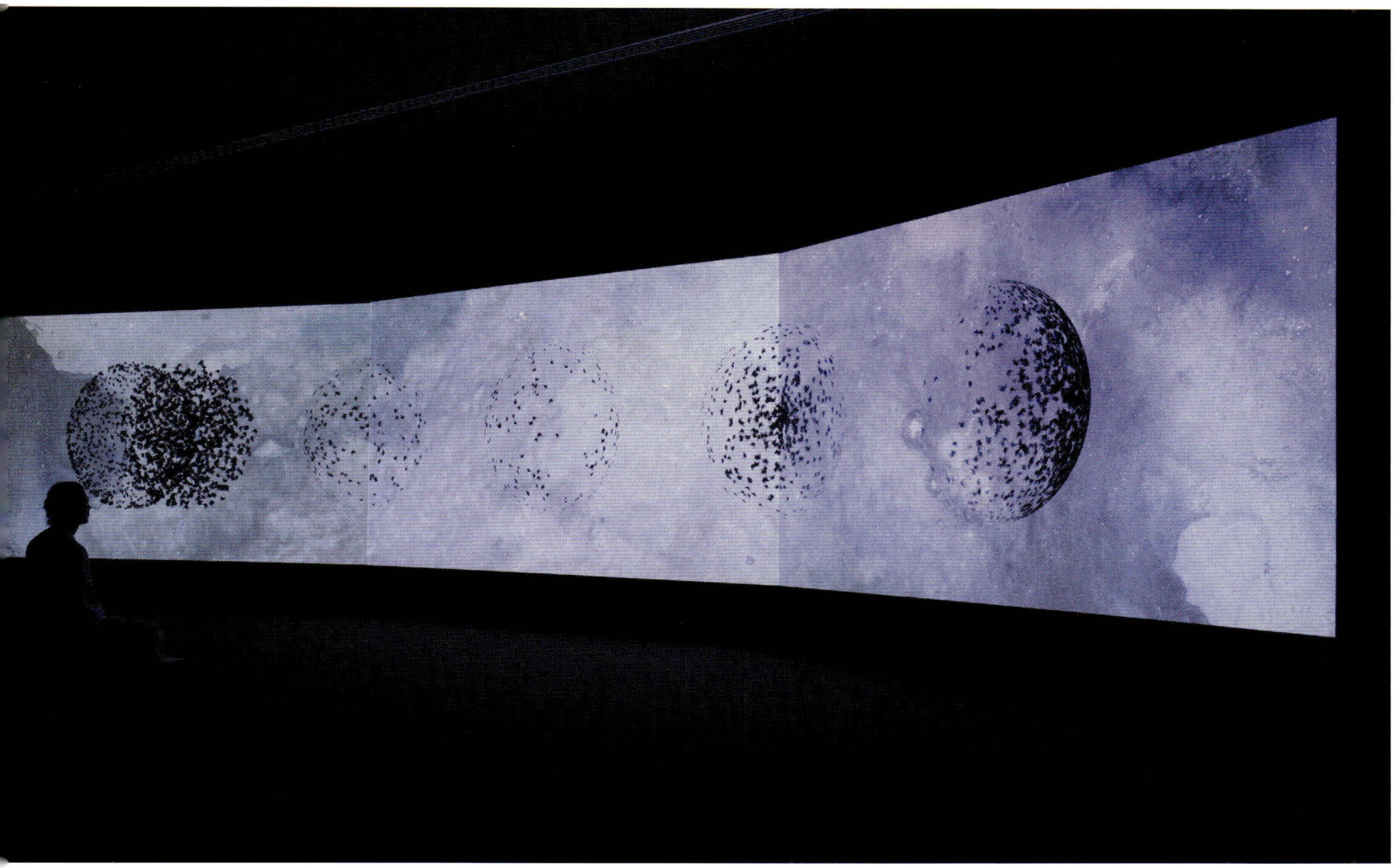

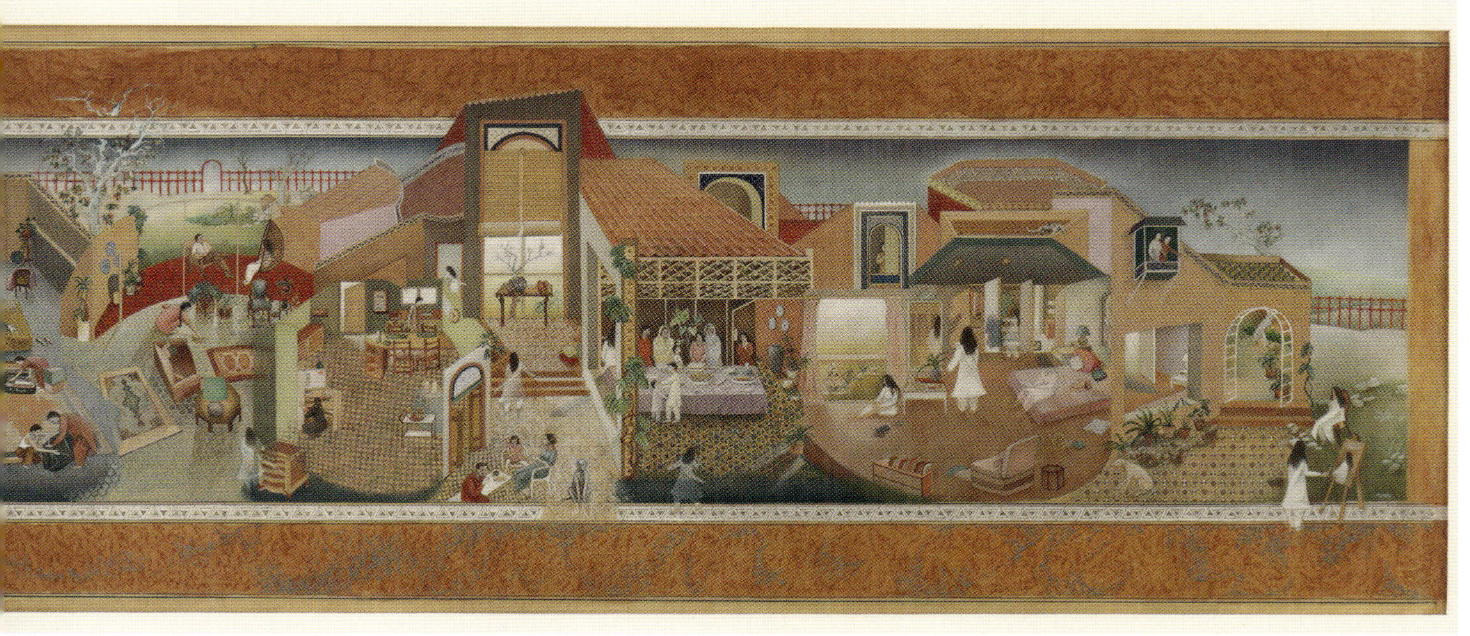

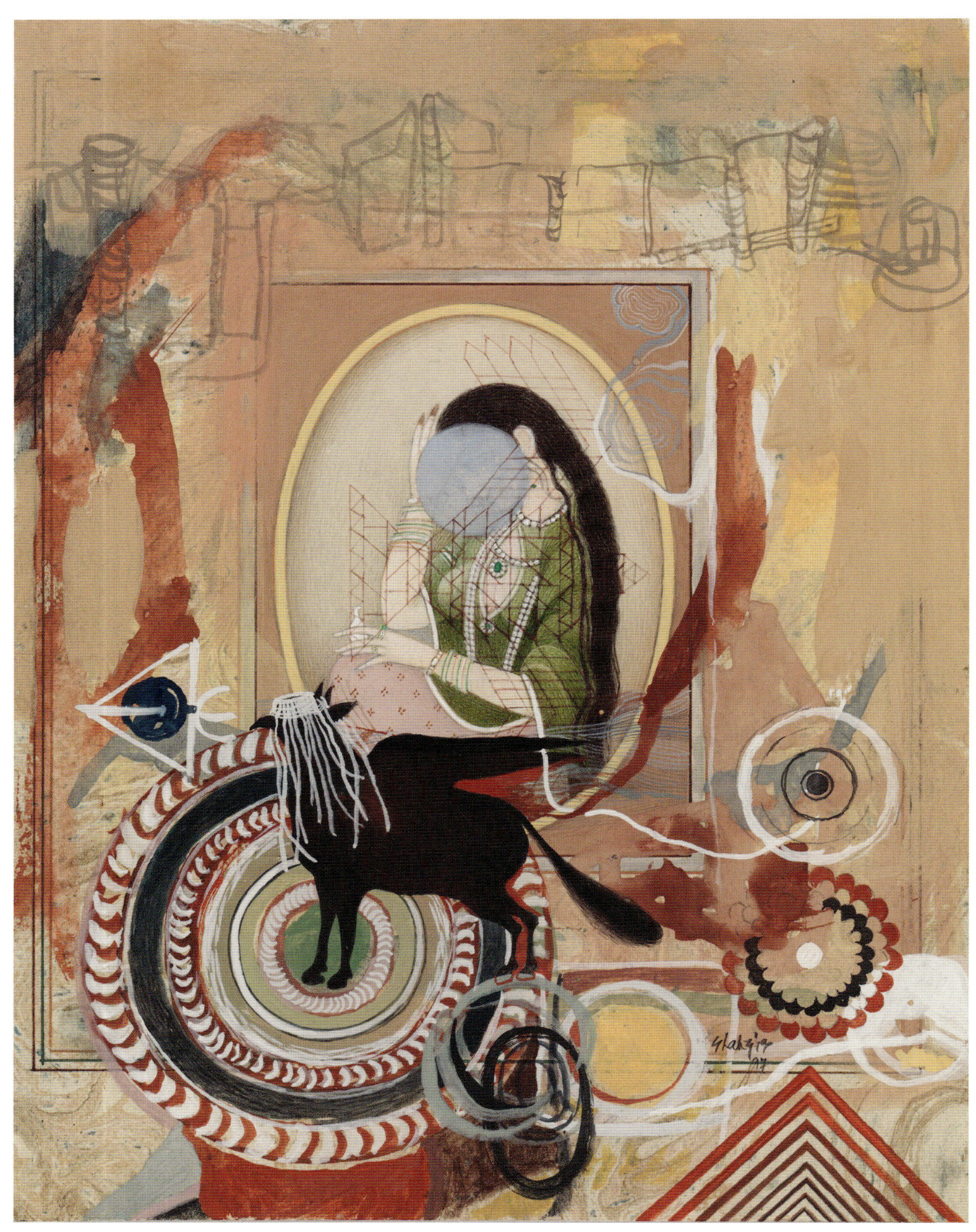

Shahzia Sikander. *Ready to Leave*, 1989–97. Vegetable color, dry pigment, watercolor, and gold-leaf on hand-prepared wasli paper: 9.88 × 7.56 inches. Whitney Museum of American Art, New York; Purchase, with funds from the Drawing Committee. 97.83.3. Image ©Shahzia Sikander. *Courtesy of the artist and Sean Kelly, New York*

SHIRIN NESHAT

Shirin Neshat is an Iranian visual artist who works in film, video, and photography. Central narratives in her work explore antipodal themes such as cultural dynamics between Islam and the West, femininity and masculinity, public life and private life, and antiquity and modernity. Her work also analyzes the female experience in Islamic societies and how identity for Muslim women is shaped through social, political, and psychological aspects.

Neshat moved to the United States in 1975, where she studied at the University of California, Berkeley, and received her BA, MA, and MFA. Afterward, she moved to New York City, where she began her artistic career in photography. Notable early photographic series are *Unveiling* and *Woman of Allah*. In 2006, she was awarded the Dorothy and Lillian Gish Prize and was named Artist of the Decade by the *Huffington Post* in 2010. Neshat has had featured solo exhibitions around the world, such as at the Museo de Arte Moderno in Mexico City; the Contemporary Arts Museum in Houston, Texas; the Walker Art Center in Minneapolis; Castello di Rivoli in Turin, Italy; the Dallas Museum of Art, Dallas, Texas; the Wexner Center for the Arts in Columbus, Ohio; the Art Institute of Chicago; the Serpentine Gallery, London; Museo de Arte Contemporáneo de Castilla y León in León, Spain; and the Hamburger Bahnhof in Berlin, Germany. Neshat has also participated in film festivals, including the Telluride Film Festival (2000), the Chicago International Film Festival (2001), the San Francisco International Film Festival (2001), the Locarno International Film Festival (2002), the Tribeca Film Festival (2003), the Sundance Film Festival (2003), and the Cannes Film Festival (2008). Notable video works by Nehsat are *Zarin*, a short video, and *Logic of the Birds*, a longer film. Her most recent exhibition, *Dreamers*, will include her two films *Roja* and *Sara* along with a series of photos called *Dreamer*. Neshat lives and works in New York City.

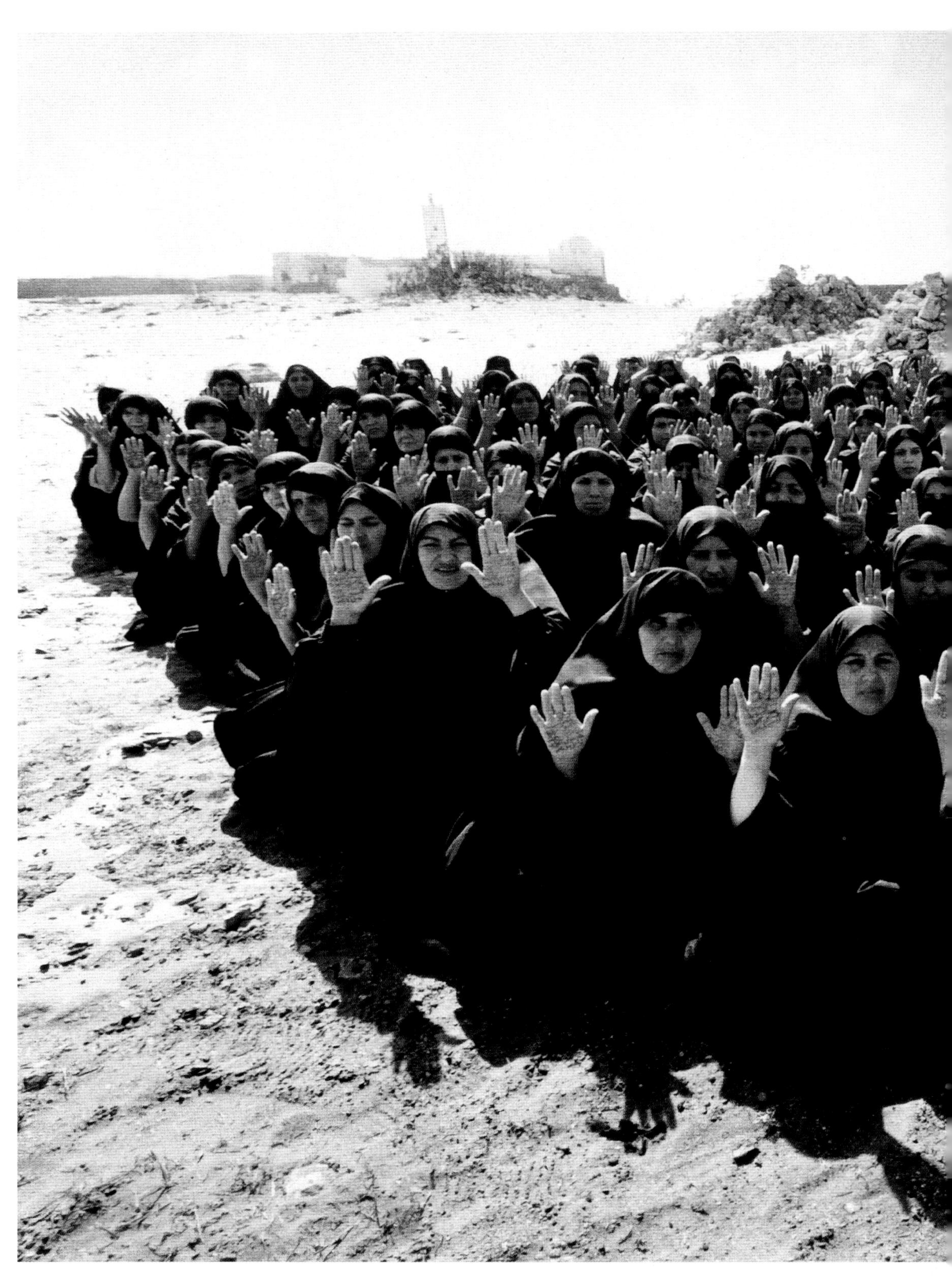

Shirin Neshat. *Rapture* (Photo by Larry Barns), 1999. Production still. Image ©Shirin Neshat. *Courtesy of the artist and Gladstone Gallery, New York and Brussels*

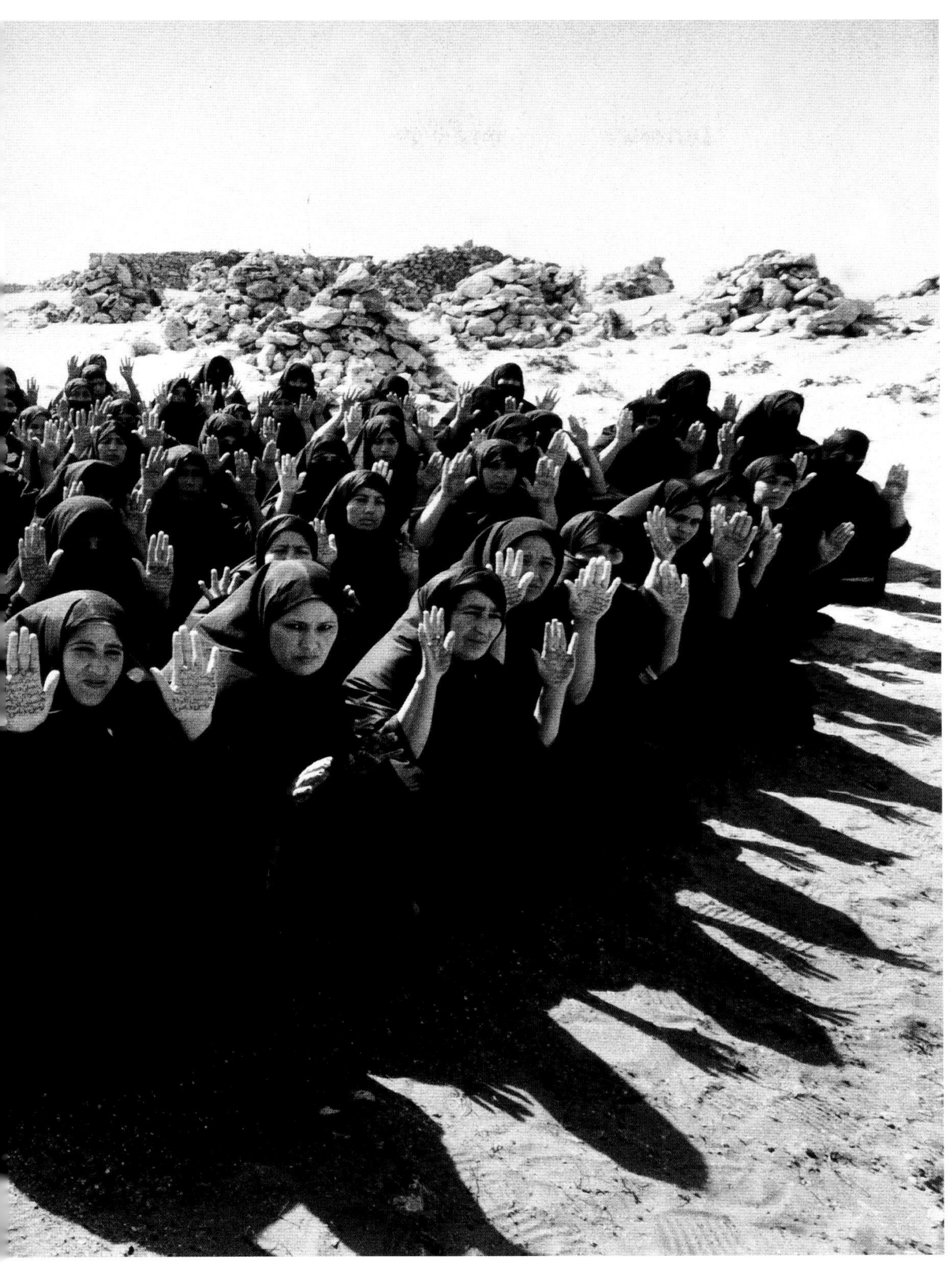

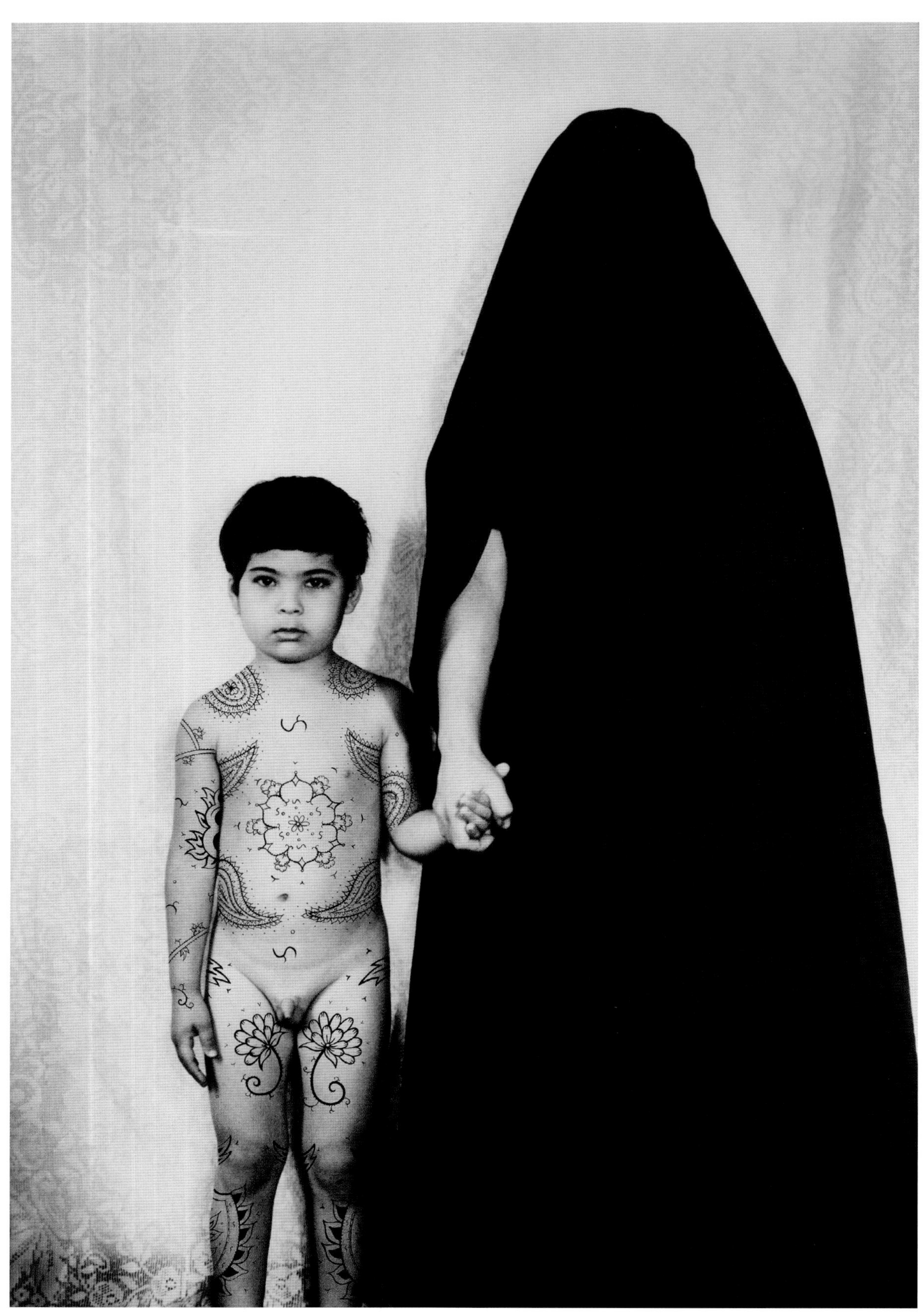

Shirin Neshat. *Untitled* (Photo by Kyong Park), 1996. RC print and ink: 53.25 × 37.75 inches. Image ©Shirin Neshat. *Courtesy of the artist and Gladstone Gallery, New York and Brussels*

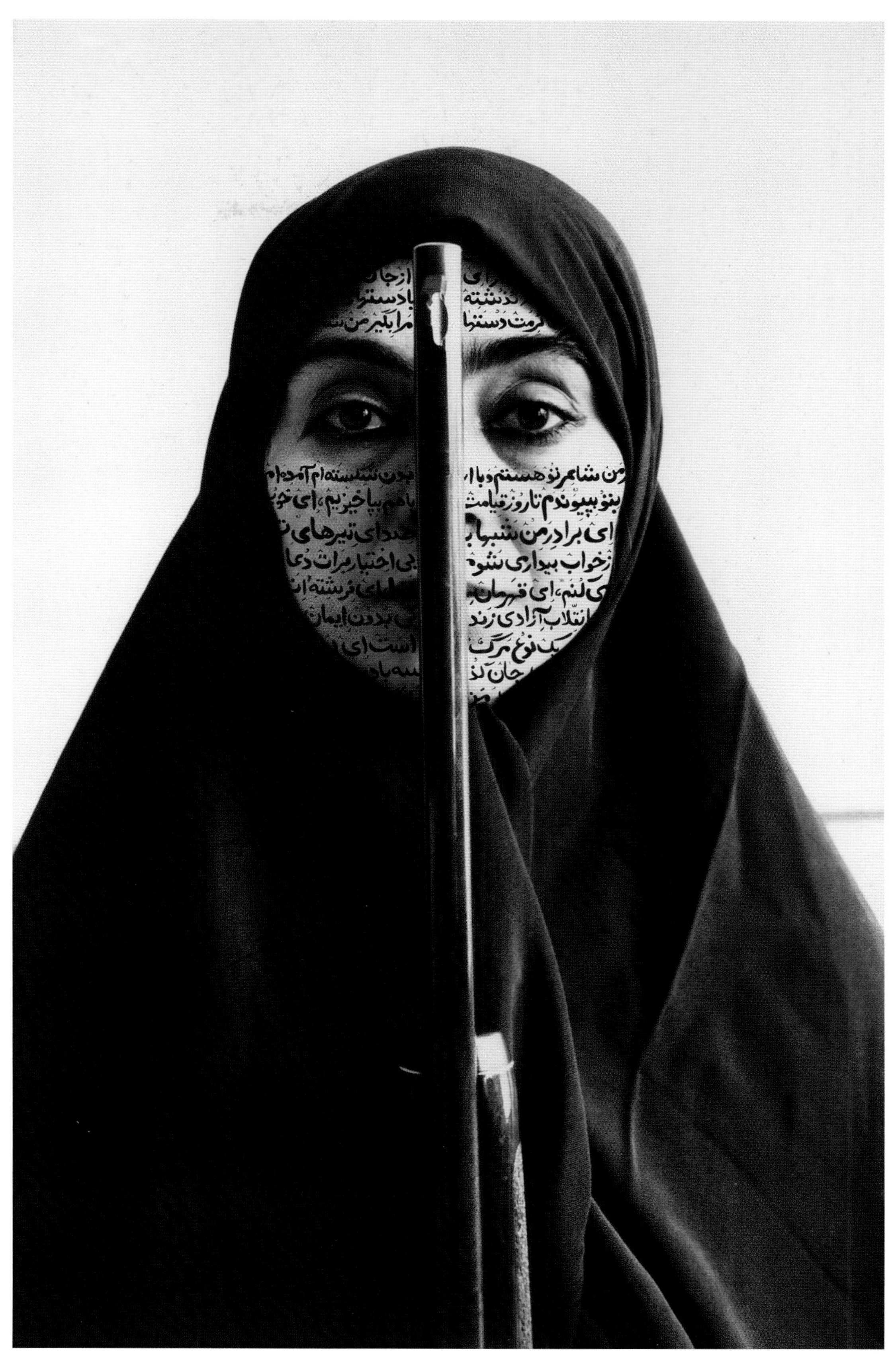

Shirin Neshat. *Rebellious Silence*, 1994. RC print and ink: 46.6 × 31.2 inches. Image ©Shirin Neshat. *Courtesy of the artist and Gladstone Gallery, New York and Brussels*

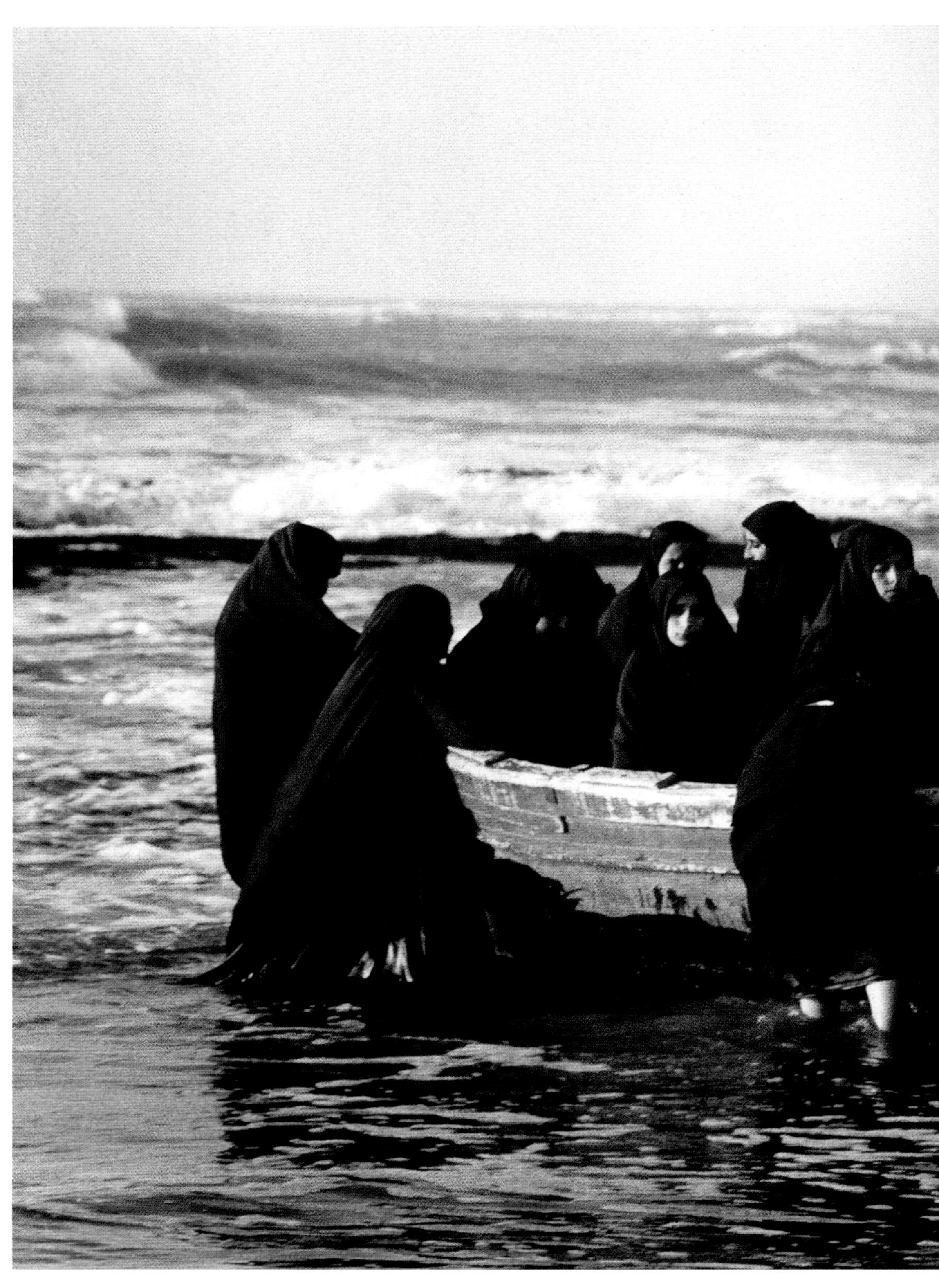

Shirin Neshat. *Untitled (Rapture* series—*Women Pushing Boat)*, 1999. Gelatin silver print: 44 × 68.25 inches. Edition of 5 + 2 AP. Image ©Shirin Neshat. *Courtesy of the artist and Gladstone Gallery, New York and Brussels*

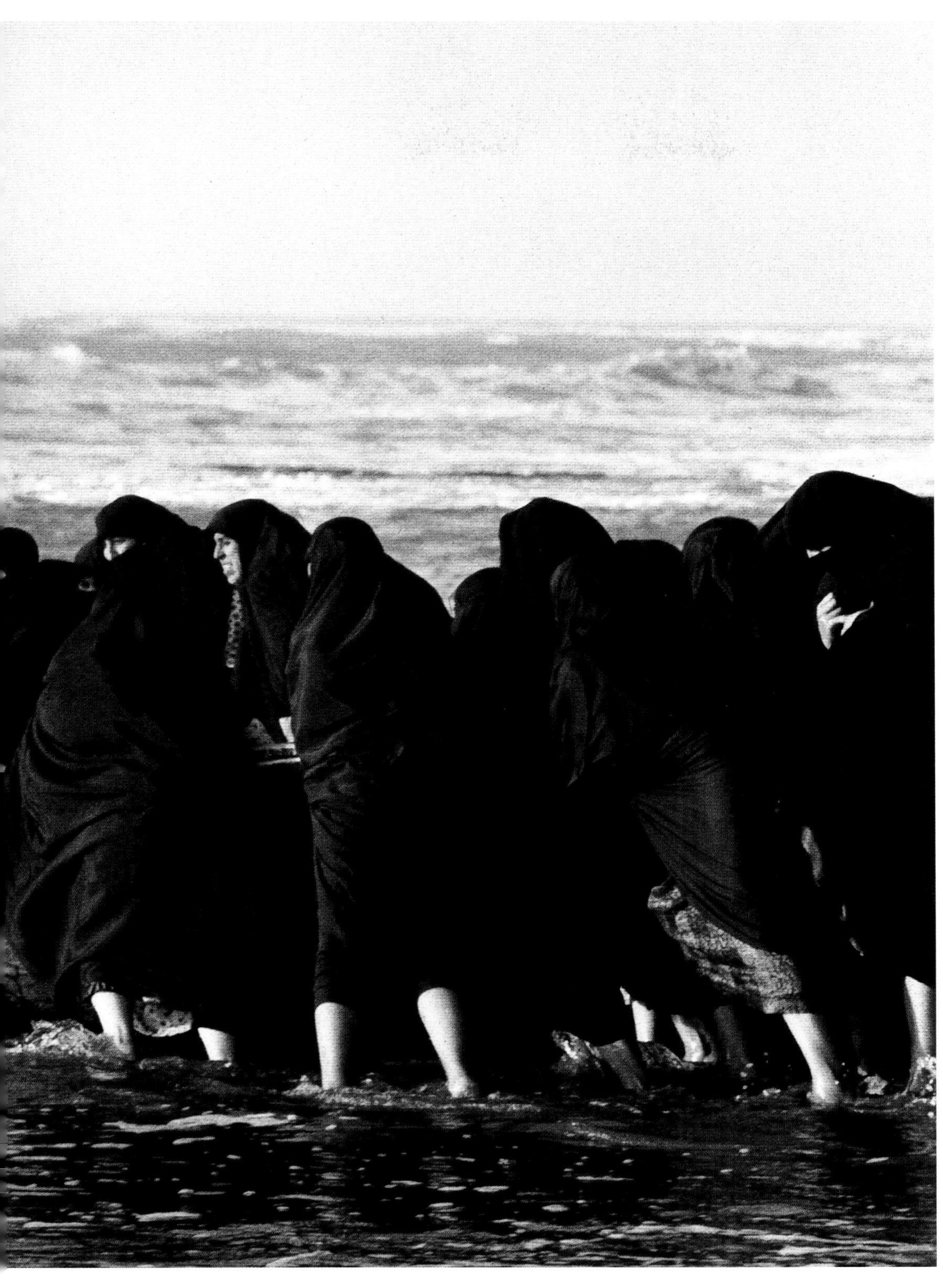

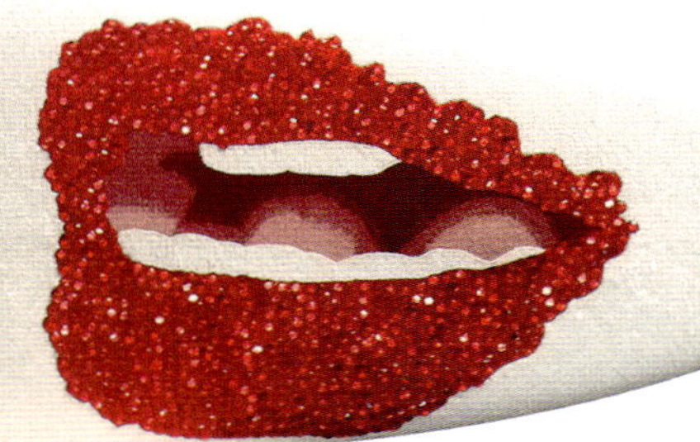

Stephanie Hirsch. *Live Deep Lips Surf*, 2015. Mixed media on surfboard: 6.8 feet. *Courtesy of the artist*

Stephanie Hirsch. *Trust the Universe Surf*, 2013. Mixed media on surfboard: 6.6 feet. *Courtesy of the artist*

Stephanie Hirsch. *Passion Is the Fire That Fuels Me Surf*, 2014. Mixed media on surfboard: 6.8 feet. *Courtesy of the artist*

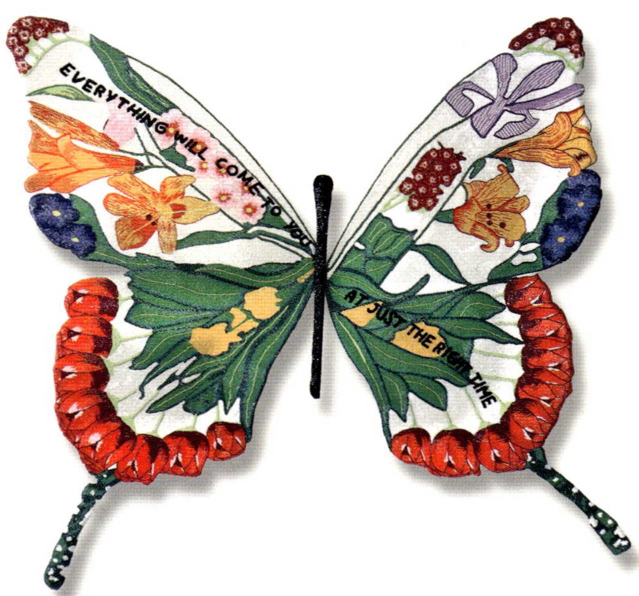

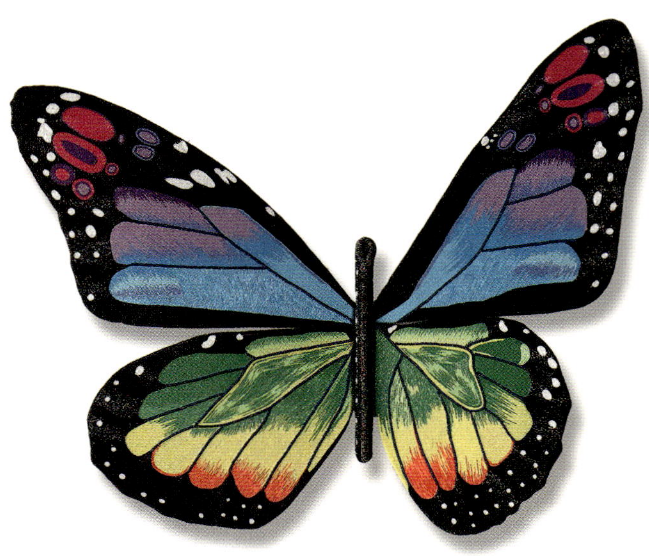

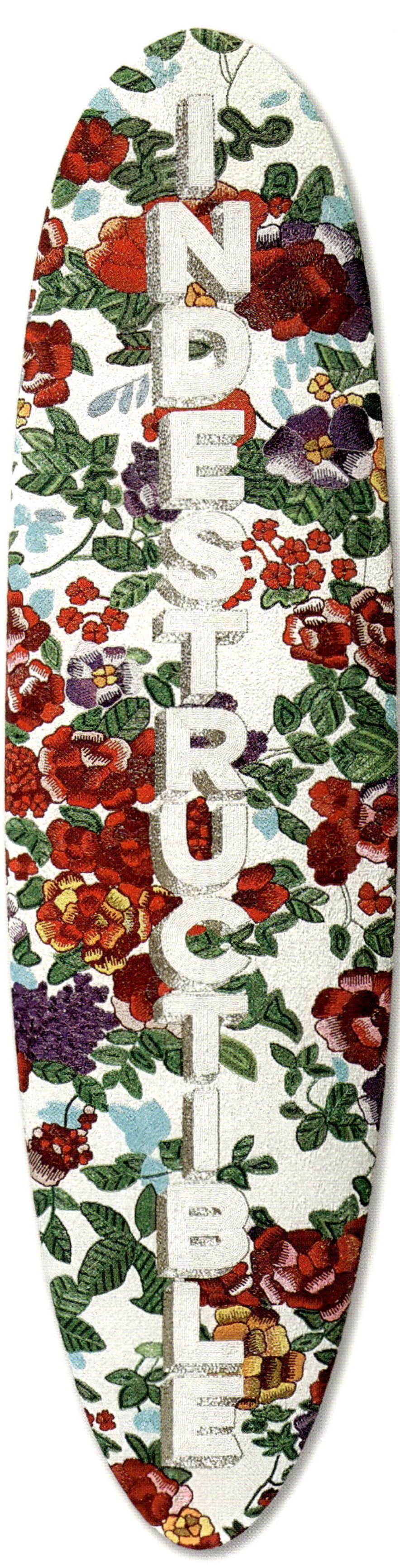

Stephanie Hirsch. *Everything Will Come to You at Just the Right Time*, 2015. Sculpted canvas and mixed media: 52 × 57 inches. *Courtesy of the artist*

Stephanie Hirsch. *Gita (Multicolored Butterfly)*, 2015. Sculpted canvas and mixed media: 49 × 56 inches. *Courtesy of the artist*

Stephanie Hirsch. *Indestructible Surf*, 2016. Mixed media on surfboard: 6.9 feet. *Courtesy of the artist*

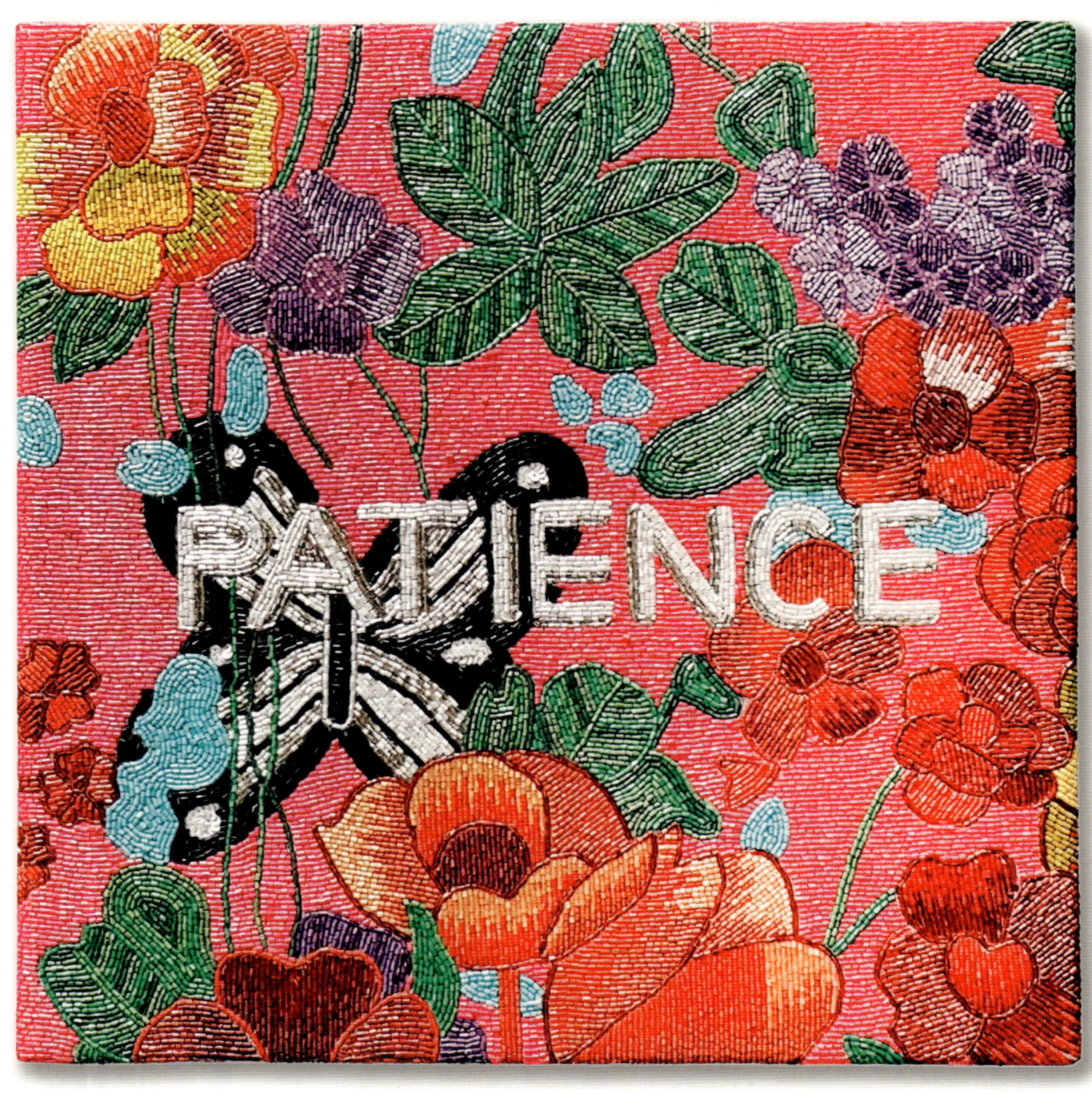

Stephanie Hirsch. *Patience*, 2016. Hand-sewn beads on canvas: 15.5 × 15.5 inches. *Courtesy of the artist*

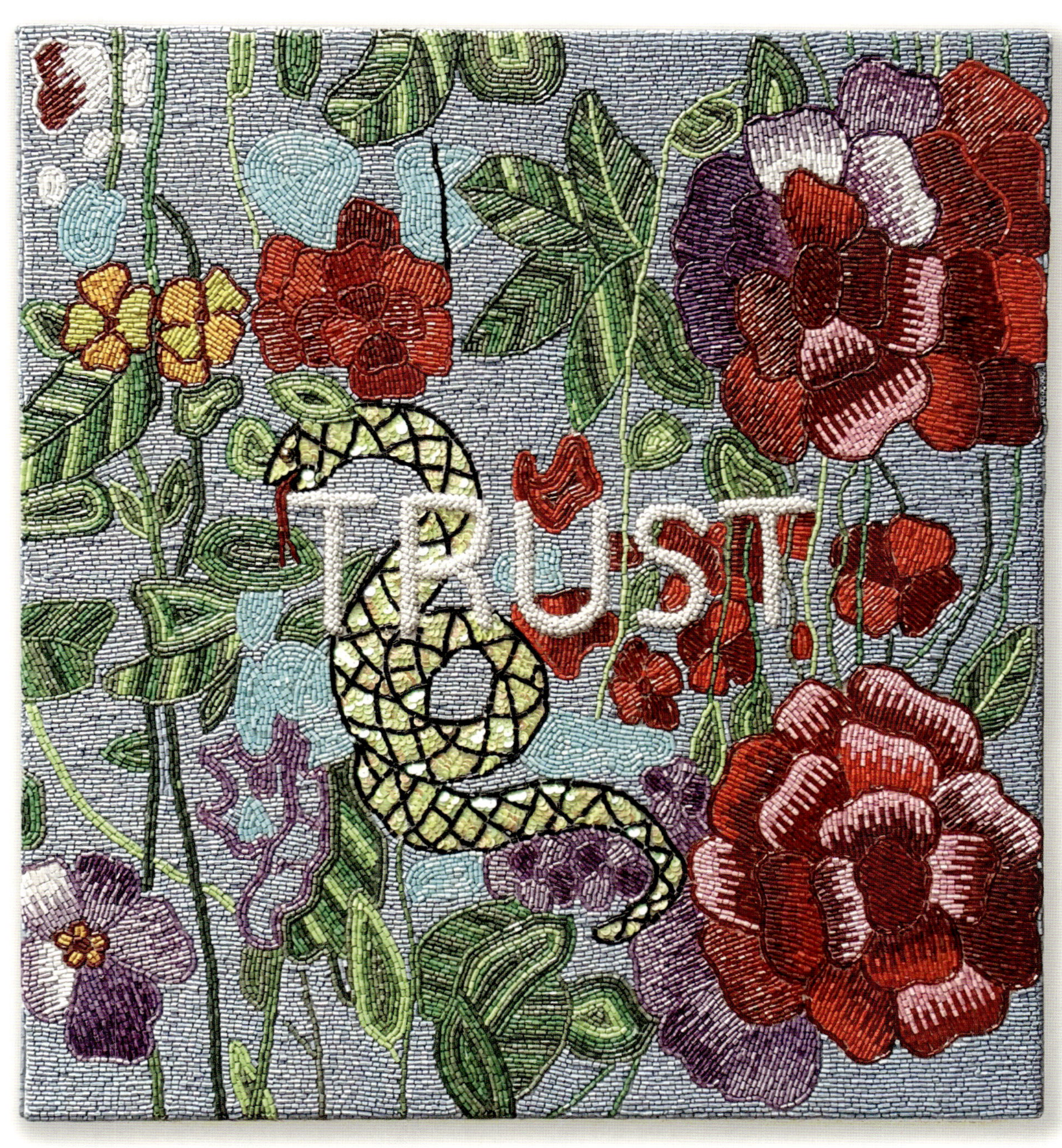

Stephanie Hirsch. *Trust*, 2016. Hand-sewn beads on canvas: 17 × 15.5 inches. *Courtesy of the artist*

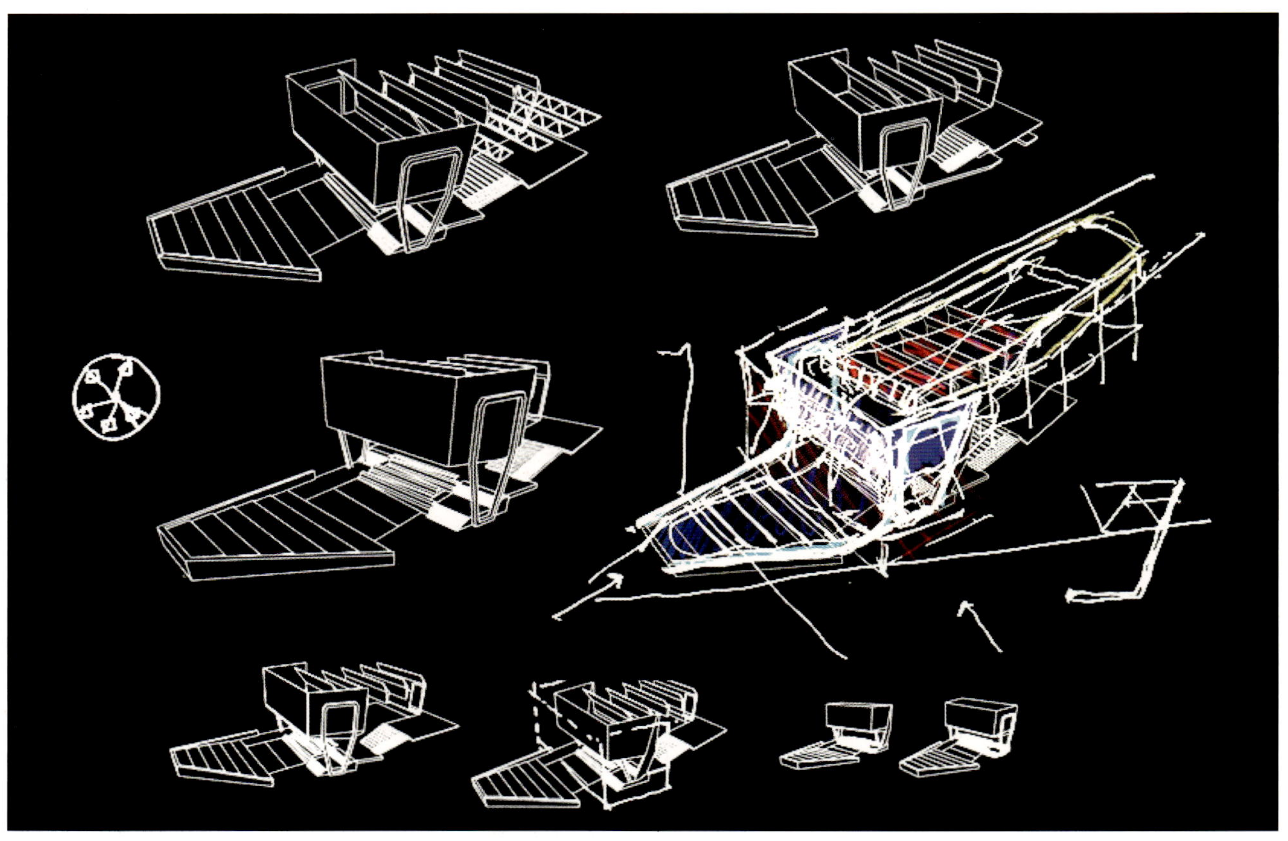

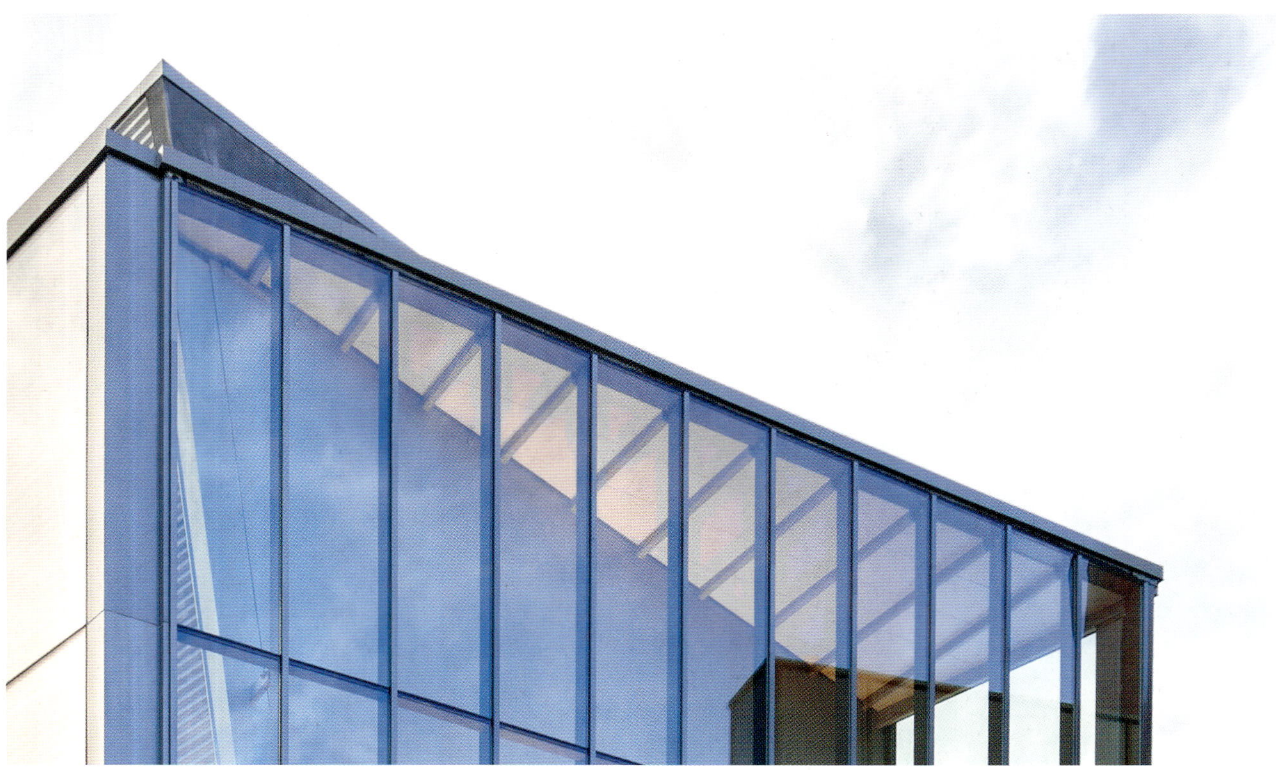

Susan T. Rodriguez. Massachusetts College of Art and Design, Design and Media Center. Sketches. *Courtesy of the artist*

Susan T. Rodriguez. Massachusetts College of Art and Design, Design and Media Center (façade detail). ©Fadi Asmar. *Courtesy of the artist*

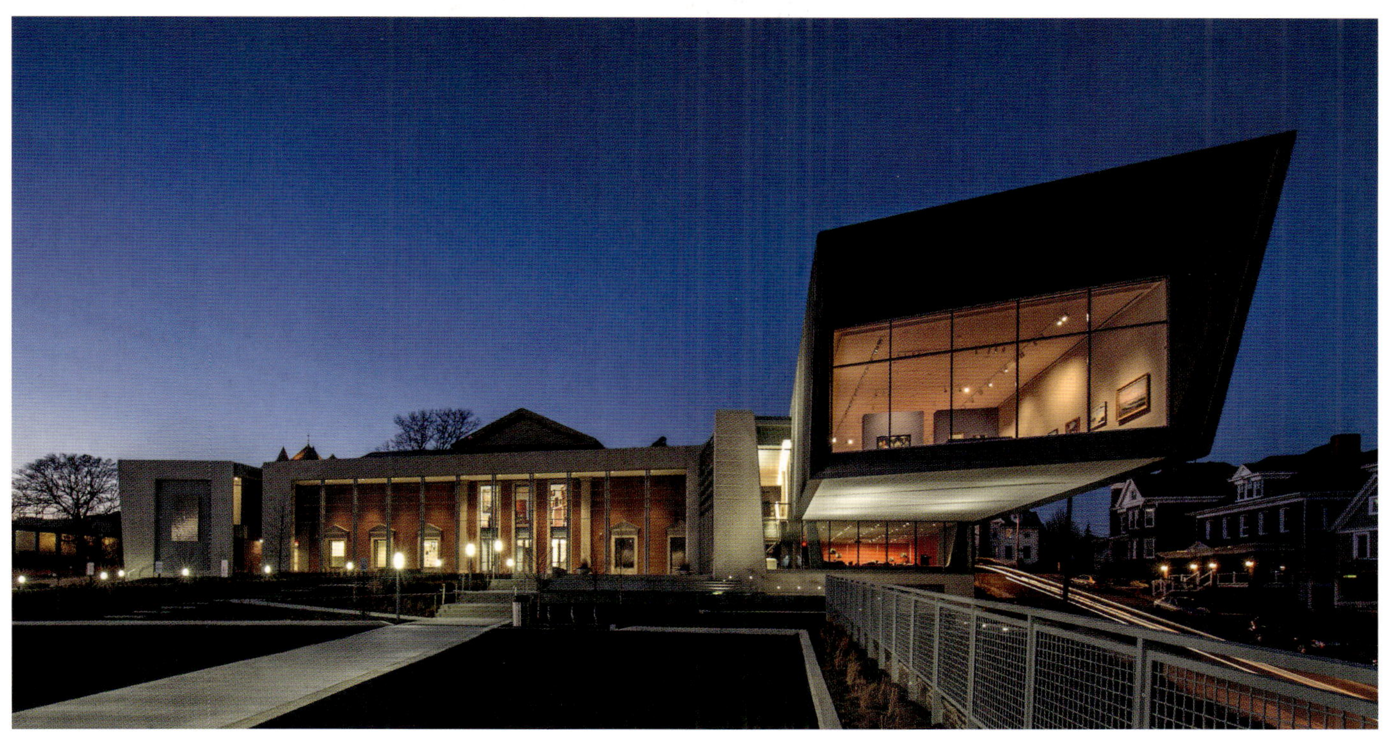

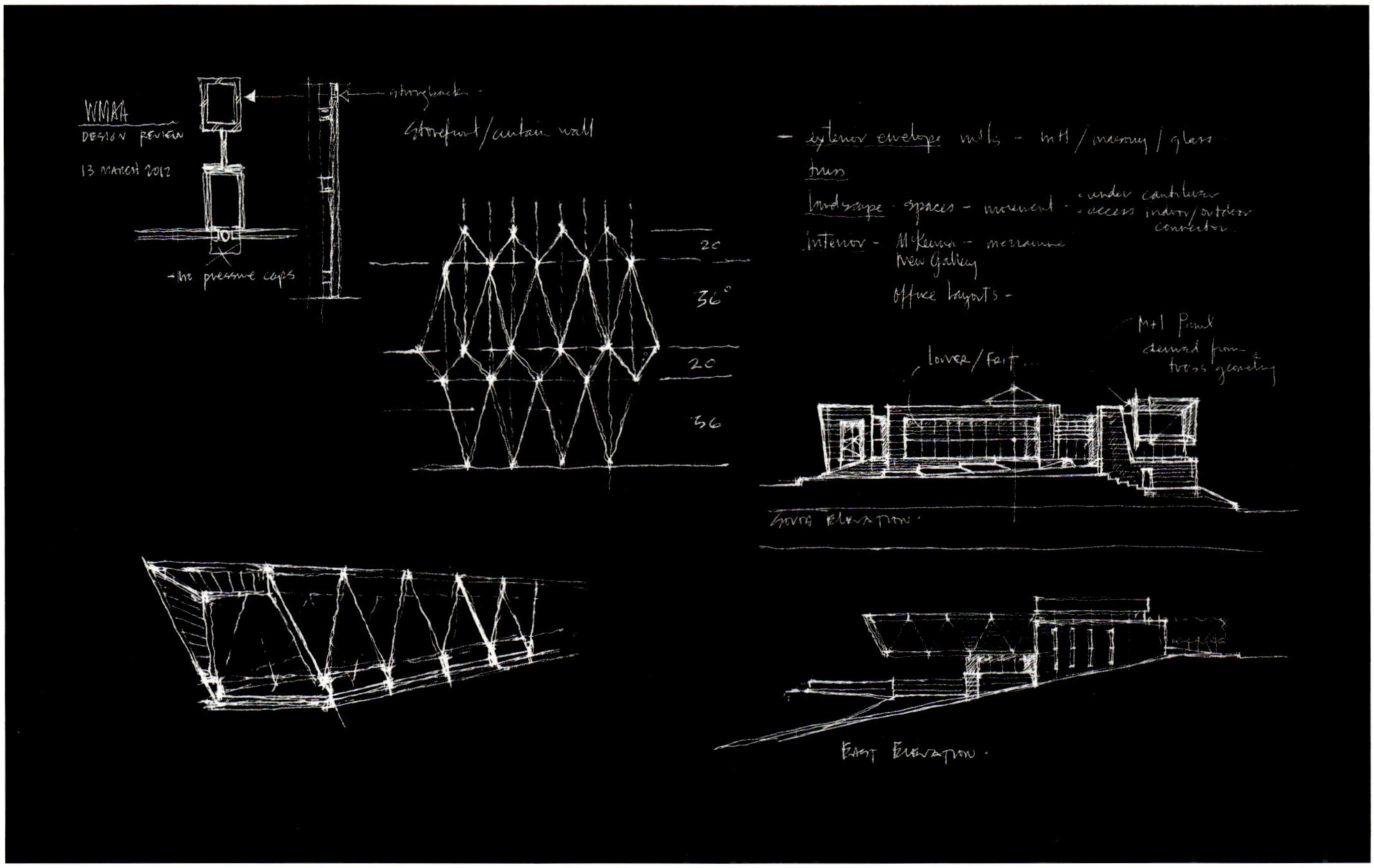

Susan T. Rodriguez. Westmoreland Museum of American Art. Elevation photograph. Image ©2015 Roy Englebrecht (www.royphoto.com). *Courtesy of the artist*

Susan T. Rodriguez. Westmoreland Museum of American Art. Sketches: left: Susan T. Rodriguez curtain wall detail sketch; upper right: Susan T. Rodriguez South Elevation sketch; lower right: Susan T. Rodriguez East Elevation sketch. *Courtesy of the artist*

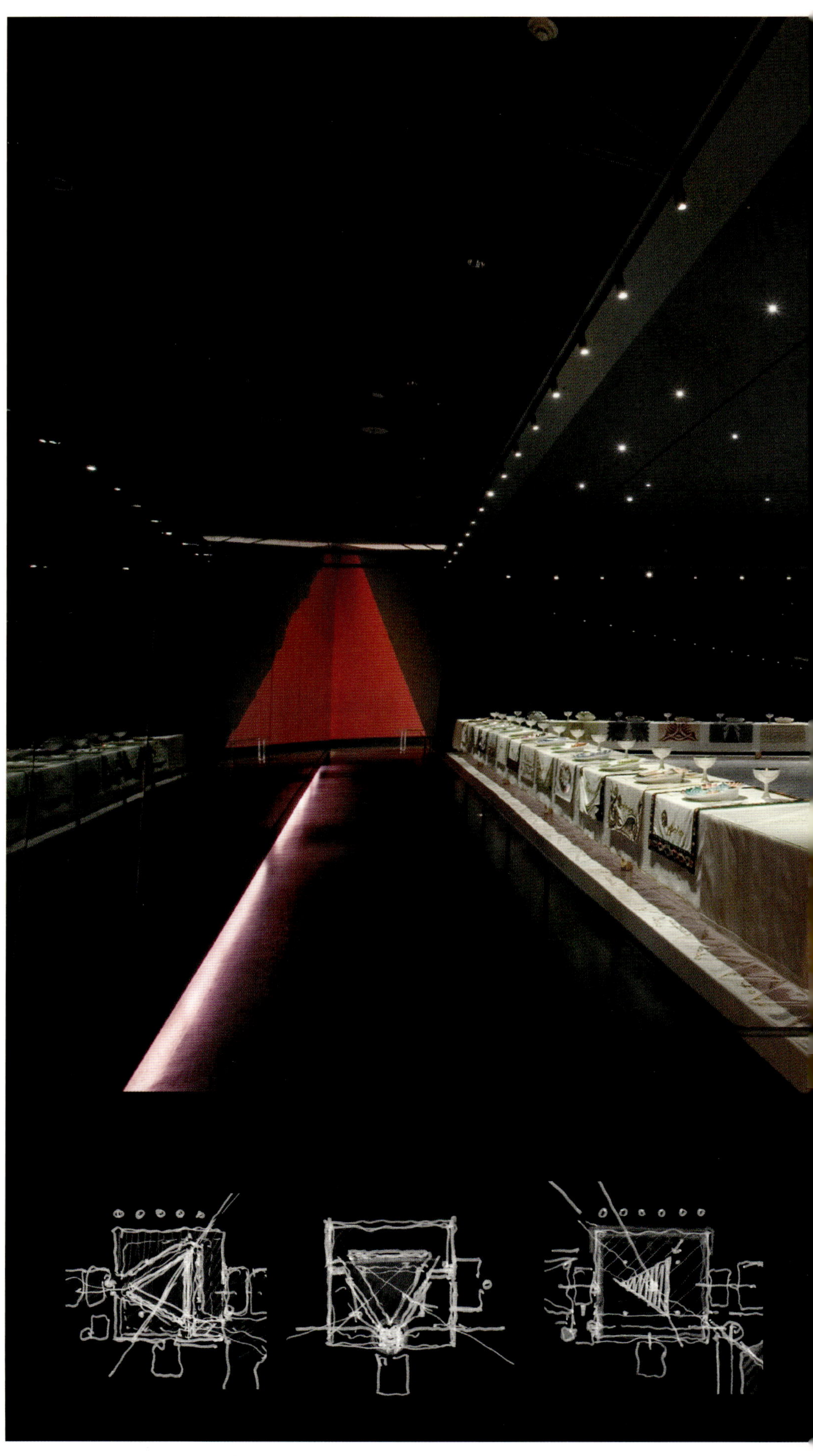

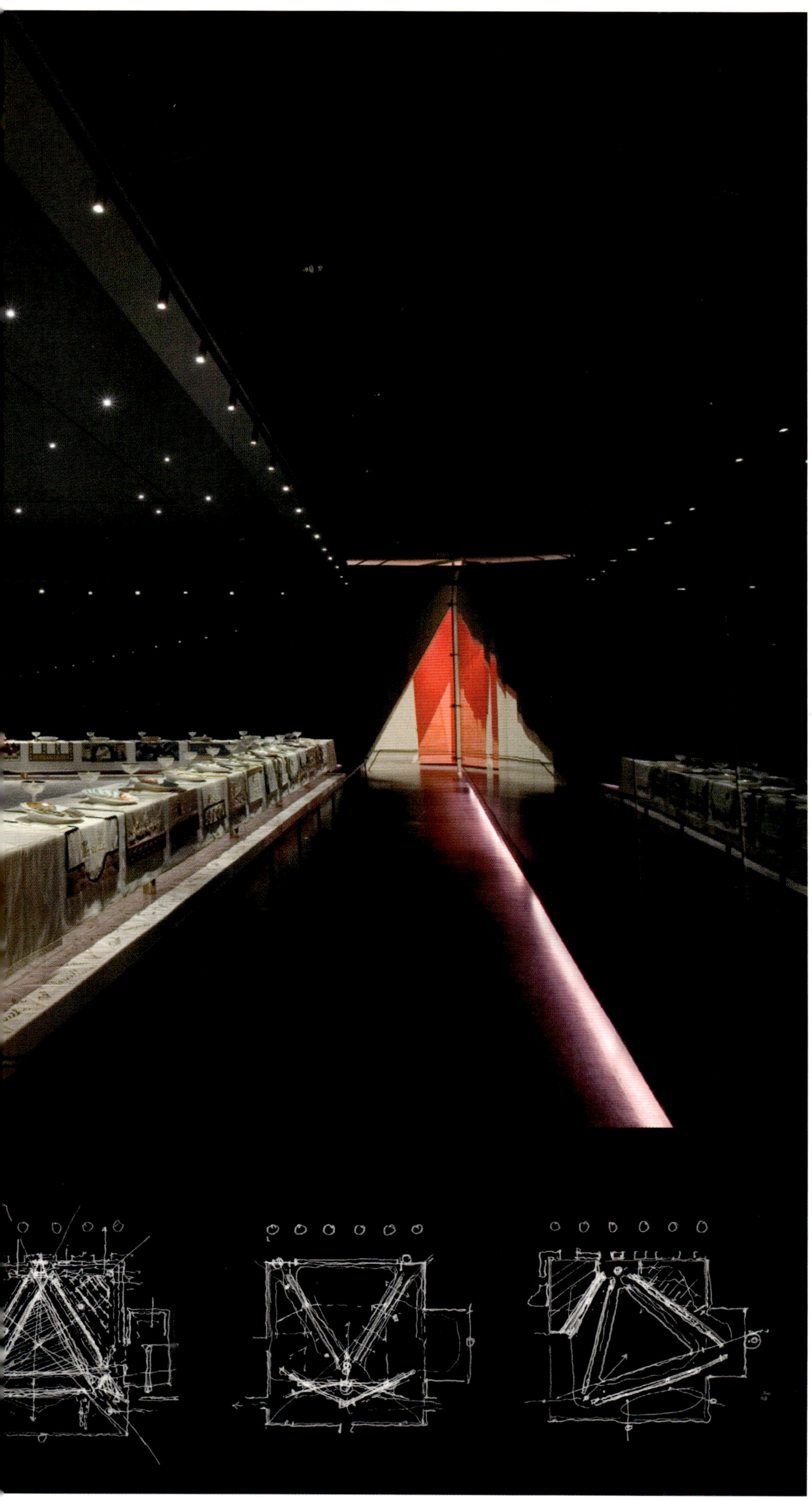

Susan T. Rodriguez. Elizabeth A. Sackler Center for Feminist Art, Brooklyn Museum. Photograph and sketches. Top photograph: ©Aislinn Weidle / Ennead Architects; bottom sketches by Susan T. Rodriguez. *Courtesy of the artist*

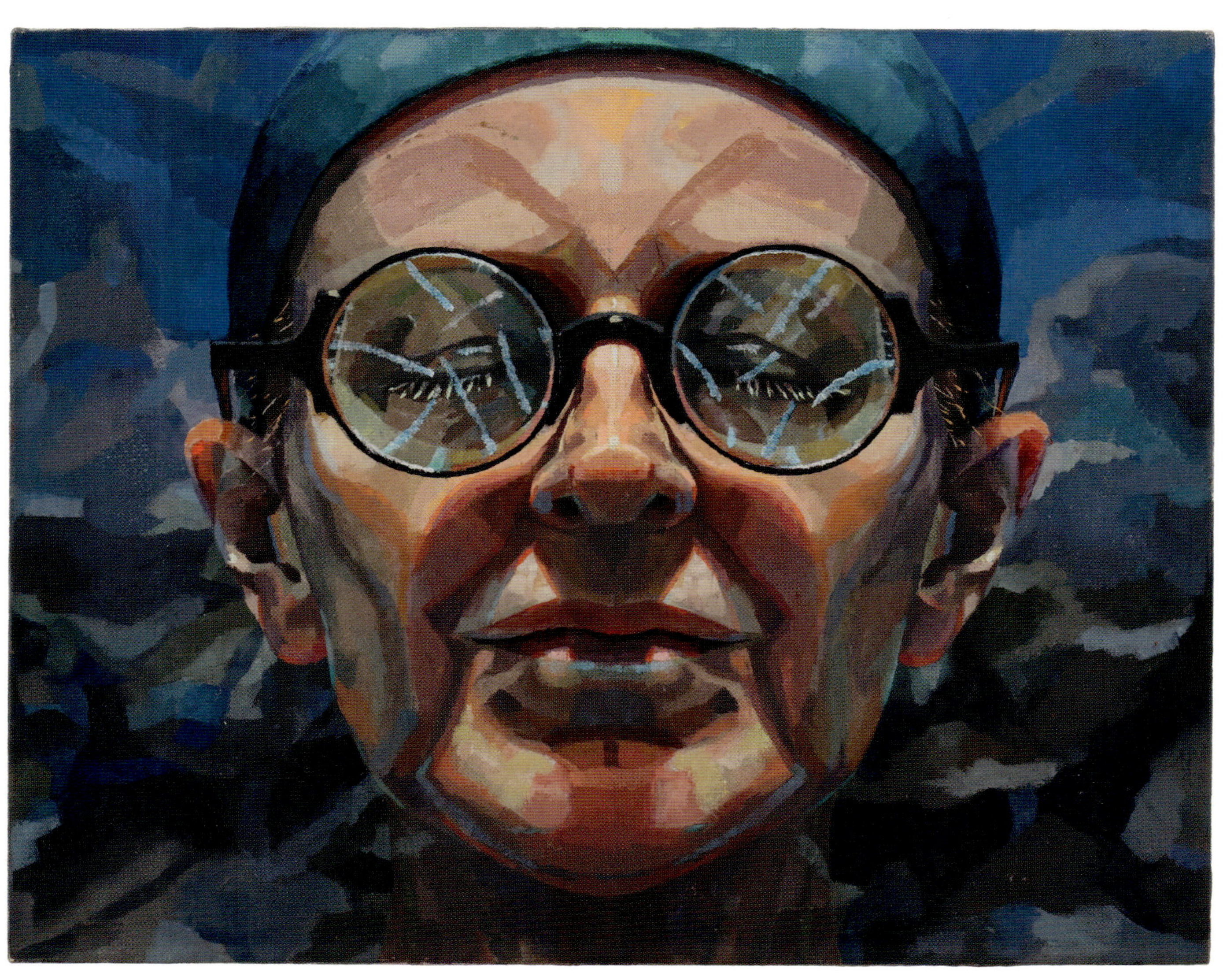

Susanna Coffey. *Slam Dunk*, 2005. Oil on panel: 12 × 14 inches. Collection of Elliot and Jacqueline Kieff. Photographer: Steve Bates. *Courtesy of the artist and Steven Harvey Fine Art Projects, New York*

TARA DONOVAN

Tara Donovan creates large-scale installations and sculptures made from everyday objects. Known for her commitment to process, she has earned acclaim for her ability to discover the inherent physical characteristics of an object and transform it into art. Donovan's many accolades include the prestigious MacArthur Foundation "Genius" Award (2008) and first annual Calder Prize (2005), among others. Donovan's solo exhibitions include the Metropolitan Museum of Art (2007–2008), the Museum of Contemporary Art, San Diego (2004 and 2009), the Institute of Contemporary Art, Boston (2008), the UCLA Hammer Museum (2004), and the Corcoran Gallery of Art, Washington, DC (1999–2000). Donovan's first European exhibition was presented in 2013 at the Louisiana Museum of Modern Art in Humlebæk, Denmark, and traveled to the Arp Museum Bahnhof Rolandseck in Remagen, Germany. Her more recent museum solo exhibitions include the Museum of Contemporary Art, Denver (2018), the Parrish Museum, Watermill, New York (2015), and Jupiter Artland, Edinburgh, Scotland (2015). Donovan's work is included in the collections of major institutions such as the Metropolitan Museum of Art, New York City; the Los Angeles County Museum of Art, Los Angeles; the Whitney Museum of American Art, New York City; and the Indianapolis Museum of Art, Indianapolis, Indiana, among many others. Donovan received a BFA (1991) from the Corcoran College of Art and Design, Washington, DC, and an MFA (1999) from Virginia Commonwealth University, Richmond. The Pace Gallery has represented Donovan since 2005.

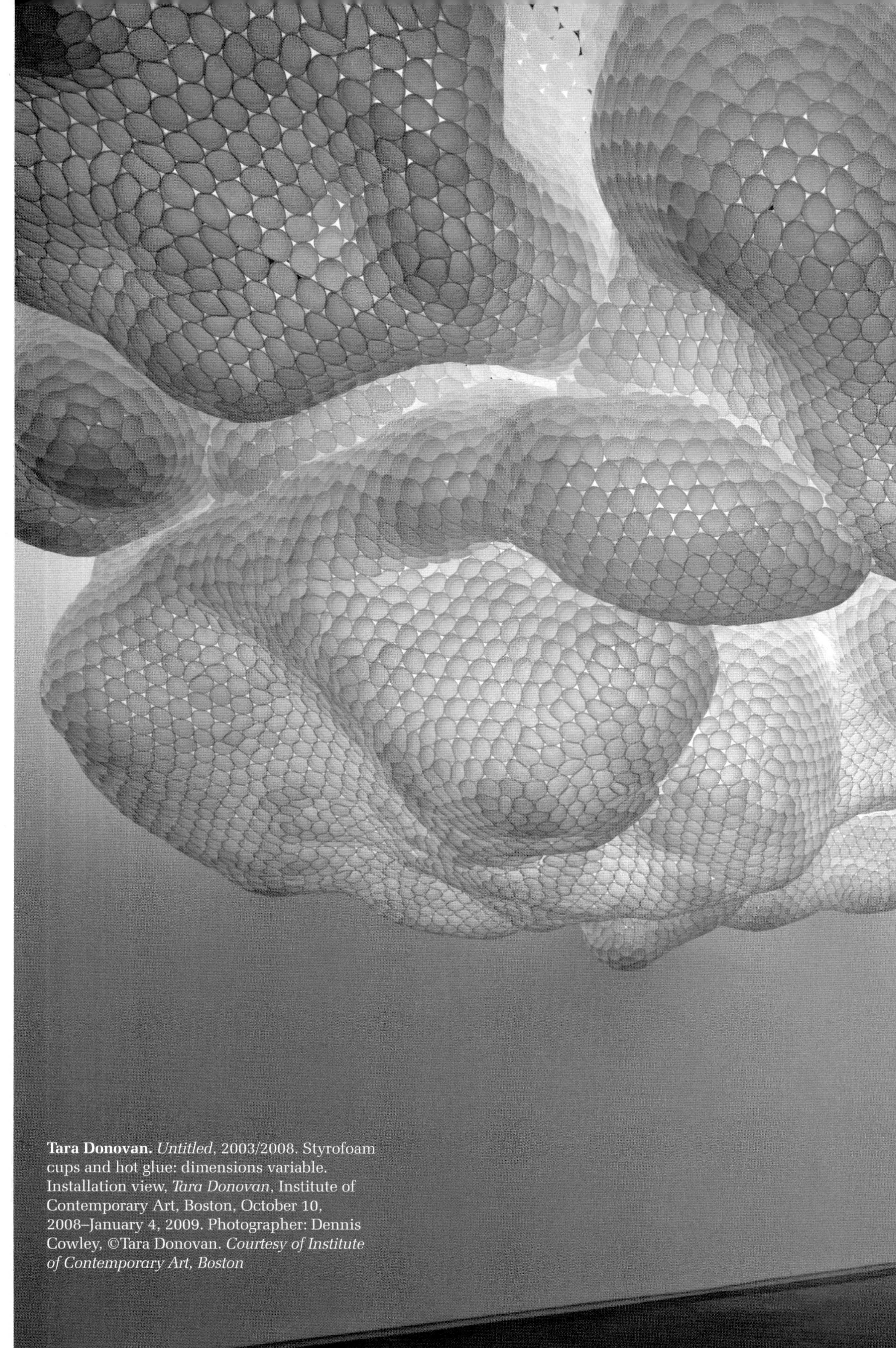

Tara Donovan. *Untitled*, 2003/2008. Styrofoam cups and hot glue: dimensions variable. Installation view, *Tara Donovan*, Institute of Contemporary Art, Boston, October 10, 2008–January 4, 2009. Photographer: Dennis Cowley, ©Tara Donovan. *Courtesy of Institute of Contemporary Art, Boston*

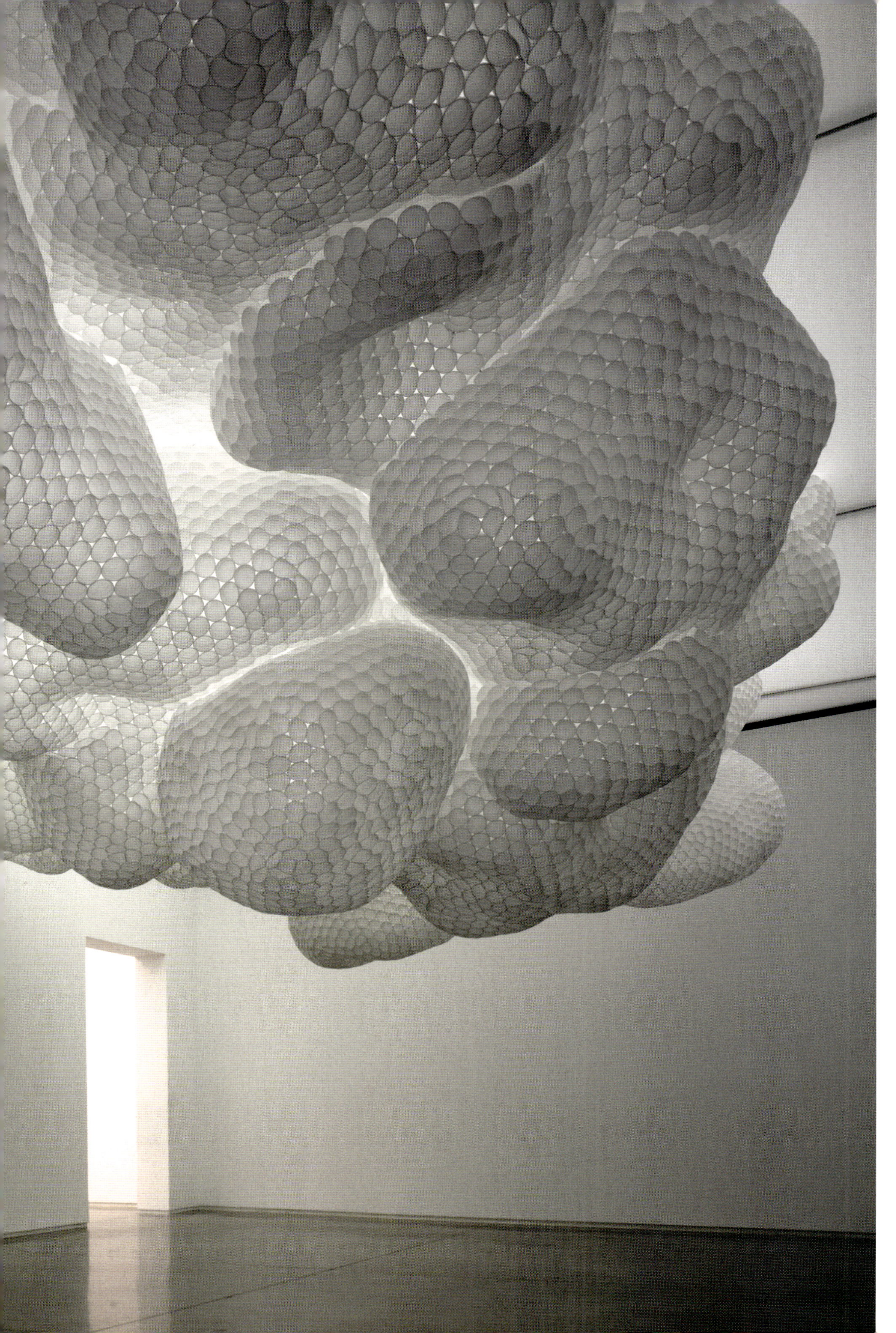

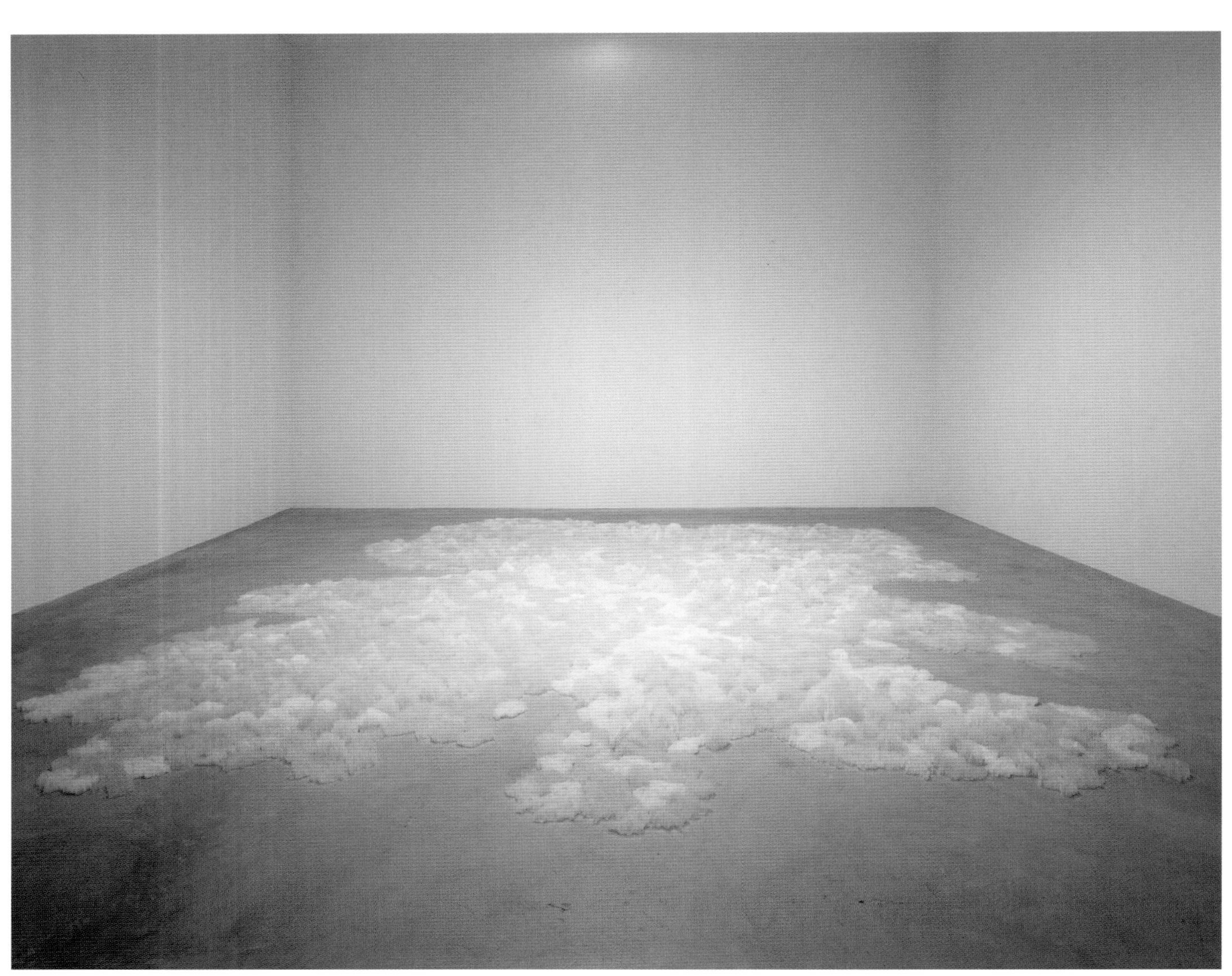

Tara Donovan. *Nebulous,* 2002/2003. Scotch tape: dimensions variable. Installation view, *Tara Donovan*, Ace Gallery, New York City, March 8–August 16, 2003. Photographer: Dennis Cowley, ©Tara Donovan. *Courtesy of Ace Gallery, New York*

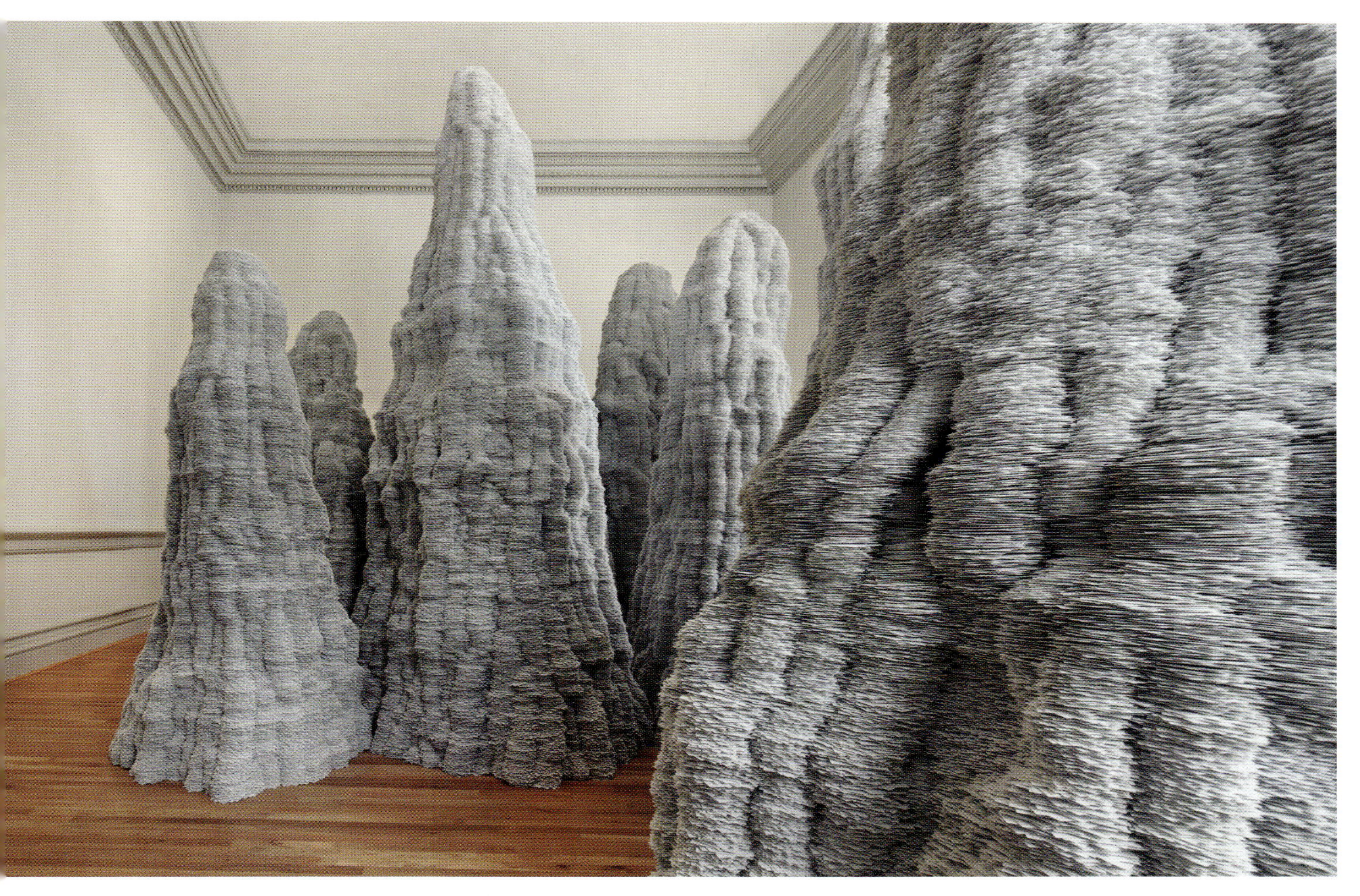

Tara Donovan. *Untitled*, 2014/2015. Styrene index cards, metal, wood, paint, and glue: dimensions variable. Installation view, *Wonder*, Renwick Gallery, Smithsonian American Art Museum, Washington, DC, November 13, 2015–July 10, 2016. Photographer: Ron Blunt, ©Tara Donovan. *Courtesy of Renwick Gallery, Smithsonian American Art Museum, Washington, DC*

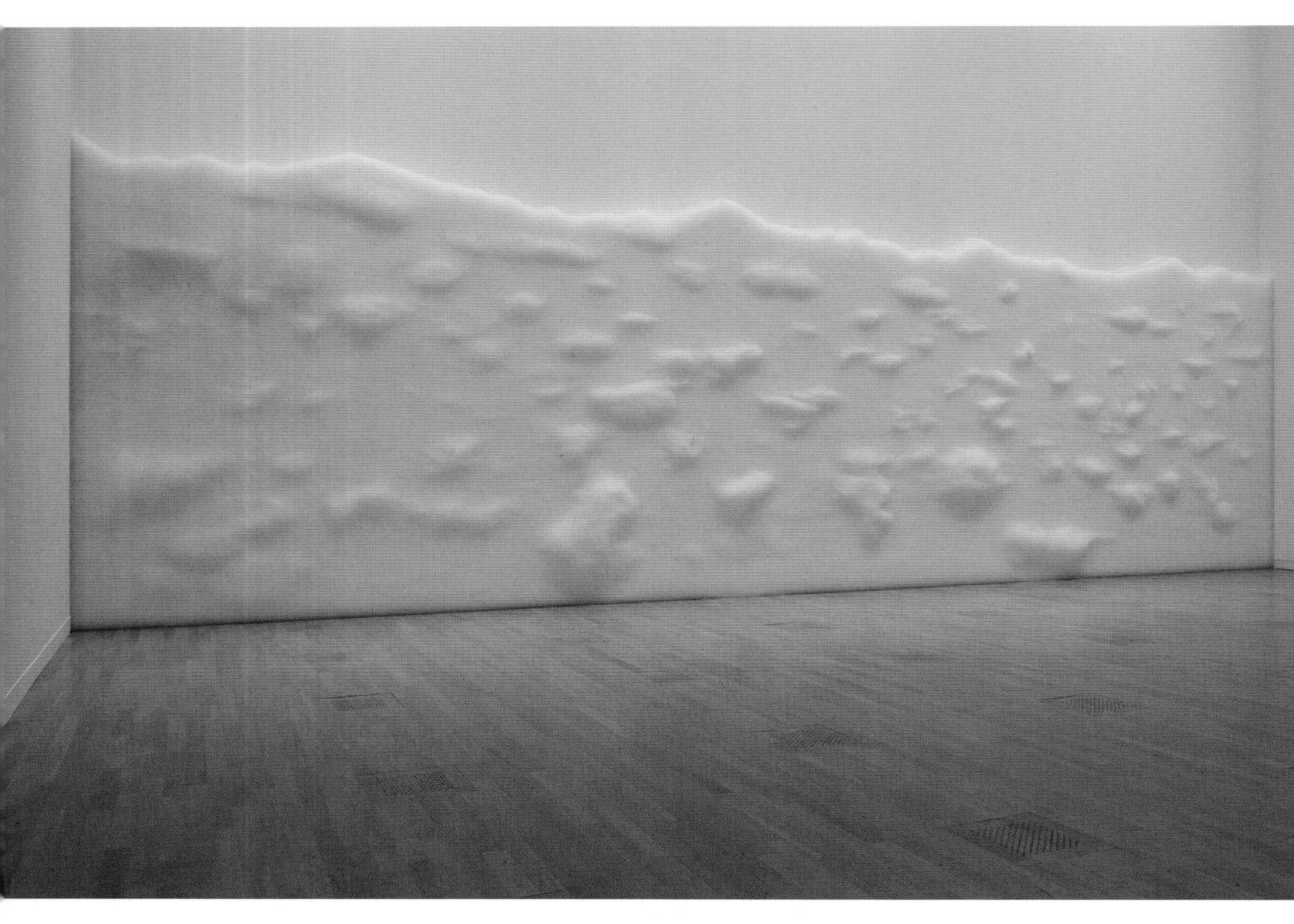

Tara Donovan. *Haze*, 2003/2011. Translucent plastic drinking straws: dimensions variable. Installation view, *Artist File 2011: The NACT Annual Show of Contemporary Art*, the National Art Center, Tokyo, March 16–June 6, 2011. Photographer: Ueno Norih, ©Tara Donovan. *Courtesy of National Art Center, Tokyo*

Tara Donovan. *Drawing (Pins)*, 2011. Gatorboard, paint, and nickel-plated steel pins: 72 × 72 × 2.5 inches. Photographer: Kerry Ryan McFate, ©Tara Donovan. *Courtesy of Pace Gallery*

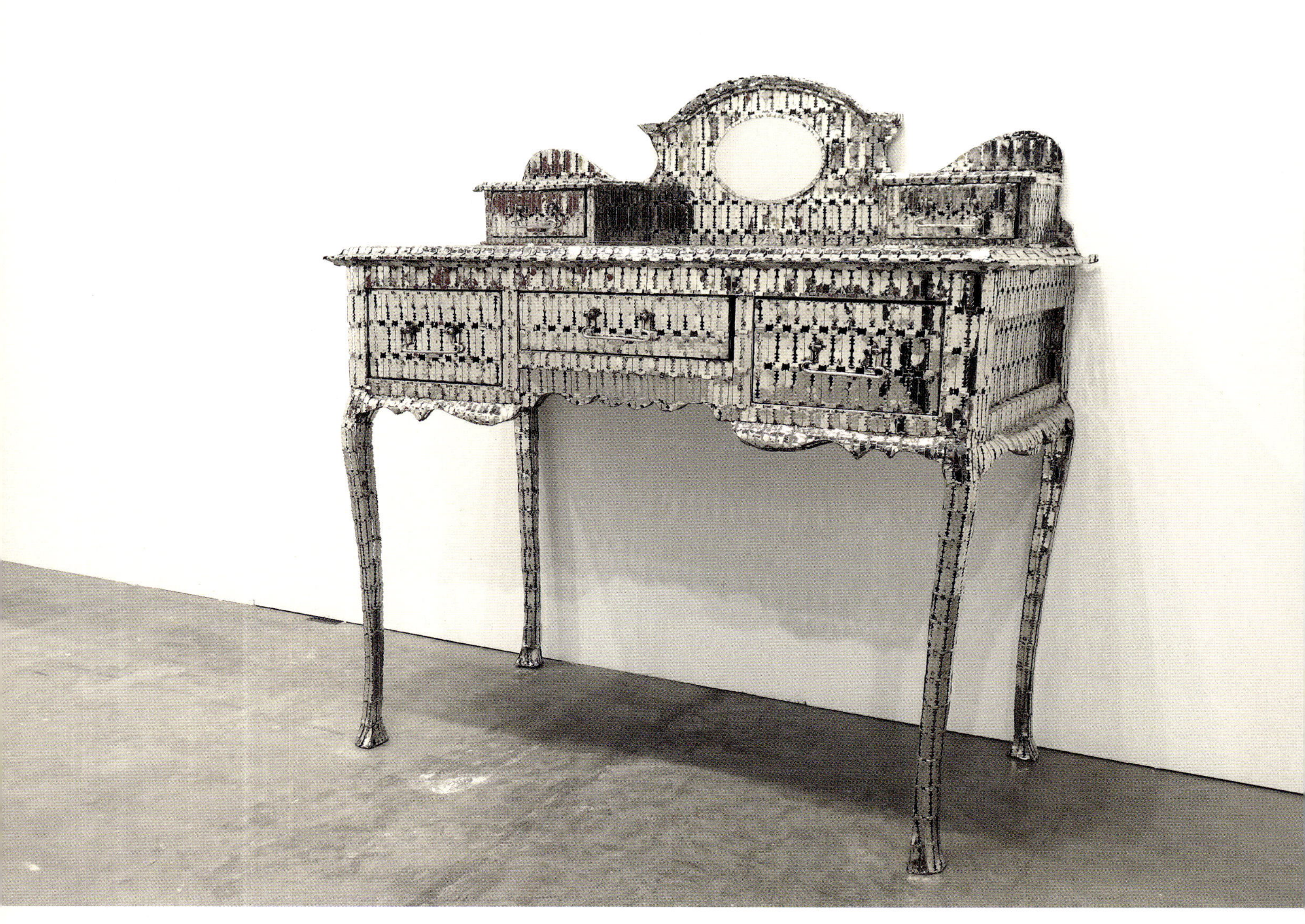

Tayeba Begum Lipi. *My Mother's Dressing Table*, 2013. Stainless-steel razor blades: 37.5 × 18.5 × 39 inches. Photographer: Tracy Szatan. *Courtesy of Sundaram Tagore Gallery, New York*

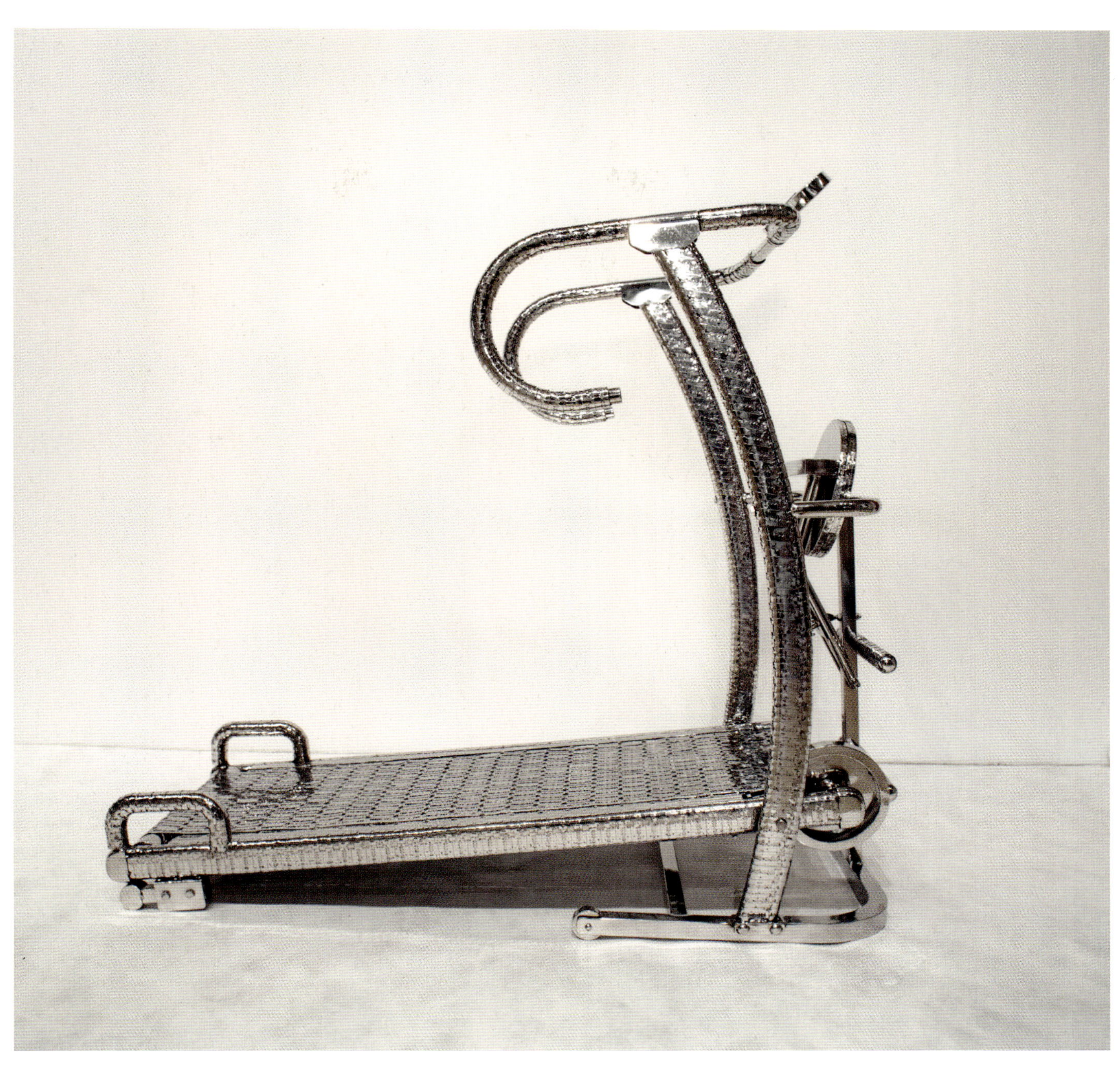

Tayeba Begum Lipi. *Time Flies*, 2015. Stainless-steel razor blades: 49.2 × 49.2 × 17.7 inches. Photographer: Tracy Szatan. *Courtesy of Sundaram Tagore Gallery, New York*

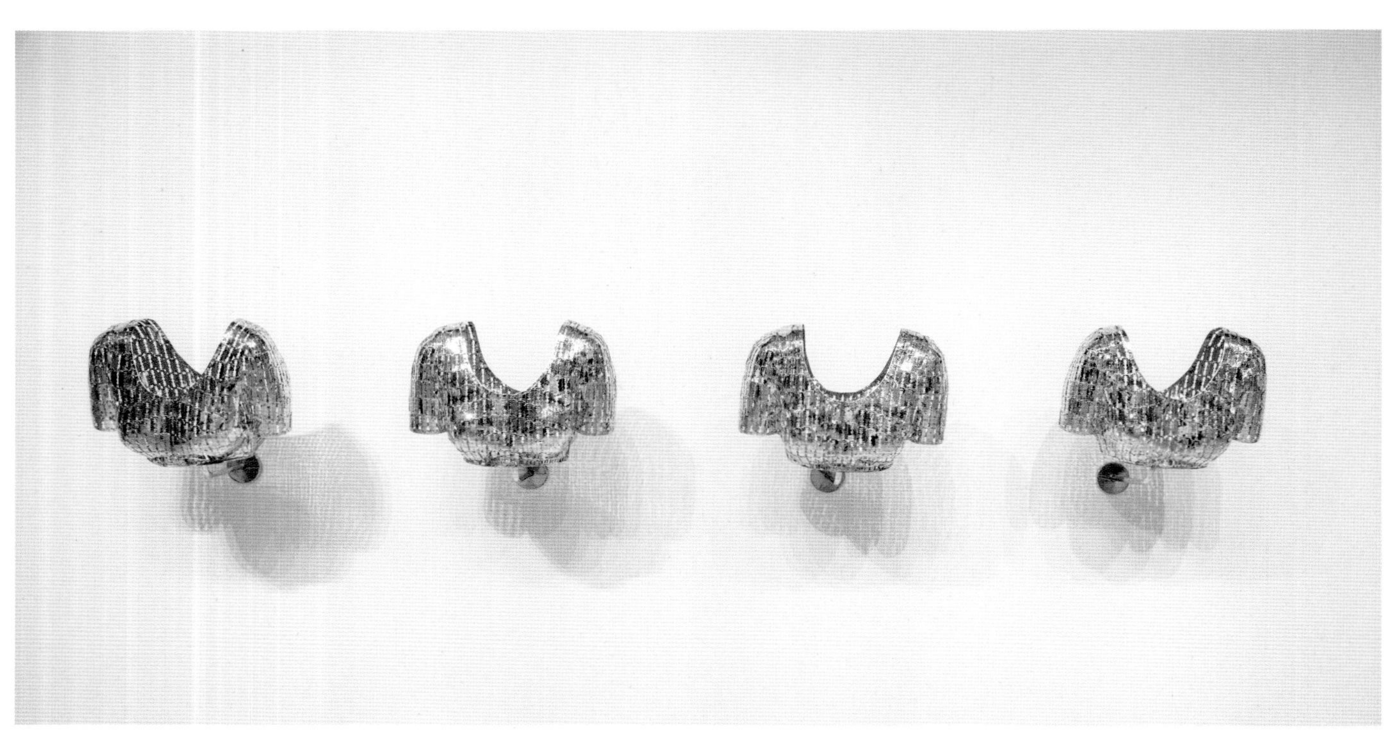

Tayeba Begum Lipi. *Womanhood*, 2015. Stainless-steel razor blades: 17.7 × 13.7 × 15.7 inches. Photographer: Tracy Szatan. *Courtesy of Sundaram Tagore Gallery, New York*

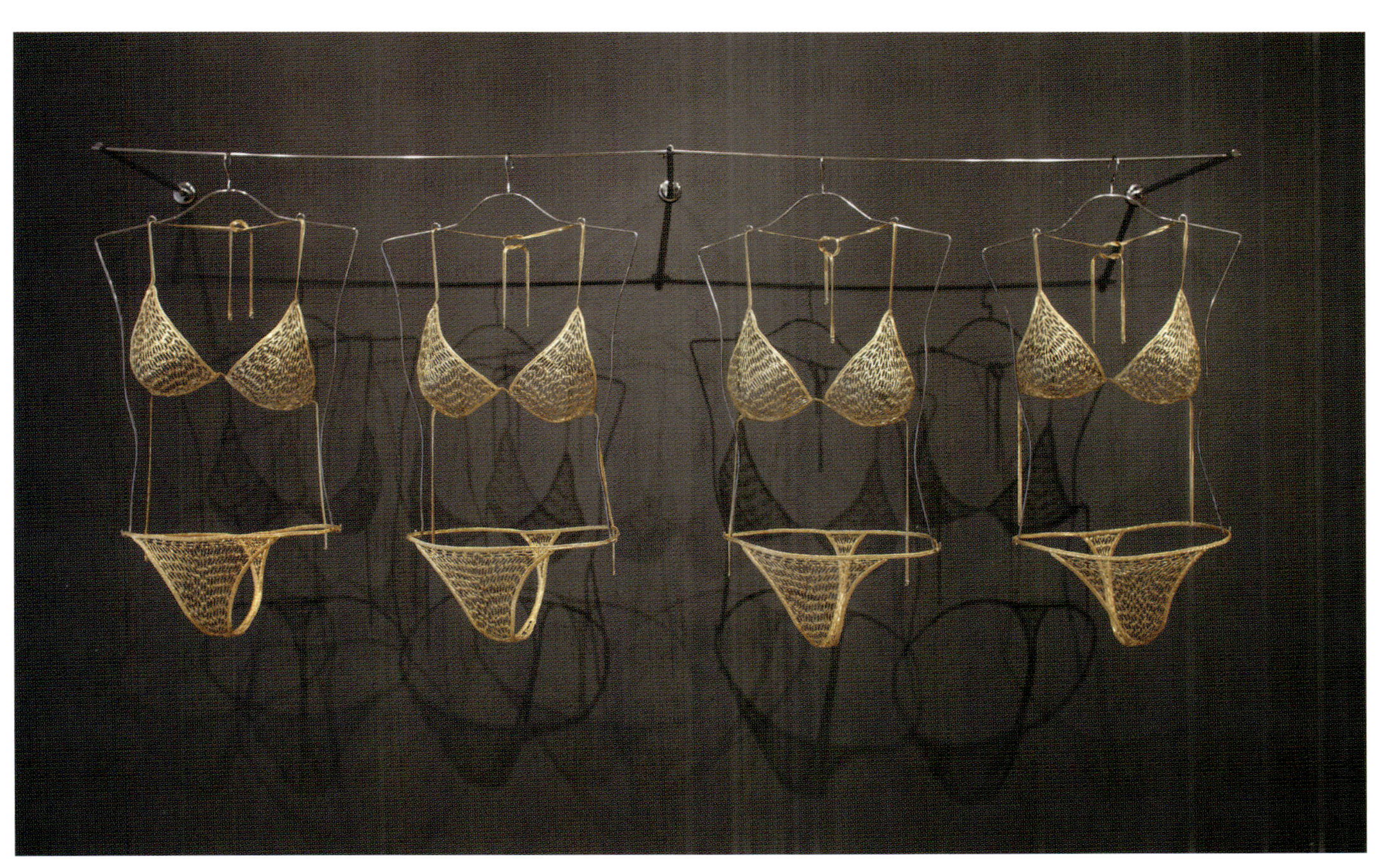

Tayeba Begum Lipi. *Comfy Bikinis*, 2013. Brass safety pins covered with electroless nickel immersion gold, stainless steel, and glass: 14.7 × 35.8 × 48 inches. Photographer: Tracy Szatan. *Courtesy of Sundaram Tagore Gallery, New York*

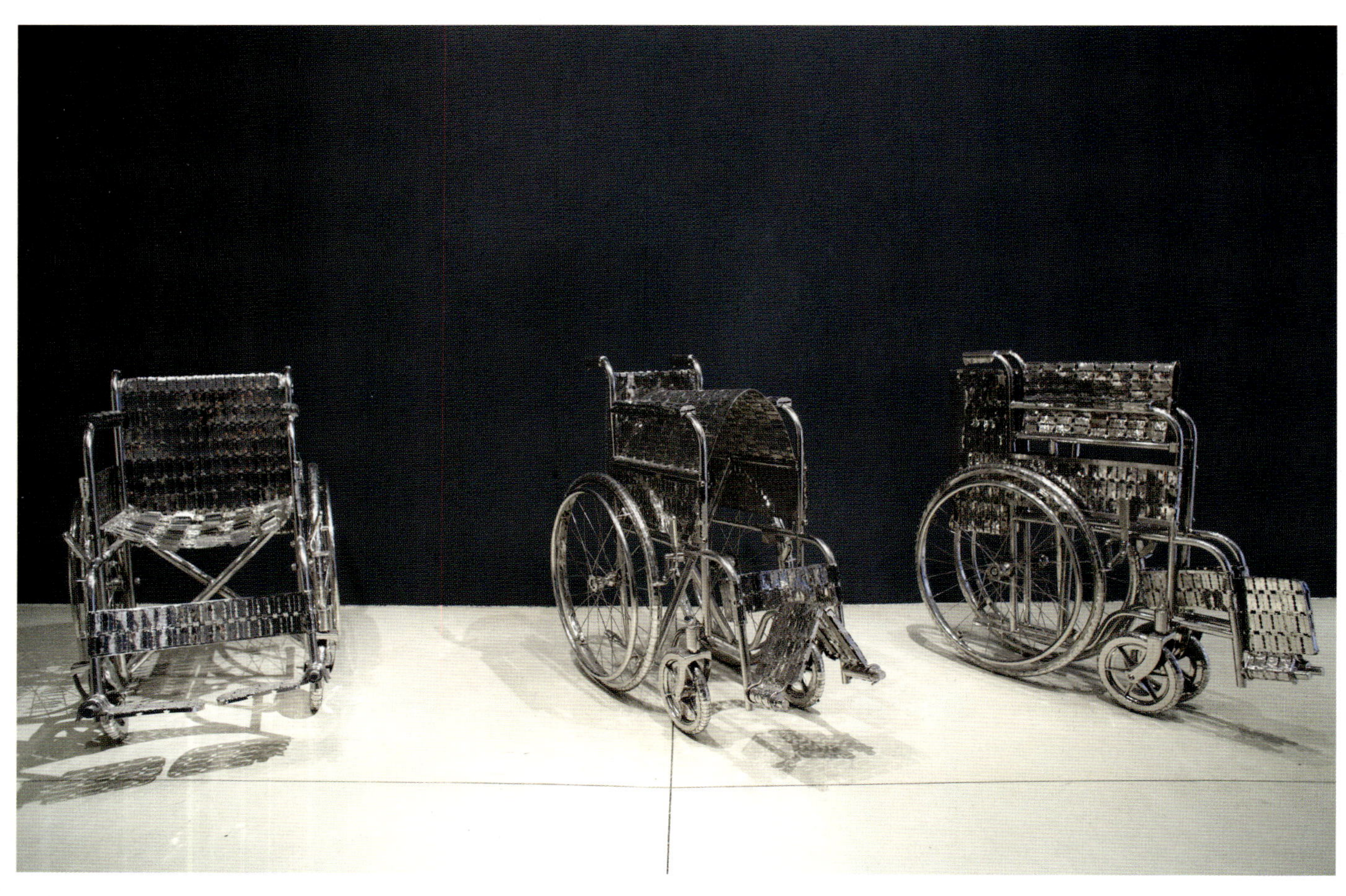

Tayeba Begum Lipi. *Agony*, 2015. Stainless-steel razor blades and stainless steel: dimensions variable. Photographer: Tracy Szatan. *Courtesy of Sundaram Tagore Gallery, New York*

TERESITA FERNÁNDEZ

Teresita Fernández is best known for her prominent public sculptures and unconventional use of materials. Her work is characterized by an interest in perception and the psychology of looking. Fernández's experiential, large-scale works are often inspired by a rethinking of the meaning of landscape and place, as well as by diverse historical and cultural references. Her sculptures present spectacular illusions that evoke natural phenomena and engage audiences in immersive art experiences and conceptual way-finding.

Fernández is a 2005 MacArthur Foundation Fellow and the recipient of numerous awards, including a Guggenheim Fellowship, an NEA Artist's Grant, and a Louis Comfort Tiffany Biennial Award. Appointed by President Obama, she is the first Latina to serve on the US Commission of Fine Arts. Fernández's works are included in many prominent collections and have been exhibited both nationally and internationally at MASS MoCA, North Adams, Massachusetts; the Museum of Modern Art, New York City; the San Francisco Museum of Modern Art; the Museum of Fine Arts, Boston; the Smithsonian Museum of American Art, Washington, DC; and Castello di Rivoli, Turin, Italy, among others. She was born in Miami, Florida, and lives in Brooklyn, New York.

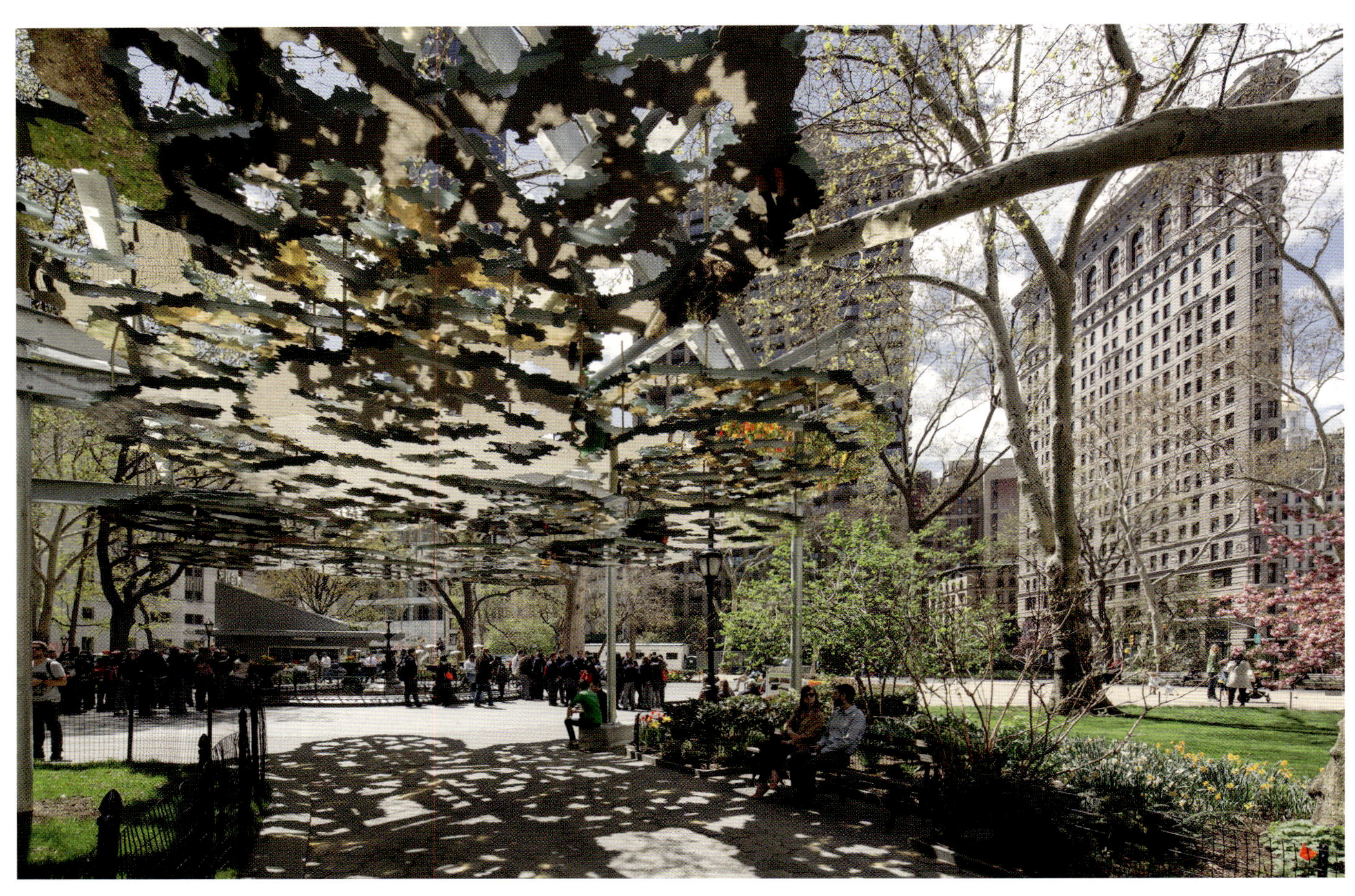

Teresita Fernández. *Fata Morgana*, 2015. Steel and gold-plated aluminum: 24,247 sq. feet (approximately). Installation view, Madison Square Park, New York City. *Courtesy of the artist and Lehmann Maupin, New York*

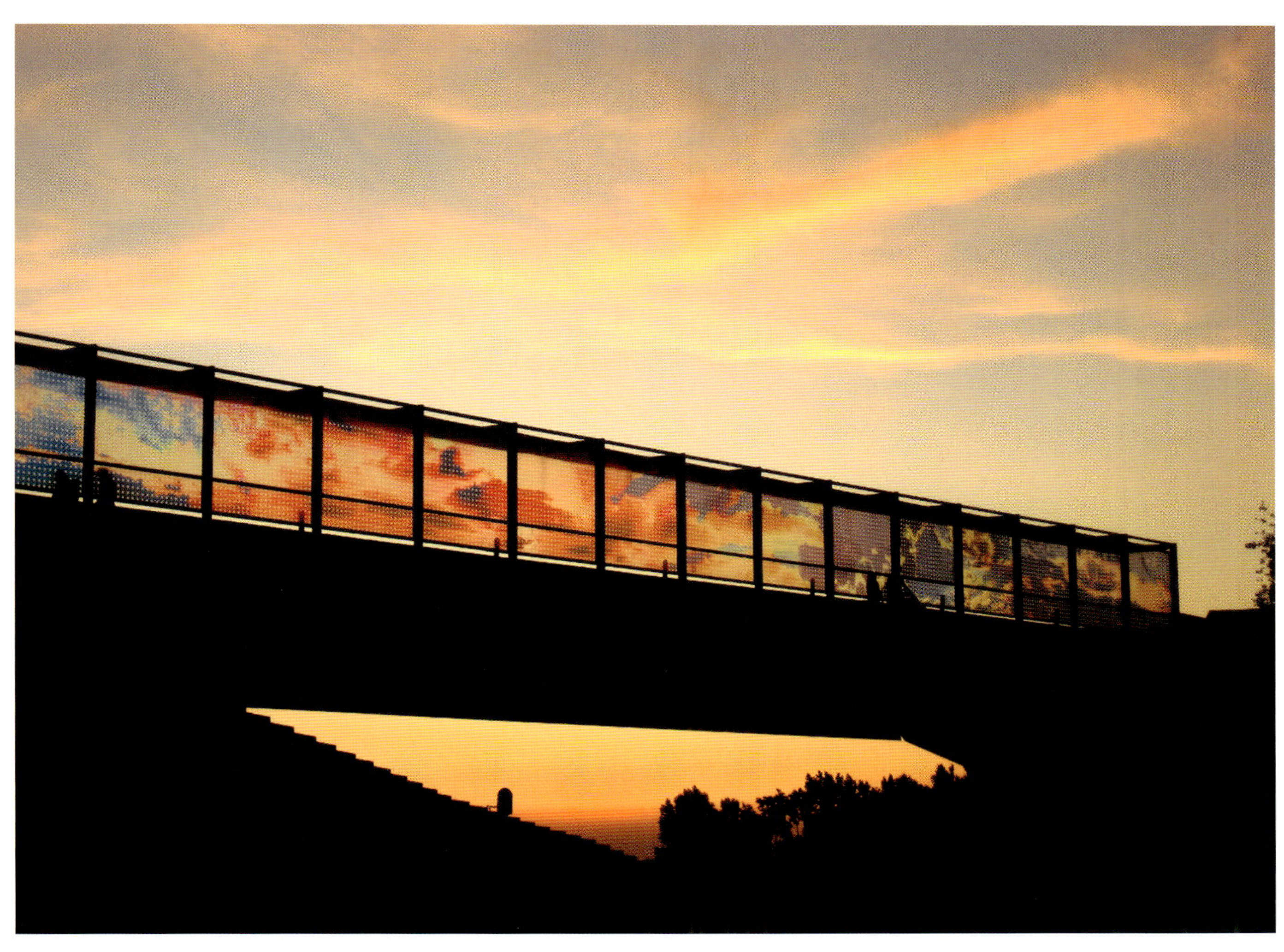

Teresita Fernández. *Seattle Cloud Cover*, 2004–2006. Laminated glass with photographic design interlay: 114 × 2,400 × 75 inches. Commissioned by the Seattle Art Museum for the Olympic Sculpture Park, Seattle, Washington. *Courtesy of the artist and Lehmann Maupin, New York*

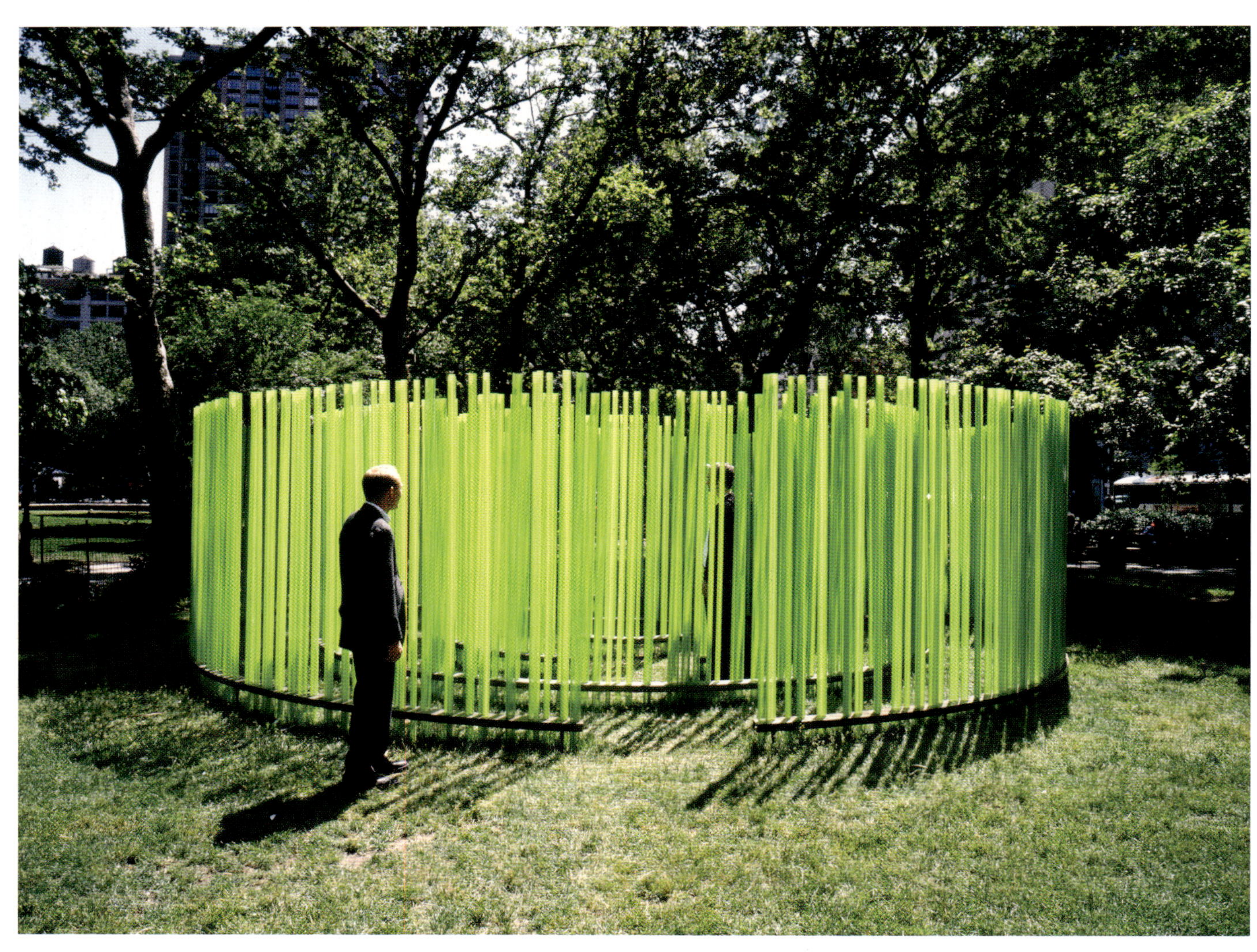

Teresita Fernández. *Bamboo Cinema*, 2001. Polycarbonate tubes and stainless steel: 96 × 332 (diameter) inches. Installation view, Madison Square Park, New York City. *Courtesy of the artist and Lehmann Maupin, New York*

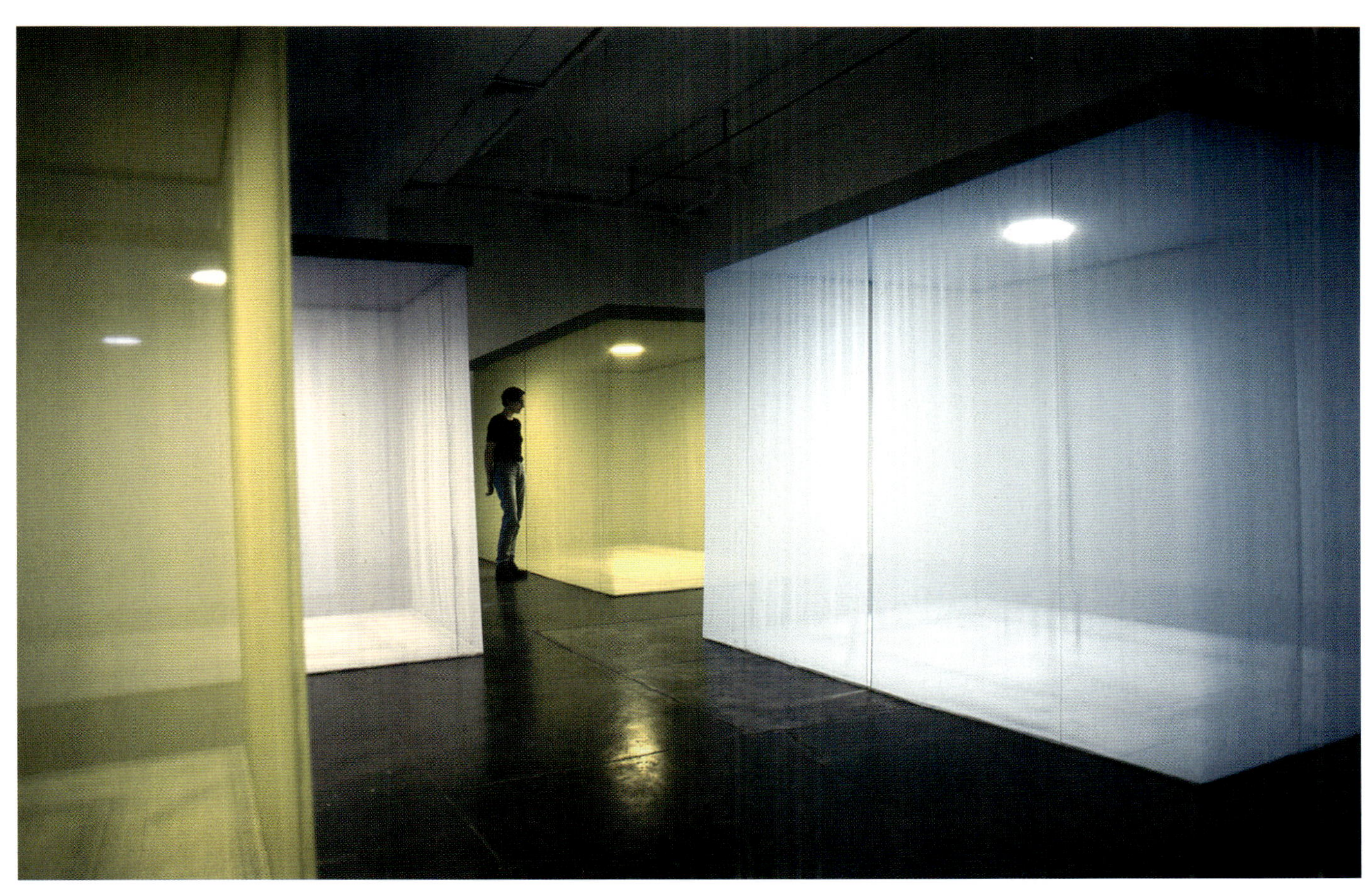

Teresita Fernández. *Borrowed Landscape,* 1998. Wood, colored fabric, light, and pencil drawing: Multiple components, each component: 90 × 84 × 120 inches. *Courtesy of the artist and Lehmann Maupin, New York*

TRICIA MIDDLETON

Tricia Middleton's sculptural practice destabilizes the boundary between what is and is not form, through experimentation with time and gravity. The inevitable movement of all material toward collapse, alongside processes of accretion and decomposition occurring in the natural world, is a significant focus of her work. Middleton seeks to mobilize these forces to manifest the interior processes of the mind, itself an abstract reflection of the creation and destruction of form. As such, Middleton's work may be considered as materialized thought at the edge of becoming something, still unknown.

Middleton was born in 1972 in Vancouver, British Columbia. Her work has been mounted in museums and galleries across Canada, including solo exhibitions at Dunlop Art Gallery (2015), Oakville Galleries (2012), and Musée d'art contemporain de Montréal (2009). Her work has been presented in many notable group exhibitions, including Misled by Nature: Contemporary Art and the Baroque at the Art Gallery of Alberta, Edmonton (2012), and the Museum of Contemporary Canadian Art, Toronto (2014); Nothing to Declare: Recent Sculpture from Canada, the Power Plant, Toronto (2010); and Dé-con-structions, the National Gallery of Canada (2007). Middleton is the winner of the Victor Martyn Lynch-Staunton Award (2010).

Tricia Middleton. *Dark Souls*, detail, *Mountains Room*, 2009. Two freestanding sculptures spanning floor to ceiling, painted and quilted false walls, demidrop ceiling with backlit textile treatment, foil appliqué on gallery ceiling, found objects, wax and hand-dyed cotton balls: dimensions variable. Installation view, *Dark Souls*, Musée d'art contemporain de Montréal, Montréal, Québec. *Courtesy of the artist*

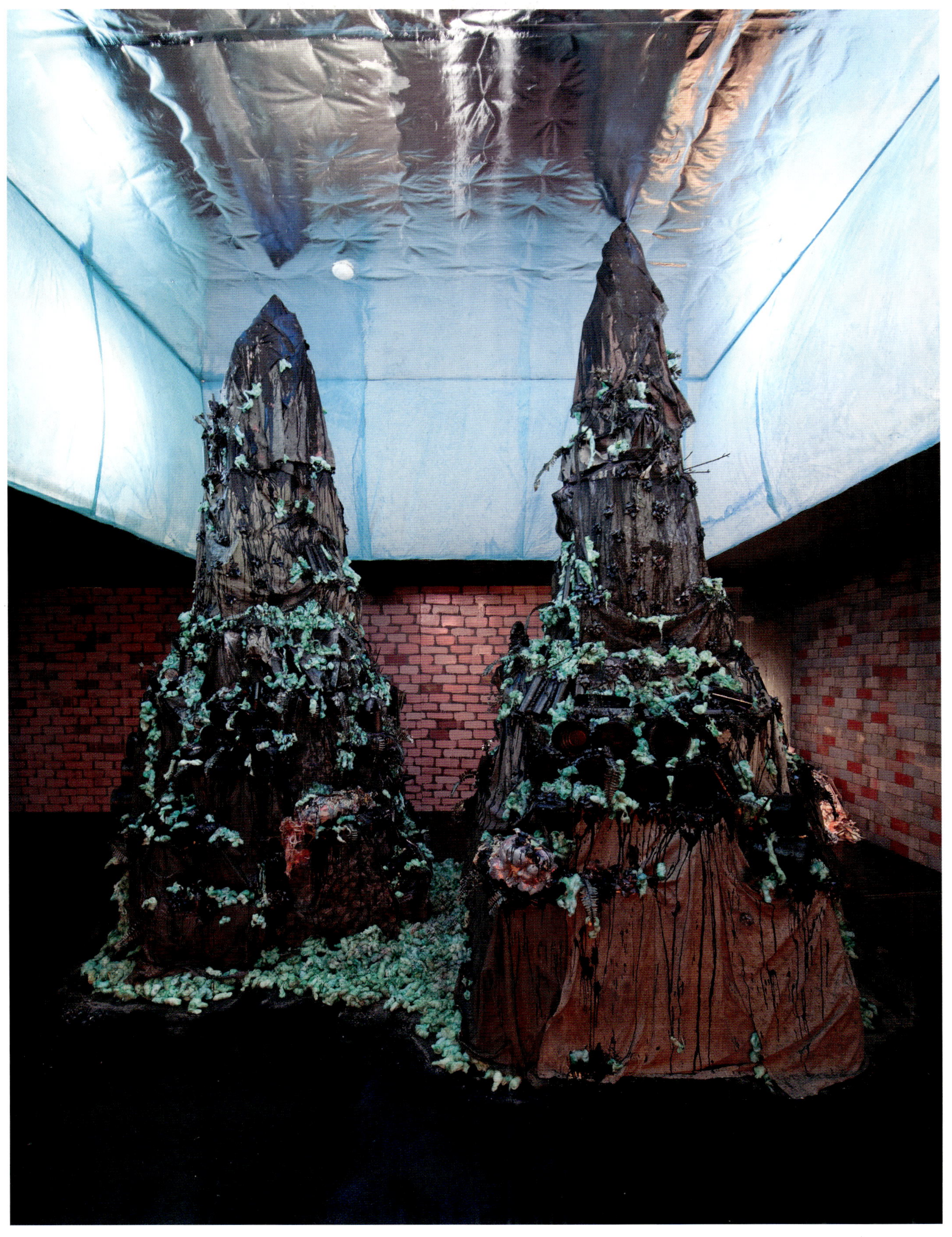

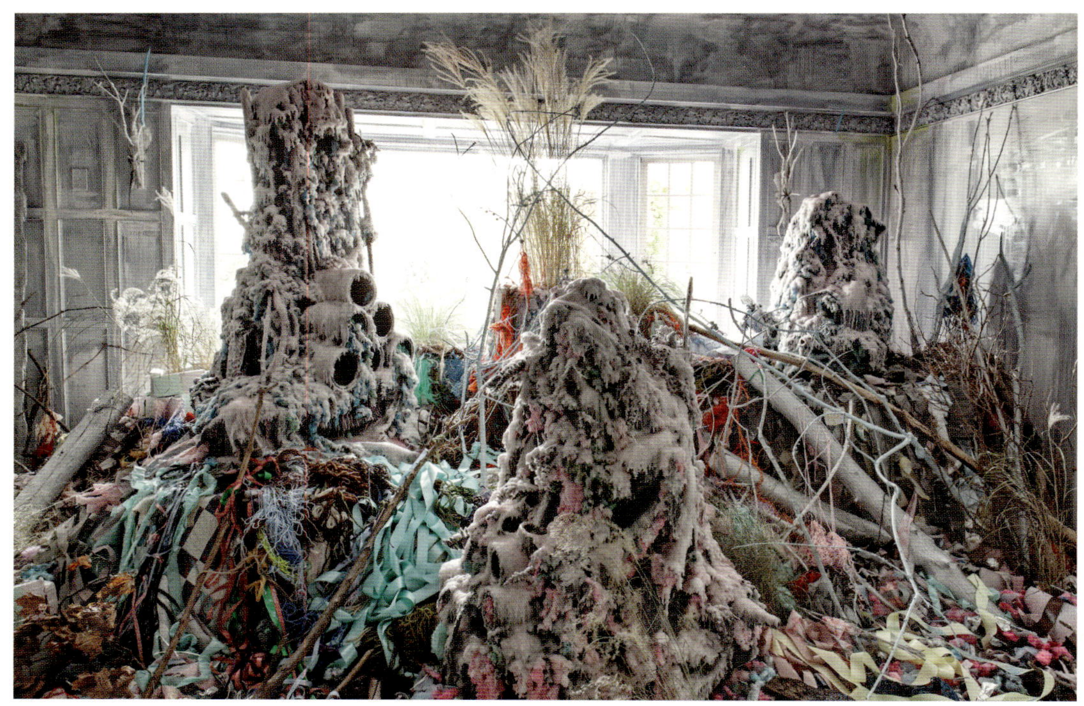

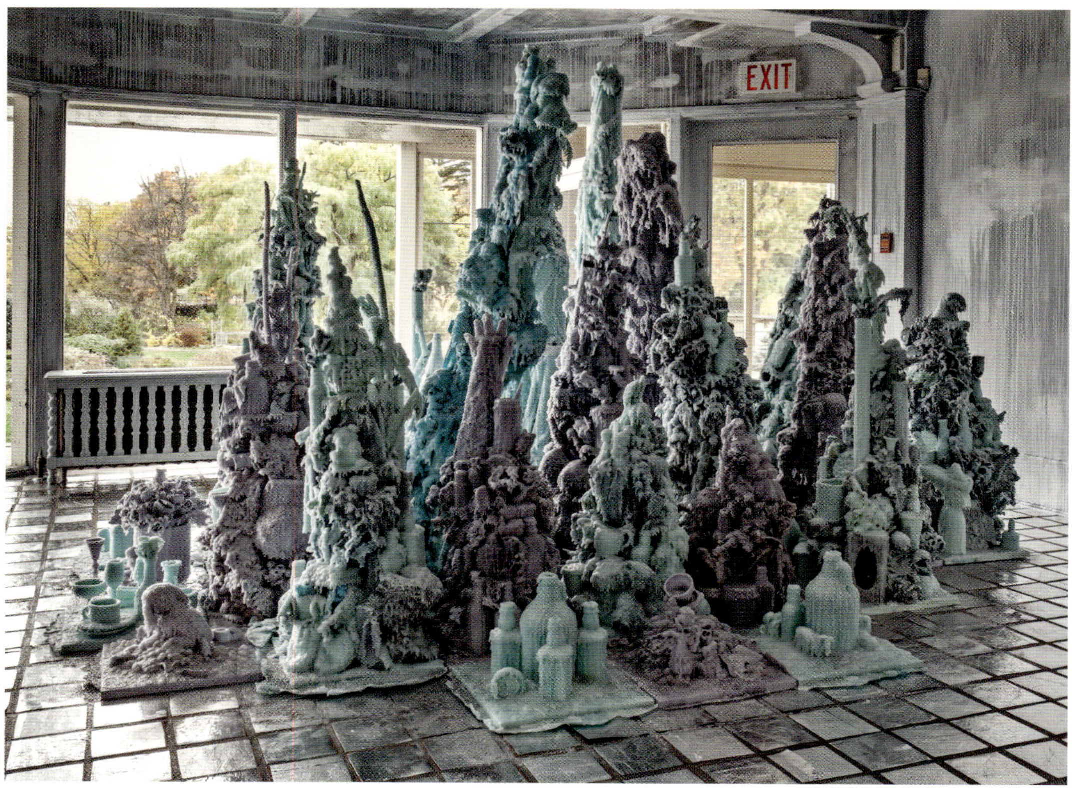

Tricia Middleton. *Form Is the Destroyer of Force, Without Severity There Can Be No Mercy*, detail, *Crones Room*, 2012. Three discrete sculptures, hand painting on décor moldings, wax, bedsheets, ribbon, grass, ceramic, paint, and branches, all materials repurposed from *Dark Souls*: dimensions variable. Installation view, *Form Is the Destroyer of Force, Without Severity There Can Be No Mercy*, Oakville Galleries, Oakville, Ontario. *Courtesy of the artist*

Tricia Middleton. *Form Is the Destroyer of Force, Without Severity There Can Be No Mercy*, detail, *Stalactites Room*, 2012. Eighteen freestanding sculptures, hand-painted walls, foil-tiling appliqué, wax, ceramic figurines, and found objects, all materials repurposed from *Dark Souls*: dimensions variable. Installation view, *Form Is the Destroyer of Force, Without Severity There Can Be No Mercy*, Oakville Galleries, Oakville, Ontario. *Courtesy of the artist*

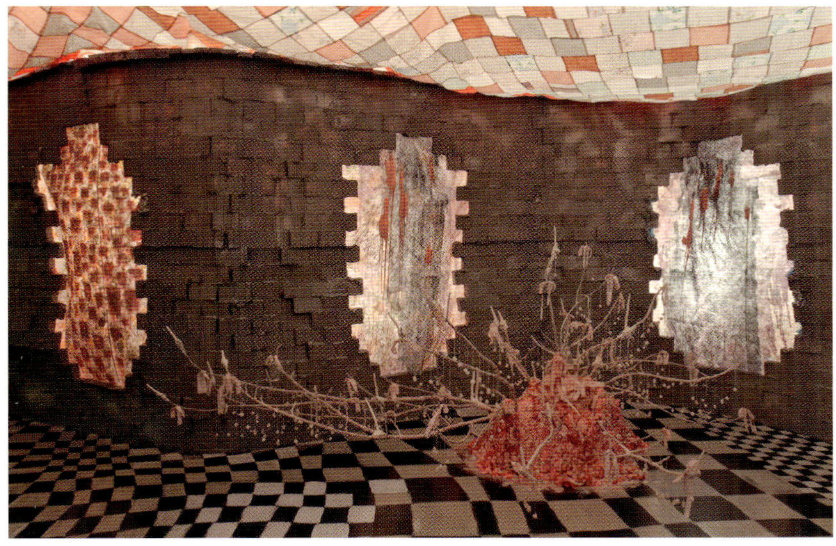

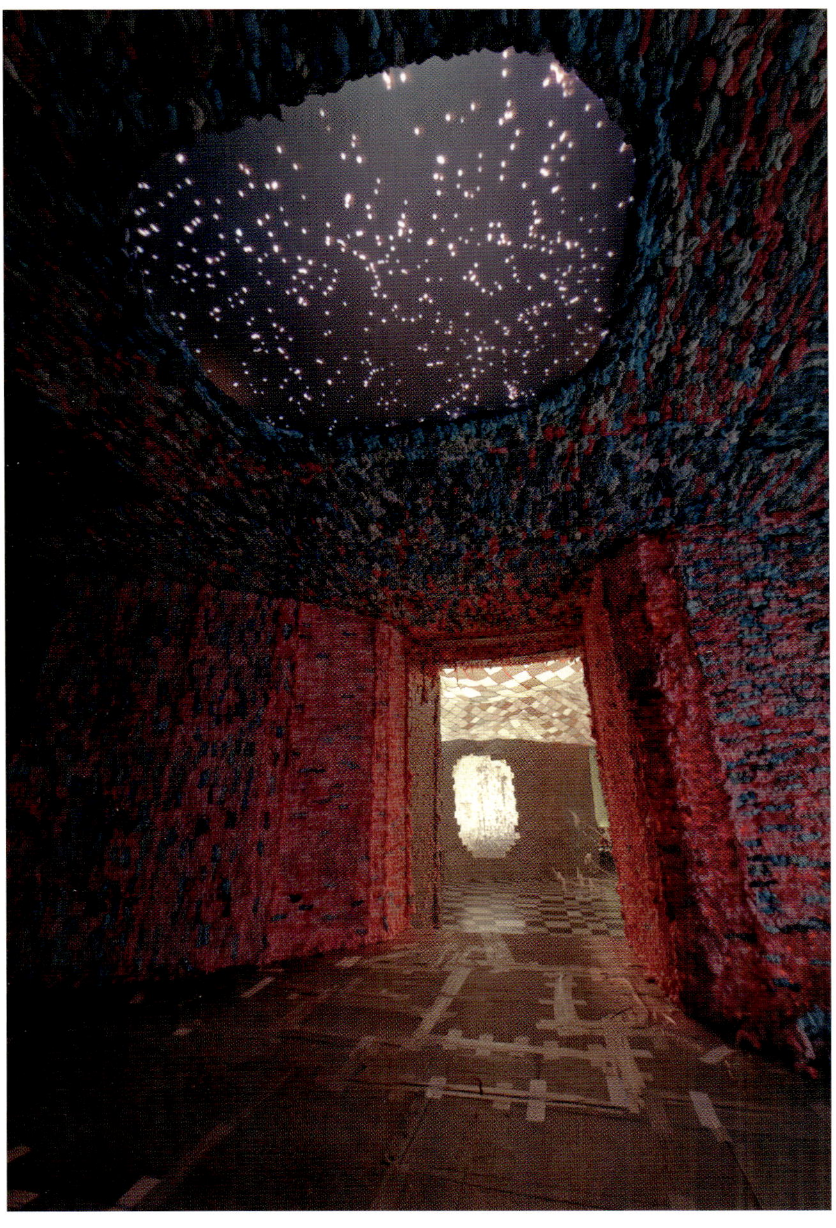

Tricia Middleton. *Dark Souls*, detail, *Chandelier Room*, 2009. Backlit drop ceiling quilted together from cut squares of various textiles, shaped false walls featuring a backlit cutout with painting on a bedsheet, and floor-mounted chandelier made from branches, wax, crystal, and hand-dyed cotton balls: dimensions variable. Installation view, *Dark Souls*, Musée d'art contemporain de Montréal, Montréal, Québec. *Courtesy of the artist*

Tricia Middleton. *Dark Souls*, detail, *Stars Room*, 2009. Rear-screen video projection, visible through a hole cut in drop ceiling, shaped walls and ceiling covered with hand-dyed cotton balls and cardboard flooring: dimensions variable. Installation view, *Dark Souls*, Musée d'art contemporain de Montréal, Montréal, Québec. *Courtesy of the artist*

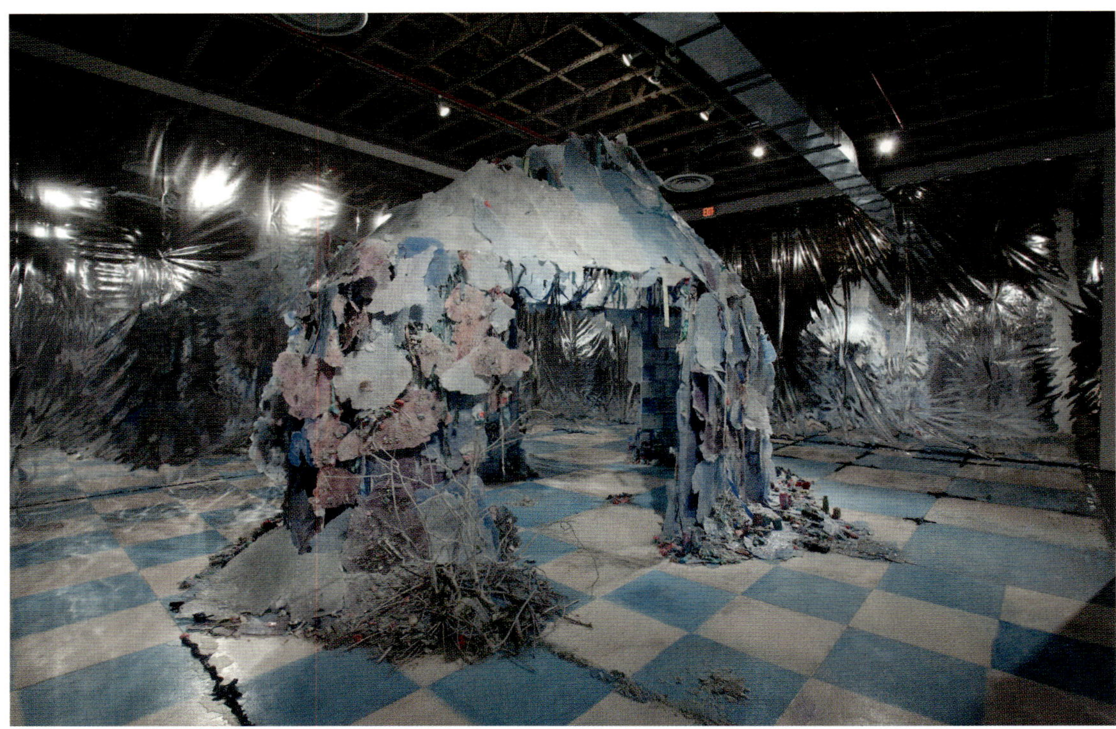

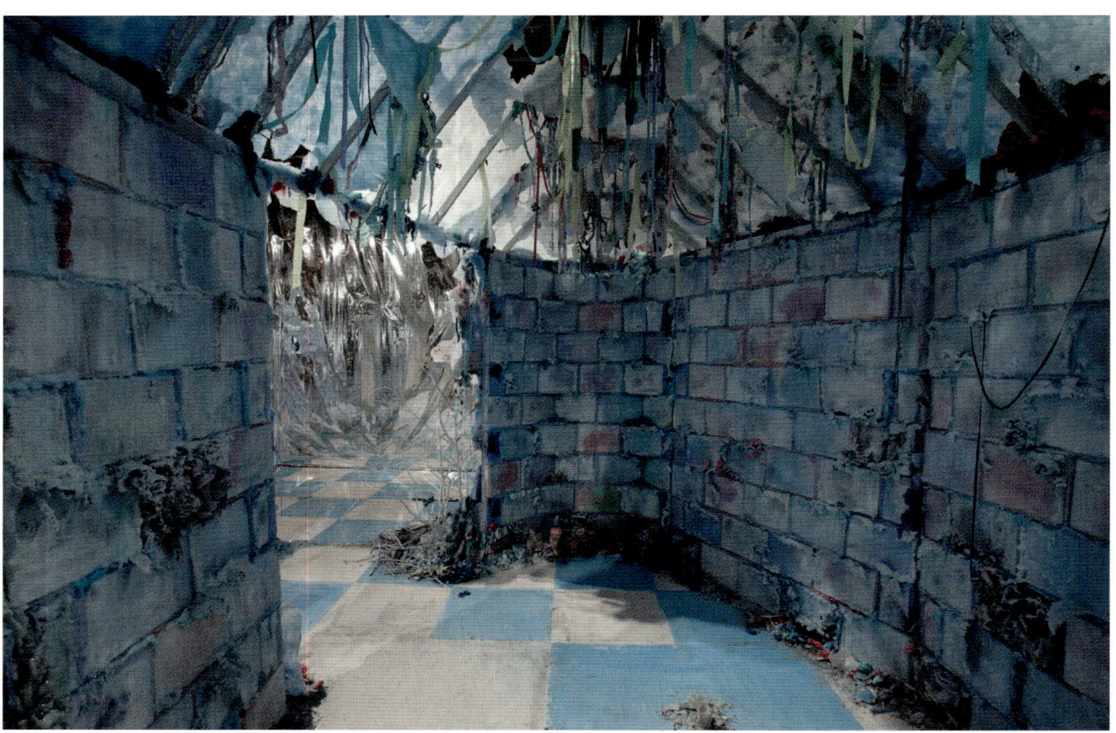

Tricia Middleton. *Embracing ruin and oblivion is the only way to live now*, 2012–14. Sculptural installation as fully functional architecture with an accessible interior, composed around the form of melting-wax "ice cap," false floor, foil appliqué, beeswax, wood, ribbon, paint, textile, ceramic, and found objects: dimensions variable. Installation view, *Embracing ruin and oblivion is the only way to live now*, Museum of Contemporary Canadian Art, Toronto, Ontario. *Courtesy of the artist*

Tricia Middleton. *Embracing ruin and oblivion is the only way to live now* (detail), 2012–14. Sculptural installation as fully functional architecture with an accessible interior, composed around the form of melting-wax "ice cap," false floor, foil appliqué, beeswax, wood, ribbon, paint, textile, ceramic, and found objects: dimensions variable. Installation view, *Embracing ruin and oblivion is the only way to live now*, Museum of Contemporary Canadian Art, Toronto, Ontario. *Courtesy of the artist*

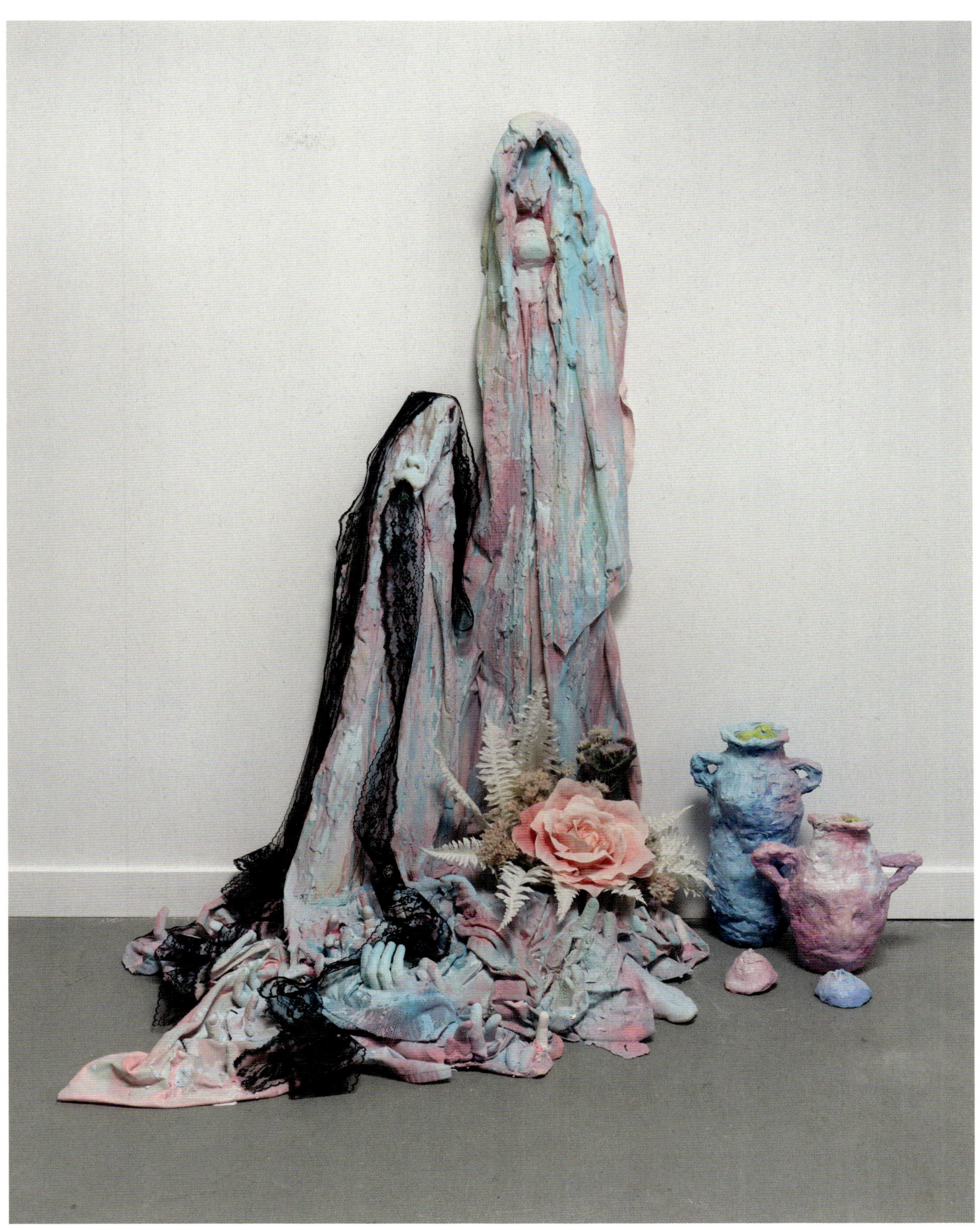

Tricia Middleton. *Heather*, 2016. Mixed media: 58 × 50 × 25 inches. *Courtesy of the artist and Galerie Antoine Ertaskiran*

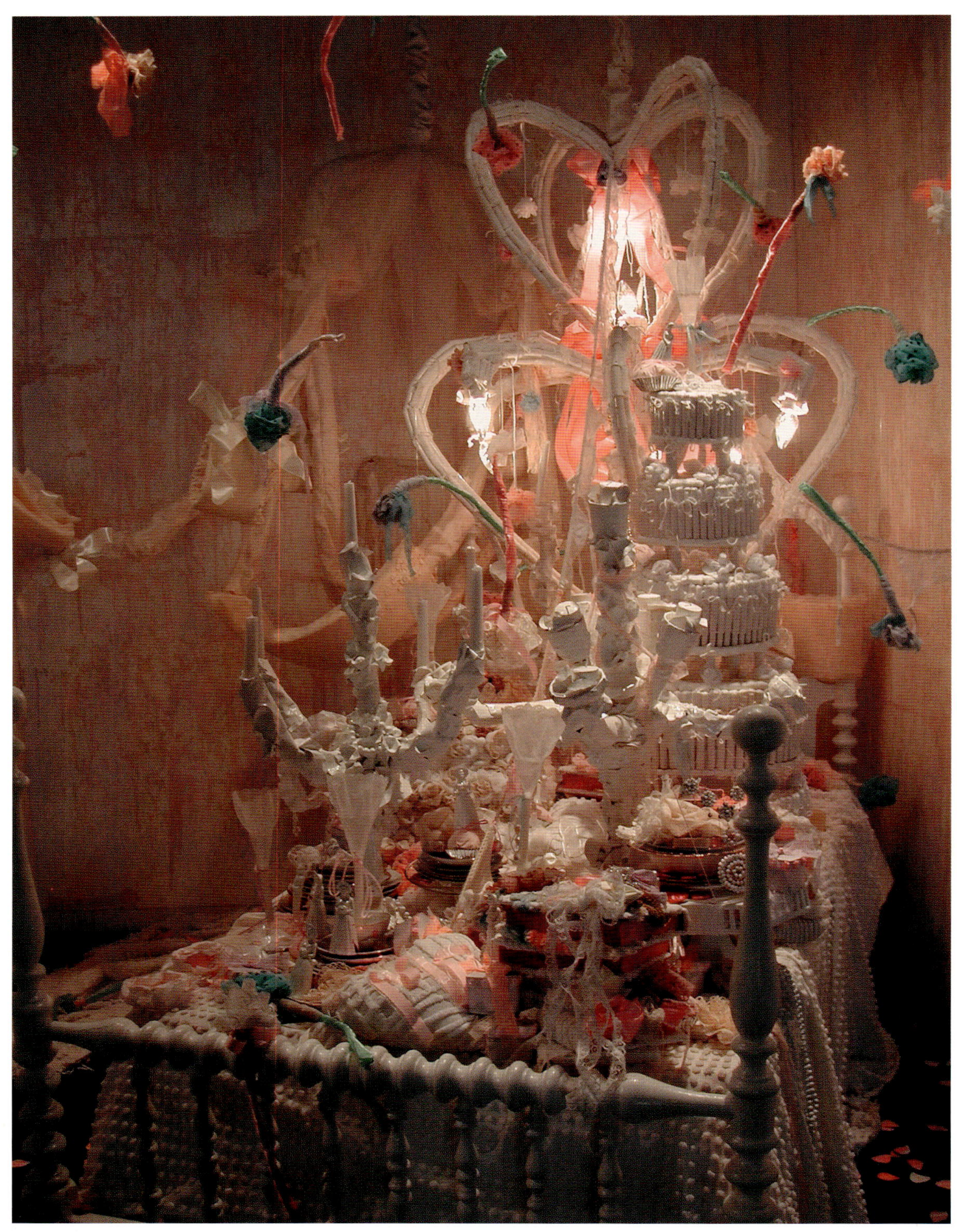

Vadis Turner. *Reception*, 2009. Bibles, tampons, birth control pills, underwear, candles, wax paper, plates, chocolate, ribbon, chenille bedspreads, paint, and mixed media: 8 × 10 feet (approximately). Installation view, Elizabeth A. Sackler Center for Feminist Art, Brooklyn Museum, Brooklyn, New York. *Courtesy of the artist and Lyons Wier Gallery, New York*

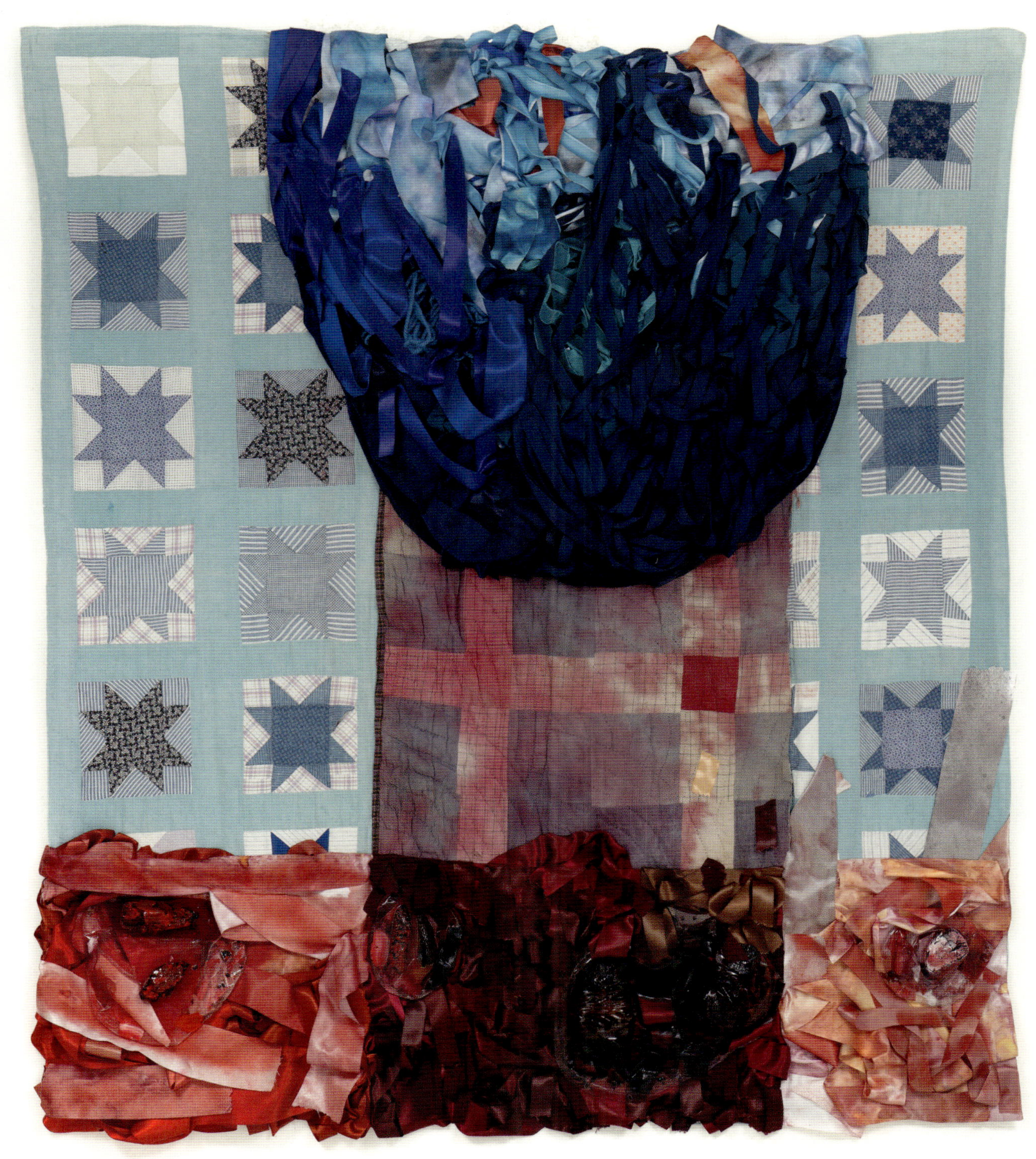

Vadis Turner. *Ritual Heirloom 1, Three Seasons and a Winter Flower*, 2017. Hand-stitched quilts, ribbon, fabric dye, charred wood, resin, acrylic paint, and mixed media: 80 × 72 inches. *Courtesy of the artist and Geary Contemporary, New York*

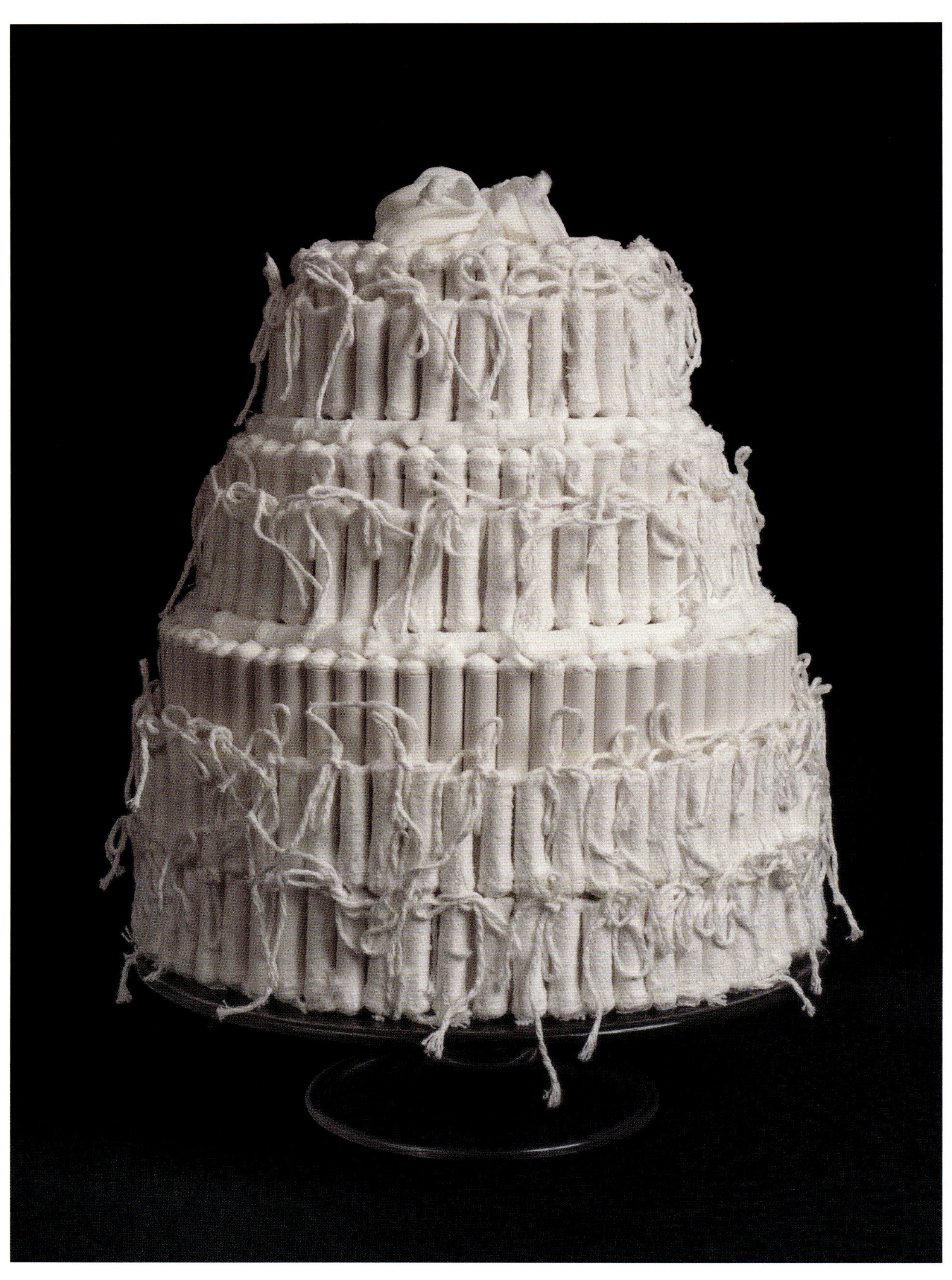

Vadis Turner. *Tampon Wedding Cake*, 2007. Tampons, applicators, panty hose, and mixed media: 12 × 12 × 15 inches. *Courtesy of the artist and Geary Contemporary, New York*

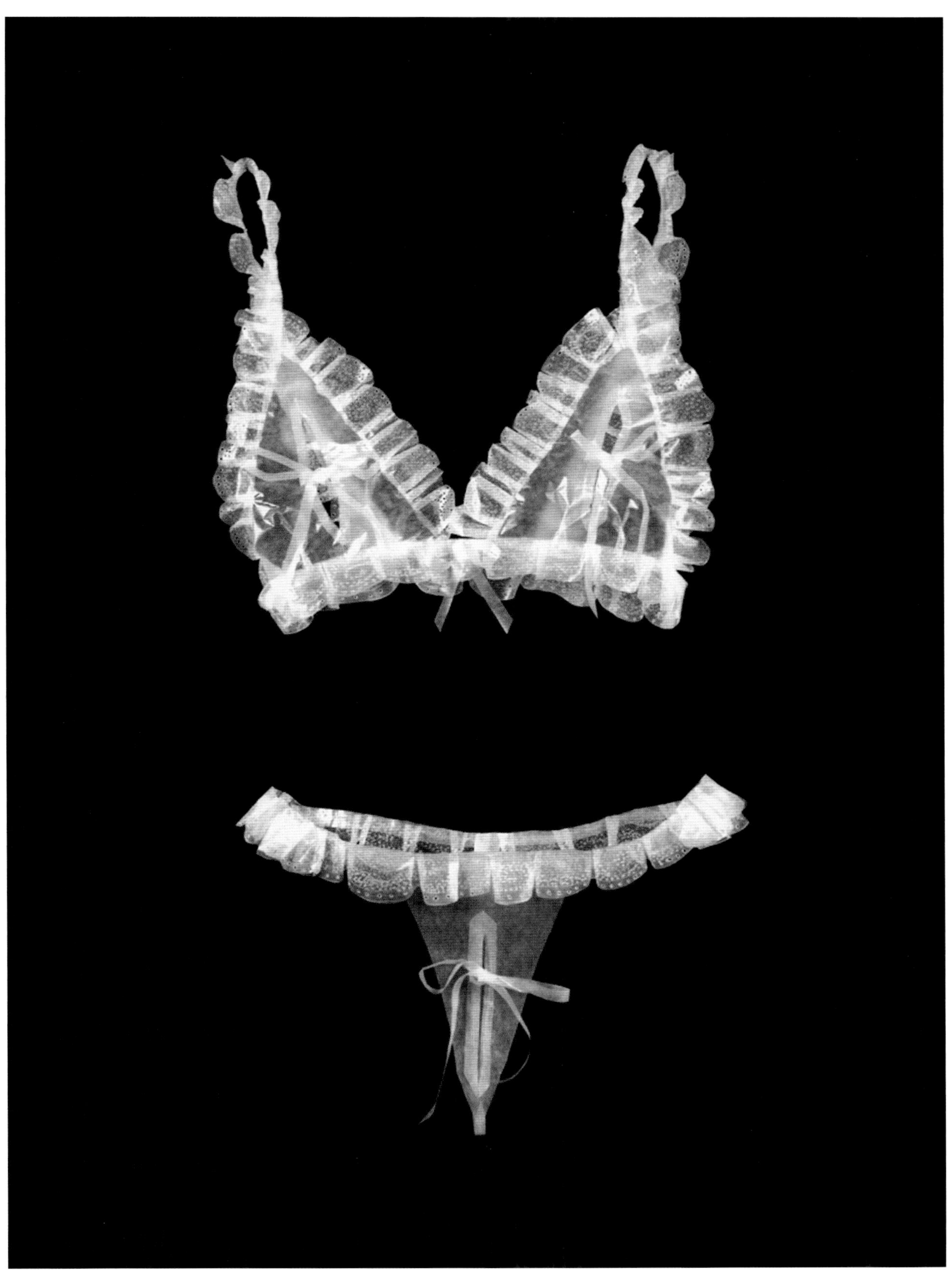

Vadis Turner. *Wax Paper Lingerie, Peek a Boo,* 2007. Wax paper: 30 × 60 inches. *Courtesy of the artist and Geary Contemporary, New York*

VAL BRITTON

Val Britton creates immersive, collaged works on paper and site-specific installations that explore physical and psychological spaces. Her fragmented, exploded landscapes draw on the language of maps, memory, history, science, and the possibilities of abstraction. Britton works in an explorative mode, employing the abstract space of the map to create a pliable structure for intuition, improvisation, and chance. Connecting paper fragments together through handmade collage, drawing, painting, staining, printing, stitching, and cutting, Britton navigates the blurry terrain of memory and imagination.

Britton's work is part of numerous collections, ranging from the Arkansas Arts Center to the Fine Arts Museums of San Francisco to the Library of Congress. In 2014, Britton completed *Voyage*, a 55-foot-long, site-specific public art commission at the San Francisco International Airport, and *Cascade*, a large-scale permanent installation at Facebook HQ, Menlo Park, California, in which a cut-paper installation references today's networked culture, organic cells, floating land masses, and perforated borders. Similarly, in 2018, Britton was commissioned by Hired, to develop a body of work in direct response to their report, *2018 The State of Wage Inequality in the Workplace*. Britton received her BFA from Rhode Island School of Design, Providence, in 1999 and her MFA from California College of the Arts, Oakland, in 2006. Britton was born in Livingston, New Jersey, and lives and works in San Francisco.

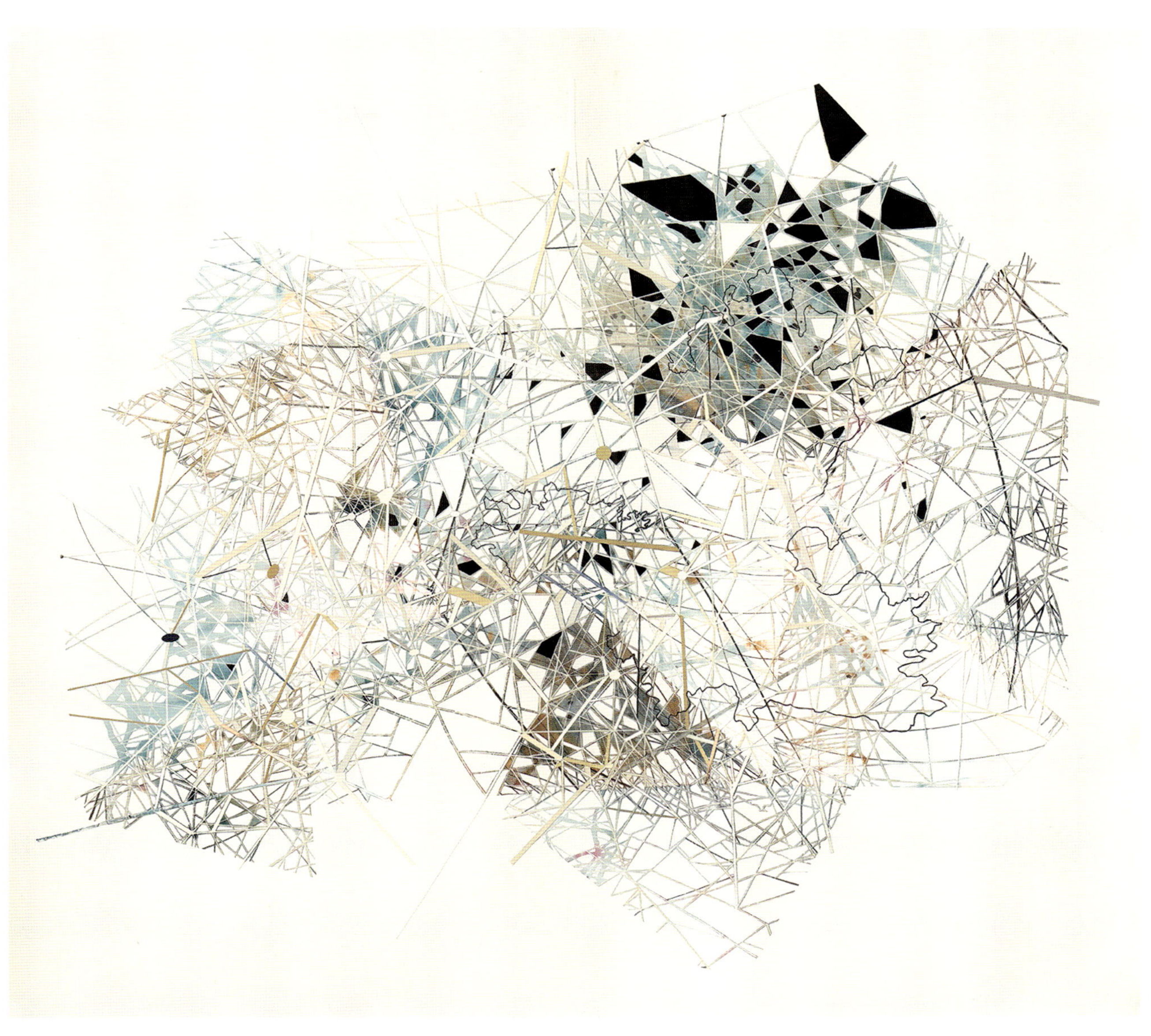

Val Britton. *Expanded Arc*, 2016. Acrylic collage on paper: 65 × 72 inches. *Courtesy of the artist and Gallery Wendi Norris, San Francisco*

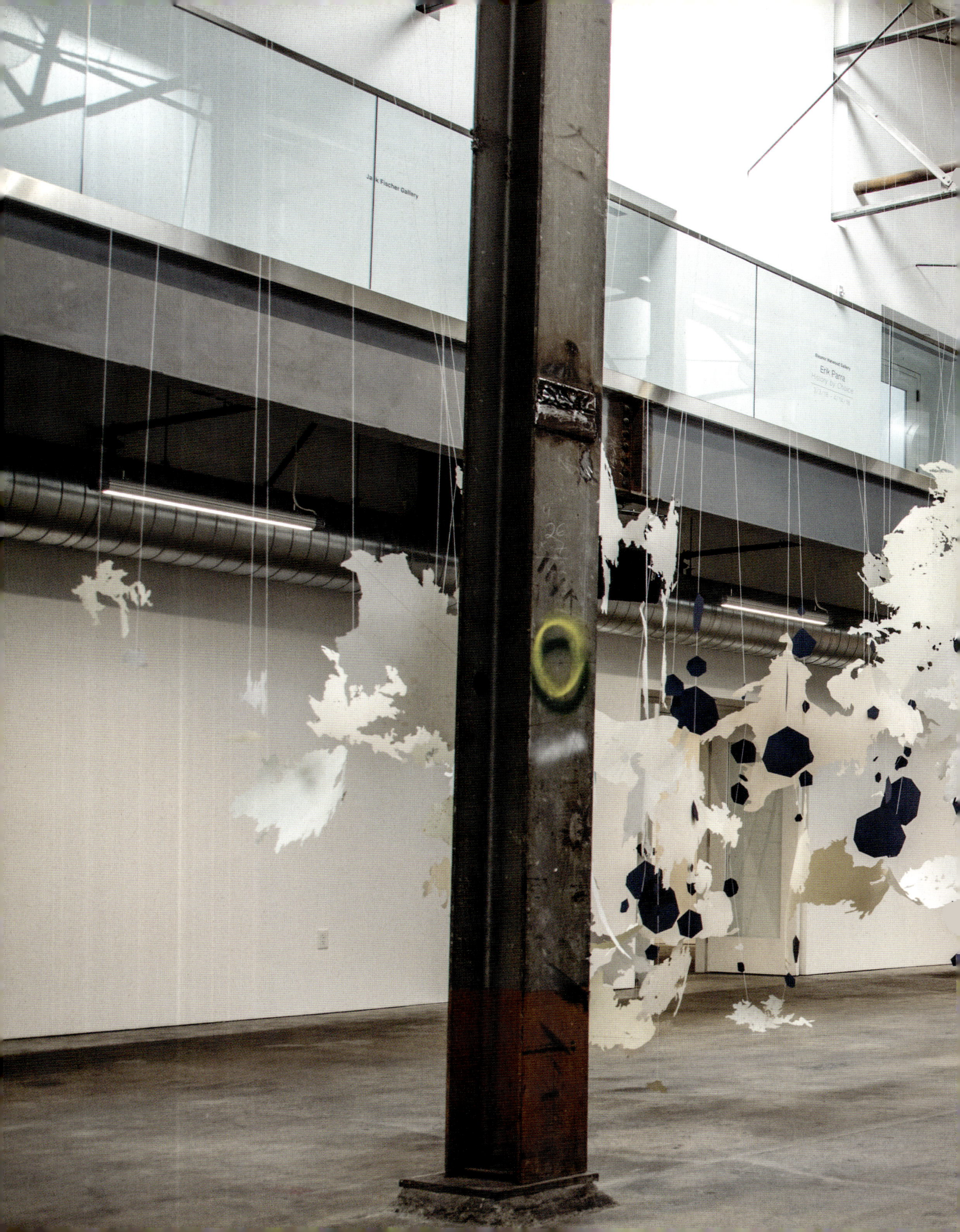
Jack Fischer Gallery
Erik Parra
History by Choice

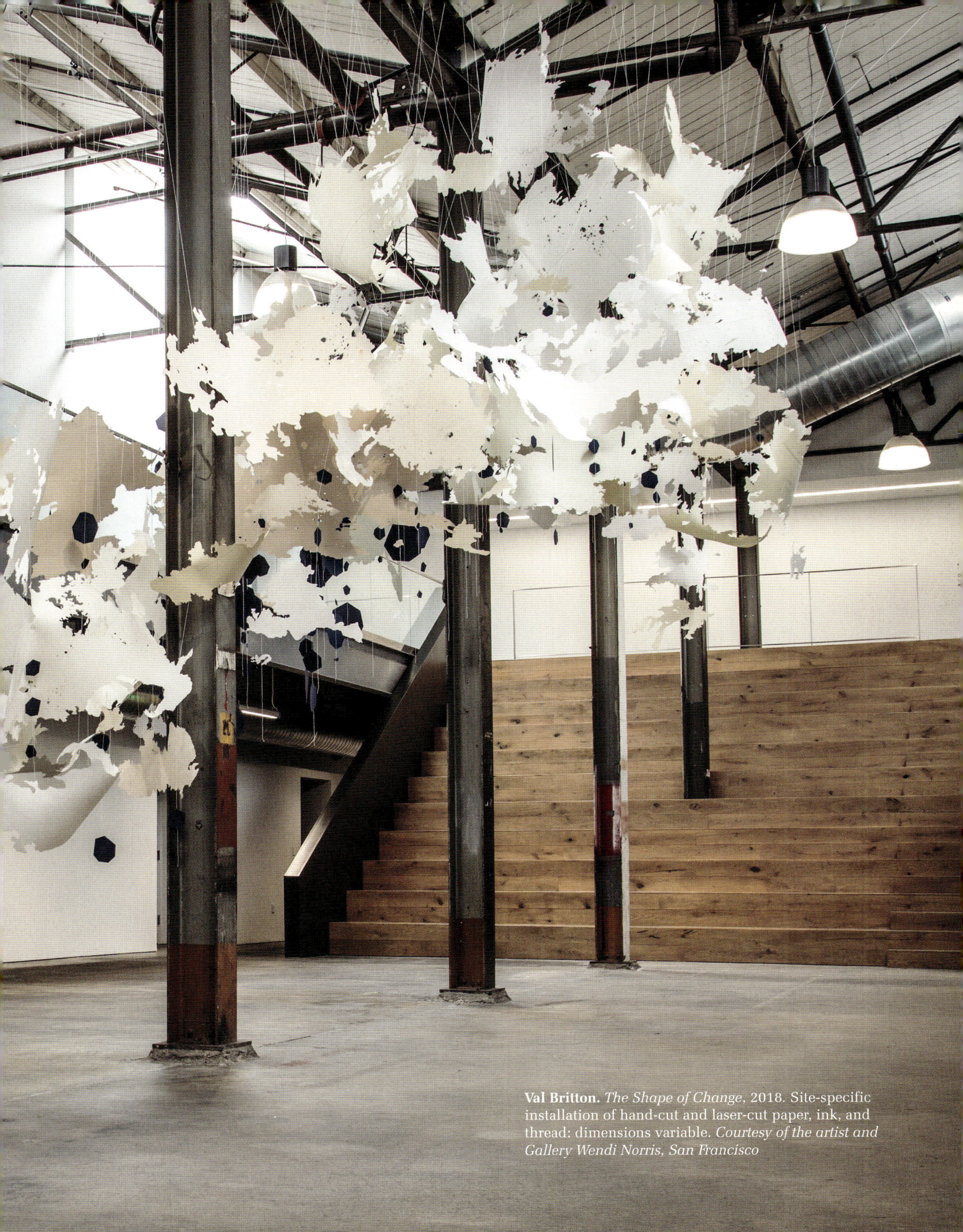

Val Britton. *The Shape of Change*, 2018. Site-specific installation of hand-cut and laser-cut paper, ink, and thread: dimensions variable. *Courtesy of the artist and Gallery Wendi Norris, San Francisco*

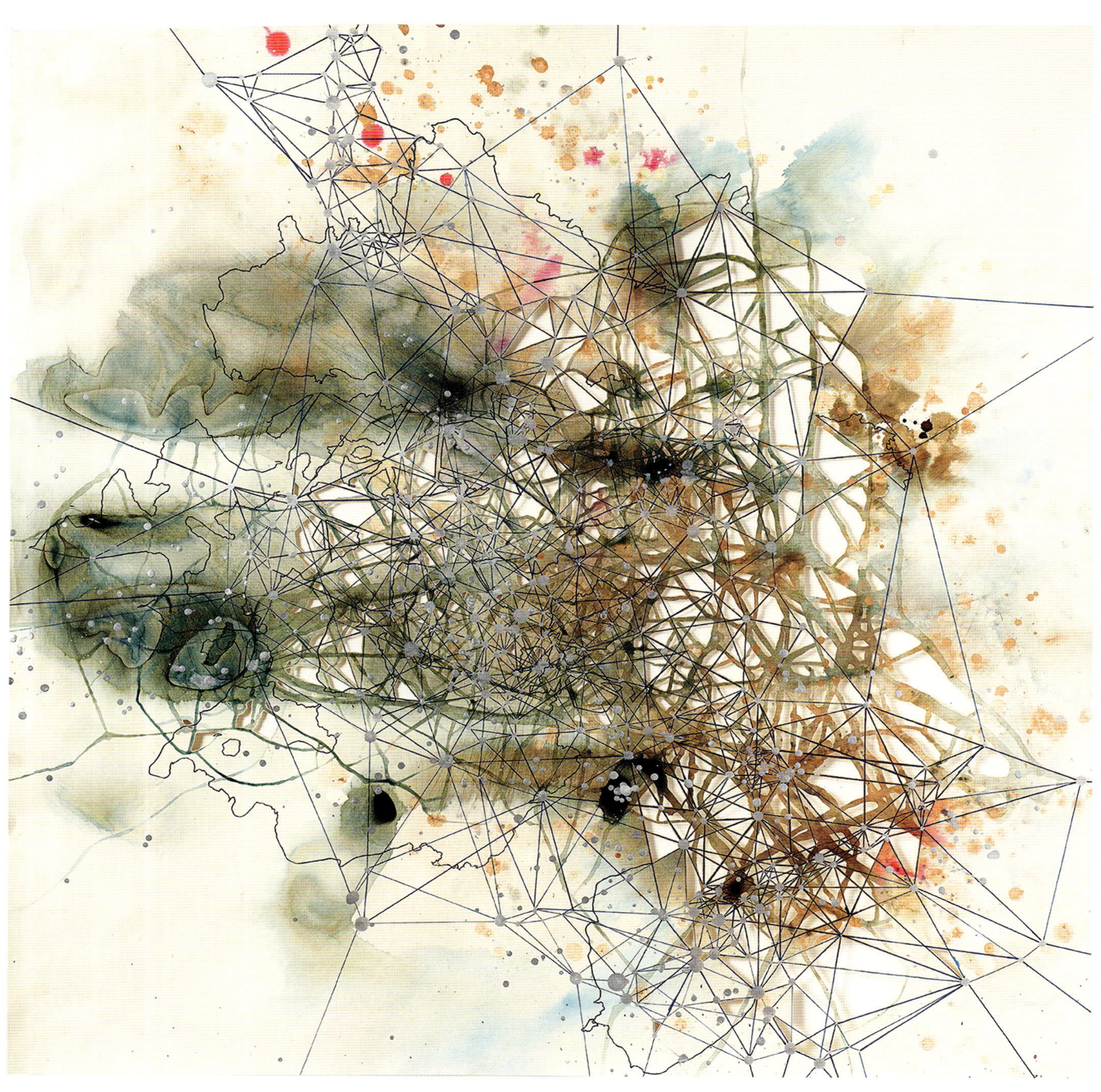

Val Britton. *Songlines*, 2015. Acrylic, collage, and cutout paper: 50 × 50 inches. *Courtesy of the artist and Gallery Wendi Norris, San Francisco*

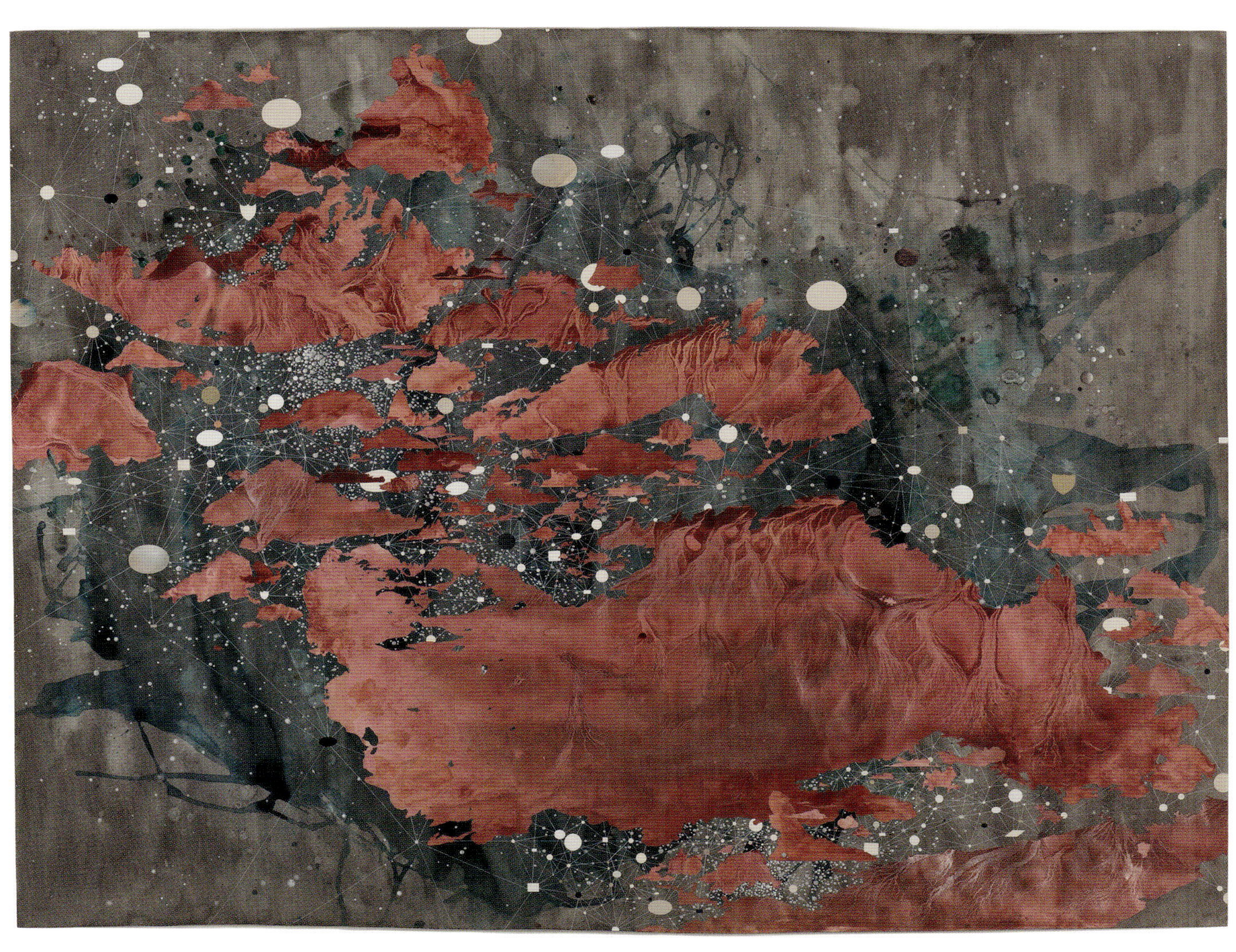

Val Britton. *Red Planet*, 2014. Ink tempera and collage on paper: 50 × 70.5 inches. *Courtesy of the artist and Gallery Wendi Norris, San Francisco*

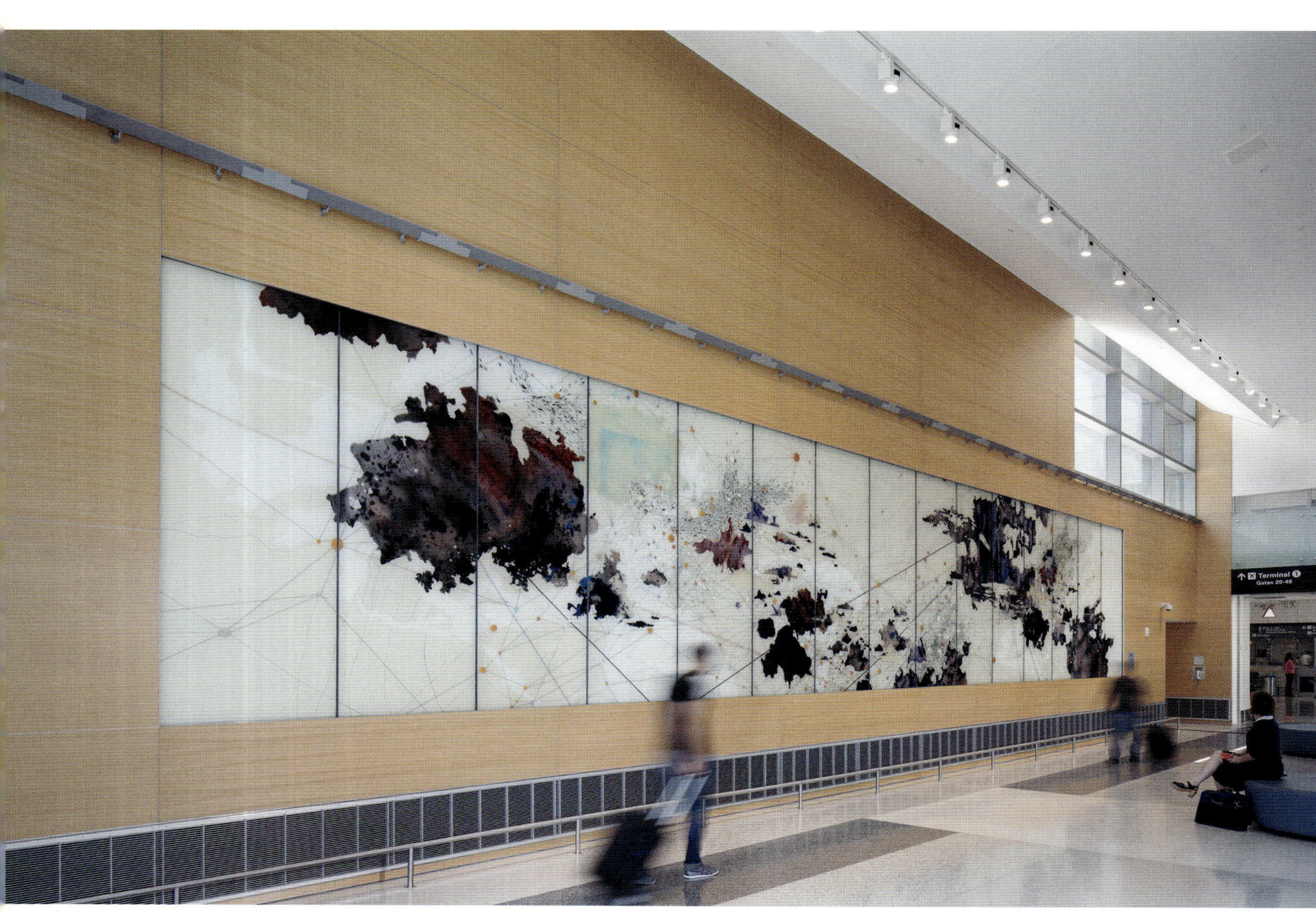

Val Britton. *Voyage*, 2014. Laminated glass panels, ceramic glass melting colors, graphite and lacquer paint. Installation view, Commissioned by the San Francisco Arts Commission at the San Francisco International Airport. *Courtesy of the artist and Gallery Wendi Norris, San Francisco*

YAEL KANAREK

Yael Kanarek's practice centers on the fundamental hypothesis that language and numerals render reality, and that this reality is an entirely subjective, unified field. Through the shuffling of physical properties that construct our use of language, such as matter, shape, and sound, Kanarek's work examines how verbal signifiers operate emotionally. Employing modes of authorship such as storytelling and multilingualism, Kanarek manipulates the biographical predisposition of cultural associations. As an Israeli American, her perception is tempered by an awareness of postnational borderlines. Her work enters spaces of meaning determined by a global network and the negotiation of identity that occurs when confronted with multiple systems. Crossing these sensibilities with her observation of the Internet as a network made of language—human and computer—her most recent projects document the consciousness shift from a modernist self to that which is networked.

Selected for the 2002 Whitney Biennial, exhibitions of Kanarek's work also include Beral Madra Contemporary Art, Istanbul; the National Museum of Contemporary Art, Athens, Greece; the University of Colorado Art Museum, Boulder; the Cantor Arts Center, Stanford University, Stanford, California; LIMN Gallery, San Francisco; Holster Projects, London; Wood Street Galleries, Pittsburgh, Pennsylvania; Nelly Aman, Tel Aviv; Boston CyberArts Festival; HVCCA, Peekskill, New York; Arena 1, Santa Monica, California; California College of the Arts, San Francisco; Orsini Palace, Bomarzo, Italy; and Sala Uno Gallery, Rome. Kanarek's work has also been shown in New York City at the Drawing Center, the Jewish Museum, Exit Art, the Kitchen, the Museum of the Moving Image, bitforms gallery, Kenny Schachter Contemporary, Silverstein Gallery, Ronald Feldman Gallery, Derek Eller Gallery, A.I.R. Gallery, 303 Gallery, and Schroeder Romero Gallery. In addition to a Rockefeller New Media Fellowship and an Eyebeam Honorary Fellowship, Kanarek is the recipient of grants from the Jerome Foundation Media Arts and New York Foundation for the Arts, and commissions from the San Francisco Museum of Modern Art, Turbulence.org, and the Alternative Museum. Kanarek's distinctions also include residencies at Civitella Ranieri, Harvestworks, and the Mamuta Art and Media Center. In 1999, she founded Upgrade! International, a network of artists and curators concerned with technology and art. Kanarek holds an MFA from Rensselaer Polytechnic Institute and lives and works in New York City.

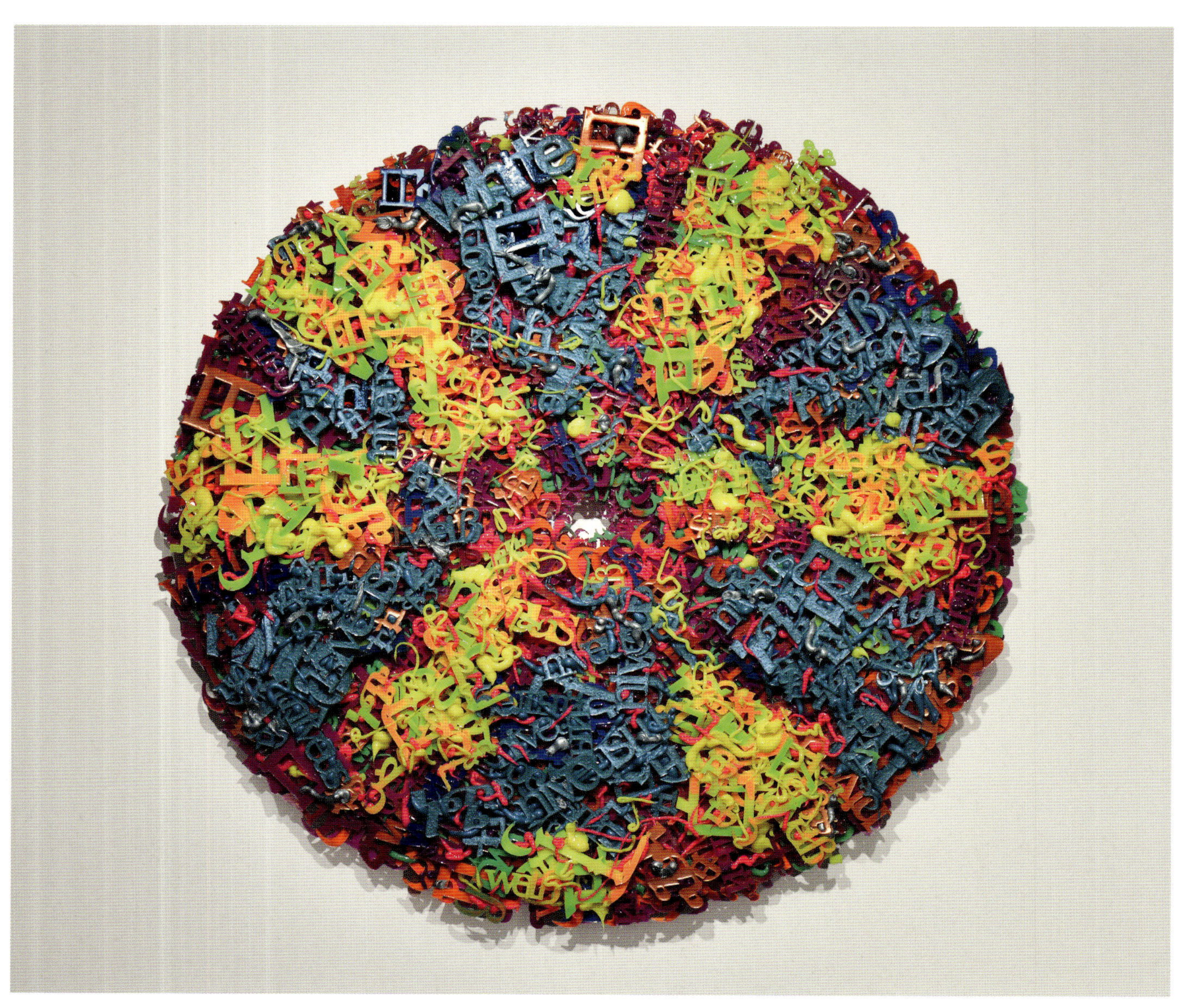

Yael Kanarek. *Rainbow, towards a New Balance (Made in the USA)*, 2013. Shoes worn by the artist, wood, and silicone words in nine languages: Amharic, Arabic, English, German, Hebrew, Japanese, Chinese, Latin, and Russian: 42 inches in diameter, 2 inches in depth. *Courtesy of the artist and bitforms gallery, New York*

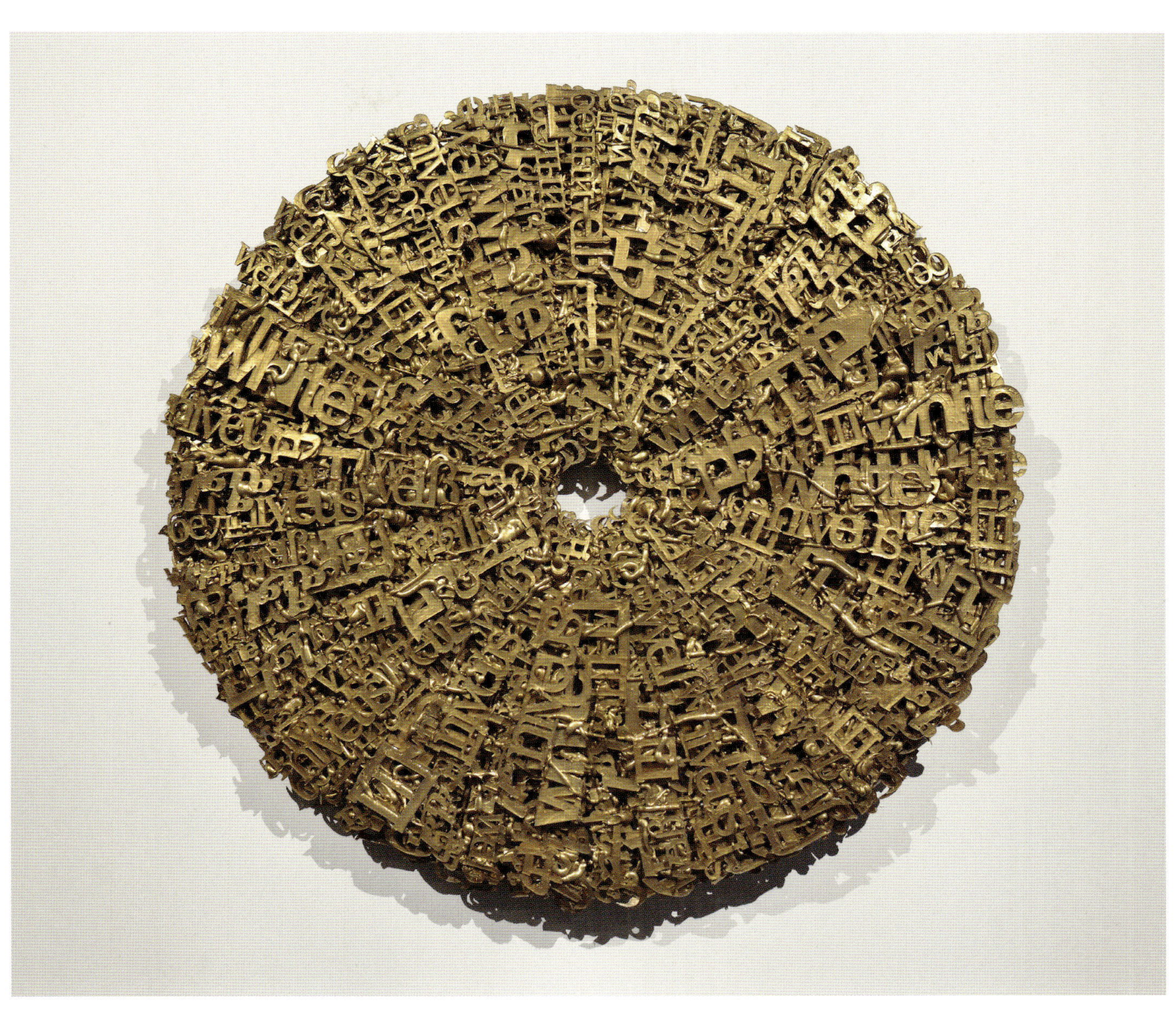

Yael Kanarek. *Sanctify Thyself, No. 1*, 2013. Wood, silicone words in nine languages: Amharic, Arabic, English, German, Hebrew, Japanese, Chinese, Latin, and Russian: 42 inches in diameter. *Courtesy of the artist and bitforms gallery, New York*

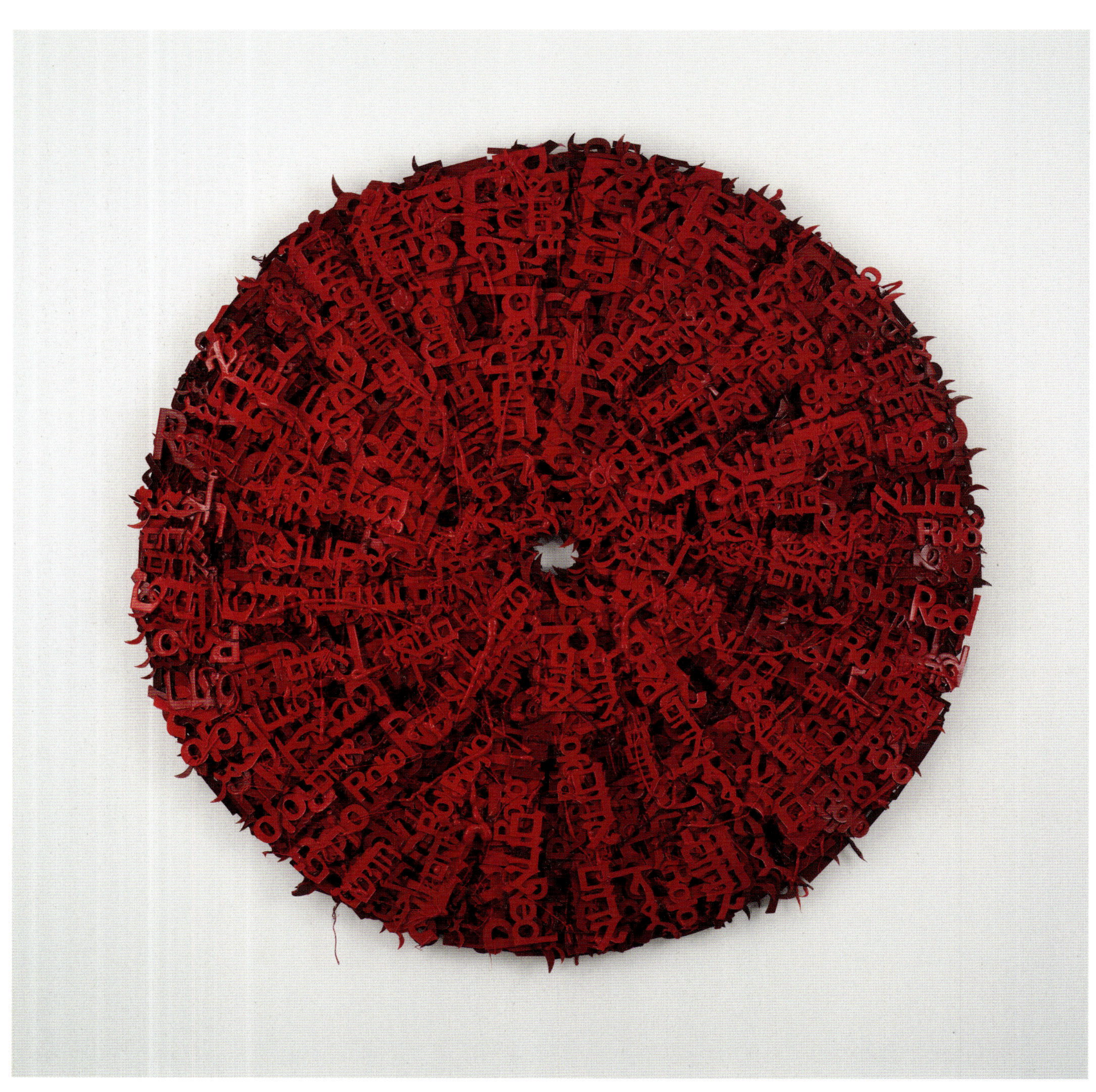

Yael Kanarek. *Wavelength Range of Roughly 630–740 nm, No. 7*, 2011. Wood, silicone words in five languages: Arabic, English, Hebrew, Spanish, and Yiddish: 72 inches in diameter. *Courtesy of the artist and bitforms gallery, New York*

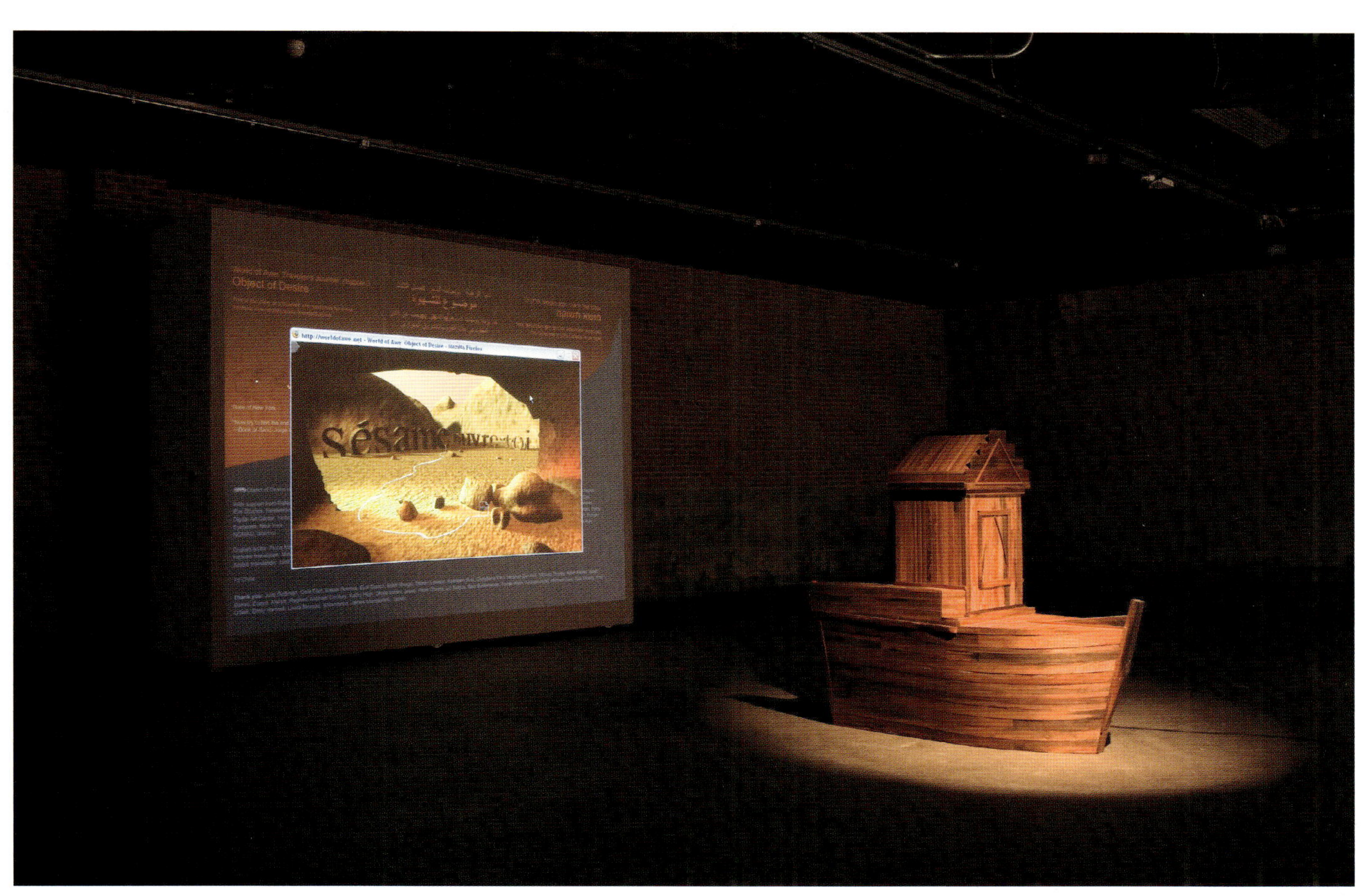

Yael Kanarek. *Object of Desire Control Chair*, 2007. Wood, plastic button and joystick, Internet connection, LCD screen or projection: 60 × 34 × 72 inches. *Courtesy of the artist and bitforms gallery, New York*

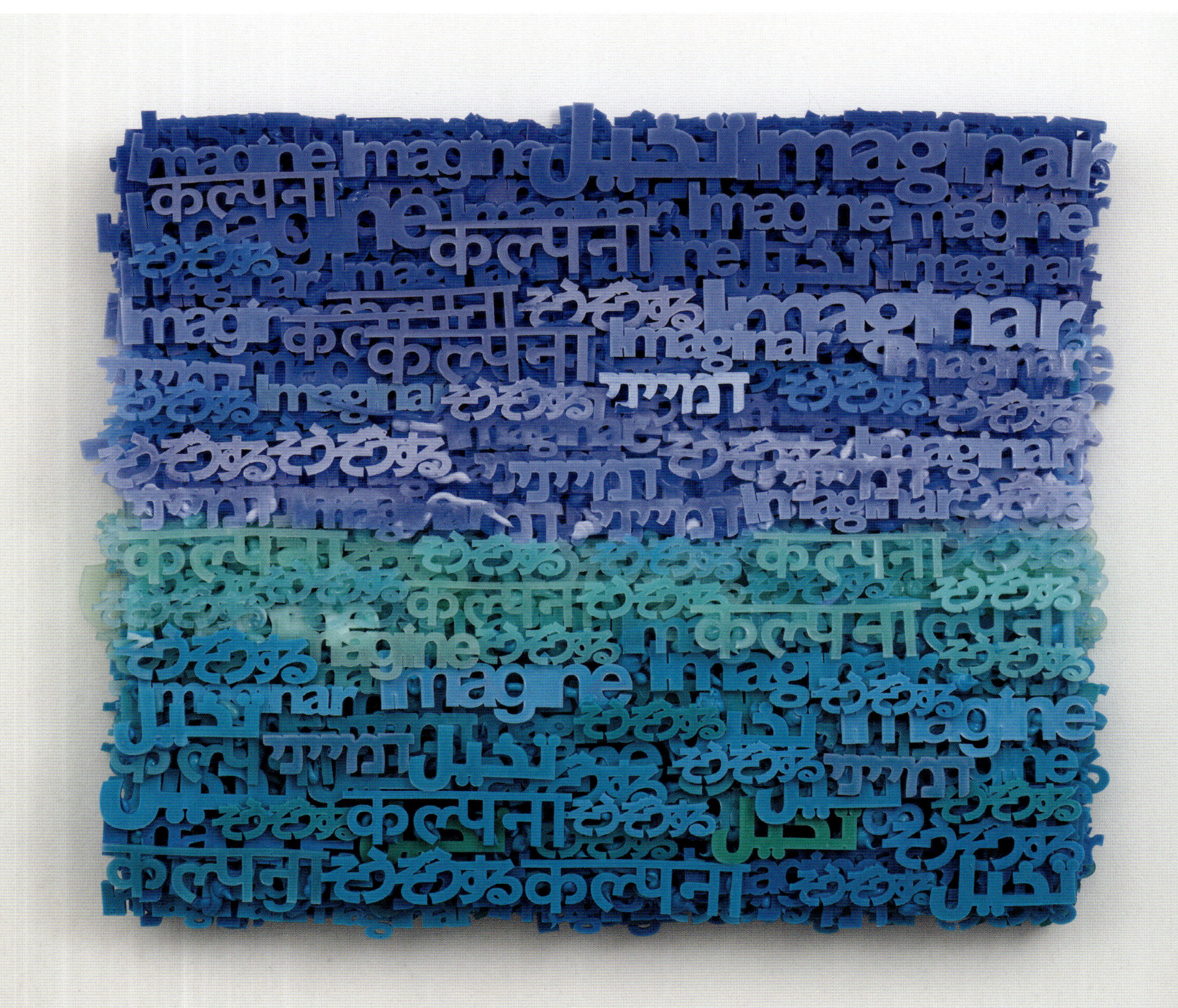

Yael Kanarek. *Damyeni*, 2015. Wood, silicone words in six languages: Arabic, English, Hindi, Hebrew, Japanese, and Portuguese: 33 × 240 inches. *Courtesy of the artist and bitforms gallery, New York*

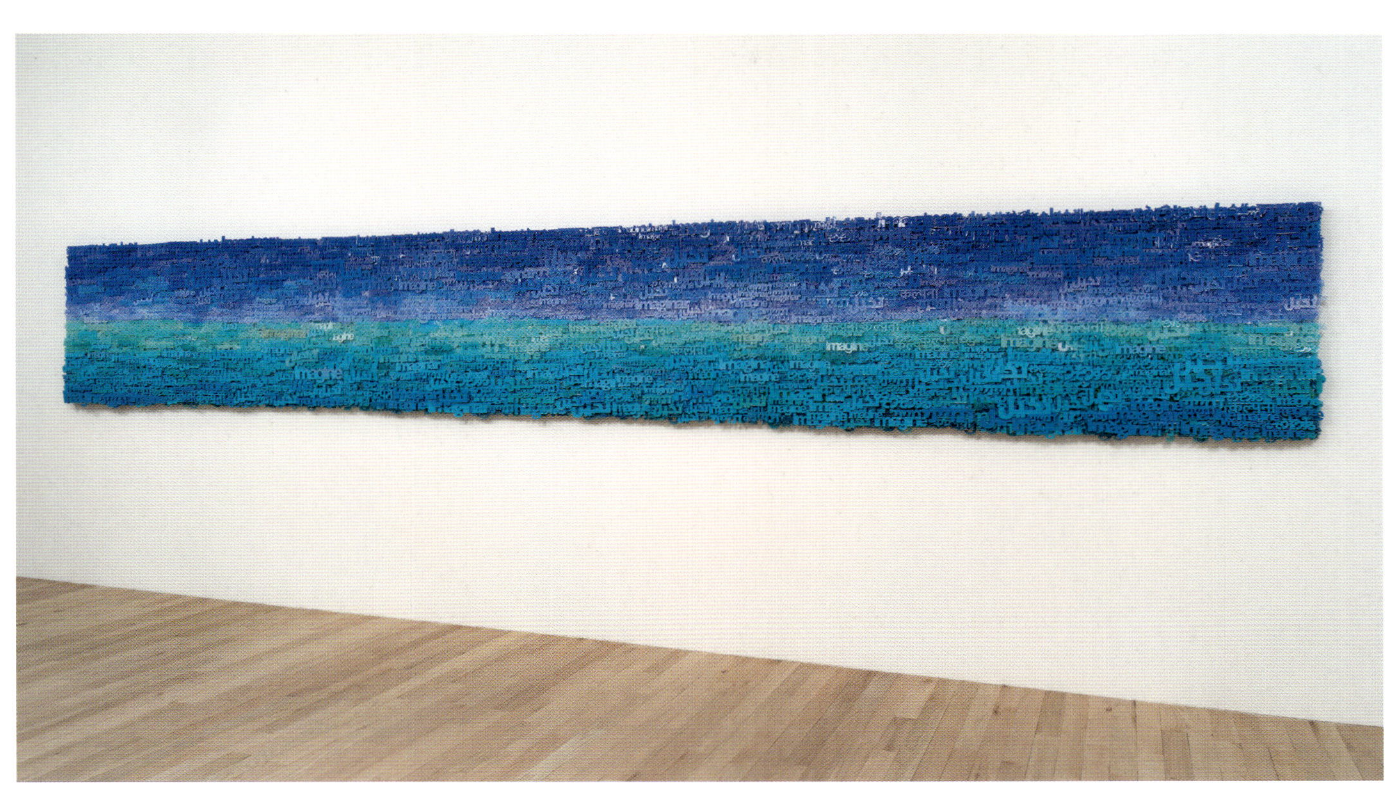

Yael Kanarek. *Image Horizon*, 2014. Wood, silicone words in six languages: Arabic, English, Hindi, Hebrew, Japanese, and Portuguese: 33 × 240 inches. *Courtesy of the artist and bitforms gallery, New York*

YEON JIN KIM

Korean multimedia artist Yeon Jin Kim's practice is based on updating the traditional techniques of scroll drawing and paper diorama construction to produce animated narrative videos. Her deliberately low-tech process, combined with animation techniques, encourages the viewer willing to engage the quintessential human muscle, the imagination. Projects include *Spaceship Grocery Store*, which documents life aboard a city-sized spaceship, where travelers are born and will die not having known their home planet and never arriving at their destination; *Zoonomia*, which occurs in a forest containing strange hybrid creatures, explores the notion of alternative evolutionary trajectories; *Ghost in the Yellow House*, which follows the disintegration of the American dream for a young Korean immigrant who experiences a hostile ghost in the form of a white woman; and *Monster Me*, which features an ancient monster emerging from Old Faithful and wreaking havoc in Jackson Hole, Wyoming. Kim has exhibited nationally and internationally, including Auburn University, Auburn, Alabama; Columbus State University, Columbus, Georgia; Hunterdon Museum, Clinton, New Jersey; Murray State University, Murray, Kentucky; Lab Gallery, New York City; Invisible-Exports, New York City; NURTUREart, Brooklyn; the Islip Museum, East Islip, New York; Boda Gallery, Seoul, Korea; and Third International Video Festival, Cairo, Egypt. Kim has participated in more than a dozen artist residency programs, including Yaddo and Wave Hill. She received her BFA in sculpture from Seoul National University, Seoul, Korea, and her MFA in combined media from Hunter College, New York City. Kim lives and works in New York City.

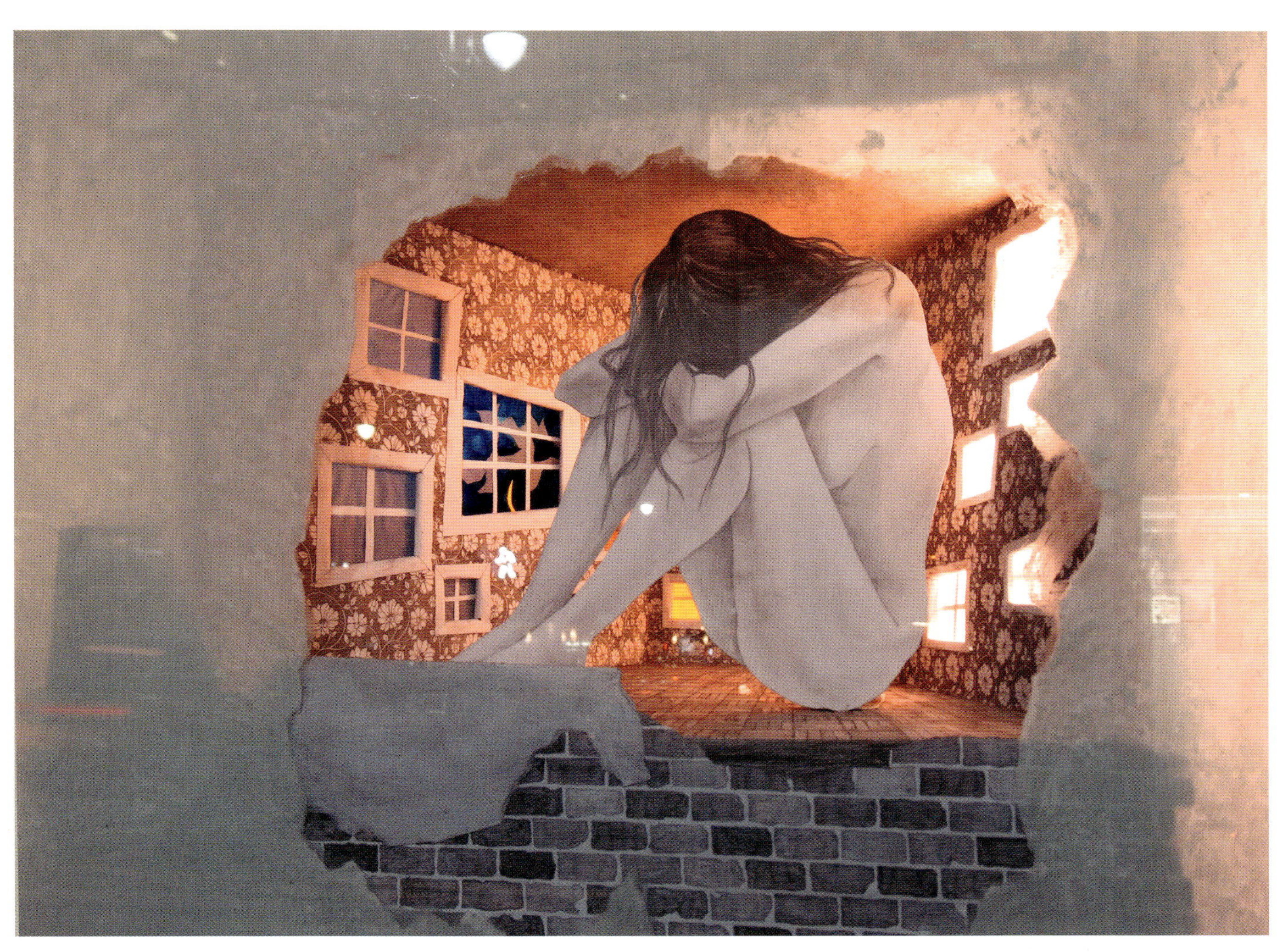

Yeon Jin Kim. *All Intellectual Animals Are Dangerous*, 2010. Paper diorama / single-channel video: 18 × 12 × 15 inches, each. Video duration: 6 minutes 31 seconds. Installation view, Lab Gallery, New York City. *Courtesy of the artist*

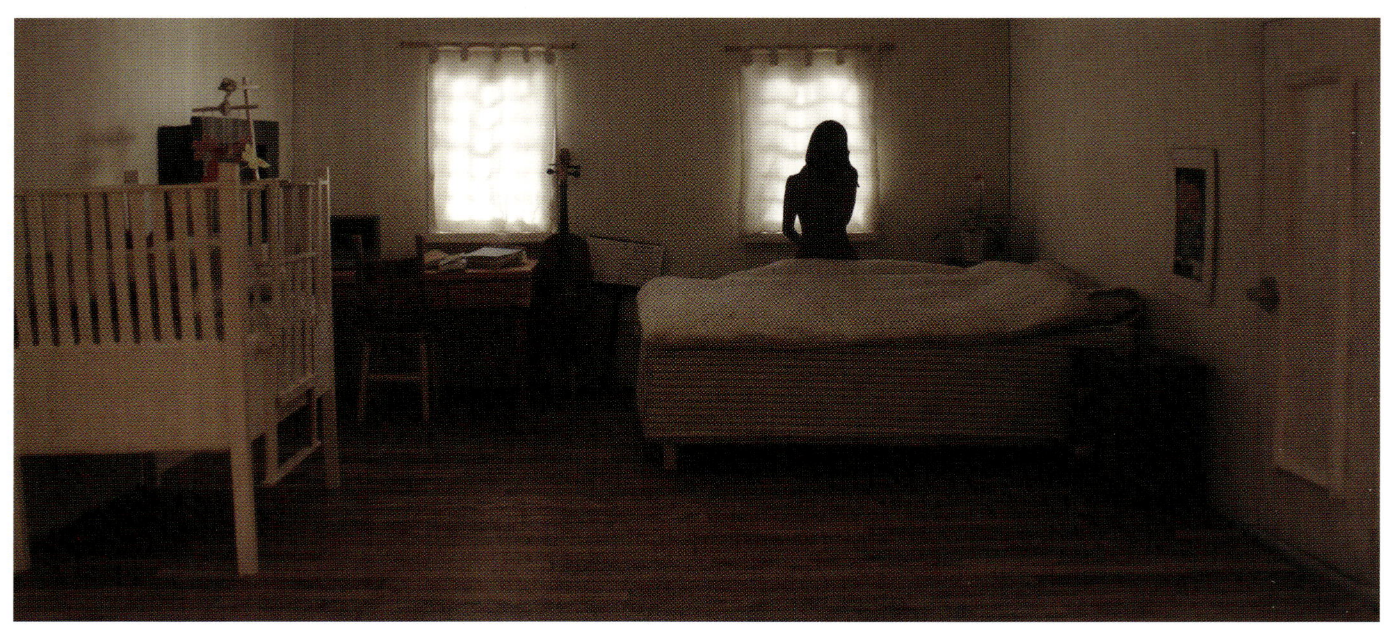

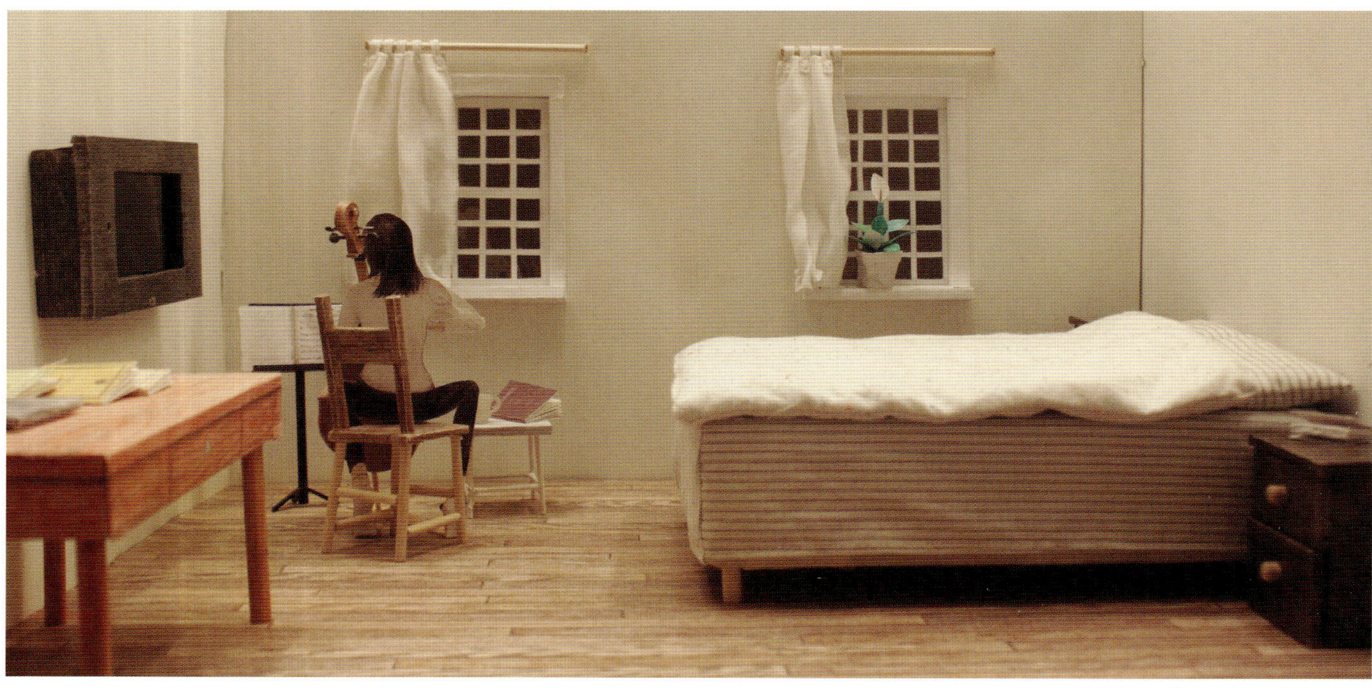

Yeon Jin Kim. *Ghost in the Yellow House*, 2016.
Paper diorama / single-channel video:
21 × 20 × 14 inches. Video duration: 20 minutes
2 seconds. *Courtesy of the artist*

Yeon Jin Kim. *Ghost in the Yellow House*, 2016.
Paper diorama / single-channel video:
21 × 20 × 14 inches. Video duration: 20 minutes
2 seconds. *Courtesy of the artist*

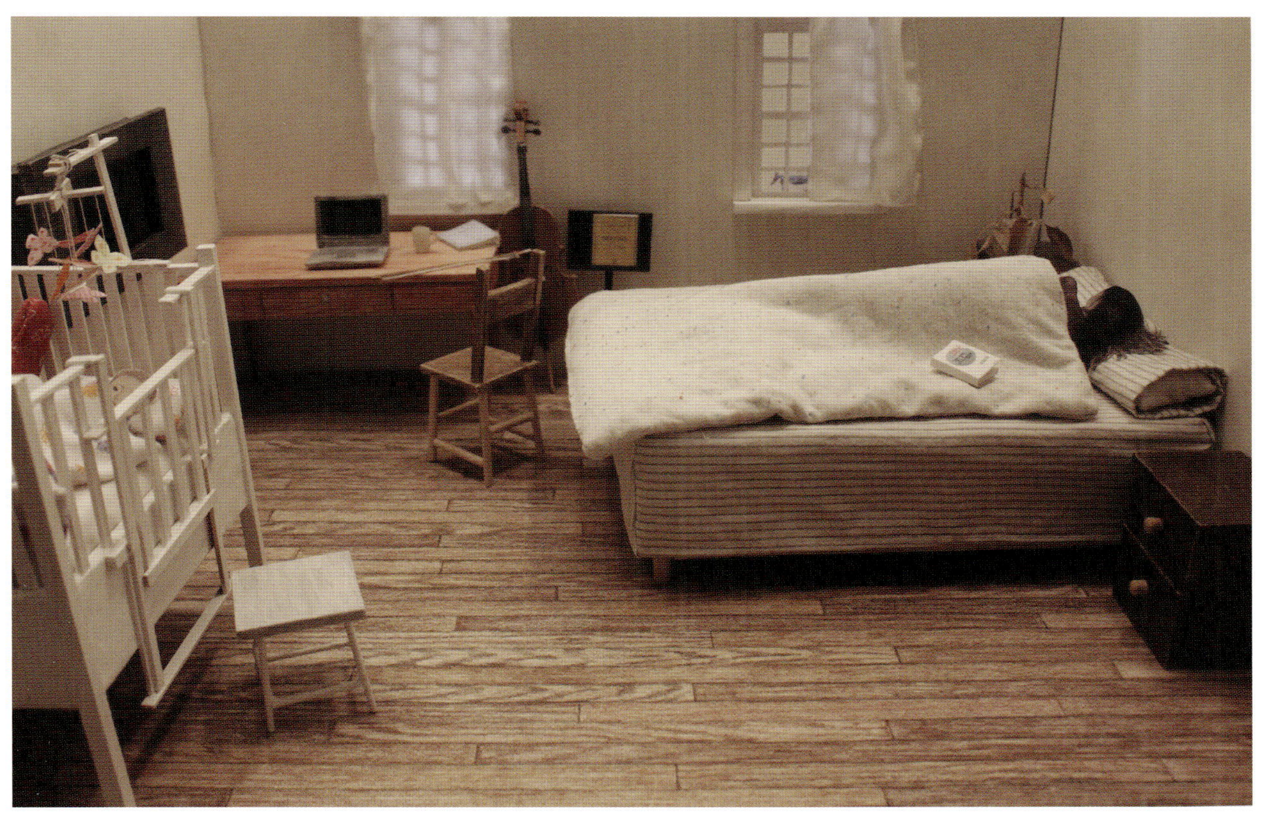

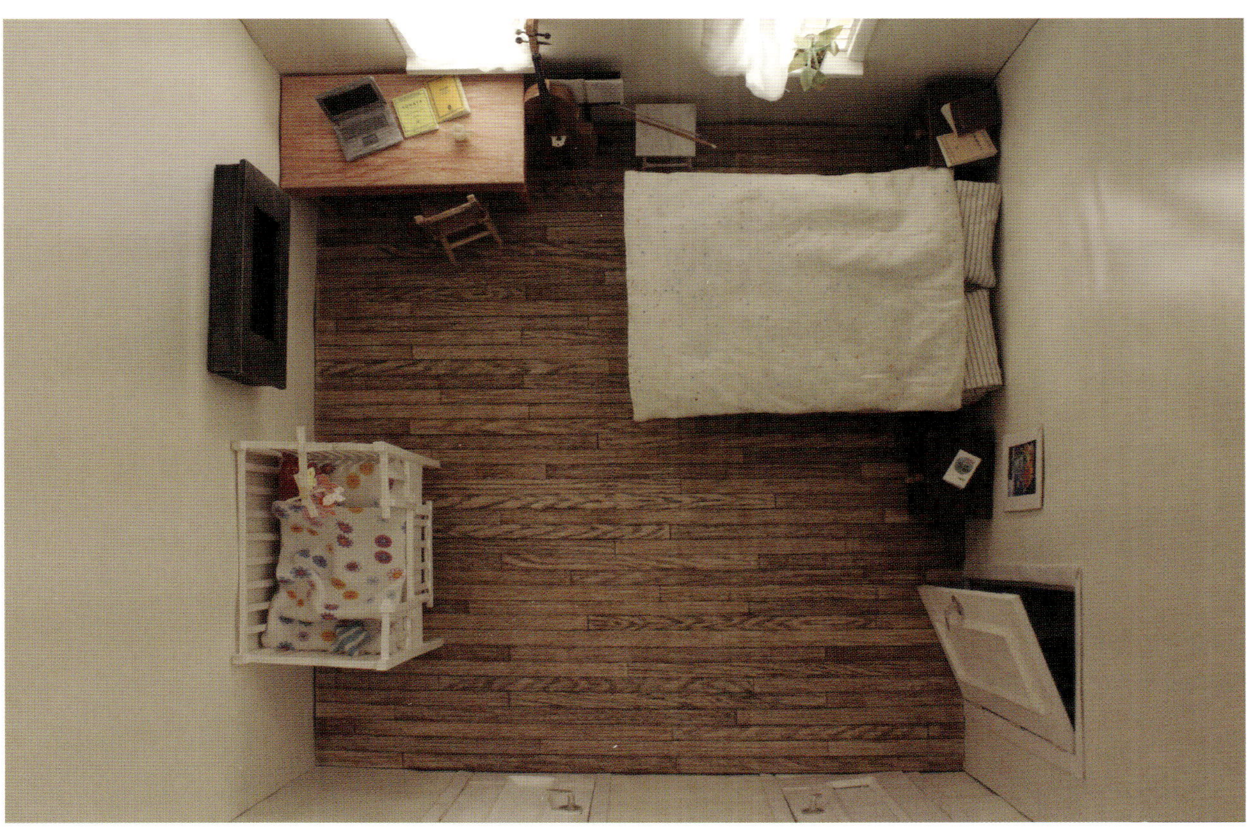

Yeon Jin Kim. *Ghost in the Yellow House*, 2016. Paper diorama / single-channel video: 21 × 20 × 14 inches. Video duration: 20 minutes 2 seconds. *Courtesy of the artist*

Yeon Jin Kim. *Ghost in the Yellow House*, 2016. Paper diorama / single-channel video: 21 × 20 × 14 inches. Video duration: 20 minutes 2 seconds. *Courtesy of the artist*

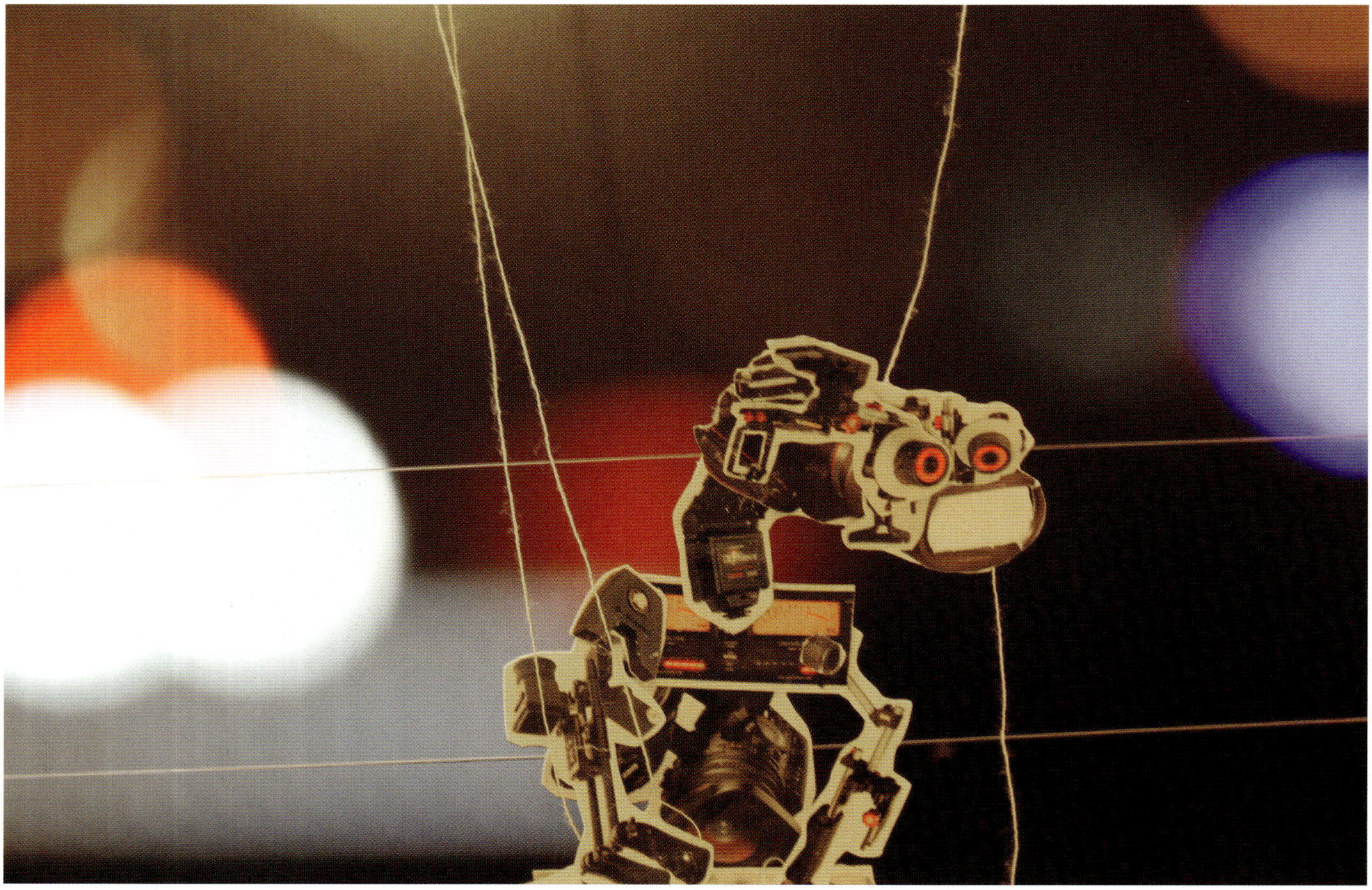

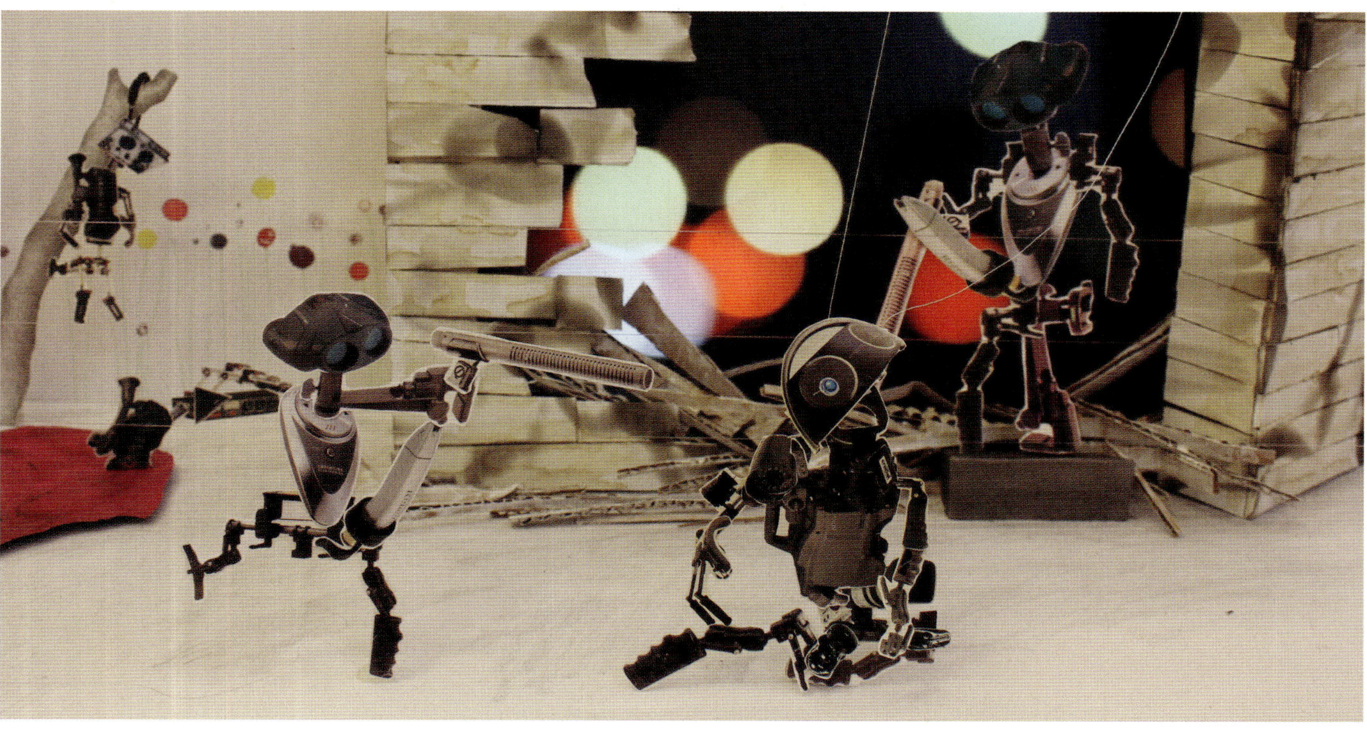

Yeon Jin Kim. *Spaceship Grocery Store*, 2012. Paper diorama / single-channel video: 532 × 15 × 12 inches. Video duration 8 minutes 21 seconds. *Courtesy of the artist*

Yeon Jin Kim. *Spaceship Grocery Store*, 2012. Paper diorama / single-channel video: 532 × 15 × 12 inches. Video duration 8 minutes 21 seconds. *Courtesy of the artist*

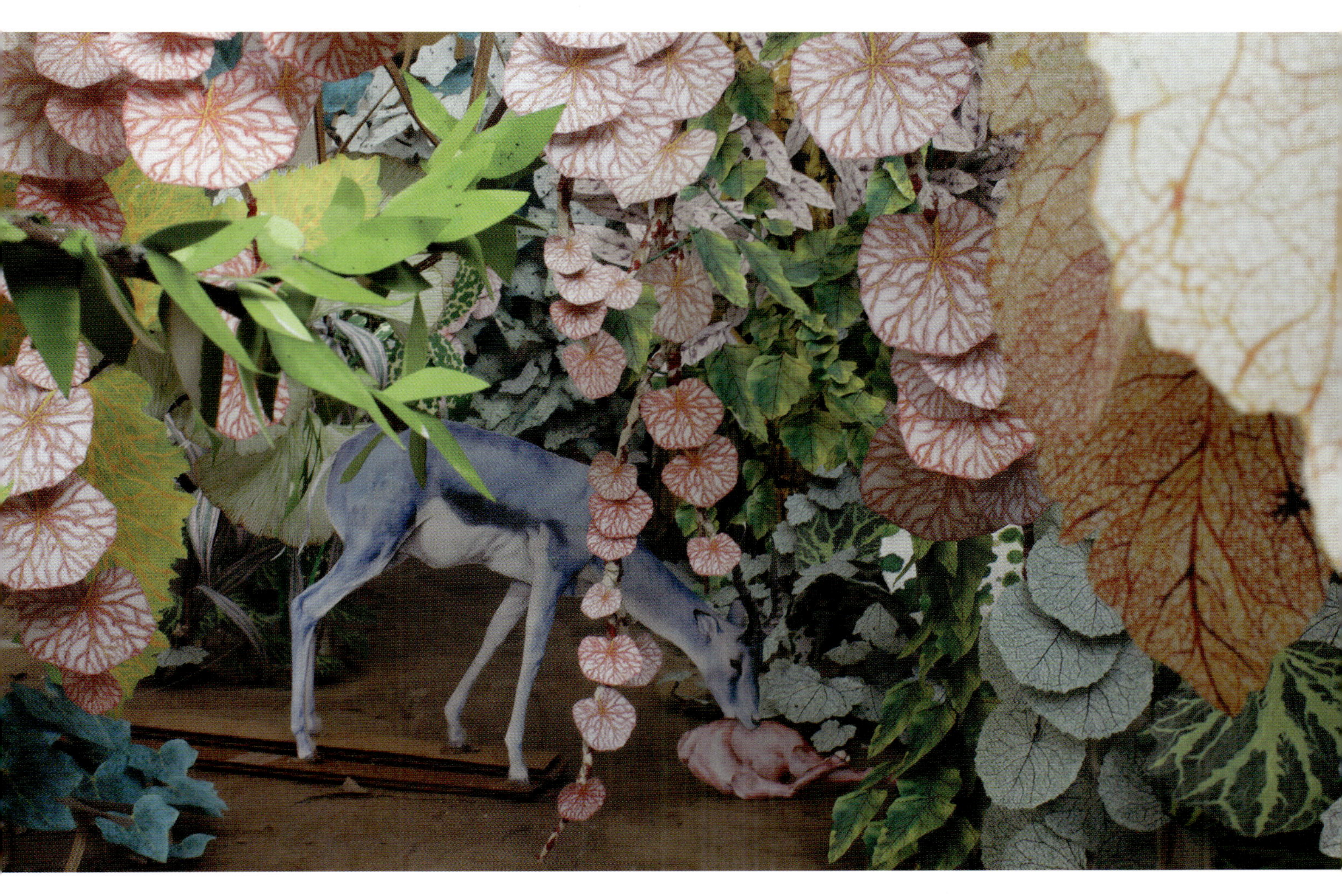

Yeon Jin Kim. *Zoonomia*, 2016. Paper diorama / single-channel video: 240 × 144 × 34 inches. Video duration: 4 minutes 11 seconds. *Courtesy of the artist*

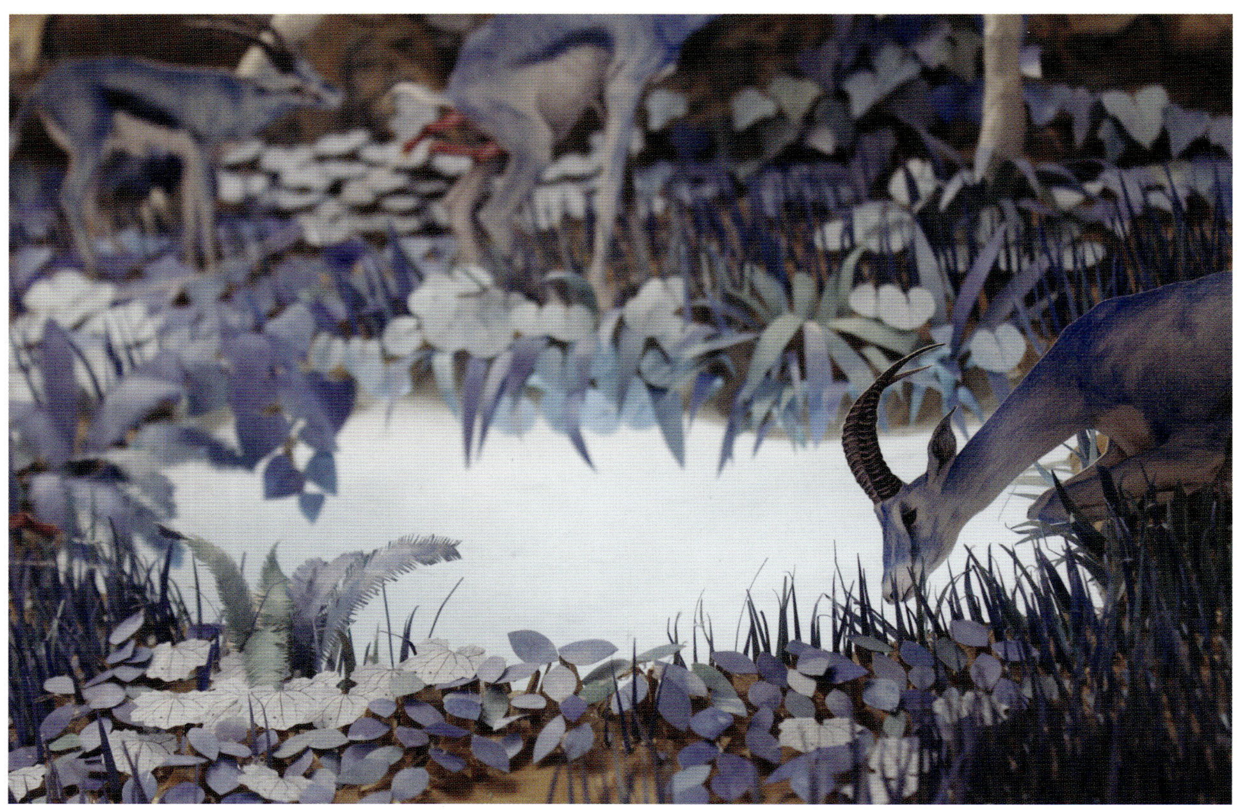

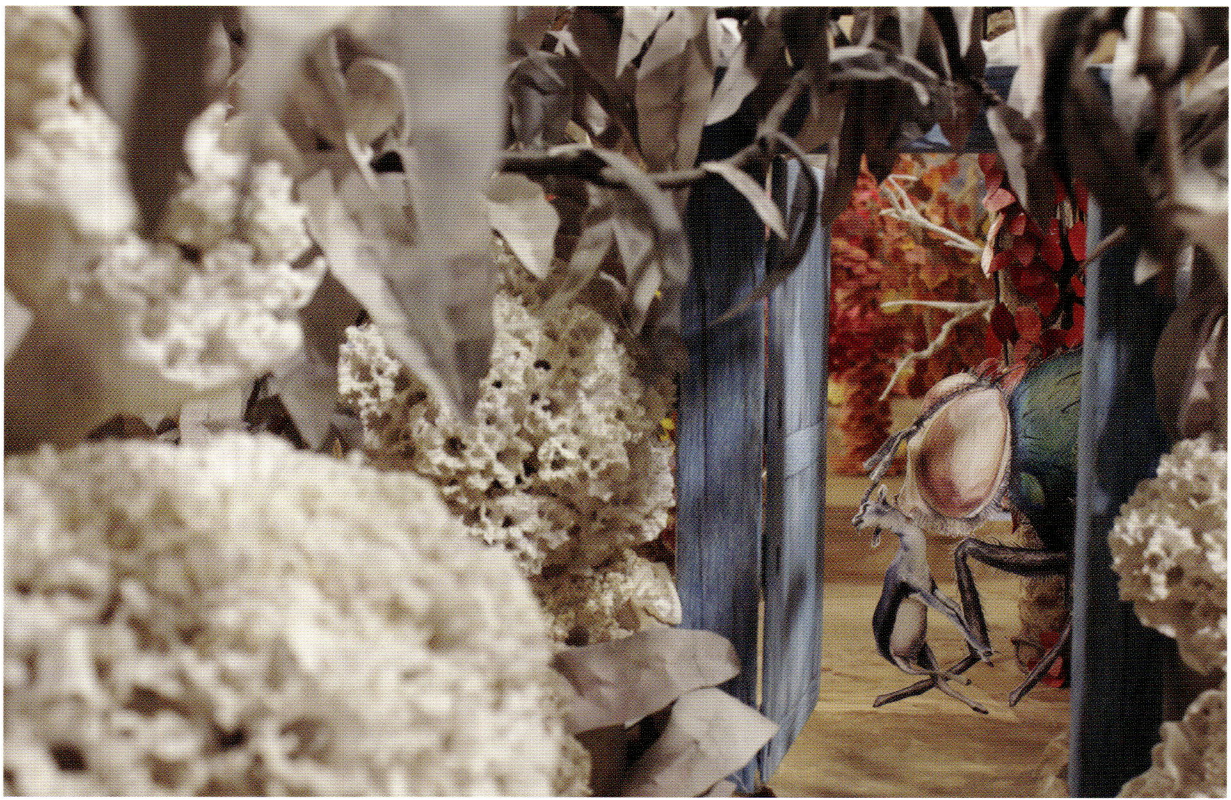

Yeon Jin Kim. *Zoonomia*, 2016. Paper diorama / single-channel video: 240 × 144 × 34 inches. Video duration: 4 minutes 11 seconds. *Courtesy of the artist*

Yeon Jin Kim. *Zoonomia*, 2016. Paper diorama / single-channel video: 240 × 144 × 34 inches. Video duration: 4 minutes 11 seconds. *Courtesy of the artist*

YIN XIUZHEN

Yin Xiuzhen is a leading female figure in Chinese contemporary art. Her career began in the early 1990s, following her graduation from Capital Normal University in Beijing, where she received a BA in oil painting from the Fine Arts Department in 1989. Her artworks have since been shown extensively in various international exhibitions. Best known for her works that incorporate secondhand objects, Yin uses her artwork to explore modern issues of globalization and homogenization. By utilizing recycled materials as sculptural documents of memory, she seeks to personalize objects and allude to the lives of specific individuals, which are often neglected in the drive toward excessive urbanization, rapid modern development, and the growing global economy. The artist explains, "In a rapidly changing China, 'memory' seems to vanish more quickly than everything else. That's why preserving memory has become an alternative way of life." Yin uses memory as a critical tool to examine the political, social, and environmental constructs that surround her.

Yin Xiuzhen has participated in many international and domestic group and solo exhibitions. Solo exhibitions include *Nowhere to Land*, Pace Beijing, Beijing (2013), *Yin Xiuzhen*, Groninger Museum, Groningen, The Netherlands; Kunstmuseum Düsseldorf, Düsseldorf, Germany (2012); and *Project 92*, Museum of Modern Art, New York City (2010). She has participated in various significant exhibitions around the world, including the *5th Moscow Contemporary Art Biennale*, Moscow (2013); *DUCHAMP and/or/in China*, UCCA, Beijing (2013); *Crossroads · Another Dimension: A Cross-Strait Four-Regions Artistic Exchange Project 2013*, He Xiangning Art Museum, Shenzhen, China; the Macao Museum of Art, Macao, China; the Kaohsiung Museum of Fine Arts, Kaohsiung, Taiwan; Hong Kong City Hall, Hong Kong (2013), the *First Kiev International Biennale of Contemporary Art*, Mystetskyi Arsenal, Kiev, Ukraine (2012); *OUR MAGIC HOUR: Yokohama Triennale*, Yokohama, Japan (2011); the *7th Shanghai Biennale*, Shanghai, China (2008); the *52nd Venice Biennale*, Venice, Italy (2007); the *14th Sydney Biennale,* Sydney, Australia (2004); the *26th Sao Paolo Biennale*, Sao Paolo, Brazil (2004); and *Inside Out: New Chinese Art*, which was organized by the Asia Society Galleries, New York City, and the San Francisco Museum of Modern Art, San Francisco (1998). The artist has received a range of prestigious awards, including the China Contemporary Art Award (CCAA) and the UNESCO/ASCHBERG award in 2000. Her work has also been acknowledged in the *New York Times* in 2006 and *Art in America* in 2003. Yin currently works and lives in Beijing.

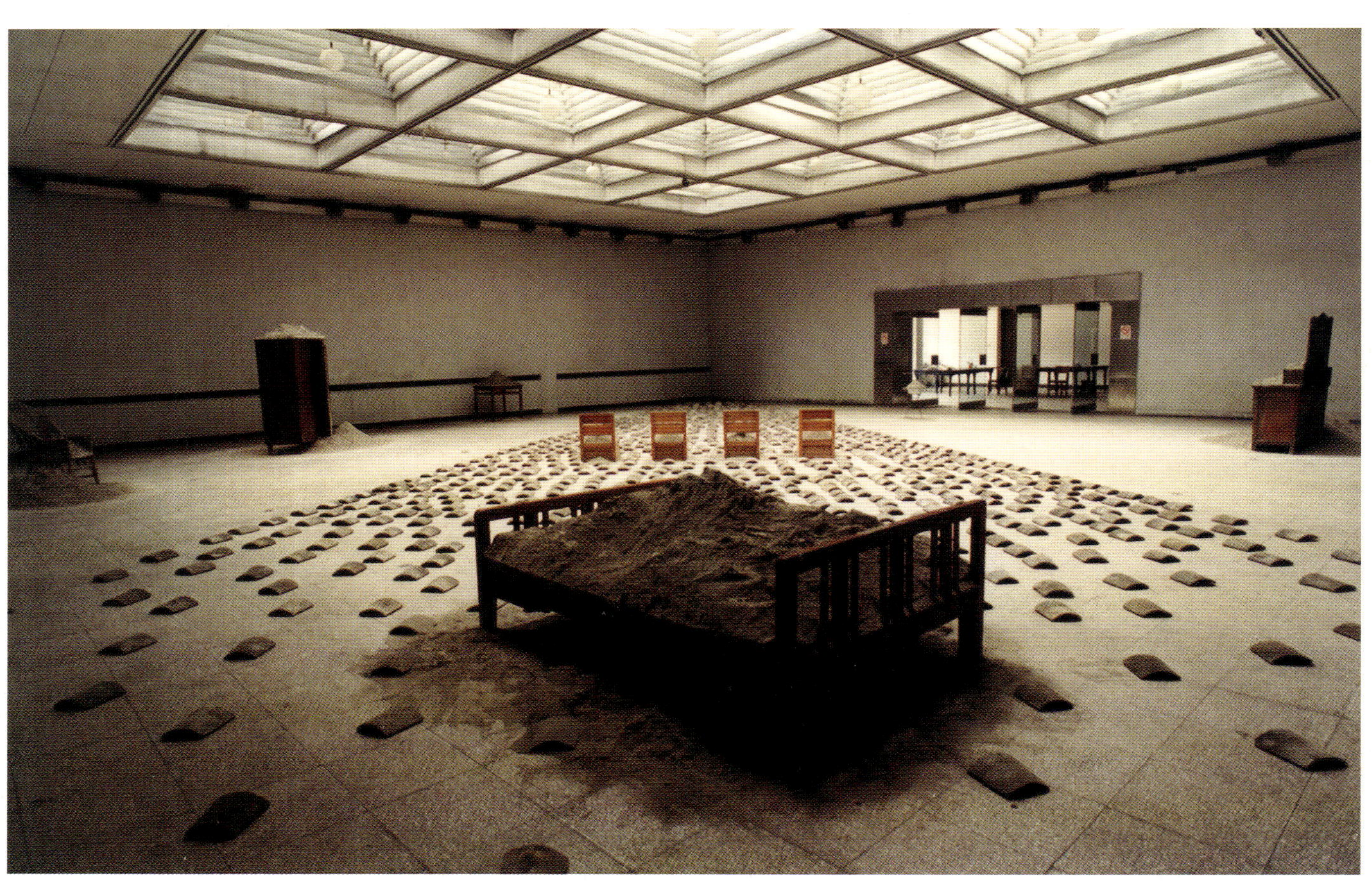

Yin Xiuzhen. *Ruined City*, 1996. Furniture, cement powder, tile, and installation bed: 22.4 × 68.8 × 68.8 inches. ©Yin Xiuzhen. *Courtesy of Pace Gallery*

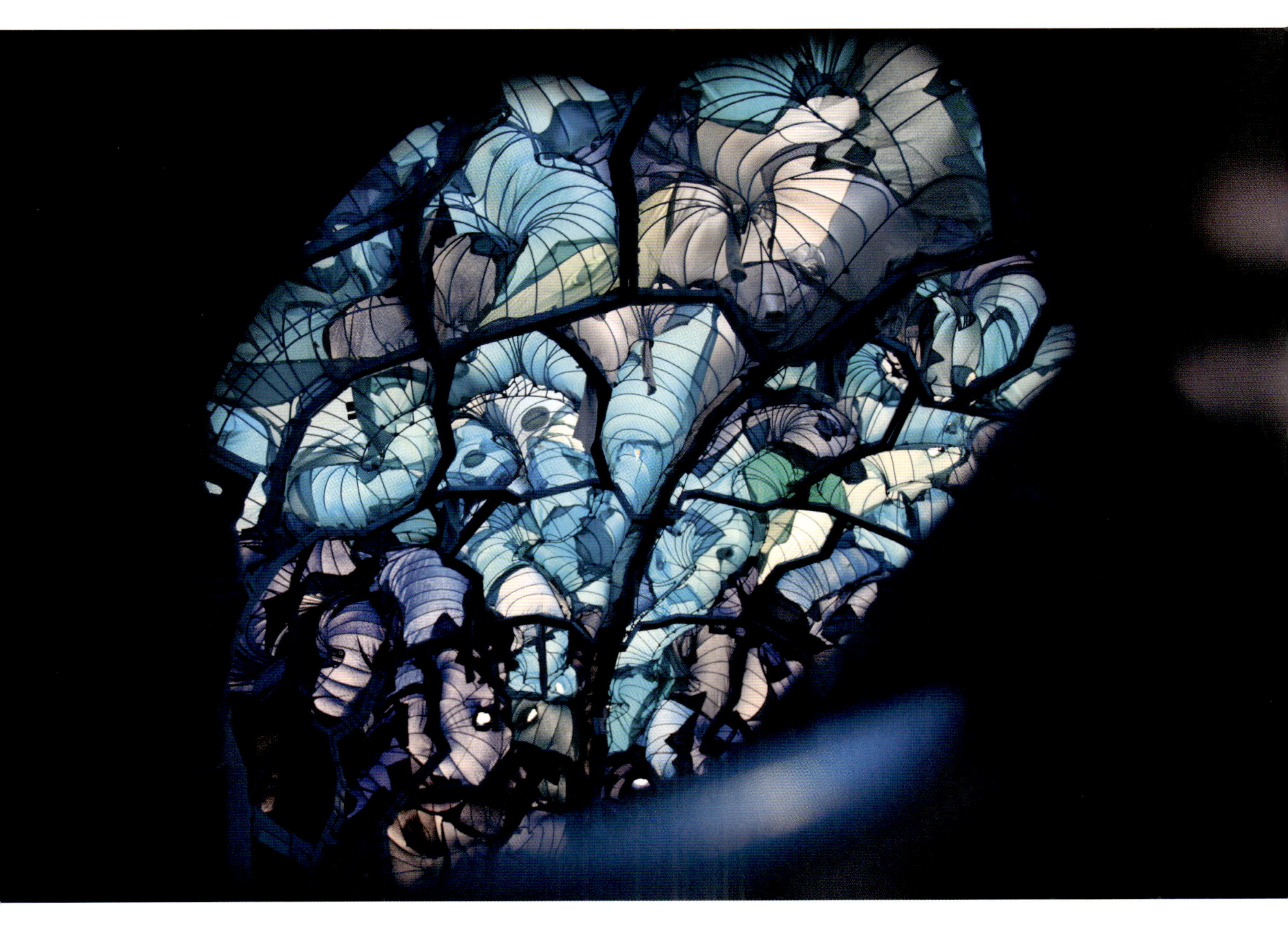

Yin Xiuzhen. *Thought*, 2009. Clothes and steel: 133.8 × 200.7 × 145.6 inches. ©Yin Xiuzhen. *Courtesy of Pace Gallery*

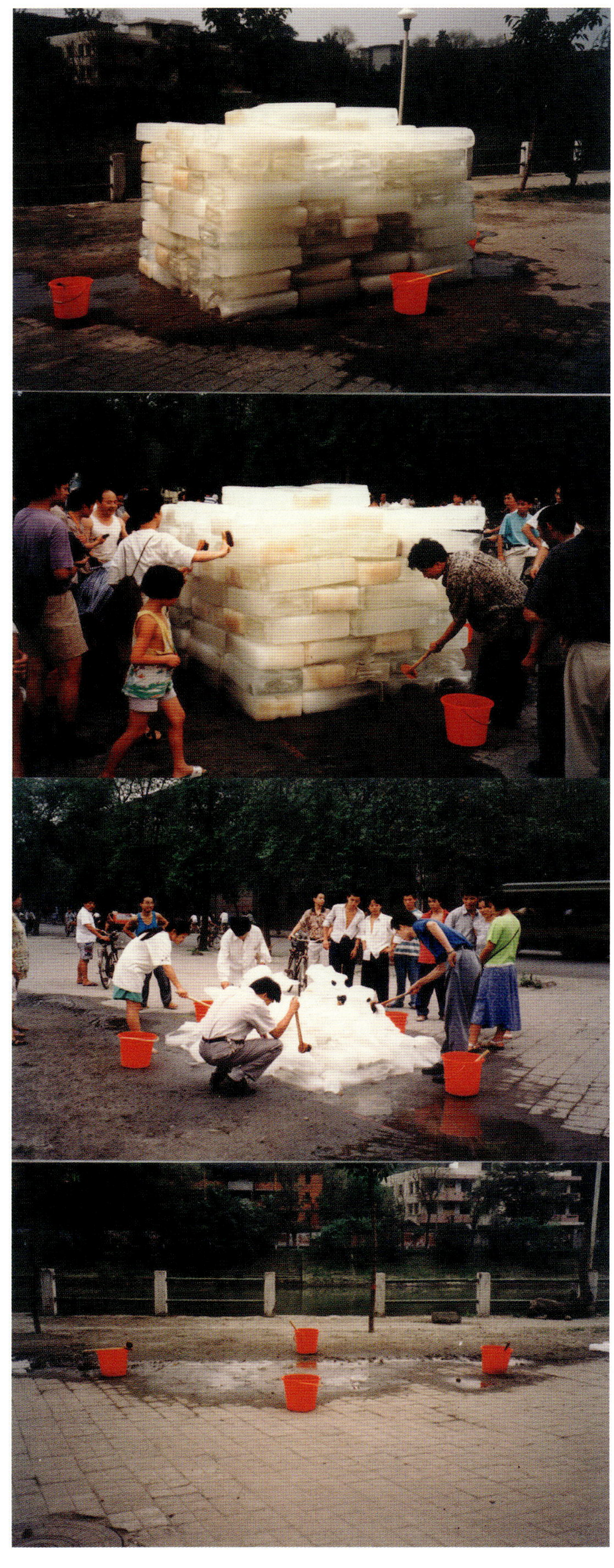

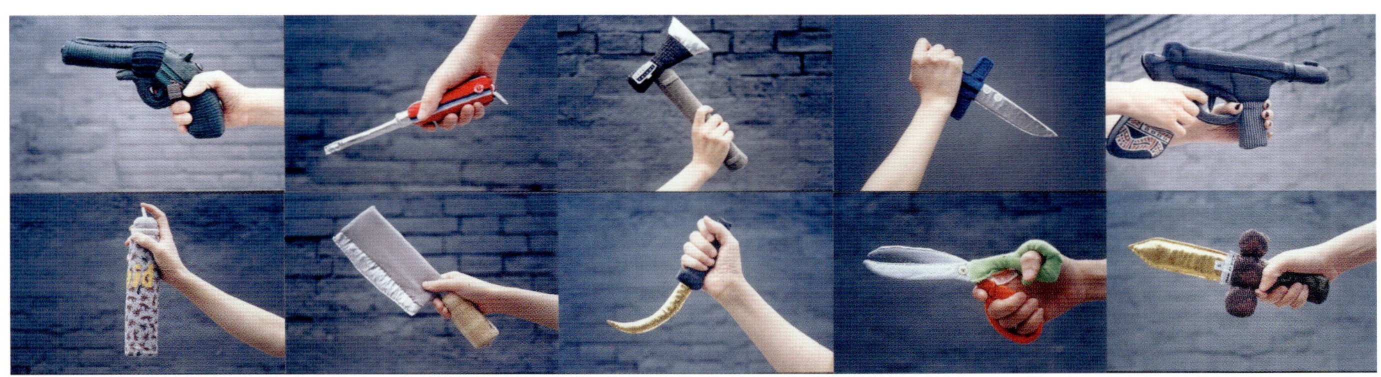

Yin Xiuzhen. *Washing River*, 1995.
Performance still: 47.2 × 70.8 inches. ©Yin Xiuzhen. *Courtesy of Pace Gallery*

Yin Xiuzhen. *Fashion Terrorism 3*, 2004.
Photographs: 70.8 × 47.2 inches, each. ©Yin Xiuzhen. *Courtesy of Pace Gallery*

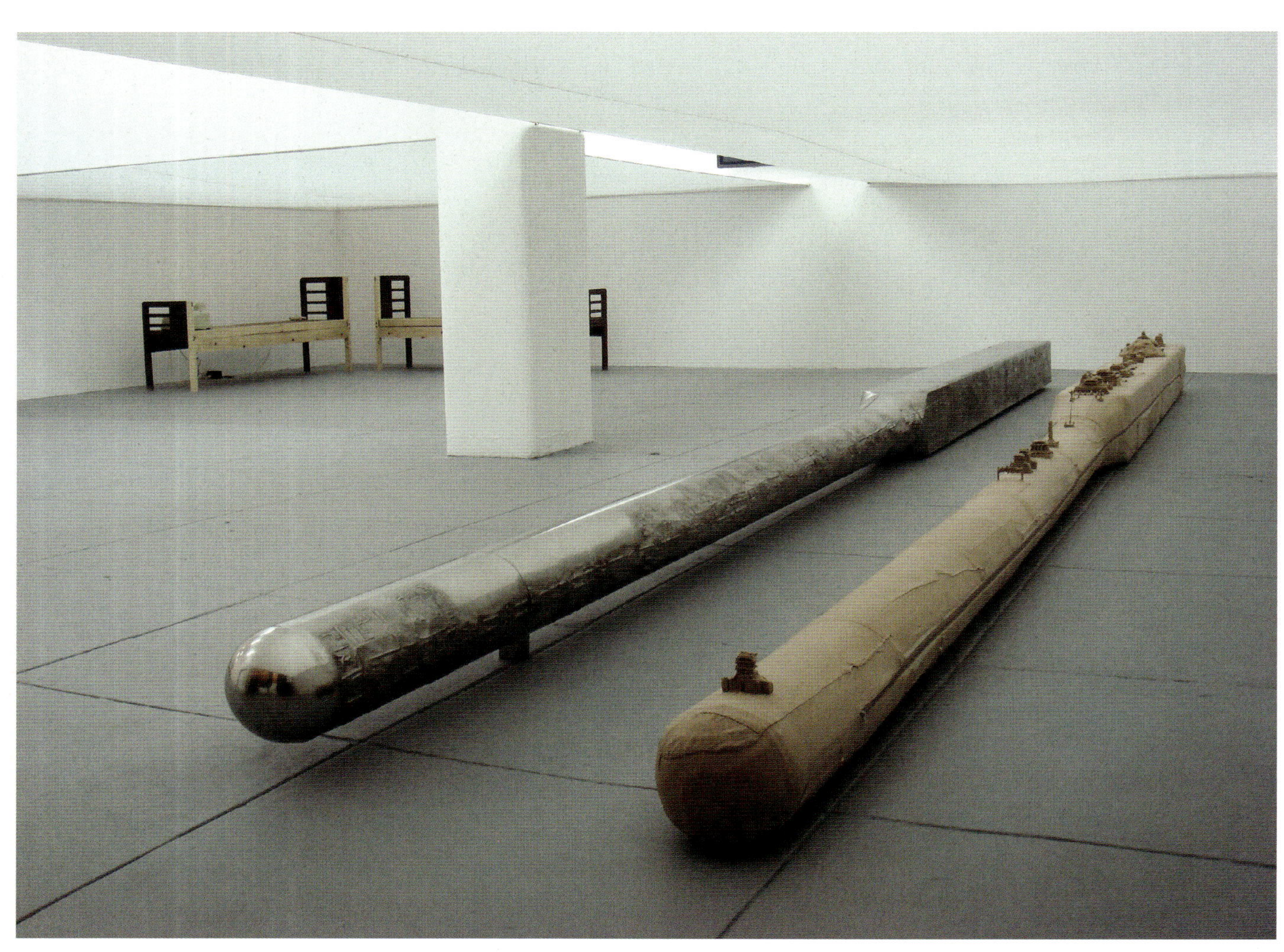

Yin Xiuzhen. *Chopsticks* (collaboration with Song Dong), 2006. Stocking, foam, thread, and stainless steel: 313 × 11.8 × 11.8 inches, each. ©Yin Xiuzhen. *Courtesy of Pace Gallery*

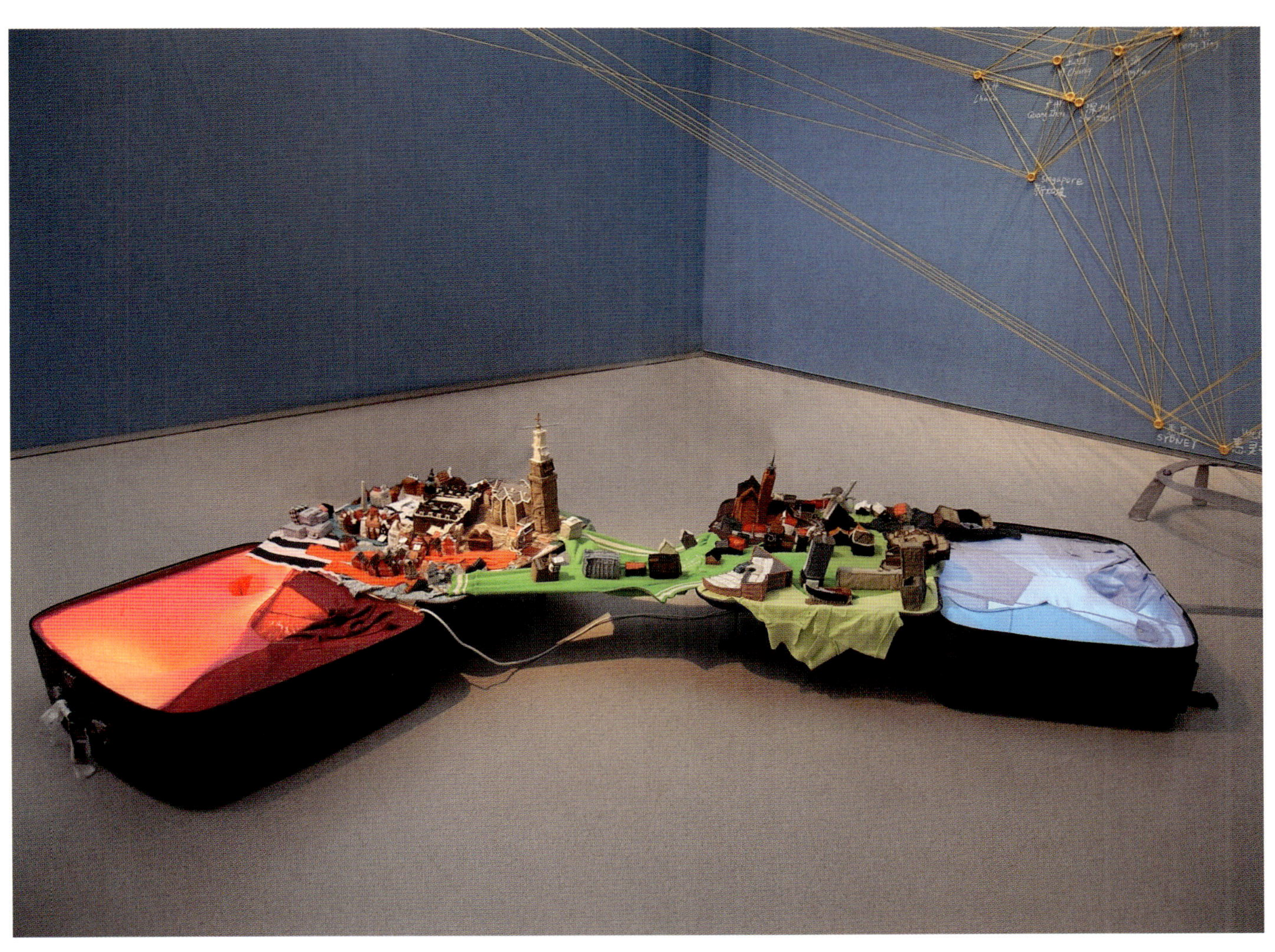

Yin Xiuzhen. *Portable Cities Amsterdam + Amsterveen*, 2007. Suitcases, used clothes, light, map, and sound: 34.2 × 31.8 × 10.6 inches (suitcase closed). ©Yin Xiuzhen. *Courtesy of Pace Gallery*

ZOË BUCKMAN

Zoë Buckman is a British multidisciplinary artist who works in sculpture, installation, and photography. Buckman's practice explores themes of feminism, mortality, and equality. Her major solo projects include *Let Her Rave* at Gavlak Gallery, Los Angeles (2018); *Imprison Her Soft Hand* at Project for Empty Space, Newark, New Jersey (2017); *Every Curve* at PAPILLION ART, Los Angeles (2016); and *Present Life* at Garis & Hahn Gallery, New York City (2015). Other notable shows include *Making and Unmaking*, curated by Duro Olowu, Camden Arts Centre, London; *For Freedoms*, Jack Shainman Gallery, New York City; and *To Be Young, Gifted, and Black*, Goodman Gallery, Johannesburg, South Africa. Buckman was a featured artist at Pulse Projects, New York City, in 2014 and Miami, Florida, in 2016, and was included in the curated Soundscape Park at Art Basel Miami Beach, Florida, in 2016. Buckman has exhibited nationally and internationally, including Paul Kasmin Gallery, New York City; Gavlak, Los Angeles; Fort Gansevoort, New York City; Nathan Cummings Foundation, New York City; the Studio Museum in Harlem, New York; Monique Meloche, Chicago; Camden Arts Centre, London; Children's Museum of the Arts, New York City; Gladstone Gallery, New York City; SPRING/BREAK Art Show, New York City (2015); and Leila Heller Gallery, New York City. Public works include a mural, *We Hold These Truths To Be Self-Evident*, in collaboration with Natalie Frank at New York Live Arts, and *Champ*, a kinetic sculpture at the Standard, Hollywood, in Los Angeles, in collaboration with Art Production Fund. Buckman is a part of *For Freedoms*, the first artist-run super PAC. She studied at the International Center of Photography, New York, and lives and works in New York City.

Zoë Buckman. *And since a Man* (from *Every Curve* series), 2014. Embroidery on vintage lingerie: dimensions variable. *Courtesy of the artist and Bethanie Brady Artist Management*

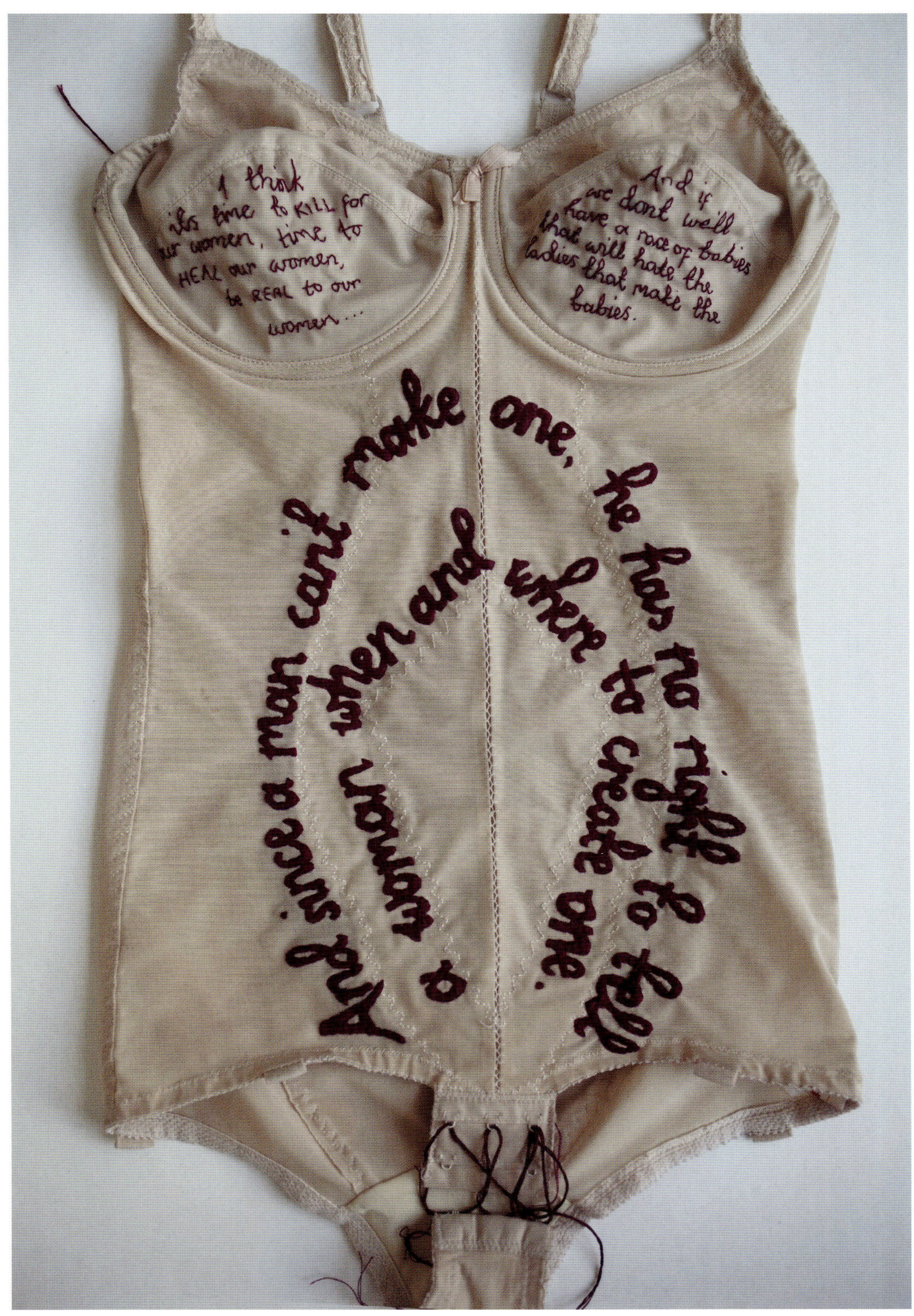
I think
its time to KILL for
ur women, time to
HEAL our women,
be REAL to our
women....
And if
we dont we'll
have a race of babies
that will hate the
ladies that make the
babies.
And since a man can't make one, he has no right to tell
a woman when and where to create one.

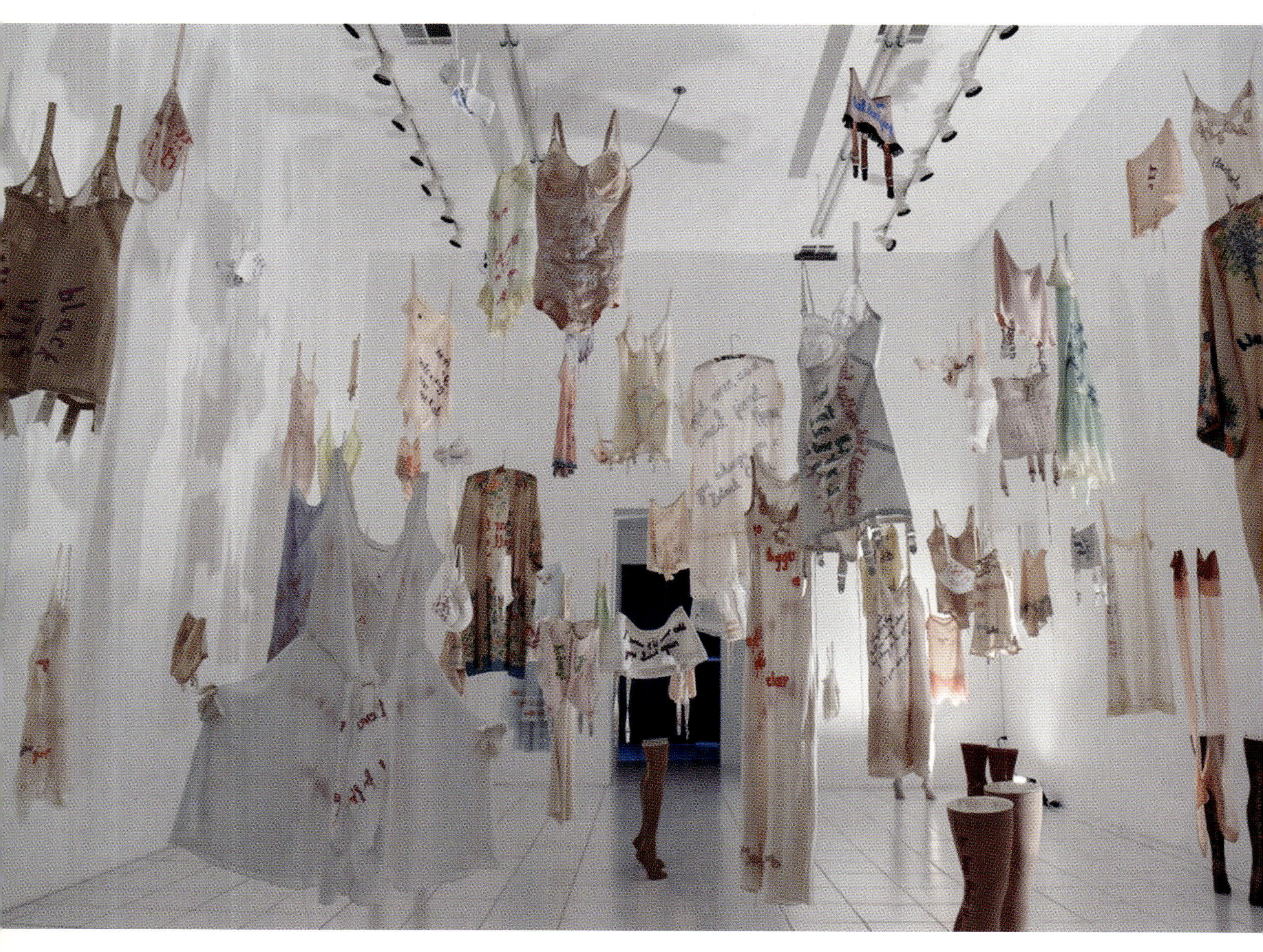

Zoë Buckman. *Every Curve*, 2016. Embroidery on vintage lingerie: dimensions variable. Installation view, *Every Curve*, PAPILLON ART, Los Angeles, CA, Spring 2016. Photography: Billy Farrell/BFA.com. *Courtesy of the artist and Bethanie Brady Artist Management*

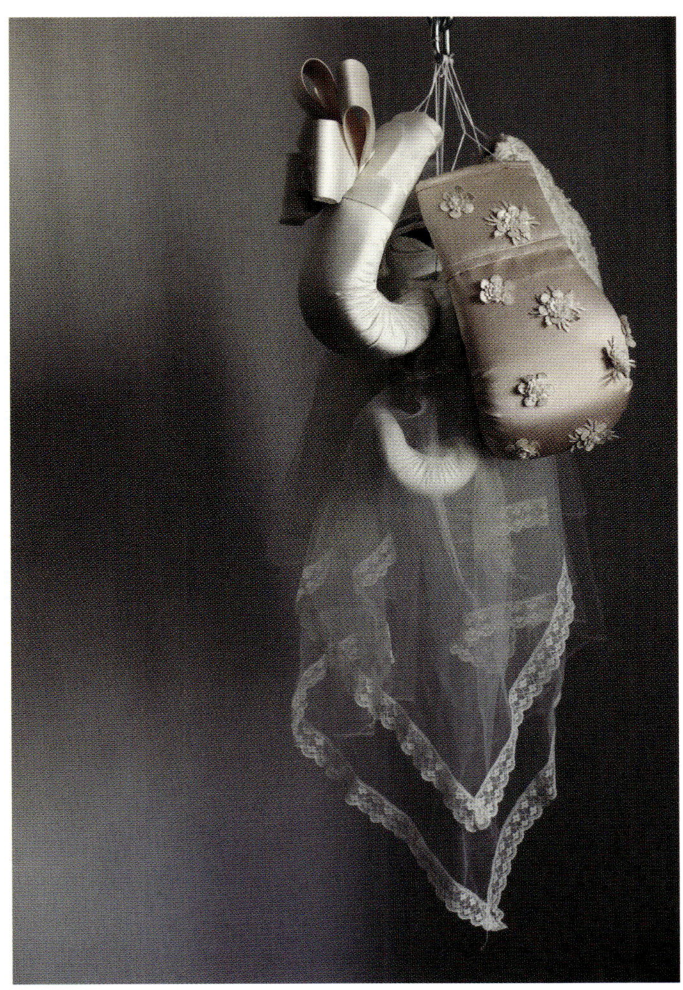

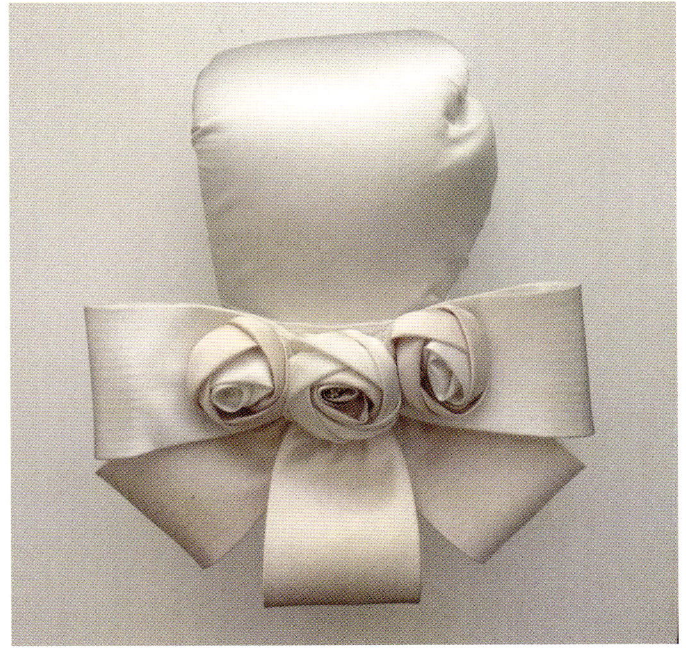

Zoë Buckman. *Ode On* (from *Let Her Rave* series), 2016. Vintage wedding dresses, boxing gloves, and chain: 41 × 16 × 17 inches. *Courtesy of the artist and Bethanie Brady Artist Management*

Zoë Buckman. *Individual Glove (Rosettes)* (from *Let Her Rave* series), 2016. Boxing glove and vintage wedding dress: dimensions variable. *Courtesy of the artist and Bethanie Brady Artist Management*

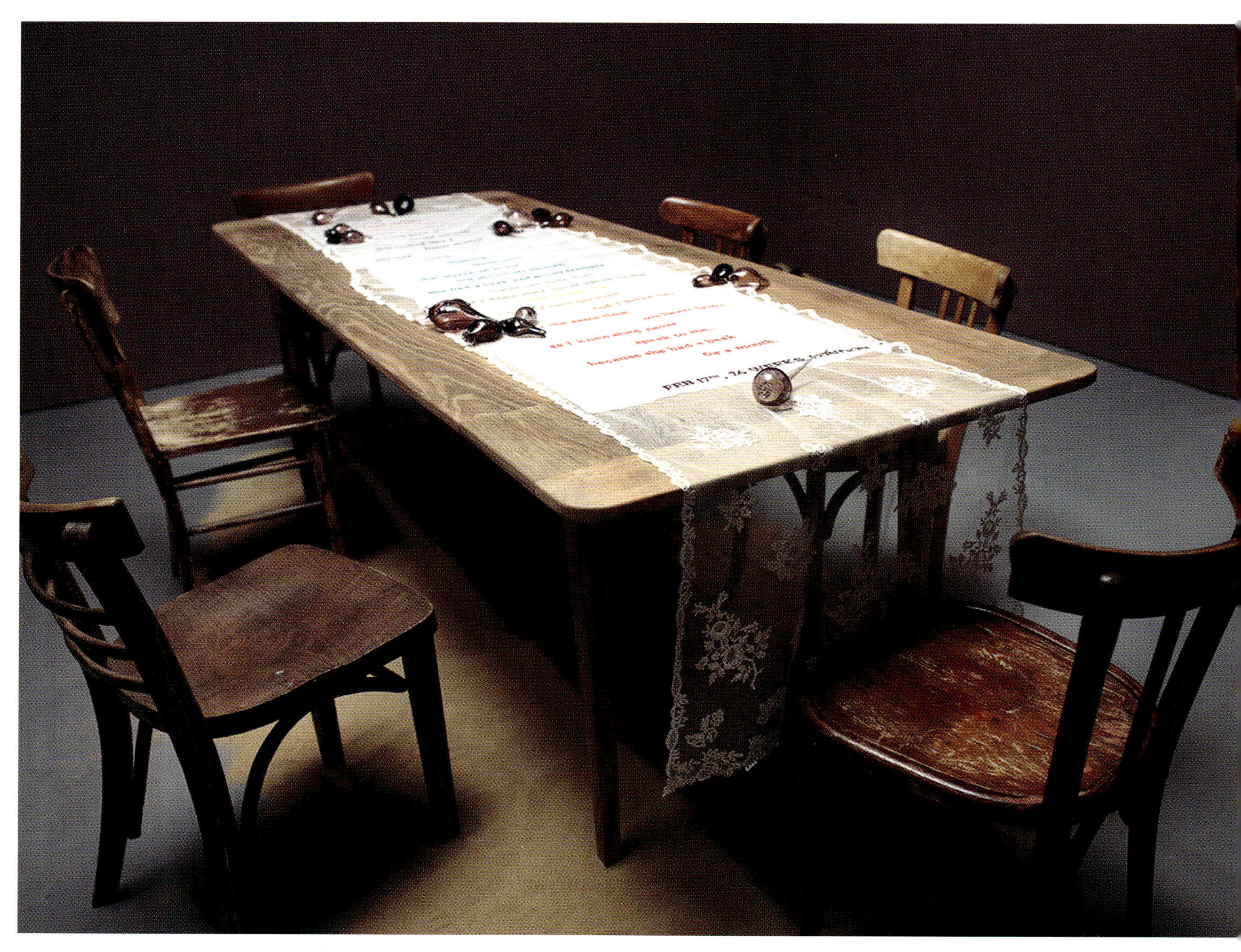

Zoë Buckman. *Untitled 15* (from *Present Life* series), 2015. Embroidery on antique lace, sand, handblown glass, farm table, chairs, and sound: dimensions variable. Installation view, *Present Life*, Garis & Hahn Gallery, New York City, spring 2015. Photography: Ben Rosser / BFA.com. *Courtesy of the artist and Bethanie Brady Artist Management*

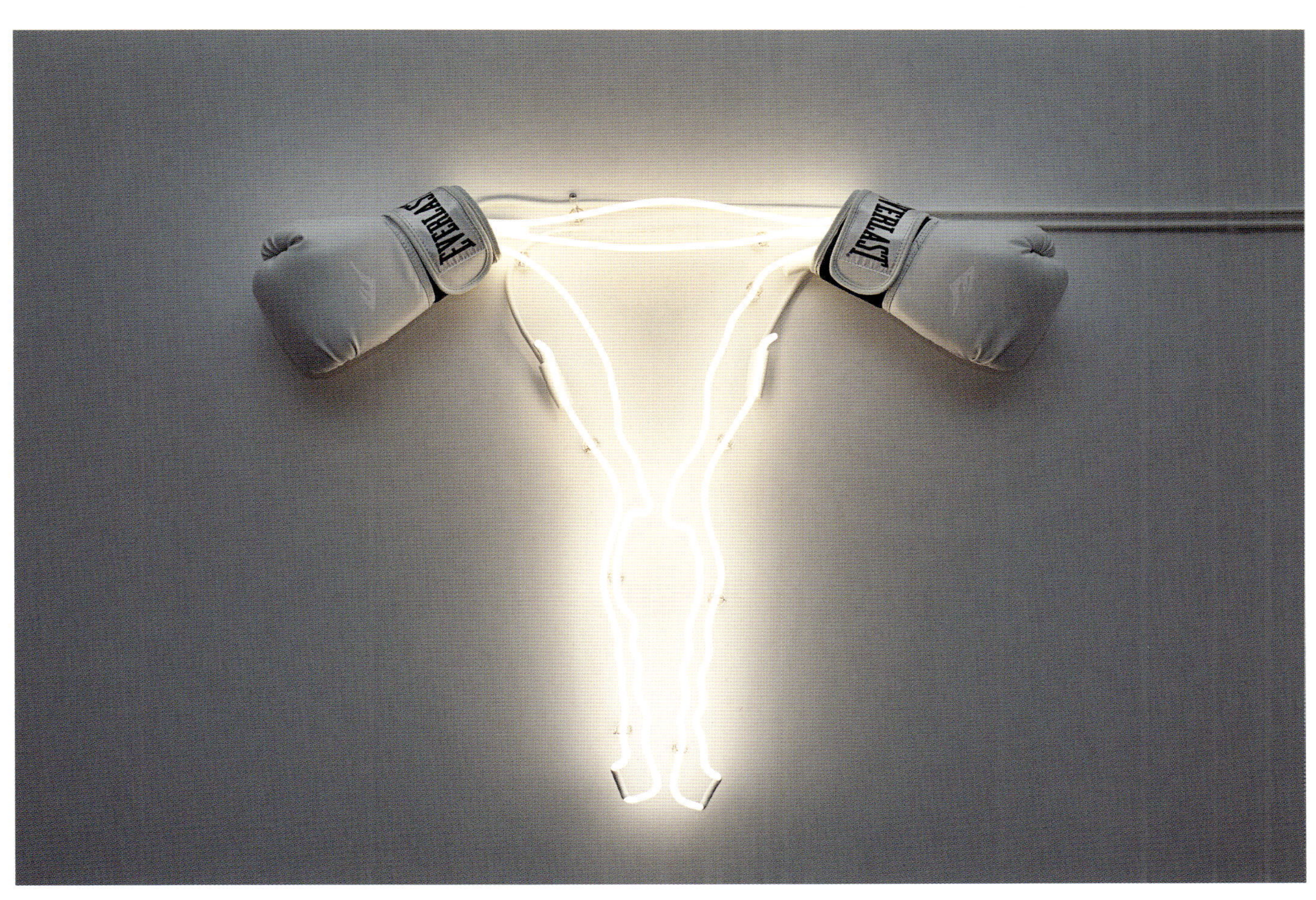

Zoë Buckman. *Champion* (from *Mostly It's Just Uncomfortable* series), 2015. Neon, fabric, and rubber: 2.5 × 3 feet. *Courtesy of the artist and Bethanie Brady Artist Management*

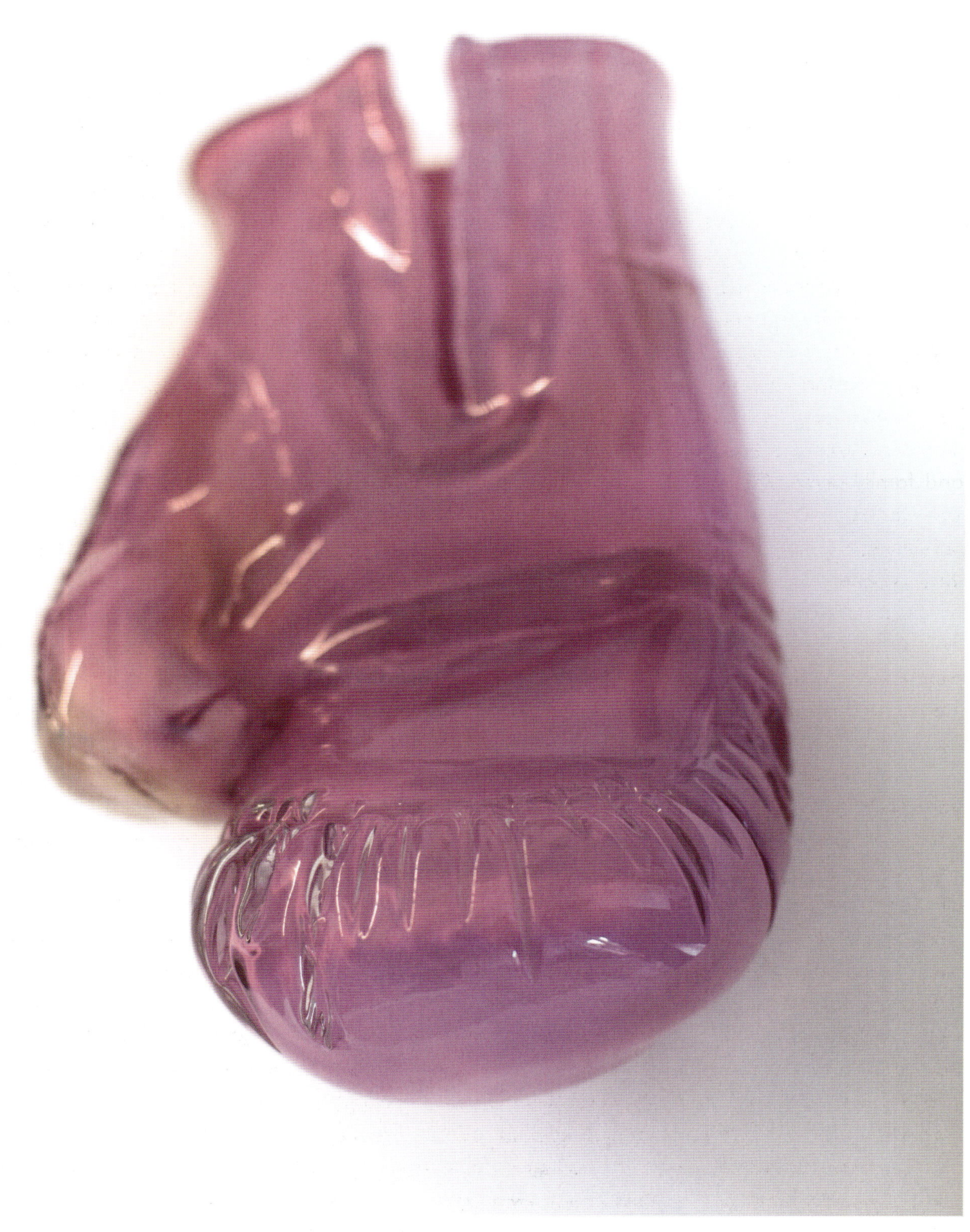

Zoë Buckman. *Bubblegum Boxing Glove* (from *Mostly It's Just Uncomfortable* series), 2014. Blown glass: 13 × 7.5 × 6 inches. *Courtesy of the artist and Bethanie Brady Artist Management*

ACKNOWLEDGMENTS

As editors, we would like to express our gratitude and reverence for the fifty participating artists and architects who embraced our book project, so we could share their work and practice with the world at large. It has been an honor and privilege getting to know each artist in this volume. Without their work, this publication would not exist.

This book is the product of three years of combined research, writing, phone calls, and shared or individual travel to galleries, institutions, artist studios, art fairs, and performances throughout the United States. Thank you to the many gallery and museum directors, mentors, curators, critics, registrars, collectors, friends, and family across the globe who made significant contributions to the creation of this book. It has been a pleasure to be in dialogue with so many individuals about women artists and feminist practices.

During the curatorial, writing, and editing process, we benefited from key assistance and guidance by experts in the field, which greatly helped us hone and improve the manuscript. As such, several people and organizations require special mention.

We thank Elizabeth Sackler, founder of the Elizabeth A. Sackler Center for Feminist Art, for her invaluable insight and contribution to this publication. As a thought leader, feminist, and activist, we could not ask for a more qualified individual to endorse the messages of this book. We appreciate her asking the thoughtful and probing questions that often steered us throughout the process.

We are grateful to Susan T. Rodriguez, one of the architects featured in this book, and the designer of the permanent gallery for Judy Chicago's *The Dinner Party* at the Sackler Center, for suggesting we meet with Elizabeth Sackler to discuss the shape of the publication. We honor her heartfelt encouragement and support throughout this project.

Thank you to Melinda Wang, founder and principal of MW Projects, founder of Equity Gallery, and former executive director of New York Artists Equity Association, who co-organized *FemiNest* in winter 2017 with editor Heather Zises, which featured five of the artists in this book (Natalie Frank, Michele Oka Doner, Barbara Segal, Page Turner, and Vadis Turner). We value her curatorial expertise, media savvy, and sage counsel.

Thank you to Amy Kisch, founder and CEO of AKArt and Collect For Change™, and Danielle Smith and Kimberly Verde, cofounders of state and FRAMEWORK, who co-organized *Object Action: The "F" Word in a Post-Truth Era* in winter 2018 with editor Heather Zises, which featured three of the artists in this book (Ana Teresa Fernández, Chitra Ganesh, and Michele Pred). We celebrate their extreme curating and fearless feminism.

Thank you to Peter D. Gerakaris, dear friend and extraordinary interdisciplinary artist, for making introductions to many of the artists in this book. We appreciate his boundless support of this project from its inception.

Thank you to Margery and David Zises, fabulous parents and exceptional editors, whose love and guidance have supported this curatorial pursuit.

Thank you to the expert staff at Schiffer Publishing and our editors, Jesse Marth and Sandra Korinchak, for their skill and precision.

Thank you to Laura Metter for author editorial assistance.

Additionally, we would like to acknowledge the galleries, museums, firms, and management companies whose commitment to their artists helped make this book possible: A.I.R. Gallery, New York; ACME Gallery, Los Angeles; Ace Gallery, Los Angeles; Baldwin Gallery, Aspen, Colorado; Bethanie Brady Artist Management, New York; bitforms gallery, New York; Causey Contemporary, New York; Cooper Cole Gallery, Toronto; David Castillo Gallery, Miami, Florida; Davidson Contemporary, New York; Deitch Projects, New York; Ennead Architects, New York; Flowers Gallery, New York; Front Room Gallery, New York; Foxy Production, New York; Galerie Antoine Ertaskiran, Montreal; Galerie Lelong & Co., New York; Galerie

Perrotin, Paris; Gallery Wendi Norris, San Francisco; Geary Contemporary, New York; Gladstone Gallery, New York; Hauser & Wirth, New York; Hirschl & Adler Modern, New York; Institute of Contemporary Art, Boston; Krakow Witkin Gallery, Boston; Lehmann Maupin, New York; Lyons Wier Gallery, New York; Marlborough Gallery, New York; Nancy Hoffman Gallery, New York; the National Art Center, Tokyo; P.P.O.W. Gallery, New York; Pace Gallery, New York; Renwick Gallery, Smithsonian American Art Museum, Washington, DC; Rhona Hoffman Gallery, Chicago; Richard Taittinger Gallery, New York; Robert Klein Gallery, Boston; Salomon Contemporary, New York; Salon94, New York; Sean Kelly, New York; Sikkema Jenkins & Co., New York; Studio C Gallery, Los Angeles; Steven Harvey Fine Art Projects, New York; Sundaram Tagore Gallery, New York; and Tracey Morgan Gallery, Asheville, North Carolina.

PHOTO CREDITS

We are also grateful to all those who assisted with sourcing and providing images for the book: Aaron Yassin / Doner Studio; Aislinn Weidle / Ennead Architects; Anne Thompson; Artists Rights Society (ARS), New York; Balthazar Korab; Ben Rosser / www.BFA.com; Billy Farrell / www.BFA.com; Colleen Chartier / ART on File; Dennis Cowley; Eric Stoner; Fadi Asmar; Graham Baring; James Cabot Ewart / Maya Lin Studio; James Dee; James Ewing; James Prinz; Jason Mandella; Jason Wyche; Jeff Goldberg / Esto; Johan Pijnappel / Nalini Malani Studio; John Lai; Jonas Hidalgo; Joshua White; Kerry Ryan McFate; Lawrence Mitchell / E. V. Day Studio; Mary Renzy / MS Renzy Studio; Nick Thomas; Paul Brewer / Tara Donovan Studios; Ron Blunt; Roy Englebrecht / www.royphoto.com; Terry Adams / National Parks Service; Tom Dubrock; Sean Cuddy / Cuddy Photography; Tracy Szatan; Steve Bates; Susan Grogan / Mickalene Thomas Studio; Ueno Norih; Victoria Sambunaris; and William MacLean.

ABOUT THE AUTHORS

John Gosslee is the editor-in-chief of New York City–based art magazine *Quiet Lunch*. He also runs *PANK* and *Fjords Review*. As a literary editor he's published more than fifty books of contemporary literature to the trade. His poetry is widely published.

Heather Zises is a Brooklyn-based curator, writer, and founder of READart, a curatorial platform for contemporary art and culture. Having launched her career at Pace Gallery and Phillips, she has curated numerous exhibitions and site-specific installations at galleries, alternative spaces, and art fairs worldwide. Heather is a contributing writer for diverse publications, including *Quiet Lunch* and *Fjords Review*, and is an art editor for *Pregame Magazine*.

Elizabeth A. Sackler, PhD is a public historian and arts activist. She is president of the Arthur M. Sackler Foundation, and founder of the Elizabeth A. Sackler Center for Feminist Art at the Brooklyn Museum and produces the public program series, "States of Denial," currently focused on state-sanctioned violence and mass incarceration. The Elizabeth A. Sackler Papers are held at the Sophia Smith Collection, Smith College.

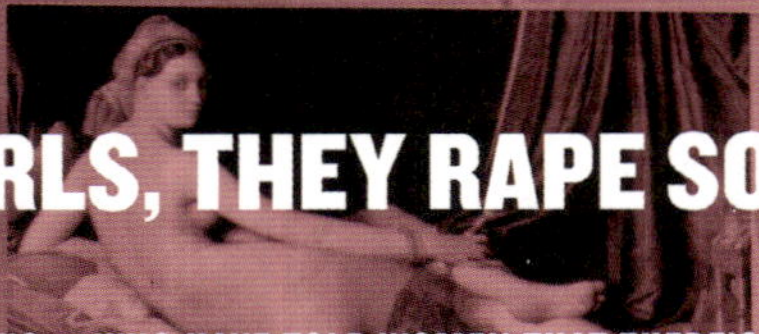

SOME GIRLS, THEY RAPE SO EASY. 1

THERE ARE THOSE OF US ... WHO HAVE TOLD WOMEN THAT THERE'S A WAR ON THEM BECAUSE THAT CUTE LITTLE BABY INSIDE OF THEM.... WE NEED TO ... RE-EDUCATE THE WOMEN TO UNDERSTAND THAT THEY ARE THE DEFENDERS OF THESE BABIES. 10

THE FACTS SHOW THAT PEOPLE WHO ARE RAPED—WHO ARE TRULY RAPED—THE JUICES DON'T FLOW ... THEY DON'T GET PREGNANT. 11

IF BABIES HAD GUNS, THEY WOULDN'T BE ABORTED. 12

THAT'S ONE OF THE UNINTENDED CONSEQUENCES OF THE WOMEN'S LIBERATION MOVEMENT—THAT, IN FACT, THE WOMEN THAT WOULD LEAD THIS COUNTRY WOULD BE FEMININE, THEY WOULD BE PRO-FAMILY, THEY WOULD HAVE HUSBANDS, THEY WOULD LOVE THEIR CHILDREN. THEY WOULDN'T BE A BUNCH OF DYKES THAT CAME FROM THE 7 SISTERS SCHOOLS. 15

BIRTH CONTROL MAKES WOMEN UNATTRACTIVE AND CRAZY. 16

THEY DON'T CALL ME TYRANNOSAURUS SEX FOR NOTHING. 17

WHEN OFFICERS ARREST CRIMINALS TODAY, THEY ARE READ THEIR RIGHTS.... IT SEEMS TO ME ONLY COMMON SENSE WE WOULD HAVE TO DO THE SAME THING FOR WOMEN BEFORE THEY...GET AN ABORTION. 18

I DID NOT HAVE SEXUAL RELATIONS WITH THAT WOMAN. 19

I MOVED ON HER LIKE A BITCH ... AND WHEN YOU'RE A STAR THEY LET YOU DO IT ... GRAB 'EM

SHE GOT A LITTLE UPSET. GIRLS DO THAT ... I DIDN'T H

UNCLE SUGAR COMING IN AND PROVIDING FOR ... BIRTH CONTROL BECAUSE THEY CANNOT C

I'M PRO LIFE WITHOUT EXCEPTION ... LIFE OF A WOMA

IF THEY'RE A MALE BABY, THEY MAY HAVE THEIR HAND BETWEEN THEIR LEGS. IF THEY FEEL PLEASURE, WHY IS IT SO HARD TO THINK THAT THEY COULD FEEL PAIN? 6

IF HILLARY CLINTON HER HUSBAND, WHA THINK SHE CAN SATI

[RAPE VICTIMS] SHOULD MAKE THE BEST OF A BAD S

[PREGNANT WOMEN ARE] LITTLE GIRLS [WHO

I GET A

MORAL OF STORY: WOMEN IN MIL

"GESTATIONAL AGE" MEANS THE AGE OF THE UNBORN CHILD AS CALCULATED FROM THE FIRST DAY OF THE LAST MENSTRUAL PERIOD OF THE PREGNANT WOMAN. 14

BUT ON THE RAPE THING ... HOW DOES PUTTING MORE VIC BODY AND TAKING THE LIFE OF AN INNOCENT CHILD ... HO

[PLANNED PARENTHOOD

YOU COULD SEE THERE WAS BLOOD CO HER EYES. BLOOD COMING OUT OF HER

[CECILE] RICHARDS IS WELL ON HER WAY

[HILLARY CLINTON] BELIEVES IN THE SYSTEMATIC MURDER OF C

RAPE IS KINDA LIKE THE WEATHER. IF IT'S INEVITAB

IF IT'S A LEGITIMATE RAPE, THE FEMALE BODY HAS WAYS TO TRY TO SHUT THE WHOLE THING DOW

[WOMEN ON WELFARE] SHOULD BE ABLE TO GET THEIR LIVES TOGETHER AND FIND A

JUST IN CASE, ANYBODY WHO'S WATCHING THRO